The

AMERICAN
BIBLE

The AMERICAN BIBLE

How Our Words Unite, Divide, and Define a Nation

Stephen Prothero

HarperOne
An Imprint of HarperCollinsPublishers

HarperOne

THE AMERICAN BIBLE: *How Our Words Unite, Divide, and Define a Nation.* Copyright © 2012 by Stephen Prothero. All rights reserved. Printed in the United States of America. No part of this book may be used or reproduced in any manner whatsoever without written permission except in the case of brief quotations embodied in critical articles and reviews. For information address HarperCollins Publishers, 10 East 53rd Street, New York, NY 10022.

HarperCollins books may be purchased for educational, business, or sales promotional use. For information please write: Special Markets Department, HarperCollins Publishers, 10 East 53rd Street, New York, NY 10022.

HarperCollins website: http://www.harpercollins.com

HarperCollins®, 📖®, and HarperOne™ are trademarks of HarperCollins Publishers.

FIRST EDITION

Designed by Terry McGrath

Library of Congress Cataloging-in-Publication Data

Prothero, Stephen R.
The American Bible: how our words unite, divide, and define a nation / by Stephen Prothero.
p. cm.
Includes bibliographical references and index.
ISBN 978–0–06–212343–5
1. National characteristics, American. 2. Speeches, addresses, etc., American—History and criticism.
3. National characteristics, American, in literature. 4. Rhetoric—Political aspects—United States—History.
5. Literature and society—United States—History. 6. Language and culture—United States.
7. Nationalism and literature—United States. 8. United States—Civilization.
9. Group identity in literature. I. Title.
E169.12.P747 2012
973—dc23   2012005054

12 13 14 15 16 RRD(H) 10 9 8 7 6 5 4 3 2 1

To Meera Subramanian

CONTENTS ❦

INTRODUCTION

ORDS MATTER. They move individuals to tears and to action. They make or break communities. In Israel and the Palestinian territories, India and Pakistan, Great Britain and the United States, words tie people together and tear them apart. Socrates lives because of Plato's dialogues. The world remembers Jesus because of the words of Matthew, Mark, Luke, and John. And what Americans recall of Paul Revere we owe to the poetry of Henry Wadsworth Longfellow.

In his Gettysburg Address, perhaps the greatest American speech ever, President Lincoln said, "The world will little note nor long remember what we say here, but it can never forget what they did here."[1] He was wrong. Americans have largely forgotten what Union and Confederate soldiers did at Gettysburg during three bloody days in July 1863, but we have not forgotten Lincoln's words, which continue to be quoted and misquoted, interpreted and misinterpreted for all sorts of purposes. In the few minutes Lincoln spoke at Gettysburg, he explained why the Civil War was being waged, why the Union was worth preserving, and why the United States was founded. His words—"conceived in liberty . . . dedicated to the proposition that all men are created equal . . . a new birth of freedom"—are now part of our lexicon. They live not because Americans agree with everything Lincoln said, but because they agree that everything he said is worth debating. What does it mean to affirm "government of the people, by the people, for the people"? It depends on whom you ask. And if you ask enough Americans you will see that the nation rests not on agreement about its core ideas and values, but on a willingness to continue to debate them.

From the beginning of the American experiment, foreign visitors noted a key difference between the United States and its European kin. It was not held together by blood or custom. Its citizens had no common history going back to the ancients. They spoke different languages and worshipped in different ways. "If there is a country in the world where concord, according to common calculation, would be least expected, it is America," wrote that great propagandist for revolution Thomas Paine. "Made up as it is of people from different nations, accustomed to different forms and habits of government, speaking different languages, and more different in their modes of worship, it would appear that the union of such a people was impracticable."[2] What constituted America, these observers argued, were ideas—a common commitment to key words such as "liberty," "equality," "constitutional-ism," and "republicanism."

But that is not quite right. At least it is not complete, because these ideas conflict with one another. Our republic of letters is a republic of conversation, constituted, divided, reconstituted, and maintained by debate over the meaning of "America" and "Americans." Whenever we say, "That is un-American" or "That is what America is all about," we are declaring our allegiance to this republic. And whenever our fellow citizens disagree with us, they are doing the same. Such declarations are charged because our unity is fragile. In every generation our *pluribus* threatens to overtake our *unum;* in every generation the nation must be imagined anew. So we are forever anxious about possible threats to our unity: immigrants, traitors, un-American ideas.

Americans agree to a surprising degree about which symbols and ideas are central to our national life, but we disagree profoundly about what these symbols and ideas mean and how they ought to be translated into public policies. The fights Americans have about who has stolen America and who is going to take it back focus, to be sure, on key words such as "liberty" and "equality"—on the ideas that energized the new nation and, for a time, rent it asunder. But this conversa-tion is also inspired by key phrases—"a city on the hill," "We the people," "one nation, under God," "I have a dream"—and by inescapable speeches, songs, and stories that carry these words and phrases down through the generations. Finally, and most important, America's conversation about itself is fueled by passion. Words have the power to make things happen, but that power is weak unless it is sparked by the passions that thinkers from David Hume to David Brooks have seen as the key drivers of political action and human history.

Perhaps because of America's strong Christian heritage, it seems natural to many U.S. citizens to imagine that our unity is creedal, resting on some political analogue to the Ten Commandments or the Nicene Creed. "To be an American is not to be someone, but to believe in something," writes historian Gordon Wood.[3]

But there is no American creed. What brings us together is a common practice. To be an American is not to agree with your fellow citizens about a set of propositions. It is to agree to argue with them, and to argue passionately. More often than not, our key words are fighting words. Here citizens disagree fiercely, even about "truths" that are supposedly "self-evident." And they do so in public, with the volume up.

This conversation is spirited because the United States isn't just a country; it is also a religion of sorts. In the hearts and minds of the faithful—those whose belief in America is strong and whose doubt marks a spiritual crisis—this land is sacred and its people are chosen. The stories we tell about our nation are sacred stories. The heroes we recall on our holy days are saints and martyrs, as ancient and permanent as granite on Mount Rushmore. Like Abraham or Moses or Jesus, they come to enter into a new covenant, to deliver a chosen people from slavery, or to shed blood to atone for our sins.

This American religion has its scripture too: the words and voices to which Americans return as they ponder the meanings and ends of their country. America's scripture includes the Bible, of course. Since colonial times, Americans have made sense of their experiences through the characters and plot points of the biblical book of Exodus—Pharaoh and Moses, slavery and deliverance, Egypt and the promised land. Contemporary American politics, on both sides of the aisle, is replete with references to the Good Samaritan, the Sermon on the Mount, and the Ten Commandments. So Americans are a "people of the book." But the Bible is not the only book Americans use to define and redefine themselves.

Over the last generation, Americans have debated, sometimes graciously, more often angrily, but always passionately, such issues as abortion, income-tax rates, and the wars in Iraq and Afghanistan. In so doing, they have asked, "What would Jefferson do?" Or MLK? Or Reagan? To answer these questions, they have returned, over and over again, to certain core texts. These core texts constitute a de facto canon of American public life. I call this canon the American Bible. Because the "real" Bible has been a prime mover of American thought, the American Bible includes portions of the Hebrew and Christian Bibles. But these biblical verses stand alongside other texts that Americans have long held sacred, such as "God Bless America," *Adventures of Huckleberry Finn,* and "I Have a Dream."

It is tempting to imagine that the American Bible speaks with one voice— the voice of the founders, perhaps. It does not. After all, the founders disagreed profoundly with one another (not least about whether to ratify the Constitution), and agreement was just as elusive in the age of Jackson as in the age of Reagan. Like the Christian and Jewish Bibles, the American Bible is multivocal—a cacophony of competing and contradictory voices. Written by different people in different times and places, it includes letters and speeches, poems and songs, memorials and novels, the decisions of justices and the proclamations of presidents. So when we ask it a hard question, it does not give us an easy answer. Instead, it invites us into an ongoing conversation between the authors of these American scriptures and their innumerable commentators (ourselves included).

The American Bible is a record of this ongoing conversation. It presents the books held sacred by the American people—the core texts to which Americans are forever returning as they reflect on what it means to be an American. Like the Catholic Bible, however, The American Bible also includes commentaries on these core texts—interpretations that keep America's scriptures vibrant by applying their time-tested truths to contemporary circumstances.

Books like this have been published before. Beginning in 1783, Noah Webster, the founding father of American English, produced a series of readers that attempted to define a new nation to its citizens by offering up a series of political, religious, and moral tracts to be read, memorized, and recited. "Begin with the infant in his cradle; let the first word he lisps be Washington," reads the title page of his earliest reader, which aimed to "transfuse" the "noble sentiments of liberty and patriotism . . . into the breasts of the rising generation."[4] In Webster's imagination, geniuses spoke, and the rest of us listened. But that isn't really how it works, because, after the speaking and the listening, we talk back. What Webster missed is what makes great books great: their ability to generate commentary and controversy. The words of Washington's Farewell Address of 1796 may be profound in their own right, but they are remembered because of the commentaries upon them. Without these commentaries and the controversies they engender, his words would be a dead letter.

Consider the writings of Thomas Jefferson, who with George Washington and Abraham Lincoln constitute a sacred trinity in the American pantheon. Novelist Gore Vidal once said of Jefferson, "If there is such a thing . . . as the American spirit, then he is it."[5] If so, that spirit is legion, and divided against itself, because America's Jeffersons are about as numerous as the stars on the American flag. As early as 1837, a Pennsylvania politician was observing that Jefferson's "opinions may be quoted on any side of almost any question."[6] Since that time, virtually every political party and social movement has created a Jefferson in its own image and then put him to work for its own purposes. Posthumously, Jefferson endorsed the Jacksonians and the Whigs, fought on both sides in the Civil War, and championed both isolationism and interventionism. Today he is a hero of liberal Democrats and conservative Republicans alike—the "Apostle of Liberty" and a champion of states' rights. But he is also a hypocrite who over the course of his life owned six hundred slaves and likely fathered children with one of them, Sally Hemings. To borrow from Lincoln's First Inaugural Address, both sides read the same Jefferson and invoke his aid against the other.

One reason Jefferson has been so malleable, and so useful, to so many American generations is that he was, in his own time, "a baffling series of contradictions: philosopher and politician, aristocrat and democrat, cosmopolitan and American."[7] But Jefferson is also legion because he must be. Societies always adapt the words and actions of their saints and heroes to changing circumstances. The Declaration of Independence, drafted by Jefferson, lives in part because, to paraphrase Walt Whitman, it is large and contains multitudes. And so it goes for Jefferson's First Inaugural Address. But Jefferson's words also live because contemporary controversies continue to breathe life into them—because they are forever being quoted and misquoted, used and abused, in an effort to divine not merely the mind of Jefferson but also the mind of America.

The Constitution is another classic in this regard. It is "the supreme Law of the Land." Presidents swear to uphold it. The Supreme Court is dedicated to interpreting it. As a result, it has generated a seemingly endless stream of commentary, both inside and outside the hallowed halls of the U.S. Supreme Court. In his 2010 commencement address at Harvard University, former Supreme Court justice David Souter spoke at length about how judges actually read the Constitution. He began by arguing that the Constitution is multivocal, so judges must read it as a whole. When they do, however, they see that it affirms many contradictory things. They also see that the Constitution itself does not offer any rules for adjudicating between the conflicting claims of, say, order and liberty or liberty and equality. So judges must do the judging, which they have done from the Supreme Court's first decision in 1791 through *Brown v. Board of Education* in 1954 and *Roe v. Wade* in 1973.

Similar observations can be made about this collection of the most influential writings of Americans, by Americans, and for Americans. Like the Constitution, *The American Bible* speaks in many voices. It includes books by Harriet Beecher

Stowe and Ayn Rand, Malcolm X and Ronald Reagan. These texts too affirm competing goods without offering a method for choosing among them. So, rather than a record of the beliefs Americans hold in common, this book is a record of what Americans value. More specifically, it is a record of what Americans value enough to fight about. And as they engage in this fight—a fight that is simultaneously political and moral, cultural and religious—they decide (provisionally, of course) what America means and who is, and who is not, authentically American.

Judaism is renowned for its traditions of controversy. Put two Jews in a room, the saying goes, and you get three (or more) opinions. The Talmud, a collection of competing rabbinic commentaries about Jewish law, ethics, and theology, is the authoritative record of this debate. A typical page from the Talmud displays a key passage in the middle, surrounded by commentary upon commentary, with no apologies for failing to arrive at *the* answer to any given dispute. The way to wisdom here lies not in affirming simple truths but in engaging in difficult discussions. To be a Jew, therefore, is not so much to have the truth as to search for it. And the method of this search is disagreement, disputation, and debate.

The American Bible began as an effort to construct an American Talmud. This origin can be seen especially in Proverbs, where key utterances in American life—"Remember that time is money," "The only thing we have to fear is fear itself," "Ain't I a woman?"—are literally surrounded on the page by commentaries about what these utterances mean. Historian Garry Wills refers to Lincoln's Gettysburg Address as a "self-referential system" in which its interlocking sentences are joined together by "a kind of hook-and-eye method."[8] The same can be said of *The American Bible,* where Lincoln conjures the Declaration of Independence, only to be conjured by the Reverend Martin Luther King Jr., who is conjured in turn by Ronald Reagan.

The aim of this book is not to create a canon but to report upon one. This is of course a controversial process. Every list by its nature includes things and excludes others; those who compile lists have to make choices. So it is important to make plain how this particular collection came to be. The dictionaries of Noah Webster, whose famous Blue-Back Speller is included here, were deeply prescriptive, focusing on what in his view American English should become. Today most dictionaries are largely descriptive—reports of the words speakers of a given language actually utter and the definitions they actually employ. This sort of "reporting" has been my goal here. I have tried to include not the books I revere but those that Americans themselves have made sacred. On this score, influence obviously matters. But my chief criterion has been the ability of a given text to generate controversy and conversation. Which words have Americans cited and recited in their ongoing debate over the meanings and ends of America? Which texts have been their touchstones?

Taking aim at "mere description" does not ward off bias, of course. Webster himself was biased toward the vocabulary and speech patterns of his native New England. I doubtless have biases of my own. Nonetheless, many of my personal favorites did not make the cut here, either because they did not take direct aim at the meaning of America or because they have not generated as strong a tradition of commentary as other books competing for inclusion. Nathaniel Philbrick refers to *Moby-Dick* as "our American Bible." What he means is that Melville's classic is a big book that carries inside its covers the "genetic code" of American life.[9] In my view, *Moby-Dick* has not been as influential as either Harriet Beecher Stowe's *Uncle Tom's Cabin* or Mark Twain's *Adventures of Huckleberry Finn*, each of which has carried considerable weight in our national conversation about race. So *Moby-Dick* is not included here.

Also slighted are more recent voices, since it is much harder to generate a vast commentary tradition for a work produced in the 1990s or 2000s than for one published during the Civil War or the American Revolution. Still, it must be admitted that most of the books in this collection are by dead white men. In fact, the only living author of an *American Bible* book is the architect of the Vietnam Veterans Memorial, Maya Lin. For better or for worse, dead white men have had outsized influence over the course of U.S. history, and among their powers has been the capacity to command an audience. Nonetheless, women, Native Americans, African Americans, and Muslims are among the authors of these core texts, and voices of the commentators—from Frederick Douglass to Rosa Parks and Gloria Steinem—are far more diverse. This collection also ranges, in both its primary and secondary texts, far and wide across the political spectrum. Radical historian Howard Zinn and consumer activist Ralph Nader are heard here, but so are conservative activists and intellectuals from William F. Buckley Jr. and Robert Bork to Rush Limbaugh and Antonin Scalia.

Throughout *The American Bible* I refer to primary texts as "books." These books are organized into sections patterned after sections of the Christian Bible (both the Old Testament and the New).

Genesis is of course the first book of that Bible. Here it headlines a selection of books that were there "in the beginning" of American culture, including the Declaration of Independence and Noah Webster's Blue-Back Speller, which has been described as America's linguistic declaration of independence. The biblical story of the Exodus of the Israelites from slavery to freedom is also included in this opening section, since many Americans during the Revolution saw themselves as reenacting this biblical story, playing the role of God's New Israel in their righteous battle with the Pharaoh George III.

The next section of *The American Bible,* Law, takes its inspiration from the legal code delivered by God through Moses on Mount Sinai. This section focuses on the American legal tradition, including the Constitution, of course, but also key Supreme Court decisions.

Chronicles presents three bestselling novels: Harriet Beecher Stowe's *Uncle Tom's Cabin,* Mark Twain's *Adventures of Huckleberry Finn,* and Ayn Rand's *Atlas Shrugged.* Classic songs—"The Star-Spangled Banner," "God Bless America," and "This Land Is Your Land"—appear here as Psalms. Shorter expressions—typically single sentences—appear as Proverbs, from Abigail Adams's admonition to her husband, John, to "remember the ladies" in crafting the Constitution to Calvin Coolidge's claim that "the business of America is business." Prophets presents the voices of those who have delivered new visions of the American experiment, from Thoreau and Eisenhower to MLK and Malcolm X. Lamentations, which borrows its name from the biblical book of loss, includes two key expressions over the loss of life in war: Lincoln's Gettysburg Address and Maya Lin's Vietnam Veterans Memorial.

Moving from the "Old Testament" to the "New," the Gospels section presents the "good news" of liberalism, conservatism, and something in between via the voices of Franklin Delano Roosevelt, Ronald Reagan, and Thomas Jefferson. The Pledge of Allegiance is the sole entry in Acts, and classic letters penned by Washington, Jefferson, and King conclude *The American Bible* as Epistles.

Each of these entries follows a three-part structure, beginning with an introduction that explains why this particular selection qualifies as American scripture and how it has served as a catalyst for later controversy. Next comes the source itself—in full or as an excerpt—so that readers can experience themselves the speeches, songs, and sayings that have united or divided us. Finally come the commentaries, either as footnotes embedded in the original text (in the case of responses to specific arguments or phrases) or, in the case of comments on the text as a whole, in the "Commentary" section that concludes each of these "books."

These commentaries, which track the "afterlife" of a given book, are the heart and soul of *The American Bible,* since it is here that the American people talk back, agreeing, disagreeing, or in many cases creatively misreading what their forebears have said. Some of these commentaries come from the lips of the rich and famous—from presidents and governors, for example. Others come from novelists, bloggers, preachers, and journalists, some well known and others obscure.

In these commentaries, which appear here in chronological order, the endless movement of American culture—its swells and breaks and ebbing and flooding tides—is on display. Standing inside any given historical moment, it is easy to imagine that the words of the American Bible are etched in stone. That is literally true in the case of the words of the Gettysburg Address at the Lincoln Memorial or those of Martin Luther King Jr. at one of the newest memorials at the National Mall. But Americans' understandings of these iconic expressions have changed over time, sometimes dividing us, sometimes uniting us, but always defining us.

To take just one example, the Declaration of Independence may tell us that "all men are created equal," but not until nearly a century later did Lincoln decide that these five words constitute the "proposition" to which America is "dedicated." And much of American public life from Lincoln on is devoted to figuring out just how far this promise of equality should extend. At the ratification of the Constitution, the vote was restricted in most states to white men with property. Since that time, suffrage has been extended to black men and to women, and, via the Twenty-Sixth Amendment, to U.S. citizens eighteen years of age and older. But suffrage does not equality make. Neither does the vote put an end to America's contentious conversation about equality. Most Americans have now accepted the proposition that "all men" extends to women and to people of all races. But does it extend to gays and lesbians? Or to the unborn?

So why this book? And why now?

American politics is broken. As the culture wars drag on and on, Americans have forgotten how to talk with one another. Our national conversation about our common life has devolved into a shouting match, with our various technologies—radio, television, and the Internet—only turning up the volume (and the heat). The Jewish tradition draws a sharp distinction between arguing for the sake of arguing (which it does not value) and "arguing for the sake of God" (which it does). Here in the United States we used to argue on behalf of the nation. Today we argue for the sake of our parties.

The first objective of *The American Bible* is to commend to readers a better way. In 2004, one hundred fifty years after the publication of Thoreau's *Walden* (another personal favorite that did *not* make the cut here), John Updike wrote: "*Walden* has become such a totem of the back-to-nature, preservationist, anti-business, civil-disobedience mind-set, and Thoreau so vivid a protester, so perfect a crank and hermit saint, that the book risks being as revered and unread as the Bible."[10] Many of the books in *The American Bible* are more revered than read. In fact, many survive almost entirely through commentaries upon them. So I hope that this book will inspire readers to go back to these sources themselves—to tune out for a moment what party leaders are telling them and to tune in to what prior Americans have said about their nation and its people. Why allow John Boehner or Nancy Pelosi to dominate your book group when Jefferson, Lincoln, and King are in the room? Whether approaching these classics for the first time or rediscovering them anew, readers will be able to clarify for themselves where they stand on issues of their day. In the process, they will be empowered to judge for themselves whether elected officials who are using Lincoln or King to support their economic or social policies know what they are talking about. Is Sarah Palin reading King's "Letter from Birmingham Jail" correctly? Does Rush Limbaugh really understand "I Have a Dream"? And what of President Obama's public statements on President Kennedy? Along the way, there should be ample surprises, as readers discover not only that their political heroes affirmed ideas they find abhorrent but also that some of their most cherished ideas originated with the leaders of another party.

Another aim of this book is to demonstrate how the course of American political, religious, moral, and cultural life can be read "rabbinically," as it were— as a series of extended commentaries on these core expressions. This is obvious in the constitutional tradition, where the Constitution gives us *Dred Scott v. Sandford,* which gives us the Fourteenth Amendment, which gives us *Brown v. Board of Education,* which provokes King's "Letter from Birmingham Jail." But it is no less true with John Winthrop's "A Model of Christian Charity," which gave Reagan his signature image of the United States as a "shining city on a hill," or with Irving Berlin's "God Bless America," which put those three words at the end of virtually every important presidential speech over the last quarter century. So I hope this book prompts American citizens to engage with not only their Constitution but also Frederick Douglass's scathing indictment of the same in his bitter yet brilliant speech "What to the Slave Is the Fourth of July?" (a classic that appears here, alas, only as a commentary).

This book also aims to provide some hope. Albert Camus once said, "He who holds hope for the human condition is a fool," proving beyond a doubt that he was French and not American. Far closer to the spirit of America are these lines by Emily Dickinson:

> *Hope is the thing with feathers*
> *That perches in the soul.*
> *And sings the tune*
> *Without the words,*
> *And never stops at all.*

It must be noted, however, that it is difficult to enter into the rough and tumble of contemporary American politics and exit with one's hope (or one's dignity) intact. Congress is obviously dysfunctional. Leaders of both parties engage all too often not in the subtle art of compromise but in the blood sport of the vendetta. They act like the Jets and the Sharks in *West Side Story*. They call each other Nazis. They accuse each other of betraying God and country. But the ills of our chosen representatives are symptomatic of our own. Forgetting the important distinction Thomas Jefferson once made between differences of opinion and differences of principle, we too characterize our political opponents as mortal enemies—socialists or Satanists at war with all that is good and godly. So incivility is our problem as well. But what ails us is not just a matter of the words we choose or the tone we adopt. There is also the matter of our collective amnesia. The chain of memory linking us to the great voices of our collective past—from Washington and Jefferson to FDR and MLK—has been broken. So when we think of political debate we do not think of Lincoln and Douglass. We think of Bill Maher and Rush Limbaugh.

Faced with these facts, it is easy to despair, and more than understandable to tune out. Many Americans are doing just that. In 2010, only 60 percent of American adults identified with either the Democratic Party (31 percent) or the Republican Party (29 percent)—the lowest aggregate figure since Gallup began following party identification in 1988.[11] In 2011, over two-thirds of Americans disapproved of the way Republicans in Congress were doing their jobs, and nearly two-thirds disapproved of congressional Democrats.[12] When asked about Congress overall, only 9 percent of Americans expressed their approval.[13]

Before we abandon all hope, however, some historical perspective may be in order. First, things have been worse. Fear and hatred ran deeper and the rhetoric was more venomous in the election of 1800 than in the debt-limit games of chicken in recent years. When partisans of Vice President Thomas Jefferson went after partisans of President John Adams in 1800, the gloves didn't just come off; they went out the window, and with them any sense of civility or propriety. Each party was convinced that a victory by the other would be the end of the world as we know it. So accusations that President Obama is a socialist or a secret Muslim are par for the course.

Second, there *is* a strong tradition of bipartisanship in American political life. The drumbeat of partisan discord has always been accompanied by a counterpoint of civility—from George Washington's stern warnings against putting the special interests of party over the common good of the nation, to President Kennedy's insistence that "civility is not a sign of weakness," to the critiques of "polarizing hate" by comedians Jon Stewart and Stephen Colbert at their 2010 "Rally to Restore Sanity and/or Fear."[14] More than anyone else in recent memory, Ronald Reagan is associated with the rise of the culture wars. But Reagan was a gracious man. Though he disagreed deeply with Democrats on foreign and domestic policy, he spoke respectfully of Jimmy Carter and kindly of President Kennedy, and on numerous occasions he expressed a deep admiration for President Roosevelt.

Unfortunately, we have largely forgotten this great tradition of conciliation, and the examples of statesmen from Washington to Reagan, who, for all of their faults, argued not to aggrandize themselves but to advance the common good. To read the proverbs and prophets of the American Bible, and the many commentaries upon them, is to reacquaint ourselves with the voices that have united us in the past and could do so again. It is to remember not just what Thoreau and Stowe and Eisenhower had to say about liberty and equality and race and nation. It is to recover how they said it. It is to reconnect ourselves with the spirit of the Talmud in American culture—a recognition that difference is endemic to social life, and that the ritual of expressing our differences may do more than we imagine to sustain community.

Third, hope can be found in the fact that neither the policies nor the principles of today's two major parties are eternal. Parties come and go, as do the positions they seem eager at any moment to defend to the death. One of the largest tax cuts in American history—a reduction in the top marginal tax rate from 91 to 70 percent—was pushed through by Democratic presidents (Kennedy and Johnson) and vigorously opposed by Republicans as fiscally irresponsible. In a 1979 op-ed, historian Henry Commager wrote about how Democrats and Republicans during Woodrow Wilson's presidency had "wrestled themselves into each other's clothes."[15] Today, Democratic and Republican leaders do the same, often unwittingly. The most controversial part of the controversial legislation now derided by Republicans as "Obamacare"—the mandate that individuals buy health insurance—was originally proposed by Republican economists, championed by the conservative Heritage Foundation, introduced in Congress by Republican politicians, and enacted in Massachusetts under Republican governor Mitt Romney.[16] Planned Parenthood, now anathema to Republicans because of its pro-choice policies, enjoyed the support of two of the biggest dynasties of Republican politics, the Goldwater and Bush families, until the rise of the Religious Right in the 1980s made the pro-life position a litmus test for the GOP. And Republican platforms from 1940 to 1976 endorsed the Equal Rights Amendment for women.

But Republicans are not the only American politicians to change their spots. Democrats have also shifted dramatically on matters they once held as unyielding principles. Rather than insisting, as Jefferson did, on a "wall of separation between church and state," Democrats over the last decade have become a religious party too, invoking Jesus at the annual National Prayer Breakfast and echoing Republicans in justifying their public policies on biblical grounds.

The point of this reminder is *not* to denounce Republicans or Democrats as "flip-floppers," but to point out that this sort of shape-shifting is nothing new. In fact, it is the American way. Things change, and the parties change with them. Therefore, it is reasonable to believe that what seems today like an eternal and unbridgeable divide is neither of those things.

So, yes, there is reason for hope. However, any honest living history of the American people must admit that a dialectic of hope and disappointment has characterized American life from before the founding. To read *The American Bible* is not just to be inspired by dreams; it is to be confronted with the realities that so often dash them. It is also to express some hope of your own—to allow yourself to imagine that these words matter, that your words matter, and that change *is* possible.

Barack Obama became America's first black president thanks in large measure to what he termed the "audacity of hope." But this audacious hope turned to disappointment when the dreams the nation held for his presidency did not come true. This quintessentially American dialectic of dreams proclaimed and dreams deferred helps to explain why U.S. citizens are so eager *both* to deify their political leaders *and* to cut them down to size. It sheds light on why American voters gravitate toward both dreamers and fearmongers—those who give voice to what Lincoln called the "better angels of our nature" and those who pander to our basest impulses (and, sometimes, to voices in between).[17]

In his play *The Trial of God* (1979), my Boston University colleague Elie Wiesel tells a story of three rabbis who indict God for cruelty for allowing the anti-Semitic pogroms that beset eastern Europe in the seventeenth century. In testimony that goes on for days, some argue for God. Many more argue against Him, dismissing as offensive and obscene simplistic justifications of God's goodness in the face of evil. In the end, God is found guilty, but after the verdict is delivered the rabbis join together in prayer.

Something of this spirit pervades American history. Here to criticize your country is not to opt out of the American experiment; it is to opt in. Americans look at historical circumstances and find it impossible to reconcile the ugliness of those realities with our lofty ideals. So we put America on trial and find it guilty. Sometimes we are tempted to put one another on trial too, contending that Catholics or Muslims are not true Americans, that the Chinese should go home, or that blacks should go back to Africa. In the end, however, we find that *we* are debating these things, and that *we* are working in the process for a less imperfect union.

Another goal of this book is to reinvigorate this work—by reminding Americans that they share a heritage of voices as deep and high and different as the Mormon Tabernacle Choir and the Boys Choir of Harlem. It is easy today to demonize our political enemies as enemies of the state—people who are forever subverting the national interest to the interests of their particular class, race, or party. These people do exist, of course. But many of our differences today are differences of interpretation. Americans on opposing sides of the aisle are reading the Constitution or the Declaration or Lincoln or King differently. The way forward, in my view, is not to anathematize as un-American those who have different interpretations, but to return together to the sources of our national life, and to do so with the recognition that Americans have never been united in our views about key issues or in our interpretations of our saints and scriptures. What has united us in the past and could bring us together again today is a chorus of voices telling us where we have been, who we are, and where we are going.

In 1915, philosopher Horace Kallen famously described the United States as a "symphony of civilization."[18] That is not quite right, unless the symphony we are discussing is made up of students from the local middle school. America's voices do not always harmonize. In fact, they are often discordant. But American life *is* a performance of sorts, with all manner of players taking the stage. To open up *The American Bible* is to sit down with an amazing cast of characters: resolute Washington, brilliant Jefferson, melancholic Lincoln, committed Stowe, satirical Twain, prophetic King. But surrounding these authors of our gospels and epistles is an even more diverse group responsible for our commentaries on the same: liberals and radicals, libertarians and conservatives, Jews and Christians, novelists and poets, women and men, blacks and Latinos, atheists and Muslims, authors and architects, representatives and voters, presidents and justices, the iconic and the unknown. And don't forget the rest of us. At the symphony we are told to sit quiet and listen, suppressing even our coughs. But here the tradition is call and response. Here we are invited to join in the conversation. This book is dedicated to the proposition that this conversation is worth having, and that the authors of these biblical books wouldn't have it any other way.

GENESIS

The Exodus Story

THE IDEA OF freedom was bequeathed to Americans by Enlightenment figures such as John Locke and Thomas Paine, who spoke of liberty as a natural right, but this idea derived more fundamentally from Christianity, which got it from Judaism, which safeguarded it in the biblical story of the Exodus. Whatever measure of freedom Americans enjoy today comes not only from the philosophical arguments of Enlightenment tracts but also from the story of a chosen people freed from bondage by the power of God. Americans have always turned to Bible stories to understand themselves and their history, and no biblical narrative has been more important in U.S. history than the Exodus. In fact, the Exodus story may be *the* American story—the narrative Americans tell themselves to make sense of their history, identity, and destiny.

This liberation tale appears chiefly in the book of Exodus, but elements are scattered throughout Numbers, Deuteronomy, and other biblical books. Jews retell the Exodus story every year at Passover, in accordance with the biblical commandment that defines remembrance as a religious obligation: "Remember this day, in which ye came out from Egypt, out of the house of bondage; for by strength of hand the Lord brought you out from this place" (Exodus 13:3).

Americans too have told and retold this story, applying its elements—escape from bondage under a cruel pharaoh, plagues on Egypt, the parting of the Red Sea, wandering in the wilderness, the covenant with God, the giving of the Law on Mount Sinai, the promise of Zion, and the idea of a chosen people—to their own circumstances. From Puritans, to founders, to slaves, to Lincoln, to "Exodusters" fleeing the South after the Reconstruction, to Martin Luther King Jr., to Malcolm X, to feminist theologians, to gay activists, Americans have made this story their own, writing themselves into its dramas and rewriting it on the American landscape. American place-names from New Canaan, Connecticut, to Zion, Illinois, literally give voice to this tendency. So do the proposals of Thomas Jefferson and Ben Franklin to depict on the great seal of the United States the children of Israel in the wilderness being led by a cloud by day and a pillar of fire by night. More recently, President Obama has been celebrated as an African-American Joshua, completing the freedom march of his people begun by civil rights pioneers.

The Exodus story is a story of movement—from Egypt to Canaan, from slavery to freedom—and the prime mover is God. This story begins with the Israelites in bondage in Egypt under the iron fist of Pharaoh. God sends Moses to liberate his chosen people. "Let my people go," Moses demands. But Pharaoh is hard of heart. So God visits ten plagues upon Egypt, not least the killing of the firstborn, commemorated today on the Jewish Passover. Finally, Pharaoh agrees to let the Israelites go, but as they flee he changes his mind, ordering his army to pursue them. At the Red Sea it seems the Israelites will be trapped and slaughtered. But Moses strikes the waters with his staff, and God parts the Red Sea just long enough for his people to cross over. When the waters return, Pharaoh's army drowns. For the next forty years, Moses and the Israelites wander in the wilderness, hoping for the Zion promised earlier by God to Abraham and his descendants. At Mount Sinai, God announces through Moses that the Israelites are his chosen people. He gives them the Ten Commandments and promises to bless them if they follow his commandments and curse them if they do not. Moses dies just before the Israelites get to the promised land, so it is Joshua who leads them into Canaan.

This is a rich narrative, and from colonial times Americans have read it typologically, bringing its plot twists to bear on their times and places. As a country, we have had our Egypt (England) and our Zion (the New World). We have put ourselves up for adoption as God's chosen people and rechristened our nation "God's New Israel," with its own special covenant to follow and destiny to fulfill. We have likened our Constitution to the law given at Sinai and seen George Washington as our own Moses. And of course we have our own sordid tale of slavery to tell, not to mention our own vexed narrative about freedom lost and found, promised and deferred, offered to some and denied to others.

The land promised by God in the Bible is of course a place of prosperity and plenty. But this promised land was not uninhabited when the Israelites arrived. In fact, part of the glory of this land was that it contained wells that had already been dug, fields that had already been plowed, and vineyards that had already been planted. And the people of Israel were told to avail themselves of these blessings. So the Exodus story is also a story of conquest, of peoples driven out by God's people. This part of the story played a major role in justifying both America's westward march under the banner of Manifest Destiny and the toll it took in human lives.

Alternative readings of this Exodus narrative—by African Americans, Mormons, and feminists, among others—undercut all pretenses to a national consensus about how it should be understood, even as they demonstrate the enduring power of the Exodus story in American life. Consider the figure of Moses. "Our true founding father," in the words of Bruce Feiler, Moses has been celebrated in American films such as *The Ten Commandments* and *The Prince of Egypt,* in Zora Neale Hurston's novel *Moses, Man of the Mountain,* and James Weldon Johnson's poem "Let My People Go."[1] But who gets to wear his mantle in U.S. history? Is George Washington America's Moses? Is Abraham Lincoln? Brigham Young? Or does this title belong to the Underground Railroad conductor Harriet Tubman, whom one biographer lauded as "the Moses of her people," or to Martin Luther King Jr., who seemed to claim the title for himself when, in his last speech, he proclaimed, "I've been to the mountaintop!"[2]

The identities of Egypt, Pharaoh, and the promised land have also shifted dramatically over time. For New England colonists and Revolutionary War patriots, Egypt was the Old World and Pharaoh was the king of England. Mormons saw the eastern United States, where their founder, Joseph Smith Jr., was killed by a mob in Carthage, Illinois, as Egypt and the West, where they would establish their headquarters in Salt Lake City, as Zion. African-American slaves saw the South as Egypt and looked for deliverance to a promised land in the North or Canada. Southern slaveholders saw the Confederate states as tribes of Israel escaping from a pharaoh—the federal government—hostile to their way of life and their rights as free and independent states. Given this clash of interpretations, it should not be surprising that Lincoln, who famously referred to Americans as God's "almost chosen people," was seen during his lifetime as both Moses and Pharaoh.[3] In later years, black nationalists sought to escape to freedom in Africa—an organization founded in the 1870s to help freed slaves settle in Liberia called itself the "Liberian Exodus

Association"—while civil rights leaders envisioned a "promised land of racial justice" at home.[4] Meanwhile, feminist theologian Mary Daly led a celebrated "Exodus" of women out of Harvard's Memorial Church, and out of patriarchal Christianity, on November 14, 1971. No wonder historian Albert Raboteau has called the Exodus story "our nation's most powerful and long lasting myth."[5]

Of course, our reading of this myth has been selective. In the Bible, the covenant between God and His people is conditional. The theme of divine deliverance is paired with the theme of Israel's obligations; God's ringing demand to Pharaoh, "Let my people go," is followed by the qualifier, "that they may serve me." After deliverance from Egypt comes the delivery of the law on Mount Sinai and the fashioning of a conditional covenant, including the terms under which Israel would either enjoy God's favor or suffer the consequences of disobedience. Early American interpreters of the Exodus story often emphasized the duties of God's New Israel and the dangers of bringing on God's wrath. This tradition, clear in early books in the American Bible, including John Winthrop's "A Model of Christian Charity," has resurfaced in recent years with the theory of televangelists Jerry Falwell and Pat Robertson that Hurricane Katrina, for example, could be understood as God's righteous retribution on a nation that continues to kill the unborn. But most recent interpreters of the Exodus story have seen America's covenant with God as unconditional—a source of blessings and never of curses. The theme of Israel's obligations has receded even as the theme of God's gift of freedom has come to the fore—freedom from tyranny, from slavery, from oppression, and from want.

To attend to the enduring power of this freedom song among Americans is to realize that much of early American history was driven more by Jewish than by Christian themes. If a religious adjective must be affixed to "America" up to and including the Civil War, that adjective would be "Hebraic" rather than "Christian." Upon his assassination, Lincoln was widely hailed as a Moses figure who led his people to the cusp of freedom, yet never saw the promised land himself. But shortly thereafter, Lincoln, who was shot on Good Friday, was being hailed as an American Christ who gave his life for the sins of his country. Lincoln's assassination redirected the nation's gaze from the story of the Exodus to the story of the crucifixion, from the Old Testament to the New, from colonial Puritanism to nineteenth-century evangelicalism, from the struggle for collective freedom to the quest for individual salvation.

After Lincoln's assassination, Christian motifs of death and resurrection began to overpower Hebraic motifs of slavery and freedom. Now the human drama was occurring inside each of us, instead of out there in the world. To be sure, the civil rights movement drew more on Moses than Jesus. Nonetheless, the therapeutic drift of the Exodus narrative after the Civil War is unmistakable. In modern America, this narrative is internalized and personalized, transformed into a story about "me" rather than "us," even as it retains its key motifs of slavery and freedom. Today the popular meaning of Exodus is not that God has chosen *us* for a collective life in the promised land, but that God has chosen *me* for salvation or health or wealth (or all of the above). The Beat, hippie, and feminist movements can all be understood as Red Sea passages out of the bondage of 1950s mores of marriage and family. "Coming out of the closet" can also be read in Exodus terms. What kind of America is delivered by this internalization of Exodus? The therapeutic culture in which we now all live.

The Exodus Story ❧

Thou art the Lord the God, who didst choose Abram, and broughtest him forth out of Ur of the Chaldees, and gavest him the name of Abraham;

And foundest his heart faithful before thee, and madest a covenant with him to give the land of the Canaanites, the Hittites, the Amorites, and the Perizzites, and the Jebusites, and the Girgashites, to give it, I say, to his seed, and hast performed thy words; for thou art righteous:

And didst see the affliction of our fathers in Egypt, and heardest their cry by the Red sea;

And shewedst signs and wonders upon Pharaoh, and on all his servants, and on all the people of his land: for thou knewest that they dealt proudly against them. So didst thou get thee a name, as it is this day.

And thou didst divide the sea before them, so that they went through the midst of the sea on the dry land; and their persecutors thou threwest into the deeps, as a stone into the mighty waters.

Moreover thou leddest them in the day by a cloudy pillar; and in the night by a pillar of fire, to give them light in the way wherein they should go.

Thou camest down also upon mount Sinai, and spakest with them from heaven, and gavest them right judgments, and true laws, good statutes and commandments:

And madest known unto them thy holy sabbath, and commandedst them precepts, statutes, and laws, by the hand of Moses thy servant:

And gavest them bread from heaven for their hunger, and broughtest forth water for them out of the rock for their thirst, and promisedst them that they should go in to possess the land which thou hadst sworn to give them.

But they and our fathers dealt proudly, and hardened their necks, and hearkened not to thy commandments,

And refused to obey, neither were mindful of thy wonders that thou didst among them; but hardened their necks, and in their rebellion appointed a captain to return to their bondage: but thou art a God ready to pardon, gracious and merciful, slow to anger, and of great kindness, and forsookest them not.

Yea, when they had made them a molten calf, and said, This is thy God that brought thee up out of Egypt, and had wrought great provocations;

Yet thou in thy manifold mercies forsookest them not in the wilderness: the pillar of the cloud departed not from them by day, to lead them in the way; neither the pillar of fire by night, to shew them light, and the way wherein they should go.

Thou gavest also thy good spirit to instruct them, and withheldest not thy manna from their mouth, and gavest them water for their thirst.

Yea, forty years didst thou sustain them in the wilderness, so that they lacked nothing; their clothes waxed not old, and their feet swelled not.

Moreover thou gavest them kingdoms and nations, and didst divide them into corners: so they possessed the land of Sihon, and the land of the king of Heshbon, and the land of Og king of Bashan.

Their children also multipliedst thou as the stars of heaven, and broughtest them into the land, concerning which thou hadst promised to their fathers, that they should go in to possess it.

So the children went in and possessed the land, and thou subduedst before them the inhabitants of the land, the Canaanites, and gavest them into their hands, with their kings, and the people of the land, that they might do with them as they would.

And they took strong cities, and a fat land, and possessed houses full of all goods, wells digged, vineyards, and oliveyards, and fruit trees in abundance: so they did eat, and were filled, and became fat, and delighted themselves in thy great goodness.[6]

COMMENTARY

"Go Down, Moses," slave spiritual, imagining slaves as God's Israel and the American South as Egypt (undated)

> When Israel was in Egypt's land
> Let my people go
> Oppressed so hard they could not stand
> Let my people go
>
> Go down (go down)
> Moses (go down Moses)
> Way down in Egypt's land
> Tell old Pharaoh
> Let my people go!
>
> Thus saith the Lord, bold Moses said
> Let my people go
> If not, I'll smite your firstborn dead
> Let my people go
>
> No more shall they in bondage toil
> Let my people go
> Let them come out with Egypt's spoil
> Let my people go

Benjamin Franklin, statesman, printer, and inventor, describing his proposed seal for the United States (1776)

> Moses standing on the Shore, and extending his Hand over the Sea, thereby causing the same to overwhelm Pharaoh who is sitting in an open Chariot, a Crown on his Head and a Sword in his Hand. Rays from the Pillar of Fire in the Clouds reaching to Moses, to express that he acts by Command of the Deity. Motto, "Rebellion to Tyrants is Obedience to God."
>
> —Benjamin Franklin, undated note, Thomas Jefferson papers, Manuscript Division, Library of Congress, quoted in Richard S. Patterson and Richard Dougall, *The Eagle and the Shield: A History of the Great Seal of the United States* (Washington, DC: U.S. Government Printing Office, 1976), p. 14.

Nicholas Street, Congregationalist minister, on Americans as a New Israel wandering in the wilderness during the Revolutionary War (1777)

> We in this land are, as it were, led out of Egypt by the hand of Moses. And now we are in the wilderness, i.e. in a state of trouble and difficulty, Egyptians pursuing us,

to overtake and reduce us. There is the Red Sea before us, I speak metaphorically, a sea of blood in your prospect before you, perhaps. And when you apprehend this in your imaginations, are you not ready to murmur against Moses and Aaron that led you out of Egypt, and to say with the people of Israel, "It had been better for us to serve the Egyptians, than that we should die in the wilderness" (Exod. 14.12). . . .

Our ill successes are owing to the sins of the people, as was the case of the people of Israel in the wilderness. We find them ten times as ready to find fault with their leaders, and to ascribe their misfortunes to them, as to recoil in upon themselves and to say, What have we done? Tho' it was owing entirely to them that they were not delivered. And thus we in this land are murmuring and complaining of our difficulties and ill successes at times, thinking our leaders to blame, and the like, not considering at the same time that we are practicing those vices that have a natural tendency to destroy us, besides the just judgments of Heaven which they tend to draw down upon us as a people. . . .

And when we are favoured with a little success, we are apt to be elated in our minds like the children of Israel after the overthrow of the Egyptians in the red sea. . . . But let the scale turn a little against us, our confidence begins to fail, and we grow distrustful of God and his providence, and begin to murmur and repine. . . .

We are apt to think that our cause is so righteous with regard to Great-Britain, that I fear we are ready to forget our unrighteousness towards God. . . . Let us look upon the ground on which we stand, consider our guilt and danger, and be humble for our sins, and under all the tokens of God's displeasure against us on account of our sins, repent and reform whatever is amiss in the midst of us, that we may be prepared for a deliverance out of our troubles; that being delivered out of the hands of our enemies, we may serve God without fear in righteousness and true holiness all the days of our lives.

—Nicholas Street, *The American States Acting Over the Part of the Children of Israel in the Wilderness* (1777), in Conrad Cherry, ed., *God's New Israel: Religious Interpretations of American Destiny* (Durham: Univ. of North Carolina Press, 1998), pp. 69, 75, 78.

Frederick Butler, historian, calling U.S. history an Exodus event (1820)

As the return of the family of Abraham to the land of their fathers, from the bondage of Egypt, forms one of the most interesting and important events of antiquity; so, in the same point of view, the emigrations of the first settlers of the United States, from the land of their fathers, to plant the Church in the wilds of America, forms one of the most interesting and important events among the moderns. The first, to open the way for the knowledge of the true God, as displayed in the formation, and government of the Jewish Church; and to prepare the way for the first advent of Jesus Christ. The second to open the way for the true knowledge of Jesus Christ, as displayed in the Gospel, by planting a pure Church, which might prepare the way for his second advent.

Had Moses attempted to detail the occurrences, and events of the Jewish Church, minutely, in their journeyings in the wilderness, or in their possessing the promised land, it would have destroyed the beauty of one of the most interesting, and important narratives that has ever appeared. Should I attempt to detail, minutely, the occurrences and events, that awaited the Pilgrims of America, in possessing this modern Canaan, it would mar the beauty of one of the most interesting and important subjects in modern story. The wisdom of the Divine plan in selecting his church from the persecutions of modern Egypt, together with the most prominent characters, and events, that became the immediate instruments of his purpose, shall be my only guide in this Narrative.

—Frederick Butler, *A Complete History of the United States of America, Embracing the Whole Period from the Discovery of North America, Down to the Year 1820* (Hartford, CT: Roberts and Burr, 1821), 1:9–10.

Henry Highland Garnet, clergyman, abolitionist, and former slave, urging slaves to confront their masters and their fears in order to fight for freedom (1843)

Brethren, the time has come when you must act for yourselves. . . . Tell [your masters] in language which they cannot misunderstand, of the exceeding sinfulness of slavery, and of a future judgment, and of the righteous retributions of an indignant God. Inform them that all you desire is FREEDOM, and that nothing else will suffice. . . . However much you and all of us may desire it, there is not much hope of redemption without the shedding of blood. If you must bleed, let it all come at once, rather *die freemen, than live to be slaves*. It is impossible like the children of Israel, to make a grand exodus from the land of bondage. The Pharaohs are on both sides of the blood-red waters! You cannot move en masse, to the dominions of the British Queen—nor can you pass through Florida and overrun Texas, and at last find peace in Mexico. . . .

You act as though, you were made for the special use of these devils. You act as though your daughters were born to pamper the lusts of your masters and overseers. And worse than all, you tamely submit while your lords tear your wives from your embraces and defile them before your eyes. In the name of God, we ask you, are you men? Where is the blood of your fathers? Has it all run out of your veins? Awake, awake; millions of voices are calling you! Your dead fathers speak to you from their graves. Heaven, as with a voice of thunder, calls on you to arise from the dust.

Let your motto be resistance! *resistance!* RESISTANCE!

—Henry Highland Garnet, "An Address to the Slaves of the United States of America," National Negro Convention, Buffalo, New York, August 16, 1843, in his *A Memorial Discourse* (Philadelphia: Wilson, 1865), pp. 44–45.

Maria Stewart, antislavery lecturer, prophesying the coming of ten plagues on America's "mighty men" (1831)

Oh, America, America, foul and indelible is thy stain! Dark and dismal is the cloud that hangs over thee for thy cruel wrongs and injuries to the fallen sons of Africa. The blood of her murdered ones cries to heaven for vengeance against thee. Thou art almost become drunken with the blood of her slain. . . .

O, ye great and mighty men of America, ye rich and powerful ones, many of you will call for the rocks and mountains to fall upon you, and to hide you from the wrath of the lamb, and from him that sitteth upon the throne; whilst many of the sable-skinned Africans you now despise, will shine in the kingdom of heaven as the stars forever and ever. Charity begins at home, and those that provide not for their own, are worse than infidels. . . . You may kill, tyrannize, and oppress as much as you choose, until our cry shall come up before the throne of God; for I am firmly persuaded that he will not suffer you to quell the proud, fearless and undaunted spirits of the Africans forever; for in his own time, he is able to plead our cause against you, and to pour out upon you the ten plagues of Egypt.

—Maria W. Stewart, *Meditations from the Pen of Mrs. Maria W. Stewart* (1831; Washington, DC: Enterprise, 1879), pp. 2–3.

Benjamin Palmer, Presbyterian pastor from New Orleans, making a Confederate covenant with the God of Israel (1861)

This day is one of surpassing solemnity. In the gravest period of our history, amidst the perils, which attend the dismemberment of a great nation and the reconstruction of a new government, we are confronted with another more instant and appalling. Our late Confederates, denying us the right of self-government, have appealed to the sword and threaten to extinguish this right in our blood. Eleven tribes sought to go forth in peace from the house of political bondage: but the heart of our modern Pharaoh is hardened, that he will not let Israel go. In their distress, with the untried sea before and the chariots of Egypt behind, ten millions of people stretch forth their hands before Jehovah's throne, imploring him to "stir up his strength before Ephraim and Benjamin and Manasseh, and come and save them." It was a memorable day when the Hebrew tribes, having crossed the Jordan, stood, the one half of them upon Mount Ebal and the other half upon Mount Gerizim, and pronounced the solemn Amen to the curses and blessings of the divine law as proclaimed by the Levites. Not less grand and awful is this scene today, when an infant nation strikes its covenant with the God of Heaven. . . .

Confessing the sins of our fathers with our own, and imploring the divine guidance through all our fortunes, the people of these Confederate States proclaim this day, "the Lord our God will we serve, and his voice will we obey." It is this sacramental feature of our worship, which lends to it such dreadful solemnity. At the moment when we are crystallizing into a nation, at the very opening of our separate career, we bend the knee together before God—appealing to his justice in the adjudication of our cause, and submitting our destiny to his supreme arbitration. The bonds of this covenant, which we seal this day to the Lord, are entered upon the register in which the Recording Angel writes up the deeds of time, before the Eternal throne.

—Benjamin M. Palmer, *National Responsibility Before God: A Discourse Delivered on the Day of Fasting, Humiliation and Prayer* (New Orleans: Price-Current Steam Book and Job Printing Office, 1861), www.confederatelegion.com/National%20Responsibility.rtf.

Edward Tullidge, writer and editor, likening Mormon leaders to Muhammad and Moses (1876)

At distant periods, as the centuries roll, Providence raises up a rare class of men to found empires and open new dispensations, thereby giving fresh life to the body of society and new forms to its institutions. Most fitly are they called men of destiny. None of the world's great characters stand out bolder in this type than do Joseph Smith and Brigham Young. They show a striking resemblance to Moses and Mohammed, two of the greatest religious empire-founders the world has yet seen. Indeed, in his lifetime the Mormon prophet was styled the Mohammed of the West; and scarcely had Brigham Young succeeded him in the leadership of the Mormon people, ever he was classed with the immortal law-giver of Israel. . . .

The period of his life that seems the most proper in which to introduce Brigham Young in action to the reader, is when he succeeded the Mormon prophet and led his people in the famous exodus from Nauvoo. Here we have him at once in the character of the modern Moses. It is no fanciful conceit of the author to thus style him to-day, after he and his people have built up a State fabric, with three hundred cities and settlements, networked with railroads and the electric telegraph; for at that very period his name rang throughout America, and reverberated in Europe, as the Moses of the "latter days," and the Mormons were likened to the children of Israel in the wilderness.

—Edward W. Tullidge, *Life of Brigham Young; or, Utah and Her Founders* (New York: n.p., 1876), pp. 1, 6.

W. E. B. Du Bois, scholar and civil rights activist, on education as the new path to the promised land (1903)

Few men ever worshipped Freedom with half such unquestioning faith as did the American Negro for two centuries. To him, so far as he thought and dreamed, slavery was the sum of all villainies, the cause of all sorrow, the root of all prejudice; Emancipation was the key to a promised land of sweeter beauty than ever stretched before the eyes of wearied Israelites. In song and exhortation swelled one refrain—Liberty; in his tears and curses the God he implored had Freedom in his right hand. At last it came,—suddenly, fearfully, like a dream. With one wild carnival of blood and passion came the message in his own plaintive cadences:—

> *"Shout, O children!*
> *Shout, you're free!*
> *For God has bought your liberty!"*

Years have passed away since then . . . [yet] the Nation has not yet found peace from its sins; the freedman has not yet found in freedom his promised land. . . .

The first decade was merely a prolongation of the vain search for freedom, the boon that seemed ever barely to elude their grasp,—like a tantalizing will-o'-the-wisp, maddening and misleading the headless host. The holocaust of war, the terrors of the Ku Klux Klan, the lies of the carpet-baggers, the disorganization of industry, and the contradictory advice of friends and foes, left the bewildered serf with no new watchword beyond the old cry for freedom. As the time flew, however, he began to grasp a new idea. The ideal of liberty demanded for its attainment powerful means, and these the Fifteenth Amendment gave him. The ballot, which before he had looked upon as a visible sign of freedom, he now regarded as the chief means of gaining and perfecting the liberty with which the war had partially endowed him. . . . Slowly but steadily, in the following years, a new vision began gradually to replace the dream of political power,—a powerful movement, the rise of another ideal to guide the unguided, another pillar of fire by night after a clouded day. It was the ideal of "book-learning"; the curiosity, born of compulsory ignorance, to know and test the power of the cabalistic letters of the white man, the longing to know. Here at last seemed to have been discovered the mountain path to Canaan; longer than the highway of Emancipation and law, steep and rugged, but straight, leading to heights high enough to overlook life.

It was weary work. . . . To the tired climbers, the horizon was ever dark, the nights were often cold, the Canaan was always dim and far away. If, however, the vistas disclosed as yet no goal, no resting-place, little but flattery and criticism, the journey at least gave leisure for reflection and self-examination; it changed the child of Emancipation to the youth with dawning self-consciousness, self-realization, self-respect. In those sombre forests of his striving his own soul rose before him, and he saw himself,—darkly as through a veil; and yet he saw in himself some faint revelation of his power, of his mission. He began to have a dim feeling that, to attain his place in the world, he must be himself, and not another.

—W. E. B. Du Bois, *The Souls of Black Folk: Essays and Sketches*, 3rd ed. (Chicago: McClurg, 1903), pp. 5–8.

Cecil B. DeMille, Hollywood film producer, speaking against Communism (1956)

The theme of [*The Ten Commandments*] is whether men ought to be ruled by God's laws or whether they are to be ruled by the whims of a dictator. . . . Are men the property of the state or are they free souls under God? This same battle continues throughout the world today.

—Cecil B. DeMille, prologue, *The Ten Commandments* (1956).

Martin Luther King Jr., Baptist pastor and civil rights leader, likening himself to Moses in his last speech (1968)

Well, I don't know what will happen now; we've got some difficult days ahead. But it really doesn't matter with me now, because I've been to the mountaintop. And I don't mind. Like anybody, I would like to live a long life—longevity has its place. But I'm not concerned about that now. I just want to do God's will. And He's allowed me to go up to the mountain. And I've looked over, and I've seen the Promised Land. I may not get there with you. But I want you to know tonight that we, as a people, will get to the Promised Land. And so I'm happy tonight; I'm not worried about anything; I'm not fearing any man. Mine eyes have seen the glory of the coming of the Lord.

—Martin Luther King Jr., "I've Been to the Mountaintop," Memphis, Tennessee, April 3, 1968, http://mlk-kpp01.stanford.edu/index.php/encyclopedia/documentsentry/ive_been_to_the_mountaintop/.

Albert Cleage, African-American theologian, on blacks as God's chosen people (1968)

We have got to find dignity somewhere because we will never be a Nation until we can first build a sense of dignity. . . . The children of Israel remembered this one thing, and struggled to keep their dignity. They remembered that God had chosen Israel.

Don't laugh at that because *we* are God's chosen people. You don't fully recognize yet what that means. When we talk about the Black Nation, we have got to remember that the Black Nation, Israel, was chosen by God. Out of the whole world God chose Israel to covenant with, to say, "You will be my people and I will be your God." What else does a man need for dignity? He didn't go to the big nations with their big armies. He went to this little nation and said, "You are my chosen people." Perhaps if we could just remember that we are God's chosen people, that we have a covenant with God, then we would know that God will not forsake us. Even in the midst of violence and oppression, we would know that we are God's chosen people. We could look the white man straight in the eye and say, "There is nothing you can do to destroy us, and you cannot take from us our dignity."

—Albert J. Cleage, *The Black Messiah* (New York: Sheed and Ward, 1968), pp. 53–54.

Mary Daly, feminist theologian, calling for an "Exodus" from Harvard's Memorial Church in the first sermon given there by a woman (1971)

We cannot really belong to institutional religion as it exists. It isn't good enough to be token preachers. . . . Singing sexist hymns, praying to a male God breaks our spirit, makes us less than human. The crushing weight of this tradition, of this power structure, tells us that *we do not even exist.*

The women's movement is an exodus community. Its basis is not merely in the promise given to our fathers thousands of years ago. Rather, its source is in the unfulfilled promise of our mothers' lives, whose history was never recorded. Its source is in the promise of our sisters, whose voices have been robbed from them, and in our own promise, our latent creativity. We can affirm *now* our promise and our exodus as we walk into a future that will be our *own* future.

Sisters—and brothers, if there are any here: Our time has come. We will take our own place in the sun. We will leave behind the centuries of silence and darkness. Let us affirm our faith in ourselves and our will to transcendence by rising and walking out together.

—Mary Daly, "Exodus Sermon," Harvard Memorial Church, November 14, 1971, in her "The Women's Movement: An Exodus Community," *Religious Education* 67.5 (September/October 1972): 332–33.

Robert Allen Warrior, English professor and Osage tribe member, applying lessons from the Exodus to the experiences of Native Americans (1989)

As a member of the Osage Nation of American Indians who stands in solidarity with other tribal people around the world, I read the Exodus stories with Canaanite eyes. . . . Israel's reward for keeping Yahweh's commandments—for building a society where the evils done to them have no place—is the continuation of life in the land. But one of the most important of Yahweh's commands is the prohibition on social relations with the Canaanites or participation in their religion. . . . In fact, the indigenes are to be destroyed. . . .

We need to be more aware of the way ideas such as those in the conquest narratives have made their way into Americans' consciousness and ideology. And only when we understand this process can those of us who have suffered from it know how to fight back. Many Puritan preachers were fond of referring to Native

Americans as Amelkites and Canaanites—in other words, people who, if they would not be converted, were worthy of annihilation. By examining such instances in theological and political writings, in sermons, and elsewhere, we can understand how America's self-image as a "chosen people" has provided a rhetoric to mystify domination.

—Robert Allen Warrior, "Canaanites, Cowboys, and Indians," *Christianity and Crisis* 49 (1989), reprinted in James Treat, ed., *Native and Christian: Indigenous Voices on Religious Identity in the United States and Canada* (New York: Routledge, 1996), pp. 93–100.

Albert Raboteau, historian, on Winthrop and King, Israel and Egypt (1994)

A period of over three hundred years stretches between John Winthrop's vision of an American Promised Land and that of Martin Luther King, Jr. The people whom Winthrop addressed long ago took possession of their Promised Land; the people whom King addressed still wait to enter theirs. For three centuries, white and black Americans have dwelt in the same land. For at least two of those centuries, they have shared the same religion. And yet, during all those years, their national and religious identities have been radically opposed. It need not have been so. After all, Winthrop's version of Exodus and King's were not so far apart. Both men understood that charity is the charter that gives title to the Promised Land. Both taught that mercy, gentleness, and justice are the terms for occupancy. Both believed that the conditions of the contract had been set by God, not by man. At times in our history, the two visions have nearly coincided, as they did in the antislavery stance of the early evangelicals, or in the abolitionist movement, or in Lincoln's profound realization that Americans were "an almost chosen people," or in the civil rights movement of our own era. Yet, despite these moments of coherence, the meaning of the Exodus story for America has remained fundamentally ambiguous. Is America Israel, or is she Egypt?

—Albert Raboteau, "African-Americans, Exodus, and the American Israel," in Paul E. Johnson, ed., *African-American Christianity: Essays in History* (Berkeley: Univ. of California Press, 1994), p. 15.

Michael Eric Dyson, Baptist minister and academic, urging President Obama to stop ignoring African Americans, and African Americans to stop confusing Obama with Moses (2010)

Black People think that Obama is Martin Luther King Jr. Excuse me. Martin Luther King Jr. shed blood in Memphis. From that blood and the soil in which that blood was mixed sprouted every ability of black people in a post-King era to survive. . . . It was forty years from King's assassination to Obama's inauguration, so don't tell me you stencil his face next to King's and they're the same. You think Obama is Moses. He is not Moses. He is Pharaoh. . . . One man is a prophet.

Another man is a politician. It is time to say to Pharaoh . . . let our resources go, let that money go, let that love flow. I know white folk don't want you to love us. But you came from us. Before they knew you, we loved you. We birthed you. We gave you acceptance. You were biracial but black folk made you a black man in America. Now represent us. Don't dog us when we need you. We love you. We just want some love back.

—Michael Eric Dyson, "Tavis Smiley Black Agenda Forum," Chicago State University, March 20, 2010, www.c-spanvideo.org/program/292635–7.

"A Model of Christian Charity"

❧ JOHN WINTHROP, 1630 ❧

*T*HE RHETORICAL centerpiece of Ronald Reagan's presidency was his image of America as a "shining city on a hill"—an example for all the world to see and emulate. Reagan borrowed this image from John Winthrop (1588–1649), the founding governor of the Massachusetts Bay Colony, who spoke of that colony as a "city upon a hill" in his 1630 sermon "A Model of Christian Charity." Winthrop himself was borrowing from the Sermon on the Mount, where Jesus says, "You are the light of the world. A city that is set on a hill cannot be hidden" (Matthew 5:14). So here we have a chain of memory linking the Bible, seventeenth-century Puritan homiletics, and twentieth-century presidential rhetoric.

The Puritans who left England in the early seventeenth century for their "errand into the wilderness" of New England understood their lives and times in the light of the Bible.[1] Like Puritans back home, they sought to "purify" Christianity of every last vestige of Roman Catholic corruption, chiefly by basing their beliefs and practices not on tradition (as Catholics did), but on the Bible alone (*sola scriptura*). Theirs was a "biblical commonwealth" in which the words of scripture circulated as freely and powerfully as the crisp New England air. Upon reading and studying the Bible, Winthrop's Puritan forbears identified two core principles: the absolute sovereignty of God and the total depravity of humans. Together these principles convinced them that God predestined every human being for either heaven or hell; before we were born and through no agency of our own, each human being was fated for either election or damnation. But God did not lord over our individual destinies only. God controlled events in human history writ large. Still, it was up to human beings to cooperate with their Creator in making both a pure church and a godly community. This was the burden that Winthrop took up in 1630.

In "A Model of Christian Charity," he spoke as a ship's captain of sorts, and as a governor, but also as an emissary of the Protestant Reformation, intent on completing the work that Martin Luther, John Calvin, and others had begun in sixteenth-century Europe. Winthrop's address took the form of a sermon, even though Winthrop was a lawyer, not a minister. Most references to this sermon suggest it was written and delivered on board the *Arbella* at some point during the Puritans' journey across the Atlantic, but the precise details are uncertain. Recent scholarship suggests that Winthrop—"America's Forgotten Founding Father"— may have given it just before the colonists set sail from Southampton, England, in March 1630.[2]

Winthrop served for twelve years as the governor of Massachusetts before his death in 1649. Since that time, his reputation has bobbed up and down, riding like a bell buoy on the swells of the reputation of Puritans as a whole. Winthrop's stature sunk as Nathaniel Hawthorne and H. L. Mencken blasted Puritans as hypocritical killjoys. It rose when scholars such as Perry Miller and Edmund Morgan attacked that stereotype with evidence from the bar bills for colonial funerals (overflowing) and the sex lives of Puritans (*not* puritanical). Nonetheless, Winthrop is saddled today with the perception that he was an intolerant theocrat who, among other things, oversaw the banishment of Anne Hutchinson from Massachusetts for "being a woman not fit for our society."[3]

Winthrop shines, however, in "A Model of Christian Charity." Though little noted by his contemporaries—it was not published during Winthrop's lifetime and there is only one surviving contemporaneous reference to it—and largely ignored well into the twentieth century, the sermon has become a classic. Identified by Harvard preacher Peter Gomes as the greatest sermon of the millennium and by literary critic Andrew Delbanco as "a kind of Ur-text of American literature," "A Model of Christian Charity" is likely the most anthologized work of colonial literature, though it is frequently chopped down (as it is here) to a manageable size. Moreover, it contains, according to Gomes, "perhaps the most enduring metaphor of the American experience—that of the exemplary nation called to virtue and mutual support."[4]

But this sermon is also a manifesto. Like King's "I Have a Dream," it articulates an ideal—"a due form of government, both civil and ecclesiastical," in this case—by which the facts on the ground will later be measured (and found wanting). In this sense, Winthrop's words represent a step toward "declension"—that unshakeable American sensibility that the nation has failed to live up to its best self, and that we are all now living with the consequences.

Winthrop appeals here to both head and heart. Anticipating Jefferson's reference to "that harmony and affection without which liberty, and even life itself, are dreary things" and Lincoln's "bonds of affection," he exhorts his fellow colonists to work to create a model Christian commonwealth, "knit together" not by freedom or equality, but by the "bond of love."[5] Employing the biblical image of the Christian community as the Body of Christ, he says that the parts of this body coexist in an intricate web of interdependence. In order to survive and thrive in their dangerous venture, Winthrop's fellow Puritans must share in each other's burdens and give generously to those in need. They must remain united, bound together as one body, by one purpose, committed as a whole to the common good rather than chasing after selfish interests. "Charity" (which for Winthrop's listeners meant not so much giving to the needy as Christian love) is the social glue required to bind this new community together.

But this sermon was not merely a brief for communitarianism. It was a plea for a "beloved community" of a hierarchical sort. As Edmund Morgan has written, "A Model of Christian Charity" is an "appeal for subjection to authority."[6] God in His wisdom has ordained for some to be rich and some poor, some "high and eminent in power and dignity" and some "mean and in submission." Christian charity requires that those on the lower rungs of the social ladder cheerfully and obediently submit to those placed in authority over them. Hanging in the balance is nothing less than the success of the colony, since social climbing and its attendant vices could swiftly bring down this holy experiment. The reasons to accept the poverty of the poor and the wealth of the wealthy are not purely pragmatic, however. They are also spiritual. According to Winthrop, social inequalities provide opportunities for all to nurture Christian virtues. The rich and powerful may exercise love, mercy, and gentleness, while the lowly and poor may cultivate faith, patience, and obedience. In this way, all are united more closely in love and "brotherly affection."

The United States has of course strayed far and wide from Winthrop's model of a community made harmonious by inequality. The Declaration of Independence declared that "all men are created equal." Then came Theodore Roosevelt and rugged individualism—the ideal of the "freedom of the solitary individual from all restraints, constraints, obligations, and relationships," which, according to Gomes, helped to produce a nation "perhaps further now from Winthrop's ideal of a city set upon a hill than at any point in our national history."[7] In fact, this dogma of individual freedom is now so entrenched that the sort of Christian efforts Winthrop insisted on to ameliorate the suffering of the poor are now widely seen as portents of tyranny and evidence of socialism. More than mutual obligation, personal liberty now defines the American dream.

But three themes from Winthrop's sermon continue to resonate. Winthrop insisted that his new colony had a unique relationship with God. Modeled on the covenant God made via Moses with the Israelites, this covenant was conditional: if His chosen people held fast to God and obeyed His commandments, God would bless them with prosperity in the promised land, but if they turned from God and violated His commandments, God would curse them and set them wandering.

Closely linked to this idea of the conditional covenant is a second key theme: the idea that this new commonwealth was to serve as an example to the rest of the world. The "city upon a hill" image implied that Europeans would be looking across the Atlantic to see what his colony was doing. And what it would be doing was merging church and state into one Christian commonwealth. This powerful image has echoed throughout U.S. history, though exactly what America is supposed to be modeling has changed over time. Is the United States a model of freedom? Equality? Capitalism? Christianity? Sounding a tone that was more cautionary than triumphant, Winthrop said that the example his colonists would set could be positive or negative. If they turned their back on God's commandments and their responsibilities to each other, then they would be made a laughingstock. But if they loved God and one another, then God would bless them and all the world would marvel.

Although "A Model of Christian Charity" appears here as a book in *The American Bible,* it also functions as an extended commentary on the Exodus story. God had delivered Winthrop's colonists from the tyranny of the English crown and the corruptions of the established Church of England. He had brought them across their own "Red Sea" into a wilderness rapidly becoming a new Canaan and commissioned them to establish a holy commonwealth based on divine law. However, these colonists were poised in Winthrop's rhetoric on the cusp of Egypt and Canaan, undertaking their own Exodus from their own pharaoh but not yet delivered into the promised land. In Winthrop's sermon, therefore, we find an early expression of a third powerful American theme—that Americans are a chosen people, God's New Israel, entrusted by providence with a unique mission to the world.

The idea of the conditional covenant so central to Winthrop's thought has faded over the course of U.S. history, replaced by an unconditional covenant in which God offers His blessing to whatever America does, at home or abroad. But the concept of America as a chosen nation with a special mission and a unique relationship to the divine has persisted, profoundly shaping American identity and American foreign and domestic policy. In short, Winthrop's rhetorical toolbox provided the building blocks for concepts such as Manifest Destiny and "American exceptionalism," which define the United States as a unique place with a unique mission to create an "empire of liberty," come what may.[8]

The biblical notion of a conditional covenant has not been entirely erased, however. Lincoln wrestled with it in his Second Inaugural Address, when he interpreted the blood flowing from Union and Confederate bayonets as God's righteous punishment for a nation sunk in the sins of slavery. Even in the twenty-first century, some have continued to warn that God was punishing (or would punish) America for its collective sins. On the right, Jerry Falwell and Pat Robertson said that 9/11 was a just punishment delivered by a righteous God on a gay and lesbian nation. On the left, the Reverend Jeremiah Wright said that God was damning America, and for good reason. The fact that such warnings have been almost universally condemned indicates how firmly the conviction that the nation deserves God's blessing, come what may, has taken hold.

"A Model of Christian Charity" 🌿

GOD ALMIGHTY in his most holy and wise providence, hath so disposed of the condition of mankind, as in all times some must be rich, some poor, some high and eminent in power and dignity; others mean and in submission.

The Reason hereof:

1st Reason. First, to hold conformity with the rest of his world, being delighted to show forth the glory of his wisdom in the variety and difference of the creatures, and the glory of his power in ordering all these differences for the preservation and good of the whole, and the glory of his greatness, that as it is the glory of princes to have many officers, so this great king will have many stewards, counting himself more honored in dispensing his gifts to man by man, than if he did it by his own immediate hands.

2nd Reason. Secondly, that he might have the more occasion to manifest the work of his Spirit: first upon the wicked in moderating and restraining them, so that the rich and mighty should not eat up the poor, nor the poor and despised rise up against and shake off their yoke. Secondly, in the regenerate, in exercising his graces in them, as in the great ones, their love, mercy, gentleness, temperance etc., and in the poor and inferior sort, their faith, patience, obedience, etc.

3rd Reason. Thirdly, that every man might have need of others, and from hence they might be all knit more nearly together in the bonds of brotherly affection. . . .

There are two rules whereby we are to walk one towards another: Justice and Mercy. These are always distinguished in their act and in their object, yet may they both concur in the same subject in each respect; as sometimes there may be an occasion of showing mercy to a rich man in some sudden danger or distress, and also doing of mere justice to a poor man in regard of some particular contract, etc.

There is likewise a double Law by which we are regulated in our conversation towards another. . . . By the first of these laws [the Law of Nature], man as he was enabled so withal is commanded to love his neighbor as himself. Upon this ground stands all the precepts of the moral law, which concerns our dealings with men. To apply this to the works of mercy, this law requires two things. First, that every man afford his help to another in every want or distress. Secondly, that he perform this out of the same affection which makes him careful of his own goods, according to the words of our Savior (from Matthew 7:12), whatsoever ye would that men should do to you. . . .

The law of Grace or of the Gospel hath some difference from the former [the law of nature], as in these respects: First, the law of nature was given to man in the estate of innocence. This of the Gospel in the estate of regeneracy. Secondly, the former propounds one man to another, as the same flesh and image of God. This as a brother in Christ also, and in the communion of the same Spirit, and so teacheth to put a difference between Christians and others. Do good to all, especially to the household of faith. . . . Thirdly, the Law of Nature would give no rules for dealing with enemies, for all are to be considered as friends in the state of innocence, but the Gospel commands love to an enemy. Proof: If thine enemy hunger, feed him; "Love your enemies . . . Do good to them that hate you" (Matt. 5:44).

This law of the Gospel propounds likewise a difference of seasons and occasions. There is a time when a Christian must sell all and give to the poor, as they did in the Apostles' times. There is a time also when Christians (though they give not all yet) must give beyond their ability, as they of Macedonia (2 Cor. 8). Likewise, community of perils calls for extraordinary liberality, and so doth community in some special service for the church.

Lastly, when there is no other means whereby our Christian brother may be relieved in his distress, we must help him beyond our ability rather than tempt God in putting him upon help by miraculous or extraordinary means. This duty of mercy is exercised in the kinds: giving, lending and forgiving (*of a debt*). . . .

The definition which the Scripture gives us of love is this: Love is the bond of perfection. First it is a bond or ligament. Secondly, it makes the work perfect. There is no body but consists of parts and that which knits these parts together, gives the body its perfection, because it makes each part so contiguous to others as thereby they do mutually participate with each other, both in strength and infirmity, in pleasure and pain. To instance in the most perfect of all bodies: Christ and his Church make one body. The several parts of this body considered a part before they were united, were as disproportionate and as much disordering as so many contrary qualities or elements, but when Christ comes, and by his spirit and love knits all these parts to himself and each to other, it is become the most perfect and best proportioned body in the world (Eph. 4:15–16). . . . So this definition is right. Love is the bond of perfection.

From hence we may frame these conclusions:

First of all, true Christians are of one body in Christ (1 Cor. 12). Ye are the body of Christ and members of their part. All the parts of this body being thus united are made so contiguous in a special relation as they must needs partake of each other's strength and infirmity; joy and sorrow, weal and woe. If one member suffers, all suffer with it, if one be in honor, all rejoice with it.

Secondly, the ligaments of this body which knit together are love.

Thirdly, no body can be perfect which wants its proper ligament.

Fourthly, all the parts of this body being thus united are made so contiguous in a special relation as they must needs partake of each other's strength and infirmity, joy and sorrow, weal and woe. (1 Cor. 12:26) If one member suffers, all suffer with it; if one be in honor, all rejoice with it.

Fifthly, this sensitivity and sympathy of each other's conditions will necessarily infuse into each part a native desire and endeavor, to strengthen, defend, preserve and comfort the other. To insist a little on this conclusion being the product of all the former, the truth hereof will appear both by precept and pattern. 1 John 3:16, "We ought to lay down our lives for the brethren." Gal. 6:2, "Bear ye one another's burden's and so fulfill the law of Christ." . . .

It rests now to make some application of this discourse. . . . Herein are four things to be propounded; first the persons, secondly the work, thirdly the end, fourthly the means.

First, for the persons. We are a company professing ourselves fellow members of Christ, in which respect only, though we were absent from each other many miles, and had our employments as far distant, yet we ought to account ourselves knit together by this bond of love and live in the exercise of it, if we would have comfort of our being in Christ. . . .

Secondly, for the work we have in hand. It is by a mutual consent, through a special overvaluing providence and a more than an ordinary approbation of the churches of Christ, to seek out a place of cohabitation and consortship under a due form of government both civil and ecclesiastical. In such cases as this, the care of the public must oversway all private respects, by which, not only conscience, but mere civil policy, doth bind us. For it is a true rule that particular estates cannot subsist in the ruin of the public.

Thirdly, the end is to improve our lives to do more service to the Lord; the comfort and increase of the body of Christ, whereof we are members, that ourselves and posterity may be the better preserved from the common corruptions of this evil world, to serve the Lord and work out our salvation under the power and purity of his holy ordinances.

Fourthly, for the means whereby this must be effected. They are twofold, a conformity with the work and end we aim at. These we see are extraordinary, therefore we must not content ourselves with usual ordinary means. Whatsoever we did, or ought to have done, when we lived in England, the same must we do, and more also, where we go. That which the most in their churches maintain as truth in profession only, we must bring into familiar and constant practice; as in this duty of love, we must love brotherly without dissimulation, we must love one another with a pure heart fervently. We must bear one another's burdens. We must not look only on our own things, but also on the things of our brethren.

Neither must we think that the Lord will bear with such failings at our hands as he doth from those among whom we have lived; and that for these three reasons:

First, in regard of the more near bond of marriage between him and us, wherein he hath taken us to be his, after a most strict and peculiar manner, which will make him the more jealous of our love and obedience. So he tells the people of Israel, you only have I known of all the families of the earth, therefore will I punish you for your transgressions.

Secondly, because the Lord will be sanctified in them that come near him. We know that there were many that corrupted the service of the Lord; some setting up altars before his own; others offering both strange fire and strange sacrifices also; yet there came no fire from heaven, or other sudden judgment upon them, as did upon Nadab and Abihu, whom yet we may think did not sin presumptuously.

Thirdly, when God gives a special commission he looks to have it strictly observed in every article. When he gave Saul a commission to destroy Amaleck, he indented with him upon certain articles, and because he failed in one of the least, and that upon a fair pretense, it lost him the kingdom, which should have been his reward, if he had observed his commission.

Thus stands the cause between God and us. We are entered into covenant with him for this work. We have taken out a commission. The Lord hath given us leave to draw our own articles. We have professed to enterprise these and those accounts, upon these and those ends. We have hereupon besought him of favor and blessing. Now if the Lord shall please to hear us, and bring us in peace to the place we desire, then hath he ratified this covenant and sealed our commission, and will expect a strict performance of the articles contained in it; but if we shall neglect the observation of these articles which are the ends we have propounded, and, dissembling with our God, shall fall to embrace this present world and prosecute our carnal intentions, seeking great things for ourselves and our posterity, the Lord will surely break out in wrath against us, and be revenged of such a people, and make us know the price of the breach of such a covenant.

Now the only way to avoid this shipwreck, and to provide for our posterity, is to follow the counsel of Micah, to do justly, to love mercy, to walk humbly with our God. For this end, we must be knit together, in this work, as one man. We must entertain each other in brotherly affection. We must be willing to abridge ourselves of our superfluities, for the supply of others' necessities. We must uphold a familiar commerce together in all meekness, gentleness, patience and liberality. We must delight in each other; make others' conditions our own; rejoice together, mourn together, labor and suffer together, always having before our eyes our commission and community in the work, as members of the same body. So shall we keep the unity of the spirit in the bond of peace. The Lord will be our God, and delight to dwell among us, as his own people, and will command a blessing upon us in all our ways, so that we shall see much more of his wisdom, power, goodness and truth, than formerly we have been acquainted with. We shall find that the God of Israel is among us, when ten of us shall be able to resist a thousand of our enemies; when he shall make us a praise and glory that men shall say of succeeding plantations, "may the Lord make it like that of New England." For we must consider that we shall be as a city upon a hill. The eyes of all people are upon us. So that if we shall deal falsely with our God in this work we have undertaken, and so cause him to withdraw his present help from us, we shall be made a story and a by-word through the world. We shall open the mouths of enemies to speak evil of the ways of God, and all professors for God's sake. We shall shame the faces of many of God's worthy servants, and cause their prayers to be turned into curses upon us till we be consumed out of the good land whither we are going.

And to shut this discourse with that exhortation of Moses, that faithful servant of the Lord, in his last farewell to Israel, Deut. 30. "Beloved, there is now set before us life and death, good and evil," in that we are commanded this day to love the Lord our God, and to love one another, to walk in his ways and to keep his Commandments and his ordinance and his laws, and the articles of our Covenant with him, that we may live and be multiplied, and that the Lord our God may bless us in the land whither we go to possess it. But if our hearts shall turn away, so that we will not obey, but shall be seduced, and worship other Gods, our pleasure and profits, and serve them; it is propounded unto us this day, we shall surely perish out of the good land whither we pass over this vast sea to possess it.

> Therefore let us choose life,
> that we and our seed may live,
> by obeying his voice and cleaving to him,
> for he is our life and our prosperity.[9]

COMMENTARY

John O'Sullivan, journalist who would later coin the term "Manifest Destiny," urging Americans to seize the western hemisphere in God's name (1839)

The far-reaching, the boundless future will be the era of American greatness. In its magnificent domain of space and time, the nation of many nations is destined to manifest to mankind the excellence of divine principles; to establish on earth the noblest temple ever dedicated to the worship of the Most High—the Sacred and the True. Its floor shall be a hemisphere—its roof the firmament of the star-studded heavens, and its congregation an Union of many Republics, comprising hundreds of happy millions, calling, owning no man master, but governed by God's natural and moral law of equality. . . .

Yes, we are the nation of progress, of individual freedom, of universal enfranchisement. . . . We must onward to the fulfilment of our mission—to the entire development of the principle of our organization—freedom of conscience, freedom of person, freedom of trade and business pursuits, universality of freedom and equality. This is our high destiny, and in nature's eternal, inevitable decree of cause and effect we must accomplish it. All this will be our future history, to establish on earth the moral dignity and salvation of man—the immutable truth and beneficence of God. For this blessed mission to the nations of the world, which are shut out from the life-giving light of truth, has America been chosen; and her high example shall smite unto death the tyranny of kings, hierarchs, and oligarchs, and carry the glad tidings of peace and good will where myriads now endure an existence scarcely more enviable than that of beasts of the field. Who, then, can doubt that our country is destined to be *the great nation of futurity*?

—John L. O'Sullivan, "The Great Nation of Futurity," *United States Democratic Review* 6.23 (November 1839): 426–30.

Oberlin Evangelist, periodical of revivalist Charles Grandison Finney, criticizing America for failing, on the question of slavery, to be "a model to the nations of the earth" (1850)

Baron Von Humboldt, now past four score, is beyond question one of the greatest men of our age. . . . [Recently] he spoke with a great deal of feeling, of his interest in American institutions; of his sojourn in the United States; of his acquaintance with Jefferson, and other great men, saying that he felt and called himself a citizen of the Union. But the more he was attached to the country and its institutions, the more he hoped from them for the world, he was the more grieved at the reckless spirit of aggression and conquest which produced and sanctioned the war with Mexico, and the Cuban expedition for more slave territory.

If Russia, if any European monarchy had done this, it would not have been such a matter of surprise; but in the United States, from which the world expected so much, it was a matter of astonishment and sorrow. He regarded Slavery as the great evil of our country—the black spot on our national reputation. . . .

Our nation is a city on a hill. It ought to be the light of freedom, a model to the nations of the earth, illustrating both the principles and the benefits of free political Institutions. How sad that instead of this, we find that in fact our oppressions of the weak are the grief of all good men to the ends of the earth! And if the good and great of earth think thus of us, what must be thought of us by the good and the great of heaven!

—"How the Great Men of Other Nations Regard Our National Character," *Oberlin Evangelist*, September 25, 1850, p. 158.

John F. Kennedy, former U.S. Senator (D-MA), speaking to Massachusetts legislators just before his presidential inauguration (1961)

During the last sixty days, I have been at the task of constructing an administration. . . . I have been guided by the standard John Winthrop set before his shipmates on the flagship *Arbella* three hundred and thirty-one years ago, as they, too, faced the task of building a new government on a perilous frontier. "We must always consider," he said, "that we shall be as a city upon a hill—the eyes of all people are upon us."

Today the eyes of all people are truly upon us—and our governments, in every branch, at every level, national, state and local, must be as a city upon a hill—constructed and inhabited by men aware of their great trust and their great responsibilities. For we are setting out upon a voyage in 1961 no less hazardous than that undertaken by the *Arbella* in 1630. We are committing ourselves to tasks of statecraft no less awesome than that of governing the Massachusetts Bay Colony, beset as it was then by terror without and disorder within. . . .

For of those to whom much is given, much is required. And when at some future date the high court of history sits in judgment on each one of us—recording whether in our brief span of service we fulfilled our responsibilities to the state—our success or failure, in whatever office we may hold, will be measured by the answers to four questions:

First, were we truly men of courage—with the courage to stand up to one's enemies—and the courage to stand up, when necessary, to one's associates—the courage to resist public pressure, as well as private greed?

Secondly, were we truly men of judgment—with perceptive judgment of the future as well as the past—of our own mistakes as well as the mistakes of others—with enough wisdom to know that we did not know, and enough candor to admit it?

Third, were we truly men of integrity—men who never ran out on either the principles in which they believed or the people who believed in them—men who believed in us—men whom neither financial gain nor political ambition could ever divert from the fulfillment of our sacred trust?

Finally, were we truly men of dedication—with an honor mortgaged to no single individual or group, and compromised by no private obligation or aim, but devoted solely to serving the public good and the national interest?

Courage—judgment—integrity—dedication—these are the historic qualities of the Bay Colony and the Bay State—the qualities which this state has consistently sent to this chamber on Beacon Hill here in Boston and to Capitol Hill back in Washington. And these are the qualities which, with God's help, this son of Massachusetts hopes will characterize our government's conduct in the four stormy years that lie ahead.

—John F. Kennedy, "Address of President-Elect John F. Kennedy Delivered to a Joint Convention of the General Court of the Commonwealth of Massachusetts," January 9, 1961, www.jfklibrary.org/Asset-Viewer/OYhUZE2Qo0-ogdV7ok900A.aspx.

Ronald Reagan, actor and former Republican California governor, invoking Winthrop in a presidential campaign debate with Jon Anderson (1980)

I've always believed that this land was placed here between the two great oceans by some divine plan. That it was placed here to be found by a special kind of people—people who had a special love for freedom and who had the courage to uproot themselves and leave hearth and homeland, and came to what, in the beginning, was the most undeveloped wilderness possible. We came from 100 different corners of the earth. We spoke a multitude of tongues. We landed on this Eastern shore and then went out over the mountains and the prairies and the deserts and the far western mountains to the Pacific, building cities and towns and farms and schools and churches. If wind, water or fire destroyed them, we built them again. And in so doing, at the same time, we built a new breed of human called an American—a proud, an independent, and a most compassionate individual, for the most part.

Two hundred years ago, Tom Paine, when the 13 tiny colonies were trying to become a nation, said, we have it in our power to begin the world over again. Today we're confronted with the horrendous problems that we've discussed here tonight. And some people in high positions of leadership tell us that the answer is to retreat. That the best is over. That we must cut back. That we must share in an ever-increasing scarcity. That we must, in the failure to be able to protect our national security as it is today, we must not be provocative to any possible adversary.

Well, we, the living Americans, have gone through four wars. We've gone through a Great Depression in our lifetime that literally was worldwide and almost brought us to our knees. But we came through all of those things and we achieved even new heights and new greatness. The living Americans today have fought harder, paid a higher price for freedom, and done more to advance the dignity of man than any people who ever lived on this earth. For 200 years, we've lived in the future, believing that tomorrow would be better than today, and today would be better than yesterday. I still believe that. I'm not running for the Presidency because I believe that I can solve the problems we've discussed tonight. I believe the people of this country can, and together, we can begin the world over again. We can meet our destiny—and that destiny to build a land here that will be, for all mankind, a shining city on a hill.

—"Presidential Debate in Baltimore (Reagan-Anderson)," September 21, 1980, www.presidency.ucsb.edu/ws/index.php?pid=29407.

Mario Cuomo, Democratic governor of New York, describing America as a "Tale of Two Cities" in his Democratic National Convention keynote address (1984)

Ten days ago, President Reagan admitted that although some people in this country seemed to be doing well nowadays, others were unhappy, even worried, about themselves, their families, and their futures. The President said that he didn't understand that fear. He said, "Why, this country is a shining city on a hill." And the President is right. In many ways we are a shining city on a hill.

But the hard truth is that not everyone is sharing in this city's splendor and glory. A shining city is perhaps all the President sees from the portico of the White House and the veranda of his ranch, where everyone seems to be doing well. But there's another city; there's another part to the shining city; the part where some people can't pay their mortgages, and most young people can't afford one; where students can't afford the education they need, and middle-class parents watch the dreams they hold for their children evaporate. In this part of the city there are more poor than ever, more families in trouble, more and more people who need help but can't find it. Even worse: There are elderly people who tremble in the basements of the houses there. And there are people who sleep in the city streets, in the gutter, where the glitter doesn't show. There are ghettos where thousands of young people, without a job or an education, give their lives away to drug dealers every day. There is despair, Mr. President, in the faces that you don't see, in the places that you don't visit in your shining city. . . .

Mr. President, you ought to know that this nation is more a "Tale of Two Cities" than it is just a "Shining City on a Hill." Maybe, maybe, Mr. President, if you visited some more places; maybe if you went to Appalachia where some people still live in sheds; maybe if you went to Lackawanna where thousands of unemployed steel workers wonder why we subsidized foreign steel. Maybe, maybe, Mr. President, if you stopped in at a shelter in Chicago and spoke to the homeless there; maybe, Mr. President, if you asked a woman who had been denied the help she needed to feed her children because you said you needed the money for a tax break for a millionaire or for a missile we couldn't afford to use.

Maybe, maybe, Mr. President. But I'm afraid not. Because the truth is, ladies and gentlemen, that this is how we were warned it would be. President Reagan told us from the very beginning that he believed in a kind of social Darwinism. Survival of the fittest. "Government can't do everything," we were told, so it should settle for taking care of the strong and hope that economic ambition and charity will do the rest. Make the rich richer, and what falls from the table will be enough for the middle class and those who are trying desperately to work their way into the middle class. You know, the Republicans called it "trickle-down" when Hoover tried it. Now they call it "supply side." But it's the same shining city for those relative few who are lucky enough to live in its good neighborhoods. But for the people who are excluded, for the people who are locked out, all they can do is stare from a distance at that city's glimmering towers. It's an old story. It's as old as our history.

—Mario Cuomo, "Democratic National Convention Keynote Address," San Francisco, California, July 16, 1984, www.americanrhetoric.com/speeches/mariocuomo1984dnc.htm.

Republican Party platform, lauding Ronald Reagan and George H. W. Bush and invoking the words of Winthrop and Lincoln (1992)

America had its rendezvous with destiny in 1980. Faced with crisis at home and abroad, Americans turned to Republican leadership in the White House. Presidents Reagan and Bush turned our Nation away from the path of over-taxation, hyper-regulation, and mega-government. Instead, we moved in a new direction. We cut taxes, reduced red tape, put people above bureaucracy. And so we vanquished the idea of the almighty state as the supervisor of our daily lives. In choosing hope over fear, Americans raised a beacon, reminding the world that we are a shining city on a hill, the last best hope for man on earth.

—"Republican Party Platform of 1992," www.presidency.ucsb.edu/ws/index.php?pid=25847.

Jerry Falwell and Pat Robertson, conservative Christian activists, discussing God's role in the 9/11 terrorist attacks and the role of liberals in provoking Him (2001)

JERRY FALWELL: And I agree totally with you that the Lord has protected us so wonderfully these 225 years. And since 1812, this is the first time that we've been attacked on our soil and by far the worst results. And I fear, as Donald Rumsfeld, the Secretary of Defense, said yesterday, that this is only the beginning. And with biological warfare available to these monsters—the Husseins, the Bin Ladens, the Arafats—what we saw on Tuesday, as terrible as it is, could be miniscule if, in fact—if, in fact—God continues to lift the curtain and allow the enemies of America to give us probably what we deserve.

PAT ROBERTSON: Jerry, that's my feeling. I think we've just seen the antechamber to terror. We haven't even begun to see what they can do to the major population.

FALWELL: The ACLU's got to take a lot of blame for this.

ROBERTSON: Well, yes.

FALWELL: And I know that I'll hear from them for this. But throwing God out successfully with the help of the federal court system, throwing God out of the public square, out of the schools. The abortionists have got to bear some burden for this because God will not be mocked. And when we destroy 40 million little innocent babies, we make God mad. I really believe that the pagans, and the abortionists, and the feminists, and the gays and the lesbians who are actively trying to make that an alternative lifestyle, the ACLU, People For the American Way—all of them who have tried to secularize America—I point the finger in their face and say "you helped this happen."

—"You Helped This Happen," *700 Club* transcript, September 13, 2001, www.beliefnet.com/Faiths/
Christianity/2001/09/You-Helped-This-Happen.aspx.

Peter Gomes, Harvard preacher, linking Winthrop's sermon to America's sense of mission (2002)

The ambition of the sermon was to establish the Christian basis for the new civilization to be established in what was then thought to be the "howling wilderness." The basis of this society was to be Christian charity, where, on the basis of those principles enunciated in the Bible, particularly in the Sermon on the Mount, the strong would bear with the weak, the rich would relieve the necessities of the poor, and all would strive to construct an exemplary society that would be like a city set upon a hill. This was not meant to be only for the comfort and consolation of the inhabitants but a beacon to the whole world, to prove to the old and tottering kingdoms of Europe that it was possible to construct a Christian society that would work. . . .

The vivid and explicitly religious sensibility in this founding metaphor . . . has been at the heart of much of our psychic identity ever since. Our wars, including the Indian Wars, the Revolutionary War, most certainly the Civil War, and the two World Wars of the twentieth century, are all in some sense Holy Wars, fought with God on our side, and in behalf of a divine mission. Our physical expansion across the continent in the nineteenth century, from sea to shining sea, was described as our Manifest Destiny, a mandate from heaven. America believes in God at a higher proportion of the population than does any other country in the West, and what is even more striking is that Americans believe that God believes in them!

—Peter J. Gomes, *The Good Book: Reading the Bible with Mind and Heart* (New York: HarperSanFrancisco, 2002), pp. 54–55.

Robert F. Kennedy, son of Attorney General Robert Kennedy, commenting on differences between the Bush and Kennedy families (2007)

There is an ancient struggle between two separate philosophies, warring for control of the American soul. The first was set forth by John Winthrop in 1630, when he made the most important speech in American history, "A Model of Christian Charity," on the deck of the sloop *Arbella*, as the Puritans approached the New World. He said this land is being given to us by God not to satisfy carnal opportunities or expand self-interest, but rather to create a shining city on a hill. This is the American ideal, working together, maintaining a spiritual mission, and creating communities for the future.

The competing vision of America comes from the conquistador side of the national character and took hold with the gold rush of 1849. That's when people began to regard the land as the source of private wealth, a place where you can get rich quick—the sort of game where whoever dies with the biggest pile wins.

—Quoted in Mark Jacobson, "American Jeremiad," *New York*, February 12, 2007, nymag.com/news/politics/27340/.

Andrew Bacevich, international relations professor, rejecting the "shining city" exceptionalism of Alaska governor Sarah Palin (2008)

But even more important is that worldview that I share with John McCain. That worldview that says that America is a nation of exceptionalism. And we are to be that shining city on a hill, as President Reagan so beautifully said, that we are a beacon of hope and that we are unapologetic here. We are not perfect as a nation. But together, we represent a perfect ideal. And that is democracy and tolerance and freedom and equal rights. —Governor Sarah Palin, October 2, 2008

In a debate filled with eminently forgettable blather, here we have a statement of genuine importance—a text that demands analysis. Where to begin? Perhaps by noting the origins of this worldview to which Governor Palin refers. The conception of America as the "city upon a hill" was not the handiwork of Ronald Reagan, or indeed of any other paladin of the Republican Party. Rather, John Winthrop, founding governor of Massachusetts Bay Colony, first voiced the conviction that God had summoned the people of the New World—or at least those settling in New England—to serve as a model for all humankind.

Speaking in Boston Harbor to a small assembly of Puritans preparing to disembark from the ship Arbella in 1630, Winthrop announced that "The eyes of all people are upon us." Should the members of his community fail in their anointed mission, a dire fate awaited them: "we shall be made a story and a by-word through the world." Winthrop described the core of that mission with great specificity. It had little to do with values such as tolerance and equal rights, in which Winthrop had little interest. It had everything to do with forging a covenant with God, who had summoned the Puritans to create a Christian commonwealth. . . .

Now there are three possibilities.

The first possibility is that God does not exist. In that case, the concept of American exceptionalism first articulated by Winthrop, employed with great political effect by Ronald Reagan, and now endorsed by Sarah Palin, is simply nonsense—a fairy tale that may once have had a certain utility, but that in our own day has become simply pernicious. To persist in this nonsense is to make it impossible either to see ourselves as we really are or to see the world as it actually is.

The second possibility is that God exists, but that he has not singled out Americans as his new Chosen People. Indeed, consult Scripture and it becomes apparent that God himself has not spoken directly on the matter. In that case, Winthrop, Reagan, and Palin are remarkably presumptuous in claiming to interpret God's purposes and will. Further investigation might be in order—perhaps consulting with priests, ministers, rabbis, imams to see what they have to say on the matter.

The third possibility is that God exists and has indeed singled out America as his New Israel. In that event, John Winthrop's charge of 1630 demands urgent attention—not least of all his warning of what will befall America should it be seduced by earthly concerns and carnal desires and tend too much to superfluities.

Today no doubt, the eyes of all people are indeed on the United States—what happens here affects the world. Yet many of those who observe us don't like what they see. The question for Governor Palin and for other believers committed to the concept of American exceptionalism is this: have we kept the Lord's covenant? If not, perhaps the time has come to mend our ways before it's too late. Who knows? The sound you hear even now on Wall Street may be God's wrath breaking out against us.

—Andrew Bacevich, "Sarah Palin and John Winthrop," *Huffington Post*, October 3, 2008, www.huffingtonpost.com/andrew-bacevich/sarah-palin-and-john-wint_b_131700.html.

Common Sense

◀ THOMAS PAINE, 1776 ▶

$\mathscr{B}$EFORE WRITING the pamphlet that would make him America's provocateur in chief, Thomas Paine (1737–1809) was an abject failure. Born Thomas Pain (the *e* came later) in 1737 in Thetford in Norfolk County, England, he learned corset making from his Quaker father. But his father could not offer him a partnership, so he left home at age nineteen to fend for himself. He worked for short stints as a sailor, shopkeeper, and English teacher before being hired as a collector of excise taxes—a job he lost, won back, and lost again. In 1774, in his late thirties, he found himself broke and out of work in London. He was also alone. His first wife and only child had died in childbirth, and he and his second wife had separated. So to say this incorrigible patriot's early years were undistinguished is to be gracious.

Then Paine met Ben Franklin in London in 1774. Buoyed by a letter of introduction from Franklin calling him "an ingenious, worthy young man," Paine set sail in November 1774 for Philadelphia.[1] There he edited *Pennsylvania Magazine*, a sleepy publication he helped turn into "the most widely read magazine published in the colonies."[2] Philadelphia was the hub of New World politics, and there Paine ran with revolutionaries, soaking up their ideas and spewing forth some of his own. One of Paine's acquaintances was the physician Benjamin Rush, who urged him to write an argument for independence and call it *Common Sense*. This pamphlet, first published anonymously on January 9, 1776, would give American politics a new sound, much as Mark Twain's *Adventures of Huckleberry Finn* bequeathed a new way of speaking to American literature. And that sound was akin to hammer on anvil.

Common Sense appeared just nine months after first blood was drawn at Lexington and Concord, so the war with England was still a rebellion without a cause. Paine gave it one, and in the process helped to turn public opinion, which largely favored reconciliation, toward the radical step of declaring the colonies "free and independent States." But *Common Sense* did more than urge independence on an ambivalent public. In a strange twist on Governor John Winthrop's image of colonial Massachusetts as a "city upon a hill," Paine saw beyond the creation of a new nation to the "birthday of a new world" in which Americans would spread the gift of freedom to unfortunates worldwide. America's second president, John Adams, would later downplay Paine's impact, insisting there was little new in *Common Sense*. "I am bold to say there is not a fact nor a reason stated in it, which had not been frequently urged in Congress," he wrote.[3] But Adams's protest attends too much to the substance of Paine's writing and too little to its style, which even Adams had to admit was "manly."[4]

As the title indicates, *Common Sense* was aimed at the common man. Previous arguments against monarchy had been advanced in legal or philosophical jargon. But Paine wrote, historian Pauline Maier observes, in the "knock-about language" of a tavern philosopher.[5] His words were plain—the working title had been *Plain Truth*—and he made the case for independence with a sledgehammer's nuance. Author Craig Nelson writes that *Common Sense* was "structured very much like a traditional pulpit sermon."[6] If so, it was a saucy one—vulgar and vituperative. It evoked throughout what Martin Luther King Jr. would later refer to as the "fierce urgency of now."[7] "The dominant tone of *Common Sense* is that of rage," writes historian Bernard Bailyn. "The aim of almost every other notable pamphlet of the Revolution was to probe difficult, urgent, and controversial questions and make appropriate recommendations. The aim of *Common Sense* was to tear the world apart."[8]

Rejecting the prevailing theory that kings ruled by divine right, Paine traces the origins of the British crown not to the Almighty, but to that "French bastard" William the Conqueror. Early English monarchs, he adds, were "nothing better than the principal ruffian of some restless gang." But *Common Sense* is not all spit and vinegar. To be sure, Paine redirects the object of American ire away from the particular missteps of George III to the general mechanisms of those "two ancient tyrannies": monarchy and aristocracy. But he does not stop at blowing up this old order. He makes recommendations for a new one, including a Congress of at least 390 representatives and a presidency that rotates among the states. "We have it in our power to begin the world over again," Paine wrote, and he was bold enough to suggest how to do it.

Many of Paine's arguments rest on analogies with nature. For example, he contends that it is unnatural for a continent to be ruled by an island. But there is a lot of theology in *Common Sense* too. Oddly, for a man Theodore Roosevelt would condemn as a "filthy little atheist," Paine draws freely not just on reason but on the "word of God" (especially the Old Testament), advancing a biblical argument for rule by ballot instead of birth.[9] In fact, the pamphlet opens with the doctrine of sin. Humans need society, Paine argues, and society needs government. Why? Because of human wickedness. So government's job is minimal: to restrain that wickedness. And this task is better accomplished by republicanism than by that "Popery of government" known as monarchy. Borrowing like so many other revolutionaries from the Exodus story, Paine speaks of "the hardened, sullen-tempered Pharaoh of England" and praises ancient Israel as a republic. Apparently God was a republican too.

Paine was overreaching when he claimed that *Common Sense* had "the greatest sale that any performance ever had since the use of letters," but it was a publishing sensation.[10] According to Josiah Bartlett, a New Hampshire Continental Congress delegate, it was "greedily bought up and read by all ranks of people."[11] In its first year, it went through at least 25 printings, sold at least 75,000 copies, and turned Paine into America's "first best-selling author."[12]

Not everyone was convinced, however, by what George Washington referred to as Paine's "sound doctrine and unanswerable reasoning."[13] Predictably, Loyalists attacked Paine's pamphlet as senseless. But so did some patriots. Ever fearful of unchecked democracy, John Adams described Paine as a "disastrous meteor" and predicted that his "crude, ignorant Notions" of government "will do more Mischief in dividing the Friends of Liberty, than all the Tory Writings together."[14] But even Adams had to admit that he lived in the "Age of Paine."[15]

This age belonged to Paine because *Common Sense* fostered a conviction among colonists that a new nation was their lot. Edmund Randolph of Virginia observed that "public sentiment, which a few weeks before had shuddered at the tremendous obstacles with which independence was environed, overleaped every barrier" after *Common Sense* appeared; George Washington credited it with "working a powerful change there in the Minds of many Men"; while Franklin called its effects "prodigious."[16] *Common Sense* thus stands with *Uncle Tom's Cabin* atop the list of books with the greatest impact on American political life.

After writing *Common Sense,* Paine joined the American army and gave virtually all of his income from his writing to the war effort. He authored *The Crisis,* a series of pro-independence pamphlets intended to boost the morale of soldiers. The first in this series, published in December 1776, begins with the famous line, "These are the times that try men's souls."

Paine was visiting England when Edmund Burke's *Reflections on the Revolution in France* (1790) appeared. He responded to Burke's criticisms of that revolution with *Rights of Man* (1791–92). This book, which historian Sean Wilentz refers to as "the most influential defense of democratic principles to appear in [Paine's] lifetime," called for a revolution in England, and made Paine persona non grata there.[17] Tried for sedition and convicted in absentia, he was banned from England for life. He fled to France, where he spent portions of 1793 and 1794 in jail. In prison he began writing *Age of Reason,* a broadside against Christianity that turned many of his former friends against him.

With the help of Thomas Jefferson, Paine returned to the United States in 1802, where he proved an embarrassment to the president and a guilty pleasure for Federalist newspapers, which blasted him as (among other things) "an object of disgust, of abhorrence, of absolute loathing to every decent man except the President of the United States."[18] Even during Jefferson's presidency, Paine's radical republicanism was widely seen as un-American. Even less forgivable was Paine's assault on Christianity, which led Adams (who made a second career of hating Paine) to describe him as "that insolent blasphemer of things sacred, and transcendent libeler of all that is good."[19] But what really ruined Paine was a public letter he wrote disparaging Washington as "treacherous in private friendship . . . and a hypocrite in publick life."[20] Not even a generation after the Revolution he helped to win, Paine had become "the best-hated man in America."[21] He spent most of his last years alone, and when he died in poverty in Manhattan in 1809 only a handful of people attended his burial.

In an odd coda to Paine's life, William Cobbett, an English radical and one of Paine's few friends, had his body dug up with the intent of returning it to England for burial. The remains were lost and never recovered. And so it went with Paine's reputation.

If he had been less a bomb thrower and more a bridge builder (ironically, he patented a design for a single-span iron bridge), and especially if he had been able to hold his tongue when it came to religion, Paine might be celebrated today as one of the most foundational of the founders. But Paine, who refused to be domesticated, never really found a home in America. In the early nineteenth century, he was shunned by both Federalists fearful of his "democratical" tendencies and Christians frightened by his freethinking. Over the course of that century, Paine's memory was kept alive by abolitionists, women's rights activists, labor leaders, socialists, utopians, and freethinkers, but historians were more likely to talk about his alleged drunkenness and infidelity than the impact of *Common Sense* on U.S. history. "To trace the curve of Paine's reputation," wrote Dixon Wecter in the early 1940s, "is to learn something about hero-worship in reverse."[22] Paine got a lift after the Civil War thanks to a two-volume fawner by biographer Moncure Conway, and at the start of the twentieth century thanks to Thomas Edison, who praised him as "our greatest political thinker."[23] Recent years have seen a Paine revival, but according to historian Jill Lepore he remains "at best, a lesser founder."[24]

The debate over Paine's place in the political pantheon has always turned largely on competing interpretations of the American Revolution. Those who ignore or attack Paine—from eighteenth-century Federalists to twenty-first century neoconservatives—are typically suspicious of the capacities of ordinary people for self-government. They also tend to draw sharp contrasts between what neoconservative Irving Kristol calls the "law-and-order" American Revolution and the "lawless" French Revolution. "To perceive the true purposes of the American Revolution," Kristol writes, "it is wise to ignore some of the more grandiloquent declamations of the moment—Tom Paine, an English radical who never really understood America, is especially worth ignoring."[25]

Not all conservatives have abandoned Paine, however. Ronald Reagan praised Paine's analysis of government as a "necessary evil" and throughout his presidency quoted the line from *Common Sense* about beginning the world anew. President George H. W. Bush quoted Paine in a 1991 speech announcing the Gulf War.[26] Christian Coalition leader Ralph Reed took pride in the fact that Paine quoted from the Bible, while atheist Christopher Hitchens, the contemporary writer whose verbal pyrotechnics most resemble Paine's, somehow managed to forgive him for that indiscretion.[27] Others have referred to Paine as "America's founding neoconservative" because of his commitment to private property rights, his conviction that the "common sense" of ordinary people is a surer guide to good government than the uncommon wisdom of elites, and his view that war is sometimes the cost of preserving liberty. According to one admirer, "Paine the free thinker would instantly have seen in the Iranian mullahs—a 21st-century religious version of the utopian Frenchmen who led the Terror—the kind of narrow-minded clerical tyranny that has to be destroyed if humanity is going to move forward."[28]

Paine's liberal admirers are convinced that these efforts to co-opt one of America's true radicals border on the criminal. Paine was in their eyes a champion of democracy, egalitarianism, and free thought—left of Jefferson, even—and ought to be returned to his rightful place in the pantheon of American heroes. President Obama concluded his 2009 Inaugural Address with a lengthy quotation from Paine—a fitting tribute to the man who is said to have been the first to refer to the country Obama would lead as the "United States of America."[29]

Common Sense

The cause of America is, in a great measure, the cause of all mankind.[a] Many circumstances have, and will arise, which are not local, but universal, and through which the principles of all lovers of mankind are affected, and in the event of which, their affections are interested. The laying a country desolate with fire and sword, declaring war against the natural rights of all mankind, and extirpating the defenders thereof from the face of the earth, is the concern of every man to whom nature hath given the power of feeling; of which class, regardless of party censure, is the AUTHOR.

a. Oscar Handlin, historian, on immigration as part and parcel of American identity (1980): The cause of America was the cause of all mankind, the Founding Fathers asserted. The republic was not, is not, like the other nations of the world, either in history or in tradition. A nation created in the wilderness by people of diverse origins could not hoard its privileges for itself. It could only be true to itself by sharing the liberty it won with all. . . . Now as then, in serving others, we serve ourselves. In providing places for the placeless, in granting freedom to the oppressed, we remind ourselves of our identity as Americans, and of the character of our republic. —Oscar Handlin, "Refugees: Should Compassion Have Limits?" *Los Angeles Times*, May 11, 1980, p. F1.

Of the Origin and Design of Government in General, with Concise Remarks on the English Constitution

SOME writers have so confounded society with government, as to leave little or no distinction between them; whereas they are not only different, but have different origins. Society is produced by our wants, and government by our wickedness; the former promotes our happiness positively by uniting our affections, the latter negatively by restraining our vices. The one encourages intercourse, the other creates distinctions. The first is a patron, the last a punisher.

Society in every state is a blessing, but government even in its best state is but a necessary evil;[b] in its worst state an intolerable one;[c,d] for when we suffer, or are exposed to the same miseries by a government, which we might expect in a country without government, our calamity is heightened

---

b. Ronald Reagan, fortieth U.S. president, on how liberals have become conservatives and vice versa (1981): The classic liberal used to be the man who believed the individual was, and should be forever, the master of his destiny. That is now the conservative position. The liberal used to believe in freedom under law. He now takes the ancient feudal position that power is everything. He believes in a stronger and stronger central government, in the philosophy that control is better than freedom. The conservative now quotes Thomas Paine, a longtime refuge of the liberals: "Government is a necessary evil; let us have as little of it as possible." —Ronald Reagan and Richard G. Hubler, *Where's the Rest of Me?* (New York: Dell, 1981), p. 337.

c. Arthur Hartley, quoting Paine against New York City's Democratic Party machine (1933): Can any more vivid expression better describe Tammany Hall than these words of Thomas Paine? —Arthur Just Hartley, letter to the editor, *New York Times*, October 27, 1933, p. 18.

d. Walter Williams, economist, on the cultural costs of big government (2011): Most of the issues that divide our nation, and give rise to conflict, are those best described as a zero-sum game where one person's or group's gain is of necessity another's loss. Examples are: racial preferences, school prayers, trade restrictions, welfare, Obamacare and a host of other government policies that benefit one American at the expense of another American. That's why political action committees, private donors and companies spend billions of dollars lobbying. Their goal is to get politicians and government officials to use the coercive power of their offices to take what belongs to one American and give it to another. . . . You might be tempted to think that the brutal domestic conflict seen in other countries can't happen here. That's nonsense. Americans are not super-humans; we possess the same frailties of other people. If there were a catastrophic economic calamity, I can imagine a political hustler exploiting those frailties, as have other tyrants, blaming it on the Jews, the blacks, the conservatives, the liberals, the Catholics or free trade. The best thing the president and Congress can do to reduce the potential for conflict and by reflecting that we furnish the means by which we suffer! Government, like dress, is the badge of lost innocence; the palaces of kings are built on the ruins of the bowers of paradise. For were the impulses of conscience clear, uniform, and irresistibly obeyed, man would need no other lawgiver; but that not being the case, he finds it necessary to surrender up a part of his property to furnish means for the protection of the rest; and this he is induced to do by the same prudence which in every other case advises him out of two evils to choose the least. Wherefore, security being the true design and end of government, it unanswerably follows that whatever form thereof appears most likely to ensure it to us, with the least expense and greatest benefit, is preferable to all others. . . .

Here then is the origin and rise of government; namely, a mode rendered necessary by the inability of moral virtue to govern the world; here too is the design and end of government, viz., freedom and security. And however our eyes may be dazzled with snow, or our ears deceived by sound; however prejudice may warp our wills, or interest darken our understanding, the simple voice of nature and of reason will say, it is right. . . .

Of Monarchy and Hereditary Succession

MANKIND being originally equals in the order of creation,[e] the equality could only be destroyed by some subsequent circumstance; the distinctions of rich, and poor, may in a great measure be

---

violence is reduce the impact of government on our lives. Doing so will not only produce a less-divided country and greater economic efficiency, but bear greater faith and allegiance to the vision of America held by our founders—a country of limited government. Our founders, in the words of Thomas Paine, recognized that "Government, even in its best state, is but a necessary evil; in its worst state, an intolerable one." —Walter E. Williams, "Why We're a Divided Nation," *Chattanooga Times Free Press*, January 23, 2011, p. F5.

e. Henry Middleton, South Carolina plantation owner, Loyalist, and former Continental Congress president, rejecting Paine's egalitarianism (1776): [This proposition], extended as far as it may lead, is a very leveling Principle. There are some natural Distinctions which cannot fail having very great Effects; one Man is born sooner than another, and all Men certainly not equal in Point of Sense and bodily Strength; some have greater Opportunities to advance themselves than others, and from such Circumstances, however accidental, some Superiority almost insensibly takes Place; and though Kings and Subjects are not a Distinction of Nature, yet that some should rule, and others obey, is essential to Society. No society can subsist without Government, and no Government without Rule and Obedience; and however Nature may put a Ridicule upon hereditary Succession, "by giving an Ass for a Lion," it must be owned that some seem by Nature formed to rule, and others to obey. —Henry Middleton, *The True Merits of a Late Treatise, Printed in America, Intitled Common Sense* (London: Nicoll, 1776), pp. 10–11.

accounted for, and that without having recourse to the harsh, ill-sounding names of oppression and avarice. Oppression is often the consequence, but seldom or never the means of riches; and though avarice will preserve a man from being necessitously poor, it generally makes him too timorous to be wealthy.

But there is another and greater distinction for which no truly natural or religious reason can be assigned, and that is, the distinction of men into KINGS and SUBJECTS. Male and female are the distinctions of nature, good and bad the distinctions of heaven; but how a race of men came into the world so exalted above the rest, and distinguished like some new species, is worth enquiring into, and whether they are the means of happiness or of misery to mankind. . . .

Government by kings was first introduced into the world by the Heathens, from whom the children of Israel copied the custom. It was the most prosperous invention the Devil ever set on foot for the promotion of idolatry. The Heathens paid divine honors to their deceased kings, and the Christian world hath improved on the plan by doing the same to their living ones. How impious is the title of sacred majesty applied to a worm, who in the midst of his splendor is crumbling into dust!

As the exalting one man so greatly above the rest cannot be justified on the equal rights of nature, so neither can it be defended on the authority of scripture; for the will of the Almighty, as declared by Gideon and the prophet Samuel, expressly disapproves of government by kings. All anti-monarchial parts of scripture have been very smoothly glossed over in monarchial governments, but they undoubtedly merit the attention of countries which have their governments yet to form. Render unto Caesar the things which are Caesar's is the scriptural doctrine of courts, yet it is no support of monarchial government, for the Jews at that time were without a king, and in a state of vassalage to the Romans.

Near three thousand years passed away from the Mosaic account of the creation, till the Jews under a national delusion requested a king. Till then their form of government (except in extraordinary cases, where the Almighty interposed) was a kind of republic administered by a judge and the elders of the tribes. Kings they had none, and it was held sinful to acknowledge any being under that title but the Lord of Hosts. And when a man seriously reflects on the idolatrous homage which is paid to the persons of kings he need not wonder, that the Almighty, ever jealous of his honor, should disapprove of a form of government which so impiously invades the prerogative of heaven. . . .

To the evil of monarchy we have added that of hereditary succession; and as the first is a degradation and lessening of ourselves, so the second, claimed as a matter of right, is an insult and an imposition on posterity. For all men being originally equals, no one by birth could have a right to set up his own family in perpetual preference to all others for ever, and though himself might deserve some decent degree of honors of his contemporaries, yet his descendants might be far too unworthy to inherit them. One of the strongest natural proofs of the folly of hereditary right in kings is that nature disapproves it, otherwise she would not so frequently turn it into ridicule by giving mankind an ass for a lion.

Secondly, as no man at first could possess any other public honors than were bestowed upon him, so the givers of those honors could have no power to give away the right of posterity, and though they might say, "We choose you for our head," they could not, without manifest injustice to their children, say, "that your children and your children's children shall reign over ours for ever." Because such an unwise, unjust, unnatural compact might (perhaps) in the next succession put them under the government of a rogue or a fool. . . .

This is supposing the present race of kings in the world to have had an honorable origin: whereas it is more than probable, that, could we take off the dark covering of antiquity and trace them to their first rise, we should find the first of them nothing better than the principal ruffian of some restless gang, whose savage manners of pre-eminence in subtilty obtained him the title of chief among plunderers; and who by increasing in power and extending his depredations, overawed the quiet and defenseless to purchase their safety by frequent contributions. . . .

England since the conquest hath known some few good monarchs, but groaned beneath a much larger number of bad ones: yet no man in his senses can say that their claim under William the Conqueror is a very honourable one. A French bastard landing with an armed Banditti and establishing himself king of England against the consent of the natives, is in plain terms a very paltry rascally original. It certainly hath no divinity in it. However it is needless to spend much time in exposing the folly of hereditary right; if there are any so weak as to believe it, let them promiscuously worship the Ass and the Lion, and welcome. I shall neither copy their humility, nor disturb their devotion. . . .

In short, monarchy and succession have laid (not this or that kingdom only) but the world in blood and ashes. 'Tis a form of government which the word of God bears testimony against, and blood will attend it. . . .

Thoughts on the Present State of American Affairs

IN the following pages I offer nothing more than simple facts, plain arguments, and common sense; and have no other preliminaries to settle with the reader, than that he will divest himself of prejudice and prepossession, and suffer his reason and his feelings to determine for themselves. . . .

Volumes have been written on the subject of the struggle between England and America. Men of all ranks have embarked in the controversy, from different motives, and with various designs; but all have been ineffectual, and the period of debate is closed. Arms, as the last resource, decide the contest; the appeal was the choice of the king, and the continent hath accepted the challenge. . . .

The sun never shined on a cause of greater worth. 'Tis not the affair of a city, a country, a province, or a kingdom, but of a continent—of at least one-eighth part of the habitable globe. 'Tis not the concern of a day, a year, or an age; posterity are virtually involved in the contest, and will be more or less affected, even to the end of time, by the proceedings now. Now is the seed time of continental union, faith and honor. The least fracture now will be like a name engraved with the point of a pin on the tender rind of a young oak; the wound will enlarge with the tree, and posterity read it in full grown characters. . . .

As much hath been said of the advantages of reconciliation, which, like an agreeable dream, hath passed away and left us as we were, it is but right, that we should examine the contrary side of the argument, and inquire into some of the many material injuries which these colonies sustain, and always will sustain, by being connected with, and dependant on Great Britain. . . .

I have heard it asserted by some, that as America hath flourished under her former connection with Great Britain, that the same connection is necessary towards her future happiness, and will always have the same effect. Nothing can be more fallacious than this kind of argument. We may as well assert, that because a child has thrived upon milk, that it is never to have meat; or that the first twenty years of our lives is to become a precedent for the next twenty. . . .

Alas! we have been long led away by ancient prejudices and made large sacrifices to superstition. We have boasted the protection of Great Britain, without considering, that her motive was interest not attachment; that she did not protect us from our enemies on our account, but from her enemies on her own account, from those who had no quarrel with us on any other account, and who will always be our enemies on the same account. Let Britain wave her pretensions to the continent, or the continent throw off the dependance, and we should be at peace with France and Spain were they at war with Britain. . . .

But Britain is the parent country, say some. Then the more shame upon her conduct. Even brutes do not devour their young; nor savages make war upon their families; wherefore the assertion, if true, turns to her reproach; but it happens not to be true, or only partly so, and the phrase parent or mother country hath been jesuitically adopted by the king and his parasites, with a low papistical design of gaining an unfair bias on the credulous weakness of our minds. Europe, and not England, is the parent country of America. This new world hath been the asylum for the persecuted lovers of civil and religious liberty from every Part of Europe. Hither have they fled, not from the tender embraces of the mother, but from the cruelty of the monster; and it is so far true of England, that the same tyranny which drove the first emigrants from home pursues their descendants still.

In this extensive quarter of the globe, we forget the narrow limits of three hundred and sixty miles (the extent of England) and carry our friendship on a larger scale; we claim brotherhood with every European Christian, and triumph in the generosity of the sentiment. . . . Not one third of the inhabitants, even of this province, are of English descent. Wherefore, I reprobate the phrase of parent or mother country applied to England only, as being false, selfish, narrow and ungenerous. . . .

I challenge the warmest advocate for reconciliation to show a single advantage that this continent can reap by being connected with Great Britain. . . . But the injuries and disadvantages we sustain by that connection are without number; and our duty to mankind at large, as well as to ourselves, instruct us to renounce the alliance: Because, any submission to, or dependance on, Great Britain tends directly to involve this continent in European wars and quarrels; and sets us at variance with nations, who would otherwise seek our friendship, and against whom, we have neither anger nor complaint. As Europe is our market for trade, we ought to form no partial connection with any part of it. It is the true interest of America to steer clear of European contentions, which she never can do, while by her dependence on Britain, she is made the make-weight in the scale of British politics.

Europe is too thickly planted with kingdoms to be long at peace, and whenever a war breaks out between England and any foreign power, the trade of America goes to ruin, because of her connection with Britain. The next war may not turn out like the Past, and should it not, the advocates for reconciliation now will be wishing for separation then, because neutrality, in that case, would be a safer convoy than a man of war. Every thing that is right or natural pleads for separation. The blood of the slain, the weeping voice of nature cries, 'tis time to part. Even the distance at which the Almighty hath placed England and America is a strong and natural proof that the authority of the one, over the other, was never the design of Heaven. The time likewise at which the continent was discovered, adds weight to the argument, and the manner in which it was peopled increases the force of it. The reformation was preceded by the discovery of America, as if the Almighty graciously meant to open a sanctuary to the persecuted in future years, when home should afford neither friendship nor safety. . . .

Men of passive tempers look somewhat lightly over the offenses of Britain, and, still hoping for the best, are apt to call out, Come we shall be friends again for all this. But examine the passions and feelings of mankind. Bring the doctrine of reconciliation to the touchstone of nature, and then tell me, whether you can hereafter love, honor, and faithfully serve the power that hath carried fire and sword into your land? If you cannot do all these, then are you only deceiving yourselves, and by your delay bringing ruin upon posterity. Your future connection with Britain, whom you can neither love nor honor, will be forced and unnatural, and being formed only on the plan of present convenience, will in a little time fall into a relapse more wretched than the first. But if you say, you can still pass the violations over, then I ask, Hath your house been burnt? Hath your property been destroyed before your face? Are your wife and children destitute of a bed to lie on, or bread to live on? Have you lost a parent or a child by their hands, and yourself the ruined and wretched survivor? If you have not, then are you not a judge of those who have. But if you have, and can still shake hands with the murderers, then are you unworthy the name of husband, father, friend, or lover, and whatever may be your rank or title in life, you have the heart of a coward, and the spirit of a sycophant. . . .

It is repugnant to reason, to the universal order of things, to all examples from the former ages, to suppose, that this continent can longer remain subject to any external power. The most sanguine in Britain does not think so. The utmost stretch of human wisdom cannot, at this time, compass a plan short of separation, which can promise the continent even a year's security. Reconciliation is now a fallacious dream. . . .

Small islands not capable of protecting themselves, are the proper objects for kingdoms to take under their care; but there is something very absurd, in supposing a continent to be perpetually governed by an island. In no instance hath nature made the satellite larger than its primary planet, and as England and America, with respect to each Other, reverses the common order of nature, it is evident they belong to different systems: England to Europe, America to itself.

I am not induced by motives of pride, party, or resentment to espouse the doctrine of separation and independence; I am clearly, positively, and conscientiously persuaded that it is the true interest of this continent to be so; that every thing short of that is mere patchwork, that it can afford no lasting felicity,—that it is leaving the sword to our children, and shrinking back at a time, when, a little more, a little farther, would have rendered this continent the glory of the earth. . . .

To bring the matter to one point. Is the power who is jealous of our prosperity, a proper power to govern us? Whoever says No to this question is an independant, for independancy means no more, than, whether we shall make our own laws, or whether the king, the greatest enemy this continent hath, or can have, shall tell us, "there shall be no laws but such as I like." . . .

If there is any true cause of fear respecting independance it is because no plan is yet laid down. Men do not see their way out; wherefore, as an opening into that business I offer the following hints; at the same time modestly affirming, that I have no other opinion of them myself, than that they may be the means of giving rise to something better. Could the straggling thoughts of individuals be collected, they would frequently form materials for wise and able men to improve to useful matter.

Let the assemblies be annual, with a President only. The representation more equal. Their business wholly domestic, and subject to the authority of a continental congress.

Let each colony be divided into six, eight, or ten convenient districts, each district to send a proper number of delegates to congress, so that each colony send at least thirty. The whole number in congress will be at least three hundred ninety. Each congress to sit and to choose a president by the following method. When the delegates are met, let a colony be taken from the whole thirteen colonies by lot, after which let the whole congress choose (by ballot) a president from out of the delegates of that province. In the next Congress, let a colony be taken by lot from twelve only, omitting that colony from which the president was taken in the former congress, and so proceeding on till the whole thirteen shall have had their proper rotation. And in order that nothing may pass into a law but what is satisfactorily just, not less than three fifths of the congress to be called a majority. He that will promote discord, under a government so equally formed as this, would join Lucifer in his revolt. . . .[f]

But where says some is the king of America? I'll tell you Friend, he reigns above, and doth not make havoc of mankind like the Royal Brute of Britain. Yet that we may not appear to be defective even in earthly honors, let a day be solemnly set apart for proclaiming the charter; let it be brought forth placed on the divine law, the word of God; let a crown be placed thereon, by which the world may know, that so far as we approve of monarchy, that in America the law is king. For as in absolute governments the king is law, so in free countries the law ought to be king;[g,h] and there ought to be no other. But lest any ill use should afterwards arise, let the crown at the conclusion of the ceremony be demolished, and scattered among the people whose right it is.

---

f. John Adams, second U.S. president, rejecting Paine's plan for a new government as unduly radical (1807): His plan was so democratical, without any restraints or even an attempt at any equilibrium or counterpoise, that it must produce confusion and every evil work. —John Adams, *Autobiography,* in Charles Francis Adams, ed., *The Works of John Adams* (Boston: Little, Brown, 1850), 2:508.

g. Henry Steele Commager, historian, lamenting Watergate-era politicians who put themselves above the law (1975): How did we get from Independence Hall to Watergate, from Yorktown to Vietnam, from Washington to Nixon? . . . How did we get from Tom Paine's proud boast, "But where is the king of America? . . . Know that in America law is king," to the official lawlessness of our own time? —Henry Steele Commager, *Jefferson, Nationalism, and the Enlightenment* (New York: Braziller, 1975), p. xviii.

h. Michael Greco, American Bar Association president, objecting to President George W. Bush's use of signing statements as unconstitutional (2006): Because Congress cannot

A government of our own is our natural right: And when a man seriously reflects on the precariousness of human affairs, he will become convinced, that it is infinitely wiser and safer, to form a constitution of our own in a cool deliberate manner, while we have it in our power, than to trust such an interesting event to time and chance. . . .

Ye that tell us of harmony and reconciliation, can ye restore to us the time that is past? Can ye give to prostitution its former innocence? Neither can ye reconcile Britain and America. The last cord now is broken, the people of England are presenting addresses against us. There are injuries which nature cannot forgive; she would cease to be nature if she did. As well can the lover forgive the ravisher of his mistress, as the continent forgive the murders of Britain. . . .

O ye that love mankind! Ye that dare oppose, not only the tyranny, but the tyrant, stand forth! Every spot of the old world is overrun with oppression. Freedom hath been hunted round the globe. Asia, and Africa, have long expelled her. Europe regards her like a stranger, and England hath given her warning to depart. O! receive the fugitive, and prepare in time an asylum for mankind.[ij]

---

veto a signing statement, and cannot now counter its very dangerous effects, the president with each signing statement issued, usurps a crucial power granted to Congress by the Constitution—the power to override a president's veto by a two-thirds majority vote. By declaring in a signing statement that a new law is unconstitutional, the president unlawfully also usurps the constitutional role of the Judiciary. He declares himself to be the chief interpreter of the Constitution, a role clearly reserved for the Supreme Court. . . . In his pamphlet "Common Sense," the colonial patriot Thomas Paine famously remarked that in England the king was the law, but in America the law is king. Yet quietly, but with devastating force, modern presidents are using signing statements to seize that which our nation's Founders purposely denied—absolute power, without any check or balance, to put themselves above the law. In America, no one is above the law—not even the president. —Michael Greco, "Opening Statement: News Conference on the Report and Recommendations of the ABA Task Force on Presidential Signing Statements and the Separation of Powers Doctrine," July 24, 2006, www.abanow.org/wordpress/wp-content/files_flutter/1273177630signstateremarks.pdf.

i. *Richmond Daily Dispatch*, the first penny paper published south of Baltimore, justifying secession at the start of the Civil War (1861): The illustrious fugitive has no longer a home in the Northern States of America. Constitutional liberty has departed from that inhospitable region, and seeks her last resting place upon the generous soil of the South. . . . It is here alone that she finds a home and a country, with the children of Washington and Jefferson, the home of Marion and Sumter and Greene. She has been

Of the Present Ability of America, with Some Miscellaneous Reflections

As to religion, I hold it to be the indispensable duty of all government, to protect all conscientious professors thereof, and I know of no other business which government hath to do therewith. Let a man throw aside that narrowness of soul, that selfishness of principle, which

---

expelled from the North. She could no longer dwell where the Higher Law proscribed the Constitution, the Bible, and God himself; where public virtue had sickened, languished and died; where honor, truth, faith, those plants of tender growth, had been eradicated from an ungenerous soil; where disinterestedness of aim and motive had become a sentiment unknown; where all education and language was cant; and indirection was the universal principle of conduct; where honesty for honesty's sake was a stranger in all public and in all private affairs; where the Government had degenerated into a job, the people into a mob, and ballot-box into a juggle. . . . With us a mob is an anomaly. We cannot run upon the evils of a pure democracy. We can have no pure democracy. Society cannot be turned bottom up by the upheaving of the masses. The slaves have no voice at the ballot box. The very presence of the negro makes a gentleman of the white, inspires him with self-respect, infuses him with a sense of his political importance and his responsibilities as a citizen. The oppressed of mankind need not despair. The experiment of free institutions is not a failure. Man's capacity for self-government will yet be vindicated. We shall fight the good fight. We shall conquer a peace. We shall establish constitutional liberty in purer forms and administer her rites in fairer temples than she has yet known. It is for her sake that we have come out from the old Union. It is for her sake that we have severed our connection with those who dishonored and repudiated her. —"Constitutional Liberty Takes Refuge in the South," *Richmond Daily Dispatch,* May 6, 1861, p. 2.

j. L. S. Stavrianos, historian, criticizing U.S. immigration policy at home and support for dictators abroad (1981): In "Common Sense," Tom Paine lamented that "Freedom hath been hunted round the globe," but he rejoiced that America would "receive the fugitive." For 200 years that was the case. Not only did America welcome fugitives, she immortalized the freedom-fighters of other lands, naming streets, parks, even cities in their honor. Today, the opposite prevails. The anonymous fugitives are turned away, while invitations are extended to Persian shahs, Korean dictators and Latin American military tyrants. Foreign revolutions that would have been hailed enthusiastically by 19th-century America are now branded as "terrorism" by 20th-century Washington; the suppression of insurrection abroad now is given precedence as a matter of America's foreign policy. The reversal of America's historic role is an outright disaster. —L. S. Stavrianos, "A Historic Role Reversed: We'll Reap Bitter Fruit in Denying Our Revolutionary Roots," *Los Angeles Times,* September 9, 1981, p. C7.

the niggards of all professions are so unwilling to part with, and he will be at once delivered of his fears on that head. Suspicion is the companion of mean souls, and the bane of all good society. For myself I fully and conscientiously believe, that it is the will of the Almighty, that there should be diversity of religious opinions among us: It affords a larger field for our Christian kindness. Were we all of one way of thinking, our religious dispositions would want matter for probation; and on this liberal principle, I look on the various denominations among us, to be like children of the same family, differing only, in what is called their Christian names. . . .

APPENDIX

I shall conclude these remarks, with the following timely and well intended hints. We ought to reflect, that there are three different ways by which an independancy may hereafter be effected; and that one of those three will, one day or other, be the fate of America, viz. By the legal voice of the people in congress; by a military power; or by a mob: It may not always happen that our soldiers are citizens, and the multitude a body of reasonable men; virtue, as I have already remarked, is not hereditary, neither is it perpetual. Should an independancy be brought about by the first of those means, we have every opportunity and every encouragement before us, to form the noblest, purest constitution on the face of the earth. We have it in our power to begin the world over again.[k,l] A situation, similar to the present, hath not happened since the days of Noah until now. The birthday of a new world is at hand, and a race of men perhaps as numerous as all Europe contains, are to receive their portion of freedom from the event of a few months. . . .

---

k. Ronald Reagan, fortieth U.S. president, invoking Paine and FDR as he accepts the Republican presidential nomination (1980): Everywhere we have met thousands of Democrats, Independents, and Republicans from all economic conditions and walks of life bound together in that community of shared values of family, work, neighborhood, peace and freedom. They are concerned, yes, but they are not frightened. They are disturbed, but not dismayed. They are the kind of men and women Tom Paine had in mind when he wrote—during the darkest days of the American Revolution—"We have it in our power to begin the world over again." Nearly 150 years after Tom Paine wrote those words, an American president told the generation of the Great Depression that it had a "rendezvous with destiny." I believe that this generation of Americans today has a rendezvous with destiny. Tonight, let us dedicate ourselves to renewing the American compact. I ask you not simply to "Trust me," but to trust your values—our values—and to hold me responsible for living up to them. I ask you to trust that American spirit which knows no ethnic, religious, social, political, regional, or economic boundaries; the spirit that burned with zeal in the hearts of millions of immigrants from every corner of the Earth who came here

In short, independance is the only bond that can tie and keep us together. We shall then see our object, and our ears will be legally shut against the schemes of an intriguing, as well as a cruel, enemy. We shall then, too, be on a proper footing to treat with Britain; for there is reason to conclude, that the pride of that court will be less hurt by treating with the American states for terms of peace, than with those whom she denominates, "rebellious subjects," for terms of accommodation. It is our delaying it that encourages her to hope for conquest, and our backwardness tends only to prolong the war. . . .

On these grounds I rest the matter. And as no offer hath yet been made to refute the doctrine contained in the former editions of this pamphlet, it is a negative proof, that either the doctrine cannot be refuted, or, that the party in favor of it are too numerous to be opposed. Wherefore, instead of gazing at each other with suspicious or doubtful curiosity, let each of us hold out to his neighbor the hearty hand of friendship, and unite in drawing a line, which, like an act of oblivion, shall bury in forgetfulness every former dissention. Let the names of Whig and Tory be extinct; and let none other be heard among us, than those of a good citizen, an open and resolute friend, and a virtuous supporter of the RIGHTS of MANKIND and of the FREE AND INDEPENDANT STATES OF AMERICA.[31]

---

in search of freedom. Some say that spirit no longer exists. But I have seen it—I have felt it—all across the land; in the big cities, the small towns and in rural America. The American spirit is still there, ready to blaze into life if you and I are willing to do what has to be done. —Ronald Reagan, "Address Accepting the Presidential Nomination at the Republican National Convention," Detroit, Michigan, July 17, 1980, www.presidency.ucsb.edu/ws/index.php?pid=25970.

l. George Will, columnist, criticizing Reagan for preferring Paine's radicalism to true conservatism (1984): Reagan is inexplicably fond of—he is constantly quoting—that stupendously dumb statement by Tom Paine: "We have it in our power to begin the world over again." Oh no, we don't. Paine's statement is the most unconservative statement that ever issued from human lips. Conservatism is grounded in an appreciation of the immense, constraining givenness of life. Conservatism is the politics of prudence, which begins with acceptance of the fact that, more often than not, and to a degree that is humbling to human beings, the inertia of society and history severely limits the pace and degree of change that human willfulness can bring about. —George Will, "The Candidates at Bay," Newsweek, October 22, 1984, p. 108.

COMMENTARY

Charles Inglis, Anglican clergyman and Loyalist, taking issue with Paine's title and predicting catastrophe (1776)

I find no Common Sense in this pamphlet, but much uncommon phrenzy. It is an outrageous insult on the common sense of Americans; an insidious attempt to poison their minds, and seduce them from their loyalty and truest interest. The principles of government laid down in it, are not only false, but too absurd to have ever entered the head of a crazy politician before. . . .

In the rotation of human affairs, a period may arrive, when (both countries being prepared for it) some terrible disaster, some dreadful convulsion in Great Britain, may transfer the seat of empire to this western hemisphere. . . . But if America should now mistake her real interest—if her sons, infatuated with romantic notions of conquest and empire, ere things are ripe, should adopt this republican's scheme: They will infallibly destroy this smiling prospect. They will dismember this happy country—make it a scene of blood and slaughter, and entail wretchedness and misery on millions yet unborn.

—Charles Inglis, *The True Interest of America Impartially Stated, in Certain Strictures on a Pamphlet Intitled Common Sense*, 2nd ed. (Philadelphia: Humphreys, 1776), pp. vi, 68–71.

John Alberger, historian of religion, defending monarchy abroad and republicanism at home (1843)

Asserting the incontestable truth that all men are by nature free and equal, [*Common Sense*] infers that there can be no state of society so artificial as to require distinctions of rank, and to need the control of what is known as absolute authority. The mind of the sober and reflective republican has no difficulty in seeing through this poor sophistry.

For ourselves, without claiming any other merit than that of sincere and conscientious devotion to our popular institutions, we are not foolish enough to deny, that there may be, and are, states of society in which democratic institutions are impracticable, or, if practicable, would be pernicious. A Muscovite, an Austrian, or a Turkish republic, no one can be insane enough to believe in. There is not a nation of Continental Europe, except, perhaps, some few of the northern, Protestant states, in which, under existing circumstances, a representative democracy could survive the year of its creation. France is, in technical language, estopped by her own deeds. And even in England, where the principles on which representative government is founded are better understood, we may be permitted to doubt, reasoning from the past and the present, if such an experiment could succeed. . . .

Here, in Anglo-Saxon America, the experiment has been made, and has succeeded; and, though a shade of doubt, a transient misgiving, may sometimes darken the minds of the most sanguine, yet it is too transient to disturb the tranquil and abiding confidence, that on this soil, and with a people educated politically as ours has been, representative republicanism is the best and only form of social institution that can exist or endure. It is, after all,—and to this point all fair reasoning brings us,—a matter of social aptitude; and, freely conceding, as we do, that a popular government is the best and most natural, the most conformable to the word of God, proclaimed in his gospel, and written in the heart of intelligent man, we deny the logic which deduces from this admission the expediency of forcing, as Paine and his disciples would have done, all existing societies, no matter how organized, into this mould. Where *self* is fit for it, self-government is best. Hence is it, that we have no sympathy with the feeling, or agreement with the reasoning, which denounces all monarchy, *per se,* as detestable and unnatural.

—John Alberger, "The Life and Character of Thomas Paine," *North American Review* 57.120 (July 1843): 16–17.

Robert Ingersoll, freethinker, applauding Common Sense (1892)

[*Common Sense*] was the first appeal for independence, the first cry for national life, for absolute separation. No pamphlet, no book, ever kindled such a sudden conflagration, a purifying flame, in which the prejudices and fears of millions were consumed. To read it now, after the lapse of more than a hundred years, hastens the blood. It is but the meagre truth to say that Thomas Paine did more for the cause of separation, to sow the seeds of independence, than any other man of his time.

—Robert G. Ingersoll, "Thomas Paine," *North American Review* 155.429 (August 1892): 183.

Bernard Bailyn, historian, on Paine's "genius" (1976)

Thomas Paine's *Common Sense* is the most brilliant pamphlet written during the American Revolution, and one of the most brilliant pamphlets ever written in the English language. How it could have been produced by a bankrupt Quaker corset-maker, a sometime teacher, preacher, and grocer, and twice-dismissed excise officer who happened to catch Benjamin Franklin's attention in England and who arrived in America only fourteen months before *Common Sense* was published is nothing one can explain without explaining genius itself. . . .

America had flourished under that benign system, and it was simply common sense to try to restore its balance. Why should one want to destroy the most successful political structure in the world, which had been constructed by generations of constitutional architects, each building on and refining the wisdom of his predecessors, simply because its present managers were vicious or criminal? . . .

Paine was certain that he knew the answers to all these questions, and the immediate impact that *Common Sense* had was in large part simply the result of the pamphlet's ringing assertiveness, its shrill unwavering declaration that all the right was on the side of independence and all the wrong on the side of loyalty to Britain.

—Bernard Bailyn, *Faces of Revolution: Personalities and Themes in the Struggle for American Independence* (New York: Vintage, 1992), pp. 67, 70–71.

Harvey Kaye, historian, castigating conservatives for simultaneously claiming Paine and selling him out (2005)

Now, after two centuries, it seems we have all become Painites. Today references to Paine abound in public debate and culture; in contrast to the past, not only the left but also the right claims him as one of their own. . . . But the truth is that not all of us are Painites. For all of their citations of Paine and his lines, conservatives do not—and truly cannot—embrace him and his arguments. Bolstered by capital, firmly in command of the Republican Party, and politically ascendant for a generation, they have initiated and instituted policies and programs that fundamentally contradict Paine's own vision and commitments. They have subordinated the Republic, the *res publica,* the commonwealth, the public good—to the marketplace and private advantage. They have furthered the interests of corporations and the rich over those of working people, their families, unions, and communities and overseen a concentration of wealth and power that, recalling the Gilded Age, has corrupted and enervated American democratic life and politics. . . . In fact, while poaching lines from Paine, they and their favorite intellectuals have disclosed their real ambitions and affections by once again declaring the "end of history" and promoting the lives of founders like John Adams and Alexander Hamilton, who in decided contrast to Paine scorned democracy and feared "the people."

—Harvey J. Kaye, *Thomas Paine and the Promise of America* (New York: Hill and Wang, 2005), pp. 259–60.

The Declaration
of Independence

❧ 1776 ❧

*T*HE Declaration of Independence is celebrated today for its soaring rhetoric of self-evident truths and inalienable rights, but most of it is given over to one long complaint. The colonists have experienced a "long train of abuses and usurpations" at the hands of Great Britain's King George III, and the Declaration describes twenty-seven distinct insults in gory detail, including: "He is at this time transporting large Armies of foreign Mercenaries to compleat the works of death, desolution, and tyranny, already begun with circumstances of Cruelty and Perfidy scarcely parallelled in the most barbarous ages, and totally unworthy the Head of a civilized nation."

So much for the facts. What is the theory? The theory is that, since government rests on "the consent of the governed," "the People" have the right to form a government, alter it, or abolish it. This right is not to be taken lightly, of course. Prudence and patience and petitions for redress are the first lines of defense. But when things get very bad, "the People" are permitted "to throw off such Government." And according to the members of the Second Continental Congress who signed this document, things had gotten very bad indeed. "The history of the present King of Great Britain is a history of repeated injuries and usurpations," the Declaration reads, so the time had come to cast aside both prudence and George III, and to "solemnly publish and declare, That these United Colonies are, and of Right ought to be Free and Independent States."

Congress did not want to seem rash, however. It did not want to enter the community of sovereign nations with the spitfire rhetoric of Thomas Paine on its lips. And it wanted to secure the support of France. So it began with the cool logic of an Enlightenment syllogism: "When in the Course of human events it becomes necessary for one people to dissolve the political bands which have connected them with another . . . a decent respect to the opinions of mankind requires that they should declare the causes which impel them to the separation." And this is what the Declaration did. It was a declaration of war, and a justification of the same. No sense of the sacred accompanied its production or publication, and there was almost no fanfare thereafter. In fact, in the years after July 4, 1776, it was largely ignored.

The representatives of the thirteen colonies who met in Philadelphia in the summer of 1776 had far more pressing concerns, not least prosecuting a war that was now over a year old. Some still hoped to reconcile with England. But since the appearance in January 1776 of Thomas Paine's *Common Sense,* public pressure was building for independence. On June 7, Richard Henry Lee of Virginia proposed a resolution to declare the colonies "free and independent states," but voting was delayed so state legislatures could be consulted and a document declaring and justifying independence drafted.

In the minds of many Americans, the Declaration of Independence is the product of the unique genius of Thomas Jefferson. The real story is more complicated. First, Congress appointed a Committee of Five to draft the document. Jefferson was assigned to write a first draft, and Adams and Franklin (both members of the Committee of Five) made some changes. On July 2, Congress passed Lee's resolution. It then made extensive changes to the draft declaration, including removing a long passage attacking George III for slavery and the slave trade. As historian Pauline Maier argues, this process, from drafting and editing to printing (on July 5) and signing (on August 2), was a "collective act," the work not only of Jefferson, the Committee of Five, and the Congress as a whole, but of a cast of thousands of nameless colonists who drafted some ninety "declarations of independence" in the months before July 4, 1776.[1]

Although the burden of the Declaration was to "declare the causes" of separation from England, it also included a remarkable second paragraph to which Americans have returned over and over, in endless cycles of interpretation and reinterpretation, as they have struggled to define themselves. This paragraph is actually one long sentence. In fact, it is the most influential sentence in U.S. history. "We hold these truths to be self-evident," it begins, before offering another litany, this time of five such truths:

That all men are created equal,

That they are endowed by their Creator with certain unalienable rights,

That among these are life, liberty and the pursuit of happiness,

That to secure these rights, governments are instituted among men, deriving their just powers from the consent of the governed,

That whenever any form of government becomes destructive of these ends, it is the right of the people to alter or to abolish it, and to institute new government, laying its foundation on such principles and organizing its powers in such form, as to them shall seem most likely to effect their safety and happiness.

The immediate effect of this document approached zero. The fact that the colonies had separated from Great Britain was historic, but the explanation had "astonishingly little immediate effect in the world of ideas, and quickly sank into . . . obscurity."[2] The Declaration was resurrected by the Jeffersonians in the 1790s and used as a cudgel to whack the Federalists and their British friends. By the time of the fiftieth-anniversary celebrations of Independence Day in 1826— a day that saw the deaths of both Jefferson and Adams—the Federalists were defunct, and Americans found themselves celebrating not merely independence but the "immortal" Declaration itself.

In the push and pull of U.S. history, one of the great debates has concerned the relative merits of the Declaration and the Constitution. Are these two voices at odds? Was the nation founded with the signing of the Declaration or with the ratification of the Constitution? Which document is preeminent today?

America's most influential interpreter of the Declaration of Independence was Abraham Lincoln, who held forth on it repeatedly. Angered by Massachusetts Senator Rufus Choate's characterization of the Declaration as so many "glittering . . . generalities," Lincoln mounted a three-pronged defense.[3] First, he reimagined the Declaration not as a practical declaration of war but as a lofty political manifesto. Second, he made equality this manifesto's central theme. Third, he made this theme the guiding light of American life and law, preeminent over even the Constitution itself.

In impromptu remarks delivered in Philadelphia's Independence Hall in 1861, just days before his inauguration, Lincoln called the Declaration his political creed. "I have never had a feeling, politically, that did not spring from the sentiments embodied in the Declaration of Independence," he said. The real American Revolution was "not the mere matter of separation of the colonies from the motherland, but that sentiment in the Declaration of Independence which gave liberty not alone to the people of this country, but hope to all the world, for all future time . . . that all should have an equal chance."[4]

Earlier, in his celebrated debates with Illinois Senator Stephen Douglas, Lincoln had insisted that the Declaration's promises were made to all Americans. "The entire records of the world, from the date of the Declaration of Independence up to within three years ago," he said at Galesburg, Illinois, in 1858, "may be searched in vain for one single affirmation, from one single man, that the negro was not included in the Declaration of Independence."[5] In 1863, in his "four score and seven years" opening at Gettysburg, Lincoln calculated that the nation was born with the Constitution, not the Declaration. No mere declaration of war, this immortal document was in Lincoln's view a declaration of equality. Through it, he asserted in another contender for the most influential sentence in U.S. history, the nation had been "dedicated to the proposition that all men are created equal."

Through Lincoln, the Declaration became dogma—*the* dogma of American life. Today this dogma is enshrined not only in American letters but also on the National Mall, where Lincoln and Martin Luther King Jr. both hold forth on what Jefferson meant by these five words. "Lincoln was the one who told us that they meant the end of slavery, and King was the one who told us that they meant racial equality," writes historian Joseph Ellis. "For this reason we can regard these three icons as an American trinity that embodies our creedal convictions in their 18th, 19th and 20th century versions."[6]

But this interpretation gives too much leverage to Lincoln and King, whose respective "magic tricks" were not quite as magical as it might seem. Decades before Lincoln and more than a century before King, American reformers were citing the Declaration's "self-evident" truths in their demands for equal rights for women, African Americans, and other minorities. A "Declaration of Sentiments" (1848) produced by women's rights activists in Seneca Falls, New York, read: "We hold these truths to be self-evident: that all men and women are created equal."[7]

In a remarkable piece of political prophesy called "What to the Slave Is the Fourth of July?" the former slave and abolitionist Frederick Douglass praised the signers of the Declaration of Independence as "truly great men" who "preferred revolution to peaceful submission to bondage." But he called July 4 celebrations a "sham" in a country that continued to practice "the great sin and shame" of slavery. "Would you have me argue that man is entitled to liberty? That he is the rightful owner of his own body?" he asked. "You have already declared it."[8]

In other words, when Martin Luther King Jr. decided that the Declaration's equality proposition meant that segregation had to end too, he was standing not only on Lincoln's shoulders but also on those of Douglass and the Seneca Falls signers and millions of other Americans who have seen the words of July 4, 1776, as an ideal toward which the nation should strive. Just as the Declaration was a "collective act," so was this egalitarian reinterpretation.[9]

But is this interpretation correct? It almost certainly wasn't the intention of the Declaration's signers, who, it should be remembered, cut Jefferson's antislavery language from the final document. But who says the framers get to freeze this document in time? The meaning of the Declaration, like the meaning of America, has always been hotly contested, with alternative interpretations competing cheek by jowl. Is it conservative? Liberal? Radical? It depends on whom you ask.

Before and during the Civil War, debates over the Declaration circled around the meaning of "all men are created equal." While antislavery activists argued for what they saw as the plain meaning of this text, proslavery thinkers contended that "all men are created equal" was self-evidently false. Inequality was a fact of life, and only dreamers and philosophers could imagine otherwise. After the Civil War, Lincoln's interpretive line took hold, and the conversation shifted to whether and where America was falling short of its egalitarian creed. Increasingly, the Declaration displaced the Constitution as the expression of the meaning of America. *It* was the soul of the American people and the spirit of American law. *It* was the ideal toward which the Constitution was striving and American history was arcing. In a classic expression of this "Declaration first" perspective, Charles Sumner of Massachusetts said that "the grandest victory of the [Civil War] was the establishment of the new rule by which the Declaration became supreme as an interpreter of the Constitution." In postbellum America, Sumner said, "every word in the Constitution must be interpreted by these primal, self-evident truths."[10]

As the twentieth century dawned, Progressive historians depicted the "revolutionary" Declaration as the hero and the "reactionary" Constitution as the villain in their retellings of the American drama. Vernon Parrington built his three-volume history around a mano a mano struggle between these two documents, one representing the "rights of man" and the other the "rights of property."[11] In this way, the Declaration came to be seen as the "ultimate expression of Revolutionary ideals, to wit, egalitarianism, popular majority rule, and human rights," while the Constitution was "cast in the role of counter-revolutionary reaction in support of monied privilege, minority rule, and property rights."[12]

Conservatives responded by contending that the Declaration was a practical rather than a philosophical document, focused on cutting the cord from Great Britain, not advancing a laundry list of human rights. Because inequality is inescapable, any effort to employ the coercive power of the state to create a nation of equals was foolhardy at best, many argued. Demands for equality do nothing but expand the powers of government and contract individual liberty. Those who made this argument insisted that the nation did not begin with the Declaration but with the Constitution. And what was created on July 4, 1776, were thirteen sovereign states. To obsess over the Declaration and its equality clause is to "derail" the American tradition of states' rights, conservatives argue. Lincoln "turned our tradition upside down."[13]

One intriguing twist in this duel between the Declaration and the Constitution is that, although the Declaration speaks of our "unalienable rights" coming from the "Creator," the Constitution is godless. As a result, the Constitution is more useful to conservatives when it comes to questions such as states' rights or the relative merits of order and equality, but the Declaration is more useful when it comes to the claim that America began as a Christian nation.

The Declaration of Independence ❧

IN CONGRESS, July 4, 1776.

The unanimous Declaration of the thirteen united States of America,

W hen in the Course of human events it becomes necessary for one people to dissolve the political bands which have connected them with another and to assume among the powers of the earth, the separate and equal station to which the Laws of Nature and of Nature's God[a,b] entitle them, a decent respect to the opinions of mankind requires that they should declare the causes which impel them to the separation.

---

a. Michael Novak, Catholic philosopher, arguing for the biblical basis of the Declaration and the American nation (1999): There are lessons in this nation's covenant with God, of which the Declaration of Independence is the primary jewel. . . . In that document, Thomas Jefferson twice referred to God in biblical terms, and before assenting to it, the Congress added two more references. The fifty-six signers were, mostly, Christians; they represented a mostly Christian people; and it was from Christian traditions that they had learned these names of God. . . . Examine closely the God of the Framers. . . . This God exercises liberty. He makes choices. He chooses "chosen" peoples and "almost chosen" peoples and loves every people with a love unique to it. —Michael Novak, *God's Country: Taking the Declaration Seriously* (Washington, DC: AEI Press, 2000), pp. 12, 15–16.

b. Alan Dershowitz, law professor, attacking the idea that the Declaration is based on biblical principles (2007): These references to "Nature's God," "Creator," "Supreme Judge," and "Divine Providence" . . . have been cited as proof of our founding fathers' commitment to the Judeo-Christian God of the Bible. But these were terms . . . employed not by conventional Christians but by Enlightenment "deists." The omission of any reference to Jesus Christ or to the specific God of Christianity or of the Bible is far more significant than the inclusion of generic words that were consistent with non-Christian deistic beliefs. . . . The Declaration was not based on the Bible, and its drafters were most definitely not "men of the Bible." On the contrary, Thomas Jefferson, its primary drafter, believed that the New Testament was written largely by "very inferior minds," and that much of it consisted of "so much absurdity, so much untruth, charlatanism and imposture" that it could aptly be characterized as "dung." He thought even less of the Old Testament, whose vengeful God he deplored and whose draconian laws he rejected. . . . Thomas Jefferson was neither a man of the Bible nor a person "of faith." —Alan Dershowitz, *Blasphemy: How the Religious Right Is Hijacking Our Declaration of Independence* (Hoboken, NJ: Wiley, 2007), pp. 12–13.

We hold these truths to be self-evident, that all men are created equal,[c,d,e,f] that they are endowed by their Creator[g] with certain unalienable Rights, that among these are Life, Liberty and the pursuit of Happiness.[h,i,j]—That to secure these rights, Governments are instituted among Men, deriving their just powers from the consent of the governed,[k,l]—That whenever any Form of

---

c. Abraham Lincoln, lawyer and Republican candidate for Senate, criticizing the *Dred Scott* decision in his famous debate with Senator Stephen Douglas (1857): Chief Justice Taney, in his opinion in the Dred Scott case, admits that the language of the Declaration is broad enough to include the whole human family, but he and Judge Douglas argue that the authors of that instrument did not intend to include negroes, by the fact that they did not at once, actually place them on an equality with the whites. Now this grave argument comes to just nothing at all, by the other fact, that they did not at once, or ever afterwards, actually place all white people on an equality with one or another. And this is the staple argument of both the Chief Justice and the Senator, for doing this obvious violence to the plain unmistakable language of the Declaration. I think the authors of that notable instrument intended to include all men, but they did not intend to declare all men equal in all respects. They did not mean to say all were equal in color, size, intellect, moral developments, or social capacity. They defined with tolerable distinctness, in what respects they did consider all men created equal—equal in "certain inalienable rights, among which are life, liberty, and the pursuit of happiness." This they said, and this meant. They did not mean to assert the obvious untruth, that all were then actually enjoying that equality, nor yet, that they were about to confer it immediately upon them. In fact they had no power to confer such a boon. They meant simply to declare the right, so that the enforcement of it might follow as fast as circumstances should permit. They meant to set up a standard maxim for free society, which should be familiar to all, and revered by all; constantly looked to, constantly labored for, and even though never perfectly attained, constantly approximated, and thereby constantly spreading and deepening its influence, and augmenting the happiness and value of life to all people of all colors everywhere. The assertion that "all men are created equal" was of no practical use in effecting our separation from Great Britain; and it was placed in the Declaration, not for that, but for future use. Its authors meant it to be, thank God, it is now proving itself, a stumbling block to those who in after times might seek to turn a free people back into the hateful paths of despotism. —Abraham Lincoln, "Speech on the Dred Scott Decision," June 26, 1857, Springfield, Illinois, http://teachingamericanhistory.org/library/index.asp?document=52.

d. Stephen Douglas, U.S. Senator from Illinois, excluding nonwhites from the Declaration's equality clause in his debate with Lincoln (1858): [Lincoln] thinks that the negro is his brother. I do not think that the negro is any kin of mine at all. And here is the difference between us. I believe that the Declaration of Independence, in the words "all men are created equal," was intended to allude only to the people of the United States, to men of European birth or descent, being white men, that they were created equal, and hence that Great Britain had no right to deprive them of their political and religious privileges; but the signers of that paper did not intend to include the Indian or the negro in that declaration, for if they had would they not have been bound to abolish slavery in every State and Colony from that day? Remember, too, that at the time the Declaration was put forth, every one of the thirteen colonies were slaveholding colonies; every man who signed that Declaration represented slaveholding constituents. Did those signers mean by that act to charge themselves, and all their constituents, with having violated the law of God, in holding the negro in an inferior condition to the white man? And yet, if they included negroes in that term, they were bound, as conscientious men, that day and that hour, not only to have abolished slavery throughout the land, but to have conferred political rights and privileges on the negro, and elevated him to an equality with the white man. . . .

The very fact that they did not shows that they did not understand the language they used to include any but the white race. Did they mean to say that the Indian, on this continent, was created equal to the white man, and that he was endowed by the Almighty with inalienable rights—rights so sacred that they could not be taken away by any Constitution or law that man could pass? Why, their whole action toward the Indian showed that they never dreamed that they were bound to put him on an equality. I am not only opposed to negro equality, but I am opposed to Indian equality. I am opposed to putting the coolies, now importing into this country, on an equality with us, or putting the Chinese or any inferior race on an equality with us. I hold that the white race, the European race, I care not whether Irish, German, French, Scotch, English, or to what nation they belong, so they are the white race, to be our equals. And I am for placing them, as our fathers did, on an equality with us. Emigrants from Europe, and their descendants, constitute the people of the United States. The Declaration of Independence only included the white people of the United States. The Constitution of the United States was framed by the white people, it ought to be administered by them, leaving each State to make such regulations concerning the negro as it chooses, allowing him political rights or not, as it chooses, and allowing him civil rights or not, as it may determine for itself. —Stephen A. Douglas, "Speech of Senator Douglas," Springfield, Illinois, July 17, 1858, in *Political Debates Between Hon. Abraham Lincoln and Hon. Stephen A. Douglas* (Columbus: Follett, Foster, 1860), pp. 51–52.

e. Clarence Manion, Notre Dame law school dean, Eisenhower Democrat, and radio personality, arguing for both spiritual equality and social inequality (1950): This is indeed a very special kind of equality. It is deliberately related to the Creator and signifies that in their "divine" endowments and in their divinely ordained purpose, men are all the same. Thus the life of any man is just as sacred as the life of any other, and each man has exactly the same natural rights and duties as every other person. . . . This equality before their Creator neither contemplates nor calls for dead level in the earthly condition of men. On the contrary each human being is by nature a distinct individual personality and is consequently and naturally different in his earthly characteristics from any other person on earth. The confusion of "inequality" with "injustice" is a fatal mistake which frustrates many well-intentioned attempts to improve human society. Injustice is vicious and must be fought unceasingly, but inequality is a natural and inescapable characteristic of the human race. There has never been nor will there ever be a time when all men are equal in their capacities and conditions here on earth. The nature of the individual as well as the nature of human society demands these unfailing differences. Without the wide diversification of talents, tastes, abilities and ambitions that now and always exist among men, society could neither feed nor clothe itself. It is consequently a wise provision of Providence that causes the perpetuation of endless variety in the desires and capabilities of human beings. —Clarence Manion, *The Key to Peace: A Formula for the Perpetuation of Real Americanism* (Chicago: Heritage Foundation, 1950), pp. 26–27.

f. Robert Bork, judge, law professor, and U.S. Supreme Court nominee, decrying the "pernicious effects" of the ever-expanding equality proposition (1996): The proposition that all men are created equal said what the colonists already believed and so, as Gordon Wood put it, equality became "the single most powerful and radical ideological force in all of American history." That is true and, though it verges on heresy to say so, it is also profoundly unfortunate. . . . The Declaration's pronouncement of equality was sweeping but sufficiently ambiguous so that even slave holders, of whom Jefferson was one, subscribed to it. The ambiguity was dangerous because it invited the continual expansion of the concept and its requirements. The Declaration was not, clearly, a document that was understood at the time to promise equality of condition, not even among white male Americans. The meaning of equality was heavily modified by the American idea of reward according to individual achievement and reverence for private property. But those modifications are hostile to the egalitarian impulse, which constantly expands the areas in which equality is thought desirable or even mandatory. . . .

The great political upsurge of equality occurred with Franklin Roosevelt's New Deal and Harry Truman's Fair Deal. The names suggest that the cards have been unfairly stacked, that there are inequalities that must be rectified. Since these were sentiments expressed in the political arena, the message was that inequality must be cured by government. No other institution is sufficiently powerful and sufficiently comprehensive in its jurisdiction to undertake the task, which means that the egalitarian passion must always lead to greater centralized power and coercion. —Robert Bork, *Slouching Towards Gomorrah: Modern Liberalism and American Decline* (New York: HarperCollins, 1996), pp. 66–67.

g. Phyllis Schlafly, lawyer and outspoken opponent of the Equal Rights Amendment, arguing that the Declaration is "America's great religious document" (2010): The

Declaration of Independence is the official and unequivocal recognition by the American people of our belief and faith in God. It affirms God's existence as a "self-evident" truth that requires no further discussion, debate or litigation. The nation created by the great Declaration is God's country. The rights it defines are God-given. The actions of its signers are God-inspired. . . . The Declaration declares that each of us was created; so if we were created, we must have had a Creator and, as the modern discovery of DNA confirms, each of God's creatures is different from every other person who has ever lived or ever will live on this earth. The Declaration proclaims that life and liberty are the unalienable gifts of God, natural rights, which no person or government can rightfully take away. It affirms that the purpose of government is to secure our God-given unalienable individual rights. —Phyllis Schlafly, "America's Great Religious Document," *Eagle Forum,* July 9, 2010, www.eagleforum.org/column/2010/july10/10-07-09.html.

h. Abraham Lincoln, lawyer and Republican candidate for Senate, arguing in the Lincoln-Douglas debates against political and social equality yet for the natural rights of African Americans (1858): I will say here, while upon this subject, that I have no purpose, directly or indirectly, to interfere with the institution of slavery in the States where it exists. I believe I have no lawful right to do so, and I have no inclination to do so. I have no purpose to introduce political and social equality between the white and the black races. There is a physical difference between the two which, in my judgment, will probably forever forbid their living together upon the footing of perfect equality, and inasmuch as it becomes a necessity that there must be a difference, I, as well as Judge Douglas, am in favor of the race to which I belong having the superior position. I have never said anything to the contrary, but I hold that, notwithstanding all this, there is no reason in the world why the negro is not entitled to all the natural rights enumerated in the Declaration of Independence, the right to life, liberty, and the pursuit of happiness. I hold that he is as much entitled to these as the white man. I agree with Judge Douglas, he is not my equal in many respects—certainly not in color, perhaps not in moral or intellectual endowment. But in the right to eat the bread, without the leave of anybody else, which his own hand earns, *he is my equal, and the equal of Judge Douglas, and the equal of every living man.* —Abraham Lincoln, first debate with Stephen Douglas, Ottawa, Illinois, August 21, 1858, in *Political Debates Between Hon. Abraham Lincoln and Hon. Stephen A. Douglas* (Columbus: Follett, Foster, 1860), pp. 240–41.

i. W. E. B. Du Bois, sociologist and civil rights activist, rejecting Booker T. Washington's view that African Americans should focus on economic advancement, not political rights (1903): The black men of America have a duty to perform, a duty stern and delicate,—a forward movement to oppose a part of the work of their greatest leader. So far as Mr. Washington preaches Thrift, Patience, and Industrial Training for the masses, we must hold up his hands and strive with him, rejoicing in his honors and glorying in the strength of this Joshua called of God and of man to lead the headless host. But so far as Mr.

Washington apologizes for injustice, North or South, does not rightly value the privilege and duty of voting, belittles the emasculating effects of caste distinctions, and opposes the higher training and ambition of our brighter minds,—so far as he, the South, or the Nation, does this,—we must unceasingly and firmly oppose them. By every civilized and peaceful method we must strive for the right which the world accords to men, clinging unwaveringly to those great words which the sons of the Fathers would fain forget: "We hold these truths to be self-evident: That all men are created equal; that they are endowed by their Creator with certain unalienable rights; that among these are life, liberty, and the pursuit of happiness." —W. E. B. Du Bois, *The Souls of Black Folk: Essays and Sketches*, 3rd ed. (Chicago: McClurg, 1903), pp. 58–59.

j. Ronald Reagan, fortieth U.S. president, marshalling the Declaration against abortion on National Sanctity of Human Life Day (1984): The values and freedoms we cherish as Americans rest on our fundamental commitment to the sanctity of human life. The first of the "unalienable rights" affirmed by our Declaration of Independence is the right to life itself, a right the Declaration states has been endowed by our Creator on all human beings—whether young or old, weak or strong, healthy or handicapped. Since 1973, however, more than 15 million unborn children have died in legalized abortions—a tragedy of stunning dimensions that stands in sad contrast to our belief that each life is sacred. These children, over tenfold the number of Americans lost in all our Nation's wars, will never laugh, never sing, never experience the joy of human love; nor will they strive to heal the sick, or feed the poor, or make peace among nations. Abortion has denied them the first and most basic of human rights, and we are infinitely poorer for their loss. —Ronald Reagan, "Proclamation 5147: National Sanctity of Human Life Day," January 13, 1984, www.presidency.ucsb.edu/ws/index.php?pid=39772.

k. Roger Taney, U.S. Supreme Court chief justice, ruling in *Dred Scott v. Sandford* that the words of the Declaration were not meant to include blacks (1857): The general words above quoted would seem to embrace the whole human family, and if they were used in a similar instrument at this day would be so understood. But it is too clear for dispute, that the enslaved African race were not intended to be included, and formed no part of the people who framed and adopted this declaration; for if the language, as understood in that day, would embrace them, the conduct of the distinguished men who framed the Declaration of Independence would have been utterly and flagrantly inconsistent with the principles they asserted; and instead of the sympathy of mankind, to which they so confidently appealed, they would have deserved and received universal rebuke and reprobation. Yet the men who framed this declaration were great men—high in literary acquirements—high in their sense of honor, and incapable of asserting principles inconsistent with those on which they were acting. They perfectly understood the meaning of the language they used, and how it would be understood by others; and they knew that it would not in any part of the civilized world be supposed to embrace the

Government becomes destructive of these ends, it is the Right of the People to alter or to abolish it, and to institute new Government, laying its foundation on such principles and organizing its powers in such form, as to them shall seem most likely to effect their Safety and Happiness. Prudence, indeed, will dictate that Governments long established should not be changed for light and transient causes; and accordingly all experience hath shewn that mankind are more disposed to suffer, while evils are sufferable, than to right themselves by abolishing the forms to which they are accustomed. But when a long train of abuses and usurpations, pursuing invariably the same Object evinces a design to reduce them under absolute Despotism, it is their right, it is their duty, to throw off such Government, and to provide new Guards for their future security.— Such has been the patient sufferance of these Colonies; and such is now the necessity which constrains them to alter their former Systems of Government. The history of the present King of Great Britain is a history of repeated injuries and usurpations, all having in direct object the

---

negro race, which, by common consent, had been excluded from civilized Governments and the family of nations, and doomed to slavery. They spoke and acted according to the then established doctrines and principles, and in the ordinary language of the day, and no one misunderstood them. The unhappy black race were separated from the white by indelible marks, and laws long before established, and were never thought of or spoken of except as property. . . . —Roger B. Taney, majority opinion, *Dred Scott v. Sandford*, 60 U.S. 393 (1857).

l. Susan B. Anthony, women's rights advocate, defending her actions prior to her June 17, 1873, trial for the crime of voting in the 1872 presidential election (1873): Here is pronounced the right of all men, and "consequently," as the Quaker preacher said, "of all women," to a voice in the government. And here, in this first paragraph of the Declaration, is the assertion of the natural right of all to the ballot; for, how can "the consent of the governed" be given, if the right to vote be denied? . . . The women, dissatisfied as they are with this form of government, that enforces taxation without representation,—that compels them to obey laws to which they have never given their consent—that imprisons and hangs them without a trial by a jury of their peers—that robs them, in marriage, of the custody of their own persons, wages and children—are this half of the people left wholly at the mercy of the other half, in direct violation of the spirit and the letter of the declarations of the framers of this government, every one of which was based on the immutable principle of equal rights to all. By those declarations, kings, priests, popes, aristocrats, were all alike dethroned, and placed on a common level, politically, with the lowliest born subject or serf. By them, too, men, as such, were deprived of their divine right to rule, and placed on a political level with women. —Susan B. Anthony, speech, Monroe and Ontario Counties, New York, in Elizabeth Cady Stanton, Susan B. Anthony, and Matilda Joslyn Gage, eds., *History of Woman Suffrage* (New York: Fowler & Wells, 1882), 2:631–32.

establishment of an absolute Tyranny over these States. To prove this, let Facts be submitted to a candid world.

He has refused his Assent to Laws, the most wholesome and necessary for the public good.

He has forbidden his Governors to pass Laws of immediate and pressing importance, unless suspended in their operation till his Assent should be obtained; and when so suspended, he has utterly neglected to attend to them.

He has refused to pass other Laws for the accommodation of large districts of people, unless those people would relinquish the right of Representation in the Legislature, a right inestimable to them and formidable to tyrants only.

He has called together legislative bodies at places unusual, uncomfortable, and distant from the depository of their public Records, for the sole purpose of fatiguing them into compliance with his measures.

He has dissolved Representative Houses repeatedly, for opposing with manly firmness his invasions on the rights of the people.

He has refused for a long time, after such dissolutions, to cause others to be elected; whereby the Legislative powers, incapable of Annihilation, have returned to the People at large for their exercise; the State remaining in the mean time exposed to all the dangers of invasion from without, and convulsions within.

He has endeavoured to prevent the population of these States; for that purpose obstructing the Laws for Naturalization of Foreigners; refusing to pass others to encourage their migrations hither, and raising the conditions of new Appropriations of Lands.

He has obstructed the Administration of Justice, by refusing his Assent to Laws for establishing Judiciary powers.

He has made Judges dependent on his Will alone, for the tenure of their offices, and the amount and payment of their salaries.

He has erected a multitude of New Offices, and sent hither swarms of Officers to harrass our people, and eat out their substance.

He has kept among us, in times of peace, Standing Armies without the Consent of our legislatures.

He has affected to render the Military independent of and superior to the Civil power.

He has combined with others to subject us to a jurisdiction foreign to our constitution, and unacknowledged by our laws; giving his Assent to their Acts of pretended Legislation:

For Quartering large bodies of armed troops among us:

For protecting them, by a mock Trial, from punishment for any Murders which they should commit on the Inhabitants of these States:

For cutting off our Trade with all parts of the world:

For imposing Taxes on us without our Consent:

For depriving us in many cases, of the benefits of Trial by Jury:

For transporting us beyond Seas to be tried for pretended offences

For abolishing the free System of English Laws in a neighbouring Province, establishing therein an Arbitrary government, and enlarging its Boundaries so as to render it at once an example and fit instrument for introducing the same absolute rule into these Colonies:

For taking away our Charters, abolishing our most valuable Laws, and altering fundamentally the Forms of our Governments:

For suspending our own Legislatures, and declaring themselves invested with power to legislate for us in all cases whatsoever.

He has abdicated Government here, by declaring us out of his Protection and waging War against us.

He has plundered our seas, ravaged our Coasts, burnt our towns, and destroyed the lives of our people.

He is at this time transporting large Armies of foreign Mercenaries to compleat the works of death, desolation and tyranny, already begun with circumstances of Cruelty and Perfidy scarcely paralleled in the most barbarous ages, and totally unworthy the Head of a civilized nation.

He has constrained our fellow Citizens taken Captive on the high Seas to bear Arms against their Country, to become the executioners of their friends and Brethren, or to fall themselves by their Hands.

He has excited domestic insurrections amongst us, and has endeavoured to bring on the inhabitants of our frontiers, the merciless Indian Savages, whose known rule of warfare, is an undistinguished destruction of all ages, sexes and conditions.

In every stage of these Oppressions We have Petitioned for Redress in the most humble terms: Our repeated Petitions have been answered only by repeated injury. A Prince whose character is thus marked by every act which may define a Tyrant, is unfit to be the ruler of a free people.

Nor have We been wanting in attentions to our Brittish brethren. We have warned them from time to time of attempts by their legislature to extend an unwarrantable jurisdiction over us. We have reminded them of the circumstances of our emigration and settlement here. We have appealed to their native justice and magnanimity, and we have conjured them by the ties of our common kindred to disavow these usurpations, which, would inevitably interrupt our connections and correspondence. They too have been deaf to the voice of justice and of consanguinity. We must, therefore, acquiesce in the necessity, which denounces our Separation, and hold them, as we hold the rest of mankind, Enemies in War, in Peace Friends.

We, therefore, the Representatives of the united States of America, in General Congress, Assembled, appealing to the Supreme Judge of the world for the rectitude of our intentions, do, in the Name, and by Authority of the good People of these Colonies, solemnly publish and declare, That these united Colonies are, and of Right ought to be Free and Independent States, that they are Absolved from all Allegiance to the British Crown, and that all political connection between them and the State of Great Britain, is and ought to be totally dissolved; and that as Free and Independent States, they have full Power to levy War, conclude Peace, contract Alliances, establish Commerce, and to do all other Acts and Things which Independent States may of right do. And for the support of this Declaration, with a firm reliance on the protection of Divine Providence, we mutually pledge to each other our Lives, our Fortunes, and our sacred Honor.[15]

COMMENTARY

Mercy Otis Warren, author and historian of the Revolution, offering an early assessment of the Declaration as a "celebrated paper" (1805)

The Declaration of Independence, which has done so much honor to the then existing congress, to the inhabitants of the United States, and to the genius and heart of the gentleman who drew it, in the belief, and under the awe, of the Divine Providence, ought to be frequently read by the rising youth of the American states, as a palladium of which they should never lose sight, so long as they wish to continue a free and independent people.

—Mercy Otis Warren, *History of the Rise, Progress, and Termination of the American Revolution* (Boston: Manning and Loring, 1805), 3:308–9.

John Quincy Adams, sixth U.S. president, arguing on Independence Day that the Declaration created one sovereign nation, not thirteen sovereign states (1837)

An error of the most dangerous character, more than once threatening the dissolution by violence of the Union itself, has occasionally found countenance and encouragement in several of the States, by an inference not only unwarranted by the language and import of the Declaration, but subversive of its fundamental principles. This inference is that because by this paper the United Colonies were declared free and independent States, therefore each of the States, separately, was free, independent and sovereign. . . . The Declaration did not proclaim the separate States free and independent; much less did it announce them as sovereign States, or affirm that they separately possessed the war-making or the peace-making power. The fact was directly the reverse. . . .

The inconsistency of the institution of domestic slavery with the principles of the Declaration of Independence was seen and lamented by all the southern patriots of the Revolution; by no one with deeper and more unalterable conviction, than by the author of the Declaration himself. No charge of insincerity or hypocrisy can be fairly laid to their charge. Never from their lips was heard one syllable of attempt to justify the institution of slavery. They universally considered it as a reproach fastened upon them by the unnatural stepmother country, and they saw that before the principles of the Declaration of Independence, slavery, in common with every other mode of oppression, was destined sooner or later to be banished from the earth. . . .

Friends and fellow citizens! I speak to you with the voice as of one risen from the dead. Were I now, as I shortly must be, cold in my grave, and could the sepulchre unbar its gates, and open to me a passage to this desk, devoted to the worship of almighty God, I would repeat the question with which this discourse was introduced:—"Why are you assembled in this place?"—And one of you would answer me for all,—Because the Declaration of Independence, with the voice of an angel from heaven, "put to his mouth the sounding alchemy," and proclaimed universal emancipation upon earth!

It is not the separation of your forefathers from their kindred race beyond the Atlantic tide. It is not the union of thirteen British Colonies into one People and the entrance of that People upon the theatre, where kingdoms, and empires, and nations are the persons of the drama. It is not that this is the birthday of the North American Union, the last and noblest offspring of time. It is that the first words uttered by the Genius of our country, in announcing his existence to the world of mankind, was,—Freedom to the slave! Liberty to the captives! Redemption! Redemption forever to the race of man, from the yoke of oppression! It is not the work of a day; it is not the labor of an age; it is not the consummation of a century, that we are assembled to commemorate. It is the emancipation of our race. It is the emancipation of man from the thralldom of man!

—John Quincy Adams, *An Oration Delivered Before the Inhabitants of the Town of Newburyport, at Their Request, on the Sixty-First Anniversary of the Declaration of Independence, July 4th, 1837* (Newburyport, MA: Morss and Brewster, 1837), n.p.

"Declaration of Sentiments," Seneca Falls Convention, rewriting the Declaration as a women's rights proclamation (1848)

When, in the course of human events, it becomes necessary for one portion of the family of man to assume among the people of the earth a position different from that which they have hitherto occupied, but one to which the laws of nature and of nature's God entitle them, a decent respect to the opinions of mankind requires that they should declare the causes that impel them to such a course.

We hold these truths to be self-evident: that all men and women are created equal; that they are endowed by their Creator with certain inalienable rights; that among these are life, liberty, and the pursuit of happiness; that to secure these rights governments are instituted, deriving their just powers from the consent of the governed. Whenever any form of government becomes destructive of these ends, it is the right of those who suffer from it to refuse allegiance to it, and to insist upon the institution of a new government, laying its foundation on such principles, and organizing its powers in such form, as to them shall seem most likely to effect their safety and happiness. Prudence, indeed, will dictate that governments long established should not be changed for light and transient causes; and accordingly all experience hath shown that mankind are more disposed to suffer, while evils are sufferable, than to right themselves by abolishing the forms to which they are accustomed. But when a long train of abuses and usurpations, pursuing invariably the same object, evinces a design to reduce them under absolute despotism, it is their duty to throw off such government, and to provide new guards for their future security. Such has been the patient sufferance of the women under this government, and such is now the necessity which constrains them to demand the equal station to which they are entitled. The history of mankind is a history of repeated injuries and usurpations on the part of man toward woman, having in direct object the establishment of an absolute tyranny over her. To prove this, let facts be submitted to a candid world. . . .

He has never permitted her to exercise her inalienable right to the elective franchise.

He has compelled her to submit to laws, in the formation of which she had no voice.

He has withheld from her rights which are given to the most ignorant and degraded men—both natives and foreigners.

Having deprived her of this first right of a citizen, the elective franchise, thereby leaving her without representation in the halls of legislation, he has oppressed her on all sides.

He has made her, if married, in the eye of the law, civilly dead.

He has taken from her all right in property, even to the wages she earns.

He has made her, morally, an irresponsible being, as she can commit many crimes with impunity, provided they be done in the presence of her husband. In the covenant of marriage, she is compelled to promise obedience to her husband, he becoming, to all intents and purposes, her master—the law giving him power to deprive her of her liberty, and to administer chastisement.

He has so framed the laws of divorce, as to what shall be the proper causes, and in case of separation, to whom the guardianship of the children shall be given, as to be wholly regardless of the happiness of women—the law, in all cases, going upon a false supposition of the supremacy of man, and giving all power into his hands.

After depriving her of all rights as a married woman, if single, and the owner of property, he has taxed her to support a government which recognizes her only when her property can be made profitable to it.

He has monopolized nearly all the profitable employments, and from those she is permitted to follow, she receives but a scanty remuneration. He closes against her all the avenues to wealth and distinction which he considers most honorable to himself. As a teacher of theology, medicine, or law, she is not known.

He has denied her the facilities for obtaining a thorough education, all colleges being closed against her.

He allows her in church, as well as state, but a subordinate position, claiming apostolic authority for her exclusion from the ministry, and, with some exceptions, from any public participation in the affairs of the church.

He has created a false public sentiment by giving to the world a different code of morals for men and women, by which moral delinquencies which exclude women from society, are not only tolerated, but deemed of little account in man.

He has usurped the prerogative of Jehovah himself, claiming it as his right to assign for her a sphere of action, when that belongs to her conscience and to her God.

He has endeavored, in every way that he could, to destroy her confidence in her own powers, to lessen her self-respect, and to make her willing to lead a dependent and abject life.

Now, in view of this entire disfranchisement of one-half the people of this country, their social and religious degradation—in view of the unjust laws above mentioned, and because women do feel themselves aggrieved, oppressed, and fraudulently deprived of their most sacred rights, we insist that they have immediate admission to all the rights and privileges which belong to them as citizens of the United States.

—"Declaration of Sentiments," in Elizabeth Cady Stanton, *A History of Woman Suffrage* (Rochester, NY: Fowler and Wells, 1881), pp. 70–71, www.fordham.edu/halsall/mod/senecafalls.asp.

Frederick Douglass, abolitionist and former slave, denouncing America's failure to live up to the "saving principles" of the Declaration (1852)

Fellow-citizens, pardon me, allow me to ask, why am I called upon to speak here to-day? What have I, or those I represent, to do with your national independence? Are the great principles of political freedom and of natural justice, embodied in that Declaration of Independence, extended to us? And am I, therefore, called upon to bring our humble offering to the national altar, and to confess the benefits and express devout gratitude for the blessings resulting from your independence to us? Would to God, both for your sakes and ours, that an affirmative answer could be truthfully returned to these questions! . . .

But, such is not the state of the case. The blessings in which you, this day, rejoice, are not enjoyed in common. The rich inheritance of justice, liberty, prosperity and independence, bequeathed by your fathers, is shared by you, not by me. The sunlight that brought life and healing to you, has brought stripes and death to me. This Fourth [of] July is yours, not mine. You may rejoice, I must mourn. To drag a man in fetters into the grand illuminated temple of liberty, and call upon him to join you in joyous anthems, were inhuman mockery and sacrilegious irony. Do you mean, citizens, to mock me, by asking me to speak to-day? . . .

Would you have me argue that man is entitled to liberty? That he is the rightful owner of his own body? You have already declared it. Must I argue the wrongfulness of slavery? Is that a question for Republicans? . . . There is not a man beneath the canopy of heaven, that does not know that slavery is wrong for him. . . .

What, to the American slave, is your 4th of July? I answer: a day that reveals to him, more than all other days in the year, the gross injustice and cruelty to which he is the constant victim. To him, your celebration is a sham; your boasted liberty, an unholy license; your national greatness, swelling vanity; your sounds of rejoicing are empty and heartless; your denunciations of tyrants, brass fronted impudence; your shouts of liberty and equality, hollow mockery; your prayers and hymns, your sermons and thanksgivings, with all your religious parade, and solemnity, are, to him, mere bombast, fraud, deception, impiety, and hypocrisy—a thin veil to cover up crimes which would disgrace a nation of savages. There is not a nation on the earth guilty of practices more shocking and bloody, than are the people of these United States, at this very hour. . . .

You declare, before the world, and are understood by the world to declare, that you "hold these truths to be self-evident, that all men are created equal; and are endowed by their Creator with certain inalienable rights; and that, among these are, life, liberty, and the pursuit of happiness"; and yet, you hold securely, in a bondage which, according to your own Thomas Jefferson, "is worse than ages of that which your fathers rose in rebellion to oppose," a seventh part of the inhabit-ants of your country. Fellow-citizens! I will not enlarge further on your national inconsistencies. The existence of slavery in this country brands your republican-ism as a sham, your humanity as a base pretence, and your Christianity as a lie.

—Frederick Douglass, "What to the Slave Is the Fourth of July?," Rochester, New York, July 5, 1852, http://teachingamericanhistory.org/library/index.asp?document=162.

W. A. Corey, socialist author and editor, offering a Declaration of Independence for the working class (1902)

When in the course of human events it becomes necessary for the enslaved class to dissolve the economic bonds which have connected them with another and to become the masters of their own destiny, it is essential that they should declare the causes which compel them to the separation.

We hold these truths to be self-evident, that all men are created equal: equal in opportunities, equal in rights, among which are life and the pursuit of happiness. That to secure these rights governments are instituted among men, deriving their just powers from the consent of the governed. That whenever any form of government becomes destructive of these ends, it is the right of the people to abolish it and to institute new government, laying its foundations on such principles and organizing its powers to such form as to them shall seem most likely to effect their safety and happiness.

Such is now the necessity which constrains the working class to abolish completely the capitalist form of government.

The history of the present capitalist rulers of the United States is a history of repeated injuries and usurpations all having for their deliberate purpose the establishment of an absolute tyranny over the people of the working class. To prove this let these facts be submitted to a candid world.

They have by the grace of the present industrial system taken four-fifths of the wealth created by our labor and cheerfully told us to be economical with the other fifth. . . .

They have wasted uncounted billions of our wealth in their wars and in suppressing capitalist-made crime and vice, and then, with characteristic hypocrisy, assumed to be our instructors in morals.

They have forced unnumbered thousands of our women to choose between the sweat-shop, suicide and dishonor and watered the tree of their prosperity with the innocent blood of millions of our little children.

They have corrupted the church, dominated the schools and subsidized the public press.

They have bought up the legislators elected by our votes like range cattle, and purchased decisions from our law courts at bargain rates; thus making new laws and interpreting old ones always in their own interest. . . .

Now therefore we, representatives of the working class of America and by their authority, do solemnly publish and declare that the working class is, and of right ought to be, free and independent; that it is absolved from all allegiance to the capitalist class; that the present capitalist industrial system is, and of right ought to be, fully abolished; and that as a free and independent people, the workers have full power to manage their own affairs both industrial and political on the basis of complete democracy.

And for the support of this declaration and with a firm reliance on the providence of our own steadfast purpose, we mutually pledge to each other our votes, our lives and our sacred honor.

All hail, the toiler's day of deliverance!

All hail, the Co-operative Commonwealth!

—W. A. Corey, "The Working Class Declaration of Independence," *Los Angeles Socialist,* June 28, 1902, reprinted in Philip S. Foner, ed., *We the Other People: Alternative Declarations of Independence by Labor Groups, Farmers, Women's Rights Advocates, Socialists, and Blacks, 1829–1975* (Urbana: Univ. of Illinois Press, 1976), pp. 151–53.

The People's Bicentennial Commission, arguing that genuine democracy requires freedom from the power of large corporations (1975)

The History of the present giant corporations is a History of repeated injuries and usurpations; all having in direct object the establishment of an absolute Tyranny over these States. To prove this, let Facts be submitted to a candid World. . . .

The Giant Corporations have pursued a policy of industrial negligence which kills 14,000 workers and permanently disables 900,000 more every year. . . .

They have used the energy crisis in order to double the price of fuel and make record gains in profit. . . .

They have turned our Nation into a weapons factory, wasting valuable labor and resources that could be utilized for basic human needs.

They have fostered tensions and conflicts between races, sexes and ethnic groups in their arbitrary and discriminatory employment practices.

They have pillaged the resources, exploited the peoples, and systematically intervened in the domestic affairs of other nations in order to profit their corporate treasuries.

The Giant Corporations have subverted the Constitution of the United States and the principle of Government of, by, and for the people

By illegally financing their own candidates for local, state and national office.

By placing their own supporters in key government commissions and regulatory agencies.

By using massive lobbying operations to virtually dictate the legislative direction of the State and Federal Governments, including the decisions on how our tax money is to be allocated.

It is the same corporate giants

That profess the strongest attachment to self-reliance, while pocketing billions of dollars of our tax money in the form of Government subsidies and special favors.

That profess their commitment to preserving their country's future, while systematically destroying our natural environment.

That herald the virtues of personal responsibility and accountability, while engaging in wholesale crime under the protection of their corporate charters. . . .

We, therefore, the Citizens of the United States of America, hereby call for the abolition of these giant institutions of tyranny and the establishment of new economic enterprises with new laws and safeguards to provide for the equal and democratic participation of all American Citizens in the economic decisions that effect the well-being of our families, our communities, and our Nation.

—People's Bicentennial Commission, "A Declaration of Economic Independence," in Philip S. Foner, ed., *We the Other People: Alternative Declarations of Independence by Labor Groups, Farmers, Women's Rights Advocates, Socialists, and Blacks, 1829–1975* (Urbana: Univ. of Illinois Press, 1976), pp. 170–74.

Pauline Maier, historian, criticizing the "idolatry" of
Declaration worship in a nation of free citizens (1997)

And the shrine up the mall at the National Archives, with its curious altar, which would seem more at home in a Baroque church somewhere in Rome? Understand it, if you will, as a reminder of what happened in the 1820s, or, better yet, as a monument to the issues and peculiarities of the twentieth century, but not to the heritage of the American Revolution. Why should the American people file by, looking up reverentially at a document that was and is their creation, as if it were handed down by God or were the work of super-human men whose talents far exceeded those of any who followed them? The symbolism is all wrong; it suggests a tradition locked in a glorious but dead past, reinforces the passive instincts of an anti-political age, and undercuts the acknowledgment and exercise of public responsibilities essential to the survival of the republic and its ideas.

Debate whether affirmative action is an anti-egalitarian bestowal of special privilege or a necessary remedy for centuries of unequal opportunity; ask whether the "individualistic character" of those passages from the Declaration of Independence on the Jefferson Memorial has helped liberate the human spirit or fostered a self-centered culture of rights at odds with the public good. Let interests clash and argument prosper. The vitality of the Declaration of Independence rests upon the readiness of the people and their leaders to discuss its implications and to make the crooked ways straight, not in the mummified paper curiosities lying in state at the Archives; in the ritual of politics, not in the worship of false gods who are at odds with our eighteenth-century origins and who war against our capacity, together, to define and realize right and justice in our time.

—Pauline Maier, *American Scripture: Making the Declaration of Independence* (New York: Knopf, 1997), p. 215.

Gordon Wood, historian, arguing for the radicalism of the
Revolution, the Declaration, and Jefferson (2011)

Jefferson's standing as the spokesman for democracy rests on his belief in equality. . . . But Jefferson went much further than simply claiming that all men were created equal—that was a cliché among the enlightened in the late eighteenth century. . . . Both he and Paine believed that people were not just created equal but were actually equal to everyone else throughout their lives. Not that Jefferson and Paine denied the obvious differences among individuals that exist—how some individuals are taller, smarter, more handsome than others—but rather both radicals posited that at bottom, every single individual, men and women, black and white, had a common moral or social sense that tied him or her to other individuals. None of the other leading Founders believed that—not Washington, not Hamilton, not Adams. And since no democracy can intelligibly exist without some such magnanimous belief that at heart everyone is the same, Jefferson's position as the apostle of American democracy seems not only legitimate but necessary to the well-being of the nation.

—Gordon S. Wood, *The Idea of America: Reflections on the Birth of the United States* (New York: Penguin, 2011), pp. 227–28.

The Blue-Back Speller

◆ NOAH WEBSTER, 1783– ◆

*N*OAH WEBSTER (1758–1843) might seem to be an unlikely candidate for inclusion in *The American Bible*. He is the man behind the dictionary, right? And wasn't he one of the most disagreeable men in the early republic, denounced by his own publisher as "a pedantic grammarian . . . full of vanity and ostentation" and by a rival editor as "a spiteful viper," a "prostitute wretch," a "demagogue coxcomb," "a great fool, and a barefaced liar."[1] Yes and yes again. The "Schoolmaster to America" was also a scolding schoolmarm—"a mere pedagogue, of very limited understanding and very strong prejudices and party passions," in the words of Thomas Jefferson.[2] But this "breathtakingly unpopular" man was also the author of the most popular secular book in American history, with the possible exception of the Harry Potter series.[3]

Webster's speller was originally published in 1783, the final year of the Revolutionary War, under the infelicitous title *A Grammatical Institute of the English Language: Part I.* (Parts II and III of this trilogy, a grammar and a reader, would follow.) It was released in 1786 as *The American Spelling Book* and, in 1829, as *The Elementary Spelling Book,* but it eventually came to be known, because of its vivid blue cloth cover, as the Blue-Back Speller. Webster hoped that this book would gradually challenge the most popular eighteenth-century speller, *A New Guide to the English Tongue* (1740), by the English cleric Thomas Dilworth. Instead, it overthrew that textbook in something of an overnight coup. Webster did not aim merely to write a bestseller, however. He meant to change the way Americans spoke and wrote and thought—to liberate the American tongue from slavery to British English.

In the wake of the American Revolution, there was a mad rush to infuse the revolutionary spirit into the American soul. "The United States cast off all things British and instead created its own holidays (the fourth of July, Washington's birthday), produced its own literature (Cooper, Emerson, and more), invented its own founding moments (including the Pilgrims' landing at Plymouth Rock), and adopted new, decidedly non-English ancestors, the noble but savage American Indian," writes historian Jill Lepore.[4] Some even considered replacing the King's English with a new official language. Hebrew, which had lent Americans a sense of themselves as God's chosen people, was one candidate. French and German were also proposed, perhaps to irritate the British. Webster insisted on English, but *American* English. "Customs, habits, and *language,* as well as government should be national," he wrote. "America should have her *own* distinct from all the world."[5] And that language should be uniform across the nation, as recognizable in Boston as in Charleston.

In order to do his orthographical work, Webster learned twenty languages, but he was a fierce nationalist who believed that "the country would be as prosperous and much more happy if no European should set his foot on our shores."[6] Like many of his fellow New Englanders (he hailed from West Hartford, Connecticut, and graduated from Yale), he was also a fervent Federalist who supported a strong central government. Like Washington, he fretted about political "factions" driving the nation apart. In fact, he saw "factions" as the gravest threat to the new nation. "We ought not to consider ourselves as inhabitants of a single state only; but as *Americans;* as the common subjects of a great empire," he wrote.[7] But a national government was not enough. To complete the revolution, Americans needed a national language, distinct from British English and shared throughout the states. To this end, Webster called for a "separation of the American tongue from the English."[8] But his speller did more than demand a divorce from the king's English. It also took aim at linguistic "factions" at home by attempting to obliterate regional, class, and racial distinctions in accents, dialects, vocabulary, and spelling—"one nation, under Webster."

Webster's effort to standardize American English by flattening out regional differences was not entirely successful. Even today, Texans sound different from natives of New Orleans (though, in the spirit of Webster, newscasters typically speak in an oddly uniform television accent). Nonetheless, Webster's goal to create an American language distinct from the English of the English was highly successful. "America must be independent in literature as she is in politics," Webster wrote.[9] And his speller, which many have described as "a cultural and linguistic Declaration of Independence," did more than any other book to advance that cause.[10]

Webster's claim to a place among America's founding fathers is strong for a man usually remembered as a wordsmith. As historian Henry Steele Commager notes, his lobbying for a strong Constitution to replace the weak Articles of Confederation helped to bring that founding document (and its federal government) into existence, while his work as editor of New York City's first daily, *American Minerva*, qualifies him as one of the fathers of American journalism. He was also the father of American copyright law and can lay claim to being a father of the census. Still, the most influential work of this "multiple American founding father" was his speller, which for nearly a century after its appearance lorded over American schoolchildren with something approaching divine authority.[11]

Webster's speller did more than introduce generations of young Americans to reading and writing, however. It also created the language in which America talked about itself. Much of the book, which appeared in 385 editions during Webster's lifetime, was devoted to lists of syllables and words. But it also included, in lieu of Dilworth's British place-names, lists of American cities, towns, rivers, and mountains. As of 1790, it also included "A Federal Catechism," which instructed its readers on the three branches of government. This catechism also held forth, in good Federalist fashion, on the "defects of democracy." "A pure democracy is generally a very bad government," wrote Webster. "It is often the most tyrannical government on earth; for a multitude is often rash, and will not hear reason."[12]

The Blue-Back Speller referred to the last letter in the alphabet by the American "zee" rather than the British "zed." It spelled the English word "honour" as "honor." It parsed words such as "nation" into two syllables rather than the customary three. It also proposed changes that were not fated to be accepted: removing the *a* from "head" and the *e* from "give"; and rendering "women" as "wimmen."

Though championed by his fellow Americans for cutting their cultural umbilical cord from England, Webster was widely criticized for removing God from American education. But Webster refused to apologize for secularizing his speller. When it first appeared, many homes had only one book, the Bible. So parents used the Good Book to instruct their children not only in ethics and theology but also in reading and spelling. Webster saw this custom as "a kind of prostitution of divine truth to secular purposes."[13] He also criticized the theological obsessions of his competitors:

Nothing has a greater tendency to lessen the reverence which mankind ought to have for the Supreme Being, than a careless repetition of his name upon every trifling occasion. Experience shows that a frequent thoughtless repetition of that sacred word, which, in our Spelling Books, often occurs two or three times in a line, renders the name as familiar to children as the name of their book, and they mention it with the same indifference. To prevent this profanation, such passages are selected from scripture, as contain some important precepts of morality and religion, in which that sacred name is seldom mentioned. Let sacred things be appropriated to sacred purposes.[14]

Although religion is more prominent in the *New England Primer,* a favorite of Puritan divines, it is wrong to describe Webster's speller as a "secular catechism."[15] To be sure, it included all manner of workaday lessons that remain with us today, including "Rome was not built in a day" and "He that lies down with dogs must rise up with fleas." But its opening lesson—the very first words millions upon millions of American children learned to read—spoke of God and sin, and a passage on the Golden Rule referred to Jesus as "Our Saviour" ("Our Savior" in later editions).[16] Not without reason do many homeschooling evangelicals today laud Webster as the "Father of American Christian Education."

This combination of piety and pedagogy turned the Blue-Back Speller into the first runaway bestseller in American history. Webster estimated that 10 million copies had been printed by 1829, and by the middle of the nineteenth century Americans were reportedly buying a million units a year. By most estimates, the book sold as many as 100 million copies over the nineteenth century, making it the bestselling book other than the Bible in the century after it appeared.[17]

Webster's speller was popular in his native New England. But J. W. Burke of Macon, Georgia, judged the book "as essential to the mental existence of the South as hog and hominy to their physical needs."[18] And the Cherokee leader Sequoyah drew on Webster's speller as he created a system of reading and writing for his native language. The Blue-Back Speller was particularly influential among African Americans. Frederick Douglass learned to write by copying letters from it, and the education of Booker T. Washington began with the same book. Sales of the speller spiked to roughly 1.5 million copies in 1866, as newly freed slaves turned to Webster to learn how to read and write. In this way, Webster's speller become "a staple American article like ham and flour"—the "volume in which the young democracy learned its A B C."[19]

Market share dropped with the appearance in 1836 of the McGuffey readers, a joint collaboration of the Reverend William McGuffey and his brother Alexander, which probably also registered sales upward of 100 million. But roughly a century of Americans learned to speak and read from Webster's speller. "Under its benign guidance," writes Commager, "generations of young Americans learned the same words, the same spelling, the same pronunciations; read the same stories; absorbed the same moral lessons."[20] Today the American conversation about "America" and "Americans" goes forth in Webster's English. "We no longer see him," writes Commager, "but we speak him and hear him."[21] His speller, beloved by homeschoolers, is still in print, and his spirit lives annually in the spelling bee, as much an American tradition today as Webster's speller was in the eighteenth and nineteenth centuries.

The Blue-Back Speller

LESSON I.
No man may put off the law of God.
My joy is in his law all the day.
O may I not go in the way of sin.
Let me not go in the way of ill men. . . .

LESSON XI.
He that came to save us will wash us from all sin; I will be glad in his name.
A good boy will do all that is just; he will flee from vice; he will do good,
    and walk in the way of life.
Love not the world, nor the things that are in the world; for they are sin.
I will not fear what flesh can do to me; for my trust is in him who made the world.
He is nigh to them that pray to him, and praise his name.

LESSON XII.
Be a good child: mind your book; love your school, and strive to learn.
Tell no tales; call no ill names; you must not lie, nor swear, nor cheat, nor steal.
Play not with bad boys; use no ill words at play; spend your time well; live in peace; and shun all strife. This is the way to make good men love you, and save your soul from pain and woe.[22]

COMMENTARY

*Jefferson Davis, U.S. Senator from Mississippi and future president of the
Confederacy, praising Webster's speller for uniting the nation (1858)*

I have spoken of diversity among the people of the United States; yet there is
probably greater similitude than is to be found elsewhere over the same extent of
country, and in the same number of people. In language, especially, our people are
one; surely much more so than those of any other country. The diversity between
the people of the different States, even those most remote from each other, is not
as great as that between inhabitants of adjoining counties of England, or departments of France or Spain, where provinces have their separate dialects. And chief
among the causes for this I would place the primary book, in which children of
my day learned their letters, and took their first lessons in spelling and reading. I
refer to the good old spelling book of Noah Webster, on which I doubt if there has
been any improvement, and which had the singular advantage of being used over
the whole country. To this unity of language and general similitude, is to be added
a community of sentiment wherever the American is brought into contrast or
opposition to any other people.

If shadows float over our disc and threaten an eclipse; if there be those who
would not avert, but desire to precipitate catastrophe to the Union, these are not
the sentiments of the American heart; they are rather the exceptions and should
not disturb our confidence in that deep seated sentiment of nationality which
aided our fathers when they entered into the compact of union, and which has
preserved it to us.

—Jefferson Davis, "Speech at the State Fair at Augusta, Maine," *Eastern Argus,* September 29, 1858, in
   Speeches of the Hon. Jefferson Davis, of Mississippi, Delivered During the Summer of 1858 (Baltimore:
   Murphy, 1859), p. 26.

The Ladies' Repository, *Methodist publication, waxing*
nostalgic about growing up with Webster (1861)

Our nation owes a great debt to Webster's Spelling Book, for I question whether
any other of man's composing has exerted so large an influence in the formation
of the national character. A vast amount of practically valuable learning was
comprised in that little and unpretending manual, and not a few of our really
great men have been indebted to it for the elementary lessons upon which their
subsequent greatness was built up. Is the good old book still used in any of the
schools? I would like to spend some quiet winter evening in reexamining its
pages, and conversing once more with its well-remembered columns of words,

and occasional reading lessons, and names of places, and those two memorable chapters near the close—the one of synonyms that were not synonymous, and the other of "abbreviations," which seemed to me to possess a kind of mystical power like the strange words of the necromancers. But then I fear they would not seem to me in the book as they do now mingled with the memories of departed joys. Ah, well, we are not so young as we once were, nor shall we be again.

—"The Editor's Repository," *The Ladies' Repository*, January 1861, p. 61.

Horace Scudder, Atlantic Monthly *editor, on Webster's moral agenda (1875)*

It is very plain, too, that Webster was a moralist and philosopher as well as a speller. He was by no means restricted in his ambition to the teaching of correct spelling, but he aimed to have a hand in the molding of the national mind and national manners. In his Preface to *The American Spelling-Book,* he says: "To diffuse an uniformity and purity of language in America, to destroy the provincial prejudices that originate in the trifling differences of dialect and produce recipro- cal ridicule, to promote the interest of literature and the harmony of the United States, is the most earnest wish of the author, and it is his highest ambition to deserve the approbation and encouragement of his countrymen."

His spelling-book, accordingly, in its early editions, contained a number of sharp little warnings in the form of foot-notes, which imply that he seized the young nation just in time to prevent the perpetuation of vulgar errors which, once becoming universal, would have required the hereditary Webster to make them the basis of orthoepic canons. Thus *ax* is reprobated when *ask* is intended; Americans were to say *wainscot,* not *winchcott; resin,* not *rozum; chimney,* not *chimbly; confiscate,* not *confisticate.* As these warnings disappeared after a few years, it may be presumed that he regarded the immediate danger as past; but the more substantial matters of good morals came to have greater prominence, and in addition to the columns of classified words, which constitute almost the sole contents of the earliest edition, there came to be inserted those fables and moral and industrial injunctions, with sly reminders of the virtue of Washington, which have sunk into the soft minds of three generations of Americans.

—Horace E. Scudder, "A Patriotic School-Master," *Atlantic Monthly*, September 1875, p. 334.

Booker T. Washington, *educator and former slave, on learning to read through Webster's speller (1901)*

From the time that I can remember having any thoughts about anything, I recall that I had an intense longing to learn to read. I determined, when quite a small child, that, if I accomplished nothing else in life, I would in some way get enough education to enable me to read common books and newspapers. Soon after we got settled in some manner in our new cabin in West Virginia, I induced my mother to get hold of a book for me.

How or where she got it I do not know, but in some way she procured an old copy of Webster's "blue-back" spelling-book, which contained the alphabet, followed by such meaningless words as "ab," "ba," "ca," "da." I began at once to devour this book, and I think that it was the first one I ever had in my hands. I had learned from somebody that the way to begin to read was to learn the alphabet, so I tried in all the ways I could think of to learn it,—all of course without a teacher, for I could find no one to teach me. At that time there was not a single member of my race anywhere near us who could read, and I was too timid to approach any of the white people. In some way, within a few weeks, I mastered the greater portion of the alphabet.

In all my efforts to learn to read my mother shared full my ambition, and sympathized with me and aided me in every way that she could. Though she was totally ignorant, so far as mere book knowledge was concerned, she had high ambitions for her children, and a large fund of good hard, common sense which seemed to enable her to meet and master every situation. If I have done anything in life worth attention, I feel sure that I inherited the disposition from my mother.

—Booker T. Washington, *Up from Slavery: An Autobiography* (Garden City, NY: Doubleday, 1901), pp. 27–28.

Henry Steele Commager, historian, doing his best to overestimate the influence of Webster's extraordinarily influential speller (1962)

It was the Speller that conquered the land. It established its sovereignty in the East; it went west with the Conestoga wagon, and in the knapsacks of countless itinerant pedagogues; it leaped the mountains and established its empire on the Pacific coast; it even invaded the South. . . . No other secular book had ever spread so wide, penetrated so deeply, lasted so long.

—Henry Steele Commager, "Schoolmaster to America," in *Noah Webster's American Spelling Book* (New York: Bureau of Publications, Teacher's College, Columbia Univ., 1962), p. 5.

Thomas Gustafson, English professor, comparing Webster to Whitman (1992)

Noah Webster spent much of a lifetime writing and revising spellers, grammars, and dictionaries. Whitman spent much of a lifetime building and rebuilding *Leaves of Grass* and collecting words in his notebooks. Neither Webster early in his career nor Whitman was afraid to embrace the forces that unsettle, amend, and reconstruct a language. The language they call for is a language open to change and open to the idioms of the people. The democratization of language that Webster propounded is advanced by Whitman. They both agree that the speech of the people must govern the language, but Whitman differs from Webster by broadening and deepening the concept of the people, whose speech should be represented in spellers, grammars, and dictionaries. . . . Whitman is at once the fulfillment of Noah Webster and the prophet of his transcendence. Like Webster, Whitman would write the speller, the grammar, and the dictionary that needed to be written to represent the people of the United States and constitute the country as a nation. But he would write them with a poet's license.

—Thomas Gustafson, *Representative Words: Politics, Literature, and the American Language, 1776–1865* (Cambridge: Cambridge Univ. Press, 1992), pp. 341–42.

LAW

The Constitution

❧ 1787 ❧

OFTEN LISTED alongside the Declaration of Independence and the Gettysburg Address as one-third of the "American testament," the Constitution is by its own acclamation the "supreme Law of the Land."[1] Presidents become presidents by swearing to uphold it. Citizens become citizens by answering questions about it. And although it is not often read, it is widely revered. At the National Archives, where it is enshrined inside a titanium and glass case filled with argon gas, pilgrims parade past it with a reverence typically associated with a fallen leader.

But the Constitution is no dead letter. In fact, it provokes more controversy than any other book in *The American Bible,* and it continues to grow via amendments. Every year the Supreme Court provides a running commentary on what the Constitution means. In 2011 alone, the Court weighed in on childhood vaccines, greenhouse-gas regulations, medical residency programs, software patents, cell phone service, and DNA testing. It decided whether female Walmart employees can sue their employer in a class-action suit (no) and whether a fundamentalist religious group that chants "Fags Doom Nations" has the right to protest at military funerals (yes). It ruled on the First Amendment and free speech, the Fourth Amendment and unreasonable searches and seizures, and the Fourteen Amendment's due process clause.

But the Constitution is not just for lawyers. America's constitutional conversation extends beyond the august deliberations of Supreme Court justices into the hardscrabble public square, where "We the people" continually revive and revise the Constitution. On television programs and websites, in schools and churches, and during presidential campaigns and Supreme Court nomination hearings, citizens ask and answer all manner of questions about the Constitution. Did the Supreme Court usurp the power of the people when it decided the 2000 presidential election in *Bush v. Gore* (2000)? And speaking of presidential elections, is it time to revisit that clunky compromise by which the nation chooses its chief executive: the Electoral College? These are not questions for judges or lawyers alone. The Constitution is, in the words of Yale professor Akhil Reed Amar, "the People's document," so ordinary Americans can and do weigh in, approving or disapproving of Supreme Court nominees, protesting or applauding Supreme Court rulings, and even denying, in the name of "popular constitutionalism," the authority of that court to serve as the final arbiter of what the Constitution means.[2]

The Constitution came into being because of the failures of the Articles of Confederation, which were passed by the Continental Congress in 1777 and ratified in 1781. In America's perennial tug of war between state and federal power, the Articles tilted sharply toward the states. Having won independence, Americans were more fearful of tyranny than chaos, and many were convinced of Montesquieu's maxim that republican government was possible only in relatively small and homogeneous societies. So they created an eighteenth-century analogue to the European Union: a "league of friendship" among thirteen sovereign states. This compact produced, according to George Washington, "a half-starved, limping Government, that appears to be always moving upon crutches, and tottering at every step."[3] It had no chief executive and no national courts. It could not tax or raise an army. Of the many ill effects of this centrifugal arrangement, spiraling inflation was the most conspicuous. Many farmers landed in prison for unpaid debts, and the United States defaulted on loans to the French. Shays's Rebellion, an armed insurrection among western Massachusetts farmers, served as a clarion call for stronger central government. "What stronger evidence can be given of the want of energy in our governments than these disorders?" Washington wrote in the midst of that uprising. "If there exists not a power to check them, what security has a man of life, liberty, or property?"[4]

In the summer of 1787, delegates convened in Philadelphia to draft a new constitution. They weighed a Virginia plan in which a powerful national government would be able to veto state legislation, and a New Jersey plan with a much weaker central government. Alexander Hamilton of New York proposed a constitution that reflected his admiration for the British, with a lifetime chief executive barely distinguishable from a king. In debating these plans, large states fought for population-based legislative representation while small states demanded equal representation for each state. Delegates also disagreed over how the chief executive would be elected. By state legislators? By the American people themselves? Virginia firebrand Patrick Henry boycotted the convention because he "smelt a rat," but delegates who, like him, prized liberty above life insisted that a nation with such a strong central government would secure only tyranny.[5]

Meanwhile, the economic interests of the North clashed with those of the South, not least over the question of slavery. The devil's bargain struck on this matter brought with it a portentous paradox: the same nation that was "conceived in liberty," as President Lincoln would later say, was also conceived in slavery. After much debate, delegates decided to permit the importation of slaves for twenty years and to count each slave as three-fifths of a person for the purposes of taxation and representation. They also agreed to the fugitive slave clause, which, by mandating that escaped slaves be returned to their owners, implicated all Americans in upholding this "peculiar institution." This compromise was a ticking time bomb. In the short term, however, it paved the way for the adoption of the Constitution—by a 38–3 margin—on September 17, 1787.

After this historic vote, a lively and learned debate ensued between Federalists, who favored the Constitution's ratification by the required three-quarters of the states, and Anti-Federalists, who opposed it. Anti-Federalists argued that the Constitution betrayed the Revolution. Pennsylvania's Samuel Bryan complained that "the United States are to be melted down" into an empire of tyranny controlled by the well-born and the wealthy.[6] The Massachusetts farmer Amos Singletary, prophesied that the elites behind the Constitution "will swallow up all us little folks, like the great *Leviathan* . . . yes, just as the whale swallowed up *Jonah*."[7]

Defenders of the Constitution responded to these "anti-federalist papers" with the now famous *Federalist Papers,* a remarkable collection of eighty-five essays published under the name of "Publius" in New York newspapers between October 1787 and May 1788. Here Alexander Hamilton, James Madison, and John Jay, who wrote these essays, argued that the Constitution would secure order against the excesses of liberty. In "Federalist No. 10," the most widely read and influential of the *Federalist Papers,* Madison turned Montesquieu's maxim on its head, arguing that large republics would be better than small republics at controlling the "dangerous vice" of factionalism.[8]

On June 21, 1788, the American people said yes to the Constitution when New Hampshire became the ninth state to ratify it. This victory was possible only because Federalists promised to append to the Constitution a Bill of Rights, which was itself ratified on December 15, 1791. The Constitution we have today consists of the original Constitution plus the ten amendments of the Bill of Rights plus seventeen additional amendments added between 1795 and 1992. The Thirteenth, Fourteenth, and Fifteenth Amendments, ratified in the aftermath of the Civil War, abolished slavery, extended citizenship to former slaves and "due process" and "equal protection" to all citizens, and provided the right to vote irrespective of race. The Sixteenth Amendment instituted the income tax. The Eighteenth dried up the manufacturing and sale of alcoholic beverages, and the Twenty-First made the United States wet again. The Nineteenth gave the vote to women, and the Twenty-Sixth lowered the voting age to eighteen.

Other proposed amendments were less successful. In 1864, Protestants who lamented God's absence from the Constitution proposed to correct "this atheistic error in our prime conceptions of Government" via a Christian amendment defining God's "revealed will as the supreme law of the land."[9] They earned an audience with President Lincoln, but their amendment stalled in Congress. An Equal Rights Amendment fared better, passing Congress in 1972, but it was ratified by only thirty-five states, just short of the necessary thirty-eight.

Unlike the Declaration of Independence, the Constitution was almost immediately sanctified as scripture. George Washington, in his 1796 Farewell Address, expressed the hope that it would "be sacredly maintained," and this hope has been realized.[10] Independence Hall, where the Constitution was debated and adopted, has become a Holy of Holies for patriotic pilgrims. The Constitution itself has been described repeatedly as an American Torah—"our Ark of Covenant."[11] And the "cult of the Constitution" remains strong today. In the twenty-first century, Tea Party politicians anointed themselves high priests of this cult after Barack Obama's inauguration in 2009, and many Republicans were sent to Congress in 2010 on the strength of promises to defend the Constitution from attacks by this "socialist" president.

Like any literary classic, "America's legal city on a hill" is sufficiently vague to sustain endless arguments about what it is trying to say.[12] At times, it speaks unambiguously, telling us that presidents must be thirty-five years old, and that each state gets two Senators. But what does "due process" mean? Or "equal protection"? More important than the ambiguity of its words and clauses is the fact that the Constitution affirms competing values without telling interpreters how to adjudicate between liberty, on the one hand, and justice, "domestic tranquility," and the "general welfare," on the other. No wonder the Constitution has spun an endless web of interpretation and reinterpretation.

Supreme Court justice Oliver Wendell Holmes Jr. famously described the Constitution as "organic"—a living document in which the words of the framers are not fixed in the past, but move into the future.[13] This approach, famously articulated in Howard McBain's *The Living Constitution* (1927), surged as liberal Supreme Courts under Chief Justices Earl Warren (1953–69) and Warren Burger (1969–86) led a "rights revolution" that vigorously protected minorities and strictly separated church and state. During the Rehnquist Court (1986–2005), conservatives pushed back. In the name of "originalism," a jurisprudence that tasks judges with judging rather than legislating, they insisted on rulings based on the "objective meaning that constitutional language had when it was adopted."[14] In *Original Meanings* (1996), Jack Rakove takes aim at this "original intent" approach, arguing that the intentions of the framers were plural from the start, with the meanings of the Constitution shifting from framer to framer and even over the course of a given framer's life. Upon careful analysis, "the notion that the Constitution had some fixed and well-known meaning at the moment of its adoption dissolves into a mirage," Rakove argues.[15]

Among the big questions taken up by Supreme Court justices and ordinary Americans alike, one of the biggest is: What did the Constitution constitute? Or, to borrow from the language of the Preamble, what precisely was this "Union" the framers aimed to make "more perfect"? And who agreed to it? A confederacy of sovereign states that could take back at will whatever authority they had ceded to the central government? Or "the people," whose authority preceded and superseded that of the states? Although the most radical implications of the former interpretation—nullification and secession—were rejected by force of arms in the Civil War, the question of the relative power of the states and the federal government remains alive, as evidenced by the conservative claim that liberal Supreme Court decisions and civil rights laws violate states' rights.

Like the original Constitution, the Bill of Rights and later amendments are not self-interpreting, so Americans have argued over what they mean. These arguments picked up in frequency and intensity in the twentieth century, and particularly after *Gitlow v. New York* (1925), when the Supreme Court, in the "incorporation doctrine," applied to the actions of states Bill of Rights restrictions previously impinging only on federal actions.[16] Controversy now swirls especially around the First Amendment, which guarantees freedom of religion, freedom of speech, freedom of the press, and the rights to assembly and to petition the government. How far do freedom of speech and of the press extend? Can you burn an American flag? Publish classified documents? Does religious liberty include the freedom to ingest illegal drugs during sacred ceremonies? And what of the First Amendment's prohibition of the establishment of religion? Do municipal displays of manger scenes, crosses, or the Ten Commandments unconstitutionally establish religion?

Debates over the twenty-seven amendments to the Constitution can be read narrowly, yet each is also pregnant with import for the meaning of America. The 2010 controversy over the so-called Ground Zero mosque in Lower Manhattan concerned religious liberty, but it was also about the character of the United States. Is this a Christian country that must be vigilant about inoculating itself against the infections of Islam? Or is it a multireligious country that opens its arms to immigrants of all religions? As these examples suggest, debates over individual amendments and individual clauses in them can and do occupy volumes. The Library of Congress lists one hundred books on the Fourteenth Amendment alone.

Given this vast literature, only the Preamble of the Constitution is reprinted here. Most of the Constitution is devoted to the nuts and bolts of the U.S. government, including congressional pay, the presidential veto, judicial terms, checks and balances, and the separation of powers. In the Preamble, the Constitution announces its purposes and in the process sets forth its vision for the United States. If the rest of the Constitution provides a blueprint for the U.S. government, the Preamble offers the ideals.

The commentaries that follow focus on the Constitution as a whole. How democratic is it? How does the central government it constitutes relate to the states? Both of these questions prompt another: How does the Constitution relate to the Declaration of Independence? Is the Constitution a revolutionary document affirming equality, or is it a counterrevolutionary project of the landed and the learned seeking to limit the power of the people and protect the property of elites? Most Americans today see considerable continuity between these two documents, reading the Constitution as a translation of the spirit of the Declaration into the day-to-day workings of government. But critics of the "reactionary" Constitution have long seen tensions between the two.

Like so much of the commentary tradition in *The American Bible*, America's conversation about the Constitution revolves around race. Proslavery writers in the Civil War era downplayed the Declaration's assertion that "all men are created equal" and took solace in the fact that the original Constitution did not proclaim equality. Some abolitionists took the same position yet evaluated it differently, condemning the Constitution as a betrayal of the Declaration's egalitarianism. On July 4, 1854, in Framingham, Massachusetts, at an antislavery rally featuring such notables as Sojourner Truth and Henry David Thoreau, William Lloyd Garrison burned a copy of the Constitution, which he denounced (in a paraphrase of Isaiah 28:15) as "a covenant with death and agreement with hell."[17] In the early twentieth century, Progressive rhetoric against the Constitution ran almost as hot. "This crowned Constitution with its halo," wrote historian Charles Beard, "has been the bulwark of every great national sin—from slavery to monopoly."[18]

Historians later challenged this Progressive interpretation, arguing that the Constitution was "essentially democratic."[19] But a stream of scholarship continues to interpret it as an effort in "taming democracy."[20] Some conservatives have agreed with this assessment, praising restrictions on democracy as prudent and applauding the fact that the Constitution mentions equality only in reference to the states. According to this line of interpretation, the arch-heretic Abraham Lincoln deserves the lion's share of the blame, because of his strategy of subordinating the wisdom of the Constitution to the pieties of the Declaration. FDR also comes in for criticism for pushing patently unconstitutional legislation during the New Deal and then trying to "pack" the Supreme Court with additional justices sympathetic to his liberal views.

Although America's conversation about the Constitution ran hottest during the Civil War, the controversy continues. And how could it be otherwise? The accommodations made to slavery in 1787 all but ensured that Americans would come to see their original Constitution as inadequate and incomplete and work to improve it. How could a document widely lauded as the "charter of liberty" simultaneously allow slavery? Or segregation? Americans eventually decided that it could not. Their collective decision to transform their Constitution, by amendment and reinterpretation, is part of the story of American constitutionalism too.

The Constitution ❧

PREAMBLE

We the people[a,b,c] of the United States, in Order to form a more perfect Union,[d] establish Justice, insure domestic Tranquility, provide for the common defense, promote the general Welfare, and secure the Blessings of Liberty to ourselves and our Posterity, do ordain and establish this Constitution for the United States of America.[e,f21]

---

a. Patrick Henry, orator, former Virginia governor, and Anti-Federalist delegate to the Virginia Constitution Ratification Convention, objecting in the name of liberty to "We the people" (1788): Have they said, we, the states? Have they made a proposal of a compact between states? If they had, this would be a confederation: It is, otherwise, most clearly, a consolidated government. The whole question turns, sir, on that poor little thing—the expression, *We the People*. . . . Here is a revolution as radical as that which separated us from Great Britain. . . . The rights of conscience, trial by jury, liberty of the press, all your immunities and franchises, all pretensions to human rights and privileges, are rendered insecure, if not lost, by this change so loudly talked of by some, and so inconsiderately by others. Is this tame relinquishment of rights worthy of freeman? Is it worthy of that manly fortitude that ought to characterize republicans? . . .

When the American spirit was in its youth, the language of America was different: liberty, sir, was then the primary object. We are descended from a people whose government was founded on liberty: our glorious forefathers of Great Britain made liberty the foundation of every thing. . . . We drew the spirit of liberty from our British ancestors: by that spirit we have triumphed over every difficulty. But now, sir, the American spirit, assisted by the ropes and chains of consolidation, is about to convert this country into a powerful and mighty empire; if you make the citizens of this country agree to become the subjects of one great consolidated empire of America, your government will not have sufficient energy to keep them together: such a government is incompatible with the genius of republicanism. There will be no checks, no real balances, in this government. What can avail your specious, imaginary balances, your rope-dancing, chain-rattling, ridiculous ideal checks and contrivances? —Patrick Henry, speech at the Virginia Constitution Ratification Convention, June 5, 1788, in William Wirt, *Patrick Henry: Life, Correspondence and Speeches* (New York: Scribner, 1891), 3:434–35, 445–46.

b. Susan B. Anthony, suffragist, defending her actions prior to her trial for voting in the 1872 election (1873): It was we, the people, not we, the white male citizens, nor yet we, the male citizens, but we, the whole people, who formed this Union. And we formed it, not to give the blessings of liberty, but to secure them; not to the half of ourselves and the half of our posterity, but to the whole people—women as well as men. And it is downright mockery to talk to women of their enjoyment of the blessings of liberty while they are denied the use of the only means of securing them provided by this democratic republican government—the ballot. —Susan B. Anthony, speech, Monroe and Ontario Counties, New York, in Elizabeth Cady Stanton, Susan B. Anthony, and Matilda Joslyn Gage, eds., *History of Woman Suffrage* (New York: Fowler & Wells, 1882), 2:632.

c. Ronald Reagan, fortieth U.S. president, praising Franklin Roosevelt as a "We the people" president (1989): I remember that voice of [Roosevelt's], as we've heard it here today, coming over the radio—its strength, its optimism. I wonder how many of us in this room know that to this day, no program in the history of radio has ever equaled the audience he had in his fireside chats. I remember how a light would snap on in the eyes of everyone in the room just hearing him, and how, because of his faith, our faith in our own capacity to overcome any crisis and any challenge was reborn. In this sense, FDR renewed the charter of the founders of our nation. The founders had created a government of "We the people." Through a depression and a great war, crises that could well have led us in another direction, FDR strengthened that charter. When others doubt, he said that we would find our salvation in our own hands—not in some elite but in ourselves. —Ronald Reagan, "Remarks at the Franklin D. Roosevelt Library 50th Anniversary Luncheon," January 10, 1989, www.presidency.ucsb.edu/ws/?pid=35350.

d. Abraham Lincoln, sixteenth U.S. president, drawing on the Preamble in his First Inaugural Address to argue that the Confederacy is still part of the Union (1861): The Union is much older than the Constitution. It was formed, in fact, by the Articles of Association in 1774. It was matured and continued by the Declaration of Independence in 1776. It was further matured, and the faith of all the then thirteen States expressly plighted and engaged that it should be perpetual, by the Articles of Confederation in 1778. And finally, in 1787, one of the declared objects for ordaining and establishing the Constitution was "to form a more perfect Union." But if destruction of the Union by one or by a part only of the States be lawfully possible, the Union is less perfect than before the Constitution, having lost the vital element of perpetuity. It follows from these views that no State upon its own mere motion can lawfully get out of the Union; that resolves and ordinances to that effect are legally void, and that acts of violence within any State or States against the authority of the United States are insurrectionary or revolutionary, according to circumstances. I therefore consider that in view of the Constitution and the laws the Union is unbroken. . . . —Abraham Lincoln, "First Inaugural Address," March 4, 1861, www.presidency.ucsb.edu/ws/index.php?pid=25818.

e. Confederate States, invoking "Almighty God" in the Preamble to their Constitution (1861): We, the people of the Confederate States, each State acting in its sovereign and independent character, in order to form a permanent federal government, establish justice,

COMMENTARY

James Madison, "Father of the Constitution" and future U.S. president, describing the Constitution as a "cure" for the "violence of faction" (1787)

There are two methods of curing the mischiefs of faction: the one, by removing its causes; the other, by controlling its effects.

There are again two methods of removing the causes of faction: the one, by destroying the liberty which is essential to its existence; the other, by giving to every citizen the same opinions, the same passions, and the same interests.

It could never be more truly said than of the first remedy, that it was worse than the disease. Liberty is to faction what air is to fire, an aliment without which it instantly expires. But it could not be less folly to abolish liberty, which is essential to political life, because it nourishes faction, than it would be to wish the annihilation of air, which is essential to animal life, because it imparts to fire its destructive agency.

The second expedient is as impracticable as the first would be unwise. As long as the reason of man continues fallible, and he is at liberty to exercise it, different opinions will be formed. As long as the connection subsists between his reason and his self-love, his opinions and his passions will have a reciprocal influence on each other; and the former will be objects to which the latter will attach themselves. . . .

The latent causes of faction are thus sown in the nature of man. . . . A zeal for different opinions concerning religion, concerning government, and many other points, as well of speculation as of practice; an attachment to different leaders

insure domestic tranquillity, and secure the blessings of liberty to ourselves and our posterity invoking the favor and guidance of Almighty God do ordain and establish this Constitution for the Confederate States of America. —"Constitution of the Confederate States," March 11, 1861, http://avalon.law.yale.edu/19th_century/csa_csa.asp.

f. H. L. Mencken, journalist and social critic, offering a new and improved Constitution for the New Deal era (1937): We, the people of the United States, in order to form a more perfect union, establish social justice, draw the fangs of privilege, effect the redistribution of property, remove the burden of liberty from ourselves and our posterity, and insure the continuance of the New Deal, do ordain and establish this Constitution. —H. L. Mencken, "A Constitution for the New Deal," *American Mercury*, June 1937, pp. 129–36.

ambitiously contending for pre-eminence and power; or to persons of other descriptions whose fortunes have been interesting to the human passions, have, in turn, divided mankind into parties, inflamed them with mutual animosity, and rendered them much more disposed to vex and oppress each other than to co-operate for their common good. . . . But the most common and durable source of factions has been the various and unequal distribution of property. Those who hold and those who are without property have ever formed distinct interests in society. Those who are creditors, and those who are debtors, fall under a like discrimination. . . .

The inference to which we are brought is, that the *causes* of faction cannot be removed, and that relief is only to be sought in the means of controlling its *effects*.

If a faction consists of less than a majority, relief is supplied by the republican principle, which enables the majority to defeat its sinister views by regular vote. It may clog the administration, it may convulse the society; but it will be unable to execute and mask its violence under the forms of the Constitution. When a majority is included in a faction, the form of popular government, on the other hand, enables it to sacrifice to its ruling passion or interest both the public good and the rights of other citizens. To secure the public good and private rights against the danger of such a faction, and at the same time to preserve the spirit and the form of popular government, is then the great object to which our inquiries are directed. . . .

By what means is this object attainable? Evidently by one of two only. Either the existence of the same passion or interest in a majority at the same time must be prevented, or the majority, having such coexistent passion or interest, must be rendered, by their number and local situation, unable to concert and carry into effect schemes of oppression. . . .

From this view of the subject it may be concluded that a pure democracy . . . can admit of no cure for the mischiefs of faction. . . . Hence it is that such democracies have ever been spectacles of turbulence and contention; have ever been found incompatible with personal security or the rights of property; and have in general been as short in their lives as they have been violent in their deaths.

A republic, by which I mean a government in which the scheme of representation takes place, opens a different prospect, and promises the cure for which we are seeking. . . .

The two great points of difference between a democracy and a republic are: first, the delegation of the government, in the latter, to a small number of citizens elected by the rest; secondly, the greater number of citizens, and greater sphere of country, over which the latter may be extended. . . .

Does the advantage consist in the substitution of representatives whose enlightened views and virtuous sentiments render them superior to local prejudices and schemes of injustice? It will not be denied that the representation of the Union will be most likely to possess these requisite endowments. Does it consist in the greater security afforded by a greater variety of parties, against the event of any one party being able to outnumber and oppress the rest? In an equal degree does the increased variety of parties comprised within the Union, increase this security. . . .

The influence of factious leaders may kindle a flame within their particular States, but will be unable to spread a general conflagration through the other States. A religious sect may degenerate into a political faction in a part of the Confederacy; but the variety of sects dispersed over the entire face of it must secure the national councils against any danger from that source. A rage for paper money, for an abolition of debts, for an equal division of property, or for any other improper or wicked project, will be less apt to pervade the whole body of the Union than a particular member of it; in the same proportion as such a malady is more likely to taint a particular county or district, than an entire State.

In the extent and proper structure of the Union, therefore, we behold a republican remedy for the diseases most incident to republican government. And according to the degree of pleasure and pride we feel in being republicans, ought to be our zeal in cherishing the spirit and supporting the character of Federalists.

—"Publius" (James Madison), "Federalist No. 10," *Daily Advertiser,* November 22, 1787, www.constitution .org/fed/federa10.htm.

Pennsylvania Anti-Federalists, on why they voted against the Constitution (1787)

We dissent, first, because it is the opinion of the most celebrated writers on government, and confirmed experience, that a very extensive territory cannot be governed on the principles of freedom, otherwise than by a confederation of republics, possessing all the powers of internal government; but united in the management of their general, and foreign concerns. . . .

We dissent, secondly, because the powers vested in Congress by this constitution, must necessarily annihilate and absorb the legislative, executive, and judicial powers of the several states, and produce from their ruins one consolidated government, which from the nature of things will be *an iron handed despotism,* as nothing short of the supremacy of despotic sway could connect and govern these United States under one government. . . .

—"The Address and Reasons of Dissent of the Minority of the Convention of Pennsylvania to Their Constituents," *Pennsylvania Packet and National Advertiser,* December 18, 1787, www.constitution.org/ afp/pennmi00.htm.

Benjamin Rush, physician and signer of the Declaration of Independence,
describing the Constitution as a compromise pleasing no one (1808)

In case of a Rupture with Britain or France, which shall we fight for? For our Constitution? I cannot meet with a man who loves it. It is considered as too weak by one half of our citizens and as too strong by the other half.

—Benjamin Rush to John Adams, June 13, 1808, in John A. Schutz and Douglass Adair, eds., *The Spur of Fame: Dialogues of John Adams and Benjamin Rush, 1805–1813* (San Marino, CA: Huntington Library, 1966), p. 108.

John Marshall, U.S. Supreme Court chief justice, finding in McCulloch v. Maryland *that the people, not the states, gave rise to the Constitution (1819)*

In discussing this question, the counsel for the State of Maryland have deemed it of some importance, in the construction of the Constitution, to consider that instrument not as emanating from the people, but as the act of sovereign and independent States. The powers of the general government, it has been said, are delegated by the States, who alone are truly sovereign; and must be exercised in subordination to the States, who alone possess supreme dominion. It would be difficult to sustain this proposition.

The Convention which framed the Constitution was indeed elected by the State legislatures. But the instrument, when it came from their hands, was a mere proposal, without obligation, or pretensions to it. It was reported to the then existing Congress of the United States, with a request that it might "be submitted to a convention of delegates, chosen in each State by the people thereof, under the recommendation of its legislature, for their assent and ratification." This mode of proceeding was adopted; and by the convention, by Congress, and by the State legislatures, the instrument was submitted to the people. They acted upon it in the only manner in which they can act safely, effectively, and wisely, on such a subject, by assembling in convention.

It is true, they assembled in their several States—and where else should they have assembled? No political dreamer was ever wild enough to think of breaking down the lines which separate the States, and of compounding the American people into one common mass. Of consequence, when they act, they act in their States. But the measures they adopt do not, on that account, cease to be the measures of the people themselves, or become the measures of the State governments.

From these conventions the Constitution derives its whole authority. The government proceeds directly from the people; is "ordained and established" in the name of the people; and is declared to be ordained, "in order to form a more perfect union, establish justice, ensure domestic tranquility, and secure the blessings of liberty to themselves and to their posterity." The assent of the States, in their sovereign capacity, is implied in calling a convention, and thus submitting that instrument to the people. But the people were at perfect liberty to accept or reject it; and their act was final. It required not the affirmance, and could not be negatived, by the State governments. The Constitution, when thus adopted, was of complete obligation, and bound the State sovereignties. . . .

The Government of the Union then (whatever may be the influence of this fact on the case) is, emphatically and truly, a Government of the people. In form and in substance, it emanates from them. Its powers are granted by them, and are to be exercised directly on them, and for their benefit.

—Chief Justice John Marshall, majority opinion, *McCulloch v. Maryland*, 17 U.S. 316 (1819).

Wendell Phillips, abolitionist, arguing in the name of the Declaration of Independence for the overthrow of the Union (1847)

Resolved, That the duty of every American is to give his sympathy and aid to the anti-slavery movement; and the first duty of every citizen is to devote himself to the destruction of the Union and the Constitution, which have already ship-wrecked the experiment of civil liberty, and bid fair to swallow up the hopes of every honest man in a worse than military despotism; assured that out of the wreck, we may confidently expect a State which will unfold, in noble proportions, the principles of the Declaration of Independence, whose promises made us once the admiration of the world.

—Quoted in William Lloyd Garrison to *The Liberator*, May 11, 1847, in Walter M. Merrill, ed., *The Letters of William Lloyd Garrison* (Cambridge, MA: Harvard Univ. Press, 1973), 3.478.

Frederick Douglass, former slave and abolitionist, denouncing the Constitution as proslavery and the Union as "inhuman" (1849)

The Constitution of the United States. — What is it? Who made it? For whom and for what was it made? Is it from heaven or from men? How, and in what light are we to understand it? . . . We hold it to be a most cunningly-devised and wicked compact, demanding the most constant and earnest efforts of the friends of righteous freedom for its complete overthrow. It was "conceived in sin, and shapen in iniquity." . . .

The parties that made the Constitution, aimed to cheat and defraud the slave, who was not himself a party to the compact or agreement. It was entered into understandingly on both sides. They both designed to purchase their freedom and safety at the expense of the imbruted slave. The North were willing to become the body guards of slavery—suppressing insurrection—returning fugitive slaves to bondage—importing slaves for twenty years, and as much longer as the Congress should see fit to leave it unprohibited, and virtually to give slaveholders three votes for every five slaves they could plunder from Africa, and all this to form a Union by which to repel invasion, and otherwise promote their interest.

—Frederick Douglass, "The Constitution and Slavery," *North Star*, March 16, 1849, http://teachingamerican history.org/library/index.asp?document=1106.

Benjamin Palmer, Confederate Presbyterian pastor and
theologian, reading the Civil War as God's righteous
response to a secular Constitution (1861)

It is true that in the eloquent paper which recited their grievances before the world, and proclaimed the Colonies independent of the British throne, the signers of the Declaration appealed to the Divine Omniscience *"for the rectitude of their intentions,"* and pledged their faith to each other *"with a firm reliance on the protection of divine Providence."* It is therefore the more remarkable that, eleven years later, in that great instrument by which the several States were linked together in a common nationality, and which was at once the public charter and the paramount law of the land, not a word is found from which one could possibly infer that such a being as God ever existed. The omission was a fearful one; and it is not surprising that He who proclaims his jealousy of his own glory, should let fall the blow which has shattered that nation.

Probable reasons may be suggested for its explanation. It certainly was not due to the irreligiousness of the masses, for they were predominantly Christian. But the public leaders of the time were largely tinctured with the free thinking and infidel spirit which swept like a pestilence over Europe in the seventeenth and eighteenth centuries, and which brought forth at last its bitter fruit in the horrors of the French Revolution. It may have been due likewise to the jealousy entertained of any union between Church and State, at a time when the novel, grand and successful experiment was first tried of an entire separation between the two.

But for whatever reasons, the fact is that the American nation stood up before the world a helpless orphan, and entered upon its career without a God. Through almost a century of unparalleled prosperity, this error has been but partially retrieved; as the religious spirit of the people has silently compelled the appointment by executive authority, of days of public thanksgiving and prayer—yet to this day, in the great national act of incorporation there is no bond which connects the old American nation with the Providence and Government of Jehovah. Thanks be unto God, my brethren, for the grace given our own Confederacy, in receding from this perilous atheism! When my eye first rested upon the Constitution adopted by the Confederate Congress, and I read in the first lines of our organic and fundamental law a clear, solemn, official recognition of Almighty God, my heart swelled with unutterable emotions of gratitude and joy. It was the return of the prodigal to the bosom of his father.

—Benjamin M. Palmer, *National Responsibility Before God: A Discourse Delivered on the Day of Fasting, Humiliation and Prayer* (New Orleans: Price-Current Steam Book and Job Printing Office, 1861), www.confederatelegion.com/National%20Responsibility.rtf.

National Reform Association, an interdenominational Protestant organization, proposing a Christian amendment to the Constitution (1864)

We, the people of the United States, humbly acknowledging Almighty God as the source of all authority and power in civil government, the Lord Jesus Christ as the Ruler among the nations, His revealed will as the supreme law of the land, in order to constitute a Christian government, and in order to form a more perfect union, establish justice, insure domestic tranquility, provide for the common defense, promote the general welfare, and secure the inalienable rights and the blessings of life, liberty, and the pursuit of happiness to ourselves, our posterity, and all the people, do ordain and establish this Constitution for the United States of America.

—National Reform Association, "Memorial to Congress" (1864), quoted in *Proceedings of the National Convention to Secure the Religious Amendment of the Constitution of the United States, Held in Pittsburg, February 4, 5, 1874* (Philadelphia: Christian Statesman Association, 1874), p. 7.

Alexander Stephens, vice president of the Confederate States of America, justifying secession on the grounds that the Constitution was a compact among "separate, distinct, and Sovereign States" (1868)

We have seen that the Union existing between these States, anterior to the formation of the Constitution, was a Compact, or as Judge Marshall expressed it, nothing but "a league" between Sovereign States. We have seen that in remodeling the Articles of the old Confederation, it was not the object, or design of any of the parties, to change the nature or character of that Union; but only to make it more perfect. . . .

Where, under the system so constituted, does Sovereignty reside? . . . Does it reside with the whole people in the mass of all the States together, or with the people of the several States separately? That is the only question. The whole subject is narrowed down to this: Where, in this country, resides the Paramount authority that can rightfully make and unmake Constitutions? In all Confederated Republics . . . it remains with the Sovereign States so Confederated. . . .

In this case the breach of plighted faith was not on the part of Georgia, or those States which withdrew or attempted to withdraw from the Union. Thirteen of their Confederates had openly and avowedly disregarded their obligations under that clause of the Constitution which covenanted for the rendition of fugitives from service, to say nothing of the acts of several of them, in a like open and palpable breach of faith, in the matter of the rendition of fugitives from justice. These are facts about which there can be no dispute. Then, by universal law, as recognized by all Nations, savage as well as civilized, the Compact, thus broken by some of the Parties, was no longer binding upon the others. The breach was not made by the seceding States.

—Alexander H. Stephens, *A Constitutional View of the Late War Between the States* (Philadelphia: National Publishing, 1868), 1:477–78, 486–87, 496–97.

*Charles Beard, Progressive historian, arguing that the Constitution was
designed to protect property rights, not popular sovereignty (1912)*

The makers of the federal Constitution represented the solid, conservative, commercial and financial interests of the country. . . . The conservative interests, made desperate by the imbecilities of the [Articles of] Confederation and harried by state legislatures . . . drew together in a mighty effort to establish a government that would be strong enough to pay the national debt, regulate interstate and foreign commerce, provide for national defense, prevent fluctuations in the currency created by paper emissions, and control the propensities of legislative majorities to attack private rights. . . .

[The framers] were not convened to write a Declaration of Independence, but to frame a government that would meet the practical issues that had arisen under the Articles of Confederation. . . . With many of the plain lessons of history before them, they naturally feared that the rights and privileges of the minority would be insecure if the principle of majority rule was definitely adopted and provisions made for its exercise. . . .

Indeed, every page of the laconic record of the proceedings . . . shows conclusively that the members of that assembly were not seeking to realize any fine notions about democracy and equality, but were striving with all the resources of political wisdom at their command to set up a system of government that would be stable and efficient, safeguarded on the one hand against the possibilities of despotism and on the other against the onslaught of majorities. . . .

By the system of checks and balances placed in the government, the convention safeguarded the interests of property against attacks by majorities. . . . This very system of checks and balances, which is undeniably the essential element of the Constitution, is built upon the doctrine that the popular branch of the government cannot be allowed full sway, and least of all in the enactment of laws touching the rights of property. The exclusion of the direct popular vote in the election of the President; the creation, again by indirect election, of a Senate which the framers hoped would represent the wealth and conservative interests of the country; and the establishment of an independent judiciary appointed by the President with the concurrence of the Senate—all these devices bear witness to the fact that the underlying purpose of the Constitution was not the establishment of popular government.

—Charles Beard, *The Supreme Court and the Constitution* (New York: Macmillan, 1912), pp. 75–96.

*Henry Hazlitt, journalist and free-market champion, arguing during the
Great Depression for radical changes to our "obsolete Constitution" (1931)*

It is no accident that American national politics is shallow, unreal, irresponsible, that intelligent European observers find it frankly uninteresting and its present party division pointless and meaningless. . . . But a far larger issue must be raised. . . . This is whether our whole constitutional system is not in need of radical revision. The result of fixed terms of office for the President and Congress and of chronological rotation in the Senate is to divorce both the legislative and executive departments from any close connection with public opinion. Our constitutional separation of executive and legislative powers, again, is ingeniously calculated to bring about constant friction, and the deadlocks are made even more frequent by the election of a new Congress every four years without the simultaneous election of a new President. It is impossible under such a system to fix real responsibility upon either the legislature or the executive. It is impossible to determine party responsibility. . . .

The result of such a system must inevitably be, as it has been, to discourage continuous interest in politics or any serious political thinking except spasmodically at election time, and to cultivate in the public an easy-going indifference to abuses. This attitude is usually, and quite shallowly, attributed to our national temperament. The fault lies with our sacrosanct Constitution itself.

It is time that we seriously considered the radical revision of our Constitution to make our government at least as responsible, as flexible, as sensitive to public opinion as the parliamentary systems of Great Britain and the leading democracies of Europe. If the biological or economic descendants of Henry Ford, 140 years from now, were still turning out the present Ford model (with perhaps a slight change in the brakes and fenders), and argued in defense of their course that Henry Ford had been a great and wise man and must have known what he was doing when he designed the model, the contemporaries of those descendants would be justified in looking on them as pure idiots.

Yet this is precisely the attitude that most Americans take toward our 1789-model Constitution today. The true heirs of Henry Ford would not really want to emulate the precise machine he designed, but his spirit of enterprise and inventiveness, and his own contempt for antiquated methods. The true heirs of the Founding Fathers will want to emulate, not their exact machinery or even their precise political philosophy, but some of their courage in founding a new form of government to meet the needs of their own time, and not least of all their sense and wisdom in abandoning their own former basic law, the original Articles of Confederation, when those had proved inadequate.

—Henry Hazlitt, "Our Obsolete Constitution," Nation 132.3422 (February 4, 1931): 124–25.

Franklin D. Roosevelt, thirty-second U.S. president, calling on Congress to pass an economic bill of rights (1944)

It is our duty now to begin to lay the plans and determine the strategy for the winning of a lasting peace and the establishment of an American standard of living higher than ever before known. We cannot be content, no matter how high that general standard of living may be, if some fraction of our people—whether it be one-third or one-fifth or one-tenth—is ill-fed, ill-clothed, ill housed, and insecure.

This Republic had its beginning, and grew to its present strength, under the protection of certain inalienable political rights—among them the right of free speech, free press, free worship, trial by jury, freedom from unreasonable searches and seizures. They were our rights to life and liberty.

As our Nation has grown in size and stature, however—as our industrial economy expanded—these political rights proved inadequate to assure us equality in the pursuit of happiness. We have come to a clear realization of the fact that true individual freedom cannot exist without economic security and independence. "Necessitous men are not free men." People who are hungry and out of a job are the stuff of which dictatorships are made.

In our day these economic truths have become accepted as self-evident. We have accepted, so to speak, a second Bill of Rights under which a new basis of security and prosperity can be established for all regardless of station, race, or creed.

Among these are:

The right to a useful and remunerative job in the industries or shops or farms or mines of the Nation;

The right to earn enough to provide adequate food and clothing and recreation;

The right of every farmer to raise and sell his products at a return which will give him and his family a decent living;

The right of every businessman, large and small, to trade in an atmosphere of freedom from unfair competition and domination by monopolies at home or abroad;

The right of every family to a decent home;

The right to adequate medical care and the opportunity to achieve and enjoy good health;

The right to adequate protection from the economic fears of old age, sickness, accident, and unemployment;

The right to a good education.

All of these rights spell security. And after this war is won we must be prepared to move forward, in the implementation of these rights, to new goals of human happiness and well-being.

—Franklin D. Roosevelt, "State of the Union Message to Congress," January 11, 1944, www.presidency.ucsb .edu/ws/index.php?pid=16518.

Rousas John Rushdoony, Christian Reconstructionist theologian, arguing that the Constitution only seems to be a secular document (1965)

The concept of a secular state was virtually *non*-existent in 1776 as well as in 1787, when the Constitution was written, and no less so when the Bill of Rights was adopted. To read the Constitution as the charter for a secular state is to misread history, and to misread it radically. The Constitution was designed to *perpetuate* a Christian order.

—Rousas John Rushdoony, *The Nature of the American System* (Nutley, NJ: Craig, 1965), p. 2.

Isaac Kramnick and R. Laurence Moore, Cornell University professors, on the "godless Constitution" (1996)

The creation of a godless Constitution was not an act of irreverence. Far from it. It was an act of confidence in religion. It intended to let religion do what it did best, to preserve the civil morality necessary to democracy, without laying upon it the burdens of being tied to the fortunes of this or that political faction. The godless Constitution must be understood as part of the American system of voluntary church support that has proved itself a much greater boon to the fortunes of organized religion than the prior systems of church establishment ever were.

—Isaac Kramnick and R. Laurence Moore, *The Godless Constitution: The Case Against Religious Correctness* (New York: Norton, 1996), p. 24.

Clarence Thomas, Supreme Court justice, rejecting the "living Constitution" idea of loose constructionists (2008)

There are really only two ways to interpret the Constitution—try to discern as best we can what the framers intended or make it up. No matter how ingenious, imaginative or artfully put, unless interpretive methodologies are tied to the original intent of the framers, they have no more basis in the Constitution than the latest football scores. To be sure, even the most conscientious effort to adhere to the original intent of the framers of our Constitution is flawed, as all methodologies and human institutions are; but at least originalism has the advantage of being legitimate and, I might add, impartial.

—Clarence Thomas, "Judging in a Government by Consent," Manhattan Institute, October 16, 2008, www.manhattan-institute.org/video/index.htm?c=10–16–2008%20Wriston%20-%20Judging%20 Government%20Consent.

David Souter, Supreme Court justice, rejecting Thomas's "fair reading" model of constitutional interpretation (2010)

The explicit terms of the Constitution, in other words, can create a conflict of approved values, and the explicit terms of the Constitution do not resolve that conflict when it arises. . . . A choice may have to be made, not because language is vague but because the Constitution embodies the desire of the American people, like most people, to have things both ways. We want order and security, and we want liberty. And we want not only liberty but equality as well. These paired desires of ours can clash, and when they do a court is forced to choose between them, between one constitutional good and another one. . . .

The Constitution is a pantheon of values, and a lot of hard cases are hard because the Constitution gives no simple rule of decision for the cases in which one of the values is truly at odds with another. Not even its most uncompromising and unconditional language can resolve every potential tension of one provision with another, tension the Constitution's Framers left to be resolved another day; and another day after that, for our cases can give no answers that fit all conflicts, and no resolutions immune to rethinking when the significance of old facts may have changed in the changing world. These are reasons enough to show how egregiously it misses the point to think of judges in constitutional cases as just sitting there reading constitutional phrases fairly and looking at reported facts objectively to produce their judgments. Judges have to choose between the good things that the Constitution approves, and when they do, they have to choose, not on the basis of measurement, but of meaning. . . .

Remember that the tensions that are the stuff of judging in so many hard constitutional cases are, after all, the creatures of our aspirations: to value liberty, as well as order, and fairness and equality, as well as liberty. And the very opportunity for conflict between one high value and another reflects our confidence that a way may be found to resolve it when a conflict arises. That is why the simplistic view of the Constitution devalues our aspirations, and attacks our confidence, and diminishes us. It is a view of judging that means to discourage our tenacity (our sometimes reluctant tenacity) to keep the constitutional promises the nation has made.

—David H. Souter, "Remarks at Harvard Commencement, May 27, 2010," *Harvard Gazette,* May 27, 2010, http://news.harvard.edu/gazette/story/2010/05/text-of-justice-david-souters-speech/.

Brown v. Board of Education

❧ 1954 ❧

WHEN PRESIDENT Barack Obama, who has two daughters, walked into the Oval Office to go to work in 2011, he passed a painting depicting a young black girl with the word "NIGGER" scrawled on a wall behind her. "The Problem We All Live With," which appeared on the *Look* magazine cover in 1964, was drawn by Norman Rockwell, an illustrator best known for his nostalgic depictions of white suburban innocence. The subject is Ruby Bridges, a six-year-old African-American girl in a starched white dress with white socks, white sneakers, and a white hair ribbon, marching on November 14, 1960, into her first day of first grade at William Frantz Elementary School in New Orleans. A tomato is splattered on the wall behind her. She is surrounded by four men in suits wearing yellow "Deputy U.S. Marshal" armbands—the officials charged with ensuring her safe entry into a formerly all-white school. One hundred fifty or so white segregationists lined the sidewalks that day to protest their school's integration. One youth chanted, "Two, four, six, eight, we don't want to integrate; eight, six, four, two, we don't want a chigeroo."[1] Housewives shouted epithets that national newscasts muffled, but novelist John Steinbeck reported in *Travels with Charley* (1962) that their words were "bestial and filthy and degenerate."[2] After Ruby Bridges enrolled, white parents took their children home (fewer than 50 of 575 pupils remained at the end of the day), so that school year she was typically the only student in her class.

Many plot points in the American story turn on the actions of presidents or the U.S. Congress. Others turn on the actions of ordinary citizens. But the Supreme

Court is another prime mover. The ugly scene in 1960 at William Frantz Elementary School, in which white segregationists clashed with black civil rights icons under the watchful eye and coercive force of federal officials, was replayed when James Meredith became the first African-American student at the University of Mississippi in 1962. Each of these confrontations was brought on by the Supreme Court's landmark decision in *Brown v. Board of Education* (1954), which ruled "separate but equal" public schooling unconstitutional.

Almost a century earlier, in *Plessy v. Ferguson* (1869), a black man named Homer Plessy had claimed that racial discrimination in railroad coaches violated the Fourteenth Amendment's equal protection clause. The Supreme Court disagreed, finding nothing unconstitutional about "separate but equal" railroad service. In the early 1950s, lawyers from the National Association for the Advancement of Colored People (NAACP), including future Supreme Court justice Thurgood Marshall, brought a series of lawsuits challenging "separate but equal" education. The Supreme Court consolidated cases brought in Kansas, South Carolina, Virginia, Delaware, and Washington, D.C., into *Oliver Brown et al. v. the Board of Education of Topeka*.[3] The case that gave *Brown* its name concerned Linda Brown, an African-American girl from Kansas who endured an hour commute every school day that took her through a railroad yard, across a busy street, and onto a bus to an all-black school miles away. In an effort to enroll her in a white school blocks from her home, Linda's father sued, arguing that segregated education was inherently unequal, even if the facilities were comparable.

The Supreme Court heard arguments in this case three times in 1952 and 1953. On May 17, 1954—a day segregationists would later call "Black Monday"—it ruled unanimously, finding for the plaintiffs in a decision one African-American paper described as "the greatest victory for the Negro people since the Emancipation Proclamation."[4]

Written by Chief Justice Earl Warren, who had been appointed only months before by President Eisenhower, this decision did not cite the "great dissent" in *Plessy v. Ferguson,* wherein Justice John Marshall Harlan had written, "In the eye of the law, there is in this country no superior, dominant, ruling class of citizens. There is no caste here."[5] But it did resurrect Harlan's egalitarian spirit. Oddly, Warren's decision "read more like an expert paper on sociology than a Supreme Court opinion."[6] It cited psychological studies of the impact of separate education on black children's self-esteem, including a controversial "doll test" proving, in the

Court's view, that race-based segregation harmed black students by instilling in them a "sense of inferiority."[7] "We conclude that, in the field of public education, the doctrine of 'separate but equal' has no place," the decision read. "Separate educational facilities are inherently unequal" and in violation of "the equal protection of the laws guaranteed by the Fourteenth Amendment."

Warren, a former Republican governor from California renowned more for political savvy than judicial acumen, was able to engineer a unanimous verdict from a deeply divided Court because he finessed the question of implementation. Though he ordered the parties to prepare to desegregate their schools, he did not mandate any concrete methods for doing so, or even any timetable. Instead, he put off the implementation question until the Court could hear a reargument of the case. As a result, *Brown* was initially viewed as an expression of the sort of lukewarm "gradualism" that Martin Luther King Jr. would later decry in his "Letter from Birmingham Jail" (1963).

After the April 1955 reargument, the Supreme Court issued on May 31 a ruling (also unanimous) now popularly known as *Brown II*. Here the Court famously wrote that school desegregation should proceed "with all deliberate speed." This may sound like a radical step, but only if you focus on "speed" rather than "deliberate." In fact, the Supreme Court acknowledged that a "period of transition" would be needed, and it put remedies and timetables alike in the hands of local school districts. In other words, desegregation would happen with as much deliberation as Southern politicians desired and none of the speed civil rights advocates demanded. Not until *Alexander v. Holmes County Board of Education* (1969) would the Supreme Court order immediate desegregation.

For all these reasons, the initial response to *Brown* was "deceptively mild" among Southern whites.[8] Many were convinced that the decision would foment racial unrest, degrade the quality of education for whites, and undercut the "Southern way of life." *Brown* turned a blind eye to the constitutional principle of states' rights in an arena (education) long recognized as a state matter, they believed. In the immediate aftermath of *Brown*, however, "most Southern spokesmen fumbled to express both opposition and acceptance" to a ruling that, to their relief, did not order immediate integration.[9] The *Richmond Times-Dispatch, Chattanooga Times,* and *Atlanta Constitution* all called for calm, and the *Louisville Courier Journal* praised the Court's "moderation and caution."[10] Meanwhile, the Southern Baptist Convention adopted a report describing the ruling as "in harmony with the constitutional guarantee of equal freedom to all citizens, and with the Christian principles of equal justice and love for all men."[11]

By the time *Brown II* was announced, however, "massive resistance" had become the Southern strategy. The pushback began with grassroots White Citizens' Councils that sprang up shortly after *Brown* and rushed into print publications refusing to recognize the decision as the law of the land. *Black Monday* (1955), a diatribe by Mississippi circuit court judge Tom Brady that would quickly become the Bible of the "massive resistance" movement, combined legal arguments, pseudo-scientific race theory, miscegenation fears, biblical interpretation, old-fashioned chivalry, and threats of a new civil war. Echoing Brady, the *Daily News* of Jackson, Mississippi, insisted that any post-*Brown* violence would not be on its readers' hands: "Human blood may stain Southern soil in many places because of this decision but the dark red stains of that blood will be on the marble steps of the United States Supreme Court building."[12]

James Kilpatrick, editor of the *Richmond News Leader* and "the most creative and influential ideologue of the segregationist cause," advanced a more reasoned argument.[13] Drawing on James Madison's Virginia Resolution of 1798 and stressing law over race, Kilpatrick argued that the "sovereign states" had a contractual right to "interpose" themselves between their citizens and a tyrannical federal government. But even he had a weakness for demagoguery. "In May of 1954, that inept fraternity of politicians and professors known as the United States Supreme Court . . . repudiated the Constitution, spit upon the Tenth Amendment, and rewrote the fundamental law of this land to suit their own gauzy concepts of sociology," he wrote. "If it be said now that the South is flouting the law, let it be said to the high court, *You taught us how.*"[14]

In an "Amen" heard across the Bible Belt, 101 of the South's 128 members of Congress endorsed in the spring of 1956 a "Southern Manifesto" denouncing *Brown* as a "clear abuse of judicial power" and pledging "to use all lawful means" to reverse it.[15] South Carolina Senator Strom Thurmond called for the impeachment of Chief Justice Warren, and billboards popped up across the South reading "Save America—Impeach Earl Warren." Meanwhile, eight states passed interposition measures along Kilpatrick's lines. But Southern segregationists did more than talk. They took concrete measures—extreme in some cases—to delay and deny segregation, including "constitutional amendments requiring school closures, substitution of private schools (with tuition subsidies) for public schools, criminal laws forbidding school integration, resolutions of interposition purporting to nullify the *Brown* decision, NAACP harassment laws, and widespread physical violence and economic coercion."[16]

This "massive resistance" worked. Ten years after *Brown*, public schools in border states (Delaware, Kentucky, Maryland, Missouri, Oklahoma, and West Virginia) had desegregated considerably, with one-third to two-thirds of their black pupils attending public schools with whites. But fewer than one in a hundred black students were going to integrated schools in Alabama, Arkansas, Georgia, and South Carolina.[17]

Brown earned a split decision nationwide. The *Cincinnati Enquirer* praised the justices for acting as the "conscience of the American nation," while the *National Review* joined Southern white critics in denouncing *Brown* as "one of the most brazen acts of judicial usurpation in our history, patently counter to the intent of the Constitution, shoddy and illegal in analysis, and invalid in sociology."[18] Overall, however, the ruling was well received. It was hailed by blacks and white liberals as a major civil rights victory. It was praised for upholding America's core values, most notably the principle of equality. It was also celebrated as a major propaganda victory in the Cold War. Before *Brown*, the Justice Department had filed a pro-*Brown* friend of the court brief arguing that "racial discrimination furnishes grist for the Communist propaganda mills, and it raises doubts even among friendly nations as to the intensity of our devotion to the democratic faith." Less than an hour after the decision, the federal radio station Voice of America was gleefully broadcasting the news worldwide. Communists had long criticized the United States as a first-class hypocrite when it came to race. How could America claim to be a land of liberty given its legacy of slavery and segregation? *Brown* undermined that argument, helping to restore America's moral authority by defining racial segregation as an un-American activity.

The Supreme Court issues dozens of decisions per year. Most are forgotten. A few are fiercely debated and become as much a part of America's conversation about itself as historic inaugural addresses and patriotic songs. *Brown v. Board of Education* is one of these landmark cases. It has been described as "the most important political, social, and legal event in America's twentieth-century history" and (more modestly) "the most widely read and quoted Supreme Court opinion of all time."[19] But the consensus is more sanguine. *Brown*'s legacy is now widely described as "ambiguous" at best and "hollow" at worst.[20] *Brown* did not integrate public education, the nay-sayers argue. Almost no progress was made on formal, de jure desegregation in the South until the passage of the Civil Rights Act in 1964. And the informal, de facto segregation of the North would not be addressed until 1971, when the Supreme Court, in *Swann v. Charlotte-Mecklenberg Board of Education,* approved busing as a remedy to the problem of residence-based school segregation. So the claim that *Brown* effected a social revolution typically hangs not on its *direct* effects on the nation's schools but on its *indirect* effects, including inspiring the civil rights movement and symbolizing America's commitment to equal opportunity for all. According to many skeptics, however, *Brown's* effect on the civil rights movement was negligible—"merely a ripple in a tidal wave."[21] Moreover, conservatives are now using *Brown* to argue against affirmative action, on the theory that treating individuals differently because of the color of their skin is unconstitutional. "They changed *Brown,*" writes Harvard law professor Lani Guinier, "from a clarion call to an excuse not to act."[22]

Nonetheless, *Brown* did play a meaningful role, both legal and symbolic, in the civil rights movement. It created a perception of the Supreme Court as a place where African Americans, women, Latinos, homosexuals, Native Americans, and the disabled could go in search of equal rights under the law. It has also served as a symbol of America's ideals and a reminder that these ideals have yet to be realized. "*Brown* is our leading authoritative symbol for the principle that the Constitution forbids a system of caste," writes one expert on constitutional law.[23] But *Brown* is also a reminder that this caste system abides. In other words, if *Brown* symbolizes the "Good Constitution" and the "Good America," it also remains a yardstick of sorts, measuring the distance the nation has fallen short of the good.[24]

During the 2004 presidential campaign, which coincided with the fiftieth anniversary of *Brown,* Democrat John Kerry and Republican George W. Bush both praised the decision. Each recognized that *Brown* had not ended segregation and that the lofty ideals it articulated had not yet changed life on the ground for all Americans. Yet each celebrated the decision as a milestone. Also in 2004, the National Park Service dedicated the *Brown v. Board of Education* National Historic Site at the grounds of the all-black school that Linda Brown had attended in Topeka. At the opening ceremonies, Cheryl Brown Henderson, the daughter of one of the *Brown* plaintiffs, called this historic site a "dream realized," but she spoke for many when she referred to this landmark case as "unfinished business."[25] Or, as Norman Rockwell might have put it, this is "The Problem We Still Live With."

Brown v. Board of Education &

These cases come to us from the States of Kansas, South Carolina, Virginia, and Delaware.... In each of the cases, minors of the Negro race, through their legal representatives, seek the aid of the courts in obtaining admission to the public schools of their community on a nonsegregated basis. In each instance, they had been denied admission to schools attended by white children under laws requiring or permitting segregation according to race. This segregation was alleged to deprive the plaintiffs of the equal protection of the laws under the Fourteenth Amendment. In each of the cases other than the Delaware case, a three-judge federal district court denied relief to the plaintiffs on the so-called "separate but equal" doctrine announced by this Court in *Plessy v. Ferguson.* Under that doctrine, equality of treatment is accorded when the races are provided substantially equal facilities, even though these facilities be separate. In the Delaware case, the Supreme Court of Delaware adhered to that doctrine, but ordered that the plaintiffs be admitted to the white schools because of their superiority to the Negro schools.

The plaintiffs contend that segregated public schools are not "equal" and cannot be made "equal," and that hence they are deprived of the equal protection of the laws....

In approaching this problem, we cannot turn the clock back to 1868, when the Amendment was adopted, or even to 1896, when *Plessy v. Ferguson* was written. We must consider public education in the light of its full development and its present place in American life throughout the Nation. Only in this way can it be determined if segregation in public schools deprives these plaintiffs of the equal protection of the laws.

Today, education is perhaps the most important function of state and local governments. Compulsory school attendance laws and the great expenditures for education both demonstrate our recognition of the importance of education to our democratic society. It is required in the performance of our most basic public responsibilities, even service in the armed forces. It is the very foundation of good citizenship. Today it is a principal instrument in awakening the child to cultural values, in preparing him for later professional training, and in helping him to adjust normally to his environment. In these days, it is doubtful that any child may reasonably be expected to succeed in life if he is denied the opportunity of an education. Such an opportunity, where the state has undertaken to provide it, is a right which must be made available to all on equal terms.

We come then to the question presented: Does segregation of children in public schools solely on the basis of race, even though the physical facilities and other "tangible" factors may be equal, deprive the children of the minority group of equal educational opportunities? We believe that it does.

In *Sweatt v. Painter, supra,* in finding that a segregated law school for Negroes could not provide them equal educational opportunities, this Court relied in large part on "those qualities which are incapable of objective measurement but which make for greatness in a law school." In *McLaurin v. Oklahoma State Regents, supra,* the Court, in requiring that a Negro admitted to a white graduate school be treated like all other students, again resorted to intangible considerations: "his ability to study, to engage in discussions and exchange views with other students, and, in general, to learn his profession." Such considerations apply with added force to children in grade and high schools. To separate them from others of similar age and qualifications solely because of their race generates a feeling of inferiority as to their status in the community that may affect their hearts and minds in a way unlikely ever to be undone. The effect of this separation on their educational opportunities was well stated by a finding in the Kansas case by a court which nevertheless felt compelled to rule against the Negro plaintiffs: Segregation of white and colored children in public schools has a detrimental effect upon the colored children. The impact is greater when it has the sanction of the law, for the policy of separating the races is usually interpreted as denoting the inferiority of the Negro group.[a] A sense of inferiority affects the motivation of a child to learn. Segregation with the sanction of law, therefore, has a tendency to [retard] the educational and mental development of Negro children and to deprive them of some of the benefits they would receive in a racial[ly] integrated school system. Whatever may have been the extent of psychological knowledge at the time of *Plessy v. Ferguson,* this finding is amply supported by modern authority. Any language in *Plessy v. Ferguson* contrary to this finding is rejected.

We conclude that, in the field of public education, the doctrine of "separate but equal" has no place. Separate educational facilities are inherently unequal. Therefore, we hold that the plaintiffs

---

a. Clarence Thomas, Supreme Court justice, taking a swipe at *Brown's* finding that separate education stamps blacks with a "feeling of inferiority" (1995): It never ceases to amaze me that the courts are so willing to assume that anything that is predominantly black must be inferior. . . . Mere *de facto* segregation (unaccompanied by discriminatory inequalities in educational resources) does not constitute a continuing harm after the end of *de jure* segregation. "Racial isolation" itself is not a harm; only state enforced segregation is. After all, if separation itself is a harm, and if integration therefore is the only way that blacks can receive a proper education, then there must be something inferior about blacks. Under this theory, segregation injures blacks because blacks, when left on their own, cannot achieve. To my way of thinking, that conclusion is the result of a jurisprudence based upon a theory of black inferiority. This misconception has drawn the courts away from the important goal in desegregation. The point of the Equal Protection Clause is not to enforce strict race mixing, but to ensure that blacks and whites are treated equally by the State without regard to their skin color. The lower courts should not be swayed by the easy answers of social science, nor should they accept the findings, and the assumptions, of sociology and psychology at the price of constitutional principle. —Justice Clarence Thomas, concurring opinion in *Missouri v. Jenkins,* 515 U.S. 70 (1995).

and others similarly situated for whom the actions have been brought are, by reason of the segregation complained of, deprived of the equal protection of the laws guaranteed by the Fourteenth Amendment. This disposition makes unnecessary any discussion whether such segregation also violates the Due Process Clause of the Fourteenth Amendment.

Because these are class actions, because of the wide applicability of this decision, and because of the great variety of local conditions, the formulation of decrees in these cases presents problems of considerable complexity. On reargument, the consideration of appropriate relief was necessarily subordinated to the primary question—the constitutionality of segregation in public education. We have now announced that such segregation is a denial of the equal protection of the laws. In order that we may have the full assistance of the parties in formulating decrees, the cases will be restored to the docket, and the parties are requested to present further argument . . . for the reargument this Term.

It is so ordered.[26]

COMMENTARY

Arthur Schlesinger Sr., historian, praising a "wonderful" decision (1954)

The Supreme Court has finally reconciled the Constitution with the Preamble of the Declaration of Independence. There will be a good many outcries against this decision and efforts to evade it by legislation. The decision will be a very great aid in clarifying to the world our conception of democracy.

—Quoted in "Historians Laud Court's Decision," *New York Times*, May 18, 1954, p. 17.

Thomas Brady, Mississippi circuit court judge and segregationist, refusing to recognize Brown *as the law of the land (1955)*

Black Monday ranks in importance with July 4th, 1776, the date upon which our Declaration of Independence was signed. May 17th, 1954, is the date upon which the declaration of socialistic doctrine was officially proclaimed throughout this nation. It was on Black Monday that the judicial branch of our government usurped the sacred privilege and right of the respective states of this union to educate their youth. This usurpation constitutes the greatest travesty of the American Constitution and jurisprudence in the history of this nation.

—Thomas P. Brady, *Black Monday: Segregation or Amalgamation . . . America Has Its Choice* (Winona, MS: Association of Citizens' Councils, 1955), foreword.

"Southern Manifesto," resolution signed by 101 of 128 Southern members of Congress, vowing to use "all lawful means" to undermine and overturn this "clear abuse of judicial power" (1956)

In the case of *Plessy v. Ferguson* in 1896 the Supreme Court expressly declared that under the Fourteenth Amendment no person was denied any of his rights if the states provided separate but equal public facilities. . . . This interpretation, restated time and again, became a part of the life of the people of many of the states and confirmed their habits, customs, traditions and way of life. . . . Though there has been no constitutional amendment or act of Congress changing this established legal principle almost a century old, the Supreme Court of the United States, with no legal basis for such action, undertook to exercise their naked judicial power and substituted their personal political and social ideas for the established law of the land.

This unwarranted exercise of power by the court, contrary to the Constitution, is creating chaos and confusion in the states principally affected. It is destroying the amicable relations between the white and Negro races that have been created through ninety years of patient effort by the good people of both races. It has planted hatred and suspicion where there has been heretofore friendship and understanding.

Without regard to the consent of the governed, outside agitators are threatening immediate and revolutionary changes in our public school systems. If done, this is certain to destroy the system of public education in some of the states.

With the gravest concern for the explosive and dangerous condition created by this decision and inflamed by outside meddlers:

We reaffirm our reliance on the Constitution as the fundamental law of the land.

We decry the Supreme Court's encroachments on rights reserved to the states and to the people, contrary to established law and to the Constitution.

We commend the motives of those states which have declared the intention to resist forced integration by any lawful means.

We appeal to the states and people who are not directly affected by these decisions to consider the constitutional principles involved against the time when they too, on issues vital to them, may be the victims of judicial encroachment. . . .

We pledge ourselves to use all lawful means to bring about a reversal of this decision which is contrary to the Constitution and to prevent the use of force in its implementation.

In this trying period, as we all seek to right this wrong, we appeal to our people not to be provoked by the agitators and troublemakers invading our states and to scrupulously refrain from disorder and lawless acts.

—"Southern Manifesto," *Congressional Record*, March 12, 1956, pp. 4459–60, www.pbs.org/wnet/ supremecourt/rights/sources_document2.html.

William Faulkner, *novelist, urging blacks to "go slow" on desegregation lest they prompt another civil war (1956)*

I don't like enforced integration any more than I like enforced segregation. . . . As long as there's a middle road, all right. I'll be on it. But if it came to fighting I'd fight for Mississippi against the United States even if it meant going out into the street and shooting Negroes.

—Russell Warren Howe, "A Talk with William Faulkner," *The Reporter*, March 22, 1956, reprinted in James B. Meriwether and Michael Millgate, *Lion in the Garden: Interviews with William Faulkner, 1926–1962* (New York: Random House, 1968), pp. 260–61.

James Kilpatrick, Richmond News Leader *editor and segregationist, urging Southern leaders to "interpose" themselves between their citizens and the Supreme Court (1957)*

The opinion of May 17, 1954, it is said, affected the eight States of the Old South and the Deep South most of all. The more accurate statement is that it affected every State equally. For the extinction of one power exercised by a few States creates precedent for the extinction of all powers exercised by all States. . . .

What is it that the Court, in effect, has commanded the South to give up? It is no less than this: The basis of the South's society, the vitality of her culture. The Southern States are ordered, subject to drastic penalties, either to abandon their schools or to breach the immutable law by which the South's character has been preserved. And the law is this: That white and black cannot come together, as equals, in any relationship that is *intimate, personal and prolonged*. And when to these guides are added further considerations of sex, and of compulsion, the barrier is complete.

Now, the only place—*the only place*—in which this line is threatened, and the law put in jeopardy, is in the field of public education. On buses, in elevators, in crowded stores, in arenas and ballparks, the races may be brought intimately together as equals, but the relation is not personal and it is not prolonged. On inter-racial boards and commissions, the relationship is of equals, it may be personal, it often is prolonged; but it is not intimate.

Public schools are something else entirely. Here the relationship is keenly intimate—as intimate as two desks touching, as two toilets in a washroom. It is personal—the social mingling of boys and girls in the same school activities. It is prolonged over the twelve-year period of elementary and secondary education. In the formative years of adolescence, the element of sex arises in its most dangerous and experimental form. And whether school attendance is required by law, or dictated by society, the element of compulsion exists. To integrate the schools of the Southern States thus is to demand a relationship forbidden by the mores of the people; and it is to risk, twenty or thirty years hence, a widespread racial amalgamation and a debasement of the society as a whole. . . .

Yet the fate of the schools, or the fate of the resisting Southern States, is not the most vital issue here. . . . The end of this process is the corruption of a constitutional Union, by judicial fiat, into a consolidated government in which the States are mere political dependencies. The end is a centralization of all meaningful powers in the hands of Federal authority. . . .

The remedy lies—it must lie—in drastic resistance by the States, *as States,* to Federal encroachment. . . . The States have submitted too long to Federal usurpations. At their grave peril, they can submit no longer. Through every device of interposition they can bring to bear—political, legislative, judicial—once more they must invoke their sovereign powers to insist that Federal encroachments be restrained.

—James Jackson Kilpatrick, *The Sovereign States: Notes of a Citizen of Virginia* (Chicago: Henry Regnery, 1957), pp. 256–57, 280–81, 286, 304–5.

Martin Luther King Jr., Baptist minister and civil rights leader, on the hope that Brown inspired (1958)

This decision brought hope to millions of disinherited Negroes who had formerly dared only to dream of freedom. It further enhanced the Negro's sense of dignity and gave him even greater determination to achieve justice.

—Martin Luther King Jr., *Stride Toward Freedom: The Montgomery Story* (Boston: Beacon, 1958), p. 191.

James Baldwin, novelist, attributing the decision to international factors rather than domestic goodwill (1960)

White Americans congratulate themselves on the 1954 Supreme Court decision outlawing segregation in the schools; they suppose, in spite of the mountain of evidence that has since accumulated to the contrary, that this was proof of a change of heart—or, as they like to say, progress. Perhaps. It all depends on how one reads the word "progress." Most of the Negroes I know do not believe that this immense concession would ever have been made if it had not been for the competition of the Cold War, and the fact that Africa was clearly liberating herself and therefore had, for political reasons, to be wooed by the descendants of her former masters. Had it been a matter of love or justice, the 1954 decision would surely have occurred sooner; were it not for the realities of power in this difficult era, it might very well not have occurred yet.

—James Baldwin, "Letter from a Region in My Mind," *New Yorker,* November 17, 1962, p. 130.

Malcolm X, black nationalist, placing Brown in the context of a dismal freedom story in the United States (1964)

One hundred years ago a civil war was fought supposedly to free us from the southern racists. We are still the victims of their racism. Lincoln's Emancipation Proclamation was supposedly to free us. We are still crying for freedom. The politicians fought for amendments to the Constitution supposedly to make us first-class citizens. We are still second-class citizens. In 1954, the U.S. Supreme Court itself issued a historic decision outlawing the segregated school system, and ten years have passed and this law is yet to be enforced even in the Northern states.

—Malcolm X, "Racism: The Cancer That Is Destroying America," *Egyptian Gazette,* August 25, 1964, reprinted in John Henrik Clarke, ed., *Malcolm X: The Man and His Times* (New York: Macmillan, 1969), pp. 305–6.

Rosa Parks, civil rights activist, on what Brown did for the civil rights struggle (1992)

You can't imagine the rejoicing among black people, and some white people, when the Supreme Court decision came down in May 1954. The Court had said that separate education could not be equal, and many of us saw how the same idea applied to other things, like public transportation. It was a very hopeful time. African Americans believed that at least there was a real chance to change the segregation laws.

—Rosa Parks, *Rosa Parks: My Story* (New York: Dial, 1992), pp. 99–100.

Michael Klarman, legal scholar, contending that Brown was "a relatively unimportant motivating factor" in the civil rights movement (1994)

The conventional view is that *Brown* instigated racial change either by pricking the conscience of northern whites or by raising the hopes and expectations of southern blacks. I shall suggest . . . that surprisingly little evidence supports either of these claims regarding *Brown's* contribution to the civil rights movement of the 1960s. The crucial link between *Brown* and the mid-1960s civil rights legislation inheres, rather, in the decision's crystalizing effect on southern white resistance to racial change. By propelling southern politics dramatically to the right on racial issues, *Brown* created a political climate conducive to the brutal suppression of civil rights demonstrations. When such violence occurred, and was vividly transmitted through the medium of television to national audiences, previously indifferent northern whites were aroused from their apathy, leading to demands for national civil rights legislation which the Kennedy and Johnson administrations no longer deemed it politically expedient to resist.

—Michael J. Klarman, "*Brown*, Racial Change, and the Civil Rights Movement," *Virginia Law Review* 80.1 (February 1994): 11.

Mark Tushnet, law professor and former law clerk to Justice Thurgood Marshall, arguing that "Brown was more important than Professor Klarman makes it out to be" (1994)

We might understand *Brown* as designed not to accomplish actual integration, but to establish a fundamental principle of constitutional law. The precise content of that principle has become controversial: It might be that race is an impermissible basis for government decisions, or that race is an impermissible basis for government decisions that subordinate African Americans. In either variant, though, the claim that *Brown* was a success is far more plausible. Government decisions relying on race (or relying on race to subordinate) rapidly became uncontroversially unconstitutional, and arguments that such decisions were acceptable rapidly became discredited.

—Mark Tushnet, "The Significance of *Brown v. Board of Education*," *Virginia Law Review* 80.1 (February 1994): 176.

Roscoe Brown, former president of Bronx Community College, on his memories of the Brown decision (2003)

I like to say that on May 17, 1954, I became a citizen of this country.

—Quoted in Michelle Fine, "The Power of the *Brown v. Board of Education* Decision: Theorizing Threats to Sustainability," *American Psychologist* 59.6 (September 2004): 502.

John Kerry, U.S. Senator (D-MA) and Democratic presidential candidate, speaking on Brown's fiftieth anniversary (2004)

In 1954, in Topeka, there were eighteen neighborhood schools for white children and just four "black only" elementary schools. Oliver Brown thought it was wrong that his seven-year-old daughter, Linda, and her friends had to walk a mile through a railroad yard every day just to catch a bus to their segregated elementary school. The trip took more than an hour, and on the way, Linda walked right past the closed doors of a white elementary school just three blocks from her house. It was separate—but it was not equal. The Supreme Court agreed and that decision became a turning point in America's long march toward equality. . . .

But we have more to do. . . . *Brown* began to tear down the walls of inequality. The next great challenge is to put up a ladder of opportunity for all. Because as far as we've come, we still have not met the promise of *Brown*. We have not met the promise of *Brown* when one-third of all African-American children are living in poverty. We have not met the promise of *Brown* when only 50 percent of African-American men in New York City have a job. We have not met the promise of *Brown* when nearly 20 million black and Hispanic Americans don't have basic health insurance. And we have certainly have not met the promise of *Brown* when, in too many parts of our country, our school systems are not separate but equal—but they are separate and unequal. . . . For America to be America for any of us, America must be America for all of us.

—John Kerry, "Remarks on the Anniversary of *Brown v. Board of Education*," Topeka, Kansas, May 17, 2004, www.presidency.ucsb.edu/ws/index.php?pid=29693.

David Garrow, civil rights historian, dismissing "revisionist" efforts to minimize Brown's importance (2004)

This year's fiftieth anniversary of *Brown v. Board of Education* ought to occasion untold praise for the courageous plaintiffs, attorneys, and jurists who helped bring about a momentous reformation of American law. Instead, anniversary celebrations and symposia have been rife with declarations that deprecate, disparage, dismiss, and otherwise dump on *Brown*. . . .

But the claim that *Brown* did not help spark greater black activism than otherwise would have occurred is not merely an abstruse historians' tussle. That argument helps advance a potentially potent political claim: that Supreme Court decisions "cannot fundamentally transform a nation," in [Michael] Klarman's words. . . . Minimizations of *Brown*, like similarly erroneous contentions that the abortion rights struggle in the United States would have fared better had the Supreme Court not handed down its far-reaching ruling in *Roe v. Wade* in 1973, argue against the political utility of constitutional reform litigation and judicial power. If *Brown's* anniversary supplies an occasion for greater attention to such claims, then commemorations may have the deleterious effect of dissuading observers from enlisting in current or future constitutional reform crusades.

The paradoxical and erroneous claim that *Brown* somehow proves that landmark judicial rulings cannot fundamentally change a society by advancing human liberty looks especially dubious at a time when the Massachusetts Supreme Judicial Court's vindication of the right to marry in *Goodridge v. Department of Public Health* is offering full legal equality to gay and lesbian citizens for the first time in American history. . . .

Brown v. Board of Education should rightfully be celebrated both as a landmark event on the continuing road to racial justice and as a judicial monument to how social reform can indeed be attained through constitutional litigation. That *Brown's* vision of racial equality remains unfulfilled is no reason to deny either its huge contribution to the modern African-American freedom struggle or its ongoing presence as a bright beacon for those who seek to use the law to advance human equality.

—David J. Garrow, "Give *Brown v. Board of Education* Its Due," *Human Rights* 31.3 (Summer 2004): 2–5.

Juan Williams, journalist, bidding good-bye to Brown *in light of a Supreme Court ruling prohibiting the assigning of students to schools by race (2007)*

It is time to acknowledge that *Brown's* time has passed. It is worthy of a send-off with fanfare for setting off the civil rights movement . . . but the decision . . . is now out of step with American political and social realities. Today a high court with a conservative majority concludes that any policy based on race—no matter how well intentioned—is a violation of every child's 14th-Amendment right to be treated as an individual without regard to race. We've come full circle.

—Juan Williams, "Don't Mourn *Brown v. Board of Education*," *New York Times*, June 29, 2007, p. 29.

Barack Obama, forty-fourth U.S. president, on Brown *as an unfulfilled dream (2009)*

There's a reason the story of the civil rights movement was written in our schools. There's a reason Thurgood Marshall took up the cause of Linda Brown. There's a reason why the Little Rock Nine defied a governor and a mob. It's because there is no stronger weapon against inequality and no better path to opportunity than an education that can unlock a child's God-given potential.

And yet, more than half a century after *Brown v. Board,* the dream of a world-class education is still being deferred all across the country. African-American students are lagging behind white classmates in reading and math, an achievement gap that is growing in states that once led the way in the civil rights movement. Over half of all African-American students are dropping out of school in some places. There are overcrowded classrooms and crumbling schools and corridors of shame in America filled with poor children, not just black children, brown and white children as well.

The state of our schools is not an African-American problem; it is an American problem, because if black and brown children cannot compete, then America cannot compete. But . . . government programs alone won't get our children to the promised land. We need a new mind-set, a new set of attitudes, because one of the most durable and destructive legacies of discrimination is the way we've internalized a sense of limitation, how so many in our community have come to expect so little from the world and from themselves.

We've got to say to our children, yes, if you're African American, the odds of growing up amid crime and gangs are higher. Yes, if you live in a poor neighborhood, you will face challenges that somebody in a wealthy suburb does not have to face. But that's not a reason to get bad grades, that's not a reason to cut class, that's not a reason to give up on your education and drop out of school. No one has written your destiny for you. Your destiny is in your hands, you cannot forget that. That's what we have to teach all of our children. No excuses—no excuses. You get that education, all those hardships will just make you stronger, better able to compete. Yes we can.

—Barack Obama, "Remarks Celebrating the 100th Anniversary of the NAACP," New York, July 16, 2009, www.presidency.ucsb.edu/ws/index.php?pid=86429.

Roe v. Wade

❦ 1973 ❧

*I*N 1969 a Texas woman named Norma McCorvey discovered that she was pregnant. Single and already the mother of two, she did not want to have another child, but abortion was illegal in Texas unless the pregnant woman's life was in danger. Assuming the name of "Jane Roe," McCorvey filed suit against Henry Wade, a Dallas County district attorney. Her lawyer, Sarah Weddington, argued that her client's right to choose an abortion was protected by a "right to privacy" secreted away in the First, Fourth, Fifth, Ninth, and Fourteenth Amendments. Later that year, a Texas court ruled in Roe's favor, locating this right to privacy in the Ninth Amendment. The State of Texas appealed. On January 2, 1973, the U.S. Supreme Court ruled for Roe by a 7–2 margin.

In the majority opinion, Justice Harry Blackmun rejected the state's claim that the fetus was a "person." He also rejected the view that women had an absolute right to end a pregnancy at any time and under any circumstances. However, he affirmed that states could not abridge a woman's choice to have an abortion during the first trimester of a pregnancy (the period, according to medical authorities at the time, when a fetus was not yet viable outside the womb).

Blackmun grounded his reasoning in the right to privacy. Although this right is not mentioned explicitly in the Constitution, Blackmun said it could be found in the Fourteenth Amendment, which says that state and local governments cannot deprive persons of life, liberty, or property without "due process." Blackmun and the rest of the majority used this right both to overturn the Texas law and to secure the right of women in all states to obtain abortions during the first trimester. This landmark decision replaced a patchwork of state abortion laws with a uniform federal abortion policy. It also sparked a firestorm of controversy that turned *Roe v. Wade* into one of the most contentious Supreme Court rulings in U.S. history.

Abortion rights advocates hailed *Roe v. Wade* as a major victory. Shortly after the ruling, Lee Gidding, Executive Director of the National Association for Repeal of Abortion Laws, said, "We haven't really gotten over it. It was such a shock. We didn't expect it to be so sweeping. It's just superb."[1] Also referring to *Roe* as "sweeping," the Committee for Pro-Life Affairs of the National Conference of Catholic Bishops described the decision as "a flagrant rejection of the unborn child's right to life," adding that the Court had made "abortion on request" U.S. policy.[2]

Soon the nation was wrestling with two newly minted rights—a woman's right to privacy and the unborn's right to life—and pondering anew the long-standing tension in American life between individual rights and collective responsibilities. Is abortion a private matter best left to the woman, her doctor, and (perhaps) the father? Or does the state have a compelling interest in protecting the life of the unborn child? If so, at what point and under what circumstances can this state interest override the mother? How Americans answered these questions depended on how they read the Constitution. But ethical, philosophical, and theological questions were also important. Does human life begin at conception? When does a fetus become a person? What is a person? And might lives (potential or otherwise) in the womb be sacrificed in order to save mothers' lives, or in cases of rape or incest?

Roe did not start today's culture wars, but it turned their skirmishes into matters of life and death, polarizing public opinion, mobilizing "pro-life" and "pro-choice" forces, and turning abortion into a litmus test of party loyalty. Many constitutional experts—liberals and conservatives alike—questioned the logic of the Court's decision. But the real venom came from conservatives, who argued that *Roe* made law rather than merely interpreting it. In *Catholic Lawyer,* two scholars blasted Blackmun for magically pulling a constitutional right out of his judicial hat:

> *The right to privacy asserted by the Court is not only absent from the express provisions of the original Constitution, the Bill of Rights, and later Amendments, it is not generally recognized by law, custom, or by majority opinion. How could such an alleged right, therefore, be "so rooted in the traditional conscience of our people to be ranked as fundamental"? The Court with equal effort could have "discovered" the unborn's right to life, invested it with "fundamental" status, and clothed it with judicial protection. This right is not explicit in any part of the*

Constitution, but unlike the right to abort, it is recognized by law, by custom, and by majority opinion.[3]

Initially, many Democrats opposed *Roe* and many Republicans supported it, but both parties quickly wrote abortion planks into their platforms and made sure their candidates were toeing the party line. Soon presidential candidates were weighing in on *Roe* in televised debates, and Supreme Court nominees were being vetted (often in code language) for their willingness to uphold or overturn it. Pro-life activists picketed clinics, and some of these protests turned violent. Several abortion providers were killed, as anti-abortion crusaders committed murder in order to stop what they saw as more of the same.

Before *Roe,* most conservative Protestants had viewed abortion, which was prohibited in the Catholic encyclical *Humanae Vitae* (1968), largely as a Catholic issue. Now they joined with Catholics to form a conservative Christian groundswell that would usher Reagan and two Bushes into the Oval Office. In this way, *Roe* lured the religious into public life, further politicizing the U.S. Catholic church and drawing evangelicals out of their self-imposed exile from politics.

Liberals hailed *Roe* for allowing women to choose whether to carry a pregnancy to term and for subtly challenging traditional gender roles at home and in the workplace. But some on the left today believe that *Roe* was, in the words of Michael Kinsley, "one of the worst things that ever happened to American liberalism."[4] Before *Roe,* public opinion and state legislators were lining up behind abortion. Afterwards, the momentum shifted to those who sought to chip away at abortion rights. And chip away they did.

Since 1973, states have passed bills requiring waiting periods, requiring minors seeking abortions to inform their parents, and requiring physicians to provide patients with anti-abortion information. In a clear repudiation of *Roe's* first trimester viability standard, at least six states have banned abortions at the twentieth week after conception, and there are efforts afoot to prohibit abortions after a fetal heartbeat can be detected (usually at six to eight weeks). Meanwhile, Congress has banned both "partial-birth" abortions and federal funding of abortion (except where the life of the mother is endangered, or in cases of rape or incest).

The pace of these restrictions is accelerating. In the first half of 2011, nineteen states enacted eighty such laws—more than double the previous record of thirty-four enacted in 2005.[5] In 2011, Texas governor Rick Perry signed an emergency measure requiring pregnant women seeking abortions to have ultrasounds and to hear descriptions of their fetuses before undergoing the procedure. In Mississippi, however, a "personhood amendment" that would have defined human life as beginning at conception was defeated that same year. All this anti-abortion activity has led some to conclude that Sandra Day O'Connor was right when she observed in 1983 that *Roe* was "on a collision course with itself."[6] Conservatives continue to subject the ruling to a death by a thousand cuts, while liberals endure the torture for fear that an increasingly conservative Supreme Court might overturn *Roe*.

Today the American public is divided over abortion, though there is considerable consensus that it should be, as President Clinton often put it, "safe, legal, and rare." Forty-nine percent of Americans now describe themselves as "pro-choice" and 45 percent as "pro-life," with 51 percent saying they favor *Roe*.[7] One opponent is "Jane Roe" herself, Norma McCorvey, who told CNN in 1997 that she now opposes abortion. The fate of this decision is not in her hands, however. Neither is it in the hands of the American public or their elected representatives. It belongs to the nine men and women who sit on the Supreme Court.

Roe v. Wade ❧

Jane Roe, a single woman who was residing in Dallas County, Texas, instituted this federal action in March 1970 against the District Attorney of the county. . . .

Roe alleged that she was unmarried and pregnant; that she wished to terminate her pregnancy by an abortion "performed by a competent, licensed physician, under safe, clinical conditions"; that she was unable to get a "legal" abortion in Texas because her life did not appear to be threatened by the continuation of her pregnancy; and that she could not afford to travel to another jurisdiction in order to secure a legal abortion under safe conditions. She claimed that the Texas statutes were unconstitutionally vague and that they abridged her right of personal privacy, protected by the First, Fourth, Fifth, Ninth, and Fourteenth Amendments. . . .

The principal thrust of appellant's attack on the Texas statutes is that they improperly invade a right, said to be possessed by the pregnant woman, to choose to terminate her pregnancy. Appellant would discover this right in the concept of personal "liberty" embodied in the Fourteenth Amendment's Due Process Clause; or in personal, marital, familial, and sexual privacy said to be protected by the Bill of Rights or its penumbras, or among those rights reserved to the people by the Ninth Amendment. . . .

It perhaps is not generally appreciated that the restrictive criminal abortion laws in effect in a majority of States today are of relatively recent vintage. Those laws, generally proscribing abortion or its attempt at any time during pregnancy except when necessary to preserve the pregnant woman's life, are not of ancient or even of common-law origin. Instead, they derive from statutory changes effected, for the most part, in the latter half of the 19th century. . . .

Three reasons have been advanced to explain historically the enactment of criminal abortion laws in the 19th century and to justify their continued existence. It has been argued occasionally that these laws were the product of a Victorian social concern to discourage illicit sexual conduct. Texas, however, does not advance this justification in the present case, and it appears that no court or commentator has taken the argument seriously. . . .

A second reason is concerned with abortion as a medical procedure. When most criminal abortion laws were first enacted, the procedure was a hazardous one for the woman. . . . Abortion mortality was high. Even after 1900, and perhaps until as late as the development of antibiotics in the 1940's, standard modern techniques such as dilation and curettage were not nearly so safe as they are today. Thus, it has been argued that a State's real concern in enacting a criminal abortion law was to protect the pregnant woman. . . .

Modern medical techniques have altered this situation. Appellants and various amici refer to medical data indicating that abortion in early pregnancy, that is, prior to the end of the first trimester, although not without its risk, is now relatively safe. . . . The State has a legitimate interest in seeing to it that abortion, like any other medical procedure, is performed under circumstances that insure maximum safety for the patient. . . . The prevalence of high mortality rates at illegal "abortion mills" strengthens, rather than weakens, the State's interest in regulating the conditions under which abortions are performed. Moreover, the risk to the woman increases as her pregnancy continues. Thus, the State retains a definite interest in protecting the woman's own health and safety when an abortion is proposed at a late stage of pregnancy.

The third reason is the State's interest—some phrase it in terms of duty—in protecting prenatal life. Some of the argument for this justification rests on the theory that a new human life is present from the moment of conception. The State's interest and general obligation to protect life then extends, it is argued, to prenatal life. Only when the life of the pregnant mother herself is at stake, balanced against the life she carries within her, should the interest of the embryo or fetus not prevail. Logically, of course, a legitimate state interest in this area need not stand or fall on acceptance of the belief that life begins at conception or at some other point prior to live birth. In assessing the State's interest, recognition may be given to the less rigid claim that as long as at least potential life is involved, the State may assert interests beyond the protection of the pregnant woman alone. It is with these interests, and the weight to be attached to them, that this case is concerned.

The Constitution does not explicitly mention any right of privacy. In a line of decisions, however, . . . the Court has recognized that a right of personal privacy, or a guarantee of certain areas or zones of privacy, does exist under the Constitution. . . .

This right of privacy, whether it be founded in the Fourteenth Amendment's concept of personal liberty and restrictions upon state action, as we feel it is, or, as the District Court determined, in the Ninth Amendment's reservation of rights to the people, is broad enough to encompass a woman's decision whether or not to terminate her pregnancy. The detriment that the State would impose upon the pregnant woman by denying this choice altogether is apparent. Specific and direct harm medically diagnosable even in early pregnancy may be involved. Maternity, or additional offspring, may force upon the woman a distressful life and future. Psychological harm may be imminent. Mental and physical health may be taxed by child care. There is also the distress, for all concerned, associated with the unwanted child, and there is the problem of bringing a child into a family already unable, psychologically and otherwise, to care for it. In other cases, as in this one, the additional difficulties and continuing stigma of unwed motherhood may be involved. . . .

On the basis of elements such as these, appellant and some amici argue that the woman's right is absolute and that she is entitled to terminate her pregnancy at whatever time, in whatever way, and for whatever reason she alone chooses. With this we do not agree. . . . As noted above, a State may properly assert important interests in safeguarding health, in maintaining medical standards, and in protecting potential life. At some point in pregnancy, these respective interests become sufficiently compelling to sustain regulation of the factors that govern the abortion decision. The privacy right involved, therefore, cannot be said to be absolute. . . .

The appellee and certain amici argue that the fetus is a "person" within the language and meaning of the Fourteenth Amendment. . . . The Constitution does not define "person" in so many words. Section 1 of the Fourteenth Amendment contains three references to "person." . . . But in nearly all these instances, the use of the word is such that it has application only postnatally. None indicates, with any assurance, that it has any possible pre-natal application.

All this, together with our observation, *supra*, that throughout the major portion of the 19th century prevailing legal abortion practices were far freer than they are today, persuades us that the word "person," as used in the Fourteenth Amendment, does not include the unborn. . . .

Texas urges that, apart from the Fourteenth Amendment, life begins at conception and is present throughout pregnancy, and that, therefore, the State has a compelling interest in protecting that life from and after conception. We need not resolve the difficult question of when life begins. When those trained in the respective disciplines of medicine, philosophy, and theology are unable to arrive at any consensus, the judiciary, at this point in the development of man's knowledge, is not in a position to speculate as to the answer. . . .[a,b]

In view of all this, we do not agree that, by adopting one theory of life, Texas may override the rights of the pregnant woman that are at stake. We repeat, however, that the State does have an important and legitimate interest in preserving and protecting the health of the pregnant woman, whether she be a resident of the State or a nonresident who seeks medical consultation and treatment there, and that it has still another important and legitimate interest in protecting the potentiality of human life. These interests are separate and distinct. Each grows in substantiality as the woman approaches term and, at a point during pregnancy, each becomes "compelling."

With respect to the State's important and legitimate interest in the health of the mother, the "compelling" point, in the light of present medical knowledge, is at approximately the end of the first trimester.[c] This is so because of the now-established medical fact . . . that until the end of the first trimester mortality in abortion may be less than mortality in normal childbirth. It follows that, from and after this point, a State may regulate the abortion procedure to the extent that the regulation reasonably relates to the preservation and protection of maternal health. Examples of permissible state regulation in this area are requirements as to the qualifications of the person

---

a. Edwin Roberts Jr., Pulitzer Prize–winning reporter, criticizing the Court's refusal to "speculate" on when human life begins (1973): Human life begins at conception—that is a fact. Medical men know it's a fact. High-school biology students know it's a fact. And the Supreme Court of the United States knows it's a fact. But it's an inconvenient fact. To recognize it would have made impossible the result the Court legislators wanted. So in their concern for unmarried pregnant women, for the miserable mothers of very large, very poor families, and for the simple convenience of housewives who want to escape the domestic routine, the Justices have declared what is known with certainty to be unknowable. —Edwin A. Roberts Jr., "High Court's Abortion Legislation," *National Observer*, March 10, 1973, in Eva R. Rubin, ed., *The Abortion Controversy: A Documentary History* (Westwood, CT: Greenwood, 1994), p. 149.

b. Ron Paul, Texas Congressman and Republican presidential candidate, speaking at the Faith and Freedom Coalition (2011): As an OB doctor, let me tell you, life does begin at conception. —Quoted in "Ron Paul Preaches a Different Kind of Conservative Gospel," *Christianity Today*, August 19, 2011, http://blog.christianitytoday.com/ctpolitics/2011/08/ron_paul_preach.html.

who is to perform the abortion; as to the licensure of that person; as to the facility in which the procedure is to be performed. . . .

This means, on the other hand, that, for the period of pregnancy prior to this "compelling" point, the attending physician, in consultation with his patient, is free to determine, without regulation by the State, that, in his medical judgment, the patient's pregnancy should be terminated. If that decision is reached, the judgment may be effectuated by an abortion free of interference by the State.

With respect to the State's important and legitimate interest in potential life, the "compelling" point is at viability. This is so because the fetus then presumably has the capability of meaningful life outside the mother's womb. State regulation protective of fetal life after viability thus has both logical and biological justifications. If the State is interested in protecting fetal life after viability, it may go so far as to proscribe abortion during that period, except when it is necessary to preserve the life or health of the mother.

Measured against these standards, Art. 1196 of the Texas Penal Code, in restricting legal abortions to those "procured or attempted by medical advice for the purpose of saving the life of the mother," sweeps too broadly. The statute makes no distinction between abortions performed early in pregnancy and those performed later, and it limits to a single reason, "saving" the mother's life, the legal justification for the procedure. The statute, therefore, cannot survive the constitutional attack made upon it here.

Our conclusion that Art. 1196 is unconstitutional means, of course, that the Texas abortion statutes, as a unit, must fall. . . .

It is so ordered.[8]

---

c. Sandra Day O'Connor, Supreme Court justice, overturning *Roe*'s trimester framework in a plurality opinion (1992): *Roe* established a trimester framework to govern abortion regulations. Under this elaborate but rigid construct, almost no regulation at all is permitted during the first trimester of pregnancy; regulations designed to protect the woman's health, but not to further the State's interest in potential life, are permitted during the second trimester; and, during the third trimester, when the fetus is viable, prohibitions are permitted provided the life or health of the mother is not at stake. . . .

We reject the trimester framework, which we do not consider to be part of the essential holding of *Roe*. . . . To promote the State's profound interest in potential life, throughout pregnancy the State may take measures to ensure that the woman's choice is informed, and measures designed to advance this interest will not be invalidated as long as their purpose is to persuade the woman to choose childbirth over abortion. These measures must not be an undue burden on the right. —Justice Sandra O'Connor, plurality opinion, *Planned Parenthood of Southeastern Pennsylvania v. Casey,* 505 U.S. 833 (1992), www.law.cornell.edu/supct/html/historics/USSC_CR_0505_0833_ZO.html.

COMMENTARY

Byron White, Supreme Court justice, dissenting in Roe (1973)

With all due respect, I dissent. I find nothing in the language or history of the Constitution to support the Court's judgment. The Court simply fashions and announces a new constitutional right for pregnant mothers and, with scarcely any reason or authority for its action, invests that right with sufficient substance to override most existing state abortion statutes. The upshot is that the people and the legislatures of the 50 States are constitutionally disentitled to weigh the relative importance of the continued existence and development of the fetus, on the one hand, against a spectrum of possible impacts on the mother, on the other hand. As an exercise of raw judicial power, the Court perhaps has authority to do what it does today; but, in my view, its judgment is an improvident and extravagant exercise of the power of judicial review that the Constitution extends to this Court. . . . This issue, for the most part, should be left with the people and to the political processes the people have devised to govern their affairs.

—Justice Byron White, dissenting opinion, *Doe v. Bolton*, 410 U.S. 179 (1973).

Michael Levi, obstetrician/gynecologist, testifying about the human cost of illegal abortions (1974)

During my years at Harlem Hospital, prior to the liberalization of the New York abortion law, I have seen women die from illegal abortions; many women die. I have watched a 20-year-old die of an infection incurred during a criminal abortion. I as a physician could not reconcile her death with my oath to preserve lives. I have seen a mother of four die leaving her children without her love and guidance, because she could not afford another child. Her act of love for her children led to her death from a self-induced abortion. I have seen a desperate 27-year-old threaten suicide if she was not given an abortion. This was in 1967, and being forbidden to help her, we denied her the abortion. She committed suicide. For these and the many, many more I remember, I cannot reconcile my conscience and the Hippocratic Oath with the tragedies that have taken place.

—Michael M. Levi, July 24, 1974, testimony, in *Abortion: Hearings Before the Subcommittee on Constitutional Amendments of the Committee on the Judiciary, United States Senate, Ninety-Third Congress, Second Session* (Washington, DC: U.S. Government Printing Office, 1976), 2:570.

Mildred Jefferson, chairman, National Right to Life Committee, on the dehumanizing effects of Roe (1974)

The Supreme Court destroyed the foundations of democracy in the abortion decisions by creating three categories of citizenship. The doctor and pregnant woman were elevated to the rank of super-citizens with the private right to kill by contract. Man, the father of the child, was reduced to the level of subcitizen with no defined right to protect the life of his unborn child. The unborn child was declared a nonperson in the eyes of the law, and, therefore, noncitizen only to allow his or her life to be taken.

—Dr. Mildred Jefferson, August 21, 1974, testimony, in *Abortion: Hearings Before the Subcommittee on Constitutional Amendments of the Committee on the Judiciary, United States Senate, Ninety-Third Congress, Second Session* (Washington, DC: U.S. Government Printing Office, 1975), 3:8.

Pat Goltz, president, Feminists for Life, testifying in favor of a constitutional amendment "for the protection of unborn children" (1974)

The only consistent philosophy a feminist can have about other instances of human life is one of granting dignity to all of them. . . . We who were once defined as less than human cannot, in claiming our rights, deny rights to others based on a subjective judgment that they are less than human. . . .

Abortion has been presented as the solution to the problems faced by women with untimely pregnancies. The vast majority of these problems can be put into one category: discrimination. We are unilaterally opposed to discrimination based on either sex or maternal status. We reserve the right to be treated as equals and to be mothers at the same time.

—Pat Goltz, August 21, 1974, testimony, in *Abortion: Hearings Before the Subcommittee on Constitutional Amendments of the Committee on the Judiciary, United States Senate, Ninety-Third Congress, Second Session* (Washington, DC: U.S. Government Printing Office, 1975), 3:108.

Sara Weddington, attorney for "Jane Roe," framing the abortion question as a matter of choice (1975)

A woman ought to have the ability to determine the course of her life. She ought to be able to determine what things will happen to her, how they will happen, and what her life will be about. She cannot make those decisions if there is a complete prohibition against abortion because, at this time, we do not have total means of avoiding pregnancy. Methods fail. Sometimes people are not informed about methods. Sometimes they do not use them well. However, when a woman is faced with an unwanted pregnancy, I see all of the questions that are involved from her life. When I look at the interest of the life of the fetus compared to the interests of the woman I . . . have to say that the basic underlying principle to me is that the woman ought to have the right to make a choice. We should not force a choice on those who do not wish an abortion. Any choice should be an informed choice, but the woman, in the last analysis, should have that choice of how her life will go.

—Sara Weddington, April 11, 1975, testimony, in *Abortion: Hearings Before the Subcommittee on Constitutional Amendments of the Committee on the Judiciary, Ninety-Fourth Congress, First Session* (Washington, DC: U.S. Government Printing Office, 1976), 4:520–21.

Democratic Party platform, affirming abortion rights (1976)

We fully recognize the religious and ethical nature of the concerns which many Americans have on the subject of abortion. We feel, however, that it is undesirable to attempt to amend the U.S. Constitution to overturn the Supreme Court decision in this area.

—"Democratic Party Platform of 1976," www.presidency.ucsb.edu/ws/index.php?pid=29606.

Republican Party platform, opposing abortion rights (1976)

The question of abortion is one of the most difficult and controversial of our time. It is undoubtedly a moral and personal issue but it also involves complex questions relating to medical science and criminal justice. There are those in our Party who favor complete support for the Supreme Court decision which permits abortion on demand. There are others who share sincere convictions that the Supreme Court's decision must be changed by a constitutional amendment prohibiting all abortions. Others have yet to take a position, or they have assumed a stance somewhere in between polar positions.

We protest the Supreme Court's intrusion into the family structure through its denial of the parents' obligation and right to guide their minor children. The Republican Party favors a continuance of the public dialogue on abortion and supports the efforts of those who seek enactment of a constitutional amendment to restore protection of the right to life for unborn children.

—"Republican Party Platform of 1976," www.presidency.ucsb.edu/ws/index.php?pid=25843.

Henry Hyde, U.S. Representative (R-IL), introducing the Hyde amendment banning federal funds for abortion (1976)

We are all exercised at the wanton killing of the porpoise, the baby seal. We urge big game hunters to save the tiger, but we somehow turn away at the specter of a million human beings being violently destroyed because this great society does not want them. . . . An innocent, defenseless human life, in a caring and human society deserves better than to be flushed down a toilet or burned in an incinerator. The promise of America is that life is not just for the privileged, the planned, or the perfect.

—Henry Hyde, *Congressional Record,* June 24, 1976, p. 20410, reprinted in Melody Rose, *Abortion: A Documentary and Reference Guide* (Westport, CT: Greenwood, 2008), pp. 118–19.

Mother Teresa, Roman Catholic nun and founder of Missionaries
of Charity, on abortion as a violation of human rights (1994)

I hope you will count it no presumption that I seek your leave to address you on behalf of the unborn child. Like that child I can be called an outsider. I am not an American citizen . . . [yet] no one in the world who prizes liberty and human rights can feel anything but a strong kinship with America. Yours is the one great nation in all of history which was founded on the precept of equal rights and respect for all humankind, for the poorest and weakest of us as well as the richest and strongest. As your Declaration of Independence put it in words which have never lost their power to stir the heart:

> *We hold these truths to be self-evident: that all men are created equal;*
> *that they are endowed by their creator with certain inalienable rights;*
> *that among these are life, liberty, and the pursuit of happiness. . . .*

It must be recognized that your model was never one of realized perfection, but of ceaseless aspiration. From the outset, for example, America denied the African slave his freedom and human dignity. But in time you righted that wrong, albeit at an incalculable cost in human suffering and loss of life. Your impetus has almost always been toward a fuller, more all-embracing conception and assurance of the rights which your founding fathers recognized as inherent and God-given. . . .

Yet there has been one infinitely tragic and destructive departure from those American ideals in recent memory. It was this Court's own decision in 1973 to exclude the unborn child from the human family. . . . Your opinion stated that you did not need to "resolve the difficult question of when life begins." That question is inescapable. If the right [to] life is an inherent and inalienable right, it must surely obtain wherever human life exists. No one can deny that the unborn child is a distinct human being, that it is human, and that it is alive. It is unjust, there-fore, to deprive the unborn child of its fundamental right to life on the basis of its age, size, or condition of dependency. . . .

America needs no words from me to see how your decision in *Roe v. Wade* has deformed a great nation. The so-called right to abortion has pitted mothers against their children and women against men. It has sown violence and discord at the heart of the most intimate human relationships. It has aggravated the derogation of the father's role in an increasingly fatherless society. It has portrayed the greatest of gifts—a child—as a competitor, an intrusion, and an inconvenience. It has nominally accorded mothers unfettered dominion over the independent lives of their physically dependent sons and daughters. And, in granting this unconscio-nable power, it has exposed many women to unjust and selfish demands from their husbands or other sexual partners.

Human rights are not a privilege conferred by government. They are every human being's entitlement by virtue of his humanity. The right to life does not depend, and must not be declared to be contingent, on the pleasure of anyone else, not even a parent or a sovereign.

—Mother Teresa and Robert P. George, "Brief Amicus Curiae of Mother Teresa of Calcutta, in Support of Petitioners' Petitions for a Writ of Certiorari," *Human Life Review* 27.2 (Spring 2001): 97–100.

Naomi Wolf, author, arguing on feminist grounds that abortion is a moral issue (1995)

At its best, feminism defends its moral high ground by being simply faithful to the truth: to women's real-life experiences. But, to its own ethical and political detriment, the pro-choice movement has relinquished the moral frame around the issue of abortion. It has ceded the language of right and wrong to abortion foes. The movement's abandonment of what Americans have always, and rightly, demanded of their movements—an ethical core—and its reliance instead on a political rhetoric in which the fetus means nothing are proving fatal.

The effects of this abandonment can be measured in two ways. First of all, such a position causes us to lose political ground. By refusing to look at abortion within a moral framework, we lose the millions of Americans who want to support abortion as a legal right, but still need to condemn it as a moral iniquity. Their ethical allegiances are then addressed by the pro-life movement, which is willing to speak about good and evil.

But we are also in danger of losing something more important than votes; we stand in jeopardy of losing what can only be called our souls. Clinging to a rhetoric about abortion in which there is no life and no death, we entangle our beliefs in a series of self-delusions, fibs and evasions. And we risk becoming precisely what our critics charge us with being: callous, selfish and casually destructive men and women who share a cheapened view of human life. . . .

It was when I was four months pregnant, sick as a dog, and in the middle of an argument, that I realized I could no longer tolerate the fetus-is-nothing paradigm of the pro-choice movement. I was being interrogated by a conservative, and the subject of abortion rights came up. "You're four months pregnant," he said. "Are you going to tell me that's not a baby you're carrying?"

The accepted pro-choice response at such a moment is to evade: to move as swiftly as possible to a discussion of "privacy" and "difficult personal decision" and "choice." Had I not been so nauseated and so cranky and so weighed down with the physical gravity of what was going on inside me, I might not have told what the truth is for me. "Of course it's a baby," I snapped. And went rashly on: "And if I found myself in circumstances in which I had to make the terrible decision to end this life, then that would be between myself and God." . . .

Now the G-word is certainly a problematic element to introduce into the debate. And yet "God" or "soul"—or, if you are secular and prefer it, "conscience"—is precisely what is missing from pro-choice discourse.

The language we use to make our case limits the way we let ourselves think about abortion. As a result of the precedents in *Roe* (including *Griswold v. Connecticut* and *Eisentadt v. Baird*), which based a woman's right to an abortion on the Ninth and Fourteenth Amendments' implied right to personal privacy, other unhelpful terms are also current in our discourse. Pro-choice advocates tend to cast an abortion as "an intensely personal decision." To which we can say, No: one's choice of *carpeting* is an intensely personal decision. One's struggles with a life-and-death issue must be understood as a matter of personal conscience. There is a world of difference between the two, and it's the difference a moral frame makes. . . .

—Naomi Wolf, "Our Bodies, Our Souls, *New Republic,* October 16, 1995, pp. 26–35.

Barack Obama, forty-fourth U.S. president, responding to critics at Notre Dame's commencement (2009)

As I considered the controversy surrounding my visit here, I was reminded of an encounter I had during my Senate campaign, one that I describe in a book I wrote called *The Audacity of Hope.* And a few days after the Democratic nomination, I received an e-mail from a doctor who told me that while he voted for me in the Illinois primary, he had a serious concern that might prevent him from voting for me in the general election. He described himself as a Christian who was strongly pro-life, but that was not what was preventing him, potentially, from voting for me.

What bothered the doctor was an entry that my campaign staff had posted on my website, an entry that said I would fight, quote, "right-wing ideologues who want to take away a woman's right to choose," unquote. The doctor said he had assumed I was a reasonable person, he supported my policy initiatives to help the poor and to lift up our educational system, but that if I truly believed that every pro-life individual was simply an ideologue who wanted to inflict suffering on women, then I was not very reasonable. He wrote, "I do not ask at this point that you oppose abortion, only that you speak about this issue in fair-minded words"—fair-minded words.

After I read the doctor's letter, I wrote back to him, and I thanked him. And I didn't change my underlying position, but I did tell my staff to change the words on my website. And I said a prayer that night that I might extend the same presumption of good faith to others that the doctor had extended to me. Because when we do that, when we open up our hearts and our minds to those who may not think precisely like we do or believe precisely what we believe, that's when we discover at least the possibility of common ground. That's when we begin to say, maybe we won't agree on abortion, but we can still agree that this heart-wrenching decision for any woman is not made casually, that it has both moral and spiritual dimensions.

So let us work together to reduce the number of women seeking abortions; let's reduce unintended pregnancies. Let's make adoption more available. Let's provide care and support for women who do carry their children to term. Let's honor the conscience of those who disagree with abortion, and draft a sensible conscience clause, and make sure that all of our health-care policies are grounded not only in sound science, but also in clear ethics, as well as respect for the equality of women. Those are things we can do.

—Barack Obama, "Commencement Address at the University of Notre Dame," May 17, 2009, www.presidency.ucsb.edu/ws/?pid=86154.

Randall Terry, founder of Operation Rescue, denouncing a murdered abortion provider as a slaughterer of the unborn (2009)

George Tiller was a mass-murderer. We grieve for him that he did not have time to properly prepare his soul to face God. I am more concerned that the Obama administration will use Tiller's killing to intimidate pro-lifers into surrendering our most effective rhetoric and actions. Murder is still murder. And we must call abortion by its proper name: murder. Those men and women who slaughter the unborn are still murderers according to the Law of God. We must continue to expose them in our communities and peacefully protest them at their offices and homes, and yes, even in their churches.

—"George Tiller Was a Mass-Murderer, Says Randall Terry," May 31, 2009, www.christiannewswire.com/news/8967610531.html.

CHRONICLES

Uncle Tom's Cabin

❧ HARRIET BEECHER STOWE, 1852 ❧

HARRIET BEECHER STOWE (1811–96) once claimed that she was merely present at the creation of *Uncle Tom's Cabin; or, Life Among the Lowly.* "God wrote it," and she "merely did his dictation."[1] Whether this antislavery novel came from God's lips or Stowe's hand (or some combination thereof), its impact was near biblical. More than anyone else in antebellum America, Stowe galvanized sentiment against slavery, cultivating sympathy for slaves by portraying them as mothers and fathers, husbands and wives, brothers and sisters. As a result, her first novel became, with the possible exception of Thomas Paine's *Common Sense,* the most influential book in U.S. history.

Uncle Tom's Cabin first appeared serially from June 1851 to April 1852 in the antislavery newspaper *The National Era.* Published in two volumes in 1852, it sold roughly 300,000 copies in the United States and perhaps 2 million worldwide in its first year. "Everybody has read it, is reading, or is about to read it," Boston's *Morning Post* reported in 1852.[2] This unprecedented readership made Stowe rich. It also made her the most famous woman of her age. Stowe toured England and was invited to the White House, where, as legend has it, President Lincoln asked, "Is this the little woman who made this great war?"[3]

Admirers praised this "little woman" (she stood no more than five feet tall) for painting a realistic picture of the human beings who suffered under slavery. Critics damned her as a liar who bore false witness against her neighbors and "an enemy to her country" who, by slandering the South, threatened the Union.[4] Others criticized "the man Harriet" as someone who "unsexed herself" by descending from the feminine art of letters to the masculine sport of politics. "She has proved herself false to her womanly mission," *The Daily Picayune* of New Orleans editorialized, "a stirrer up of strife, rather than a 'peace maker'; deficient in the delicacy and purity of a woman."[5]

Commenting on this controversy, Unitarian minister Theodore Parker observed in January 1853 that the novel had "excited more attention than any book since the invention of printing."[6] Parker's critics routinely accused him of neglecting the Bible, and he obviously did so here. But Stowe's "family values" novel was an unprecedented event in American publishing. For the first time in popular literature, African Americans appeared as living, breathing people with families of their own.

In an era before film and television spin-offs, *Uncle Tom's Cabin* also lived in popular plays referred to as "Tom shows," which brought Stowe's characters to the stage for nearly a century. Although banned in some Southern states, many of these shows actually reinforced racial stereotypes, with white actors playing African-American characters in blackface, and directors playing many of the novel's tragic scenes for laughs. One of these Tom shows, produced by George Aiken, became the longest-running play in America, spreading Stowe's antislavery gospel to standing-room-only crowds and making "theater, once reviled, a holier place than the church in America."[7] Stowe's characters—the young slave Topsy, the angelic blonde girl Eva, the dastardly Simon Legree, and the Christlike martyr Uncle Tom—appeared in card games and jigsaw puzzles, and on root-beer bottles and Cream of Wheat boxes. Illustrations of key scenes in the novel abounded, as did popular songs. And when cinema came to America, there were film adaptations too. In a 1933 Walt Disney cartoon, "The Meller Drama," Mickey (in blackface) and Minnie dance together as Uncle Tom and Little Eva.

Uncle Tom's Cabin was also a sensation in Great Britain, where it sold over a million copies in its first year. Eventually translated into roughly sixty languages, the book, according to historian David Reynolds, "gave impetus to revolutions in Russia, China, Brazil, Cuba, and elsewhere." Vladimir Lenin said it was his favorite book as a child. Leo Tolstoy called it an example of the "highest art" because of its demonstration of the "brotherhood of God and man."[8]

Harriet Beecher Stowe was born in 1811 in Litchfield, Connecticut, to one of America's most famous families. Her father, Lyman Beecher, was a Presbyterian minister, a Second Great Awakening revivalist, and one of the emperors of the "benevolent empire" of social reform and missionary organizations dedicated to remaking America in the image of Christ. A staunch anti-Catholic, Beecher took a job as president of Lane Theological Seminary in Cincinnati, Ohio, in an effort to win the West for Protestantism. Though opposed to slavery, he also opposed the abolitionism of some of his Lane seminarians, prompting them to leave to found Oberlin College. As a member of the American Colonization Society, he proposed sending free blacks back to Africa. Harriet's siblings in the Beecher household included Catharine Beecher, an author best known for *A Treatise on Domestic Economy* (1841), and Henry Ward Beecher, the most famous preacher of his day. Unlike his predecessors in the pulpit, who stressed biblical exegesis, he specialized in story sermons that captured the imagination of his parishioners in Brooklyn's Plymouth Church. But the family's greatest story sermon was *Uncle Tom's Cabin*.

Research for this sermon began when the Beecher family moved to Cincinnati in 1832. Cincinnati abuts the Ohio River, and on the far bank was the slave state of Kentucky. So runaway slaves were an everyday reality in Stowe's new Midwestern life, as was the Underground Railroad. But the catalyst for the novel came more than a decade later, with the passage of the Fugitive Slave Law in 1850. The Constitution had required the return of runaway slaves, but this law had teeth, including six months in prison and a $1,000 fine for anyone caught harboring a runaway slave.

Though opposed to slavery, Stowe, like her father, believed that the "moral monomaniacs" calling for immediate emancipation were jeopardizing the Union.[9] But the Fugitive Slave Law moved Stowe to appeal to a Higher Law to justify breaking lower ones. Instead of advancing an argument for this Higher Law, as Henry David Thoreau did in "Civil Disobedience" (1849), Stowe told a story. She wrote this story in Maine, where she and her husband, Lane Bible professor Calvin Stowe, had moved in 1850 so he could take a job at Bowdoin College and they could escape the sadness of the cholera death of their son Charley one year earlier.

Like the Beecher family, Stowe's novel was through-and-through theological. It too was perched between the harsh Puritanism of the early republic and the religion of love of Victorian-era liberal Protestantism. And in crafting her characters Stowe drew on both traditions. She found the innate goodness prized by liberal Protestants in Uncle Tom and other black characters, and the total depravity emphasized by Puritans in white characters such as the sadistic slave owner Simon Legree.

Addressing itself to *the* great question in American life, *Uncle Tom's Cabin* opens on a Kentucky plantation with the sale of two slaves—a middle-aged man named Uncle Tom and a four-year-old boy named Harry. It then follows two main narratives: a Northern plot in which Harry's mother, Eliza Harris, attempts to flee to join her husband George (who has already escaped) in Canada; and a Southern plot in which Uncle Tom is sold ever deeper into the Deep South and into the hands of increasingly cruel slave masters. The Northern plot includes one of the most famous scenes in American literature: Eliza's daring dash, baby in arms, across Ohio River ice floes. It ends with the Harris family reunited in Canada. The Southern plot ends with one of American literature's saddest scenes: Uncle Tom's Christlike death by lashing upon the orders of Simon Legree. Both of these plots attack the institution of slavery as immoral and unchristian. But that had been done before. What Stowe added was a genius for cultivating empathy for her African-American characters, and for laying bear the suffering slavery inflicted on black families in a way that somehow seemed both melodramatic and authentic.

Uncle Tom's Cabin ends on a prophetic note. In her "Concluding Remarks," Stowe challenges her mostly white audience to "read the signs of the times":

> *A day of grace is yet held out to us. Both North and South have been guilty before God; and the Christian church has a heavy account to answer. Not by combining together, to protect injustice and cruelty, and making a common capital of sin, is this Union to be saved,—but by repentance, justice and mercy; for, not surer is the eternal law by which the millstone sinks in the ocean, than that stronger law, by which injustice and cruelty shall bring on nations the wrath of Almighty God!*[10]

In keeping with her moderate antislavery position, Stowe did not intend to portray the slavery debate as an apocalyptic battle between good and evil. Many Southerners in the novel are portrayed quite favorably—Uncle Tom's masters range from cruel (Legree) to kind (Shelby)—and the horrors of slavery are told more than shown. But the effects of the book did not always obey Stowe's orders. Because it appealed to the heart over the head, the novel did more than conventional antislavery arguments to commend abolitionism to Northerners. But it also steeled the resolve of many Southerners, who read it as a divisive broadside against the Constitution and their way of life.

Early criticism of *Uncle Tom's Cabin* centered on whether Stowe's characters were real to life and her depiction of American slavery accurate. African Americans for the most part applauded the book—*Frederick Douglass' Paper* called it "the wonder of wonders"—though many lamented a chapter advocating colonization.[11] Defenders of the novel said it was the truest account of slavery ever written, while detractors denounced it as a lie—an "immaculate encyclopaedia of fictitious crimes."[12] The *New York Observer* complained about stereotypes: "The Uncle Tom of the authoress is a perfect angel, and her blacks generally are half-angels; her Simon Legree is a perfect demon, and her whites generally are half-demons."[13] One of the most exhaustive critiques came from George Graham of *Graham's Magazine* who besmirched the title character in this "vastly overrated" novel as "an exaggeration—a monster of perfection." The plot was in Graham's view "feeble." As for Stowe's motive, it was "*business,* and nothing more . . . a question of dollars and cents, not of slavery or liberty."[14]

Critics also responded to the novel's popular acclaim with proslavery tracts defending an institution they saw as biblical. Sociologist George Fitzhugh argued that life in the slaveholding South was far better for slaves under the care of their masters than life in the North was for "slaves without masters"—workers under the thumb of their capitalist exploiters.[15] Others published anti-Tom novels, such as W. L. G. Smith's *Life at the South; or, "Uncle Tom's Cabin" As It Is* (1852). Stowe pushed back with *The Key to Uncle Tom's Cabin* (1853), which documented the facts and characters in her novel. It sold 100,000 copies in its first year.

Later critics of *Uncle Tom's Cabin* asked whether racism animated the book and its author. Historian George Fredrickson saw Stowe's characterization of Uncle Tom as an example of "romantic racialism."[16] But most twentieth-century critics attacked the book on literary grounds. Its writing was in their view sensational, sentimental, and preachy, while its characters were one-dimensional—types of good or evil rather than the messy mix typically found walking this earth. In "Everybody's Protest Novel" (1949), James Baldwin labeled *Uncle Tom's Cabin* a "very bad novel" and Stowe "not so much a novelist as an impassioned pamphleteer."[17] Why did her black characters have to be so pious, and so cloyingly good? In the strangest turn in the novel's afterlife, the term "Uncle Tom" became, largely thanks to the Tom shows, a racial slur referring to a black man who is only half black and half a man and would do anything to kowtow to whites. According to Reynolds, Frederick Douglass may have been the first to use "Uncle Tom" in this way. Later, Malcolm X employed it against Martin Luther King Jr.[18]

As a result of the nay-sayers, Stowe's page-turner largely disappeared from the American literary canon, only to reemerge in the 1960s and 1970s when civil rights and feminist activists resurrected it as an eloquent protest against racism written "in a woman's voice." Alfred Kazin called it "the most powerful and enduring work of art ever written about American slavery."[19] But as this line suggests, the novel was praised largely as a political tract, not literature.

In an 1868 *Nation* essay that coined the term "the Great American Novel," John W. De Forest named *Uncle Tom's Cabin* his prime candidate for this honor, praising its "national breadth" as well as its "truthful outlining of character, natural speaking, and plenty of strong feeling."[20] Echoing De Forest, Jane Tompkins wrote in 1985 that Stowe's novel "retells the culture's central religious myth—the story of the crucifixion—in terms of the nation's greatest political conflict—slavery—and of its most cherished social beliefs—the sanctity of motherhood and the family."[21] At least as the phrase is now understood, *Uncle Tom's Cabin* does not qualify as "the Great American Novel." Melville's *Moby-Dick* is by most lights a greater work of art, but Stowe's *Uncle Tom's Cabin* had a bigger impact. Like Thomas Paine's *Common Sense* it was an unprecedented bestseller that packed a powerful political punch. It addressed itself to *the* defining issue in U.S. history and, even if it didn't bring on the Civil War, it convinced millions of Americans that slavery belonged in the nation's past.

Uncle Tom's Cabin 🍃

Chapter 40: The Martyr

"Deem not the just by Heaven forgot!
Though life its common gifts deny,—
Though, with a crushed and bleeding heart,
And spurned of man, he goes to die!
For God hath marked each sorrowing day,
And numbered every bitter tear,
And heaven's long years of bliss shall pay
For all his children suffer here."

—Bryant

The longest way must have its close,—the gloomiest night will wear on to a morning. An eternal, inexorable lapse of moments is ever hurrying the day of the evil to an eternal night, and the night of the just to an eternal day. We have walked with our humble friend thus far in the valley of slavery; first through flowery fields of ease and indulgence, then through heart-breaking separations from all that man holds dear. Again, we have waited with him in a sunny island, where generous hands concealed his chains with flowers; and, lastly, we have followed him when the last ray of earthly hope went out in night, and seen how, in the blackness of earthly darkness, the firmament of the unseen has blazed with stars of new and significant lustre.

The morning-star now stands over the tops of the mountains, and gales and breezes, not of earth, show that the gates of day are unclosing.

The escape of Cassy and Emmeline irritated the before surly temper of Legree to the last degree; and his fury, as was to be expected, fell upon the defenceless head of Tom. When he hurriedly announced the tidings among his hands, there was a sudden light in Tom's eye, a sudden uprais-ing of his hands, that did not escape him. He saw that he did not join the muster of the pursuers. He thought of forcing him to do it; but, having had, of old, experience of his inflexibility when commanded to take part in any deed of inhumanity, he would not, in his hurry, stop to enter into any conflict with him.

Tom, therefore, remained behind, with a few who had learned of him to pray, and offered up prayers for the escape of the fugitives.

When Legree returned, baffled and disappointed, all the long-working hatred of his soul towards his slave began to gather in a deadly and desperate form. Had not this man braved him,—steadily, powerfully, resistlessly,—ever since he bought him? Was there not a spirit in him which, silent as it was, burned on him like the fires of perdition?

"I *hate* him!" said Legree, that night, as he sat up in his bed; "I *hate* him! And isn't he MINE? Can't I do what I like with him? Who's to hinder, I wonder?" And Legree clenched his fist, and shook it, as if he had something in his hands that he could rend in pieces.

But, then, Tom was a faithful, valuable servant; and, although Legree hated him the more for that, yet the consideration was still somewhat of a restraint to him.

The next morning, he determined to say nothing, as yet; to assemble a party, from some neighboring plantations, with dogs and guns; to surround the swamp, and go about the hunt systematically. If it succeeded, well and good; if not, he would summon Tom before him, and—his teeth clenched and his blood boiled—*then* he would break the fellow down, or—there was a dire inward whisper, to which his soul assented.

Ye say that the *interest* of the master is a sufficient safeguard for the slave. In the fury of man's mad will, he will wittingly, and with open eye, sell his own soul to the devil to gain his ends; and will he be more careful of his neighbor's body?

"Well," said Cassy, the next day, from the garret, as she reconnoitered through the knot-hole, "the hunt's going to begin again, to-day!"

Three or four mounted horsemen were curvetting about, on the space in front of the house; and one or two leashes of strange dogs were struggling with the negroes who held them, baying and barking at each other.

The men are, two of them, overseers of plantations in the vicinity; and others were some of Legree's associates at the tavern-bar of a neighboring city, who had come for the interest of the sport. A more hard-favored set, perhaps, could not be imagined. Legree was serving brandy, profusely, round among them, as also among the negroes, who had been detailed from the various plantations for this service; for it was an object to make every service of this kind, among the negroes, as much of a holiday as possible.

Cassy placed her ear at the knot-hole; and, as the morning air blew directly towards the house, she could overhear a good deal of the conversation. A grave sneer overcast the dark, severe gravity of her face, as she listened, and heard them divide out the ground, discuss the rival merits of the dogs, give orders about firing, and the treatment of each, in case of capture.

Cassy drew back; and, clasping her hands, looked upward, and said, "O, great Almighty God! we are *all* sinners; but what have *we* done, more than all the rest of the world, that we should be treated so?"

There was a terrible earnestness in her face and voice, as she spoke.

"If it wasn't for *you*, child," she said, looking at Emmeline, "I'd *go* out to them; and I'd thank any one of them that *would* shoot me down; for what use will freedom be to me? Can it give me back my children, or make me what I used to be?"

Emmeline, in her child-like simplicity, was half afraid of the dark moods of Cassy. She looked perplexed, but made no answer. She only took her hand, with a gentle, caressing movement.

"Don't!" said Cassy, trying to draw it away; "you'll get me to loving you; and I never mean to love anything, again!"

"Poor Cassy!" said Emmeline, "don't feel so! If the Lord gives us liberty, perhaps he'll give you back your daughter; at any rate, I'll be like a daughter to you. I know I'll never see my poor old mother again! I shall love you, Cassy, whether you love me or not!"

The gentle, child-like spirit conquered. Cassy sat down by her, put her arm round her neck, stroked her soft, brown hair; and Emmeline then wondered at the beauty of her magnificent eyes, now soft with tears.

"O, Em!" said Cassy, "I've hungered for my children, and thirsted for them, and my eyes fail with longing for them! Here! here!" she said, striking her breast, "it's all desolate, all empty! If God would give me back my children, then I could pray."

"You must trust him, Cassy," said Emmeline; "he is our Father!"

"His wrath is upon us," said Cassy; "he has turned away in anger."

"No, Cassy! He will be good to us! Let us hope in Him," said Emmeline,—"I always have had hope."

The hunt was long, animated, and thorough, but unsuccessful; and, with grave, ironic exultation, Cassy looked down on Legree, as, weary and dispirited, he alighted from his horse.

"Now, Quimbo," said Legree, as he stretched himself down in the sitting-room, "you jest go and walk that Tom up here, right away! The old cuss is at the bottom of this yer whole matter; and I'll have it out of his old black hide, or I'll know the reason why!"

Sambo and Quimbo, both, though hating each other, were joined in one mind by a no less cordial hatred of Tom. Legree had told them, at first, that he had bought him for a general overseer, in his absence; and this had begun an ill will, on their part, which had increased, in their debased and servile natures, as they saw him becoming obnoxious to their master's displeasure. Quimbo, therefore, departed, with a will, to execute his orders.

Tom heard the message with a forewarning heart; for he knew all the plan of the fugitives' escape, and the place of their present concealment;—he knew the deadly character of the man he had to deal with, and his despotic power. But he felt strong in God to meet death, rather than betray the helpless.

He sat his basket down by the row, and, looking up, said, "Into thy hands I commend my spirit! Thou hast redeemed me, oh Lord God of truth!" and then quietly yielded himself to the rough, brutal grasp with which Quimbo seized him.

"Ay, ay!" said the giant, as he dragged him along; "ye'll cotch it, now! I'll boun' Mas'r's back's up *high!* No sneaking out, now! Tell ye, ye'll get it, and no mistake! See how ye'll look, now, helpin' Mas'r's niggers to run away! See what ye'll get!"

The savage words none of them reached that ear!—a higher voice there was saying, "Fear not them that kill the body, and, after that, have no more that they can do." Nerve and bone of that poor man's body vibrated to those words, as if touched by the finger of God; and he felt the strength of a thousand souls in one. As he passed along, the trees and bushes, the huts of his servitude, the whole scene of his degradation, seemed to whirl by him as the landscape by the rushing ear. His soul throbbed,—his home was in sight,—and the hour of release seemed at hand.

"Well, Tom!" said Legree, walking up, and seizing him grimly by the collar of his coat, and speaking through his teeth, in a paroxysm of determined rage, "do you know I've made up my mind to KILL YOU?"

"It's very likely, Mas'r," said Tom, calmly.

"I *have*," said Legree, with a grim, terrible calmness, "*done—just—that—thing*, Tom, unless you'll tell me what you know about these yer gals!"

Tom stood silent.

"D'ye hear?" said Legree, stamping, with a roar like that of an incensed lion. "Speak!"

"*I han't got nothing to tell, Mas'r*," said Tom, with a slow, firm, deliberate utterance.

"Do you dare to tell me, ye old black Christian, ye don't *know*?" said Legree.

Tom was silent.

"Speak!" thundered Legree, striking him furiously. "Do you know anything?"

"I know, Mas'r; but I can't tell anything. *I can die!*"

Legree drew in a long breath; and, suppressing his rage, took Tom by the arm, and, approaching his face almost to his, said, in a terrible voice, "Hark 'e, Tom!—ye think, 'cause I've let you off before, I don't mean what I say; but, this time, *I've made up my mind*, and counted the cost. You've always stood it out again' me: now, *I'll conquer ye, or kill ye!*—one or t' other. I'll count every drop of blood there is in you, and take 'em, one by one, till ye give up!"

Tom looked up to his master, and answered, "Mas'r, if you was sick, or in trouble, or dying, and I could save ye, I'd *give* ye my heart's blood; and, if taking every drop of blood in this poor old body would save your precious soul, I'd give 'em freely, as the Lord gave his for me. O, Mas'r! don't bring this great sin on your soul! It will hurt you more than 't will me! Do the worst you can, my troubles'll be over soon; but, if ye don't repent, yours won't *never* end!"

Like a strange snatch of heavenly music, heard in the lull of a tempest, this burst of feeling made a moment's blank pause. Legree stood aghast, and looked at Tom; and there was such a silence, that the tick of the old clock could be heard, measuring, with silent touch, the last moments of mercy and probation to that hardened heart.

It was but a moment. There was one hesitating pause,—one irresolute, relenting thrill,—and the spirit of evil came back, with seven-fold vehemence; and Legree, foaming with rage, smote his victim to the ground.

Scenes of blood and cruelty are shocking to our ear and heart. What man has nerve to do, man has not nerve to hear. What brother-man and brother-Christian must suffer, cannot be told us, even in our secret chamber, it so harrows the soul! And yet, oh my country! these things are done under the shadow of thy laws! O, Christ! thy church sees them, almost in silence!

But, of old, there was One whose suffering changed an instrument of torture, degradation and shame, into a symbol of glory, honor, and immortal life; and, where His spirit is, neither degrading stripes, nor blood, nor insults, can make the Christian's last struggle less than glorious.

Was he alone, that long night, whose brave, loving spirit was bearing up, in that old shed, against buffeting and brutal stripes?

Nay! There stood by him ONE,—seen by him alone,—"like unto the Son of God."

The tempter stood by him, too,—blinded by furious, despotic will,—every moment pressing him to shun that agony by the betrayal of the innocent. But the brave, true heart was firm on the Eternal Rock. Like his Master, he knew that, if he saved others, himself he could not save; nor could utmost extremity wring from him words, save of prayers and holy trust.

"He's most gone, Mas'r," said Sambo, touched, in spite of himself, by the patience of his victim.

"Pay away, till he gives up! Give it to him!—give it to him!" shouted Legree. "I'll take every drop of blood he has, unless he confesses!"

Tom opened his eyes, and looked upon his master. "Ye poor miserable critter!" he said, "there ain't no more ye can do! I forgive ye, with all my soul!" and he fainted entirely away.

"I b'lieve, my soul, he's done for, finally," said Legree, stepping forward, to look at him. "Yes, he is! Well, his mouth's shut up, at last,—that's one comfort!"

Yes, Legree; but who shall shut up that voice in thy soul—that soul, past repentance, past prayer, past hope, in whom the fire that never shall be quenched is already burning!

Yet Tom was not quite gone. His wondrous words and pious prayers had struck upon the hearts of the imbruted blacks, who had been the instruments of cruelty upon him; and, the instant Legree withdrew, they took him down, and, in their ignorance, sought to call him back to life,—as if *that* were any favor to him.

"Sartin, we's been doin' a drefful wicked thing!" said Sambo; "hopes Mas'r'll have to 'count for it, and not we."

They washed his wounds,—they provided a rude bed, of some refuse cotton, for him to lie down on; and one of them, stealing up to the house, begged a drink of brandy of Legree, pretending that he was tired, and wanted it for himself. He brought it back, and poured it down Tom's throat.

"O, Tom!" said Quimbo, "we's been awful wicked to ye!"

"I forgive ye, with all my heart!" said Tom, faintly.

"O, Tom! do tell us who is *Jesus*, anyhow?" said Sambo;—"Jesus, that's been a standin' by you so, all this night!—Who is he?"

The word roused the failing, fainting spirit. He poured forth a few energetic sentences of that wondrous One,—his life, his death, his everlasting presence, and power to save.

They wept,—both the two savage men.

"Why didn't I never hear this before?" said Sambo; "but I do believe!—I can't help it! Lord Jesus, have mercy on us!"

"Poor critters!" said Tom, "I'd be willing to bar' all I have, if it'll only bring ye to Christ! O, Lord! give me these two more souls, I pray!"

That prayer was answered![22]

COMMENTARY

Charles Sumner, U.S. Senator from Massachusetts, referring to Uncle Tom's Cabin *in a speech urging the repeal of the Fugitive Slave Law (1852)*

But the great heart of the people recoils from this enactment. It palpitates for the fugitive, and rejoices in his escape. Sir, I am telling you facts. The literature of the age is all on his side. Songs, more potent than laws, are for him. Poets, with voices of melody, sing for Freedom. . . . And now, Sir, behold a new and heavenly ally. A woman, inspired by Christian genius, enters the lists, like another Joan of Arc, and with marvelous power sweeps the popular heart. Now melting to tears, and now inspiring to rage, her work everywhere touches the conscience, and makes the Slave-Hunter more hateful. In a brief period, nearly one hundred thousand copies of "Uncle Tom's Cabin" have been already circulated. But this extraordinary and sudden success, surpassing all other instances in the records of literature, cannot be regarded as but the triumph of genius. Better far, it is the testimony of the people, by an unprecedented act, against the Fugitive Slave Bill.

—Charles Sumner, "Freedom National, Slavery Sectional," U.S. Senate speech, August 26, 1852, in *The Works of Charles Sumner* (Boston: Lee and Shepard, 1871), p. 182.

George Frederick Holmes, scholar, denouncing Stowe in a florid, novella-length critique for libel, slander, fraud, defamation, sedition, sophistry, hypocrisy, perjury, and "Pharisaical self-sanctification" (1852)

We have said that Uncle Tom's Cabin is a fiction. It is a fiction throughout; a fiction in form; a fiction in its facts; a fiction in its representations and coloring; a fiction in its statements; a fiction in its sentiments; a fiction in its morals; a fiction in its religion; a fiction in its inferences; a fiction equally with regard to the subjects it is designed to expound, and with respect to the manner of their exposition. . . . Every fact is distorted, every incident discolored, in order to awaken rancorous hatred and malignant jealousies between the citizens of the same republic, the fellow-countrymen whose interests and happiness are linked with the perpetuity of a common union, and with the prosperity of a common government.

—George Frederick Holmes, "Uncle Tom's Cabin," *Southern Literary Messenger,* December 1852, pp. 722–30, http://utc.iath.virginia.edu/reviews/rere24bt.html.

Harriet Beecher Stowe, author, commenting on her Uncle Tom character and laying bare her own racial stereotypes (1853)

The vision attributed to Uncle Tom introduces quite a curious chapter of psychology with regard to the negro race, and indicates a peculiarity which goes far to show how very different they are from the white race. They are possessed of a nervous organisation peculiarly susceptible and impressible. Their sensations and impressions are very vivid, and their fancy and imagination lively. In this respect the race has an Oriental character, and betrays its tropical origin. Like the Hebrews of old and the Oriental nations of the present, they give vent to their emotions with the utmost vivacity of expression, and their whole bodily system sympathises with the movements of their minds. When in distress, they actually lift up their voices to weep, and "cry with an exceeding bitter cry." When alarmed, they are often paralysed, and rendered entirely helpless. Their religious exercises are all coloured by this sensitive and exceedingly vivacious temperament. Like Oriental nations, they incline much to outward expressions, violent gesticulations, and agitating movements of the body. Sometimes in their religious meetings they will spring from the floor many times in succession, with a violence and rapidity which is perfectly astonishing. They will laugh, weep, and embrace each other convulsively, and sometimes become entirely paralysed and cataleptic.

Considering those distinctive traits of the race, it is no matter of surprise to find . . . almost constantly, in the narrations of their religious histories, accounts of visions, of heavenly voices, of mysterious sympathies and transmissions of knowledge from heart to heart without the intervention of the senses, or what the Quakers call being "baptized into the spirit" of those who are distant.

—Harriet Beecher Stowe, *The Key to Uncle Tom's Cabin* (London: Clarke, Beeton, 1853), pp. 45–46.

A. Woodward, medical doctor, attacking Stowe for casting "vile aspersions" on Southerners and threatening the union (1853)

Southern people have their faults; they err in many things: and far be it from me, under such circumstances, to become their apologist. It is not as a defender of the South I appear before the public, but in defense of my country, North and South. We are all brethren; we are all citizens of the same heaven-favored country; and how residents of one part of it can spend their life's in vilifying, traducing, and misrepresenting those of another portion of it, is, to me, unaccountable. . . . If such productions as Uncle Tom's Cabin are to give tone to public sentiment in the North, then assuredly we are in danger. Should Mrs. Stowe's vile aspersion of southern character, and her loose, reckless and wicked misrepresentations of the institution of slavery in the southern States ever become accredited in the northern section of the Union I fear the consequence.

—A. Woodward, *A Review of Uncle Tom's Cabin; or, an Essay on Slavery* (Cincinnati: Applegate, 1853), pp. 9, 11–12.

The Weekly Call, *African-American periodical from Topeka, Kansas, eulogizing Stowe (1896)*

In the passing of Mrs. Harriet Beecher Stowe, the Negro race loses one of its greatest benefactors. It is probable that no other American woman has done so much for this country. Mrs. Stowe was a member of the famous Beecher family, celebrated every where for intellect and genius, and she occupies a place in the front rank of American literature.

In literary efforts, as in all her other endeavors, her one purpose was to do good. Being of a reflective turn of mind, and of a kind, generous and sympathetic nature, and living in a part of the country that afforded her exceptional opportunities for seeing the traits of slavery, she was naturally affected by a system so vile and pernicious and so inhuman in its practices. As a result she wrote the most widely published of all American books.

"Uncle Tom's Cabin," the book and the story it relates are too well known to need any further mention here. It has been translated into nearly every language, and being dramatized, it has been played upon nearly every stage in the civilized world. The advent of this book did more than any other agency to arouse the lethargic spirit of the people of the north against the system of slavery. If the merits of the book are to be determined by the nobleness of its aim and the purity of its purpose, and the extent to which they are accomplished, "Uncle Tom's Cabin" is the greatest production in American literature.

—*The Weekly Call,* July 3, 1896, http://utc.iath.virginia.edu/africam/afar58at.html.

James King, Stowe's Methodist pastor, on Uncle Tom's Cabin *and the Declaration of Independence (1896)*

The Declaration of Independence read that all men were created free and equal, but it was not for eighty-eight years that the free and liberty-loving American people saw the great hypocrisy of this statement. It was Mrs. Stowe's grand work, conceived in the Lord, that drove this great lie out of our Declaration of Independence. No permanent victory crowned the Union forces until the proclamation abolishing slavery was issued. It was the story of "Uncle Tom's Cabin" that quickened the spirit of the North, and many a mother gave up her son to her country with tears in her eyes but with the story of Uncle Tom's wrongs in her heart.

The secret of the success of Mrs. Stowe's work was simple. It came from the heart. . . . The book was conceived and born in the sacrament of the Lord's Supper. It was during the solemn service that the inspiration came to her. I believe that Mrs. Stowe was called, as Lincoln was, by God to come forward in the great crisis, in our Nation's history. The story of "Uncle Tom's Cabin" served admirably to quicken the National conscience until the great blot of slavery was removed from our escutcheon.

—Quoted in "Mrs. Stowe Eulogized," *New York Times*, July 6, 1896, p. 8.

F. Hopkinson Smith, author, blaming the Civil War on Stowe's "criminal" novel in a speech delivered in Newton, Massachusetts (1901)

[*Uncle Tom's Cabin*] is the most vicious book that ever appeared. It compares with Kennan's first book on Russia. I could go into the prisons of the North today and write a similar book. The book precipitated the war and made the North believe nothing but the worst of the South. We are not an inhuman people; we are all alike, we are Americans. It was an outrage to raise the North against the South. The book was an appalling, awful, and criminal mistake.

—F. Hopkinson Smith, "Scores Mrs. Stowe's Book," *Chicago Daily Tribune*, January 11, 1901, p. 1.

James Weldon Johnson, author, praising Uncle Tom's Cabin for making sense of the Civil War and of his own experience (1912)

This work of Harriet Beecher Stowe has been the object of much unfavorable criticism. It has been assailed, not only as fiction of the most imaginative sort, but as being a direct misrepresentation. Several successful attempts have lately been made to displace the book from Northern school libraries. Its critics would brush it aside with the remark that there never was a Negro as good as Uncle Tom, nor a slave-holder as bad as Legree. For my part, I was never an admirer of Uncle Tom, nor of his type of goodness; but I believe that there were lots of old Negroes as foolishly good as he; the proof of which is that they knowingly stayed and worked the plantations that furnished sinews for the army which was fighting to keep them enslaved. . . .

I do not think it takes any great stretch of the imagination to believe there was a fairly large class of slave-holders typified in Legree. And we must also remember that the author depicted a number of worthless if not vicious Negroes, and a slave-holder who was as much of a Christian and a gentleman as it was possible for one in his position to be; that she pictured the happy, singing, shuffling "darkey" as well as the mother waiting for her child sold "down river." I do not think it is claiming too much to say that *Uncle Tom's Cabin* was a fair and truthful panorama of slavery; however that may be, it opened my eyes as to who and what I was and what my country considered me; in fact, it gave me my bearing.

—James Weldon Johnson, *Autobiography of an Ex-Colored Man* (1912), in Rudolph P. Byrd, ed., *The Essential Writings of James Weldon Johnson* (New York: Modern Library, 2008), p. 49.

James Baldwin, novelist, denouncing "protest novels" as "fantasies" that are "trapped and immobilized in the sunlit prison of the American dream" (1949)

> *Uncle Tom's Cabin* is a very bad novel, having, in its self-righteous, virtuous sentimentality, much in common with *Little Women*. Sentimentality, the ostentatious parading of excessive and spurious emotion, is the mark of dishonesty, the inability to feel; the wet eyes of the sentimentalist betray his aversion to experience, his fear of life, his arid heart; and it is always, therefore, the signal of secret and violent inhumanity, the mask of cruelty.

> —James Baldwin, "Everybody's Protest Novel" (1949), in *Notes of a Native Son* (Boston: Beacon, 1955), p. 14.

Jane Tompkins, English professor, praising both Uncle Tom's Cabin *and the sentimental novel for empowering women (1978)*

> The thesis I will argue . . . holds that the popular domestic novel of the nineteenth century represents a monumental effort to reorganize culture from the woman's point of view; that this body of work is remarkable for its intellectual complexity, ambition, and resourcefulness; and that, in certain cases, it offers a critique of American society far more devastating than any delivered by better-known critics such as Hawthorne and Melville. Finally, it suggests that the enormous popularity of these novels, which has been cause for suspicion bordering on disgust, is a reason for paying close attention to them.

> *Uncle Tom's Cabin* was, in almost any terms one can think of, the most important book of the century. It was the first American novel ever to sell over a million copies and its impact is generally thought to have been incalculable. Expressive of and responsible for the values of its time, it also belongs to a genre, the sentimental novel, whose chief characteristic is that it is written by, for, and about women. In this respect, *Uncle Tom's Cabin* is not exceptional but representative. It is the *summa theologica* of nineteenth-century America's religion of domesticity, a brilliant redaction of the culture's favorite story about itself—the story of salvation through motherly love. Out of the ideological materials at their disposal, the sentimental novelists elaborated a myth that gave women the central position of power and authority in the culture; and of these efforts *Uncle Tom's Cabin* is the most dazzling exemplar.

> —Jane P. Tompkins, *Sentimental Designs: The Cultural Work of American Fiction, 1790–1860* (New York: Oxford Univ. Press, 1985), pp. 124–25.

Jane Smiley, novelist, on her preference for Uncle Tom's Cabin *over* Huckleberry Finn *(1996)*

> Ernest Hemingway, thinking of himself, as always, once said that all American literature grew out of *Huck Finn*. It undoubtedly would have been better for

American literature, and American culture, if our literature had grown out of one of the best-selling novels of all time, another American work of the nineteenth century, *Uncle Tom's Cabin,* which for its portrayal of an array of thoughtful, autonomous, and passionate black characters leaves *Huck Finn* far behind. . . .

The novel was immediately read and acclaimed by any number of excellent judges: Charles Dickens, George Eliot, Leo Tolstoy, George Sand—the whole roster of nineteenth-century liberals whose work we read today and try to persuade ourselves that *Huck Finn* is equal to. English novelist and critic Charles Kingsley thought *Uncle Tom's Cabin* the best novel ever written. These writers honored Stowe's book for all its myriad virtues. One of these was her adept characterization of a whole world of whites and blacks who find themselves gripped by slavery, many of whose names have entered the American language as expressions—not only Uncle Tom himself, but Simon Legree and, to a lesser extent, little Eva and the black child Topsy. . . .

The power of *Uncle Tom's Cabin* is the power of brilliant analysis married to great wisdom of feeling. Stowe never forgets the logical end of any relationship in which one person is the subject and the other is the object. No matter how the two people feel, or what their intentions are, the logic of the relationship is inherently tragic and traps both parties until the false subject/object relationship is ended. Stowe's most oft-repeated and potent representation of this inexorable logic is the forcible separation of family members, especially of mothers from children. Eliza, faced with the sale of her child, Harry, escapes across the breaking ice of the Ohio River. Lucy, whose ten-month-old is sold behind her back, kills herself. Prue, who has been used for breeding, must listen to her last child cry itself to death because her mistress won't let her save it; she falls into alcoholism and thievery and is finally whipped to death. Cassy, prefiguring a choice made by one of the characters in Toni Morrison's *Beloved,* kills her last child so that it won't grow up in slavery. . . .

Obviously, *Uncle Tom's Cabin* is no more the last word on race relations than *The Brothers Karamazov* or *David Copperfield* is on any number of characteristically Russian or English themes and social questions. Some of Stowe's ideas about inherent racial characteristics (whites: cold, heartless; blacks: naturally religious and warm) are bad and have been exploded. One of her solutions to the American racial conflicts that she foresaw, a colony in Africa, she later repudiated. Nevertheless, her views about many issues were brilliant, and her heart was wise. She gained the respect and friendship of many men and women of goodwill, black and white, such as Frederick Douglass, the civil rights activist Mary Church Terrill, the writer and social activist James Weldon Johnson, and W. E. B. Du Bois.

What she did was find a way to talk about slavery and family, power and law, life and death, good and evil, North and South. She truly believed that all

Americans together had to find a solution to the problem of slavery, in which all were implicated. When her voice, a courageously public voice—as demonstrated by the public arguments about slavery that race throughout *Uncle Tom's Cabin*—fell silent in our culture and was replaced by the secretive voice of Huck Finn, who acknowledges Jim only when they are alone on the raft together out in the middle of the big river, racism fell out of the public world and into the private one, where whites think it really is but blacks know it really isn't.

Should *Huckleberry Finn* be taught in the schools? . . . I would rather my children read *Uncle Tom's Cabin*, even though it is far more vivid in its depiction of cruelty than *Huck Finn*, and this is because Stowe's novel is clearly and unmistakably a tragedy. No whitewash, no secrets, but evil, suffering, imagination, endurance, and redemption—just like life. Like little Eva, who eagerly but fearfully listens to the stories of the slaves that her family tries to keep from her, our children want to know what is going on, what has gone on, and what we intend to do about it. If "great" literature has any purpose, it is to help us face up to our responsibilities instead of enabling us to avoid them once again by lighting out for the territory.

—Jane Smiley, "Say It Ain't So, Huck: Second Thoughts on Mark Twain's 'Masterpiece,'" *Harper's*, January 1996, pp. 64–67.

Adventures of Huckleberry Finn

❦ MARK TWAIN, 1884 ❦

ON HIS television show *The Colbert Report,* comedian Stephen Colbert is fond of asking his guests, "George W. Bush—great president or the greatest president?" Generations of admirers have played a similar game with Samuel Clemens, a.k.a. Mark Twain (1835–1910). Weighing in on the "greatest" side of this debate, journalist H. L. Mencken lauded Twain as "the true father of our national literature, the first genuinely American artist of the royal blood." Twain's most popular and controversial novel, *Adventures of Huckleberry Finn,* was, in Mencken's estimation, "the great work of the imagination yet produced in America" and "the one most likely to endure."[1] Not long after its appearance in 1884, *Huck Finn* was being hailed as the "great American novel."[2] Today it is required reading in high schools nationwide. As with the legacy of President Bush, however, dissenters abound. Literature scholar Jonathan Arac, who has criticized the "idolatry" that has built up around the novel, complains that "to question *Huckleberry Finn* is to be *un*-American."[3] Not quite. What is un-American is to ignore it.

Like *Gilgamesh* (the world's first great narrative) and *Don Quixote* (the world's first great novel), *Huckleberry Finn* is a picaresque tale of male comradeship "on the road." It is the story of a boy, a man, a river, and an escape—the rebellion of youthful exuberance against the props of polite society. But because the boy, the narrator Huck, is white and the man, Jim, is a runaway black slave, this is also a story of freedom from slavery, which is to say it is a story about America and an occasion for debating the meaning of the same. In this "fresh-water *Moby Dick,*" we see a "community of saints" drifting on a raft down the Mississippi River, but we also see the contradictions of American society—the not so peaceful coexistence of individual liberty and community responsibility, freedom and slavery, equality and hierarchy, property rights and human rights.[4] How does America look through Huck's eyes? Jim's? What are the norms and values of "the United States of Huckdom"?[5] Some say *Huck Finn* excoriates slavery and champions democracy. Others insist it is immoral, obscene, irreverent, elitist, and racist.

In 2011, literary critics fumed over the publication of a bowdlerized *Huck Finn,* which had been whitewashed of over two hundred usages (one on almost every page) of the word "nigger." But this book has always been controversial. It was published in England in December 1884, but its U.S. appearance was delayed until February 1885 after a mischievous engraver snuck an obscene illustration onto the printer's plates.

Early reviews were mixed. Lauding Twain as "the Edison of our literature," the *San Francisco Sunday Chronicle* called the novel a *"tour de force . . .* in which the most unlikely materials are transmuted into a work of literary art."[6] Joel Chandler Harris, of Brer Rabbit fame, viewed *Huck Finn* as "the most original contribution that has yet been made to American literature."[7] But one newspaper called the book "cheap and pernicious stuff"—"a piece of careless hack-work in which a few good things are dropped amid a mass of rubbish."[8] Another editorialized, "It is doubtful if the edition could be disposed of to people of average intellect at anything short of the point of the bayonet."[9] Readers faulted Twain the humorist for failing to make them laugh, and Twain the opportunist for laughing all the way to the bank. But most early criticisms were moral and theological rather than literary. *Huck Finn* was according to many reviewers both irreverent and uncouth—an affront to the piety and propriety of genteel culture. *Huck Finn,* according to a *New York World* headline, was "a Pitiable Exhibition of Irreverence and Vulgarity."[10]

In March 1885, the public library in Concord, Massachusetts, banned the book as "the veriest trash." According to one library committee member, *Huck Finn* was "rough, coarse and inelegant, dealing with a series of experiences not elevating, the whole book being more suited to the slums than to intelligent, respectable people."[11] Other libraries—in Denver, Omaha, Brooklyn—followed suit, but not everyone concurred with the verdict. "In regard to the charge of grossness," wrote the *San Francisco Chronicle,* "there is not a line in it which cannot be read by a pure-minded woman."[12] The *Boston Daily Globe,* which also opposed the ban, offered Twain some tongue-in-cheek advice about how to sneak his next novel past Concord's scions of Transcendentalist nonsense: "When Mark writes another book he should think of the Concord School of Philosophy and put a little more whenceness of the hereafter among his nowness of the here."[13] Twain himself weighed in on the controversy by labeling members of Concord's library committee "moral icebergs."[14]

Writing in 1935, Ernest Hemingway couldn't bring himself to like the much-maligned ending (also known as the "evasion") in which Tom Sawyer's return to center stage banishes Huck to the wings and in the process turns Jim's freedom quest into farce. Nonetheless, he lauded the book as both the foundation and the pinnacle of his craft. "All modern American literature comes from one book by Mark Twain called *Huckleberry Finn,*" he wrote. "There was nothing before. There has been nothing as good since."[15]

This "greatness" thesis became gospel after World War II, when literary lights praised Huck as one of America's inescapable voices and the novel as "an icon of integration."[16] Columbia professor Lionel Trilling's stamp of approval in a 1948 edition of the novel—"an almost perfect work," he wrote, "one of the world's great books and one of the central documents of American culture"—made *Huck Finn* a fixture in America's literary firmament.[17] In 1953, Nobel Laureate T. S. Eliot furthered this "hypercanonization" by comparing Huck to Ulysses and calling the book a "masterpiece" in which Twain's "genius is completely realized." Unlike Hemingway, Eliot praised the conclusion: "I do not think that any book ever written ends more certainly with the right words."[18] *Huck Finn,* Eliot later added, had secured Twain's place as "one of those writers, of whom there are not a great many in any literature, who have discovered a new way of writing, valid not only for themselves but for others."[19] This new way was the vernacular—the "Huckspeech" of the book's narrator and later seized upon (in different dialects of course) by Hemingway, Faulkner, Salinger, and O'Connor.[20]

Today some critics employ *Huck Finn* as a prism for examining sexuality in American life and literature. Do Huck and Jim stand in a tradition of deep affection between white and nonwhite males? But recent work on the novel focuses on race: Twain's depiction of Jim and his repeated use of the epithet "nigger." This conversation is not new. In 1957 the NAACP called *Huck Finn* "racially offensive," and the New York City Board of Education removed it from its list of approved text-books. And in 1982 John Wallace, an African-American educator at the Mark Twain Intermediate School in Fairfax, Virginia, called for the book's removal from the curriculum on the grounds that it was "racist trash."[21] "The book is poison," Wallace argued. "It is anti-American; it works against the melting pot theory of our country; it works against the idea that all men are created equal; it works against the Fourteenth Amendment to the Constitution and against the preamble that guarantees all men life, liberty and the pursuit of happiness."[22]

Defenders of the book argued that Wallace and like-minded critics were missing the obvious irony and satire in the story. Far from a racist tract, *Huck Finn* was according to one champion "a savage indictment of a society that accepted slavery as a way of life."[23] Its power, Twain's partisans argued, derives from its realism, including its use of the idioms and folkways of ordinary people along the Mississippi River in the 1830s or 1840s, when the action is set.

In an oft quoted passage late in the novel, Huck is regaling his Aunt Sally with a tall tale about how he was delayed because a riverboat blew out its engine. The key exchange follows, beginning with Aunt Sally:

> *"Good gracious! Anybody hurt?"*
> *"No'm. Killed a nigger."*
> *"Well, it's lucky; because sometimes people do get hurt."*

Is this racist drivel? Of course. But is it Twain's? Huck's? More important, is it America's own? According to columnist George Will, "only someone suffering terminal solemnity can take offense" at this passage. "Accusing Huck of racism is cuckoo."[24]

Although much of the recent criticism of the novel has been prosecuted in the name of the sensibilities of black children, some black writers have come to its defense. Ralph Ellison judged it a "great classic."[25] Toni Morrison wrote that the "fatal ending" of the book works by demonstrating how much the freedom of Huck depends on his relationship with Jim: "In that sense the book may indeed be 'great' because in its structure, in the hell it puts its readers through at the end, the frontal debate it forces, it simulates and describes the parasitical nature of white freedom."[26]

All this is to say that for over a century Americans have used *Huck Finn* to debate the central paradox of the American experiment: the coexistence of the ideal of equality in the Declaration of Independence with the realities of slavery, segregation, and racism. Huck and Jim and the Mississippi River itself have all been conscripted into this debate, as has Mark Twain. Is Twain, as literary critic William Dean Howells wrote, "the Lincoln of our literature"?[27] Or is he the Jefferson Davis?

When we ask whether *Huck Finn* is racist or antiracist (or something in between), we are of course asking the same thing about the country that produced it, canonized it, and continues to revere it. The fact that Americans continue to debate this novel so passionately indicates that the question of race is *the* great question of American history and that this question remains unresolved. Or, as *New Yorker* writer William Styron puts it, " 'Huckleberry Finn' has never really struggled up out of a continuous vortex of discord, and probably never will, as long as its enchanting central figures, with their confused and incalculable feelings for each other, remain symbols of our own racial confusion."[28]

The following excerpt comes from Chapter 31, where Huck wrestles with whether to follow the law and community customs by turning Jim in. Like Thoreau in "Civil Disobedience" (1849), Huck decides to follow his conscience instead.

Adventures of Huckleberry Finn ❧

Chapter 31[a]

We dasn't stop again at any town for days and days; kept right along down the river. We was down south in the warm weather now, and a mighty long ways from home. We begun to come to trees with Spanish moss on them, hanging down from the limbs like long, gray beards. It was the first I ever see it growing, and it made the woods look

---

a. Ralph Ellison, novelist, weighing in on this key chapter (1953): [In Chapter 31] we have arrived at a key point of the novel and, by an ironic reversal, of American fiction, a pivotal moment announcing a change of direction in the plot, a reversal as well as a recognition scene (like that in which Oedipus discovers his true identity) wherein a new definition of necessity is being formulated. Huck Finn has struggled with the problem poised by the clash between property rights and human rights, between what the community considered to be the proper attitude toward an escaped slave and his knowledge of Jim's humanity, gained through their adventures as fugitives together. He has made his decision on the side of humanity. In this passage Twain has stated the basic moral issue centering around Negroes and the white American's democratic ethics. It dramatizes as well the highest point of tension generated by the clash between the direct, human relationships of the frontier and the abstract, inhuman, market-dominated relationships fostered by the rising middle class which in Twain's day was already compromising dangerously with the most inhuman aspects of the defeated slave system. And just as politically these forces reached their sharpest tension in the outbreak of the Civil War, in Huckleberry Finn (both the boy and the novel) their human implications come to sharpest focus around the figure of the Negro.

Huckleberry Finn knew, as did Mark Twain, that Jim was not only a slave but a human being, a man who in some ways was to be envied, and who expressed his essential humanity in his desire for freedom, his will to possess his own labor, in his loyalty and capacity for friendship and in his love for his wife and child. Yet Twain, though guilty of the sentimentality common to humorists, does not idealize the slave. Jim is drawn in all his ignorance and superstition, with his good traits and his bad. He, like all men, is ambiguous, limited in circumstance but not in possibility. And it will be noted that when Huck makes his decision he identifies himself with Jim and accepts the judgment of his superego—that internalized representative of the community—that his action is evil. Like Prometheus, who for mankind stole fire from the gods, he embraces the evil implicit in his act in order to affirm his belief in humanity. Jim, therefore, is not simply a slave, he is a symbol of humanity, and in freeing Jim, Huck makes a bid to free himself of the conventionalized evil taken for civilization by the town. —Ralph Ellison, "Twentieth-Century Fiction and the Black Mask of Humanity," *Confluence* (December 1953): 3–21.

solemn and dismal. So now the frauds reckoned they was out of danger, and they begun to work the villages again.

First they done a lecture on temperance; but they didn't make enough for them both to get drunk on. Then in another village they started a dancing-school; but they didn't know no more how to dance than a kangaroo does; so the first prance they made the general public jumped in and pranced them out of town. Another time they tried to go at yellocution; but they didn't yellocute long till the audience got up and give them a solid good cussing, and made them skip out. They tackled missionarying, and mesmerizing, and doctoring, and telling fortunes, and a little of everything; but they couldn't seem to have no luck. So at last they got just about dead broke, and laid around the raft as she floated along, thinking and thinking, and never saying nothing, by the half a day at a time, and dreadful blue and desperate.

And at last they took a change and begun to lay their heads together in the wigwam and talk low and confidential two or three hours at a time. Jim and me got uneasy. We didn't like the look of it. We judged they was studying up some kind of worse deviltry than ever. We turned it over and over, and at last we made up our minds they was going to break into somebody's house or store, or was going into the counterfeit-money business, or something. So then we was pretty scared, and made up an agreement that we wouldn't have nothing in the world to do with such actions, and if we ever got the least show we would give them the cold shake and clear out and leave them behind. Well, early one morning we hid the raft in a good, safe place about two mile below a little bit of a shabby village named Pikesville, and the king he went ashore and told us all to stay hid whilst he went up to town and smelt around to see if anybody had got any wind of the Royal Nonesuch there yet. ("House to rob, you *mean*," says I to myself; "and when you get through robbing it you'll come back here and wonder what has become of me and Jim and the raft—and you'll have to take it out in wondering.") And he said if he warn't back by midday the duke and me would know it was all right, and we was to come along.

So we stayed where we was. The duke he fretted and sweated around, and was in a mighty sour way. He scolded us for everything, and we couldn't seem to do nothing right; he found fault with every little thing. Something was a-brewing, sure. I was good and glad when midday come and no king; we could have a change, anyway—and maybe a chance for *the* chance on top of it. So me and the duke went up to the village, and hunted around there for the king, and by and by we found him in the back room of a little low doggery, very tight, and a lot of loafers bullyragging him for sport, and he a-cussing and a-threatening with all his might, and so tight he couldn't walk, and couldn't do nothing to them. The duke he begun to abuse him for an old fool, and the king begun to sass back, and the minute they was fairly at it I lit out and shook the reefs out of my hind legs, and spun down the river road like a deer, for I see our chance; and I made up my mind that it would be a long day before they ever see me and Jim again. I got down there all out of breath but loaded up with joy, and sung out:

"Set her loose, Jim! we're all right now!"

But there warn't no answer, and nobody come out of the wigwam. Jim was gone! I set up a shout—and then another—and then another one; and run this way and that in the woods, whooping and screeching; but it warn't no use—old Jim was gone. Then I set down and cried; I couldn't help it. But I couldn't set still long. Pretty soon I went out on the road, trying to think what I better do, and I run across a boy walking, and asked him if he'd seen a strange nigger[b] dressed so and so, and he says:

"Yes."

"Whereabouts?" says I.

"Down to Silas Phelps' place, two mile below here. He's a runaway nigger, and they've got him. Was you looking for him?"

"You bet I ain't! I run across him in the woods about an hour or two ago, and he said if I hollered he'd cut my livers out—and told me to lay down and stay where I was; and I done it. Been there ever since; afeard to come out."

"Well," he says, "you needn't be afeard no more, becuz they've got him. He run off f'm down South, som'ers."

"It's a good job they got him."

"Well, I *reckon!* There's two hunderd dollars reward on him. It's like picking up money out'n the road."

"Yes, it is—and I could a had it if I'd been big enough; I see him *first*. Who nailed him?"

"It was an old fellow—a stranger—and he sold out his chance in him for forty dollars, becuz he's got to go up the river and can't wait. Think o' that, now! You bet *I'd* wait, if it was seven year."

---

b. Jonathan Arac, English professor, criticizing the novel for keeping the term "nigger" in circulation (1997): Liberal white American opinion identifies with the wonderful boy Huck. Even though his society was racist, he was not, and so "we" are not. For African Americans to challenge this view is to challenge "us" just where "we" feel ourselves most intimately virtuous, and it is also to challenge Mark Twain, and thereby the American he "quintessentially" represents. . . . Even though *Huckleberry Finn* is claimed as a talisman of racially progressive thought and action, one of its major effects is actually to license and authorize the continued honored circulation of a term that is both explosive and degrading. —Jonathan Arac, *Huckleberry Finn as Idol and Target: The Functions of Criticism in Our Time* (Madison: Univ. of Wisconsin Press, 1997), pp. 9, 28–29.

"That's me, every time," says I. "But maybe his chance ain't worth no more than that, if he'll sell it so cheap. Maybe there's something ain't straight about it."

"But it *is*, though—straight as a string. I see the handbill myself. It tells all about him, to a dot—paints him like a picture, and tells the plantation he's frum, below New*rleans*. No-sirree-*bob*, they ain't no trouble 'bout *that* speculation, you bet you. Say, gimme a chaw tobacker, won't ye?"

I didn't have none, so he left. I went to the raft, and set down in the wigwam to think. But I couldn't come to nothing. I thought till I wore my head sore, but I couldn't see no way out of the trouble. After all this long journey, and after all we'd done for them scoundrels, here it was all come to nothing, everything all busted up and ruined, because they could have the heart to serve Jim such a trick as that, and make him a slave again all his life, and amongst strangers, too, for forty dirty dollars.

Once I said to myself it would be a thousand times better for Jim to be a slave at home where his family was, as long as he'd *got* to be a slave, and so I'd better write a letter to Tom Sawyer and tell him to tell Miss Watson where he was. But I soon give up that notion for two things: she'd be mad and disgusted at his rascality and ungratefulness for leaving her, and so she'd sell him straight down the river again; and if she didn't, everybody naturally despises an ungrateful nigger, and they'd make Jim feel it all the time, and so he'd feel ornery and disgraced. And then think of *me!* It would get all around that Huck Finn helped a nigger to get his freedom; and if I was ever to see anybody from that town again I'd be ready to get down and lick his boots for shame. That's just the way: a person does a low-down thing, and then he don't want to take no consequences of it. Thinks as long as he can hide, it ain't no disgrace. That was my fix exactly. The more I studied about this the more my conscience went to grinding me, and the more wicked and low-down and ornery I got to feeling. And at last, when it hit me all of a sudden that here was the plain hand of Providence slapping me in the face and letting me know my wickedness was being watched all the time from up there in heaven, whilst I was stealing a poor old woman's nigger that hadn't ever done me no harm, and now was showing me there's One that's always on the lookout, and ain't a-going to allow no such miserable doings to go only just so fur and no further, I most dropped in my tracks I was so scared. Well, I tried the best I could to kinder soften it up somehow for myself by saying I was brung up wicked, and so I warn't so much to blame; but something inside of me kept saying, "There was the Sunday-school, you could a gone to it; and if you'd a done it they'd a learnt you there that people that acts as I'd been acting about that nigger goes to everlasting fire."

It made me shiver. And I about made up my mind to pray, and see if I couldn't try to quit being the kind of a boy I was and be better. So I kneeled down. But the words wouldn't come. Why wouldn't they? It warn't no use to try and hide it from Him. Nor from *me*, neither. I knowed very well why they wouldn't come. It was because my heart warn't right; it was because I warn't square;

it was because I was playing double. I was letting *on* to give up sin, but away inside of me I was holding on to the biggest one of all. I was trying to make my mouth *say* I would do the right thing and the clean thing, and go and write to that nigger's owner and tell where he was; but deep down in me I knowed it was a lie, and He knowed it. You can't pray a lie—I found that out.

So I was full of trouble, full as I could be; and didn't know what to do. At last I had an idea; and I says, I'll go and write the letter—and *then* see if I can pray. Why, it was astonishing, the way I felt as light as a feather right straight off, and my troubles all gone. So I got a piece of paper and a pencil, all glad and excited, and set down and wrote:

> Miss Watson, your runaway nigger Jim is down here two mile below Pikesville, and Mr. Phelps has got him and he will give him up for the reward if you send.
> HUCK FINN.

I felt good and all washed clean of sin for the first time I had ever felt so in my life, and I knowed I could pray now. But I didn't do it straight off, but laid the paper down and set there thinking—thinking how good it was all this happened so, and how near I come to being lost and going to hell. And went on thinking. And got to thinking over our trip down the river; and I see Jim before me all the time: in the day and in the night-time, sometimes moonlight, sometimes storms, and we a-floating along, talking and singing and laughing. But somehow I couldn't seem to strike no places to harden me against him, but only the other kind. I'd see him standing my watch on top of his'n, 'stead of calling me, so I could go on sleeping; and see him how glad he was when I come back out of the fog; and when I come to him again in the swamp, up there where the feud was; and such-like times; and would always call me honey, and pet me and do everything he could think of for me, and how good he always was; and at last I struck the time I saved him by telling the men we had small-pox aboard, and he was so grateful, and said I was the best friend old Jim ever had in the world, and the *only* one he's got now; and then I happened to look around and see that paper.

It was a close place. I took it up, and held it in my hand. I was a-trembling, because I'd got to decide, forever, betwixt two things, and I knowed it. I studied a minute, sort of holding my breath, and then says to myself:

"All right, then, I'll *go* to hell"—and tore it up.[c]

It was awful thoughts and awful words, but they was said. And I let them stay said; and never thought no more about reforming. I shoved the whole thing out of my head, and said I would

---

c. Arthur Schlesinger Jr., historian, reading Huck's decision as a dramatization of "the essential American struggle of the individual against absolutes" (1989): That, it may be said, is what America is all about. —Arthur Schlesinger Jr., *The Disuniting of America: Reflections on a Multicultural Society*, rev. ed. (New York: Norton, 1998), p. 174.

take up wickedness again, which was in my line, being brung up to it, and the other warn't. And for a starter I would go to work and steal Jim out of slavery again; and if I could think up anything worse, I would do that, too; because as long as I was in, and in for good, I might as well go the whole hog.

Then I set to thinking over how to get at it, and turned over some considerable many ways in my mind; and at last fixed up a plan that suited me. So then I took the bearings of a woody island that was down the river a piece, and as soon as it was fairly dark I crept out with my raft and went for it, and hid it there, and then turned in. I slept the night through, and got up before it was light, and had my breakfast, and put on my store clothes, and tied up some others and one thing or another in a bundle, and took the canoe and cleared for shore. I landed below where I judged was Phelps's place, and hid my bundle in the woods, and then filled up the canoe with water, and loaded rocks into her and sunk her where I could find her again when I wanted her, about a quarter of a mile below a little steam sawmill that was on the bank.

Then I struck up the road, and when I passed the mill I see a sign on it, "Phelps's Sawmill," and when I come to the farm-houses, two or three hundred yards further along, I kept my eyes peeled, but didn't see nobody around, though it was good daylight now. But I didn't mind, because I didn't want to see nobody just yet—I only wanted to get the lay of the land. According to my plan, I was going to turn up there from the village, not from below. So I just took a look, and shoved along, straight for town. Well, the very first man I see when I got there was the duke. He was sticking up a bill for the Royal Nonesuch—three-night performance—like that other time. *They* had the cheek, them frauds! I was right on him before I could shirk. He looked astonished, and says:

"Hel-*lo!* Where'd *you* come from?" Then he says, kind of glad and eager, "Where's the raft?—got her in a good place?"

I says: "Why, that's just what I was going to ask your grace."

Then he didn't look so joyful, and says: "What was your idea for asking *me?*" he says.

"Well," I says, "when I see the king in that doggery yesterday I says to myself, we can't get him home for hours, till he's soberer; so I went a-loafing around town to put in the time and wait. A man up and offered me ten cents to help him pull a skiff over the river and back to fetch a sheep, and so I went along; but when we was dragging him to the boat, and the man left me a-holt of the rope and went behind him to shove him along, he was too strong for me and jerked loose and run, and we after him. We didn't have no dog, and so we had to chase him all over the country till we tired him out. We never got him till dark; then we fetched him over, and I started down for the raft. When I got there and see it was gone, I says to myself, 'They've got into trouble and had to leave; and they've took my nigger, which is the only nigger I've got in the world, and now I'm in a strange country, and ain't got no property no more, nor nothing, and no way to make my living;' so I set down and cried. I slept in the woods all night. But what *did* become of the raft, then?—and Jim—poor Jim!"

"Blamed if *I* know—that is, what's become of the raft. That old fool had made a trade and got forty dollars, and when we found him in the doggery the loafers had matched half-dollars with him and got every cent but what he'd spent for whisky; and when I got him home late last night and found the raft gone, we said, 'That little rascal has stole our raft and shook us, and run off down the river.'"

"I wouldn't shake my *nigger*, would I?—the only nigger I had in the world, and the only property."

"We never thought of that. Fact is, I reckon we'd come to consider him *our* nigger; yes, we did consider him so—goodness knows we had trouble enough for him. So when we see the raft was gone and we flat broke, there warn't anything for it but to try the Royal Nonesuch another shake. And I've pegged along ever since, dry as a powder-horn. Where's that ten cents? Give it here."

I had considerable money, so I give him ten cents, but begged him to spend it for something to eat, and give me some, because it was all the money I had, and I hadn't had nothing to eat since yesterday. He never said nothing. The next minute he whirls on me and says:

"Do you reckon that nigger would blow on us? We'd skin him if he done that!"

"How can he blow? Hain't he run off?"

"No! That old fool sold him, and never divided with me, and the money's gone."

"*Sold* him?" I says, and begun to cry; "why, he was *my* nigger, and that was my money. Where is he?—I want my nigger."

"Well, you can't *get* your nigger, that's all—so dry up your blubbering. Looky here—do you think *you'd* venture to blow on us? Blamed if I think I'd trust you. Why, if you *was* to blow on us—"

He stopped, but I never see the duke look so ugly out of his eyes before. I went on a-whimpering, and says:

"I don't want to blow on nobody; and I ain't got no time to blow, nohow. I got to turn out and find my nigger."

He looked kinder bothered, and stood there with his bills fluttering on his arm, thinking, and wrinkling up his forehead. At last he says:

"I'll tell you something. We got to be here three days. If you'll promise you won't blow, and won't let the nigger blow, I'll tell you where to find him."

So I promised, and he says:

"A farmer by the name of Silas Ph—" and then he stopped. You see, he started to tell me the truth; but when he stopped that way, and begun to study and think again, I reckoned he was changing his mind. And so he was. He wouldn't trust me; he wanted to make sure of having me out of the way the whole three days. So pretty soon he says:

"The man that bought him is named Abram Foster—Abram G. Foster—and he lives forty mile back here in the country, on the road to Lafayette."

"All right," I says, "I can walk it in three days. And I'll start this very afternoon."

"No you wont, you'll start *now*; and don't you lose any time about it, neither, nor do any gabbling by the way. Just keep a tight tongue in your head and move right along, and then you won't get into trouble with *us*, d'ye hear?"

That was the order I wanted, and that was the one I played for. I wanted to be left free to work my plans.

"So clear out," he says; "and you can tell Mr. Foster whatever you want to. Maybe you can get him to believe that Jim *is* your nigger—some idiots don't require documents—leastways I've heard there's such down South here. And when you tell him the handbill and the reward's bogus, maybe he'll believe you when you explain to him what the idea was for getting 'em out. Go 'long now, and tell him anything you want to; but mind you don't work your jaw any *between* here and there."

So I left, and struck for the back country. I didn't look around, but I kinder felt like he was watching me. But I knowed I could tire him out at that. I went straight out in the country as much as a mile before I stopped; then I doubled back through the woods towards Phelps'. I reckoned I better start in on my plan straight off without fooling around, because I wanted to stop Jim's mouth till these fellows could get away. I didn't want no trouble with their kind. I'd seen all I wanted to of them, and wanted to get entirely shut of them.[29]

COMMENTARY

H. L. Mencken, journalist, on the "Americanism" of Huck Finn (1917)

[Twain] was a literary artist of the very first rank, and incomparably the greatest ever hatched in these states.

One reads with something akin to astonishment of his superstitious reverence for Emerson—of how he stood silent and bare-headed before the great transcendentalist's house at Concord. One hears of him, with amazement, courting Whittier, Longfellow and Holmes. One is staggered by the news, reported by Traubel, that Walt Whitman thought "he mainly misses fire." The simple fact is that *Huckleberry Finn* is worth the whole work of Emerson with two-thirds of the work of Whitman thrown in for make-weight, and that one chapter of it is worth the whole work of Whittier, Longfellow and Holmes.

Mark was not only a great artist; he was pre-eminently a great American artist. No other writer that we have produced has ever been more extravagantly national. Whitman dreamed of an America that never was and never will be; Poe was a foreigner in every line he wrote; even Emerson was no more than an American spigot for European, and especially German, ideas. But Mark was wholly of the soil. His humor was American. His incurable Philistinism was American. His very English was American. Above all, he was an American in his curious mixture of sentimentality and cynicism, his mingling of romanticist and iconoclast.

English Traits might have been written by any one of half a dozen Germans. The tales of Poe, printed as translations from the French, would have deceived even Frenchmen. And *Leaves of Grass* might have been written in London quite as well as in Brooklyn. But in *Huckleberry Finn,* in *A Connecticut Yankee* and in most of the short sketches there is a quality that is unmistakably and overwhelmingly national. They belong to our country and our time quite as obviously as the skyscraper or the quick lunch counter. They are as magnificently American as the Brooklyn Bridge or Tammany Hall.

—H. L. Mencken, "Mark Twain's Americanism," *Evening Mail* (New York), November 1, 1917, www.etsu.edu/cas/history/documents/menckentwain.htm.

Leo Marx, American Studies scholar, loving the book, hating the ending (1953)

Huckleberry Finn is a masterpiece because it brings Western humor to perfection and yet transcends the narrow limits of its conventions. But the ending does not. During the final extravaganza we are forced to put aside many of the mature emotions evoked earlier by the vivid rendering of Jim's fear of capture, the tenderness of Huck's and Jim's regard for each other, and Huck's excruciating moments of wavering between honesty and respectability. None of these emotions are called forth by the anticlimactic final sequence. . . . Moreover, the most serious motive in the novel, Jim's yearning for freedom, is made the object of nonsense. The conclusion, in short, is farce, but the rest of the novel is not. . . . It should be added at once that Jim doesn't mind too much. The fact is that he has undergone a similar transformation. On the raft he was an individual, man enough to denounce Huck when Huck made him the victim of a practical joke. In the closing episode, however, we lose sight of Jim in the maze of farcical invention. He ceases to be a man.

—Leo Marx, "Mr. Eliot, Mr. Trilling, and *Huckleberry Finn*," *American Scholar* 22 (Autumn 1953): 423–40, reprinted in M. Thomas Inge, ed., *Huck Finn Among the Critics: A Centennial Selection* (Frederick, MD: Univ. Publications of America, 1985), pp. 117, 119.

Norman Podhoretz, writer, on Twain's exorcism of European culture (1959)

Sooner or later, it seems, all discussions of "Huckleberry Finn" turn into discussions of America—and with good reason. Mark Twain was the quintessential American writer, quintessential because he was more or less untutored—"a natural," as Wright Morris puts it, "who learned to write the way a river pilot learns the feel of a channel." And Richard Chase, in his remarkable book on the American novel, observes that "Huckleberry Finn" is constantly engaged in an "exorcism of false forms" through parody and burlesque, and that the chief exorcism performed by the novel is done upon "European culture itself." . . .

Someone once quipped that the whole of philosophy is a footnote to Plato, and it might be remarked with equal justice that the whole of European literature is a commentary on the first sentence of Aristotle's "Politics." Man, says European literature in a thousand different ways and in tones ranging from dismay to jubilation—man is by nature a social animal. To conceive of the individual as existing apart from society is an illusion or at best a convenient fiction; there is no State of Nature and there never was one. It was this idea more than anything else, I believe, that Mark Twain was trying to exorcise in "Huckleberry Finn." He was asserting through the image of life on the raft that the State of Nature is a reality, and he was asserting through the character of Huck that the distinction between the individual and society is a true distinction and a necessary one.

—Norman Podhoretz, "The Literary Adventures of Huck Finn," *New York Times*, December 6, 1959, p. BR5.

Justin Kaplan, biographer, praising Twain for fighting racism with satire (1985)

It seems unlikely that anyone, of any color, who had actually read *Huckleberry Finn*, instead of merely reading or hearing about it, and who had allowed himself or herself even the barest minimum of intelligent response to its underlying spirit and intention, could accuse it of being "racist" because some of its characters use offensive racial epithets. These characters belong to their time and place, which is the Mississippi Valley thirty years before Emancipation.

As a historical portrait of slaveholding society, Mark Twain's novel is probably more faithful as well as less stereotypical than Harriet Beecher Stowe's beloved *Uncle Tom's Cabin*. And it is worth recalling that Mrs. Stowe, like most of her fellow abolitionists, believed that there was no place for free blacks in American society—they advocated colonization and repatriation to Africa. Mark Twain, "the most de-southernized of southerners," according to his friend William Dean Howells, believed that it was henceforward the duty of white people to make amends for the crime of slavery. He may have been the least "racist" of all the major writers of his time, Herman Melville excepted. *Huckleberry Finn* is a matchless satire on racism, bigotry, and property rights in human beings.

—Justin Kaplan, *Born to Trouble: One Hundred Years of Huckleberry Finn* (Washington, DC: Library of Congress, 1985).

Wendell Berry, Kentucky farmer and writer, urging Twain, Huck, and America to grow up (1987)

The book ends with Huck's determination to "light out for the Territory" to escape being adopted and "sivilized" by Tom's Aunt Sally. And here, I think, we are left face to face with a flaw in Mark Twain's character that is also a flaw in our national character, a flaw in our history, and a flaw in much of our literature.

As I have said, Huck's point about Miss Watson is well taken and well made. There is an extremity, an enclosure, of conventional piety and propriety that needs to be escaped. A part of the business of young people is to escape it. But this point, having been made once, does not need to be made again. . . .

Something is badly awry here. At the end of this great book we are asked to believe, or to believe that Huck believes, that there are no choices between the "civilization" represented by pious slave-owners such as Miss Watson or lethal "gentleman" such as Col. Sherburn, and lighting out for the Territory. This hopeless polarity marks the exit of Mark Twain's highest imagination from his work. . . .

It is arguable, I think, that our country's culture is still suspended as if at the end of *Huckleberry Finn*, assuming that its only choices are either a deadly "civilization" of piety and violence or an escape into some "Territory" where we may remain free of adulthood and community obligation. We want to be free; we want to have rights; we want to have power; we do not yet want much to do with responsibility. We have imagined the great and estimable freedom of boyhood, of which Huck Finn remains the finest spokesman. We have imagined the bachelorhoods of nature and genius and power: the contemplative, the artist, the hunter, the cowboy, the general, the president—lives dedicated and solitary in the Territory of individual adventure or responsibility. But boyhood and bachelorhood have remained our norms of "liberation," for women as well as men. We have hardly begun to imagine the coming to responsibility that is the meaning, and the liberation, of growing up. We have hardly begun to imagine community, and the tragedy that is at the heart of community life. . . .

The real "evasion" of the last chapter is Huck's, or Mark Twain's, evasion of the community responsibility which would have been a natural and expectable next step after his declaration of loyalty to his friend. Mark Twain's failure or inability to imagine this possibility was a disaster for his finest character, Huck, whom we next see, not as a grown man but as a partner in another boyish evasion. . . .

I am supposing, then, that *Huckleberry Finn* fails in failing to imagine a responsible, adult community life. And I am supposing further that this is the failure of Mark Twain's life, and of our life, so far, as a society.

—Wendell Berry, "Writer and Region," *Hudson Review* 40.1 (Spring 1987): 18–20.

Jane Smiley, novelist, casting a vote for Uncle Tom's Cabin *over* Huck Finn *(1996)*

I closed the cover stunned. Yes, stunned. Not, by any means, by the artistry of the book, but by the notion that this is the novel all American literature grows out of, that this is a great novel, that this is even a serious novel.

The sort of meretricious critical reasoning that has raised Huck's paltry good intentions to a "strategy of subversion" (David L. Smith) and a "convincing indictment of slavery" (Eliot) precisely mirrors the same sort of meretricious reasoning that white people use to convince themselves that they are not "racist." If Huck *feels* positive toward Jim, and *loves* him, and *thinks* of him as a man, then that's enough. He doesn't actually have to act in accordance with his feelings. White Americans always think racism is a feeling, and they reject it or they embrace it. To most Americans, it seems more honorable and nicer to reject it, so they do, but they almost invariably fail to understand that how they *feel* means very little to black Americans, who understand racism as a way of structuring American culture, American politics, and the American economy.

To invest *The Adventures of Huckleberry Finn* with "greatness" is to underwrite a very simplistic and evasive theory of what racism is and to promulgate it, philosophically, in schools and the media as well as in academic journals. Surely the discomfort of many readers, black and white, and the censorship battles that have dogged *Huck Finn* in the last twenty years are understandable in this context. No matter how often the critics "place in context" Huck's use of the word "nigger," they can never excuse or fully hide the deeper racism of the novel—the way Twain and Huck use Jim because they really don't care enough about his desire for freedom to let that desire change their plans. And to give credit to Huck suggests that the only racial insight Americans of the nineteenth or twentieth century are capable of is a recognition of the obvious—that blacks, slave and free, are human. . . .

Scholar Nina Baym has already detailed how the canonization of a very narrow range of white, Protestant, middle-class male authors (Twain, Hawthorne, Melville, Emerson, etc.) has misrepresented our literary life—first by defining the only worthy American literary subject as "the struggle of the individual against society [in which] the essential quality of America comes to reside in its unsettled wilderness and the opportunities that such a wilderness offers to the individual as the medium on which he may inscribe, unhindered, his own destiny and his own nature," and then by casting women, and especially women writers (specialists in the "flagrantly bad best-seller," according to Leslie Fiedler), as the enemy. In such critical readings, all other themes and modes of literary expression fall out of consideration as "un-American." There goes *Uncle Tom's Cabin,* there goes Edith Wharton, there goes domestic life as a subject, there go almost all the best-selling novelists of the nineteenth century and their readers, who were mostly women. The real loss, though, is not to our literature, but to our culture and ourselves, because we have lost the subject of how the various social groups who may not escape to the wilderness are to get along in society; and, in the case of *Uncle Tom's Cabin,* the hard-nosed, unsentimental dialogue about race that we should have been having since before the Civil War.

—Jane Smiley, "Say It Ain't So, Huck: Second Thoughts on Mark Twain's 'Masterpiece,'" *Harper's,* January 1996, pp. 61–67.

Christopher Hitchens, journalist, on Twain as an American founder (2003)

Twain was not just a founding author but a founding American. Until his appearance, even writers as adventurous as Hawthorne and Melville would have been gratified to receive the praise of a comparison to Walter Scott. (A boat named the *Walter Scott* is sunk with some ignominy in Chapter 13 of *Huckleberry Finn.*) Twain originated in the riverine, slaveholding heartland; compromised almost as much as Missouri itself when it came to the Civil War; headed out to California (the "Lincoln of our literature" made a name in the state that Lincoln always hoped to see and never did); and conquered the eastern seaboard in his own sweet time. But though he had an unimpeachable claim to be from native ground, there was nothing provincial or crabbed about his declaration of independence for American letters.

—Christopher Hitchens, "American Radical," *Atlantic Monthly,* November 2003, www.theatlantic.com/past/docs/issues/2003/11/hitchens.htm.

Atlas Shrugged

◖ AYN RAND, 1957 ◗

*T*HERE IS no more polarizing novel in American literature than *Atlas Shrugged* by the libertarian icon and atheist philosopher Ayn Rand (1905–82). Hate may not be too strong a word to describe how literary critics feel about this epic ode to "rational selfishness," which is routinely dismissed as juvenile, humorless, and preachy. Christopher Hitchens called it "transcendentally awful" and William F. Buckley Jr. described it as "a thousand pages of ideological fabulism."[1] Meanwhile, the *Chicago Tribune* named it the second worst novel of the millennium—after Edward Bulwer-Lytton's *Paul Clifford* (1830), which infamously begins, "It was a dark and stormy night."[2]

However, thanks to the word of mouth of millions of ordinary readers who love the book beyond compare, *Atlas Shrugged* has become a perennial bestseller, shipping over one hundred thousand units annually. In a 1991 Library of Congress survey of the books that made the biggest difference in readers' lives, it finished second (after the Bible).[3] It did not appear on the Modern Library's "board's list" of the one hundred greatest novels of the twentieth century (where James Joyce's *Ulysses* was number one), but it topped the "readers' list" (which put *Ulysses* in its place—behind no fewer than three Rand novels).[4]

Atlas Shrugged does not just set readers against critics, however. It sets left and right alike on edge—by insisting (to the annoyance of liberals) that laissez-faire capitalism is more moral than the welfare state and by rejecting (to the annoyance of conservatives) both God and tradition. Upon its publication, *Atlas Shrugged* received what may be "the definitive poison-pen review"—a takedown in the *National Review,* in which the anti-Communist Whittaker Chambers found a disquieting measure of Marx in Rand, and a bit of Hitler too.[5]

In recent years, however, and especially after the United States bailed out banks and automakers during the late, great financial crisis, Rand has become a darling of conservative Republicans. Glenn Beck and Rush Limbaugh tout her genius. The opening line of *Atlas Shrugged*—"Who is John Galt?"—pops up on signs at Tea Party rallies. Among Rand's adoring acolytes in the House of Representatives, Paul Ryan (R-WI) has called her "the reason I got involved in public service."[6] Libertarian Ron Paul, a Texas congressman and perennial presidential candidate, has invoked Rand in the House on matters as disparate as NASA and the post office. Even Supreme Court justice Clarence Thomas has said, "I tend really to be partial to Ayn Rand."[7]

Who is this controversial "radical for capitalism"? Is she "a traitor to her own sex," as feminist Susan Brownmiller claims? "One of the most evil figures of modern intellectual history," as MIT professor Noam Chomsky writes? Or is she the creative genius behind "America's Second Declaration of Independence"?[8]

Born Alisa Rosenbaum to a well-to-do Jewish family in St. Petersburg, Russia, in 1905, Rand lived through and was traumatized by the Russian Revolution of 1917. The formative moment in her life came one year later when the Red Guard seized her father's chemistry shop in the name of the Russian people. In many respects, Rand's career can be understood as an extended scream over this outrage, which gave her both a lifelong hatred of Communism and an unshakeable suspicion that Soviet-style Death Eaters were lurking around every corner. More to the point, the taking of her father's business gave Rand's fiction its grand theme: the life-and-death struggle between free individuals and the "parasites" ever conspiring to exploit them.

As a student at the University of Petrograd, Rand came to admire the United States, which she saw not as a Christian nation offering salvation but as a land of liberty offering political and economic freedom, including the freedom to reinvent oneself. Immigrating to the United States in 1926, Rand made her way to America's Mecca of reinvention, where, thanks to a chance meeting with Cecil B. DeMille, she found work as an extra and then as a screenwriter in Hollywood. She also found her husband, actor Frank O'Connor, whom she married in 1929. For the next two decades, they would shuttle back and forth between New York and Los Angeles.

Rand's first bestseller, *The Fountainhead* (1943), a paean to heroic individualism in the person of architect Howard Roark, set down themes that would recur in

Atlas Shrugged. The climax comes when Roark blows up a building he had designed rather than allow his inferiors to compromise his vision. After the movie, which starred Gary Cooper, was released in 1949, Rand and her husband settled in New York, gathering a circle of devotees known (ironically) as "The Collective." One member, Nathaniel Branden, would become Rand's secret lover and the Paul to her Jesus in the movement now known as Objectivism. Another acolyte, Alan Greenspan, would go on to serve as chairman of the Federal Reserve.

In Greek mythology, Atlas carries the weight of the world on his shoulders. In *Atlas Shrugged,* the people who hold up the world are the entrepreneurs, scientists, artists, and captains of industry who cultivate the ideas and produce the things that expand the economy. But the taxes and regulations imposed on their factories, railroads, and mines by welfare state "parasites" eventually grow intolerable, and when their businesses are nationalized they decide to "shrug." In the Shinto mythology of Japan, the sun goddess Amaterasu withdraws to a cave and plunges the earth into darkness in protest over the actions of her brother (or husband, in some versions). In *Atlas Shrugged,* the Amaterasu role is played by "traders" ("job creators," in modern parlance), and the results are nearly as catastrophic. Inspired by the novel's hero, John Galt, the inventor of a revolutionary motor that runs on static electricity, the best and the brightest go on strike to protest their exploitation at the hands of "moochers" and "looters"—people who by hook (guilt) or by crook (government coercion) steal from the hard-won earnings of their moral and intellectual superiors.

In a secular version of the apocalyptic theology of today's *Left Behind* series (in which Christians are "raptured" into heaven as the end times begin), Rand's heroes vanish, "stopping the motor of the world" and plunging the nation into a dark dystopia. Withdrawing to "Galt's Gulch" in Colorado, the novel's heroes begin to fashion for themselves a utopia in which the currency is gold, the verb "to give" dares not speak its name, and the only "revelation" is reason. Their goals? An end to income taxes, foreign aid, and the welfare state, and a return to the gold standard. Their oath? "I swear by my life and my love of it that I will never live for the sake of another man, nor ask another man to live for mine."

Eventually, government bureaucrats beg Galt to return and cure what ails the economy. At the climax of the book, Galt responds with a radio address detailing his political philosophy. In the upside-down kingdom of God of the Christian gospels, the last will be first and the first will be last. Galt's godless gospel effects an equally radical inversion of values. Here egoism is a virtue, and altruism is a vice. Greed is good, and the evildoers are "do-gooders" who in the name of the "public interest" threaten to bankrupt heroes such as railroad owner Dagny Taggart and steel magnate Henry Reardon. "Man—every man—is an end in himself, he exists for his own sake," Galt proclaims, "and the achievement of his own happiness is his highest moral purpose." Rand's editors demanded that she cut Galt's rambling and repetitive speech, which in the first edition ran to seventy pages. "Would you cut the Bible?" she responded, and refused. So she sacrificed seven cents per copy in royalties, and the speech ran in full.[9]

Like Harriet Beecher Stowe, whose *Uncle Tom's Cabin* helped to turn the American public against slavery, Rand wrote political novels. In fact, she was, by her own description, "the chief living writer of propaganda fiction."[10] She was also an antislavery writer of sorts, railing against enslavement by the welfare state. History was on Stowe's side and, at least according to President Lincoln, so were "the better angels of our nature." But the civil war between the "traders" and the "looters" is not yet over, so history's verdict will have to wait, as will any definitive judgment on whether Rand stands with Stowe among the "better angels." Still, one difference between these two massively popular writers is plain. Stowe appealed most fundamentally to emotion, and Rand to reason. As a result, Rand's audience has been limited (like her characters) to a certain sort of thinker, while Stowe's extended to those whose hearts were bigger than their plantations.

After the publication of *Atlas Shrugged,* Rand turned to writing nonfiction, including *The Virtue of Selfishness* (1964), and to speaking on college campuses, where she became something of a cult figure—"the Camille Paglia of the early sixties."[11] The 1960s was doubtless the decade of the hippie, but it was also a time in which conservatism ceased to be square. Not every college student in this era danced naked at Woodstock. Rand's "do what you want" heroes became role models for the abstainers: conservative youth who didn't want to be doing whatever Jack Kerouac was doing. These counter-countercultural thinkers were thrilled to hear Rand justify all manner of things they thought were unjustifiable—and on moral grounds no less. In this way, Rand's ideas entered the conservative mainstream in the 1970s and 1980s (a number of Nixon and Reagan appointees were devotees).

Modern American conservatism, which rose from the ashes of Republican Barry Goldwater's embarrassing defeat at the hands of President Lyndon Johnson in 1964, knits together at least three different strands: traditionalism, which follows Edmund Burke in defending custom and tradition against liberal reforms;

libertarianism, which follows John Stuart Mill in safeguarding individual liberty against the coercion of the state; and social conservatism, which follows the Christian Right in championing so-called family values. Rand took her libertarianism neat, clashing with traditionalists in her refusal to credit the wisdom of the dead, and with social conservatives—"militant mystics," she called them—on abortion rights (which she favored) and God, "family values," revelation, and Reagan (which she did not).[12] But Rand, who never fit neatly into any political philosophy other than their own, also locked horns with libertarians, in part because the limited state of her imagining was, in their imagining, never quite limited enough. In other words, Rand maintained at best an uneasy relationship with the conservative movement. Whereas Buckley and Reagan insisted that the freedoms so prized in Western civilization were an inheritance from Christianity, Rand saw Christian dogma as a threat to those freedoms.

As time has passed since Rand's death in New York in 1982, admirers have smoothed down her rough edges, remaking her in their own image. Rand's recent resurgence within the Republican Party helped bring to life a film adaptation of *Atlas Shrugged* in 2011. It also scared up a backlash among social conservatives who rode to power on the wings of precisely the sort of faith she despised. Real conservatism is about sacrifice, as is authentic Christianity, they argue. But Rand's "I, me, mine" Objectivism brooks no self-sacrifice. Serve yourself, and save yourself as well, Rand insists. There is no higher purpose than individual happiness. This "idolatry of self and selfishness," concludes the evangelical leader Chuck Colson, is "the antithesis of Christianity."[13]

During Rand's funeral, mourners laid out her body next to a floral dollar sign. The image was apt. In the ongoing debate over what America was, is, and should become, Rand put economic considerations front and center. For her, America's key word was not "democracy" but "capitalism." "We the people" did not make America rich. Captains of industry did that. And their only true god was the "Almighty Dollar."

The pages that follow were going to include an *Atlas Shrugged* speech by Francisco d'Anconia, a copper magnate and Patrick Henry University graduate whose words translate Rand's funerary tableau into her most beloved medium: the argument. In the 1987 film *Wall Street,* Gordon Gekko preached the goodness of greed. But d'Anconia did the same decades earlier. "So you think that money is the root of all evil?" he begins, and before he has finished he has made the most heartfelt case in American literature for money as "the root of all good." "The proudest distinction of Americans [is] . . . the fact that they were the people who created the phrase 'to make money,'" he says. "Americans were the first to understand that wealth has to be created. The words 'to make money' hold the essence of human morality." Unfortunately, the Estate of Ayn Rand refused to allow this excerpt to be included here amid the controversy that continues to swirl around her many characters, not least herself.

Atlas Shrugged

Permission to reprint denied by the Estate of Ayn Rand.

COMMENTARY

Granville Hicks, writer, on the hateful spirit of Atlas Shrugged *(1957)*

Not in any literary sense a serious novel, it is an earnest one, belligerent and unremitting in its earnestness. It howls in the reader's ear and beats him about the head in order to secure his attention, and then, when it has him subdued, harangues him for page upon page. It has only two moods, the melodramatic and the didactic, and in both it knows no bounds. . . .

It would be pointless to discuss the logic or the feasibility of the program Miss Rand so vehemently puts forth. What is important is the spirit in which the book is written. Like "The Fountainhead," "Atlas Shrugged" is a defense of and a tribute to the superior individual, who is, in Miss Rand's view, superior in every way—in body as well as mind and especially in his capacity for life. . . . Yet, loudly as Miss Rand proclaims her love of life, it seems clear that the book is written out of hate. . . . Perhaps most of us have moments when we feel that it might be a good idea if the whole human race, except for us and the few nice people we know, were wiped out; but one wonders about a person who sustains such a mood through the writing of 1,168 pages and some fourteen years of work.

—Granville Hicks, "A Parable of Buried Talents," *New York Times*, October 13, 1957, pp. 4–5.

Alan Greenspan, economist, future chairman of the Federal Reserve, and Rand follower, responding to the Hicks review (1957)

"Atlas Shrugged" is a celebration of life and happiness. Justice is unrelenting. Creative individuals and undeviating purpose and rationality achieve joy and fulfillment. Parasites who persistently avoid either purpose or reason perish as they should. Mr. Hicks suspiciously wonders "about a person who sustains such a mood through the writing of 1,168 pages and some fourteen years of work." This reader wonders about a person who finds unrelenting justice personally disturbing.

—Alan Greenspan, letter to the editor, *New York Times*, November 3, 1957.

Whittaker Chambers, writer, denouncing the "dictatorial tone" of "Big Sister" in a famous review of her "silly book" (1957)

Atlas Shrugged can be called a novel only by devaluing the term. It is a massive tract for the times. Its story merely serves Miss Rand to get the customers inside the tent, and as a soapbox for delivering her Message. The Message is the thing. It is, in sum, a forthright philosophic materialism. . . . Like any consistent materialism, this one begins by rejecting God, religion, original sin. . . . Thus, Randian Man, like Marxian Man, is made the center of a godless world. . . .

It is when a system of materialist ideas presumes to give positive answers to real problems of our real life that mischief starts. In an age like ours, in which a highly complex technological society is everywhere in a high state of instability, such answers, however philosophic, translate quickly into political realities. And in the degree to which problems of complexity and instability are most bewildering to masses of men, a temptation sets in to let some species of Big Brother solve and supervise them.

One Big Brother is, of course, a socializing elite (as we know, several cut-rate brands are on the shelves). Miss Rand, as the enemy of any socializing force, calls in a Big Brother of her own contriving to do battle with the other. In the name of free enterprise, therefore, she plumps for a technocratic elite (I find no more inclusive word than technocratic to bracket the industrial-financial-engineering caste she seems to have in mind). When she calls "productive achievement" man's "noblest activity," she means, almost exclusively, technological achievement, supervised by such a managerial political bureau. . . . And in reality, too, by contrast with fiction, this can only head into a dictatorship. . . .

Something of this implication is fixed in the book's dictatorial tone, which is much its most striking feature. Out of a lifetime of reading, I can recall no other book in which a tone of overriding arrogance was so implacably sustained. Its shrillness is without reprieve. Its dogmatism is without appeal. . . . It supposes itself to be the bringer of a final revelation. Therefore, resistance to the Message cannot be tolerated because disagreement can never be merely honest, prudent or just humanly fallible. Dissent from revelation so final (because, the author would say, so reasonable) can only be willfully wicked. There are ways of dealing with such wickedness, and, in fact, right reason itself enjoins them. From almost any page of *Atlas Shrugged*, a voice can be heard, from painful necessity, commanding: "To a gas chamber—go!"

—Whittaker Chambers, "Big Sister Is Watching You," *National Review*, December 28, 1957, pp. 594–96.

Daryn Kent, member of Rand's "Collective," responding to Chambers (1958)

[Whittaker Chambers's] review is a monument to the mind-blanking, life-hating, unreasoning, less-than-human being which Miss Rand proves undeniably is the cause of the tragic situation the world now faces. . . . If I wanted to understand why my rights are being taken from me and in what manner the life-blood is being squeezed from this country and from the world, I had only to read Whittaker Chambers in the *National Review*.

—Daryn Kent, letter to the editor, *National Review*, January 18, 1958, p. 71.

Billie Jean King, tennis champion and women's rights activist, on how an Atlas Shrugged *heroine helped her game (1975)*

The book really turned me around, because, at the time, I was going through a bad period in tennis and thinking about quitting. People were constantly calling me and making me feel rotten if I didn't play in their tournament or help them out. I realized then that people were . . . using me as a pawn to help their own ends and if I wasn't careful, I'd end up losing myself. So, like Dagny Taggart, I had to learn how to be selfish, although selfish has the wrong connotation. As I see it, being selfish is really doing your own thing. Now I know that if I can make myself happy, I can make other people happy—and if that's being selfish, so be it. That's what I am.

—"Playboy Interview: Billie Jean King," *Playboy*, March 1975, pp. 55–70, 194–96.

Mimi Gladstein, English professor, reading Rand as a feminist (1978)

Atlas Shrugged . . . is not generally considered to be philosophically feminist. In fact, it may not be on anyone's reading list for women's courses, except mine. But close analysis of the book's themes and theories will prove that it should be. . . . The novel has a protagonist who is a good example of a woman who is active, assertive, successful, and still retains the love and sexual admiration of three heroic men. Though the situation is highly romantic, and science fiction to boot, how refreshing it is to find a female protagonist in American fiction who emerges triumphant.

Rand's attack on altruism . . . is especially relevant to women because they have been the chief internalizers of this concept [which] has encouraged women to view themselves as sacrificial animals whose desires and talents are forfeited for the good of children, family and society.

—Mimi R. Gladstein, "Ayn Rand and Feminism: An Unlikely Alliance," *College English* 39.6 (February 1978): 681–83.

Terry Teachout, author, accounting for the outsized influence of this "awful" novel on American conservatives (1982)

Sure, it's a preposterous book; sure, the reviewers demolished it; sure, virtually every reputable conservative from Russell Kirk to Frank Meyer rushed to repudiate it. . . . There's no graceful way to get around it: *Atlas Shrugged,* awful as it is, has left its mark on the history of American conservatism. . . . I spent a delightful month out of my 16th year plowing through every book I could find by the author of *Atlas Shrugged.* . . . It didn't last, thank God, and I had a terrible mental hangover when it was all over; but, as Dr. Johnson would have said, my mind had been cleared of a great deal of liberal cant. . . . It seems likely that most people who read it are 16-year-olds (of various ages) who find themselves carried away by the sheer mind-clearing exhilaration of unrestrained adolescent individualism; and I know a sizable number of readers, myself included, who have gone on from there to the infinitely greener pastures of true conservatism.

—Terry Teachout, "Farewell, Dagny Taggart," *National Review*, May 14, 1982, pp. 566–67.

Peter Berger, *sociologist, on the awkward fit between* Rand's philosophy and American culture *(1986)*

Rand's novels are ponderous, filled with characters that are, indeed, embodiments of principles rather than living human beings. Her philosophy is a vulgarized cross between Adam Smith and Friedrich Nietzsche, a flat Enlightenment rationalism aspiring to an ethic of heroism. Her epistemology of "objectivity" is roughly as sophisticated as Lenin's dialectical materialism, her morality is based on selfishness and her political program could not be realized in any modern society.

Yet Rand did understand some central realities—precisely realities that a good number of contemporary American intellectuals fail to see. Foremost among these is the reality that capitalism alone provides the institutional foundation for individual rights, which is why all forms of modern collectivism, of whatever ideological coloration, detest capitalism. . . .

Rand was passionately patriotic about her adopted country. There are many things about America, though, that she never understood, and the pervasiveness of religion in this country was certainly one of them. She imagined America as she imagined capitalism, and her success is evidence of the fact that her own fantasies coincided with those of others—and probably that her own simplicities met the need of others for one simple, all-embracing explanation of everything. This makes for a movement, but it doesn't make for good philosophy or viable politics. Capitalism is part and parcel of an inevitably messy empirical reality that can never be captured in a system of axioms. A defense of capitalism that can claim to be both moral and rational will have to take cognizance of its empirical reality— something Rand was temperamentally unable to do.

—Peter L. Berger, "Adam Smith Meets Nietzsche," *New York Times*, July 6, 1986, p. BR13.

Stephen Moore, Wall Street Journal *economics writer, denouncing the "economic lunacy" of bailouts and stimulus programs (2009)*

The current economic strategy is right out of "Atlas Shrugged": The more incompetent you are in business, the more handouts the politicians will bestow on you. That's the justification for the $2 trillion of subsidies doled out already to keep afloat distressed insurance companies, banks, Wall Street investment houses, and auto companies. . . . As "Atlas" grimly foretold, we now treat the incompetent who wreck their companies as victims, while those resourceful business owners who manage to make a profit are portrayed as recipients of illegitimate "windfalls."

—Stephen Moore, "'Atlas Shrugged': From Fiction to Fact in 52 Years," *Wall Street Journal,* January 9, 2009, p. W11.

Ralph Nader, consumer activist, declaiming Atlas Shrugged *as dangerous (2010)*

I find [*Atlas Shrugged*] abhorrent. . . . I find the idea of maximum narcissism destructive of any sense of community, basically omnicidal, if you extrapolate it across the globe.

—Ralph Nader, "In Depth," C-Span2/BookTV, August 1, 2010, www.booktv.org/Watch/11751/In+Depth +Ralph+Nader.aspx.

Michael Gerson, columnist and former speechwriter for President George W. Bush, reviewing the film Atlas Shrugged *(2011)*

Rand's distinctive mix of expressive egotism, free love and free-market metallurgy does not hold up very well on the screen. . . . All of the characters are ideological puppets. Visionary, comely capitalists are assaulted by sniveling government planners, smirking lobbyists, nagging wives, rented scientists and cynical humanitarians. When characters begin disappearing—on strike against the servility and inferiority of the masses—one does not question their wisdom in leaving the movie.

None of the characters expresses a hint of sympathetic human emotion—which is precisely the point. Rand's novels are vehicles for a system of thought known as Objectivism. Rand developed this philosophy at the length of Tolstoy, with the intellectual pretensions of Hegel, but it can be summarized on a napkin. Reason is everything. Religion is a fraud. Selfishness is a virtue. Altruism is a crime against human excellence. Self-sacrifice is weakness. . . .

If Objectivism seems familiar, it is because most people know it under another name: adolescence. Many of us experienced a few unfortunate years of invincible self-involvement, testing moral boundaries and prone to stormy egotism and hero worship. Usually one grows out of it, eventually discovering that the quality of our lives is tied to the benefit of others. Rand's achievement was to turn a phase into a philosophy as attractive as an outbreak of acne.

The appeal of Ayn Rand to conservatives is both considerable and inexplicable. Modern conservatism was largely defined by Ronald Reagan's faith in the people instead of elites. Rand regarded the people as "looters" and "parasites." She was a strenuous advocate for class warfare, except that she took the side of a mythical class of capitalist supermen. Rand, in fact, pronounced herself "profoundly opposed" to Reagan's presidential candidacy, since he did not meet her exacting ideological standards. . . .

Reaction to Rand draws a line in political theory. Some believe with Rand that all government is coercion and theft—the tearing-down of the strong for the benefit of the undeserving. Others believe that government has a limited but noble role in helping the most vulnerable in society—not motivated by egalitarianism, which is destructive, but by compassion, which is human. And some root this duty in God's particular concern for the vulnerable and undeserving, which eventually includes us all. This is the message of Easter, and it is inconsistent with the gospel of Rand.

—Michael Gerson, "Ayn Rand's Adult-Onset Adolescence," *Virginian-Pilot* (Norfolk, VA), April 24, 2011, p. B9.

Onkar Ghate, senior fellow at the Ayn Rand Institute, arguing that the plot of Atlas Shrugged *was being lived out in contemporary America (2011)*

"Atlas Shrugged" has finally reached the big screen and, especially among Tea Partiers, Ayn Rand is being hailed a prophet. How could she have anticipated, more than 50 years ago, a United States spinning out of financial control, plagued by soaring spending and crippling regulations? How could she have painted villains who seem ripped from today's headlines? . . .

"You have cried that man's sins are destroying the world and you have cursed human nature for its unwillingness to practice the virtues you demanded," novel hero John Galt declares to a country in crisis. "Since virtue, to you, consists of sacrifice, you have demanded more sacrifices at every successive disaster."

He elaborates: "You have sacrificed justice to mercy." (For example, calls to make homeownership "accessible" to those who could not afford it and then bailouts and foreclosure freezes to spare them when they couldn't pay.)

"You have sacrificed reason to faith." (For example, attempts to prevent stem-cell research on Biblical grounds or blind faith that Mr. Obama's deliberately empty rhetoric about hope and change will magically produce prosperity.)

"You have sacrificed wealth to need." (For example, Bush's prescription drug benefit and Obamacare, both enacted because people needed "free" health care.)

"You have sacrificed self-esteem to self-denial." (For example, attacks on Bill Gates for making a fortune; applause when he gives that fortune away.)

"You have sacrificed happiness to duty." (For example, every president's Kennedyesque exhortations to "Ask not what your country can do for you—ask what you can do for your country.")

—Onkar Ghate, " 'Atlas Shrugged': With America on the Brink, Should You 'Go Galt' and Strike?" *Christian Science Monitor,* April 29, 2011, www.csmonitor.com/Commentary/Opinion/2011/0429/Atlas-Shrugged-With-America-on-the-brink-should-you-go-Galt-and-strike.

Charles Colson, Watergate criminal and evangelical commentator, choosing Jesus over Rand (2011)

The book's aggressive atheism grows out of this materialism, which places man at the center of a godless world, a world in which self-satisfaction becomes the moral purpose of his life. It's hard for me to imagine a worldview more antithetical to Christianity. Also difficult to imagine a more juvenile one. . . . Don't be fooled by Rand's phony conservatism or by her followers that claim to be true conservatives. Her philosophy of life, called objectivism, is nothing more than the idolatry of self and selfishness.

—Charles Colson, "Two-Minute Warning: Atlas Shrugged and So Should You," May 10, 2011, www.youtube.com/watch?v=ZhbE8NDTY0c.

PSALMS

"The Star-Spangled Banner"

❧ FRANCIS SCOTT KEY, 1814 ❧

URING THE War of 1812, a medical doctor named William Beanes was captured by the British and held as a prisoner of war. In September 1814, President James Madison dispatched two lawyers, Francis Scott Key and Colonel John Skinner, to the British flagship the *Tonnant* in Chesapeake Bay to negotiate for the doctor's release on the grounds that he was an unarmed civilian. Key and Skinner won Beanes his freedom, but while on board they learned of British plans to attack Baltimore, so the British refused to allow them to go ashore until the attack was over. As a result, the three Americans watched the twenty-five-hour bombardment of Fort McHenry from a sloop on the evening of September 13, 1814, and into the next day.

In a letter to a friend, John Randolph of Roanoke, Key wrote of watching the battle in "a state of anxiety," because he had heard from a British admiral that Baltimore was to be "given up to plunder." "It seemed as though mother earth had opened and was vomiting shot and shell in a sheet of fire and brimstone," Key wrote. "The heavens aglow were a seething sea of flame, and the waters of the harbor rode and tossed as though in a tempest."[1] When the bombs stopped bursting, the Americans didn't know who had won. The British had burned Washington, D.C. Were they about to do the same to Baltimore? But at dawn the Americans saw their flag flying over Fort McHenry. The British were retreating, and they allowed Skinner, Key, and Beanes to go.

Key, a pious Episcopalian and an opponent of the war, saw the hand of God in the outcome of the Battle of Fort McHenry, and he began work immediately on a poem describing "this most merciful deliverance."[2] At the Fountain Inn in Baltimore, he finished the four-stanza poem, which Colonel Skinner later described as "a versified and almost literal transcript of our expressed hopes and apprehensions, through that ever-memorable period of anxiety to all."[3] Under the title, "Defence of Fort McHenry," it found its way to the offices of the *Baltimore American,* which published it as a handbill on September 15, 1814. Five days later it appeared in the *Baltimore Patriot.* Before the year was out, it was being sung under its current name, "The Star-Spangled Banner," to the tune of an old British drinking song, "To Anacreon in Heaven."

Used during the presidential campaign of General William Henry Harrison in 1840 and at the presidential inauguration of Abraham Lincoln in 1861, this song grew in popularity over the course of the nineteenth century, particularly in wartime. It was a Union standard during the Civil War, and the Confederacy claimed it too. In the end, efforts to appropriate this song for one region or party failed. Widely used by both the army and the navy at the beginning of the twentieth century, "The Star-Spangled Banner" became the nation's unofficial national anthem during World War I.

Legislative efforts during the 1920s to make this designation official flushed out partisans of alternative anthems, including "Yankee Doodle," "The Battle Hymn of the Republic," and "America the Beautiful." Critics also appeared in droves. Temperance advocates objected to using an old drinking song as the national melody, while Anglophiles objected to canonizing a song about bashing the British. Others echoed the sentiments of conductor John Philip Sousa, who opposed the song on nationalist grounds. "We ought not to adopt as our national air the work of a foreigner," Sousa said. "The words of the 'Star-Spangled Banner' are American, but the music is English."[4]

The most strident opposition came from pacifists, who objected to canonizing a war song. Was America fated to memorialize forever its martial spirit and its antagonism toward Great Britain? In 1922, in an effort members of the Grand Army of the Republic would later denounce as a "pernicious anti-American campaign," a series of newspaper advertisements paid for by Christian Scientist Augusta Stetson denounced "The Star-Spangled Banner" as an "outgrown ballad of venom and hatred." Wrote Stetson: "Christian Americans who have imbibed the spirit of Washington and Lincoln" will not learn or sing a song masquerading as patriotic which expresses the lowest qualities of human sentiment—hatred, boastful pride, and murder."[5]

Because of their city's association with "The Star-Spangled Banner," Baltimore newspapers had long advocated the song, and this time Baltimore's *Sun* jumped to its defense. "'The Star-Spangled Banner' has undergone fiercer bombardments at the hands of Americans of late years than it sustained from the British ships on the occasion of the famous attack that inspired Key's fervent poetic outburst," it editorialized. "And it may be remarked that now, as then, 'the flag is still there,' in spite of both literary and pacifist critics."[6] In the early 1930s, such advocacy won the day in Washington, in part because of strong support for "The Star-Spangled Banner" among veterans groups such as the Veterans of Foreign Wars and the American Legion. On March 3, 1931, Congress and President Herbert Hoover made this war song the official national anthem.

The selection remains controversial, however. As anyone who saw Christina Aguilera fumble the lyrics at the 2011 Super Bowl can attest, the lyrics are confusing and hard to memorize. Like answers on the television show *Jeopardy,* the first stanza (the only one that is regularly sung today) is phrased in the form of a question. Meanwhile, the tune, which ranges over an octave and a half, is harder to carry than your average opera singer. In 1976, in the midst of America's bicentennial, Key's great-great-great-granddaughter, Constance Allard, joined the naysayers. "Frankly, I think it's an awful song for a national anthem," she said. "It's practically impossible for anybody to sing it."[7]

Americans do not confine their debates over the song to its lyrics or melody, however. Controversies abound concerning *how* it is sung. When Aretha Franklin performed a soulful version at the Democratic National Convention in 1968, a letter to Washington's *Evening Star* called it a "sacrilege"—"a new low in musical taste and an affront to all Americans."[8] After comedian Roseanne Barr screeched her way through the song (and then grabbed her crotch and spat for good measure) at a major league baseball game in 1990, President George W. Bush denounced her performance as "disgraceful" and "disgusting." But an op-ed piece in the *New York Times* called it "high art"—"a profoundly funny statement about the average American who can't sing the tune and doesn't know the words anyway."[9]

The most talked-about versions of "The Star-Spangled Banner" didn't include any singing. A bluesy instrumental version performed by Jose Feliciano in Detroit before Game 5 of the 1968 World Series—"The Lexington and Concord of *Star-Spangled Banner* controversies"—started a revolution in inventive interpretations of the national anthem.[10] But nothing surpassed the performance at Woodstock by the rock icon Jimi Hendrix, whose electric guitar transported the song to the Vietnamese battlefield, complete with incoming ordnance and exploding grenades.

The biggest "Star-Spangled Banner" controversy came at the 1968 Summer Olympics in Mexico City, when sprinters Tommie Smith and John Carlos lowered their heads and raised their fists in a black power salute during the medals ceremony for the 200-meter dash. It was an era of protests, but sympathy for these men was scarce. They were kicked off the Olympic team, stripped of their gold (Smith) and bronze (Carlos) medals, and sent home to death threats.

In 2006, a group of Latin pop stars recorded "Nuestro Himno," a Spanish-language version written to express solidarity with undocumented migrant workers. Critics said the national anthem should be sung in English and saw this "illegal alien anthem" as further evidence of the refusal of immigrants to assimilate. Supporters argued that "Nuestro Himno" was actually a *means* of assimilation. "The first step to understanding something is to understand it in the language you understand, and then you can understand it in another language," said Leo Chavez, a professor of Chicano/Latino Studies at the University of California. "What this song represents at this moment is a communal shout, that the dream of America, which is represented by the song, is their dream, too."[11] This controversy made its way to the White House, where President George W. Bush spoke against the new anthem. "I think people who want to be citizens of this country . . . ought to learn to sing the national anthem in English," he said.[12]

Today the flag remains the nation's most enduring symbol in part because of the power of "The Star-Spangled Banner." The Star-Spangled Banner itself—the flag that flew over Fort McHenry on the morning of September 14, 1814—is one of the most treasured holdings of the Smithsonian's National Museum of American History.

"The Star-Spangled Banner" 🕊

Oh, say, can you see, by the dawn's early light,
What so proudly we hailed at the twilight's last gleaming?
Whose broad stripes and bright stars, through the perilous fight,
O'er the ramparts we watched, were so gallantly streaming?
And the rockets' red glare, the bombs bursting in air,
Gave proof through the night that our flag was still there.
O say, does that star-spangled banner yet wave
O'er the land of the free and the home of the brave?[a,b]

---

a. Robert Owen, utopian, socialist, and U.S. Representative (D-IN), arguing that naturalized citizens are full citizens (1844): But the gentleman from Maryland takes exception to it that I, a naturalized citizen only, should have opened such a debate as this. . . . Sorry am I, sir, to recognize this bastard spirit of native Americanism here. I know that it has had its brief hour in New York, but I did not know that it was to find its advocate, its partisan, in a member of this House. Unworthy, sir—utterly unworthy is that narrow and illiberal spirit to find a representative in any legislative body—least of all on the floor of the Congress of America. America is the land—not of one class, of one tribe, of one people—a home, not to those only to whom favoring fortune has granted birth within its borders. The world claims birth right in America! The world admits America's own claim to be "the land of the free, and the home of the brave." The free claim this for their country; I, foreign born, though I be—I rightfully claim it for my country. It is mine by free selection, by deliberate preference; the gentleman's by accident only. —Quoted in "A Noble Reply," *Democratic Free Press* (Detroit), May 30, 1844.

b. Frederick Douglass, abolitionist and former slave, on finding more freedom abroad than at home (1846): I remember, about two years ago, there was in Boston, near the southwest corner of Boston Common, a menagerie. I had long desired to see such a collection as I understood was being exhibited there. Never having had an opportunity while a slave, I resolved to seize this, my first, since my escape. I went, and as I approached the entrance to gain admission, I was met and told by the door-keeper, in a harsh and contemptuous tone, "We don't allow niggers in here." I also remember attending a revival meeting in the Rev. Henry Jackson's meeting-house, at New Bedford, and going up the broad aisle to find a seat, I was met by a good deacon, who told me, in a pious tone, "We don't allow niggers in here!" . . .

Thank heaven for the respite I now enjoy! I had been in Dublin but a few days, when a gentleman of great respectability kindly offered to conduct me through all the public buildings of that beautiful city; and a little afterward, I found myself dining with the lord mayor of Dublin. What a pity there was not some American democratic Christian

On the shore dimly seen through the mists of the deep,
Where the foe's haughty host in dread silence reposes,
What is that which the breeze, o'er the towering steep,
As it fitfully blows, half conceals, half discloses?
Now it catches the gleam of the morning's first beam,
In full glory reflected, now shines on the stream:
'Tis the star-spangled banner: O, long may it wave
O'er the land of the free and the home of the brave![c,d]

at the door of his splendid mansion, to bark out at my approach, "They don't allow niggers in here!" The truth is, the people here know nothing of the republican negro hate prevalent in our glorious land. They measure and esteem men according to their moral and intellectual worth, and not according to the color of their skin. Whatever may be said of the aristocracies here, there is none based on the color of a man's skin. This species of aristocracy belongs preëminently to "the land of the free, and the home of the brave." I have never found it abroad, in any but Americans. It sticks to them wherever they go. They find it almost as hard to get rid of, as to get rid of their skins. —Frederick Douglass to William Lloyd Garrison, January 1, 1846, reprinted in *My Bondage and My Freedom* (New York: Miller, Orgon & Mulligan, 1855), pp. 371–72.

c. *Chicago Daily Tribune*, editorializing for restrictions on Chinese immigration (1879): The Chinese question is rapidly assuming a national importance. . . . Many people start out in a consideration of this subject on false premises. Assuming this country to be the "land of the free and the home of the brave," they are inclined to think its mission is to open all its doors to all who knock, without any regard to the welfare of those who are already in possession. From this they reach the false generalization that the Government has no right to exclude men of any race or limit immigration from any quarter of the globe. It is true that the spirit of the Government is largely missionary, since, from the earliest days of independence, it offered the inducements of self-government and declared itself the chosen refuge of the oppressed of all nations. But it must not be overlooked that a selfish interest has been served along with the philanthropic pretense, and that, while America has offered a free home and full equality to the people of all the world, the millions who have been plucky and enterprising enough to avail themselves of this offer have contributed to the growth and progress of the nation, and have given as well as partaken of the common benefits of development. Whenever immigration threatens loss or disaster instead of an increase of material or political prosperity, there is no doubt that the American Republic has the same moral right to exclude, limit, or regulate such immigration as pertains to the sovereign power of every nation. —"The Chinese Question," *Chicago Daily Tribune*, January 7, 1879, p. 4.

d. John James Ingalls, U.S. Senator (R-KS), railing against income inequality (1891): Our population is sixty-two and one-half millions, and by some means, by some device,

And where is that band who so vauntingly swore
That the havoc of war and the battle's confusion
A home and a country should leave us no more?
Their blood has washed out their foul footsteps' pollution.
No refuge could save the hireling and slave
From the terror of flight or the gloom of the grave:
And the star-spangled banner in triumph doth wave
O'er the land of the free and the home of the brave.[e,f]

---

by some machination, by some incantation, honest or otherwise, by some process that cannot be defined, less than a two-thousandth part of our population have obtained possession, and have kept out of the penitentiary in spite of the means they have adopted to acquire it, of more than one-half of the entire accumulated wealth of the country. That is not the worst, Mr. President. It has been largely acquired by men who have contributed little to the material welfare of the country and by processes that I do not care in appropriate terms to describe, by the wrecking of the fortunes of innocent men, women, and children, by jugglery, by bookkeeping, by financiering, by what the Senator from Ohio calls "speculation," and this process is going on with frightful and constantly accelerating rapidity. . . . So it happens, Mr. President, that our society is becoming rapidly stratified, almost hopelessly stratified, into a condition of superfluously rich and helplessly poor. We are accustomed to speak of this as the land of the free and the home of the brave. It will soon be the home of the rich and the land of the slave. —John James Ingalls, "The Image and Superscription of Caesar," January 14, 1891, speech, in William Elsey Connelley, ed., *A Collection of the Writings of John James Ingalls: Essays, Addresses, and Orations* (Kansas City, MO: Hudson-Kimberly, 1902), pp. 321–24.

e. Fannie Lou Hamer, civil rights activist, calling on the Democratic National Convention to integrate her state's all-white delegation by seating black delegates from the Mississippi Freedom Democratic Party (1964): All of this [harassment and abuse] is on account of we want to register [to vote], to become first-class citizens, and if the Freedom Democratic Party is not seated now, I question America. Is this America, the land of the free and the home of the brave, where we have to sleep with our telephones off the hooks because our lives be threatened daily, because we want to live as decent human beings, in America? —Fannie Lou Hamer, "Testimony Before the Credentials Committee," Democratic National Convention, Atlantic City, New Jersey, August 22, 1964, http://americanradioworks.pub licradio.org/features/sayitplain/flhamer.html.

f. Leonard Pitts Jr., columnist, addressing Wake Forest graduates on the relationship between freedom and bravery post-9/11 (2006): That struck me as a telling conjunction

O, thus be it ever when freemen shall stand,
Between their loved home and the war's desolation!
Blest with victory and peace, may the heav'n-rescued land
Praise the Power that hath made and preserved us a nation!
Then conquer we must, when our cause it is just,
And this be our motto: "In God is our trust."
And the star-spangled banner in triumph shall wave
O'er the land of the free and the home of the brave!

---

of words: "the land of the free and the home of the brave." I don't think we have distinguished ourselves by our bravery in this era. Fifty-one percent of the electorate (is) willing to suspend its own civil rights, willing to suspend the things that make America, America because they are scared of terrorists? It is time all of us grew a spine. Because, there is one undeniable truth about being the land of the free and the home of the brave; if you do not have the guts to be the one, you will soon cease to be the other.
—Leonard Pitts Jr., "Wake Forest Convocation Speech," October 12, 2006, quoted in "Columnist Pitts at Wake Forest Convocation: Freedom Requires 'Guts,'" www.wfu.edu/news/release/2006.10.12.p.php.

COMMENTARY

Oliver Wendell Holmes, writer, offering a new stanza in response to the Confederate attack on Fort Sumter (1861)

When our land is illumined with liberty's smile,
If a foe from within strike a blow at her glory,
Down, down with the traitor that dares to defile
The flag of her stars and the page of her story!
By the millions unchained who their birthright have gained,
We will keep her bright blazon forever unstained!
And the Star-Spangled Banner in triumph shall wave
While the land of the free is the home of the brave!

—Quoted in George Henry Preble, *Origin and History of the American Flag* (Philadelphia: Brown, 1917), 2:730.

Richmond Examiner, *claiming "The Star-Spangled Banner" for the Confederacy (1861)*

Let us never surrender to the north the noble song, "the Star-Spangled Banner." It is Southern in its origin, its sentiments, poetry, and song; in its associations with chivalrous deeds, it is ours; and the time, I trust is not remote when the broad stripes and brilliant stars of the Confederate flag of the South will wave triumphantly over our capitol, Fortress Monroe, and every fort within our borders.

—*Richmond Examiner,* April 4, 1861, quoted in George Henry Preble, *Origin and History of the American Flag* (Philadelphia: Brown, 1917), 2:510.

North American Review, *pleading for a new "national hymn" (1906)*

Will not someone kindly compose a new national hymn? We should dislike to lose "The Star-Spangled Banner" chiefly because of its patriotic origin on board an American frigate during a British bombardment. . . . But, after all, only the words are American, the atrocious music being that of "Anacreon in Heaven," composed by an Englishman. It is therefore distinctively national only in part, and after nearly a century of trying service might well be laid upon the shelf. A yet more efficient reason for seeking a substitute is found in the fact that the American people have been trying in vain for nearly a century to sing it. Despite the general cultivation of voices, the endeavor of an audience to-day to respond to the demand upon their patriotic spirit continues to be as pathetic as it has ever been desperate. . . . For double-quick marching "Yankee Doodle" continues to be satisfactory and "Hail, Columbia" is not without merit; but "America" is of too common use among the nations and "The Star-Spangled Banner" too throat-rending; so again we ask, Will not someone kindly present us with a new distinctively American national hymn?

—"For a New National Hymn," *North American Review,* November 2, 1906, pp. 947–48.

John Phillip Hill, *U.S. Representative (R-MD), defending the militarism of the song in congressional hearings (1924)*

I do not care where "The Star-Spangled Banner" came from. "The Star-Spangled Banner" is essentially American. It belongs to the American people. It is the only American anthem, and whenever I hear "The Star-Spangled Banner" or think of "The Star-Spangled Banner," I think of the men who died in France, the men who died in the War of the Revolution, the Spanish-American War, and the men who died in the War of 1812. It is inseparably bound up with the ideals of the American flag and the ideal of American nationality.

As to the suggestion that it would be taken as an insult to England, the chairman and the members of the committee entirely dispensed with that thought.

The war with England is an incident. The patriotic impulses and the patriotic expression of "The Star-Spangled Banner" are the national spirit, and I agree with Theodore Roosevelt that the man who does not raise his boy to be a soldier is like the woman who does not raise her daughter to be a woman in America.

You cannot have a national anthem that has not got a militant spirit. We do not want a national anthem that has not got a militant spirit. Why would we have an Army, why should we have a Navy, if we want to sing some psalm like "Brighten the Corner Where You Are" or some other piffle as a national anthem?

—"Statement of Honorable John Phillip Hull," in *Legislation to Make "The Star-Spangled Banner" the National Anthem: Hearing Before the Committee on the Judiciary, House of Representatives* (Washington, DC: U.S. Government Printing Office, 1924), pp. 17–18.

Francis S. Key-Smith, attorney, commending his great-grandfather's song as an anthem of sanctified sacrifice (1930)

What about the national anthem, and I call it so advisedly, because it has been that, having for 100 years commanded such respect and such adoration and allegiance in the hearts of the American people. It is not a war-like measure, neither does it repudiate war. It is a tribute to the glorious sacrifice, to the patriotic devotion which made possible the great victory of American arms that gave it birth. It is sanctified, gentlemen, in the blood of martyrs, and its words breathe American independence and freedom as no other poem that has ever been written breathes and, furthermore, it says this, that when freemen shall stand in a just cause between their loved home and the war's desolation, with the trust placed in Divine Providence, the Stars and Stripes will forever wave over that land which it characterizes, which "The Star-Spangled Banner" characterizes, as the land of the free and the home of the brave.

—"Statement of Mr. Francis S. Key-Smith," *Legislation to Make "The Star-Spangled Banner" the National Anthem: Hearing Before the Committee on the Judiciary, House of Representatives* (Washington, DC: U.S. Government Printing Office, 1930), p. 27.

Kitty Cheatham, singer and actress, denouncing the song as "un-Christian" and "un-American" (1930)

I do think it is a shameful thing, it is un-American, it is un-Christian, it is illogical, it is unthinking, particularly at this moment when we are having a peace conference abroad and peace is being talked about in the world, to plant in the virgin soil of the consciences of little children such sentiment as bombs bursting in air, rockets' red glare, the foul footsteps' pollution, the foes horrid hosts, the gloom of the grave. . . .

Now we are certainly the Nation to hold up the torch of light to a starving world and we want to usher in that great millennium time which has been foreseen for centuries, when the lion can lie down with the lamb and a little child can lead them. The song of the Star-Spangled Banner is certainly retarding it and is not doing anything to usher in the days of "Peace on earth, good will toward men," to which the whole world is assembled, trying to direct their efforts.

—"Statement of Miss Kitty Cheatham," *Legislation to Make "The Star-Spangled Banner" the National Anthem: Hearing Before the Committee on the Judiciary, House of Representatives* (Washington, DC: U.S. Government Printing Office, 1930), pp. 37–38.

Caldwell Titcomb, music professor, objecting to this "earache" of a song on musicological grounds (1985)

Is our nation so poverty-stricken that we must rule out homegrown music? The tune is a constant stumbling block. Technically, it covers a span of a twelfth—that is, an octave plus a perfect fifth. Not only is it difficult for the general public to sing, but it has repeatedly caused trouble even for professional opera singers. Some people assert that this problem could be solved by selecting the right key for performance. But the point is that *all* 12 possible keys are poor. No matter what the key, the tune goes either too high or too low (and both, for some people). What's more, the tune is irregular in its phrasing, and does not always fit the text well. In "Whose broad stripes," for instance, assigning "broad" to a tiny sixteenth note is bad.

Finally, Francis Scott Key's poem (1814) is not suitable. It is of low quality as poetry, and its subject matter is too specific and too militaristic, dealing with a one-day incident in a war. Are glaring rockets and bursting bombs the essence of the nation? . . . The poem has little to recommend it except for the single line, "The land of the free and the home of the brave."

—Caldwell Titcomb, "Star Spangled Earache," *New Republic*, December 16, 1985, p. 11.

Tony Kushner, playwright, reflecting on the song through the voice of a character (1992)

I hate America, Louis. I hate this country. It's just big ideas, and stories, and people dying, and people like you. The white cracker who wrote the national anthem knew what he was doing. He set the word "free" to a note so high nobody can reach it. That was deliberate. Nothing on Earth sounds less like freedom to me. You come to room 1013 over at the hospital, I'll show you America. Terminal, crazy and mean. I live in America, Louis, that's hard enough, I don't have to love it. You do that. Everybody's got to love something.

—"Belize," in Tony Kushner, *Angels in America: A Gay Fantasia on National Themes: Part II, Perestroika* (New York: Theater Communications Group, 1992), pp. 246–47.

Stanley Hauerwas, ethicist, reflecting on the national anthem, post-9/11 (2002)

I never really wanted to be a pacifist. I had learned from Reinhold Niebuhr that if you desire justice, you had better be ready to kill someone along the way. But then [John Howard Yoder's] *The Politics of Jesus* . . . convinced me that if there is anything to this Christian "stuff," it must surely involve the conviction that the Son would rather die on the cross than for the world to be redeemed by violence. . . .

But what does a pacifist have to say in the face of the terror September 11, 2001, names? I vaguely knew when I first declared I was a pacifist that there might be some serious consequences. To be nonviolent might even change my life. But I do not really think I understood what that change might entail until September 11. For example after I declared I was a pacifist, I quit singing "The Star-Spangled Banner." I will stand when it is sung, particularly at baseball games, but I do not sing. Not to sing "The Star-Spangled Banner" is a small thing that reminds me that my first loyalty is not to the United States, but to God and God's church. I confess it never crossed my mind that such small acts might over the years make my response to September 11 quite different from that of the good people who sing "God Bless America"—so different that I am left in saddened silence.

—Stanley Hauerwas, "September 11, 2001: A Pacifist Response," *South Atlantic Quarterly* 101.2 (Spring 2002): 427.

"God Bless America"

❧ IRVING BERLIN, 1938 ❧

ON THE AFTERNOON of Tuesday, September 11, 2001, in Washington, D.C., members of the House and Senate gathered in solidarity on the Capitol steps. Someone started to sing "God Bless America" and soon the U.S. Congress became the U.S. Chorus, with Democrats and Republicans belting out one of America's most beloved patriotic songs. The next day, President George W. Bush joined employees at the Pentagon in petitioning the blessings of the Almighty in song. On Thursday, when the lights came back up on Broadway, cast members led "God Bless America" sing-alongs. On Friday, a National Day of Prayer and Remembrance, at the National Cathedral, the U.S. Army Orchestra played "God Bless America." And at the New York Stock Exchange the following Monday, a Marine officer sang "God Bless America" before firefighters and police officers rang the bell to resume trading.

In the days and weeks after 9/11, this song became the nation's song. For the remainder of the 2001 season, it was performed during the seventh-inning stretch at Major League Baseball games. In November a benefit album called "God Bless America" featuring Canadian pop star Celine Dion debuted at the top of the Billboard charts. "God Bless America" was the anthem of the moment because the star-spangled imagery of America's official national anthem—"rockets' red glare" and "bombs bursting in air"—seemed inappropriate after jets had burst over Lower Manhattan, and because the nation, weary for the moment of irony and sarcasm, was desperate for nostalgia and sincerity.

"God Bless America" was written by Irving Berlin (1888–1989), a Russian immigrant and cantor's son whose vast contributions to the American songbook include "Alexander's Ragtime Band," "White Christmas," and "Easter Parade." Berlin wrote an early version of "God Bless America" on Long Island in 1918, in the midst of World War I, for a revue—"Yip, Yip Yaphank"—put on for the benefit of his army camp near Yaphank, New York. Berlin thought the song—a prayer set to music—was too heavy for such lighthearted entertainment, so he put it away, only to dust it off in 1938.

Berlin added an introductory verse, now rarely performed, that refers to portents of war in Europe and the Pledge of Allegiance at home. But for the most part he demilitarized his lyrics. "Make her victorious on land and foam" became "From the mountains, to the prairies, / To the oceans white with foam"; and "guide her / To the right" became "guide her / Through the night."

On November 10, 1938, on the eve of Armistice Day, the twentieth anniversary of the end of World War I, Kate Smith sang these new lyrics during her CBS radio show. Soon "God Bless America," which Smith referred to as "one of the most beautiful compositions ever written, a song that will never die," was being sung in public schools and Sunday schools, at meetings of the American Legion and the Daughters of the American Revolution, and at baseball and football games.[1] It made its Hollywood debut in *This Is the Army* (1943), a movie featuring Ronald Reagan, who would later turn Berlin's prayer into a political mantra.

Like Woody Guthrie's "This Land Is Your Land," Berlin's song has been appropriated by liberals and conservatives alike. In 1940, both Democrats and Republicans asked Berlin to allow them to play it at their conventions. But this song has not escaped controversy.

"God Bless America" sounds nonpartisan—"an expression of gratitude for what this country has done for its citizens, of what home really means," as Berlin told the *New York Times*.[2] But what is this "American home"? What does it stand for? At the time Berlin and Smith debuted the song, the nation was fractured. Democrats supported President Roosevelt's progressive reforms, while Republicans denounced the New Deal as a raw deal for the U.S. economy. Isolationists wanted the United States to stay out of European conflicts with the Nazis, while interventionists called for action in the name of justice. Americans were further divided between nativists, who insisted on immigration restrictions, and pluralists, who gloried in America as a melting pot of races, ethnicities, and religions. Berlin was at the time a New Deal Democrat, an internationalist, and a pluralist, so it should not be surprising that his song was initially identified with the left—an impression reinforced when Berlin played it on January 19, 1941, at an inauguration party for FDR, and when Ku Klux Klan leaders called for a boycott of the song because of its author's heritage. What right did a Jewish immigrant have to craft America's song?

Not everyone on the left applauded, however. Folk singer Woody Guthrie, who saw the song as saccharine pap, crafted "This Land Is Your Land" in protest. "God Bless America" was not a celebration of a nation of immigrants, in his view, but a cloying cover-up of America's ills. Others denounced the song as chauvinistic, for presuming that the Almighty had some special relationship with America. Bob Dylan's "With God on Our Side"—a powerful rejection of the view that America's interests could be blithely identified with those of the divine—was probably crafted in response to "God Bless America."

In the late 1960s, as the bloom on the counterculture started to fade, "God Bless America" came to be associated with the right. Whereas the song had previously been embraced by labor unions and civil rights activists, it was now sung by people in favor of segregation and the Vietnam War. In an episode of the 1970s sitcom *All in the Family,* the irrepressibly bigoted Archie Bunker cuts through an argument with his liberal son-in-law, Mike "Meathead" Stivic, first, by reciting the words to "God Bless America" and then singing them (off-key) with gusto. In June 2002, after a U.S. appeals court ruled that the words "under God" in the Pledge of Allegiance were unconstitutional, protesters took to the Capitol and sang "God Bless America." According to Sheryl Kaskowitz, whose Harvard dissertation focuses on the song, "'God Bless America' was their 'We Shall Overcome.'"[3]

As Kaskowitz observes, the post-9/11 revival of "God Bless America" began as a way for Americans to mourn collectively for those who lost their lives (or their innocence) on 9/11. So for a time it transcended its ties with religious and political conservatism. With the 2003 U.S. invasion of Iraq, however, the song shifted "from 9/11 tribute to pro-war anthem." It was played not to remember the firefighters and restaurant workers who died on 9/11, but to support the troops in Iraq and Afghanistan. In this way, "God Bless America" has served both as "a unifying symbol" and as a "wedge."[4]

Recent years have seen some pushback against "God Bless America," based on both principle and simple fatigue. There were few complaints when Major

League Baseball had "God Bless America" pinch-hit for "Take Me Out to the Ball Game" through the end of the 2001 baseball season, but as this tradition wore on (a handful of teams were still playing the song at every home game in 2011), some waxed nostalgic for that old-time religion of peanuts, Cracker Jacks, and the old ball game. According to a 2009 online survey done by Kaskowitz, the overwhelming majority of baseball fans either "dislike" or "strongly dislike" the singing of "God Bless America" at baseball games. As one survey participant said:

> I am an American who is an agnostic, liberal Democrat who loves baseball and its traditions. Playing "God Bless America" at baseball games offends me in three ways: forced worship of a God I don't believe in, forced participation in a political "rally" whose views I don't share, and the extended interruption of a sport that I love.[5]

Others are irked about the intrusion of the phrase "God bless America" into American political rhetoric. Beginning with the Reagan presidency, this salutation has become all but obligatory in presidential speeches, as George H. W. Bush, Bill Clinton, George W. Bush, and Barack Obama all echoed Reagan in concluding many presidential addresses with some variation on this theme. In 1992, *New York Times* columnist William Safire finished a column on this subject with a mock prayer: "Thank you. God bless each and every reader of this column, even you lefties. And God bless America (which is not to say that God should not also bless the rest of the world)."[6] In a similar piece in *Slate* (which also ended with a mock prayer), Michael Kinsley complained in 2001 about what he called "our Official Patriotic Sentiment," noting that "in another disturbing trend, God is being called on to bless you and then bless various individual states."[7]

"God Bless America" 🐦

> While the storm clouds gather far across the sea,
> Let us swear allegiance to a land that's free;
> Let us all be grateful for a land so fair,
> As we raise our voices in a solemn prayer:
>
> God bless America, land that I love.
> Stand beside her and guide her
> Through the night with a light from above.
> From the mountains, to the prairies,
> To the oceans white with foam,
> God bless America, my home sweet home.

COMMENTARY

Peter Marshall, Presbyterian minister, arguing for real prayer over sentimental singing (1940)

Singing "God Bless America" is not enough. Waving our flag is not enough. A maudlin, sticky, sentimental, pseudo-patriotism is not enough. God is not going to bless America just because a nation sings the song.

Why *should* God bless America? Why should we be blessed of God more than Germany, or Poland, or France, or Great Britain, or Denmark, or China? Have we any racial superiority, or rare intelligence, or moral excellence? Are we more deserving in the sight of God? Are we better than other nations? Are our morals higher? Are we Gentiles, are we Protestants, are we Presbyterians, any better than other peoples? Can we show any reason why God should bless us? . . .

We can sing "God Bless America" until we are blue in the face . . . but unless we do what God has indicated, His blessings will be withheld.

—Peter Marshall, "Why Should God Bless America?," sermon, New York Avenue Presbyterian Church, Washington, D.C., September 15, 1940, in Peter J. Marshall, ed., *The Wartime Sermons of Dr. Peter Marshall* (Dallas: Clarion Call Marketing, 2005), pp. 6–7, 17.

Richard Nixon, thirty-seventh U.S. president, transforming Berlin's
lyrics into a standard sign-off for a presidential address (1973)

Tonight, I ask for your prayers to help me in everything that I do throughout the days of my Presidency to be worthy of their hopes and of yours. God bless America and God bless each and every one of you.

—Richard Nixon, "Address to the Nation About the Watergate Investigations," April 30, 1973, in *Public Papers of the Presidents of the United States, Richard Nixon, 1973* (Washington, DC: U.S. Government Printing Office, 1975), p. 328.

Ronald Reagan, fortieth U.S. president, invoking
God in the Capitol Rotunda (1985)

Now we're standing inside this symbol of our democracy, and we see and hear again the echoes of our past: a general falls to his knees in the hard snow of Valley Forge; a lonely President paces the darkened halls and ponders his struggle to preserve the Union; the men of the Alamo call out encouragement to each other; a settler pushes west and sings a song, and the song echoes out forever and fills the unknowing air.

It is the American sound. It is hopeful, big-hearted, idealistic, daring, decent, and fair. That's our heritage, that's our song. We sing it still. For all our problems, our differences, we are together as of old. We raise our voices to the God who is the Author of this most tender music. And may He continue to hold us close as we fill the world with our sound—in unity, affection, and love—one people under God, dedicated to the dream of freedom that He has placed in the human heart, called upon now to pass that dream on to a waiting and hopeful world.

God bless you, and God bless America.

—Ronald Reagan, "Second Inaugural Address," January 21, 1985, www.presidency.ucsb.edu/ws/index .php?pid=38688#axzz1ZMzcQ7tL.

William Safire, columnist, on efforts to draft God into politics (1992)

Remember when politicians concluded their speeches with "Thank you and good night"? Gone are those secular days.

At the Republican Convention, Pat Buchanan ended with "God bless you, and God bless America." Ronald Reagan followed with greater specificity: "God bless each and every one of you, and God bless this country we love." . . .

Democrats cannot really complain about this G.O.P. enlistment of G.O.D. because this generation's recruitment of the Deity in politics began with born-again Jimmy Carter's 1976 campaign. And in New York last month, Bill Clinton nine times evoked a religious image with his new "covenant," and concluded his acceptance address with "God bless you, and God bless America."

But the voter-viewer can ask: Why has "God bless you" become the universal, politically required sign-off? And by what ecclesiastical authority do politicians, in holy alliance, bestow God's blessing on us and our country?

The answer is that the name of the Lord is being used as a symbol for the other side's immorality, much as the American flag was used in previous campaigns as a symbol for the other side's lack of patriotism. A few years ago, Democrats answered the Nixonite flag lapel pin with heavy flag drapery. Are Democrats now to counter Mr. Bush's wooing of the religious right with fervent protestations of morality, displaying red, white and blue crosses and stars?

I hope not. The more effective response is to challenge the religious propriety of any political organization's claim to having God on its side.

Lincoln addressed that in his Second Inaugural. The North, fighting against slavery, was certain it was doing God's will. Why, the Emancipator wondered, did God let the terrible bloodshed go on and on?

Lincoln's conclusion was that God might not be on either side: "The Almighty has his own purposes." He later wrote to a political ally about that speech: " I believe it is not immediately popular. Men are not flattered by being shown that there has been a difference of purpose between the Almighty and them."

That Inaugural, with its "malice toward none" peroration, is now popular, but its troubling theological point is missed: God is not in moral bondage to Man. His design is not for us to discern. As the biblical Job learned, God does not have to do justice on earth—nor need He explain the suffering of innocent babes in Somalia, Bosnia or Kurdistan.

Believers may properly refer to God with respect in every activity, including politics, but it is the height of presumption—irreverence to the point of blasphemy—for any political or religious leader to arrogate the right to cast God's vote. His is the most secret ballot of all.

Whose side is God on in the 1992 Presidential race? His side.

Thank you. God bless each and every reader of this column, even you lefties. And God bless America (which is not to say that God should not also bless the rest of the world).

—William Safire, "God Bless Us," *New York Times*, August 27, 1992, p. A23.

William Sloane Coffin, preacher, calling down God's blessings on other countries (2001)

In church we are always singing that "there's a wideness in God's mercy," of "one great fellowship divine throughout the whole wide earth," about how "other lands have sunshine too, and clover, and skies are everywhere as blue as mine." In all these hymns we are affirming God's same impartial love for all people, with no special privileges in it for only some. In other words, "God Bless America" means "God bless Afghanistan" too, not to mention Iraq and North Korea.

—William Sloane Coffin, "God Bless America," October 14, 2001, in *A Passion for the Possible: A Message to U.S. Churches* (Louisville: Westminster John Knox, 2004), p. 92.

James Carroll, columnist, on the mutation of "God Bless America" into a "truth-claim" (2003)

The suicide-murderers of Al Qaeda (and of Hezbollah, for that matter) are not the only ones to justify violent absolutism by appeals to the divine. America's War on Terrorism is itself defined by a fervent Manichaeanism that divides the world between good and evil. "God bless America," a formerly innocuous patriotic piety, has taken on the character of a truth-claim, an open assertion of the long-dormant exceptionalism that assumes a national anointing—a sacred destiny that elevates America above other nations. A religious self-understanding informs our nation's new imperial impulse, explicitly articulated in the Bush administration's 2002 "National Security Strategy." The result is a drastic reordering of American relations not only with an Islamic adversary that is perceived univocally (Iraq is "evil," and so is Iraq's mortal enemy Iran), but also with an openly skeptical Europe, and an increasingly alienated Asia.

—James Carroll, "Why Religion Still Matters," *Daedalus* 132.3 (Summer 2003): 9.

Jeremiah Wright, United Church of Christ minister, asking God to damn America instead (2003)

The government gives them the drugs, builds bigger prisons, passes a three-strike law, and then wants us to sing "God Bless America." No, no, no. Not God bless America. God damn America. That's in the Bible for killing innocent people. God damn America for treating our citizens as less than human. God damn America for as long as she acts like she is God and she is supreme.

—"Jeremiah Wright," sermon, April 13, 2003, www.youtube.com/watch?v=36T1fnIafC0.

Gersh Kuntzman, journalist, asking God not to bless America during baseball games (2003)

As we celebrate our national holiday on Tuesday—the baseball All-Star Game— I have just one prayer for our nation: If God insists on blessing America, can He please, for Pete's sake, stop doing it during the seventh-inning stretch? . . .

Since September 18, 2001—when Major League Baseball returned after the terror attacks—the song "God Bless America" has pushed aside "Take Me Out to the Ball Game" as the new seventh-inning tradition. For the first few months, who could object? It provided catharsis and comfort—a way for Americans to grieve together.

Most teams have continued the "tradition" to this day. My beloved Mets and the hated Yankees still play "God Bless America" at all home games. Even my minor league team, the Brooklyn Cyclones, which fills the between-inning breaks with racing hot dogs and old ladies dancing the "Cha-Cha Slide" on the dugout roof, plays a somber version of the song at every game. . . .

The seventh-inning stretch renditions of "God Bless America" still embody some great things about America—the community, the notion of shared sacrifice—and all of the worst things: the self-righteous pride, the forced piety, the earnest self-reverence, the smugness.

It offends a broad section of people, such as:

Atheists!: "As a patriotic American, I'd love to be able to join my fellow countrymen in song, but 'God Bless America' brings politics and religion to a baseball game," says Ellen Johnson, president of American Atheists. "I don't go to a baseball game to get aggravated." (Obviously, she's not a Mets fan.)

Non-Atheists!: "The song is dumb," says Charlie Pillsbury, who ran for Congress in Connecticut as a Green Party candidate last year (and got 5 percent of the vote). One of his campaign issues was his objection to "God Bless America." "If you believe in God, as I do, you believe that God shows no partiality towards nations," he said. "God blesses the whole world." . . .

Some British guy!: At a recent Cyclones game, I ran into James Silver, a British journalist who's studying his country's former colonists. When "God Bless America" was being played, Silver smiled. "It's exactly what I expect from Americans," he says. "The self-righteousness, the patriotism. It's always nice to see my opinions confirmed." . . .

Most important, of course, is that "God Bless America" is a bully that has pushed aside a song that actually should be the National Anthem, namely, "Take Me Out to the Ball Game."

Written in 1908—by a guy who'd never even attended a game—this song embodies everything that is good about America, from the notion of losing yourself to something bigger than earthly concerns ("I don't care if I ever get back") to the assertion that Vince Lombardi was wrong about winning ("if they don't win it's a shame") to, finally, the joy of fair play ("It's one, two, three strikes you're out at the old ball game"). . . .

So, give me back my "Take Me Out to the Ball Game." If God wants to bless America, He can save it until after the game.

—Gersh Kuntzman, "American Beat: Play Ball, Not Prayers," *Newsweek*, July 14, 2003, www.thedailybeast.com/newsweek/2003/07/13/american-beat-play-ball-not-prayers.html.

J. C. Watts, U.S. Representative (R-OK), eulogizing President Reagan (2005)

When we lost our friend early in the summer of 2004, I didn't mourn President Reagan's death. Rather, I celebrated his life. While our nation continues its journey toward that "shining city on a hill," there is no doubt in my mind that President

Reagan is now there watching, head cocked to the side with that signature infectious smile, pulling for that great goodness that is the place others call America, and we call home. President Reagan often closed his speeches with the words "God bless you, and God bless America." God answered that prayer—for America and the world—by giving us the gift of Ronald Reagan.

—J. C. Watts, "Remembering Ronald Reagan," in Michael K. Deaver, ed., *Why I Am a Reagan Conservative* (New York: HarperCollins, 2005), p. 49.

Billboard, central Indiana (2011)

When Americans worship God, God will bless America.

"This Land Is Your Land"

❧ WOODY GUTHRIE, 1940 ❧

FOLKSINGER Woody Guthrie (1912–67) initially conceived of "This Land Is Your Land" as a protest against Irving Berlin's "God Bless America." Like Berlin, who cast his gaze "from the mountains, to the prairies, to the oceans white with foam," Guthrie set his ballad "from the redwood forest, to the Gulf Stream waters." But Guthrie, who wrote "God Blessed America for Me" (as he initially called this song) in New York City on February 23, 1940, sang of the bitterness as well as the sweetness of his American home, and he did not request God's blessing. A habitual tinkerer, Guthrie played around with the words and the title, and when he finally recorded it in April 1944 it had become "This Land Is Your Land."

Popularized in the 1960s, this "singable, hand-clappingly lively and populist" ballad has been embraced by Americans of all political persuasions.[1] Rock 'n' roll legend Bruce Springsteen has called it "perhaps the greatest song ever written about our home."[2] To author Studs Terkel, it is America's unofficial national anthem, and far superior to both "The Star-Spangled Banner" and "God Bless America." "It has nothing to do with bombs bursting in air nor with sanctimonious blessing," writes Terkel. "It has to do with what this country is all about."[3]

Woodrow Wilson Guthrie, the man behind the legend behind this song, was a folksinger, wanderer, radio personality, newspaper columnist, and prairie radical who, upon his death in 1967 at the age of fifty-five, left behind more than three thousand songs plus a first-rate autobiography, *Bound for Glory* (1943). Born in

Oklahoma, Guthrie led a hardscrabble life, which included a sister and a daughter who burned to death, a father who abandoned him, and a mother who gradually succumbed, body and mind, to Huntington's disease—a degenerative illness that would eventually claim Guthrie's life as well.

Ever an activist, Guthrie defined the folk song as "what's wrong and how to fix it," and his songs gave voice to the troubles he saw in the Great Depression, the Dust Bowl, and World War II.[4] For these songs, Guthrie was being praised as early as 1940 as a "rusty-voiced Homer."[5] In that same year, *Grapes of Wrath* author John Steinbeck welcomed him as America's troubadour:

> *Harsh voiced and nasal, his guitar hanging like a tire iron on a rusty rim, there is nothing sweet about Woody, and there is nothing sweet about the songs he sings. But there is something more important for those who will listen. There is the will of a people to endure and fight against oppression. I think we call this the American spirit.*[6]

Bob Dylan, who memorialized Guthrie in "Song for Woody" (1962), wrote that Guthrie's songs were "beyond category. They had the infinite sweep of humanity in them."[7]

Because of his left-wing politics (he contributed columns and cartoons to the Communist newspaper the *People's World* and was tracked by the FBI during the Red Scare of the 1950s), Guthrie has always been controversial. When Senator Fred Harris (D-OK) introduced a congressional resolution proposing a national Woody Guthrie Day in the early 1970s, the Chamber of Commerce in Guthrie's hometown of Okemah, Oklahoma, opposed it on the grounds that such a celebration would amount to "the commemoration of a Communist."[8] Meanwhile, some on the left thought that Guthrie was too cozy with the establishment. When asked to comment on his politics, Guthrie reportedly said, "I ain't a Communist necessarily, but I been in the red all my life."[9]

"This Land Is Your Land" has been less controversial. It was featured at the 1960 Republican National Convention, which nominated Richard Nixon, and at the 1972 Democratic National Convention, which nominated George McGovern. It has been performed by folksingers, country stars, and rock 'n' roll and punk legends, including Peter, Paul, and Mary, Dave Matthews, Joan Baez, Johnny Cash, Lou Reed, Billy Bragg, and the Mormon Tabernacle Choir. It has also been played at the Miss America pageant, and in advertisements for Ford and Target. Like other American originals, "This Land Is Your Land" has inspired many parodies. During the 2004 presidential campaign, a YouTube spoof appeared, featuring George Bush and John Kerry each singing "this land will surely vote for me."[10]

During his lifetime, Guthrie was largely unknown outside of folk music circles, but today he is widely regarded as a national treasure. He was glorified in a 1976 biopic called *Bound for Glory,* praised at his induction into the Rock and Roll Hall of Fame in 1988, and remembered in the late 1990s and early 2000s in a Smithsonian Institution traveling exhibition called "This Land Is Your Land: The Life and Legacy of Woody Guthrie." Even Okemah has come to embrace its native son. It is now home to an annual Woody Guthrie Folk Festival and to a statue commemorating Guthrie, complete with a guitar that reads (as Guthrie's did), "This machine kills fascists."

Like many other books in *The American Bible,* "This Land Is Your Land" can be interpreted as either celebratory or prophetic—a hymn of praise to the promise of America or a lament over the inability of Americans to live up to that promise. In this case, however, how it is interpreted depends on what "it" is. The most popular version of the song contains three verses and a chorus celebrating the American landscape and the American highway. But early versions of the song include two additional verses—about landowners trying to keep wanderers out in the name of "Private Property" and hungry people standing at "the relief office" hoping for assistance. These protest verses were largely forgotten until the late 1960s, when Arlo Guthrie (Woody's son), Pete Seeger, and other folksingers began to sing them in concerts.

In part because of the resurgence of these more pointed lyrics, "This Land Is Your Land" has been associated in recent years with the left. Bruce Springsteen and Pete Seeger sang it (complete with the "lost verses") during the inaugural concert for President Barack Obama held on the steps of the Lincoln Memorial in January 2009. The song also opened the 2009 film *Up in the Air* starring George Clooney. Today a Facebook page urges Americans to adopt it as their national anthem.

"This Land Is Your Land" 🕊

This land is your land, this land is my land,
From California to the New York island;
From the redwood forest to the Gulf Stream waters,
This land was made for you and me.

As I was walking that ribbon of highway,
I saw above me that endless skyway.
I saw below me that golden valley.
This land was made for you and me.

I've roamed and rambled and I followed my footsteps
To the sparkling sands of her diamond deserts;
And all around me a voice was sounding:
This land was made for you and me.

When the sun came shining, and I was strolling,
And the wheat fields waving and the dust clouds rolling,
As the fog was lifting a voice was chanting:
"This land was made for you and me."

As I went walking I saw a sign there,
And on the sign it said, "No Trespassing."
But on the other side it didn't say nothing.
That side was made for you and me.

In the shadow of the steeple I saw my people,
By the relief office I seen my people;
As they stood there hungry, I stood there asking,
"Is this land made for you and me?"

Nobody living can ever stop me,
As I go walking that freedom highway;
Nobody living can ever make me turn back
This land was made for you and me.

COMMENTARY

The Folksinger's Wordbook, *imagining how "this land" looks to Native Americans, environmentalists, and GIs (1973)*

Native American Version

This land is your land, it once was my land,
Before we sold you Manhattan Island,
You pushed our nations to the reservations
This land was stole by you from me.

Ecology Version

I've roamed and rambled and followed the beer cans,
From the toxic cities to the flooded canyons.
And all around me were the billboards reading:
This land was made for you and me!

As I was walking that ribbon of highway,
I heard the buzzing of a hundred chain saws,
And the redwoods falling, and the loggers calling:
This land was made for you and me.

GI Vietnam Version

This land is your land, but it isn't my land,
From the Mekong Delta to the Pleiku Highland,
When we get shot at the ARVN flee,
This land was meant for the V.C.!

—Fred and Irwin Silber, eds., *The Folksinger's Wordbook* (New York: Oak, 1973), p. 315.

Jesse Jackson, *Baptist preacher running for president (1988)*

If I get your vote, I can win. If I can win, any American can become President. If I cannot win, most Americans cannot become President. If I can win, it means never again will race, sex or religion stand between you and the White House. If I cannot win, most of you can never win. Together we can win. Workers united will never be defeated. I know it's been tough, but hold on to your faith. Don't turn to drugs, hold on to your faith. Don't turn on your wives and your children—hold on. I know it's been tough, but don't give up. Above all, keep your dignity, keep your self-respect. Hold your head high, stick your chest out. Be proud. You built America. You built the world. This land is your land.

—Jesse Jackson, "From a Tradition of Marching for Jobs and Rights," *New York Times*, January 19, 1988, p. B6.

Douglas Applegate, U.S. Representative (D-OH), preaching protectionism (1991)

Mr. Speaker, the trade deficit with Japan continues to soar. The only trade policy that we have in this country is to allow all these foreign products to come in with no restrictions, and then we allow them to restrict our goods into their country. . . .

The other day I saw a cartoon where there was this group of Japanese sitting in their boardroom around a big table and they were singing, they were toasting, "This land is my land, this land is your land, from California to the New York Islands." I am telling you, that is what it is coming down to now. We spend billions of dollars to defend this island of billionaires, and then they turn it into profit at our expense. I think it is time for a trade policy that is going to be fair to American industry and American workers.

—Douglas Applegate, "Our Trade Policy with Japan," *Congressional Record,* March 6, 1991, p. H1425.

Michael Kelly, author, on how CEOs and billionaires have taken over this land (2002)

Woody Guthrie carries a nice tune, but this land is not your land, unless you are Trump or Tisch.

—Michael Kelly, "Getting Hip to Squareness: We Want Our Virginity Back," *Atlantic Monthly,* February 2002, pp. 20–21.

J. Mark Fox, nondenominational Christian minister, on who really owns America (2008)

The Bible says: "The earth is the Lord's and all its fullness, the world and those who dwell therein." The truth is, with all due respect to Woody Guthrie, this land is not your land or my land. It is His land. The Lord owns it all.

—J. Mark Fox, *Real Life Moments: A Dad's Devotional* (Indianapolis, IN: Dog Ear, 2008), p. 30.

Barbara Ehrenreich, author, criticizing the colonization of America's most beautiful places by mansions and millionaires (2008)

I recently took a little break—nine hours in Sun Valley before an evening speaking engagement. The sky was deep blue, the air crystalline, the hills green and, unlike much of the West, not yet on fire. . . . But things started to get a little sinister—maybe I had wandered into a movie set or Paris Hilton's closet?—because even at a 60 percent discount, I couldn't find a sleeveless cotton shirt for less than $100. These items shouldn't have been outdoors; they should have been in locked glass cases. Then I remembered the general rule, which has been in place since sometime in the nineties: *if a place is truly beautiful, you can't afford to be there.* All right,

I'm sure there are still exceptions, a few scenic spots not yet eaten up by mansions. But they're going fast. . . .

When I was a child, I sang "America the Beautiful" and meant it. I was born in the Rocky Mountains and raised, at various times, on the coasts. The Big Sky, the rolling surf, the jagged, snowcapped mountains—all this seemed to be my birthright. But now I flinch when I hear Woody Guthrie's line "This land was made for you and me." Somehow, I don't think it was meant to be sung by a chorus of hedge-fund operators.

—Barbara Ehrenreich, *This Land Is Their Land: Reports from a Divided Nation* (New York: Metropolitan, 2008), pp. 11–13.

Ted Poe, U.S. Representative (R-TX), arguing for private sales of public lands (2011)

Mr. Speaker, we've heard ["This Land Is Your Land"]. But we need to understand that, in America, the greatest, largest landowner is Uncle Sam. . . . He owns 27 percent of all the land in America. . . . Maybe we should sell some of that.

So I introduced the American Land Act, which will do this: It will require that the Bureau of Land Management and the Forestry Service sell a portion of their land for the next 5 years, and that will be a 26 percent decrease in total land in the United States owned by Uncle Sam. . . . Plus, it would do other things. It would put the land in the hands of Americans. Americans would own the land, and they would pay taxes. They could pay taxes not only to local and State governments, but when they build a business or make a business, they would bring in more Federal income tax. It will save the Federal Government the cost of maintaining ownership, and it will raise revenue and pay down the debt. . . .

Uncle Sam shouldn't prevent Americans from having a stake, or a share, in America. The United States owns most of the grand estate of our great country, and it's time to let more Americans own it—because this land was made for you and me.

—Ted Poe, "Uncle Sam—The Great Landowner," *Congressional Record,* July 20, 2011, p. H5241.

PROVERBS

B ENJAMIN FRANKLIN (1706–90), printer, inventor, and founding father, gave the world many things, but few so enduring or influential as his aphorisms, which provide as good a summary as any of the American ethos in the early republic. In these pithy sayings, Franklin plays the part of a secular preacher, exhorting his congregation to cultivate the virtues of temperance and frugality, sincerity and moderation, cleanliness and humility. In "Advice to a Young Tradesman" (1748), Franklin writes, "Remember that time is money. He that can earn ten shillings a day by his labor, and goes abroad, or sits idle, one half of that day, though he spends but sixpence during his diversion or idleness, ought not to reckon that the only expense; he has really spent, or rather thrown away, five shillings besides."[1] In other words, if you aren't working you are wasting your time. Franklin lived in an era when most Americans earned a living off land or sea, and time was measured not so much by clocks as by ebbing and flowing tides and the rising and setting sun. With the emergence of industrial capitalism in the early nineteenth century, clocks began to dominate American life, both at home and in factories. By the middle of the nineteenth century, Franklin's aphorism had "grown to a proverb"— "penciled on our time-pieces, placed conspicuously in our mechanic shops, and heralded in our public journals."[2] With the invention of the railroad, telegraph, airplane, and Internet, "time is money" became truer than ever. A century ago, the German sociologist Max Weber wrote that Franklin's aphorism summed up the "spirit of capitalism" in "almost classical purity."[3] The point of this early form of capitalism, Weber observed, was to amass capital, not to spend it. So time not spent in raising capital was time wasted. Today America is possessed of a new spirit of capitalism, one focused on spending and consuming. But like the hundred-dollar bill, which features Franklin's portrait, Franklin's wisdom still circulates, reminding Americans that hard work is a duty of sorts, and productivity an end in itself.

"A Farmer," letter to the editor (1825): Both time and money are valuable. Let them not be wasted in the training stable and on the race course.

Louis Agassiz, Harvard natural history professor (1858): I cannot afford to waste my time in making money.

Mark Twain, author (1870): Time is money. Now, I haven't got any money, but, as regards time, I am in affluent circumstances, and if you will receipt that bill, I will give you a check for as much time as you think equivalent, and throw you in a couple of hours for your trouble.

Austin Phelps, Congregationalist minister (1899): It is a wretched burlesque to say that time is money. It would be as truthful to say that light is money, that air is money, that sleep is money. Time is thought, time is knowledge, time is character, time is power, time is the threshold of eternity.

Abraham Heschel, rabbi (1951): We usually think that the earth is our mother, that time is money and profit our mate. The seventh day is a reminder that God is our father, that time is life and the spirit our mate.

Peter Drucker, management guru (1966): One cannot buy, rent or hire more time. The supply of time is totally inelastic. No matter how high the demand, the supply will not increase. There is no price for it and no marginal utility curve for it. Moreover, time is totally perishable and cannot be stored. Yesterday's time is gone forever, and will never come back. Time is, therefore, always in exceedingly short supply.

Richard Callahan Jr., religious studies professor (2003): If, in America, time is money, then sacred time might be considered time that is not commodified, time that is valued for something other than its monetary value alone. Activities that make time sacred today are those that remind Americans that money is not the final measure of value. People talk about quality time spent with family or loved ones as "sacred time." Walks in the forest or on the beach, travel unrelated to business, personal retreats, meditation, and exercise have all been called sacred time. Yet, ironically, the perceived scarcity of such times and experiences has made them the perfect commodity. The market for sacred time in the form of retreats, meditation centers, pilgrimage packages, massages, healing arts, and more continues to grow.

David Marcus, editor (2010): Time is money—an adage well-worn by last century's entrepreneurial and managerial classes—has lost much of its resonance these days. We have lots of time; little of it is becoming money.[4]

> ## "Remember that time is money"
> BENJAMIN FRANKLIN, 1748

THE OVERWHELMING majority of Americans—including the overwhelming majority of born-again Christians—believe that "God helps those who help themselves" is biblical. In fact, in some surveys this is the most frequently cited Bible verse in the United States. Unfortunately, the Bible never says, "God helps those who help themselves." In fact, one of the core teachings of the New Testament is quite the opposite—that God helps the helpless. One reason why this saying seems biblical is its aphoristic quality. Another is that it elegantly distills the now "self-evident" American value of self-reliance. An ancient sentiment, "God helps those who help themselves" appears in writing by the sixteenth-century British author John Heywood and the seventeenth-century English politician Algernon Sidney, but it was popularized among Americans by Benjamin Franklin, who included "God helps them that help themselves" in "The Way to Wealth," a preface to the 1758 edition of his *Poor Richard Improved*.[1] As a Deist, Franklin did not actually believe that God meddled in human affairs. So this was his way of saying that hard work, not prayer, was the way to get ahead in the rough-and-tumble of colonial America. In recent years this saying has been used by Nation of Islam leader Elijah Muhammad and among self-help gurus and startup CEOs. It is also a favorite of politically conservative Christians, who quote it to support their opposition to welfare, and of prosperity gospel preachers, for whom Jesus comes to bring health and wealth as well as otherworldly salvation. An alternative view is presented on a Facebook page called "God Helps Those Who Help Others." Still, this plea for self-reliance packs a punch in American popular culture. Franklin's words may not be biblical, but they are part of *The American Bible* nonetheless.

Orson Hyde, Mormon pioneer and LDS Church president (1854): I have been showing you what will be done for His elect in the last days; but will He do it for them who will do nothing for themselves? I say no; God helps those who help themselves. I recollect when I was in Potawatomie [Iowa] I was determined to raise a crop if I could. I commenced and plowed up the land, and went into the woods when it was hot enough in the summer season almost to unsolder a skellet, and hauled out my rails, and fenced and sowed the land; when snow came, there was a fleece of wheat over the land like wool on a sheep's back. President [Brigham] Young saw it, and he said it pleased him; and he said, "I know that God helps those who help themselves." We may sit down and persuade ourselves that it is God's will we should do nothing for ourselves, and we may go to beggary; but if we help ourselves, and bestow the labor for nature to bring forth, we shall have an abundance, and God will be faithful in blessing our labors.

Malcolm X, black nationalist leader (1965): I felt that Allah would be more inclined to help those who helped themselves.

Bill McKibben, journalist (2005): Three out of four Americans believe that this uber-American idea, a notion at the core of our current individualist politics and culture, which was in fact uttered by Ben Franklin, actually appears in Holy Scripture. The thing is, not only is Franklin's wisdom not biblical; it's counter-biblical. Few ideas could be further from the gospel message, with its radical summons to love of neighbor.

Bill O'Reilly, television personality (2010): Every fair-minded person should support government safety nets for people who need assistance through no fault of their own. But [liberal Democrats] don't make distinctions like that. For them, the baby Jesus wants us to "provide," no matter what the circumstance. But being a Christian, I know that while Jesus promoted charity at the highest level, he was not self-destructive. The Lord helps those who help themselves. Does he not?

Barack Obama, forty-fourth U.S. president (2011): If you want to put teachers back in the classroom, pass this bill. If you want construction workers back on the job, pass this bill. . . . Now is the time to act. We are not people who sit back in tough times. We step up in tough times. We make things happen in tough times. We've been through tougher times before, and we got through them. We're going to get through these to a brighter day, but we're going to have to act. God helps those who help themselves. We need to help ourselves right now.[2]

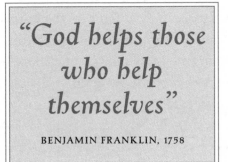

"God helps those who help themselves"

BENJAMIN FRANKLIN, 1758

$\mathbf{I}$N THE SPRING of 1775, events were building, economically, politically, and militarily, toward the "shot heard round the world." About a month before that shot was fired, the Virginia House of Burgesses met at St. John's Church in Richmond, Virginia, to consider whether Virginians should raise a militia to prepare for war. Thomas Jefferson and George Washington were there. So was the orator and statesman Patrick Henry (1736–99), who rose to speak for mobilization. Henry's speech, delivered on March 23, 1775, was neither recorded nor published in his lifetime, but his biographer, William Wirt (who was *not* there), later reconstructed it, likely with the help of Judge St. George Tucker (who was). Henry addressed his remarks, which referred repeatedly to scripture (including Judas betraying Jesus with a kiss), to moderates who still hoped for reconciliation with the British. He told them not to be deceived; it was time to fight. Attempts to resolve peacefully the decade-long power struggle between the Crown and its colonies had failed. "Our petitions have been slighted; our remonstrances have produced additional violence and insult; our supplications have been disregarded," he said in words that would later echo in the Declaration of Independence. "Is life so dear, or peace so sweet, as to be purchased at the price of chains and slavery?" he asked. "Forbid it, Almighty God! I know not what course others may take; but as for me, give me liberty or give me death!"[1] Virginia's delegates voted with Henry, and his passionate call to arms in the name of liberty has resounded through the American centuries, particularly among those who see liberty as *the* American ideal and its preservation as *the* obligation of government. In a speech announcing the Voting Rights Act (1965), President Lyndon Johnson placed Henry in a long line of long-suffering American champions of freedom, including Minutemen, Union soldiers, and civil rights protesters. Henry's words "are a promise to every citizen . . . that he shall share in freedom, he shall choose his leaders, educate his children, and provide for his family according to his ability and his merits as a human being," he said.[2] Today Henry is remembered on New Hampshire license plates, which read "Live free or die," in Patrick Henry public schools, and in the bestselling U.S. history textbook *Give Me Liberty!* His words continue to be used to champion civil liberties at home and democracy abroad. In the centerpiece of the Arab Spring in Cairo's Tahrir Square in 2011, many protesters held Henry's words high, demanding liberty and offering their lives in return.

Henry Highland Garnet, Presbyterian minister and former slave (1843): Fellow men! Patient sufferers! Behold your dearest rights crushed to the earth! See your sons murdered, and your wives, mothers and sisters doomed to prostitution. In the name of the merciful God, and by all that life is worth, let it no longer be a debatable question, whether it is better to choose liberty or death.

William Jennings Bryan, anti-imperialist and Democratic nominee for president (1900): If the Republicans are prepared to censure all who have used language calculated to make the Filipinos hate foreign domination [by the United States], let them condemn the speech of Patrick Henry. When he uttered that passionate appeal, "Give me liberty or give me death," he expressed a sentiment which still echoes in the hearts of men. . . . Let them censure Lincoln, whose Gettysburg speech will be quoted in defense of popular government when the present advocates of force and conquest are forgotten. Someone has said that a truth, once spoken, can never be recalled. It goes on and on, and no one can set a limit to its ever-widening influence. But if it were possible to obliterate every word written or spoken in defense of the principles set forth in the Declaration of Independence, a war of conquest would still leave its legacy of perpetual hatred, for it was God himself who placed in every human heart the love of liberty. He never made a race of people so low in the scale of civilization or intelligence that it would welcome a foreign master.

Harry Truman, thirty-third U.S. president (1950): I had a card from Los Angeles this morning, in which the writer suggested to me in all seriousness that the proper thing to do was to surrender to Russia. He said we may lose our freedom, but it is better to lose our freedom than to lose our lives. Now, what do you think of that? That is Patrick Henry in reverse, if I know anything.

> ## "Give me liberty or give me death"
>
> PATRICK HENRY, 1775

Kiplinger's Personal Finance magazine (1950): The Republicans are promising liberty, and the Democrats are promising dollars. There was a time when patriots cried, "Give me liberty or give me death." . . . [Now a] good many seem inclined to say, "Give me liberty and at the same time give me enough dollars to live on comfortably up to the time of my death."

John F. Kennedy, U.S. Senator (D-MA) (1960): We should not fear the 20th century, for this worldwide revolution which we see all around us is part of the original American Revolution. When the Indonesians revolted after the end of World War II, they scrawled on the walls, "Give me liberty or give me death." They scrawled on the walls "All men are created equal." Not Russian slogans but American slogans.[3]

ᴇ ARLY ɪɴ 1776 in the throes of the Revolutionary War, John and Abigail Adams exchanged letters between their home outside Boston and the Continental Congress in Philadelphia. The immortal line in this correspondence came when Abigail (1744–1818) urged her husband to "remember the ladies" while drafting new laws for the aborning nation. Half-jokingly reminding him that men are "naturally tyrannical," she urged him not to "treat us only as the vassals of your sex." "If particular care and attention is not paid to the ladies," she warned, "we are determined to foment a rebellion, and will not hold ourselves bound by any laws in which we have no voice or representation."[1] John responded playfully, chuckling at the "despotism of the petticoat."[2] In a later letter, Abigail redeployed the revolutionary rhetoric in the air: "But you must remember that arbitrary power is like most other things which are very hard, very liable to be broken; and, notwithstanding all your wise laws and maxims, we have it in our power, not only to free ourselves, but to subdue our masters, and, without violence, throw both your natural and legal authority at our feet."[3] Abigail's words have been described as "the boldest statement written by an American woman in the 18th century."[4] Her private letter had little public effect, however. John did raise the question of women's rights with the governor of Massachusetts a few weeks later: "Whence arises the Right of the Men to govern Women, without their Consent?"[5] But this question hung in the air. The framers did not extend the "rights of man" to women, who would not get the vote until the ratification of the Nineteenth Amendment in 1920. Today "remember the ladies" lives on as a sort of Magna Carta for the women's movement and as an ongoing reminder that gender equality remains a dream deferred. Women have served as heads of state in India, Israel, and Argentina. Though the United States has in Abigail Adams an icon for liberals and conservatives alike, it has yet to elect a female chief executive.

John Adams, second U.S. president (1776): As to your extraordinary code of laws, I cannot but laugh. . . . Depend upon it, we know better than to repeal our masculine systems. Although they are in full force, you know they are little more than theory. We dare not exert our power in its full latitude. We are obliged to go fair and softly, and, in practice, you know we are the subjects. We have only the name of masters, and rather than give up this, which would completely subject us to the despotism of the petticoat, I hope General Washington and all our brave heroes would fight.

Elizabeth Stanton, Susan Anthony, and Matilda Gage, suffragists (1881): [Abigail Adams] was the first American woman who threatened rebellion unless the rights of her sex were secured. . . . Thus our country started into governmental life freighted with the protests of the Revolutionary Mothers against being ruled without their consent. From that hour to the present, women have been continually raising their voices against political tyranny, and demanding for themselves equality of opportunity in every department of life.

Emily Taft Douglas, U.S. Representative (D-IL) (1966): In contrast to the professional literary ladies, only one American woman, Abigail Adams, is still of interest for what she said—as well as when she said it. She never patterned herself on foreign writers, but spoke quite simply from her New England heart. . . . Abigail Adams was right in connecting the woman's revolt with the American Revolu-

tion. . . . She had looked into the future, but what she saw was not for her day.

Letty Cottin Pogrebin, Ms. Magazine editor (1976): Maybe women should use 1976 to challenge the American dream, not celebrate it. After all, 1776 was the year women's powerlessness was first enshrined in the Constitution. In response to . . . "Remember the Ladies," the otherwise enlightened John Adams wrote, "I cannot but laugh." . . . In 1976, the laughter has faded, but women's grievances are still being dismissed as boring and trivial. . . . Thanks to Abigail Adams . . . we have learned that we cannot marry power; we must have it ourselves.

> ## "Remember the ladies"
> ABIGAIL ADAMS, 1776

Carl Degler, historian (1980): Abigail Adams's famous admonition . . . was far from a feminist plea. . . . Rather than denying in any way wifehood or motherhood as the role of women, Abigail Adams asked merely for an improvement in the traditional relationships with husbands.

Abigail Adams Tea Party Patriots, conservative political organization (2011): Dear John, Our announcement is official. A calling of Patriot Ladies: wives, mothers, grandmothers, aunts, and sisters, inspired by your wife, Abigail Adams. The most recognized Founding Mother of this great country! Our primary focus and actions will be in support of the United States of America, the Constitution, and speaking out about threats to our freedoms and liberties. God Bless America, Abigail Adams Tea Party Patriots.[6]

Dᴇᴄᴀᴅᴇs before Horace Greeley was urging young men to "Go West," a former slave from Ulster County, New York, heard God's call to leave New York City and "Go East" as a traveling preacher.[1] Taking the name Sojourner Truth (c. 1797–1883), she did just that. She found her calling in politics rather than religion, however, becoming one of America's foremost advocates for abolitionism and women's rights. In a country that valued individualism, Truth was one of a kind. Standing nearly six feet tall, she typically sported a sun bonnet and a pipe, and she spoke in a deep voice, layered with the Dutch she spoke for the first decade of her life. On May 29, 1851, at a women's rights conference in Akron, Ohio, she delivered her most famous speech.[2] According to Frances Gage, who organized the event, sexist men and racist women alike voiced objections to allowing Truth (the only black woman on the program) to speak. Reports differ over just what Truth said, but clearly she appealed to her womanhood, arguing that neither her race nor her strength disqualified her from being a woman.[3] "That man over there says that women need to be helped into carriages, and lifted over ditches, and to have the best place everywhere," she said, according to Gage's account. "Nobody ever helps me into carriages, or over mud puddles, or gives me any best place! And ain't I a woman?" This question—perhaps a reworking of the women's rights slogan "Am I not a woman and a sister?" (itself a reworking of the abolitionist slogan "Am I not a man and a brother?")—represented "a historic joining of abolitionism and feminism bodied forth in her own person."[4] It also became Truth's refrain, reenacted on stage and screen, and reprinted in countless anthologies. Some remember Truth for another pointed question. After Frederick Douglass finished a depressing speech in Boston, she asked in her booming voice, "Frederick, is God dead?" These words of hope and faith, retold by novelist Harriet Beecher Stowe, among others, became another "dominant symbol for Truth" and are etched today on her tombstone.[5] One hundred and twenty-six years after her death in 1883, Truth was memorialized with a bust in the U.S. Capitol—the first African-American woman to be so honored. Secretary of State Hillary Clinton called her an indefatigable fighter for "the rights and protections of our democracy" and a true believer in "the promise of liberty."[6] First Lady Michelle Obama praised her as an "outspoken, tell-it-like-it-is kind of woman."[7]

Gloria Steinem, feminist activist (1968): To accuse someone of not being a "real man" or "real woman" is a potent social weapon in preserving the status quo. During each war, women discover that they can do "masculine" jobs and wield power without losing their femininity, and after each war, they are sent back home. . . . Even those who keep their jobs are often apologetic about it, insisting that they just work so the family can have a few more luxuries; an easy way to avoid disapproval that might come from admitting they liked the independence, and even the power. In the women's rights movement, one of the few instances of taking this emotional blackmail head-on came from a distinguished Negro freedwoman named Sojourner Truth. "Nobody ever helps me into carriages or over puddles, or gives me the best place," she said, letting a male critic have it between the eyes, "and ain't I a woman?" . . . That was more than 100 years ago, and now, women are defensive about commanding office staffs, much less ploughing.

Donna Haraway, postmodern theorist (1992): Why does her question have more power for feminist theory 150 years later than any number of affirmative and declarative sentences?

Nell Painter, historian (1994): It may seem ironic that Sojourner Truth is known for words she did not say, but American history is full of symbols that do their work without a basis in life. As a black and feminist talisman rather than a text, Sojourner Truth is still selling. She remains more sign than lived existence, like Betsy Ross, Chief Seattle, and Mason ("Parson") Weems's George Washington, who are also best remembered for deeds they did not perform and words they did not utter. Like other invented greats, Truth is consumed as a signifier and beloved for what we need her to have said. It is no accident that other people writing well after the fact made up what we see as most meaningful about each of those greats.

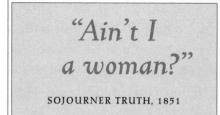

"Ain't I a woman?"

SOJOURNER TRUTH, 1851

Gwen Moore, U.S. Representative (D-WI) (2010): With regard to health care, I would paraphrase Sojourner Truth and say, "Ain't I a human being?" It's not an understatement to say that the lack of affordable health coverage has contributed to keeping women in poverty, not to mention keeping too many women in poor health. . . . Isn't it about time we stood up and said, "Ain't I a woman?" Or, even, "Ain't I a human being?" . . . Health care reform here will provide women the care that they need; the economic security they need; prohibit plans from charging women more than men; ban the insurance practice of rejecting women with a preexisting condition; and include maternity services. Yes, we are women; and, yes, we are human beings.[8]

ABRAHAM LINCOLN's Second Inaugural Address[1] is, as Theodore Roosevelt said, "a speech which will be read as long as the memory of this nation endures," but it is not, as some have argued, his "greatest speech."[2] That honor belongs to the Gettysburg Address. But the Second Inaugural contains his most profound thinking. The Civil War, which would claim over 600,000 lives (ten times more than the U.S. servicemen lost in Vietnam), was nearly over when Lincoln was inaugurated on March 4, 1865. But the president sounded no trumpet of triumphalism. He did not call for revenge. Instead, he waxed theological—"Let us judge not that we be not judged"—in a six-minute speech that, according to Frederick Douglass, "sounded more like a sermon than a state paper."[3] America's theologian in chief did not call God to his side, however. He did not call his opponents evildoers. Instead, he struggled to make sense of "this terrible war" and, failing, humbly confessed his confusion. In keeping with his Calvinist education in the mysteries of God, he did not pretend to know God's will, but he allowed himself to wonder whether slavery had set God's teeth on edge. Even as he prayed for the war to end, he prepared his fellow citizens for the possibility that Providence might prolong it "until every drop of blood drawn with the lash, shall be paid by another drawn with the sword." In his final sentence—"one of the finest sentences ever written by an American president"—he turned from theology to ethics, calling on Americans to forgo the anger of war for the benevolence of peace—to proceed "with malice toward none, with charity for all."[4] Lincoln was assassinated six weeks later—shot on Good Friday, April 14, 1865, he died the next day—and many of his eulogists quoted these words. "He lived as he died: the last of his public utterances closed with the words, 'With malice toward none, with charity for all,'" said one minister. "This phrase will fall hereafter into that small number of phrases, not Scripture, but which men often cite, unwittingly, as though they were."[5] Lincoln's hope for a nation undivided by race or region was not realized, but this coda to forgiveness became a touchstone for those seeking to transcend petty politics. As Americans fought over the place in their society for Catholics and Muslims, blacks and women, the unborn and the elderly, the words of "the Forgiver," as Melville called him, resounded among new generations.[6] Lincoln's Second Inaugural now stands alongside Washington's Farewell Address and Jefferson's First Inaugural as one of our great invocations of the common good.

Chicago Times, proslavery newspaper (1865): We did not conceive it possible that even Mr. Lincoln could produce a paper so slip shod, so loose-joined, so puerile, not alone in literary construction, but in its ideas, its sentiments, its grasp. . . . By the side of it, mediocrity is superb.

Abraham Lincoln, sixteenth U.S. president (1865): I believe it is not immediately popular. Men are not flattered by being shown that there has been a difference of purpose between the Almighty and them.

Wendell Willkie, Republican presidential candidate (1944): We need a new leader. . . . A leader who does not think of a nation as made up of groups of people who can be played against each other to insure his continuing power. A leader who recognizes that all groups are an essential part of America. A leader with malice toward none. For as Lincoln so well knew, malice is the very essence of disunity. . . . Disunity has been the Nazi game, and even if we beat Hitler we can still lose the war if we lay ourselves open, by disunity at home, to conquest by the Nazi spirit.

Jonathan Alter, journalist (1998): After Matthew Shepard was murdered for being gay, many conservatives were quick to call for the death penalty for his assailant—so quick that they sounded a trifle defensive. . . . The Party of Lincoln should follow . . . Honest Abe's lead, by projecting moral conduct without moral fervor. Lincoln was uncomfortable with impassioned abolitionism, and urged "malice toward none" when it came to dealing with immoral Southerners. The danger of theo-conservatives is not that they are trying to bring a moral compass into politics. It's that they are doing so without the generosity of spirit that has always been essential for any navigation of public life.

Ronald White, historian (2002): In the short weeks left before his assassination, "With malice toward none; with charity for all" became the watchwords written in newspapers, inscribed upon badges. And after his assassination, they came to represent Lincoln's legacy to the nation. They would become some of our sacred words. Other words of his, from the Gettysburg Address—"of the people, by the people, for the people"—endure because they forever define America. "With malice toward none; with charity for all" defined Lincoln's vision for a post–Civil War America.

Jonathan Zimmerman, historian (2011): Yes, we feel the need to exact revenge from our enemies. But our key religious scriptures as well as our greatest political leaders warn us against this dark human desire. . . . That's why Lincoln concluded his second inaugural address . . . by promising "malice toward none" and "charity for all." . . . Lincoln rejected calls for revenge against the soon-to-be-defeated Confederacy. Instead, he called upon all Americans to recognize the essential humanity of us all. . . . Last night, in celebrating the death of Osama bin Laden, we lost sight of that responsibility.[7]

> ## "With malice toward none, with charity for all"
>
> ABRAHAM LINCOLN, 1865

Before encountering white men in 1805 during the Lewis and Clark expedition, the Nimiipuu, or Nez Perce Indians, were gatherers of fish, game, and wild plants in the Pacific Northwest's Wallowa Valley. In 1855 their leader, Old Joseph, signed a treaty restricting them to 6.4 million acres in today's Oregon, Washington, and Idaho. After gold was discovered there, U.S. government officials proposed in 1863 a new treaty cutting this reservation to one-tenth its prior size. Old Joseph refused to sign. In 1877, the U.S. army demanded that "non-treaty" Nez Perce (those who refused to sign the "steal treaty") relocate inside the 1863 lines. Young Joseph (Old Joseph's son and successor) said no. But after General Oliver O. Howard threatened to attack, he relented. Before his people could leave, however, some young warriors killed white settlers to avenge an earlier Nez Perce killing. So Chief Joseph (1840–1904) fled, heading to Canada with roughly seven hundred men, women, and children. Interpreting the killings as an act of war, the army pursued the Nez Perce for three months and fifteen hundred miles. This long retreat, punctuated by many engagements and four pitched battles, ended when Chief Joseph surrendered a day's ride from Canada in Montana's Bear Paw Mountains. As legend has it, he handed over his rifle before delivering one of the greatest short speeches in U.S. history.[1] He said he was tired of fighting. He took an inventory of the dead. Then he said, "From where the sun now stands I will fight no more forever." Or did he? Chief Joseph did not speak English, so at best this is a translation. Most scholars now believe that the speech was written after the fact by General Howard's aide, Charles Erskine Scott Wood, a writer who later became Chief Joseph's friend.[2] Nonetheless, the speech became "the most famous, controversial, and intercultural text in nineteenth-century western American literature."[3] It has been quoted in song lyrics, memorialized in a Ken Burns documentary, immortalized in a book-length poem by Robert Penn Warren, and widely anthologized. Although Chief Joseph was more statesman than general, he was lionized after the war as the "Red Napoleon"—a military genius. His words were celebrated then because they called attention to the human costs of westward expansion and Manifest Destiny. They live now because they symbolize the corruption of American ideals and the tragedies of Native American history. Confined after his surrender to the Indian Territory in present-day Oklahoma, Chief Joseph was eventually allowed to return home. He died at the Colville Reservation in eastern Washington in 1904.

George Truman Kercheval, author (1890): O my friends! Had Joseph been other than an Indian you would have raised a monument to perpetuate in our minds his noble deeds, valor, and heroic kindness. We love the story of Joseph who forgave his brothers for thinking to slay him, for driving him from his father's home; we admire him for releasing them when they were his prisoners, for giving them back their lives. The story of both Josephs is much the same; the Israelite is a hero, but not more great a man than Joseph, the Nez Perce.

J. W. Powell, explorer (1896): In all our sad Indian history there is nothing to exceed in pathetic eloquence the surrender speech of the Nez Perce chief.

Helen Howard, writer of western U.S. history (1941): In the simplicity of its dramatic intensity the speech is without parallel in aboriginal oration.

Mark Brown, historian (1972): The cold truth is that there was no surrender speech, nor is there any proof that these words were actually spoken by Joseph. . . . The statement that Joseph spoke even one sentence is open to serious question.

Marlon Brando, actor (1994): Chief Joseph surrendered in a speech that summarized poignantly how a great and proud people had been devastated by the United States. . . . After their lands were stolen from them and [they] were herded onto reservations, the government sent out missionaries from seven or eight religious denominations who tried to force the Indians to become Christians. . . . Yet these crimes are almost invisible in our national consciousness. If they give any thought to the Indians, most Americans project a montage of images from the movies; few conjure up anguish, suffering or murder when they think of Native Americans. Indians are simply a vague, colorful chapter in our country's past, deserving no more interest than might be devoted to the building of the Erie Canal or the transcontinental railroad.

Bill Clinton, forty-second U.S. president (2000): When I was just a very young boy, I used to go to the county public library in my hometown in Arkansas. . . . I remember once I read in the biography of Chief Joseph of the Nez Perce that incredible statement he made, "From this day, I will fight no more, forever." It was a noble, powerful, brave thing to do. . . . But as we all know, though many of your ancestors gave up fighting and gave up land and water and mineral rights in exchange for peace, security, health care, and education, the Federal Government did not live up to its end of the deal. That was wrong.

Gerald Vizenor, Native American writer (2005): [Chief Joseph's] eloquent statement was reported widely, and has become a romantic signifier of a Native vanishing point in art, literature and history. . . . The Nez Perce created a great narrative of resistance, tragic retreat, surrender, and survivance. . . . [They] are truly the patriots of a continental Native liberty.[4]

> "I will fight no more forever"
>
> CHIEF JOSEPH, 1877

CALVIN COOLIDGE (1872–1933), a Massachusetts Republican who served in the White House for much of the Roaring Twenties, never actually uttered the six words that have come to define his presidency. In an address he delivered to the American Society of Newspaper Editors in Washington, D.C., on January 17, 1925, Coolidge said, "After all, the chief business of the American people is business. They are profoundly concerned with producing, buying, selling, investing and prospering in the world. I am strongly of the opinion that the great majority of people will always find these are moving impulses of our life." Later commentators distilled this saying down to "The business of America is business." But what is America's business? It depends on whom you ask. Critics of Coolidge on the left have insisted that the business of America is actually freedom or justice or revolution. Meanwhile, television commentator Pat Buchanan has insisted from the political right that the business of America is not business or even politics, but culture and morality—preserving Christian civilization and protecting the unborn. Coolidge's saying lives, however, because Americans *have* moved over time from worshipping the Almighty God to worshipping the almighty dollar. To be fair, Coolidge did not say that America should or would sell out its ideals to business interests. "It is only those who do not understand our people, who believe that our national life is entirely absorbed by material motives," he told the American Society of Newspaper Editors. "We make no concealment of the fact that we want wealth, but there are many other things that we want very much more. We want peace and honor, and that charity which is so strong an element of all civilization. The chief ideal of the American people is idealism."[1]

William Allen White, author (1925): "The business of America is business" says it all. Lincoln's whole life was devoted to showing that the business of America is freedom. Roosevelt's life was consecrated to the theory that the business of America is justice. Wilson's one life-long message to the world is that the business of America is peace.

Stephen Wise, rabbi (1928): The choice [in the Hoover/Smith presidential election] is really between . . . the conception of the present President of the United States, who has said that the business of America is business, and the conception of the next President of the United States, who believes that the business of America is America!

Shirley Chisholm, U.S. Representative (D-NY) (1969): We are now spending $80 billion a year on defense. That is two-thirds of every tax dollar. At this time, gentlemen, the business of America is war, and it is time for a change.

Russell Baker, columnist (1972): Nowadays the business of America is government, and the business of government is business.

Arthur Ochs Sulzberger, New York Times publisher (1977): Fifty years ago, an American president could say, with much justification, that "the business of America is business." We've gone beyond that. The business of America is freedom. For the journalist, that means the freedom to get to the root of the truth, the freedom to criticize. . . . For the businessman, that means the freedom to compete fairly, on the basis of value and service.

Tom Shales, reporter (1988): On Super Bowl Sunday, the business of America is football, yes, but the business of America is television, too.

George Will, columnist (1991): The business of America is not business. Neither is it war. The business of America is justice, and securing the blessings of liberty.

Wendell Berry, Kentucky farmer and poet (1993): "The business of America is business," a prophet of our era too correctly said. Two corollaries are clearly implied: that the business of the American government is to serve, protect, and defend business; and that the business of the American people is to serve the government, which means to serve business. The costs of this state of things are incalculable.

> "The business of America is business"
>
> CALVIN COOLIDGE, 1925

Ralph Nader, consumer activist (2004): Surely, there are grander purposes of our collective life than a simple measuring of the gross national product. The commercial imperative permeates every aspect of our lives. Our food, entertainment, our electoral and political institutions—all of this and much more is controlled by corporations which care most about their bottom line. The mercantile juggernaut has moved into area after area once wholly or largely off limits to commerce, including our schools and colleges, amateur sports, the arts, our holidays and rituals, religious institutions, and environment. Our major "public space" is the corporate shopping mall, which bars civic activity like petitioning. . . . If we take our Constitution and founding ideals seriously, the business of America is democracy.[2]

WHEN Franklin Delano Roosevelt (1882–1945) was picked to represent the Democratic Party in the 1932 presidential race, the United States was still choking on the fumes of the Great Depression, the multiyear economic burnout that smothered the prosperity and frivolity of the Roaring Twenties. The unemployment rate stood at 24 percent. The stock market, which had crashed nearly three years earlier, in October 1929, had not yet bottomed out. In his nomination speech, which he called a "call to arms," FDR unleashed a blistering attack on laissez-faire capitalism and promised a "new deal for the American people."[1] He won forty-two states and 57 percent of the popular vote, trouncing the incumbent Republican Herbert Hoover. In his first hundred days in office, he and a cooperative Congress made good on his "crusade to restore America to its own people" with fifteen pieces of landmark legislation, including the Social Security Act. This blitzkrieg of bills created what President Reagan would later call an "alphabet soup of federal agencies" (the FDIC, CCC, WPA, TVA, etc.) and prompted humorist Will Rogers to quip, "Congress doesn't pass legislation anymore; they just wave at the bills as they go by."[2] The New Deal also reinvented the term "liberal," which had previously referred to people who, like Jefferson, sought to maximize liberty by minimizing government. FDR's efforts at "Relief, Recovery, and Reform" have been widely credited with returning the nation to prosperity, and he was rewarded with an unprecedented four presidential terms. During his twelve years as commander in chief (he died in office in 1945), he remade the modern presidency and modern America. Today, many conservatives argue that the New Deal, far from ending the Great Depression, actually extended it, by shackling corporations with regulations, mandating a job-killing minimum wage, and otherwise increasing the cost of doing business. The Reagan Revolution, a repudiation of 1960s libertinism, was perhaps more fundamentally a rejection of the New Deal (though Reagan himself voted for FDR four times). In his 1996 State of the Union address, President Clinton famously declared the death of big government. Then came the Great Recession and new efforts to stimulate the economy ("the New New Deal") by "Franklin Delano Obama."[3] Today Democrats and Republicans disagree about whether Roosevelt's revolution was a good deal. Neither party seems willing to speak ill of FDR or to pull up his "safety nets," but hardly anyone in politics speaks anymore the way Roosevelt and his supporters once did about the glories of good government.

Harold Ickes, FDR's secretary of the interior (1933): It's more than a New Deal. It's a new world. People feel free again. They can breathe naturally. It's like quitting a morgue for the open woods.

Herbert Hoover, thirty-first U.S. president (1934): [The New Deal] is the most stupendous invasion of the whole spirit of liberty that the nation has witnessed since the days of colonial America.

Charles Coughlin, populist Catholic priest (1935): [The New Deal is] a government of the bankers, by the bankers, and for the bankers.

Carl Degler, historian (1959): [The New Deal] was a revolutionary response to a revolutionary situation. . . . The searing ordeal of the Great Depression purged the American people of their belief in the limited powers of the federal government and convinced them of the necessity of the guarantor state.

William Leuchtenburg, historian (1963): The New Deal [was] a halfway revolution; it swelled the ranks of the bourgeoisie but left many Americans—sharecroppers, slum dwellers, most Negroes—outside of the new equilibrium.

Barton Bernstein, historian (1968): The New Deal failed to solve the problem of depression, it failed to raise the impoverished, it failed to redistribute income, it failed to extend equality and generally countenanced racial discrimination and segregation. . . . In this sense, the New Deal . . . was profoundly conservative and continuous with the 1920's.

Samuel Eliot Morison, historian (1972): The New Deal was just what the term implied—a new deal of old cards, no longer stacked against the common man. Opponents called it near-fascism or near-communism, but it was American as a bale of hay—an opportunist, rule-of-thumb method of curing deep-seated ills. Probably it saved the capitalist system in the United States.

Ronald Reagan, fortieth U.S. president (1989): The months before FDR took office are far behind us now. We forget what they were like— the pink slips handed out at factories across the land with no jobs anywhere if you lost yours, the soup kitchens in every major city, the look of desperation in people's eyes. And we forget that, in the unprecedented economic crisis, many had begun to question our most basic institutions, including our democracy itself. And then along came FDR, who put his faith, as he said, "in the forgotten man," the ordinary American.

Amity Shlaes, author (2007): Roosevelt's work on behalf of his version of the forgotten man generated a new tradition. To justify giving to one forgotten man, the administration found, it had to make a scapegoat of another. Businessmen and businesses were the targets.

Jim Powell, Cato Institute senior fellow (2011): President Obama's New New Deal of massive government intervention was inspired by FDR's New Deal, and both have been plagued by chronic high unemployment. . . . We need very different policies, not more of the same.[4]

> "I pledge you, I pledge myself, to a new deal for the American people"
>
> FRANKLIN DELANO ROOSEVELT, 1932

On January 20, 1961, in his first and only inaugural address, John F. Kennedy offered the nation something more than its first Catholic president. Just days after an aging President Eisenhower had warned in his farewell speech of the dangers of the "military-industrial complex," Kennedy, who at forty-three was the youngest man ever elected president, offered the nation youth, vigor, and (thanks to his wife, Jacqueline) some glamour to wash away the winter gray. As he spoke, hatless and coatless and invigorated by the cold, he ushered in both a new presidency and a new decade, which would not end until a man had walked on the moon and a president had been assassinated. His short speech—"the best inaugural address since Lincoln," wrote poet Carl Sandburg[1]—focused on foreign policy, but it is remembered for one line: "Ask not what your country can do for you—ask what you can do for your country." Similar sentiments had been expressed as early as 1884 by future Supreme Court justice Oliver Wendell Holmes Jr., but now the moment—Camelot's opening act—was appropriate to the message.[2] Written in the imperative voice and delivered with a series of emphatic forward thrusts of Kennedy's right hand, this line drew on a rich vein in the bedrock of America. Its message—to put nation above the interests of region, party, and even self—would give America the Peace Corps and inspire a generation of youth to enter public service. Columnist James Reston was deeply moved by Kennedy's call but wondered whether those who applauded it were "willing to go along with the sacrifices implied."[3] The answer, of course, is no. As the hosannas went up for Kennedy's "inspiring," "eloquent," "magnificent," "brilliant," and "historic" address, so did his approval ratings, which averaged over 70 percent during his thousand days in office—the highest figure for any U.S. president.[4] But politicians today rarely call for sacrifice. They tell us what our country can do for us, or they demand that our country leave us alone. In the age-old battle between two conservative impulses in American life—the impulse to sacrifice for your country and the impulse to pursue your self-interest—self-interest has triumphed, in part because there appear to be more votes in lowering taxes than in raising them, even in wartime.[5] Still, Kennedy's voice lives on. His inaugural address was recited at his funeral in 1963, and "ask not" is inscribed into his Arlington National Cemetery memorial, which is warmed by an eternal flame. The idea for this flame came from another classic line from this classic speech: "Let the word go forth from this time and place, to friend and foe alike, that the torch has been passed to a new generation of Americans."

Milton Friedman, economist (1962): The paternalistic "what your country can do for you" implies that government is the patron, the citizen the ward, a view that is at odds with the free man's belief in his own responsibility for his own destiny. The organismic "what you can do for your country" implies the government is the master or the deity, the citizen, the servant or the votary. The free man will ask neither what his country can do for him nor what he can do for his country. He will ask rather: What can I and my compatriots do through government to help us discharge our individual responsibilities, to achieve our several goals and purposes, and above all, to protect our freedom?

Robert Bellah, sociologist (1967): The whole address can be understood as only the most recent statement of a theme that lies very deep in the American tradition, namely the obligation, both collective and individual, to carry out God's will on earth. This was the motivating spirit of those who founded America, and it has been present in every generation since. . . . That this very activist and non-contemplative conception of the fundamental religious obligation, which has been historically associated with the Protestant position, should be enunciated so clearly in the first major statement of the first Catholic president seems to underline how deeply established it is in the American outlook.

Richard Nixon, thirty-seventh U.S. president (1973): Let us remember that America was built not by government, but by people;

> "Ask not what your country can do for you— ask what you can do for your country"
>
> JOHN F. KENNEDY, 1961

not by welfare, but by work; not by shirking responsibility, but by seeking responsibility. In our own lives, let each of us ask—not just what will government do for me, but what can I do for myself? In the challenges we face together, let each of us ask—not just how can government help, but how can I help?

Ronald Reagan, fortieth U.S. president (1985): He was a patriot who summoned patriotism from the heart of a sated country. It is a matter of pride to me that so many men and women who were inspired by his bracing vision and moved by his call to "ask not" serve now in the White House doing the business of government.

Mark McKinnon, Republican political adviser (2011): Unfortunately, in today's environment, speeches are more likely to say, "Ask not what you can do for your country, ask what you can do for your party."

Barack Obama, forty-fourth U.S. president (2011): There he is, the handsome Bostonian, summoning a generation to service and a nation to greatness in a speech that would become part of the American canon. And there's the crowd, bundled up for the cold, making their way through streets white with snow, full of expectation; a nation feeling young again, its mood brightened by the promise of a new decade. Because of his vision, more people prospered, more people served, our Union was made more perfect. Because of that vision, I can stand here tonight as President of the United States.[6]

T HE SIGNATURE SPEECH of Ronald Reagan's presidency could have been a throwaway. Reagan had agreed to address the National Association of Evangelicals in Orlando, Florida, in 1983. Speechwriter Anthony Dolan had drafted remarks for the Religious Right, which had helped to punch Reagan's ticket to the Oval Office. But this draft called the Soviet empire "evil," so a tug-of-war ensued between administration pragmatists (who wanted the tough language to go) and hard-liners (who wanted it to stay). Reagan—"with malice aforethought," in his words—sided with the hard-liners.[1] "There is sin and evil in the world," he told the NAE, and its "focus" was the Soviet Union. "So in your discussions of the nuclear freeze proposals I urge you to beware the temptation . . . to ignore the facts of history and the aggressive impulses of an evil empire, to simply call the arms race a giant misunderstanding and thereby remove yourself from the struggle between right and wrong and good and evil."[2] The blowback was immediate. Historian Henry Steele Commager called it "the worst speech in American history," and even First Lady Nancy Reagan "blanched."[3] Others complained that Reagan's black-and-white world view was naive, and his incendiary rhetoric near suicidal in a world where nuclear weapons could flatten the capital in a flash. But critics objected especially to Reagan's overstepping of the church/state wall. "We elected a President, not a priest," fumed the *New Republic*."[4] But "The Right Rev. Ronald Reagan," as *Time* magazine called him, was convinced that America would win the Cold War if only it continued to wage it.[5] Rejecting Nixon's détente strategy as "a one-way street the Soviet Union has used to pursue its own aims," Reagan worked not to contain Communism but to push it back.[6] He did negotiate with the Soviets, however. On May 31, 1988, while walking in Red Square during a nuclear arms treaty summit with Soviet leader Mikhail Gorbachev, a reporter asked him, "Do you still think you're in an evil empire?" "No," he answered, "I was talking about another time and another era."[7] After Reagan urged Gorbachev to "tear down this wall," and he did, some critics came around, admitting that Reagan's mix of incendiary rhetoric, cowboy diplomacy, and massive military spending had won the Cold War.[8] President George W. Bush used a similar phrase—"axis of evil"—to describe Iraq, Iran, and North Korea.[9] "Evil empire" is now a generic term, used to refer to Iran in politics, Microsoft in business, and the Yankees in baseball.

Anthony Lewis, New York Times columnist (1983): What is the world to think when the greatest of powers is led by a man who applies to the most difficult human problem a simplistic theology?

Tom Wicker, New York Times columnist (1983): Are we so clearly a God-directed, chosen people that we have no need to question our virtue, or the evil of our rivals?

Patriarch Pimen, Russian Orthodox Church leader (1983): It is with bitterness and grief in my heart that I read your belligerent calls which sow the seeds of hatred and hostility against my motherland and threaten peace all over the world. These calls are the more so sinful as they are wrapped in the attire of Christian morals.

Tip O'Neill, House Speaker (D-MA) (1984): The evil is in the White House at the present time. And that evil is a man who has no care and no concern for the working class of America.

National Review *editorial* (1984): "Evil empire" sticks in the liberal craw. But an "evil empire" is precisely what the Soviet Union

actually is. One thinks of the gulag, the infamous mental hospitals, slave labor building the Siberian gas pipeline . . . the ongoing war against poetry, art, religion, and all forms of free thought—well, if that's not an evil empire, it will certainly do until the real thing comes along.

Strobe Talbott, journalist (1984): [Reagan] may have been impolitic, but he was not wrong. After all, the Soviets do lie, cheat, and reserve the right to commit any crime.

William F. Buckley Jr., journalist (1988): Mr. Reagan does well to encourage changes in the Soviet system. . . . But to greet it as if it were no longer evil is on the order of changing our entire position toward Adolf Hitler on receiving news that he had abolished one extermination camp. . . . [The Soviet Union] continues to be an evil empire.

Richard Cizik, president of Evangelical Partnership for the Common Good (2010): *There are those today who want to make Islam the new Evil Empire. . . . To those who would exercise derision, bigotry, open rejection of our fellow Americans of a different faith, I say, shame on you.*[10]

> ## "evil empire"
> RONALD REAGAN, 1983

PROPHETS

"Civil Disobedience"

❧ HENRY DAVID THOREAU, 1849 ❧

ESSAYIST, surveyor, yogi, and nonconformist, Henry David Thoreau (1817–62) is best known for *Walden* (1854), a love letter to solitude, simplicity, and the wild that recalls his two years living in a one-room cabin near Walden Pond in Concord, Massachusetts. Philosopher Stanley Cavell referred to *Walden* as "scripture," and historian Vernon Parrington praised it as a "transcendental declaration of independence."[1] But Thoreau's most influential work is "Civil Disobedience," an essay originally published in 1849 as "Resistance to Civil Government."[2] This "bible of protesting minorities" was rarely read during Thoreau's life, and by the end of the nineteenth century it was "less a living document than a work on life support."[3] Its standing today as perhaps the most influential political essay written by an American rests largely on its use by Mohandas Gandhi and Martin Luther King Jr. Through these two men, the essay played a role in the movements for independence in India and civil rights in the United States.

Thoreau (who pronounced his surname "thorough") moved into his Walden cabin on July 4, 1845. The following July, he was arrested and jailed for refusing to pay a poll tax. "Civil Disobedience" explains and justifies this refusal, arguing that each citizen has a duty to resist a government whose actions—in this case, supporting slavery, prosecuting the Mexican war, and mistreating Indians—offend his conscience.

Like his fellow Transcendentalist Ralph Waldo Emerson (whose land he squatted on at Walden Pond, whose ideas he freely borrowed, and whose alma mater—Harvard—he also shared), Thoreau was the sort of man we now refer to as "spiritual, but not religious." Like his Puritan forebears, he sought first and foremost to save his soul, but in so doing he turned to Asian scriptures and the everyday revelations of ants and woodchucks, beans and chokeberries. As "Civil Disobedience" indicates, however, neither his spirituality nor his self-reliance cordoned him off from politics. Thoreau acted as a "conductor" on the Underground Railroad, and "Civil Disobedience" weighs in on many of the great themes in America's conversation about itself, including the right to revolution, the tyranny of majority rule, and the existence of a higher law above even the Constitution.

Thoreau's reputation has waxed and waned since his death from tuberculosis in 1862 at the age of forty-four. Throughout the nineteenth century, he was typically catalogued among the "lesser Transcendentalists"—a dud to the firecracker that was Emerson. Judging him "unmanly," "coldly cruel in the pursuit of goodness, and morbid even in the pursuit of health," Robert Louis Stevenson dismissed Thoreau as a "skulker."[4] Henry James called him "imperfect, unfinished, inartistic," and "parochial."[5] Others reckoned him egotistical, arrogant, judgmental, humorless, anarchic, lazy, escapist, priggish, adolescent, dishonest, and misanthropic.

In his eulogy to his friend, Emerson said, "No truer American existed than Thoreau," and over the last century Thoreau has become an American icon, widely read in high-school and college courses, hallowed on a postage stamp, roasted in the *National Lampoon,* and revered as an "ecological prophet"—the progenitor of environmental writers from John Muir to Annie Dillard.[6] As early as 1907, the *New York Times* was writing of Thoreau "in the full flood of popularity," and in 1927 it was basking in his "genius."[7] Initially, the compliments were directed toward Thoreau the naturalist and (especially during the Depression) Thoreau the oracle of simple living, but readers gradually warmed to his politics too, lauding him as the "incarnation of the independence that has been our national watchword."[8] "As a political writer," wrote Stanley Edgar Hyman of the *New Yorker,* "he was the most ringing and magnificent polemicist America has ever produced."[9]

During World War II, "Civil Disobedience" inspired resistance to the Nazis in Denmark and emboldened American pacifists to affirm their conscientious objection to war. During the 1960s and 1970s, Thoreau was lionized by Beat Generation writers, civil rights agitators, Vietnam War protesters, hippies, and environmental activists. In 1960, a rowboat used to protest nuclear submarines in Groton, Connecticut, was christened *Henry David Thoreau,* and in 1962 President Kennedy praised "Thoreau's pervasive and universal influence on social thinking and political action."[10] *The Night Thoreau Spent in Jail,* a play based on "Civil Disobedience," was performed to packed houses at hundreds of colleges in the early 1970s. Today this essay is used to justify the eco-radicalism of groups such as Earth First!, and some tax resisters send a copy of "Civil Disobedience" each year to the IRS in lieu of a 1040 form.

Not everyone joined in the hosannas, however. Senator Joseph McCarthy had "Civil Disobedience" removed from United States Information Service libraries. Hannah Arendt and John Rawls dismissed Thoreau's thought as apolitical and naive. But this remains a minority report on a man who is now among the American beloved and on an essay that contains some of the most memorable lines in American political thought.

The first line of "Civil Disobedience"—"That government is best which governs least"—would seem to be catnip to contemporary conservatives, and Thoreau was featured in the early twenty-first century on a YouTube video in support of the libertarian politician Ron Paul.[11] But Thoreau's reputation as a countercultural saint and a critic of imperialism and industrial capitalism has stymied his adoption on the right. "Civil Disobedience" endures not for its call for limited government but for its reimagining of the American covenant as a contract between nation and citizen. The "consent of the governed" articulated in the Declaration of Independence has typically been interpreted as issuing from either the states or "we the people" as a whole. Thoreau believed it derived from each person, so individuals could secede from the national compact whenever its laws offended their conscience. The American Revolution championed the sovereignty of the people over the sovereignty of the king, but Thoreau's solocratic rebellion championed the sovereignty of the individual over both. Thoreau would later come to the defense of John Brown, who led a bloody slave revolt in 1859 at Harpers Ferry, Virginia (now West Virginia), but the resistance he champions here has typically been read as nonviolent.

A fair portion of "Civil Disobedience" mimics *Walden*, as Thoreau reflects on his experience apart from society in a Concord jail. "It was like travelling into a far country, such as I had never expected to behold, to lie there for one night," he writes, before going on to describe the revelations that the sounds of nighttime Concord offered to his imagination. When some unnamed benefactor paid his poll tax, Thoreau was released after one night with a new vision of his town and townspeople. He did not like what he saw:

> *I saw yet more distinctly the State in which I lived. I saw to what extent the people among whom I lived could be trusted as good neighbors and friends; that their friendship was for summer weather only; that they did not greatly purpose to do right; that they were a distinct race from me by their prejudices and superstitions, as the China men and Malays are; that, in their sacrifices to humanity, they ran no risks, not even to their property.*

After conceding that he may have been judging his neighbors harshly—he says he believes that most of them were not aware that they had "such an institution as the jail" in their village—Thoreau returns in this essay to the errand that had called him away from his Walden idylls: getting a shoe mended. He then proceeds to place the government under a cloak of invisibility through a means no more (or less) revolutionary than a "huckleberry party":

> *When I was let out the next morning, I proceeded to finish my errand, and, having put on my mended shoe, joined a huckleberry party, who were impatient to put themselves under my conduct; and in half an hour—for the horse was soon tackled—was in the midst of a huckleberry field, on one of our highest hills, two miles off; and then the State was nowhere to be seen.*

"Civil Disobedience" 🌿

I HEARTILY accept the motto, "That government is best which governs least;"[a,b,c] and I should like to see it acted up to more rapidly and systematically. Carried out, it finally amounts to this, which also I believe, "That government is best which governs not at all";

---

a. George Sutherland, former Utah Senator, calling for "just enough" government (1921): A very distinguished political philosopher of a bygone generation . . . summed up one of the cardinal doctrines of his faith in the phrase: "That government is best which governs least." The aphorism is as fallacious in one direction as the counter-assertion, "that government is best which governs most," would be fallacious in the opposite direction. The government which governs least is that of the savage tribe, while the government which governs most is a despotism. Too little government and too much government lie at the opposite extremities of social management, and both are bad; for if too little government tends toward anarchy, too much government carries us in the opposite direction of tyranny and oppression, and, in the language of Wendell Phillips, "kills the self-help and energy of the governed." Obviously, therefore, that government is best which governs neither least nor most, but just enough. —George Sutherland, "Principle or Expedient?" *Constitutional Review* 5.4 (October 1921): 195.

b. Douglas MacArthur, army general, opposing the income tax (1957): There seems to be no restraint in this lust for taxes. It began with the Federal Income Tax Law of 1914, which gave unlimited access to the people's wealth, and the power for the first time to levy taxes not for revenue only but for social purposes. Since then the sphere of government has increased with a kind of explosive force. Thomas Jefferson's wise aphorism, "That government is best which governs least," has been tossed into the wastebasket with ridicule and sarcasm. Whether we want it or not, we pay now for almost unlimited government; a government which limits our lives by dictating how we are fed and clothed and housed; how to provide for old age; how the national income, which is the product of our labor, shall be divided among us; how we shall buy and sell; how long and how hard and under what circumstances we shall work. There is only scorn for the one who dares to say, "The government should not be infinite." —Douglas MacArthur, "Excerpts from an Address to the Annual Stockholder's Meeting of the Sperry Rand Corporation," New York, July 30, 1957, in Edward T. Imparato, ed., *General MacArthur Speeches and Reports: 1908–1964* (Paducah, KY: Turner, 2000), p. 227.

c. Bill Clinton, forty-second U.S. president, affirming limited government (1996): The era of big government is over. —William Jefferson Clinton, "State of the Union Address," January 23, 1996, http://clinton4.nara.gov/WH/New/other/sotu.html.

and when men are prepared for it, that will be the kind of government which they will have. Government is at best but an expedient; but most governments are usually, and all governments are sometimes, inexpedient. The objections which have been brought against a standing army, and they are many and weighty, and deserve to prevail, may also at last be brought against a standing government. The standing army is only an arm of the standing government. The government itself, which is only the mode which the people have chosen to execute their will, is equally liable to be abused and perverted before the people can act through it. Witness the present Mexican war, the work of comparatively a few individuals using the standing government as their tool; for, in the outset, the people would not have consented to this measure.

This American government, what is it but a tradition, though a recent one, endeavoring to transmit itself unimpaired to posterity, but each instant losing some of its integrity? It has not the vitality and force of a single living man; for a single man can bend it to his will. It is a sort of wooden gun to the people themselves; and, if ever they should use it in earnest as a real one against each other, it will surely split. But it is not the less necessary for this; for the people must have some complicated machinery or other, and hear its din, to satisfy that idea of government which they have. Governments show thus how successfully men can be imposed on, even impose on themselves, for their own advantage. It is excellent, we must all allow; yet this government never of itself furthered any enterprise, but by the alacrity with which it got out of its way. It does not keep the country free. It does not settle the West. It does not educate. The character inherent in the American people has done all that has been accomplished; and it would have done somewhat more, if the government had not sometimes got in its way. For government is an expedient by which men would fain succeed in letting one another alone; and, as has been said, when it is most expedient, the governed are most let alone by it. . . .

But, to speak practically and as a citizen, unlike those who call themselves no-government men, I ask for, not at once no government, but at once a better government. Let every man make known what kind of government would command his respect, and that will be one step toward obtaining it.

After all, the practical reason why, when the power is once in the hands of the people, a majority are permitted, and for a long period continue, to rule, is not because they are most likely to be in the right, nor because this seems fairest to the minority, but because they are physically the strongest. But a government in which the majority rule in all cases cannot be based on justice, even as far as men understand it. Can there not be a government in which majorities do not virtually decide right and wrong, but conscience?—in which majorities decide only those questions to which the rule of expediency is applicable? Must the citizen ever for a moment, or in the least degree, resign his conscience to the legislator? Why has every man a conscience, then? I think that we should be men first, and subjects afterward. It is not desirable to cultivate a respect for the law, so much as for the right. The only obligation which I have a right to assume, is to do at any time what I think right.[d] It is truly enough said, that a corporation has no conscience; but a corporation of conscientious men is a corporation with a conscience. Law never made men a whit more just; and, by means of their respect for it, even the well-disposed are daily made the agents of injustice.

The mass of men serve the State thus, not as men mainly, but as machines, with their bodies. They are the standing army, and the militia, jailers, constables, *posse comitatus*, etc. In most cases there is no free exercise whatever of the judgment or of the moral sense; but they put themselves on a level with wood and earth and stones; and wooden men can perhaps be manufactured that will serve the purpose as well. Such command no more respect than men of straw, or a lump of dirt. They have the same sort of worth only as horses and dogs.[e] Yet such as these even are commonly esteemed good citizens. Others, as most legislators, politicians, lawyers, ministers, and office-holders, serve the State chiefly with their heads; and, as they rarely make any moral distinctions, they are as likely

---

d. Vincent Buranelli, writer, decrying Thoreau's elevation of conscience over law (1957): There is no more insidious political theory than this. When consciences conflict—and antagonism is never worse than when it involves two men each of whom is convinced that he speaks for goodness and rectitude—what then? Who is to decide? Who except the Leader with a capital *L*? Thoreau's theory has overtones of Rousseau's Legislator who can do what he pleases with the people under his control because he alone can fathom the holy intentions of the General Will. It points forward to Lenin, the "genius theoretician" whose right it is to force a suitable class consciousness on those who do not have it, and to the horrors that resulted from Hitler's "intuition" of what is best for Germany. Thoreau had as profound a disdain for ordinary law as these tyrants. Of course he would have insisted that he meant only "bad" law, and that they erected the most monstrous legislation into a system as soon as they had seized power. But this is no answer, for in subordinating law to conscience as he did, by denigrating majority rule and institutional checks, he opened the door to the agile demagogue who generally does not defer to the author of *Civil Disobedience* when it comes to claiming infallibility. For the Concord Transcendentalists peculiar notions like Thoreau's may have sounded pleasantly philosophical and intellectually titillating. For the world of the twentieth century they have been politically scarifying. —Vincent Buranelli, "The Case Against Thoreau," *Ethics* 67.4 (July 1957): 266–67.

e. George Hochfield, English professor, criticizing Thoreau's condescension toward those who lead the "unexamined life" (1988): So much for "the mass of men." Such a passage, characteristic of Thoreau, does not have the tone or purpose of satire: his imagination is too inflexible to encompass a vision of humanity as grotesque or ridiculous, and he never laughs. He is essentially a Puritan in decadent form, and all imperfection is for him depravity. —George Hochfield, "Anti-Thoreau," *Sewanee Review* 96.3 (Summer 1988): 434–35.

to serve the devil, without intending it, as God. A very few, as heroes, patriots, martyrs, reformers in the great sense, and men, serve the State with their consciences also, and so necessarily resist it for the most part; and they are commonly treated by it as enemies. . . .

All men recognize the right of revolution; that is, the right to refuse allegiance to and to resist the government, when its tyranny or its inefficiency are great and unendurable. But almost all say that such is not the case now. But such was the case, they think, in the Revolution of '75. If one were to tell me that this was a bad government because it taxed certain foreign commodities brought to its ports, it is most probable that I should not make an ado about it, for I can do without them: all machines have their friction; and possibly this does enough good to counterbalance the evil. At any rate, it is a great evil to make a stir about it. But when the friction comes to have its machine, and oppression and robbery are organized, I say, let us not have such a machine any longer. In other words, when a sixth of the population of a nation which has undertaken to be the refuge of liberty are slaves, and a whole country is unjustly overrun and conquered by a foreign army, and subjected to military law, I think that it is not too soon for honest men to rebel and revolutionize. . . .

All voting is a sort of gaming, like chequers or backgammon, with a slight moral tinge to it, a playing with right and wrong, with moral questions; and betting naturally accompanies it. The character of the voters is not staked. I cast my vote, perchance, as I think right; but I am not vitally concerned that that right should prevail. I am willing to leave it to the majority. Its obligation, therefore, never exceeds that of expediency. Even voting for the right is doing nothing for it. It is only expressing to men feebly your desire that it should prevail. A wise man will not leave the right to the mercy of chance, nor wish it to prevail through the power of the majority. There is but little virtue in the action of masses of men. When the majority shall at length vote for the abolition of slavery, it will be because they are indifferent to slavery, or because there is but little slavery left to be abolished by their vote. They will then be the only slaves. Only his vote can hasten the abolition of slavery who asserts his own freedom by his vote.

It is not a man's duty, as a matter of course, to devote himself to the eradication of any, even the most enormous wrong; he may still properly have other concerns to engage him; but it is his duty, at least, to wash his hands of it, and, if he gives it no thought longer, not to give it practically his support. If I devote myself to other pursuits and contemplations, I must first see, at least, that I do not pursue them sitting upon another man's shoulders. I must get off him first, that he may pursue his contemplations too. . . .

Some are petitioning the State to dissolve the Union, to disregard the requisitions of the President. Why do they not dissolve it themselves, the union between themselves and the State, and refuse to pay their quota into its treasury? Do not they stand in the same relation to the State, that the

State does to the Union? And have not the same reasons prevented the State from resisting the Union, which have prevented them from resisting the State?

Action from principle, the perception and the performance of right, changes things and relations; it is essentially revolutionary, and does not consist wholly with any thing which was. It not only divides states and churches, it divides families; aye, it divides the individual, separating the diabolical in him from the divine.

Unjust laws exist: shall we be content to obey them, or shall we endeavor to amend them, and obey them until we have succeeded, or shall we transgress them at once? Men generally, under such a government as this, think that they ought to wait until they have persuaded the majority to alter them. They think that, if they should resist, the remedy would be worse than the evil. But it is the fault of the government itself that the remedy is worse than the evil. It makes it worse. Why is it not more apt to anticipate and provide for reform? Why does it not cherish its wise minority? Why does it cry and resist before it is hurt? Why does it not encourage its citizens to be on the alert to point out its faults, and do better than it would have them? Why does it always crucify Christ, and excommunicate Copernicus and Luther, and pronounce Washington and Franklin rebels?

If the injustice is part of the necessary friction of the machine of government, let it go, let it go: perchance it will wear smooth, certainly the machine will wear out. If the injustice has a spring, or a pulley, or a rope, or a crank, exclusively for itself, then perhaps you may consider whether the remedy will not be worse than the evil; but if it is of such a nature that it requires you to be the agent of injustice to another, then, I say, break the law. Let your life be a counter friction to stop the machine. What I have to do is to see, at any rate, that I do not lend myself to the wrong which I condemn.

As for adopting the ways which the State has provided for remedying the evil, I know not of such ways. They take too much time, and a man's life will be gone. I have other affairs to attend to. I came into this world, not chiefly to make this a good place to live in, but to live in it, be it good or bad. A man has not every thing to do, but something; and because he cannot do everything, it is not necessary that he should do something wrong. It is not my business to be petitioning the governor or the legislature any more than it is theirs to petition me; and, if they should not hear my petition, what should I do then? But in this case the State has provided no way: its very Constitution is the evil.

I do not hesitate to say, that those who call themselves abolitionists should at once effectually withdraw their support, both in person and property, from the government of Massachusetts, and not wait till they constitute a majority of one, before they suffer the right to prevail through them. I think that it is enough if they have God on their side, without waiting for that other one. Moreover, any man more right than his neighbors, constitutes a majority of one already. . . .

I know this well, that if one thousand, if one hundred, if ten men whom I could name, if ten honest men only, aye, if *one* HONEST man, in this State of Massachusetts, *ceasing to hold slaves*, were actually to withdraw from this copartnership, and be locked up in the county jail therefor, it would be the abolition of slavery in America. For it matters not how small the beginning may seem to be: what is once well done is done for ever. . . .

Under a government which imprisons any unjustly, the true place for a just man is also a prison. The proper place to-day, the only place which Massachusetts has provided for her freer and less desponding spirits, is in her prisons, to be put out and locked out of the State by her own act, as they have already put themselves out by their principles. It is there that the fugitive slave, and the Mexican prisoner on parole, and the Indian come to plead the wrongs of his race, should find them; on that separate, but more free and honorable ground, where the State places those who are not with her but against her, the only house in a slave-state in which a free man can abide with honor. If any think that their influence would be lost there, and their voices no longer afflict the ear of the State, that they would not be as an enemy within its walls, they do not know by how much truth is stronger than error, nor how much more eloquently and effectively he can combat injustice who has experienced a little in his own person. Cast your whole vote, not a strip of paper merely, but your whole influence. A minority is powerless while it conforms to the majority; it is not even a minority then; but it is irresistible when it clogs by its whole weight. If the alternative is to keep all just men in prison, or give up war and slavery, the State will not hesitate which to choose. If a thousand men were not to pay their tax-bills this year, that would not be a violent and bloody measure, as it would be to pay them, and enable the State to commit violence and shed innocent blood. This is, in fact, the definition of a peaceable revolution, if any such is possible. If the tax-gatherer, or any other public officer, asks me, as one has done, "But what shall I do?" my answer is, "If you really wish to do any thing, resign your office." When the subject has refused allegiance, and the officer has resigned his office, then the revolution is accomplished. But even suppose blood should flow. Is there not a sort of blood shed when the conscience is wounded? Through this wound a man's real manhood and immortality flow out, and he bleeds to an everlasting death. I see this blood flowing now. . . .

Thus the State never intentionally confronts a man's sense, intellectual or moral, but only his body, his senses. It is not armed with superior wit or honesty, but with superior physical strength. I was not born to be forced. I will breathe after my own fashion. Let us see who is the strongest. What force has a multitude? They only can force me who obey a higher law than I. They force me to become like themselves. I do not hear of men being forced to live this way or that by masses of men. What sort of life were that to live? When I meet a government which says to me, "Your money or your life," why should I be in haste to give it my money? It may be in a great strait, and not know what to do: I cannot help that. It must help itself; do as I do. It is not worth the while to snivel about it. I am not responsible for the successful working of the machinery of society. I am not the son of the engineer. I perceive that, when an acorn and a chestnut fall side by side, the one does not remain inert to make way for the other, but both obey their own laws, and spring and grow and flourish as best they can, till one, perchance, overshadows and destroys the other. If a plant cannot live according to its nature, it dies; and so a man.

It is for no particular item in the tax-bill that I refuse to pay it. I simply wish to refuse allegiance to the State, to withdraw and stand aloof from it effectually. I do not care to trace the course of my dollar, if I could, till it buys a man, or a musket to shoot one with—the dollar is innocent— but I am concerned to trace the effects of my allegiance. In fact, I quietly declare war with the State, after any fashion, though I will still make what use and get what advantage of her I can, as is usual in such cases.

Seen from a lower point of view, the Constitution, with all its faults, is very good; the law and the courts are very respectable; even this State and this American government are, in many respects, very admirable and rare things, to be thankful for, such as a great many have described them; but seen from a point of view a little higher, they are what I have described them; seen from a higher still, and the highest, who shall say what they are, or that they are worth looking at or thinking of at all? . . .

The authority of government, even such as I am willing to submit to, for I will cheerfully obey those who know and can do better than I, and in many things even those who neither know nor can do so well, is still an impure one: to be strictly just, it must have the sanction and consent of the governed. It can have no pure right over my person and property but what I concede to it. The progress from an absolute to a limited monarchy, from a limited monarchy to a democracy, is a progress toward a true respect for the individual. Is a democracy, such as we know it, the last improvement possible in government? Is it not possible to take a step further towards recogniz- ing and organizing the rights of man? There will never be a really free and enlightened State, until the State comes to recognize the individual as a higher and independent power, from which all its own power and authority are derived, and treats him accordingly. I please myself with imagin- ing a State at last which can afford to be just to all men, and to treat the individual with respect as a neighbor; which even would not think it inconsistent with its own repose, if a few were to live aloof from it, not meddling with it, nor embraced by it, who fulfilled all the duties of neighbors and fellow-men. A State which bore this kind of fruit, and suffered it to drop off as fast as it rip- ened, would prepare the way for a still more perfect and glorious State, which also I have imagined, but not yet anywhere seen.[12]

COMMENTARY

John Macy, writer, summoning "Civil Disobedience" out of the critical woods (1913)

"Walden" and "A Week on the Concord and Merrimac Rivers" have been accepted as classics. The essays on "Forest Trees" and "Wild Apples" were to be found in a school reader twenty-five years ago. But the ringing revolt of the essay on "Civil Disobedience" is still silenced under the thick respectability of our times. The ideas in it could not today be printed in the magazine which was for years owned by the publishers of Thoreau's complete works. Boston Back Bay would shiver! . . . The application of Thoreau's principles to the injustices of our present political and industrial life would be condemned as disloyally "un-American" in the community where he lived and which is now owned, body and soul, factory and college, by State Street. Thoreau's intellectual kinsmen are not there.

—John Macy, *The Spirit of American Literature* (Garden City, NY: Doubleday, 1913), pp. 173–74.

Mohandas Gandhi, Indian independence leader, crediting Thoreau with influencing his freedom movement (1931)

Why, of course, I read Thoreau. I read *Walden* first in Johannesburg in South Africa in 1906 and his ideas influenced me greatly. I adopted some of them and recommended the study of Thoreau to all my friends who were helping me in the cause of Indian independence. Why, I actually took the name of my movement from Thoreau's essay, "On the Duty of Civil Disobedience," written about eighty years ago. Until I read that essay I never found a suitable English translation for my Indian word, *Satyagraha*. . . . There is no doubt that Thoreau's ideas greatly influenced my movement in India.

—Mohandas Gandhi, remarks at the Second Round Table Conference, London, 1931, quoted in Webb Miller, *I Found No Peace: The Journal of a Foreign Correspondent* (New York: Simon & Schuster, 1936), pp. 238–39.

Martin Luther King Jr., Baptist minister and civil rights leader, on his first encounter with Thoreau and "nonviolent resistance" (1958)

During my student days at Morehouse I read Thoreau's *Essay on Civil Disobedience* for the first time. Fascinated by the idea of refusing to cooperate with an evil system, I was so deeply moved that I reread the work several times. This was my first intellectual contact with the theory of nonviolent resistance.

—Martin Luther King Jr., *Stride Toward Freedom: The Montgomery Story* (1958; New York: Harper & Row, 1986), p. 91.

Ernest Earnest, writer, blasting Thoreau for providing aid and comfort to segregationists (1959)

The intellectual who praises Thoreau as a political thinker is about as realistic as the exurbanite who believes himself to be a spiritual inhabitant of Walden. Both are victims of their own neurotic compulsions and of Thoreau's charming literary style. The fact remains that Henry Thoreau is the spiritual ancestor of [Arkansas segregationist] Governor Orval Fabus.

—Ernest Earnest, "Thoreau and Little Rock," *Best Articles and Stories* 3 (November 1959): 42–43.

Henry Miller, novelist, invoking Thoreau against the atom bomb (1962)

Had [Thoreau] been told of the atom bomb, of the good and bad that it was capable of producing, he would have had something memorable to say about its use. And he would have said it in defiance of the prevalent attitude. He would not have rejoiced that the secret of its manufacture was in the hands of the righteous ones. He would have asked immediately: "Who is righteous enough to employ such a diabolical instrument destructively?" He would have had no more faith in the wisdom and sanctity of this present government of the United States than he had of our government in the days of slavery. . . . No, Thoreau would have been the first to say that no government on earth is good enough or wise enough to be entrusted with such powers for good and evil.

—Henry Miller, *Stand Still Like the Hummingbird* (Norfolk, CT: New Directions, 1962), p. 113.

Edwin Griswold, solicitor general of the United States, blaming 1960s hippiedom on Thoreau's myopia (1968)

Today, much protest seems reflexive rather than cerebral, motivated more by the desire to reject established positions and policies than by deliberate preference for some alternatives. Perhaps I am not perceptive enough to discern the latent wisdom and goals of movements that seek the elevation of dirty words on campus, or that exalt the virtues of "flower power," or that conduct a "strip-in" in a public park. The message, if there is one, escapes me. . . .

I cannot distinguish in principle the legal quality of the determination to halt a troop train to protest the Vietnam war or to block workmen from entering a segregated job site to protest employment discrimination, from the determination to fire shots into a civil rights leader's home to protest integration. The right to disagree—and to manifest disagreement—which the Constitution allows to the individuals in those situations—does not authorize them to carry on their campaign of education and persuasion at the expense of someone else's liberty, or in violation of some laws whose independent validity is unquestionable. . . .

Henry David Thoreau is generally regarded as the most notable American exponent of civil disobedience, and all of us share admiration for his determination. But we must not ignore the vital aspect of Thoreau's non-conformity—his passionate attempt to dissociate himself from society. He was, as Henry Kalven has put it, "a man who does not see himself as belonging very intensely to the community in which he was raised," and who sought constantly but futilely to reject the society to which he had not voluntarily adhered.

Thoreau's poignant attitude was charming enough in mid-nineteenth-century America. But it was, essentially, an effort to withdraw from the realities of life, and it was, I suggest, myopic even then, for it was painfully inconsistent with the fact that man is a part of society by nature, by geography, and by citizenship. Unlike a member of a purely artificial group, like a bar association or country club, a citizen cannot resign from the "social compact" because he protests policies of the regime. Now in the last third of the twentieth century, we must be even more cognizant that there is nothing noble or salutary about foredoomed attempts to abdicate membership in society. Complex problems demand rational attention that can come only from personal focus on solutions and never from stubbornly turning one's back on harsh and unpleasant realities.

This is precisely what non-conformity as a way of life is. It is the essential irrationality of the "hippie movement"—a mass endeavor to drop out of life. It is a protest of sorts, of course, but one that can bear no fruit, because it takes issue with what is not only inevitable, but more importantly, indispensable—social regulation of individual behavior.

—Edwin N. Griswold, "Dissent—1968," *Tulane Law Review* 42.4 (June 1968): 730, 733–34, 737.

Howard Zinn, historian and activist, insisting that America's problem is civil obedience (1970)

As soon as you say the topic is civil disobedience, you are saying our problem is civil disobedience. That is not our problem. . . . Our problem is civil obedience. Our problem is the numbers of people all over the world who have obeyed the dictates of the leaders of their government and have gone to war, and millions have been killed because of this obedience. And our problem is that scene in *All Quiet on the Western Front* where the schoolboys march off dutifully in a line to war. Our problem is that people are obedient all over the world, in the face of poverty and starvation and stupidity, and war and cruelty. Our problem is that people are obedient while the jails are full of petty thieves, and all the while the grand thieves are running the country. That's our problem. . . .

We are asked, "What if everyone disobeyed the law?" But a better question is, "What if everyone obeyed the law?" And the answer to that question is much easier to come by, because we have a lot of empirical evidence about what happens if everyone obeys the law, or if even most people obey the law. What happens is what has happened, what is happening. . . .

[The United States] then was founded on disrespect for the law, and then came the Constitution and the notion of stability which Madison and Hamilton liked. But then we found in certain crucial times in our history that the legal framework did not suffice, and in order to end slavery we had to go outside the legal framework, as we had to do at the time of the American Revolution or the Civil War. . . .

What we are trying to do, I assume, is really to get back to the principles and aims and spirit of the Declaration of Independence. This spirit is resistance to illegitimate authority and to forces that deprive people of their life and liberty and right to pursue happiness, and therefore under these conditions, it urges the right to alter or abolish their current form of government—and the stress had been on abolish. But to establish the principles of the Declaration of Independence, we are going to need to go outside the law, to stop obeying the laws that demand killing or that allocate wealth the way it has been done, or that put people in jail for petty technical offenses and keep other people out of jail for enormous crimes. My hope is that this kind of spirit will take place not just in this country but in other countries because they all need it. People in all countries need the spirit of disobedience to the state, which is not a metaphysical thing but a thing of force and wealth. And we need a kind of declaration of interdependence among people in all countries of the world who are striving for the same thing.

—Howard Zinn, "The Problem Is Civil Obedience," in *The Zinn Reader: Writings on Disobedience and Democracy* (New York: Seven Stories, 1997), pp. 405–7, 410–11.

Alfred Kazin, literary critic, on the futility of Thoreau's "literary anarchism" (1984)

"Civil Disobedience" stirs us by the urgency of its personal morality. As is usual with Thoreau, he seems to be putting his whole soul into the protest against injustice committed by the State. He affirms the absolute right of the individual to obey his own conscience in defiance of an unknown law. But despite his compelling personal heat, he tends to moralize all political relationships and make them not really serious. He turns the State into a totally ridiculous object, its demands on him into a pure affront, and then archly tells it to stop being so overbearing and please to disappear. . . .

The significantly political passages in the essay have to do with what Thoreau calls "slavery in Massachusetts." He of all people could not grant that property is the greatest passion and the root of most social conflicts and wars. Yet he insisted "that if one thousand, if one hundred, if ten men whom I could name—if ten *honest* men only—ay, if *one* Honest man, in this State of Massachusetts, *ceasing to hold slaves,* were actually to withdraw from this co-partnership, and be locked up in the county jail therefore, it would be the abolition of slavery in America." With his marvelous instinct for justice, for pure Christianity, and for the deep-rooted rights of the individual soul, he said: "Under a government which imprisons any unjustly, the true place for a just man is also a prison." Morally invigorating as this is, it would perhaps not have helped the fugitive slave, or the Mexican prisoner on parole, or the Indian come to plead the wrongs of his race when, as Thoreau said, they came to prison and found the best spirits of Massachusetts there. Thoreau estimated the power of individual example to be beyond any other device in politics, but he did not explain how the usefulness of example could communicate itself to people who were in fact slaves and were not free.

—Alfred Kazin, *An American Procession* (New York: Knopf, 1984), pp. 75–76.

Wendell Berry, Kentucky farmer and novelist, on Thoreau as a bad friend and a worse political activist (1985)

Thoreau has been adopted by the American environment movement as a figure-head; he is customarily quoted and invoked as if he were in some simple way a forerunner of environmentalism. This is possible, obviously, only because Thoreau has been dead since 1862. Thoreau was an environmentalist in exactly the sense that Edward Abbey is: he was for some things that environmentalists are for. And in his own time he was just as much of an embarrassment to movements, just as uncongenial to the group spirit, as Edward Abbey is, and for the same reasons: he was working as an autobiographer, and his great effort was to conserve himself as a human being in the best and fullest sense. As a political activist, he was a poor excuse. What was the political value of his forlorn, solitary taxpayer's revolt against the Mexican War? What was politic about his defense of John Brown or his insistence that abolitionists should free the *wage* slaves of Massachusetts? Who could trust the diplomacy of a man who would pray:

> *Great God, I ask thee for no other pelf*
> *Than that I may not disappoint myself; . . .*
> *And next in value, which thy kindness lends,*
> *That I may greatly disappoint my friends.*

—Wendell Berry, "A Few Words in Favor of Edward Abbey," in *What Are People For?* (New York: North Point, 1990), pp. 40–41.

Farewell Address

❦ DWIGHT EISENHOWER, 1961 ❦

*D*WIGHT DAVID EISENHOWER (1890–1969) was obviously a man of action. A five-star general, he led the Allies to victory in World War II before serving two presidential terms. But "Ike," as he was popularly known, also delivered the most influential farewell address in modern America.

The farewell address of another general turned president, George Washington, is remembered for its stern warning against the emerging party system. But Washington also spoke against "overgrown military establishments which, under any form of government, are inauspicious to liberty."[1] Eisenhower, in a speech delivered on January 17, 1961, just days before President Kennedy's inauguration, issued a similar warning, in this case against the "unwarranted influence" of the "military-industrial complex."[2]

This was not Eisenhower's first alert about the dangers posed by this powerful nexus of military and business interests. In a 1953 speech to the American Society of Newspaper Editors, he delivered what *Time* called "one of the most notable policy statements of U.S. history."[3] Russian leader Joseph Stalin had just died, but the Cold War lived on, so Eisenhower addressed his remarks to the realities of a newly nuclear world divided into Communists and capitalists. About the costs of the Cold War, Eisenhower spoke bluntly. In fact, he referred to military spending as a sort of plunder: "Every gun that is made, every warship launched, every rocket fired signifies, in the final sense, a theft from those who hunger and are not fed, those who are cold and are not clothed." But Eisenhower also did the math:

The cost of one modern heavy bomber is this: a modern brick school in more than 30 cities. It is two electric power plants, each serving a town of 60,000 population. . . . We pay for a single fighter with a half-million bushels of wheat. We pay for a single destroyer with new homes that could have housed more than 8,000 people.

"This is the best way of life to be found on the road the world has been taking," he continued, yet "this is not a way of life at all, in any true sense. Under the cloud of threatening war, it is humanity hanging from a cross of iron."[4]

This stern warning was ignored in 1953 because of "military Keynsianism," the theory that military expenditures, by stimulating the economy, would pay for themselves.[5] In other words, Americans could have their guns and eat their butter too. The new guns, of course, were nuclear weapons, which multiplied from 1,000 warheads upon Eisenhower's election in 1952 to 24,000 upon Kennedy's inauguration in 1961. Over this same period, military spending accounted for roughly half of all federal spending. So Eisenhower was no dove. But his role as a key player in the "military-industrial complex" made his criticism of it in his 1961 farewell address all the more noteworthy—like hearing of the dangers of ballet shoes from George Balanchine.

Once again, Eisenhower sounded an alarm about military theft. This time the stealing was being done not by heavy bombers but by a nexus of special-interest groups (Washington would have called them "factions"), including arms manufacturers and military elites. And what was now at stake was America's soul. A powerful network of military and industrial leaders threatened individual liberty and popular sovereignty:

In the councils of government, we must guard against the acquisition of unwarranted influence, whether sought or unsought, by the military-industrial complex. The potential for the disastrous rise of misplaced power exists and will persist. We must never let the weight of this combination endanger our liberties or democratic processes. We should take nothing for granted.

The power of "this conjunction of an immense military establishment and a large arms industry," he argued, should not be underestimated. Its "total influence—economic, political, even spiritual—is felt in every city, every State house, every office of the Federal government." In other words, the business of America was becoming war.

This farewell address was in some respects a response to allegations that Eisenhower, whose commitment to a balanced budget had led him to cut some defense appropriations, had allowed the Soviets to bypass the United States in the arms race. Kennedy had campaigned, and won, on a promise to close this "missile gap." According to Eisenhower, however, federal budget decisions should not be driven by fear. They should be made by an "engaged citizenry" looking after America's common good, not by self-aggrandizing special interests.

Initially, Eisenhower's words were lost in the moment, which belonged to President Kennedy and the Camelot myth. But Eisenhower aide Bryce Harlow, in a perceptive March 17, 1961, memo to Eisenhower and his vice president Richard Nixon, rightly saw that the military-industrial complex theme was "yeasty."[6] It took some time, but eventually debate over Ike's coinage would heat up and rise.

By the late 1960s, allegations that "merchants of death" were holding the country hostage was a staple of Vietnam War protesters. To them, Eisenhower was an "antimilitarist" prophet, and the war without end in Vietnam was proof positive that military men and defense CEOs were running the country for profit.[7] The "mounting influence of the military-industrial complex" is "the most serious internal threat facing the United States," said Senator George McGovern (D-SD) in 1968.[8] "The Economy of Life in America has been starved to feed the Economy of Death," added Richard Barnet of the Institute for Policy Studies one year later.[9]

Hawks responded by insisting that these peaceniks were taking Eisenhower's remarks out of context. President Nixon called the military-industrial complex a "strawman" and an excuse for isolationism.[10] Others insisted that Eisenhower never deviated from the view that the need for military might outweighed its perils.

By the mid-1980s, it had become obvious that doors of influence and employment were swinging freely for not only military officers and defense contractors but also academics and legislators. "Today, the military-industrial complex . . . is larger and more pervasive than [Eisenhower] could have imagined. Linked by profit and patriotism, the armed services, corporations, scientists, engineers, consultants and members of Congress form a loose confederation that reaches almost every corner of American society," wrote the *Washington Post* in 1986. "It's no longer a question of controlling a military-industrial complex," added former MIT president Jerome Weisner, "but rather of keeping the United States from becoming a total military culture."[11]

This notion of a "warfare state" has now been invoked in debates over the B-1 bomber, the MX missile, and the SALT Treaty. Since 9/11, however, "the military industrial complex has had a field day," with profits at the Big Five defense contractors jumping from $6.7 billion in 2001 to $24.8 billion in 2010.[12] The intelligence community has also grown by leaps and bounds, as has the newly created Department of Homeland Security. According to Boston University professor Andrew Bacevich, "annual U.S. military outlays now approximate those of all other nations, friends as well as foes, combined."[13]

Farewell Address ❧

My fellow Americans:

Three days from now, after half a century in the service of our country, I shall lay down the responsibilities of office as, in traditional and solemn ceremony, the authority of the Presidency is vested in my successor. This evening I come to you with a message of leave-taking and farewell, and to share a few final thoughts with you, my countrymen. . . .

We now stand ten years past the midpoint of a century that has witnessed four major wars among great nations. Three of these involved our own country. Despite these holocausts America is today the strongest, the most influential and most productive nation in the world. Understandably proud of this pre-eminence, we yet realize that America's leadership and prestige depend, not merely upon our unmatched material progress, riches and military strength, but on how we use our power in the interests of world peace and human betterment.

Throughout America's adventure in free government, our basic purposes have been to keep the peace, to foster progress in human achievement, and to enhance liberty, dignity and integrity among people and among nations. To strive for less would be unworthy of a free and religious people. Any failure traceable to arrogance or our lack of comprehension or readiness to sacrifice would inflict upon us grievous hurt both at home and abroad.

Progress toward these noble goals is persistently threatened by the conflict now engulfing the world. It commands our whole attention, absorbs our very beings. We face a hostile ideology—global in scope, atheistic in character, ruthless in purpose, and insidious in method. Unhappily, the danger it poses promises to be of indefinite duration. To meet it successfully, there is called for, not so much the emotional and transitory sacrifices of crisis, but rather those which enable us to carry forward steadily, surely, and without complaint the burdens of a prolonged and complex struggle—with liberty the stake. Only thus shall we remain, despite every provocation, on our charted course toward permanent peace and human betterment.

Crises there will continue to be. In meeting them, whether foreign or domestic, great or small, there is a recurring temptation to feel that some spectacular and costly action could become the miraculous solution to all current difficulties. A huge increase in newer elements of our defense; development of unrealistic programs to cure every ill in agriculture; a dramatic expansion in basic and applied research—these and many other possibilities, each possibly promising in itself, may be suggested as the only way to the road we wish to travel.

But each proposal must be weighed in the light of a broader consideration: the need to maintain balance in and among national programs—balance between the private and the public economy, balance between cost and hoped for advantage—balance between the clearly necessary and the comfortably desirable; balance between our essential requirements as a nation and the duties imposed by the nation upon the individual; balance between actions of the moment and the national welfare of the future. Good judgment seeks balance and progress; lack of it eventually finds imbalance and frustration.

The record of many decades stands as proof that our people and their government have, in the main, understood these truths and have responded to them well, in the face of stress and threat. But threats, new in kind or degree, constantly arise. I mention two only.

A vital element in keeping the peace is our military establishment. Our arms must be mighty, ready for instant action, so that no potential aggressor may be tempted to risk his own destruction.

Our military organization today bears little relation to that known by any of my predecessors in peacetime, or indeed by the fighting men of World War II or Korea. Until the latest of our world conflicts, the United States had no armaments industry. American makers of plowshares could, with time and as required, make swords as well. But now we can no longer risk emergency improvisation of national defense; we have been compelled to create a permanent armaments industry of vast proportions. Added to this, three and a half million men and women are directly engaged in the defense establishment. We annually spend on military security more than the net income of all United States corporations.

This conjunction of an immense military establishment and a large arms industry is new in the American experience. The total influence—economic, political, even spiritual—is felt in every city, every State house, every office of the Federal government. We recognize the imperative need for this development. Yet we must not fail to comprehend its grave implications. Our toil, resources and livelihood are all involved; so is the very structure of our society.

In the councils of government, we must guard against the acquisition of unwarranted influence, whether sought or unsought, by the military-industrial complex. The potential for the disastrous rise of misplaced power exists and will persist. We must never let the weight of this combination endanger our liberties or democratic processes. We should take nothing for granted. Only an alert and knowledgeable citizenry can compel the proper meshing of the huge industrial and military machinery of defense with our peaceful methods and goals, so that security and liberty may prosper together.

Akin to, and largely responsible for, the sweeping changes in our industrial-military posture has been the technological revolution during recent decades. In this revolution, research has become central; it also becomes more formalized, complex, and costly. A steadily increasing share is conducted for, by, or at the direction of, the Federal government.

Today, the solitary inventor, tinkering in his shop, has been overshadowed by task forces of scientists in laboratories and testing fields. In the same fashion, the free university, historically the fountainhead of free ideas and scientific discovery, has experienced a revolution in the conduct of research. Partly because of the huge costs involved, a government contract becomes virtually a substitute for intellectual curiosity. For every old blackboard there are now hundreds of new electronic computers.

The prospect of domination of the nation's scholars by Federal employment, project allocations, and the power of money is ever present—and is gravely to be regarded. Yet, in holding scientific research and discovery in respect, as we should, we must also be alert to the equal and opposite danger that public policy could itself become the captive of a scientific-technological elite. It is the task of statesmanship to mold, to balance, and to integrate these and other forces, new and old, within the principles of our democratic system—ever aiming toward the supreme goals of our free society.

Another factor in maintaining balance involves the element of time. As we peer into society's future, we—you and I, and our government—must avoid the impulse to live only for today, plundering, for our own ease and convenience, the precious resources of tomorrow. We cannot mortgage the material assets of our grandchildren without risking the loss also of their political and spiritual heritage. We want democracy to survive for all generations to come, not to become the insolvent phantom of tomorrow.

Down the long lane of the history yet to be written America knows that this world of ours, ever growing smaller, must avoid becoming a community of dreadful fear and hate, and be, instead, a proud confederation of mutual trust and respect. Such a confederation must be one of equals. The weakest must come to the conference table with the same confidence as do we, protected as we are by our moral, economic, and military strength. That table, though scarred by many past frustrations, cannot be abandoned for the certain agony of the battlefield.

Disarmament, with mutual honor and confidence, is a continuing imperative. Together we must learn how to compose differences, not with arms, but with intellect and decent purpose. Because this need is so sharp and apparent I confess that I lay down my official responsibilities in this field with a definite sense of disappointment. As one who has witnessed the horror and the lingering sadness of war—as one who knows that another war could utterly destroy this civilization which has been so slowly and painfully built over thousands of years—I wish I could say tonight that a lasting peace is in sight.

Happily, I can say that war has been avoided. Steady progress toward our ultimate goal has been made. But, so much remains to be done. As a private citizen, I shall never cease to do what little I can to help the world advance along that road. . . .

To all the peoples of the world, I once more give expression to America's prayerful and continuing aspiration: We pray that peoples of all faiths, all races, all nations, may have their great human needs satisfied; that those now denied opportunity shall come to enjoy it to the full; that all who yearn for freedom may experience its spiritual blessings; that those who have freedom will understand, also, its heavy responsibilities; that all who are insensitive to the needs of others will learn charity; that the scourges of poverty, disease and ignorance will be made to disappear from the earth, and that, in the goodness of time, all peoples will come to live together in a peace guaranteed by the binding force of mutual respect and love.[14]

COMMENTARY

J. W. Fulbright, U.S. Senator (D-AR), on how ordinary citizens create and sustain the military-industrial complex (1967)

I do not think the military-industrial complex is the conspiratorial invention of a band of "merchants of death." . . . It is rather the inevitable result of the creation of a huge, permanent military establishment, whose needs have given rise to a vast private defense industry tied to the armed forces by a natural bond of common interest. . . . Unplanned though it was, this complex has become a major political force. It is the result rather than the cause of American military involvements around the world; but, composed as it is of a vast number of citizens—not tycoons or "merchants of death" but ordinary, good American citizens—whose livelihood depends on defense production, the military-industrial complex has become an indirect force for the perpetuation of our global military commitments.

This is not—and I emphasize "not"—because anyone favors war but because every one of us has a natural and proper desire to preserve the sources of his livelihood. For the defense worker this means preserving or obtaining some local factory or installation and obtaining new defense orders; for the labor union leader it means jobs for his members at abnormally high wages; for the politician it means preserving the good will of his constituents by helping them to get what they want. . . . The constituency-building process is further advanced by the perspicacity of Defense officials and contractors in locating installations and plants in the districts of influential key members of Congress. In this natural way, generals, industrialists, businessmen, labor leaders, workers, and politicians have joined together in a military-industrial complex—a complex which, for all the inadvertency of its creation and the innocent intentions of its participants, has nonetheless become a powerful new force for the perpetuation of foreign military commitments, for the introduction of an expansion of expensive weapons systems, and, as a result, for the militarization of large segments of our national life.

—J. W. Fulbright, *Congressional Record,* December 13, 1967, quoted in Mike Moore, "A Counterweight,"
  The Bulletin of the Atomic Scientists 51.5 (September/October 1995): 2.

George McGovern, U.S. Senator (D-SD), declaring his candidacy for the Democratic presidential nomination (1968)

For nearly five years I have warned, on the floor of the Senate, against our deepening involvement in Vietnam—the most disastrous political, moral, diplomatic blunder in our national history. . . . Beyond this, I have long advocated a systematic reduction of our overgrown military-industrial complex about which President Eisenhower warned us some eight years ago. It is imperative that we scale down the military waste that weakens rather than strengthens the nation, so that those urgently needed excess resources may be diverted to long-neglected areas of our national life, the reconstruction of our rural America.

—"Transcript of Statement of Candidacy by Senator McGovern," *New York Times,* August 11, 1968, p. 62.

Richard Nixon, thirty-seventh U.S. president, opposing the "new isolationists" in a speech at the Air Force Academy (1969)

I worked closely with President Eisenhower for 8 years. I know what he meant when he said: "we must guard against the acquisition of unwarranted influence, whether sought or unsought, by the military-industrial complex." Many people conveniently forget that he followed that warning with another: "we must also be alert to the equal and opposite danger that public policy could itself become the captive of a scientific-technological elite." We sometimes forget that in that same farewell address, President Eisenhower spoke of the need for national security. He said: "A vital element in keeping the peace is our military establishment. Our arms must be mighty, ready for instant action, so that no potential aggressor may be tempted to risk his own destruction."

I say to you, my fellow Americans, let us never forget those wise words of one of America's greatest leaders. The American defense establishment should never be a sacred cow, but on the other hand, the American military should never be anybody's scapegoat. . . .

The question, I submit, in defense spending is a very simple one: "How much is necessary?" The President of the United States is the man charged with making that judgment. After a complete review of our foreign and defense policies I have submitted requests to the Congress for military appropriations. . . . I do not consider my recommendations infallible. But if I have made a mistake, I pray that it is on the side of too much and not too little. If we do too much it will cost us our money. If we do too little, it may cost us our lives.

—Richard Nixon, "Air Force Academy Commencement Address," June 4, 1969, www.presidency.ucsb.edu/ws/index.php?pid=2081#axzz1YzNDMpZX.

Barry Goldwater, U.S. Senator (R-AZ), thanking God for the military-industrial complex (1969)

If I were a psychologist, I might be tempted to the conclusion that the left wing in American politics has developed a "complex over a complex." Judging from the views expressed by many of our public officials and commentators, the so-called military-industrial complex would seem to be responsible for almost all of the world's evils. Certainly, a determined effort is under way to place at its doorstep almost full responsibility for the unfortunate war in Vietnam and the high cost of American defense. . . .

Mr. President, do these critics of what they term a military-industrial complex really want us to default on our worldwide responsibilities, turn our back on aggression and slavery, and develop a national policy of selfish isolation?

Rather than deploring the existence of a military-industrial complex, I say we should thank heavens for it. That complex gives us our protective shield. It is the bubble under which our nation thrives and prospers. It is the armor which is unfortunately required in a world divided.

—Barry Goldwater, *Congressional Record*, April 15, 1969, quoted in "Arms and the Man: Senator Goldwater Salutes the Military-Industrial Complex," *Barron's*, April 21, 1969, pp. 1, 10.

Ronald Reagan, former governor of California and Republican presidential candidate, defending U.S. military personnel against "libel" (1980)

The American people are prepared for a large and definite purpose: . . . to begin the moral and military rearmament of the United States for the difficult, dangerous decade ahead, and to tune out those cynics, pacifists, and appeasers who tell us the Army and Navy of this country are nothing but the extensions of some malevolent military-industrial complex. We reject that libel—that lie—against millions of American men and women who are serving in the armed forces of the United States. There is only one military-industrial complex whose operations should concern us and it is located not in Arlington, Virginia, but in Moscow in the Soviet Union.

—"The Basic Speech: Ronald Reagan," *New York Times*, February 29, 1980, p. B4.

Jack Shor, letter to the editor, saying Ike was right (1990)

How sad that we have lived to see his worst fears realized: our economic strength sapped by an apparently uncontrollable "defense" budget; billion-dollar planes that don't fly; trillion-dollar fantasy weapons systems that will never see the light of day and a Congress with no idea what to do about it. Ike would have wept.

—Jack Shor, "Ike Would Have Wept to See State of Nation," *New York Times*, April 20, 1990, p. A32.

George W. Bush, forty-third U.S. president, justifying skyrocketing defense outlays (2002)

My budget includes the largest increase in defense spending in two decades, because while the price of freedom and security is high, it is never too high. Whatever it costs to defend our country, we will pay.

—George W. Bush, "Address Before a Joint Session of the Congress on the State of the Union," January 29, 2002, www.presidency.ucsb.edu/ws/index.php?pid=29644.

Robert Gates, secretary of defense, raising questions Eisenhower might ask today (2010)

Before making claims of requirements not being met or alleged "gaps"—in ships, tactical fighters, personnel, or anything else—we need to evaluate the criteria upon which requirements are based and the wider real world context. For example, should we really be up in arms over a temporary projected shortfall of about 100 Navy and Marine strike fighters relative to the number of carrier wings, when America's military possesses more than 3,200 tactical combat aircraft of all kinds? Does the number of warships we have and are building really put America at risk when the U.S. battle fleet is larger than the next 13 navies combined, 11 of which belong to allies and partners? Is it a dire threat that by 2020 the United States will have only 20 times more advanced stealth fighters than China? These are the kinds of questions Eisenhower asked as commander-in-chief. They are the kinds of questions I believe he would ask today.

—Robert M. Gates, speech, Abilene, Kansas, May 8, 2010, www.defense.gov/Speeches/Speech.aspx?SpeechID=1467.

"I Have a Dream"

❧ MARTIN LUTHER KING JR., 1963 ❧

*T*HE LINCOLN MEMORIAL is one of the great gathering places for America's conversation about itself. We go there alone or with friends or family members to remember our most iconic president. We go there en masse to protest when our nation has fallen short of Lincoln's ideals, and our own. After the Daughters of the American Revolution barred the African-American contralto Marian Anderson from performing at Constitution Hall in Washington, D.C., in 1939, Anderson sang on the steps of the Lincoln Memorial. Beyoncé, Bono, and Bruce Springsteen performed there in 2009 during the inauguration festivities for President Barack Obama. One year later talk-show host Glenn Beck held a "Restoring Honor" rally at the same site. Of all these Memorial moments, however, the most celebrated came on the afternoon of August 28, 1963, when Martin Luther King Jr. (1929–68) stepped up to the microphone at the March on Washington for Jobs and Freedom and delivered one of the most powerful speeches in American history.

On June 11, 1963, the same day President Kennedy would address the nation on desegregation, leaders in the civil rights movement had announced plans to march on Washington in order "to arouse the conscience of the nation over the economic plight of the Negro."[1] On June 22, President Kennedy met with leaders of the "Big Six" civil rights groups behind the march—the Congress of Racial Equality (CORE), the Southern Christian Leadership Conference (SCLC), the Student Nonviolent Coordinating Committee (SNCC), the Brotherhood of Sleeping Car Porters, the National Association of Colored People (NAACP), and the National Urban League—to urge them to cancel the protest. They refused. After a series of labor and religious groups joined the organizing team, the president gave the march his blessing. But he and his brother, Attorney General Robert Kennedy, worked behind the scenes to moderate it.

Young black militants worried that the event would turn into nothing more than a picnic. Older civil rights veterans worried that it might turn into a blood-bath. Many in D.C. feared violence too. On the day of the march, all bars and liquor stores in the District were closed, a baseball game between the Minnesota Twins and the Washington Senators was cancelled, and the D.C. police, reinforced by twenty-five hundred members of the National Guard, were on high alert. "The general feeling is that the Vandals are coming to sack Rome," wrote the *Washington Daily News*.[2]

Meanwhile, King and his colleagues fretted about a low turnout. But supporters came by planes, buses, and trains, and on August 28, 1963, a crowd of perhaps 300,000 marched from the Washington Monument to the Lincoln Memorial in the largest demonstration in U.S. history. The gathering was peaceful, the mood buoyant. At the Lincoln Memorial, Marian Anderson reprised her 1939 performance by singing "The Star-Spangled Banner." There were songs by Bob Dylan and Joan Baez, and speeches by representatives of each of the Big Six.

John Lewis, a SNCC leader who would go on to represent Georgia's fifth congressional district, had prepared a fiery speech that damned Kennedy's civil rights bill as "too little and too late." A draft found its way into the hands of Washington's Archbishop Patrick O'Boyle and through him to the White House. Efforts to persuade SNCC to tone it down were unsuccessful until A. Philip Randolph, who had first imagined a march on Washington to protest segregation in 1941, personally prevailed on Lewis. "I have waited twenty-two years for this. I've waited all my *life* for this opportunity," he said. "Please don't ruin it."[3] Lewis still spoke against Kennedy's bill, but he did not promise to "march through the South, through the heart of Dixie, the way Sherman did . . . and burn Jim Crow to the ground."[4]

King, the last of the main speakers, began by noting the moment: "five score years ago," he calculated, in language reminiscent of Lincoln, after the Emancipation Proclamation. And yet, he observed, "the Negro is still not free," shackled by segregation, discrimination, and poverty. King spoke of those who gave us the Declaration of Independence and the Constitution as "signing a promissory note" guaranteeing to all Americans "the inalienable rights of life, liberty, and the pursuit of happiness." But America had not made good on this promise, he said, "So we have come to cash this check, a check that will give us upon demand the riches of freedom and the security of justice."

Drawing on the prophetic tradition of Jeremiah, Amos, and Isaiah, who had chastised the people of Israel for their sinful ways and called upon them to repent and return to their covenant with God, King laid bare the sins of America. Throughout U.S. history, Americans have been tempted to turn the conditional covenant invoked by Massachusetts governor John Winthrop in his 1630 *Arbella* sermon into an unconditional covenant in which God blesses America come what may. But King called for a revitalization of the more venerable tradition in which God would bless Americans only if they heeded God's call to "do justly, and to love mercy" (Micah 6:8). Like the Hebrew prophets, King saw no clear demarcation between the sacred world of the spirit and the secular world of politics. Like Winthrop, he saw no clear line between biblical times and his own.

In words drawn from Amos that would later grace Maya Lin's Civil Rights Memorial in Montgomery, Alabama, King said, "We will not be satisfied until justice rolls down like waters and righteousness like a mighty stream." And in words based on the passion of Jesus on the cross, he urged those who had been "battered by the storms of persecution and staggered by the winds of police brutality" to stand firm in "the faith that unearned suffering is redemptive."

As King was delivering these prepared remarks, the gospel singer Mahalia Jackson reportedly cried out for him to talk about his dream for America. Two months earlier, in Detroit, King had given a speech about this dream. Few had remarked upon it, but it had moved Jackson, and soon King was moving millions of Americans watching him on national television. Setting aside his written speech, King metamorphosed from prophet to visionary, hewing "a stone of hope" out of "the mountain of despair." Improvising on his vision of the American dream to the cadences of the Bible, he "turned the Lincoln Memorial into a Baptist sanctuary and preached an inspiring sermon."[5]

As his words picked up speed and urgency, he shared his vision of an America in which the equality promised in the Declaration would be made manifest in the South and the freedom promised in "My Country, 'Tis of Thee" would ring from hilltop to mountaintop. He concluded his speech by raising his hands and allowing himself to imagine "that day when all of God's children, black men and white men, Jews and Gentiles, Protestants and Catholics, will be able to join hands and sing in the words of the old Negro spiritual, 'Free at last! Free at last! Thank God Almighty, we are free at last!' "

The next day the news was neither the record turnout nor King's speech, but the fact that the city had not been laid waste by rioting. Nonetheless, the march gave the civil rights movement a huge lift, pressuring Congress to pass the Civil Rights Act in 1964 (when there were only five African Americans in the House) and the Voting Rights Act of 1965 (when there were only six). America, it seemed, was willing to make good on the bounced check. But then the movement lost its momentum. King, named *Time* magazine's Man of the Year in 1964, turned increasingly to economic issues and to protesting the Vietnam war.[6] More militant black voices gained ground, including that of the Nation of Islam leader Malcolm X, who famously dismissed the March on Washington as the "Farce on Washington."[7] Then came the assassinations of Malcolm X in 1965, and those of King and Robert Kennedy in 1968. In ensuing decades, anniversaries of the March on Washington were reprised by rallies in Washington, D.C., and King's speech emerged as a yardstick to measure America's progress on racial equality, economic justice, and freedom for all.

Since his death, King has morphed from man to martyr, honored with a national holiday in 1986 and with a memorial of his own on the Mall in 2011. So it should not be surprising that his most famous speech has been appropriated and misappropriated, both at home and abroad. According to scholar and activist Drew Hansen, by the early 1980s, "it was excerpted in countless American studies textbooks, reprinted on posters sold in college bookstores, and emblazoned on pins and T-shirts sold at civil rights rallies. . . . In Nelson Mandela's victory speech after South Africa's first multiracial elections, he declared that black Africans were 'Free at last.' Protestors in Tiananmen Square held up billboards with pictures of King and the words, 'I have a dream.' "[8]

King's speech, which pastor-politician Andrew Young describes as "our Declaration of Independence, our declaration of freedom, and our Gettysburg Address," has inspired gay rights activists to dream of a day in which "the sons of homosexuals and the sons of heterosexuals will be able to sit down together at the table of brotherhood."[9] King's dream of a day when his children "will not be judged by the color of their skin but by the content of their character" has also been used by William Bennett, Rush Limbaugh, and other conservatives to criticize affirmative action as "reverse discrimination," despite the fact that King advocated "special, compensatory measures which could be regarded as a settlement in accordance with the accepted practice of common law."[10]

In 2000, a panel of 137 academics named "I Have a Dream" the greatest political speech of the twentieth century.[11] In 2009, with the inauguration of Barack Obama as America's first African-American president, there was much talk of King's dream, and of Obama playing Joshua to his Moses. But according to a study entitled *State of the Dream 2009: The Silent Depression,* the incarceration rate for black men that year was more than six times that for white men. The unemployment rate for young black men was 33 percent. The portion of all blacks in poverty was 24 percent, versus 8 percent of whites.[12] So Americans are still struggling to answer the question posed by Harlem Renaissance poet Langston Hughes: "What happens to a dream deferred?"[13]

"I Have a Dream"

I am happy to join with you today in what will go down in history as the greatest demonstration for freedom in the history of our nation.

Five score years ago, a great American, in whose symbolic shadow we stand, signed the Emancipation Proclamation. This momentous decree came as a great beacon light of hope to millions of Negro slaves who had been seared in the flames of withering injustice. It came as a joyous daybreak to end the long night of captivity.

But one hundred years later, we must face the tragic fact that the Negro is still not free. One hundred years later, the life of the Negro is still sadly crippled by the manacles of segregation and the chains of discrimination. One hundred years later, the Negro lives on a lonely island of poverty in the midst of a vast ocean of material prosperity. One hundred years later, the Negro is still languishing in the corners of American society and finds himself an exile in his own land. So we have come here today to dramatize an appalling condition.

In a sense we have come to our nation's capital to cash a check. When the architects of our republic wrote the magnificent words of the Constitution and the Declaration of Independence, they were signing a promissory note to which every American was to fall heir. This note was a promise that all men would be guaranteed the inalienable rights of life, liberty, and the pursuit of happiness.

It is obvious today that America has defaulted on this promissory note insofar as her citizens of color are concerned. Instead of honoring this sacred obligation, America has given the Negro people a bad check which has come back marked "insufficient funds." But we refuse to believe that the bank of justice is bankrupt. We refuse to believe that there are insufficient funds in the great vaults of opportunity of this nation. So we have come to cash this check—a check that will give us upon demand the riches of freedom and the security of justice. We have also come to this hallowed spot to remind America of the fierce urgency of now. This is no time to engage in the luxury of cooling off or to take the tranquilizing drug of gradualism. Now is the time to rise from the dark and desolate valley of segregation to the sunlit path of racial justice. Now is the time to open the doors of opportunity to all of God's children. Now is the time to lift our nation from the quicksands of racial injustice to the solid rock of brotherhood.

It would be fatal for the nation to overlook the urgency of the moment and to underestimate the determination of the Negro. This sweltering summer of the Negro's legitimate discontent will not pass until there is an invigorating autumn of freedom and equality. 1963 is not an end, but a beginning. Those who hope that the Negro needed to blow off steam and will now be content will have a rude awakening if the nation returns to business as usual. There will be neither rest nor tranquility in America until the Negro is granted his citizenship rights. The whirlwinds of revolt will continue to shake the foundations of our nation until the bright day of justice emerges.

But there is something that I must say to my people who stand on the warm threshold which leads into the palace of justice. In the process of gaining our rightful place we must not be guilty of wrongful deeds. Let us not seek to satisfy our thirst for freedom by drinking from the cup of bitterness and hatred.

We must forever conduct our struggle on the high plane of dignity and discipline. We must not allow our creative protest to degenerate into physical violence. Again and again we must rise to the majestic heights of meeting physical force with soul force. The marvelous new militancy which has engulfed the Negro community must not lead us to distrust of all white people, for many of our white brothers, as evidenced by their presence here today, have come to realize that their destiny is tied up with our destiny and their freedom is inextricably bound to our freedom. We cannot walk alone.

And as we walk, we must make the pledge that we shall march ahead. We cannot turn back. There are those who are asking the devotees of civil rights, "When will you be satisfied?" We can never be satisfied as long as our bodies, heavy with the fatigue of travel, cannot gain lodging in the motels of the highways and the hotels of the cities. We cannot be satisfied as long as the Negro's basic mobility is from a smaller ghetto to a larger one. We can never be satisfied as long as a Negro in Mississippi cannot vote and a Negro in New York believes he has nothing for which to vote. No, no, we are not satisfied, and we will not be satisfied until justice rolls down like waters and righteousness like a mighty stream.

I am not unmindful that some of you have come here out of great trials and tribulations. Some of you have come fresh from narrow cells. Some of you have come from areas where your quest for freedom left you battered by the storms of persecution and staggered by the winds of police brutality. You have been the veterans of creative suffering. Continue to work with the faith that unearned suffering is redemptive.

Go back to Mississippi, go back to Alabama, go back to Georgia, go back to Louisiana, go back to the slums and ghettos of our northern cities, knowing that somehow this situation can and will be changed. Let us not wallow in the valley of despair.

I say to you today, my friends, that in spite of the difficulties and frustrations of the moment, I still have a dream. It is a dream deeply rooted in the American dream.

I have a dream that one day this nation will rise up and live out the true meaning of its creed: "We hold these truths to be self-evident: that all men are created equal."

I have a dream that one day on the red hills of Georgia the sons of former slaves and the sons of former slave owners will be able to sit down together at a table of brotherhood.

I have a dream that one day even the state of Mississippi, a desert state, sweltering with the heat of injustice and oppression, will be transformed into an oasis of freedom and justice.

I have a dream that my four children will one day live in a nation where they will not be judged by the color of their skin but by the content of their character.

I have a dream today.

I have a dream that one day the state of Alabama, whose governor's lips are presently dripping with the words of interposition and nullification, will be transformed into a situation where little black boys and black girls will be able to join hands with little white boys and white girls and walk together as sisters and brothers.

I have a dream today.

I have a dream that one day every valley shall be exalted, every hill and mountain shall be made low, the rough places will be made plain, and the crooked places will be made straight, and the glory of the Lord shall be revealed, and all flesh shall see it together.

This is our hope. This is the faith with which I return to the South. With this faith we will be able to hew out of the mountain of despair a stone of hope. With this faith we will be able to transform the jangling discords of our nation into a beautiful symphony of brotherhood. With this faith we will be able to work together, to pray together, to struggle together, to go to jail together, to stand up for freedom together, knowing that we will be free one day.

This will be the day when all of God's children will be able to sing with a new meaning, "My country, 'tis of thee, sweet land of liberty, of thee I sing. Land where my fathers died, land of the pilgrim's pride, from every mountainside, let freedom ring."

And if America is to be a great nation this must become true. So let freedom ring from the prodigious hilltops of New Hampshire. Let freedom ring from the mighty mountains of New York. Let freedom ring from the heightening Alleghenies of Pennsylvania!

Let freedom ring from the snowcapped Rockies of Colorado!

Let freedom ring from the curvaceous peaks of California!

But not only that; let freedom ring from Stone Mountain of Georgia!

Let freedom ring from Lookout Mountain of Tennessee!

Let freedom ring from every hill and every molehill of Mississippi. From every mountainside, let freedom ring.

When we let freedom ring, when we let it ring from every village and every hamlet, from every state and every city, we will be able to speed up that day when all of God's children, black men and white men, Jews and Gentiles, Protestants and Catholics, will be able to join hands and sing in the words of the old Negro spiritual, "Free at last! free at last! Thank God Almighty, we are free at last!"[14]

COMMENTARY

Malcolm X, Nation of Islam leader, speaking to March on Washington organizer Bayard Rustin (1963)

You know, this dream of King's is going to be a nightmare before it's over.

—Quoted in Drew D. Hansen, *The Dream: Martin Luther King and the Speech That Inspired a Nation* (New York: HarperCollins, 2003), p. 172.

Martin Luther King Jr., Baptist minister and civil rights leader, echoing Malcolm X (1967)

I remember the first time I saw that dream turn into a nightmare, just a few weeks after I had talked about it. It was when four beautiful, unoffending, innocent Negro girls were murdered in a church in Birmingham, Alabama. I watched that dream turn into a nightmare as I moved through the ghettos of the nation and saw my black brothers and sisters perishing on a lonely island of poverty in the midst of a vast ocean of material prosperity, and saw the nation do nothing to grapple with the Negroes' problem of poverty. . . . I saw that dream turn into a nightmare as I watched the war in Vietnam escalating, and as I saw so-called military advisors, 16,000 strong, turn into fighting soldiers until today over 500,000 American boys are fighting on Asian soil. Yes, I am personally the victim of deferred dreams, of blasted hopes, but in spite of that I close today by saying I still have a dream, because, you know, you can't give up in life.

—Martin Luther King Jr., "A Christmas Sermon on Peace," in Martin Luther King Jr., *The Trumpet of Conscience* (New York: Harper & Row, 1967), p. 76.

Bill Bradley, U.S. Senator (D-NJ), objecting to a Senate filibuster of a bill to create a Martin Luther King Jr. holiday (1983)

The dream he shared that hot August afternoon in 1963 on the steps of the Lincoln Memorial—the dream he gave his life for—was a dream shared by millions of Americans black and white alike. It was a dream that challenged America to live up to its ideals, to rise above the assumed rights of prejudice and to assert the inherent rights of humanity once again, just as 100 years earlier Abraham Lincoln had urged Americans to rise above the assumed rights of property and to assert the inherent rights of humanity. Dr. King taught what any good family North or South taught—there is no room for hate in this house. He preached that America was still an idea becoming—becoming what its people would have it be. And he labored for an America in which men and women were not judged by color, but stood equal in the eyes and practices of the State just as they do in the eyes of God. His message told us what we knew, that America was incomplete without addressing the injustice, festering in our national soul, of a dual society of black and white. But he believed that even in the face of blatant discrimination, America—its institutions and its people—had the capacity for righting the wrong course. His message offered redemption from our original sin. His message spawned the civil rights revolution of the 1960s—the 1964 Civil Rights Act, 1965 Voting Rights Act, the 1968 Fair Housing Act. These laws secured long withheld civil rights for black Americans, but they also changed the attitudes of white Americans, and led to a legitimate moral awakening, and made America a better place. . . .

This is the American we seek to honor with a national holiday. . . .

I want to give the Senators of North Carolina the due respect of a colleague, but I must say it is just not possible in this case. When I listen to the senior Senator from North Carolina talk about Dr. King and Communism and when I listen to the junior Senator from North Carolina construe Dr. King's words so that he implies Dr. King called American soldiers Nazis—two images swirl up in my imagination, one trivial, one ominous. The first image is that of a shriveled persimmon, small and bitter, drying up, ready to blow away when exposed to a winter wind. The second image is hot, flashing across my mind in rapid frames— Bull Connor and his dogs; George Wallace at the school door; three civil rights workers murdered; marches and sit-ins; Medgar Evers struggling to stand, shot in the back in front of his own home; and Dr. Martin Luther King dead in his coffin.

—Bill Bradley, *Congressional Record*, October 19, 1983, pp. 28359–60.

Ronald Reagan, fortieth U.S. president, employing "I Have a Dream" against affirmative action "quotas" (1985)

When the Civil Rights Act of 1964 was being debated in the Congress, Senator Hubert Humphrey, one of its leading advocates, said he'd start eating the pages of the act if it contained any language which provides that an employer will have to hire on the basis of percentage or quota. But I think if Senator Humphrey saw how some people today are interpreting that act, he'd get a severe case of indigestion. The truth is, quotas deny jobs to many who would have gotten them otherwise, but who weren't born a specified race or sex. That's discrimination pure and simple and is exactly what the civil rights laws were designed to stop. . . .

Twenty-two years ago Martin Luther King proclaimed his dream of a society rid of discrimination and prejudice, a society where people would be judged on the content of their character, not by the color of their skin. That's the vision our entire administration is committed to—a society that keeps faith with the promise of our Declaration of Independence, a proud society in which all men and women truly are created free and equal under God.

—Ronald Reagan, "Radio Address to the Nation on Civil Rights," June 15, 1985, www.presidency.ucsb.edu/ ws/index.php?pid=38782.

Keith Miller, English professor, locating "I Have a Dream" in the American imagination (1992)

In "I Have a Dream" King argues from the authority of Jefferson, Lincoln, "America," and the Bible—all of which he applies deductively to the situation of black America. According to the logic of "I Have a Dream," segregation is wrong, but not for the reasons unveiled in a detailed analysis, which never surfaces in the speech. Rather, segregation is wrong because it eviscerates the Emancipation Proclamation, scandalizes Jefferson's vision, violates Amos's demand, stymies Isaiah's longings, and contaminates the freedom celebrated in "America." Essentially "I Have a Dream" contends that segregation is wrong because it prevents the highest deductive truths of the nation and the Bible from governing human relations. Enacting these deductive truths means eradicating segregation.

—Keith D. Miller, *Voice of Deliverance: The Language of Martin Luther King, Jr. and Its Sources* (New York: Free Press, 1992), p. 149.

Michael Eric Dyson, Baptist minister and religious studies professor, refusing to see "I Have a Dream" as King's "definitive statement on race" (2000)

In ways that King could never have imagined—indeed, in a fashion that might make him spin in his grave—"I Have a Dream" has been used to chip away at King's enduring social legacy. One phrase has been pinched from King's speech to justify assaults on civil rights in the name of color-blind policies. Moreover, we have frozen King in a timeless mood of optimism that later *that very year* he grew to question. That's because we have selectively listened to what King had to say to us that muggy afternoon. It is easier for us to embrace the day's warm memories than to confront the cold realities that led to the March on Washington in the first place. August 28, 1963, was a single moment in time that captured the suffering of centuries. It was an afternoon shaped as much by white brutality and black oppression as by uplifting rhetoric. We have chosen to forget how our nation achieved the racial progress we now enjoy.

In the light of the determined misuse of King's rhetoric, a modest proposal appears in order: a ten-year moratorium on listening to or reading "I Have a Dream." At first blush, such a proposal seems absurd and counterproductive. After all, King's words have convinced many Americans that racial justice should be aggressively pursued. The sad truth is, however, that our political climate has eroded the real point of King's beautiful words. We have been ambushed by bizarre and sophisticated distortions of King's true meaning. If we are to recover the authentic purposes of King's address, we must dig beneath his words into our own social and moral habits. Only then can the animating spirit behind his words be truly restored.

—Michael Eric Dyson, *I May Not Get There with You: The True Martin Luther King, Jr.* (New York: Free Press, 2000), pp. 15–16.

Rush Limbaugh, conservative talk-show host, using King's words against President Obama's Supreme Court nominee Sonia Sotomayor (2009)

How do you get promoted in a Barack Obama administration? By hating white people. . . . Make white people the new oppressed minority, and they're going right along about it 'cause they're shutting up. They're moving to the back of the bus. They're saying, "I can't use that drinking fountain? Okay! I can't use that restroom? Okay!" That's the modern day Republican Party, the equivalent of the Old South: the new oppressed minority. Whatever happened to the content of one's character as the basis of judging people?

Whatever happened to that? And when someone—a judge, no less—uses race to demean and dismiss people, that is not to be condemned? We're supposed to understand the rage? We're supposed to understand the roots where that came from? . . . I did a fundraiser in Texas last night. There were 250 people there. I made a point. . . . I'm looking out in the audience and I say, "Okay, let me see. I count. I look at all of you women, so I make sure I say something that doesn't offend you. I'm looking at all you men. Let's see, are there any black people here? Do I see any gays?"

That's how liberals look at people. It's not how we used to look at people. We look at people as individuals. I don't care what race she is. I don't care what gender she is. She is one of nine people with a lifetime appointment to the United States Supreme Court. I care about whether she's qualified, and I think she's disqualified herself. Not only does she lack the often-discussed appropriate "judicial temperament," it's worse than that. She brings a form of bigotry or racism to the court!

—Rush Limbaugh, "America's Pinata Strikes Back: We Won't Shut Up on Sotomayor," May 29, 2009, www .rushlimbaugh.com/daily/2009/05/29/america_s_pi_ata_strikes_back_we_won_t_shut_up_on_sotomayor.

Jesse Jackson Jr., U.S. Representative (D-IL), rewriting King's speech on the day Congress passed "the budget cutting, insufficient funds and bounced check deal" (2011)

Let us not wallow in the valley of despair, I say to you today, my friends.

And so even though we face the difficulties of today and tomorrow, I still have a dream. It is a dream deeply rooted in the American Dream. I have a dream that one day this nation will rise up and live out the true meaning of its creed: "We hold these truths to be self-evident, that all men are created equal." I have a dream that one day on the red hills of Georgia, the sons of former slaves and the sons of former slave owners will be able to sit down together around a table of brotherhood where full employment, high-quality health care for all Americans, excellence in education for every child, and safe, sanitary and affordable housing for every family is their natural experience.

I have a dream that one day, absent the false excuse of sweltering deficits and debt and the heat of economic injustice, America will be transformed into an oasis of full employment, freedom and economic justice.

I have a dream that my two little children will one day live in a Nation where they will not be judged by the color of their skin but by the content of their character, and that voting will be as natural as breathing, and no trickery or legal obstacles will be thrown in their path.

I have a dream today.

I have a dream that one day over Michigan, over Ohio, Illinois and Indiana, with its wicked unemployment and suffering families, that one day right there in Michigan, Ohio, Illinois and Indiana, all of these families will be able to enjoy full employment, social and economic justice, and all will be able to join hands as sisters and brothers.

I have a dream today.

I have a dream that one day every valley shall be exalted, and every hill and mountain shall be made low, the rough places will be made plain and the crooked places will be made straight "and the glory of the Lord shall be revealed and all flesh shall see it together."

This is my hope, and this is the faith that I go forward with every day.

With this faith, we will be able to hew out of the mountain of deficits and debt a stone of economic hope and justice for all Americans. With this faith, we will be able to transform the jangling discords of unemployment and home foreclosures into a beautiful symphony of full employment and affordable housing. With this faith, we will be able to work together, to pray together, to struggle together, to go to jail together, to stand up for freedom together, knowing that we will be free and fully employed one day. . . .

And when this happens, when we allow freedom, full employment, social and economic justice to ring, when we let it ring from every village and every hamlet, from every State and every city, we will be able to speed up that day when all of God's children, black men, white men, women, Jews, Gentiles, and Muslims, Protestants and Catholics, gays and straights, those who are whole and those who are handicapped, will be able to join hands and sing in the words of the old Negro spiritual: "Free at last, free at last, thank God Almighty, we are free at last."

—Jesse Jackson Jr., "I Have a Dream," *Congressional Record*, August 1, 2011, pp. H5877–78.

Janet Murguía, National Council of La Raza president, on the power of King's dream in the Latino community (2012)

In his iconic "I Have a Dream" speech, whose anniversary we commemorate this week, [King] spoke eloquently about the Declaration of Independence. Part of his dream, in fact, was that this nation would one day live up to the creed, "We hold these truths to be self-evident: that all men are created equal."

I believe that he did this, in part, to demonstrate that these core tenets of our democracy do not belong just to a few, or to just one party, or to just one group of

Americans. They belong to all of us. And I think there is no better time to remind us all of that than right now.

He quoted from these cherished documents to reaffirm to other Americans that democracy and living up to our ideals are not simply abstract concepts but a living, breathing reality. It is why his words also resonated so deeply with the Latino community. Thousands were on the Mall that day, including my predecessor Raul Yzaguirre, who marched with Dr. King.

I am a child of Dr. King's hope. I know the power of his dream.

—"NCLR Welcomes the Dr. Martin Luther King, Jr. Memorial to the National Mall," August 25, 2011, www.nclr.org/index.php/about_us/news/news_releases/nclr_welcomes_the_dr_martin_luther_king_jr _memorial_to_the_national_mall/.

The Autobiography of Malcolm X

◆❯ MALCOLM X, 1965 ❮◆

As THE 1950s of Eisenhower and the "man in the gray flannel suit" yielded to the 1960s of Kennedy and the hippies, Malcolm X (1925–65) was not widely known. A 1959 television documentary called *The Hate That Hate Produced* had shined a harsh spotlight on this self-described "angriest black man in America," but whatever attention white Americans had to devote to nonwhites in the early 1960s was being lavished on Protestant civil rights leaders like Martin Luther King Jr., not Nation of Islam black nationalists like Malcolm X. That changed on February 21, 1965, at the Audubon Ballroom in New York City's Washington Heights neighborhood. Malcolm X was scheduled to address his new Organization of Afro-American Unity. But before he could speak, rival Black Muslims pumped bullet after bullet into his thirty-nine-year-old body. Later that year, Grove Press published *The Autobiography of Malcolm X,* a collaboration with the African-American writer (and future *Roots* author) Alex Haley. It was, according to *Time* magazine, Modern Library, and the New York Public Library, one of the twentieth century's ten most important nonfiction books.[1]

It is now commonplace to observe that this assassination made a martyr of Malcolm X. At his funeral, actor Ossie Davis famously called him "our own black shining Prince."[2] More recently, he was celebrated in the 1992 Spike Lee biopic *Malcolm X* and honored with a 1999 postage stamp. But immediately after his assassination, the media consensus was that Malcolm had gotten his just desserts. In 1963, he had referred to President Kennedy's assassination as a case of "the chickens coming home to roost."[3] Now the same thing was being said about him.

Time called him "an unashamed demagogue" whose "gospel was hatred" and whose "creed was violence." A *New York Times* obituary called him "an extraordinary and twisted man" who had used his "true gifts to evil purpose." "The world he saw through those horn-rimmed glasses of his was distorted and dark," the *Times* continued. "Yesterday someone came out of that darkness that he spawned, and killed him."[4] But attitudes changed with the appearance of the autobiography, which sold six million copies between 1965 and 1977 and detailed in searing prose the depredations he endured and the causes to which he gave his life.

"Our quintessential story about the ordeal of being black in America," *The Autobiography of Malcolm X* tells a tale of the metamorphosis of a black kid in Michigan into street hustler in the ghettos of Boston and Harlem, a prisoner, a minister and "nation builder" for Elijah Muhammad's Nation of Islam (NOI), and, finally, a practitioner of mainstream Sunni Islam.[5] But this book is also a "jihad of words"—a prophetic condemnation of the racism of American society—that challenges the black reader not to become a "twentieth-century Uncle Thomas," more concerned with currying the favor of whites than with pressing for the human rights of blacks.[6] The *Autobiography* also challenges white readers to see themselves through new eyes and to confront a national history dedicated to the proposition of slavery. "Before the Pilgrims landed at Plymouth Rock, we were here," King writes.[7] "We didn't land on Plymouth Rock," Malcolm responds, "Plymouth Rock landed on *us*!"

The first part of this autobiography turns its protagonist into an orphan of sorts. At the age of six, Malcolm loses his father, a Baptist preacher enamored of black nationalist Marcus Garvey, at the murderous hands of white racists. When Malcolm is thirteen, his mother is committed to a mental institution, which sets him adrift in the flotsam of foster homes and the jetsam of reform schools. Like so many protagonists in films and fairy tales before him, Malcolm is left to his own devices. In his struggle to survive and succeed in a society that seems dead set against him, he reinvents himself and reimagines the world.

The *Autobiography* has been described as a *sui generis* classic with a voice unique in American letters—"the *Urtext* of contemporary black nationalism."[8] More than any other book in *The American Bible,* this one speaks its own language, quite apart from the words and phrases that have traditionally united, divided, and defined Americans. The *Autobiography* doesn't just reject Christianity. It almost entirely ignores America's founding documents. In his last speech, King challenged

America to "be true to what you said on paper."[9] There is very little of that in this book, which rejects American culture as racist in both design and realization. Neither Thomas Jefferson nor the Declaration of Independence is ever mentioned. There is one reference to the Constitution—when Malcolm asks why the Second Amendment guarantees guns to white Americans but not to blacks.[10] "Coffee," Malcolm wrote, "is the only thing I like integrated."[11]

But "this eloquent testament," as one reviewer called it, is not cut entirely out of its own cloth.[12] It draws on American themes such as self-reliance, self-determination, and self-improvement and on the Exodus story of liberation from bondage and escape to freedom. (Though here, significantly, the United States is Egypt, not some promised land in the making.) The *Autobiography* is part of an African-American "up from slavery" tradition that includes *Narrative of the Life of Frederick Douglass, an American Slave* (1845) and *Incidents in the Life of a Slave Girl* (1861) by Harriet Jacobs. It is also indebted to the African-American autobiographical tradition of Richard Wright (*Black Boy,* 1945) and James Baldwin (*Notes of a Native Son,* 1955) and to the outlaw oratory of black separatists such as David Walker, Henry McNeal Turner, and Marcus Garvey. It does not take too much stretching to draw a fairly straight line from *The Education of Henry Adams* (1918) or from the self-made-man stories of Horatio Alger to this account of self-education and self-improvement. The *Autobiography* also stands as a "political testament"— a witness to Malcolm's thought.[13] Finally, and most important, it is steeped in the tradition of American spiritual autobiography that runs from the conversion "relations" of New England Puritans through such contemporary classics as Thomas Merton's *The Seven Storey Mountain* (1948).

In *Varieties of Religious Experience* (1902), psychologist William James divided people of faith into the "once-born," who inherited their religious traditions from their parents, and the "twice-born," who, via conversion, crafted a religious identity for themselves. But one dramatic conversion was not enough for Malcolm X. Born Malcolm Little in Omaha, Nebraska, in 1925, he became a member of the Nation of Islam in 1952 and took the name by which he is known today. In 1964, after a life-altering pilgrimage to Mecca, he left the Nation of Islam and its leader Elijah Muhammad for a more orthodox version of Sunni Islam.

Along the way, he played a vast cast of characters, each brought to life in his autobiography. After leaving Lansing, Michigan, he makes his way to Boston where, as Homeboy, he works as a shoeshine boy, soda jerk, and railroad dining-car attendant. In Harlem he becomes Detroit Red—a zoot-suiting, lindy-hopping street hustler who scratches out a living as a pimp, drug pusher, numbers runner, and confidence man. In 1946, before he even needs to shave, he is arrested, convicted, and sent for six and a half years to prison, where he becomes "Satan" (because of his conviction that Christianity is the opiate of the black masses).

A prison autodidact inspires him to make something of himself by improving on his eighth-grade education, so he takes correspondence courses in English grammar and Latin. In one of the great sketches in the book—and in all of America's literature on self-improvement—he doesn't just read the dictionary from cover to cover, he copies it, word for word. His voracious reading (he reportedly made his way through the prison library) eventually leads him to read Elijah Muhammad and convert to his Nation of Islam.

Upon his release from prison in 1952 he takes the name of Malcolm X (to symbolize his lost African surname), becoming an NOI minister and, eventually, its chief spokesman and organizer. Like every religion, the NOI preaches things that to outsiders sound like they sprang not from the mouth of God but from the spittle of drug-induced psychosis. There is, for example, the view that the Black Man is trillions of years old whereas the White Man, only 6,000 years old, is the creation of one Mr. Yakub (a mad scientist). But there is also a strict moral code far removed from the ethos of Malcolm's zoot-suiting days—no alcohol, no smoking, no drugs, no gambling, no extramarital sex—which he credits with saving him from a life of crime and debauchery. So this first conversion is not just an awakening to faith; it is also an awakening to self-discipline.

Over time, tensions build between Malcolm and his new father figure, Elijah Muhammad—regarding Malcolm's growing celebrity, Elijah Muhammad's affairs (one with a former girlfriend of Malcolm), and disagreements over the NOI's policy of nonengagement in politics. In December 1963, Muhammad suspends Malcolm, and in March 1964 Malcolm walks away.

The most dramatic plot point in the autobiography comes in April 1964 when Malcolm goes on pilgrimage to Mecca. There he is embarrassed at how little the NOI's ersatz Islam has taught him about "true Islam." He stands shoulder to shoulder with Muslims of all colors, including white believers who treat him with respect. As a result, he renounces Elijah Muhammad's racial theories and comes to see himself as "a human being first and foremost." He also takes yet another new name: El-Hajj Malik El-Shabazz. Back in the United States, he starts to describe whiteness as an attitude, not a skin color. The solution to America's race problem now lies not with the NOI's denunciation of whites as "blue-eyed devils" but with Islam's color-blind understanding of all human beings as Allah's children.

How much Mecca really changed Malcolm is a subject of intense debate. The *Autobiography* was a partnership based on thousands of hours of taped conversations that took place between Malcolm and Haley in 1963 and 1964. And like every life story, both fact and fancy live in it.[14] But two competing agendas work here to bend nonfiction into fiction: Haley's desire to portray his subject to white readers (and editors) as somewhat likeable and not entirely scary; and Malcolm's desires, initially, to laud Elijah Muhammad and the NOI and, later, to present himself as a new man, both religiously and politically.

In the push and pull between Haley and Malcolm, Malcolm exaggerated the vices of his life as a street hustler in order to accentuate the drama of his conversion to Islam. Haley, a liberal Republican and integrationist, muted his subject's anti-Semitism, misogyny, and socialism while amplifying his post-Mecca turn away from black separatism. "If Malcolm's Americanization culminated with the release of a commemorative stamp in 1999, then the process arguably began in earnest with the publication of *The Autobiography of Malcolm X* in 1965," biographer Manning Marable writes. "The individual most responsible for removing the radical and revolutionary context from the image of Malcolm X was Alex Haley."[15] What Marable neglects to mention is that this autobiographical process itself began only when Malcolm agreed to participate. At least in this case, the medium made the man. Or, as American Studies scholar Albert Stone puts it, "It is possible that the most important act of the Black Muslim preacher's life was telling his story to Alex Haley."[16]

This debate over the Malcolm/Haley relationship is closely tied to an even more contentious matter: the relationship between Malcolm and Martin Luther King Jr. This debate will never be settled, but many have embraced a convergence thesis that describes the two as alter egos: Martin as the yin to Malcolm's yang. This thesis has two parts. The first is that these two men, in the words of theologian James Cone, "complemented and corrected each other." Yes, one was a Christian and the other a Muslim. Yes, one was a nonviolent integrationist from the Southern middle-class and the other a "by any means necessary" black nationalist from the Northern underclass. But both were "soldiers fighting their enemies from different angles of vision, each pointing out the other's blind spots and correcting the other's errors."[17] More to the point, it was Malcolm's hate that made King's hope attractive, and his threats of violence that gave King's nonviolent strategy force. This perspective seems to have been endorsed by Malcolm himself, who told King's wife, Coretta Scott King, in February 1965 in Selma, Alabama, "I want Dr. King to know that I didn't come to Selma to make his job difficult. I really did come thinking that I could make it easier. If the white people realize what the alternative is, perhaps they will be more willing to hear Dr. King."[18]

The second part of this convergence thesis is that over time the perspectives of these two sons of Baptist preachers converged. "By the time each met his death," writes James Baldwin, "there was practically no difference between them."[19] Toward the end of his life, King focused on ending poverty and fighting the Vietnam War. Toward the end of his life, Malcolm came to believe in the universal brotherhood of humanity. "This view is not only wrong, but unfair to both Malcolm and Martin," writes Marable, who sees a series of irreconcilable differences between these men: "King saw himself, like Frederick Douglass, first and foremost as an American, who pursued the civil rights and civic privileges enjoyed by other Americans. . . . In striking contrast, Malcolm perceived himself first and foremost as a black man, a person of African descent who happened to be a United States citizen."[20] "I'm not an American. I'm one of the 22 million black people who are victims of Americanism," he said in his famous "The Ballot or the Bullet" speech shortly before leaving for Mecca in April 1964. "I don't see any American dream; I see an American nightmare."[21]

This Malcolm versus Martin debate is impossible to judge definitively because neither man lived to the far side of forty and because each changed over time. Even more than Martin, however, Malcolm is hard to pin down. His autobiography doesn't just contain many Malcolms; it makes no effort to reconcile them. Malcolm began working with Haley on the autobiography in May 1963 when he was a devoted follower of Elijah Muhammad, so the early chapters are quite pious. But by the time the later chapters were taking shape, Malcolm had broken from his mentor. "My whole life has been a chronicle of changes," he told Haley during one of their interviews, and the autobiography these two men produced makes no attempt to freeze him in time. Instead, it glories in the chameleon-like quality of its protagonist. As a result, the book seems dedicated *both* to Elijah Muhammad *and* to his repudiation. And when it comes to the protagonist himself, it echoes

Walt Whitman: "Do I contradict myself? / Very well then I contradict myself, / (I am large, I contain multitudes.)"[22]

Ever since the appearance of *The Autobiography of Malcolm X*, readers have attempted to do what Haley refused to do: find the one true Malcolm hidden within. Black nationalists and hip-hop artists embraced the militant "prophet of black rage"—the macho Malcolm of the Harlem streets and the fiery NOI orator.[23] White liberals and black civil rights activists decided that the kinder, gentler, post-Mecca Malcolm was the real deal. Others portrayed him as first and foremost a socialist, a spiritual leader, a Pan-Africanist, a public moralist, or an example of "feminist manhood."[24] Still others tried to read him psychoanalytically, as an angry child displacing rage at his parents onto white society. A few have even tried to make a conservative out of him, focusing on his rejection of integration, his strict moral code, and his emphasis on self-help and "family values."

Part of what makes any book a classic is its openness to varying interpretations. The Bible and the Constitution can be criticized for being vague and amorphous and at odds with themselves, but they are classics precisely because of these so-called "defects." Although it is certainly sensible to criticize the *Autobiography* for not giving us a stable and authoritative Malcolm, the book has survived for roughly half a century precisely because of this open-ended quality, which offers readers all sorts of interpretive puddles to splash around in. Who is the *real* Malcolm? This book does not say. So readers must struggle to answer this question themselves.

As America fell in love with Ronald Reagan in the 1980s, interest in the *Autobiography* flagged, but it picked up again in the early 1990s, when the opening of Spike Lee's *Malcolm X* in 1992 sparked an era of "Malcolmania" that saw hip-hop artists sampling his words, young people of all races sporting "X" baseball caps, and politicians of both major parties praising its author. Bill Clinton wore an "X" cap after his election in 1992, and in a sure sign that the demonization was over and the beatification had begun, Malcolm was praised by the Republican Vice President Dan Quayle and the conservative justice Clarence Thomas (whose "high-tech lynching" sounds like something Malcolm might have said).

Americans enshrined St. Malcolm in the pantheon of civil rights heroes because of his willingness to stare down reality—to experience life not as he might have hoped it would be (the dream), but as it actually was (the nightmare). Above all, they praised him for being true to himself. "He is still hailed by many as the most authentic voice of America's vast black underclass," writes Marshall Frady. "In this he was actually ahead of King."[25]

Of all the mysteries to solve in examining the life, death, and afterlife of Malcolm X, perhaps the most vexing is how this "messiah of hate," *the* demon to many Americans in the 1960s, has come to stand alongside (and, for some, above) King as an icon of America's unfinished struggle against racism.[26] His life is now remembered on street signs, and in the names of public schools and community centers across the country. His autobiography is required reading for millions of high-school and college students. In 2012, *Time* magazine argued that he deserves a federal holiday.[27] Says a convenience store owner in Watts, "It seems like Malcolm is more alive today than when he was alive."[28]

Philosopher George Santayana once wrote: "American life is a powerful solvent. It seems to neutralize every intellectual element, however tough and alien it may be, and to fuse it in the native good-will, complacency, thoughtlessness, and optimism."[29] In the decades after his death, this solvent seems to have worn the sharp edges off of Malcolm. "The angriest black man in America" has become a man almost nobody hates.

The Autobiography of Malcolm X {❧}

From Chapter 12, Savior

I n early 1953 . . . Minister Lemuel Hassan urged me to address the brothers and sisters [of the Nation of Islam in Detroit] with an extemporaneous lecture. I was uncertain, and hesitant—but at least I had debated in prison, and I tried my best. (Of course, I can't remember exactly what I said, but I do know that in my beginning efforts my favorite subject was Christianity and the horrors of slavery, where I felt well-equipped from so much reading in prison.)

"My brothers and sisters, our white slavemaster's Christian religion has taught us black people here in the wilderness of North America that we will sprout wings when we die and fly up into the sky where God will have for us a special place called heaven. This is white man's Christian religion used to *brain-wash* us black people! We have *accepted* it! We have *embraced* it! We have *believed* it! We have *practiced* it! And while we are doing all of that, for himself, this blue-eyed devil has *twisted* his Christianity, to keep his *foot* on our backs . . . to keep our eyes fixed on the pie in the sky and heaven in the hereafter . . . while *he* enjoys *his* heaven right *here* . . . on *this earth* . . . in *this life*." . . .

In the summer of 1953—all praise is due to Allah—I was named Detroit Temple Number One's Assistant Minister.

Every day after work, I walked, "fishing" for potential converts in the Detroit black ghetto. I saw the African features of my black brothers and sisters whom the devilish white man had brainwashed. I saw the hair as mine had been for years, conked by cooking it with lye until it lay limp, looking straight like the white man's hair. Time and again Mr. Muhammad's teachings were rebuffed and even ridiculed. . . . "Aw, man, get out of my face, you niggers are crazy!" My head would reel sometimes, with mingled anger and pity for my poor blind black brothers. I couldn't wait for the next time our Minister Lemuel Hassan would let me speak:

"We didn't land on Plymouth Rock, my brothers and sisters—Plymouth Rock landed on *us!* . . . Give *all* you can to help Messenger Elijah Muhammad's independence program for the black man! . . . This white man always has controlled us black people by keeping us running to him begging, 'Please, lawdy, please, Mr. White Man, boss, would you push me off another crumb down from your table that's sagging with riches.' . . .

"My *beautiful* black brothers and sisters! And when we say 'black,' we mean everything not white, brothers and sisters! Because *look* at your skins! We're all black to the white man, but we're a thousand and one different colors. Turn around, *look* at each other! What shade of black African polluted by devil white man are you? You see me—well, in the streets they used to call me Detroit Red. Yes! Yes, that raping, red-headed devil was my *grandfather!* That close, yes! My *mother's* father! She didn't like to speak of it, can you blame her? She said she never laid eyes on him! She was *glad* for that! I'm *glad* for her! If I could drain away *his* blood that pollutes *my* body, and pollutes *my* complexion, I'd do it! Because I hate every drop of the rapist's blood that's in me!

"And it's not just me, it's *all* of us! During slavery, *think* of it, it was a *rare* one of our black grandmothers, our great-grandmothers and our great-great-grandmothers who escaped the white rapist slavemaster. That rapist slavemaster who emasculated the black man . . . with threats, with fear . . . until even today the black man lives with fear of the white man in his heart! Lives even today still under the heel of the white man! . . .

"Turn around and look at each other, brothers and sisters, and *think* of this! You and me, polluted all these colors—and this devil has the arrogance and the gall to think we, his victims, should *love* him!"

From Chapter 17, Mecca

About twenty of us Muslims who had finished the Hajj were sitting in a huge tent on Mount Arafat. As a Muslim from America, I was the center of attention. They asked me what about the Hajj had impressed me the most. . . .

I said, "The *brotherhood!* The people of all races, colors, from all over the world coming together as *one!* It has proved to me the power of the One God."

It may have been out of taste, but that gave me an opportunity, and I used it, to preach them a quick little sermon on America's racism, and its evils.

I could tell the impact of this upon them. They had been aware that the plight of the black man in America was "bad," but they had not been aware that it was inhuman, that it was a psychological castration. These people from elsewhere around the world were shocked. As Muslims, they had a very tender heart for all unfortunates, and very sensitive feelings for truth and justice. And in everything I said to them, as long as we talked, they were aware of the yardstick that I was using to measure everything—that to me the earth's most explosive and pernicious evil is racism, the inability of God's creatures to live as One, especially in the Western world. . . .

I wrote to my loyal assistants at my newly formed Muslim Mosque, Inc., in Harlem, with a note appended, asking that my letter be duplicated and distributed to the press.

I knew that when my letter became public knowledge back in America, many would be astounded—loved ones, friends, and enemies alike. And no less astounded would be millions whom I did not know—who had gained during my twelve years with Elijah Muhammad a "hate" image of Malcolm X.

Even I was myself astounded. But there was precedent in my life for this letter. My whole life had been a chronology of—*changes.*

Here is what I wrote . . . from my heart:

> *Never have I witnessed such sincere hospitality and the overwhelming spirit of true brotherhood as is practiced by people of all colors and races here in this Ancient Holy Land, the home of Abraham, Muhammad, and all the other prophets of the Holy Scriptures. For the past week, I have been utterly speechless and spellbound by the graciousness I see displayed all around me by people of all colors.*
>
> *I have been blessed to visit the Holy City of Mecca. I have made my seven circuits around the Ka'ba, led by a young Mutawaf named Muhammad. I drank water from the well of Zem Zem. I ran seven times back and forth between the hills of Mt. Al-Safa and Al-Marwah. I have prayed in the ancient city of Mina, and I have prayed on Mt. Arafat.*

There were tens of thousands of pilgrims, from all over the world. They were of all colors, from blue-eyed blonds to black-skinned Africans. But we were all participating in the same ritual, displaying a spirit of unity and brotherhood that my experiences in America had led me to believe never could exist between the white and the non-white.

America needs to understand Islam, because this is the one religion that erases from its society the race problem. Throughout my travels in the Muslim world, I have met, talked to, and even eaten with people who in America would have been considered "white"—but the "white" attitude was removed from their minds by the religion of Islam. I have never before seen sincere and true brotherhood practiced by all colors together, irrespective of their color.

You may be shocked by these words coming from me. But on this pilgrimage, what I have seen, and experienced, has forced me to re-arrange much of my thought-patterns previously held, and to toss aside some of my previous conclusions. This was not too difficult for me. Despite my firm convictions, I have been always a man who tries to face facts, and to accept the reality of life as new experience and new knowledge unfolds it. I have always kept an open mind, which is necessary to the flexibility that must go hand in hand with every form of intelligent search for truth.

During the past eleven days here in the Muslim world, I have eaten from the same plate, drunk from the same glass, and slept in the same bed (or on the same rug)—while praying to the same God—with fellow Muslims, whose eyes were the bluest of blue, whose hair was the blondest of blond, and whose skin was the whitest of white. And in the words and in the actions and in the deeds of the "white" Muslims, I felt the same sincerity that I felt among the black African Muslims of Nigeria, Sudan, and Ghana.

We were truly all the same (brothers)—because their belief in one God had removed the "white" from their minds, the "white" from their behavior, and the "white" from their attitude.

I could see from this, that perhaps if white Americans could accept the Oneness of God, then perhaps, too, they could accept in reality the Oneness of Man—and cease to measure, and hinder, and harm others in terms of their "differences" in color.

With racism plaguing America like an incurable cancer, the so-called "Christian" white American heart should be more receptive to a proven solution to such a destructive problem. Perhaps it could be in time to save America from imminent disaster—the same destruction brought upon Germany by racism that eventually destroyed the Germans themselves.

Each hour here in the Holy Land enables me to have greater spiritual insights into what is happening in America between black and white. The American Negro never can be blamed for his racial animosities—he is only reacting to four hundred years of the conscious racism of the American whites. But as racism leads America up the suicide path, I do believe, from the experiences that I have had with them, that the whites of the younger generation, in the colleges and universities, will see the hand-writing on the wall and many of them will turn to the spiritual *path* of truth—the only *way* left to America to ward off the disaster that racism inevitably must lead to.

Never have I been so highly honored. Never have I been made to feel more humble and unworthy. Who would believe the blessings that have been heaped upon an American Negro? A few nights ago, a man who would be called in America a "white" man, a United Nations diplomat, an ambassador, a companion of kings, gave me his hotel suite, his bed. By this man, His Excellency Prince Faisal, who rules this Holy Land, was made aware of my presence here in Jedda. The very next morning, Prince Faisal's son, in person, informed me that by the will and decree of his esteemed father, I was to be a State Guest.

The Deputy Chief of Protocol himself took me before the Hajj Court. His Holiness Sheikh Muhammad Harkon himself okayed my visit to Mecca. His Holiness gave me two books on Islam, with his personal seal and autograph, and he told me that he prayed that I would be a successful preacher of Islam in America. A car, a driver, and a guide have been placed at my disposal, making it possible for me to travel about this Holy Land almost at will. The government provides air-conditioned quarters and servants in each city that I visit. Never would I have even thought of dreaming that I would ever be a recipient of such honors—honors that in America would be bestowed upon a King—not a Negro.

All praise is due to Allah, the Lord of all the Worlds.

Sincerely,

El-Hajj Malik El-Shabazz

(Malcolm X)

From Chapter 19, 1965

Largely, the American white man's press refused to convey that I was now attempting to teach Negroes a new direction. With the 1964 "long, hot summer" steadily producing new incidents, I was constantly accused of "stirring up Negroes." Every time I had another radio or television microphone at my mouth, when I was asked about "stirring up Negroes" or "inciting violence," I'd get hot.

"It takes no one to stir up the sociological dynamite that stems from the unemployment, bad housing, and inferior education already in the ghettoes. This explosively criminal condition has existed for so long, it needs no fuse; it fuses itself; it spontaneously combusts from within itself. . . ."

They called me "the angriest Negro in America." I wouldn't deny that charge. I spoke exactly as I felt. "I *believe* in anger. The Bible says there is a *time* for anger." They called me "a teacher, a fomenter of violence." I would say point blank, "That is a lie. I'm not for wanton violence, I'm for justice. I feel that if white people were attacked by Negroes—if the forces of law prove unable, or inadequate, or reluctant to protect those whites from those Negroes—then those white people should protect and defend themselves from those Negroes, using arms if necessary. And I feel that when the law fails to protect Negroes from whites' attack, then those Negroes should use arms, if necessary, to defend themselves." . . .

What was wrong with that? I'll tell you what was wrong. I was a black man talking about physical defense against the white man. The white man can lynch and burn and bomb and beat Negroes—that's all right: "Have patience." . . . "The customs are entrenched." . . . "Things are getting better."

Well, I believe it's a crime for anyone who is being brutalized to continue to accept that brutality without doing something to defend himself. If that's how "Christian" philosophy is interpreted, if that's what Gandhian philosophy teaches, well, then, I will call them criminal philosophies.

I tried in every speech I made to clarify my new position regarding white people—"I don't speak against the sincere, well-meaning, good white people. I have learned that there *are* some. I have learned that not all white people are racists. I am speaking against and my fight is against the white *racists*. I firmly believe that Negroes have the right to fight against these racists, by any means that are necessary."

But the white reporters kept wanting me linked with that word "violence." I doubt if I had one interview without having to deal with that accusation.

I *am* for violence if non-violence means we continue postponing a solution to the American black man's problem—just to *avoid* violence. I don't go for non-violence if it also means a delayed solution. To me a delayed solution is a non-solution. . . .

White society *hates* to hear anybody, especially a black man, talk about the crime the white man has perpetrated on the black man. I have always understood that's why I have been so frequently called "a revolutionist." It sounds as if *I* have done some crime! Well, it may be the American black man does need to become involved in a *real* revolution. . . . The Negro's so-called "revolt" is merely an asking to be *accepted* into the existing system! A *true* Negro revolt might entail, for instance, fighting for separate black states within this country—which several groups and individuals have advocated, long before Elijah Muhammad came along. . . .

I am in agreement one hundred percent with those racists who say that no government laws ever can *force* brotherhood. The only true world solution today is governments guided by true religion—of the spirit. Here in race-torn America, I am convinced that the Islam religion is desperately needed, particularly by the American black man. The black man needs to reflect that he has been America's most fervent Christian—and where has it gotten him? In fact, in the white man's hands, in the white man's interpretation . . . where has Christianity brought this *world*? . . .

As the Christian Crusade once went East, now the Islamic Crusade is going West. With the East—Asia—closed to Christianity, with Africa rapidly being converted to Islam, with Europe rapidly becoming un-Christian, generally today it is accepted that the "Christian" civilization of America—which is propping up the white race around the world—is Christianity's remaining strongest bastion.

Well, if *this* is so—if the so-called "Christianity" now being practiced in America displays the best that world Christianity has left to offer—no one in his right mind should need any much greater proof that very close at hand is the *end* of Christianity. . . .

And what is the greatest single reason for this Christian church's failure? It is its failure to combat racism. It is the old "You sow, you reap" story. The Christian church sowed racism—blasphemously; now it reaps racism. . . .

I believe that God now is giving the world's so-called "Christian" white society its last opportunity to repent and atone for the crimes of exploiting and enslaving the world's non-white peoples. It is exactly as when God gave Pharaoh a chance to repent. But Pharaoh persisted in his refusal to give justice to those whom he oppressed. And, we know, God finally destroyed Pharaoh.

Is white America really sorry for her crimes against the black people? Does white America have the capacity to repent—and to atone? Does the capacity to repent, to atone, exist in a majority, in one-half, in even one-third of American white society? . . .

Indeed, how *can* white society atone for enslaving, for raping, for unmanning, for otherwise brutalizing *millions* of human beings, for centuries? What atonement would the God of Justice demand for the robbery of the black people's labor, their lives, their true identities, their culture, their history—and even their human dignity?

A desegregated cup of coffee, a theater, public toilets—the whole range of hypocritical "integration"—these are not atonement. . . .

I tell sincere white people, "Work in conjunction with us—each of us working among our own kind." Let sincere white individuals find all other white people they can who feel as they do—and let them form their own all-white groups, to work trying to convert other white people who are thinking and acting so racist. Let sincere whites go and teach non-violence to white people!

We will completely respect our white co-workers. They will deserve every credit. We will give them every credit. We will meanwhile be working among our own kind, in our own black communities—showing and teaching black men in ways that only other black men can—that the black man has got to help himself. Working separately, the sincere white people and sincere black people actually will be working together.

In our mutual sincerity we might be able to show a road to the salvation of America's very soul. It can only be salvaged if human rights and dignity, in full, are extended to black men. Only such real, meaningful actions as those which are sincerely motivated from a deep sense of humanism and moral responsibility can get at the basic causes that produce the racial explosions in America today. Otherwise, the racial explosions are only going to grow worse. Certainly nothing is ever going to be solved by throwing upon me and other so-called black "extremists" and "demagogues" the blame for the racism that is in America.

Sometimes, I have dared to dream to myself that one day history may even say that my voice—which disturbed the white man's smugness, and his arrogance, and his complacency—that my voice helped to save America from a grave, possibly even a fatal catastrophe. . . .

In the 1964 "long, hot summer" riots in major cities across the United States, the socially dis-inherited black ghetto youth were always at the forefront. In this year, 1965, I am certain that more—and worse—riots are going to erupt, in yet more cities, in spite of the conscience-salving Civil Rights Bill. The reason is that the *cause* of these riots, the racist malignancy in America, has been too long unattended. . . .

Anyway, now, each day I live as if I am already dead, and I tell you what I would like for you to do. When I *am* dead—I say it that way because from the things I *know*, I do not expect to live long enough to read this book in its finished form—I want you to just watch and see if I'm not right in what I say: that the white man, in his press, is going to identify me with "hate."

He will make use of me dead, as he has made use of me alive, as a convenient symbol of "hatred"—and that will help him to escape facing the truth that all I have been doing is holding up a mirror to reflect, to show, the history of unspeakable crimes that his race has committed against my race. . . .

You watch. I will be labeled as, at best, an "irresponsible" black man. I have always felt about this accusation that the black "leader" whom white men consider to be "responsible" is invariably the black "leader" who never gets any results. You only get action as a black man if you are regarded by the white man as "irresponsible." . . .

Yes, I have cherished my "demagogue" role. I know that societies often have killed the people who have helped to change those societies. And if I can die having brought any light, having exposed any meaningful truth that will help to destroy the racist cancer that is malignant in the body of America—then, all of the credit is due to Allah. Only the mistakes have been mine.[30]

COMMENTARY

Saturday Evening Post *editorial accompanying an extended*
excerpt of the forthcoming Autobiography *(1964)*

If Malcolm X were not a Negro, his autobiography would be little more than a
journal of abnormal psychology, the story of a burglar, dope pusher, addict and
jailbird—with a family history of insanity—who acquires messianic delusions and
sets forth to preach an upside-down religion of "brotherly" hatred. What lends
importance to Malcolm's otherwise depressing tale is that he is a leader of the
Black Muslims, a sort of Negro Ku Klux Klan. Nobody knows just how large a
following he has, but unquestionably the militant hatred he preaches was behind
some of the violence of the summer riots in the North.

Society must share the blame for making Malcolm X the angry and possibly
dangerous man that he is. His story is the story of all the injustice still inflicted
on his race; it begins in senseless cruelty and violence, moves through poverty
and deprivation to the capricious murder of his father and his mother's insanity,
through his own easy drift into crime and long imprisonment, to—finally—the
catharsis of a pseudoreligious revelation. He is, in truth, the product of a world he
never made. But he is also, like every other man, self-made. The same unjust world
has also turned out a Martin Luther King, who has had to face the same depriva-
tions and senseless cruelties, yet through them has reached a personal serenity and
religious revelation founded on the idea of brotherly love. America may consider
itself lucky that in a large poll which the *New York Times* took in Harlem—by
coincidence, just before the riots—King had more than 12 times as many followers
as Malcolm X. We say lucky, because this fact shows more patience, forbearance
and trust among Negroes than their past treatment has justified. . . .

The lesson of Malcolm X . . . is that 19 million Negro Americans, who are
equally taxed in all respects, still do not get equal representation, politically or
otherwise. Taxation without representation is still tyranny, and until all Americans
join in providing every citizen with the rights of citizenship, we shall be lucky if
Malcolm X is not succeeded by even weirder and more virulent extremists.

—"The Lesson of Malcolm X," *Saturday Evening Post*, September 12, 1964, p. 84.

Robert R. Kirsch, Los Angeles Times *book critic, warning*
readers of the dangers of Malcolm X (1965)

Judging from this book . . . Malcolm X was demagogic, opinionated, hypocritical,
opportunistic, and in many areas, either ignorant or deliberately blind to the facts

of history. . . . His remarks about women, Jews, Christianity, Negroes (other than the Black Nationalists), and a variety of other topics are as biased, mischievous and incendiary as anything out of the Ku Klux Klan. As a symbol, Malcolm X ought to be examined very, very carefully. For he represents a dangerous, authoritarian impulse in America.

—Robert R. Kirsch, "The Real and Imagined Faces of Malcolm X," *Los Angeles Times,* November 5, 1965, p. C6.

Truman Nelson, author and social activist, praising the book as a modern-day Pilgrim's Progress (1965)

Viewed in its complete historical context, this is indeed a great book. Its deadlevel honesty, its passion, its exalted purpose, even its manifold unresolved ambiguities will make it stand as a monument to the most painful of truths: that this country, this people, this Western world had practiced unspeakable cruelty against a race, an individual, who might have made its fraudulent humanism a reality.

—Truman Nelson, "Delinquent's Progress," *Nation,* November 8, 1965, p. 336.

Robert Penn Warren, poet, placing Malcolm in the American tradition of the self-made man (1966)

[Malcolm X] was a latter-day example of an old-fashioned type of American celebrated in grammar school readers, commencement addresses, and speeches at Rotary Club lunches—the man who "makes it," the man who, from humble origins and with meager education, converts, by will, intelligence, and sterling character, his liabilities into assets. Malcolm X was of that breed of Americans, autodidacts and homemade successes, that has included Benjamin Franklin, Abraham Lincoln, P. T. Barnum, Thomas Alva Edison, Booker T. Washington, Mark Twain, Henry Ford, and the Wright brothers.

—Robert Penn Warren, "Malcolm X: Mission and Meaning," *Yale Review* 56.2 (1966): 161–71, reprinted in Douglas A. Hughes, *The Way It Is: Readings in Contemporary American Prose* (New York: Holt, Rinehart, and Winston, 1970), pp. 116–17.

Albert Cleage, black theologian and proponent of a black Jesus, rejecting the integrationist "Malcolm myth" (1967)

Brother Malcolm has become a symbol, a dream, a hope, a nostalgia for the past, a mystique, a shadow sometimes without substance, "our shining black prince," to whom we do obeisance, about whom we write heroic poems. But I think Brother Malcolm the man is in danger of being lost in a vast tissue of distortions which now constitute the Malcolm myth. . . .

The Malcolm myth or myths depend for substance upon the last chaotic and confusing year or two of his life—fragmentary statements growing out of his trip to Mecca and his efforts to bring the problems of black people in America to the attention of African leaders. . . . According to the myth, his pilgrimage to Mecca turned Brother Malcolm into an integrationist. I've heard that seriously stated by people who claim to be scholars and students of the life of Brother Malcolm. In Mecca, they say, he saw blue-eyed whites and blacks worshipping and living together, in love, for the first time in his 39 years—and his whole concept of white people changed. This is the myth. And he rejected his former position that the white man is the enemy and that separation is inescapable. This is the myth.

The implication here is that this new insight changed his orientation; that with this new insight he was now free to join the NAACP, or to sing "We Shall Overcome" with Martin Luther King, or to become a Marxist and join the Socialist Workers Party. . . .

I do not believe this myth. I reject it completely, totally and absolutely. I say if Malcolm X, Brother Malcolm, had undergone this kind of transformation, if in Mecca he had decided that blacks and whites can unite, then his life at that moment would have become meaningless in terms of the world struggle of black people. . . . So I say I do not believe it.

—Albert Cleage, "Myths About Malcolm X: A Speech," Detroit, Michigan, February 24, 1967, published in *International Socialist Review* 28.5 (September/October 1967): 33–42, www.marx.org/history/etol/newspape/isr/vol28/no05/cleage.htm.

Carol Ohmann, English professor, comparing Benjamin Franklin and Malcolm X as autobiographers (1970)

The Autobiography of Malcolm X testifies to the black experience in America. More precisely, it testifies to the personal cost of the black experience in America. . . . And yet, at the same time . . . the *Autobiography* is in many ways a traditionally American work. . . . Despite the fact that Benjamin Franklin could not have bought a bottle of Red Devil lye, and would have no need or wish to, his *Autobiography* and *The Autobiography of Malcolm X* resemble each other in the conceptions of the self they convey, in the categories by which they apprehend men and events, in the standards by which they judge them, and in the ways, looking backward as autobiographers do, they pattern or structure the raw materials in their own lives. . . . To put this in a practical academic way, *The Autobiography of Malcolm X* belongs not only in an Afro-American course but in a course in American literature or American autobiography. Both Benjamin Franklin and Malcolm X testify to certain strengths and certain weaknesses in our national ethos.

—Carol Ohmann, "The Autobiography of Malcolm X: A Revolutionary Use of the Franklin Tradition," *American Quarterly* 22.2 (Summer 1970): 131–32.

Howard Zinn, radical historian and social activist, on autobiography as a spur to action (1970)

Both the *Autobiography of Malcolm X* and the *Autobiography of Frederick Douglass* are history, one more recent than the other. Both assault our complacency. So do the photos on television of blacks burning buildings in the ghetto today, but the autobiographies do something special: they let us look closely, carefully, personally behind the impersonality of those blacks on the screen. They invade our homes, as the blacks in the ghetto have not yet done; and our minds, which we tend to harden against the demands of *now*. They tell us, in some small degree, what it is like to be black, in a way that all the liberal clichés about the downtrodden Negro could never match. And thus they insist that we act; they explain why blacks are acting. They prepare us, if not to initiate, to respond.

—Howard Zinn, "What Is Radical History?" in *The Politics of History* (Boston: Beacon, 1970), pp. 37–38.

Giles Gunn, American literature scholar, praising the Autobiography as "an American classic" (1981)

The Autobiography of Malcolm X is already an American classic, not only because it is a powerful narrative of an ordinary life, but because it depicts that life as following certain American patterns and supporting a variety of distinctive American values. The *Autobiography* traces Malcolm X's journey from obscurity to fame, from solitude to society, from provinciality to cosmopolitanism, and from estrangement to cautious accommodation, and embraces on its own terms such inherited American values as the importance of self-improvement, the need for self-criticism, the moral responsibility for public service, and the spiritual significance of human brotherhood.

—Giles Gunn, *New World Metaphysics: Readings on the Religious Meaning of the American Experience* (New York: Oxford Univ. Press, 1981), p. 437.

Kevin Pritchett, Wall Street Journal *correspondent, hailing a fellow "conservative" as Spike Lee's film is about to debut (1992)*

Malcolm's most important legacy and the reason for his new popularity is this: He stood for action. In the high-stakes battle of Malcolm X revisionism, the Spike Lee side wants to interpret "action" to include revolutionary—illegal—action of the kind we saw in the Los Angeles riots (fasten your seatbelts, inner cities). But Malcolm X really stood for another kind of action more useful to black Americans— the "action" of taking control of one's own life, of voting, or starting a business, or of giving up a life of welfare. . . . He believed that blacks should control their own destinies: become producers, not just consumers, and fix their own neighborhoods.

—Kevin Pritchett, "Malcolm X, Conservative Hero," *Wall Street Journal*, November 10, 1992, p. A24.

Colman McCarthy, journalist and pacifist, condemning Malcolm X's stance on violence (1992)

I've read . . . plenty to reach a conclusion that this was no giant of racial justice. Malcolm should be listened to but not heeded. He pushed violence. Other victims of American racism [from Thurgood Marshall to Clarence Thomas] have written and spoken powerfully about the social and economic violence they endured. None even hints that retaliatory violence is a solution. Compared with these pillars, and large numbers of others, Malcolm X was a second-rate mind spouting a third-rate agenda.

—Colman McCarthy, "Malcolm X's Ruinous Message," *Washington Post*, November 21, 1992, p. A25.

Barack Obama, forty-fourth U.S. president, recalling the mark made by the Autobiography on his early life (1995)

Only Malcolm X's autobiography seemed to offer something different. His repeated acts of self-creation spoke to me; the blunt poetry of his words, his unadorned insistence on respect promised a new and uncompromising order, martial in its discipline, forged through sheer force of will. All the other stuff, the talk of blue-eyed devils and apocalypse, was incidental to that program, I decided, religious baggage that Malcolm himself seemed to have safely abandoned toward the end of his life. And yet, even as I imagined myself following Malcolm's call, one line in the book stayed with me. He spoke of a wish he'd once had, the wish that the white blood that ran through him, there by an act of violence, might somehow be expunged. I knew that, for Malcolm, that wish would never be incidental. I knew as well that traveling down the road to self-respect my own white blood would never recede into mere abstraction. I was left to wonder what else I would be severing if and when I left my mother and my grandparents at some uncharted border.

—Barack Obama, *Dreams from My Father: A Story of Race and Inheritance* (1995; New York: Crown, 2004), p. 86.

Stephen Whitfield, American Studies scholar, blaming Malcolm for introducing a new form of anti-Semitism to black America (2001)

Hostility to Jews took an ideological turn among some blacks only in the 1960s, and no one was more responsible for that change than Malcolm X (albeit posthumously through his autobiography). Before this, black anti-Semitism consisted mainly of snippets of Christian folklore concerning who was to blame for deicide, alongside class-based resentment at the exploitation, greed, and cunning ascribed to Jewish merchants, landlords, and creditors. (Farrakhan's phrase for them was "bloodsuckers.") Malcolm X introduced a couple of novelty items to this list of accusations. More forcefully than any previous black spokesman, he scorned the Jewish invocation of the Holocaust. *After* breaking with Elijah Muhammad, Malcolm X told a Harlem crowd how tiresome it was to keep hearing about the Six Million. "I was reading a book the other day that showed that one hundred million of us were kidnapped and brought to this country," the autodidact announced. "Now everybody's wet-eyed over a handful of Jews who brought it on themselves. What about our one hundred million?" . . .

But above all, he pioneered in injecting into black public discourse a third world ideology that defined his own country as the chief source of evil in the world and located Israel as the only source of evil in the Middle East. Tapping ancient myths about Jews, Malcolm X made black militancy geopolitical even as he professed a racial solidarity with Arabs, especially Palestinians, whose land, he charged, Zionists had "stolen." The impact that his 1965 autobiography exerted can scarcely be exaggerated.

—Stephen J. Whitfield, "Asymmetries in America: Recent Work on Jews and Blacks," in Eli Lederhendler, ed., *Who Owns Judaism? Public Religion and Private Faith in America and Israel* (New York: Oxford Univ. Press, 2001), p. 199.

Eddie Glaude, *African-American Studies scholar, on the impact the* Autobiography *had on him as a child (2010)*

I remember as a young country boy from Mississippi, crying out, "Oh My God." I have my goatee to this day because of that book. I will never shave it off. He revealed the secret. What's the secret? That maybe black folk really don't like white people. You can't help but be a little bit giddy when you read that.

—Quoted on *Studio 360*, "American Icons: The Autobiography of Malcolm X," September 24, 2010, www.studio360.org/2011/aug/26/transcript.

LAMENTATIONS

Gettysburg Address

❧ ABRAHAM LINCOLN, 1863 ❧

O N November 19, 1863, in Gettysburg, Pennsylvania, at the dedication of America's first national cemetery, on the site of the battle that had turned the course of the Civil War decisively toward the Union, Edward Everett of Massachusetts delivered the keynote address. A former Harvard president and heir to Massachusetts Senator Daniel Webster as the leading orator of the day, Everett offered an exhaustive lecture on this battle, comparing it to the Battle of Marathon in 490 BCE, in which the Greeks defeated the Persians and thereby saved democracy. In the presence of the living and the dead (many of the 50,000 or so slain soldiers lay unburied), Everett also advanced a learned constitutional thesis on the supremacy of the nation over the states. His "classic but frigid oration," as *New York Tribune* editor Horace Greeley termed it, lasted over two hours.[1] It has been almost entirely forgotten. The "dedicatory remarks" of Abraham Lincoln (1809–65) lasted three minutes. Today *they* are the Gettysburg Address.

Most of this address is dedicated to the men who died there—those who, in Lincoln's memorable phrase, "gave the last full measure of devotion." It is not up to the living to consecrate this battlefield. Soldiers' blood has already made this place holy. But it is up to Lincoln and his listeners to ensure that these men did not die in vain. They "gave their lives that this nation might live," Lincoln says. So the living must see to it that the United States experiences "a new birth of freedom."

These sentiments are pitch-perfect, as might be expected from America's most eloquent president. But the underlying message about wartime sacrifice is also the sort of thing a president is expected to say in a moment like this. What Lincoln said about the Declaration of Independence and the Constitution is an entirely different matter.

There is a recurring tension in American thought between the Declaration of Independence and the Constitution. The Declaration is a revolutionary document, but it is also in many respects a radical one, affirming as "self-evident" a host of "truths" that in 1776 most colonists would have denied. The Constitution is far more conservative, a product of tortured negotiations among thirteen states. In short, if the Declaration is an outburst on behalf of liberty, the Constitution is a compromise by committee on behalf of order. Or so it went in the 1700s.

Secreted inside Lincoln's "dedicatory remarks" is a new interpretation of Declaration and Constitution alike, and of the relationship between them. The first hint of this reinterpretation comes at the start of the opening sentence, when Lincoln dates America's birth not to the ratification of the Constitution in 1788 but to the promulgation of the Declaration in 1776. (1863 minus 86 is 1776.) But Lincoln does more than calculate America's birthday. He distills its project down to one idea. This bombshell comes in the second part of the first sentence, when Lincoln asserts that the United States, though "conceived in liberty," is dedicated to a single proposition: "that all men are created equal."

In his last sentence, Lincoln states that these men have died so that republicanism might live—"that government of the people, by the people, for the people shall not perish from the earth." Here Lincoln is borrowing from Daniel Webster and Unitarian minister Theodore Parker, both of whom had defined democracy in similar terms. In so doing, Lincoln is interpreting the federal government as a covenant of people rather than a compact of states.

What is Lincoln up to? First, he is subordinating the Constitution to the Declaration, which had long stood at the center of his political thought. The Declaration was in his view America's Genesis, the founding book of the American Bible and the core expression of the aspirations of the American people. It was *this* text that constituted the nation. According to historian Garry Wills, "Lincoln distinguished between the Declaration as the statement of a permanent ideal and the Constitution as an early and provisional embodiment of that ideal, to be tested against it, kept in motion toward it."[2] Second, Lincoln is reading the "equality clause" of the Declaration—the obvious truth "that all men are created equal"— as the heart and soul of this founding expression and employing equality (a word never mentioned in the Constitution) as the principle by which American society is to be judged. Third, he is, by context and implication, reading African Americans into this clause. They too are created equal. Finally, he is reimagining the United States not as a collection of states but as a people. "Up to the Civil War, 'the United States' was invariably a plural noun: 'The United States are a free government,'" Wills explains. "After Gettysburg, it became a singular: 'The United States is a free government.'"[3]

But this Gettysburg revolution did not just place the American people over the states and the spirit of the Declaration before the letter of the Constitution. It also elevated the Gettysburg Address above the Declaration. Here the same eyes Lincoln used to gaze over the battlefield became the eyes through which subsequent generations read the Declaration. "For most people now," Wills concludes, "the Declaration means what Lincoln told us it means."[4]

This new gospel of Gettysburg—a new version of the "good news" of the American story—had huge implications for the question that was above all other questions at the time, since the Constitution would seem, on any simple reading, to favor slavery, whereas the Declaration's "self-evident" truths would seem to protest most emphatically against it.[5] Lincoln did not take up this question at Gettysburg. Neither did he address the Almighty in his working draft. But he added the words "under God" under the impress of the moment and to subsequent copies he produced. Roughly a century later, in 1954, this last-minute insertion would become a winning argument for adding "under God" to the Pledge of Allegiance.

After Lincoln finished speaking, he was met, first, with a hushed silence and then with "immense applause."[6] Not everyone in attendance was happy, however. The *Chicago Times* complained about the president's "silly, flat, and dishwatery utterances," while the *Harrisburg Patriot and Union* allowed itself to hope that a "veil of oblivion shall be dropped over [Lincoln's remarks] and that they shall no more be repeated or thought of." The Massachusetts-based *Springfield Republican*, however, got its first draft of history right: "His little speech is a perfect gem, deep in feeling, compact in thought and expression, and tasteful and elegant in every word and comma."[7]

What this "perfect gem" did was define the Civil War to succeeding generations, and in the process redefine America. Still, many took exception, both before and after his 1865 assassination, to Lincoln's interpretations of war and nation.

The *Chicago Times* called the Gettysburg Address "a perversion of history so flagrant that the most extended charity cannot regard it as otherwise than willful."[8] Others insisted that the Constitution, not the Declaration, was the law of the land and the basis for the national compact. Many Northerners, chafing at any suggestion that the Civil War was being fought for racial equality, insisted that the war's purpose was to preserve the Union. Who said that blacks were heirs to the Declaration's promises?

This debate has never been settled, but the legend of the Gettysburg Address has swelled over time. The popular elementary-school readers of the McGuffey brothers started to include it in the 1890s, and it was first cast in bronze in 1896. By the start of the twentieth century it had become American scripture—"the nation's political Sermon on the Mount."[9] Over the last hundred years, Americans have invoked Lincoln's words to justify all sorts of causes— new wars, of course, but also the New Deal, the Equal Rights Amendment, and the civil rights movement. In 2011, economist Joseph Stiglitz married Lincoln to the Occupy Wall Street movement with a *Vanity Fair* essay on income inequality called "Of the 1 Percent, by the 1 Percent, for the 1 Percent."[10]

The Gettysburg Address has also been used to chasten America. In 1984 South African archbishop Desmond Tutu blasted the United States for abstaining from a U.N. Security Council vote condemning apartheid in South Africa: "I believed, naively perhaps, that the United States lived by the precepts of the Declaration of Independence and the Gettysburg Address."[11] In 1985, the Soviet state newspaper *Pravda,* noting that the large corporations that had picked up much of the $12.5 million tab for President Reagan's second inauguration would expect to be repaid, said the United States was becoming "a government of millionaires, for millionaires and by millionaires."[12]

As the civil rights movement went from success to success in the 1960s, Lincoln's views of the Constitution, the Declaration, the Civil War, and the origins and ends of America came to predominate. Or, to be more precise, an even more audacious interpretation of the Declaration's equality clause triumphed, because Lincoln, who in his famous debate with Senator Stephen Douglas denied that he was "in favor of bringing about in any way, the social and political equality of the white and black races," never imagined the sort of racial integration the 1960s wrought.[13]

During and after the Reagan Revolution of the 1980s, conservative advocates of states' rights and an "original intent" approach to constitutional interpretation challenged Lincoln's Gettysburg gospel. The Declaration did nothing more than declare thirteen colonies independent from the British crown, they argued. It did not found a new nation; the Constitution did that. Moreover, the equality clause in the Declaration could not possibly have created a national commitment to realize equality for all. "All men" could not have meant "all people" to the founders, since the vote was kept from slaves, women, and the landless. Lincoln's "second founding," in short, lured the country away from first principles and toward untold dangers. Far from the pinnacle of American political thought, these critics now argue, the Gettysburg Address is a nadir.

Despite these criticisms, the Gettysburg Address is now widely recognized as the greatest American speech, challenged only by Martin Luther King Jr.'s "I Have a Dream," which shares with it a vision, soaring rhetoric, and a historic moment appropriate to the task. In recent years, the most quoted phrase from the Gettysburg Address, perhaps because of its resonance with resurgent evangelicalism, is "a new birth of freedom." Bob Dole, Jack Kemp, and Steve Forbes used this phrase in their Republican campaigns for president, and Ronald Reagan used it at least ten times during his presidency. In 2009, the theme of Barack Obama's inauguration was "A New Birth of Freedom."

Gettysburg Address &

Four score and seven years ago our fathers brought forth on this continent, a new nation, conceived in Liberty, and dedicated to the proposition that all men are created equal.[a,b]

Now we are engaged in a great civil war, testing whether that nation, or any nation so conceived and so dedicated, can long endure. We are met on a great battle field of that war. We have come

---

a. *Chicago Times*, Democratic newspaper, denouncing Lincoln's interpretation of America's founding documents (1863): As a refutation of this statement, we copy certain clauses in the Federal Constitution: "Representatives and direct taxes shall be apportioned among the several States which may be included in this Union, according to their respective numbers, which shall be determined by adding to the whole number of *free* persons, including those bound to service for a term of years, and excluding Indians not taxed, three-fifths of *all other persons*."

to dedicate a portion of that field, as a final resting place for those who here gave their lives that that nation might live. It is altogether fitting and proper that we should do this.

But, in a larger sense, we cannot dedicate—we cannot consecrate—we cannot hallow—this ground. The brave men, living and dead, who struggled here, have consecrated it, far above our poor power to add or detract. The world will little note, nor long remember what we say here, but it can never forget what they did here. It is for us the living, rather, to be dedicated here to the unfinished work which they who fought here have thus far so nobly advanced. It is rather for us to be here dedicated to the great task remaining before us—that from these honored dead we

---

"The migration or importation of such persons as any of the States now existing shall think proper to admit shall not be prohibited by the Congress prior to the year 1808, but a tax or duty may be imposed on such importation, not exceeding ten dollars for each person."

"No amendment to the constitution, made prior to 1808, shall affect the preceding clause."

"No person held to service or labor in one State under the laws thereof, escaping into another, shall, in consequence of any law or regulation therein, be discharged from such service or labor, but shall be delivered up on claim of the party to whom such service or labor may be due."

Do these provisions in the Constitution dedicate the nation to "the proposition that all men are created equal"? Mr. Lincoln occupies his present position by virtue of this Constitution, and is sworn to the maintenance and enforcement of these provisions. It was to uphold this Constitution, and the Union created by it, that our officers and soldiers gave their lives at Gettysburg. How dared he, then, standing on their graves, misstate the cause for which they died, and libel the statesmen who founded the government? They were men possessing too much self-respect to declare that negroes were their equals. —"The President at Gettysburg," *Chicago Times*, November 23, 1863, http://teachingamericanhistory.org/library/index.asp?document=1721.

b. John F. Kennedy, thirty-fifth U.S. president, addressing the American people on civil rights (1963): This Nation was founded by men of many nations and backgrounds. It was founded on the principle that all men are created equal, and that the rights of every man are diminished when the rights of one man are threatened. Today we are committed to a worldwide struggle to promote and protect the rights of all who wish to be free. And when Americans are sent to Viet-Nam or West Berlin, we do not ask for whites only. It ought to be possible, therefore, for American students of any color to attend any public institution they select without having to be backed up by troops. It ought to be possible for American consumers of any color to receive equal service in places of public accommodation, such as hotels and restaurants and theaters and retail stores, without being forced to resort to demonstrations in the street, and it ought to be possible for American citizens of any color take increased devotion to that cause for which they gave the last full measure of devotion—that we here highly resolve that these dead shall not have died in vain, that this nation, under God,[c] shall have a new birth of freedom[d,e]—and that government of the people, by the people, for the people, shall not perish from the earth.[14]

---

to register and to vote in a free election without interference or fear of reprisal. . . . In short, every American ought to have the right to be treated as he would wish to be treated, as one would wish his children to be treated. But this is not the case. . . .

Next week I shall ask the Congress of the United States to act, to make a commitment it has not fully made in this century to the proposition that race has no place in American life or law. The Federal judiciary has upheld that proposition in a series of forthright cases. The executive branch has adopted that proposition in the conduct of its affairs, including the employment of Federal personnel, the use of Federal facilities, and the sale of federally financed housing. But there are other necessary measures which only the Congress can provide, and they must be provided at this session. The old code of equity law under which we live commands for every wrong a remedy, but in too many communities, in too many parts of the country, wrongs are inflicted on Negro citizens and there are no remedies at law. Unless the Congress acts, their only remedy is in the street. —John F. Kennedy, "Radio and Television Report to the American People on Civil Rights," June 11, 1963, www.presidency.ucsb.edu/ws/index.php?pid=9271.

c. Dwight Eisenhower, thirty-fourth U.S. president, recruiting Lincoln into the postwar religious revival (1954): Out of faith in God, and through faith in themselves as His children, our forefathers designed and built this Republic. We remember from school days that, aboard a tiny ship of destiny called the Mayflower, self-government on our continent was first conceived by the Pilgrim Fathers. Their immortal compact began with the words, "In the name of God, Amen." We remember the picture of the Father of our Country, on his knees at Valley Forge seeking divine guidance in the cold gloom of a bitter winter. Thus Washington gained strength to lead to independence a nation dedicated to the belief that each of us is divinely endowed with indestructible rights. We remember, too, that three-fourths of a century later, on the battle-torn field of Gettysburg, and in the silence of many a wartime night, Abraham Lincoln recognized that only under God could this Nation win a new birth of freedom. —Dwight D. Eisenhower, "Remarks Broadcast as Part of the American Legion 'Back to God'" Program, January 7, 1954, www.presidency.ucsb.edu/ws/index.php?pid=10119.

d. *Washington Post*, welcoming the Supreme Court's *Brown v. Board of Education* decision against public school desegregation (1954): It is not too much to speak of the Court's decision as a new birth of freedom. . . . Abroad as well as at home, this decision will engender a renewal of faith in democratic institutions and ideals. —*Washington Post* editorial, May 19, 1954, quoted in Juan Williams, *Eyes on the Prize: America's Civil Rights Years, 1954–1965* (New York: Penguin, 1988), p. 35.

COMMENTARY

New York World, *attacking Lincoln's interpretation of U.S. history and the Civil War (1863)*

This United States is not the United States which fought the War of Independence. *This* United States is the result of the ratification of a compact known as the Constitution by eleven States originally, and such as have acceded since.

The *States* met in convention to form a government for themselves. They framed a plan which was to go into operation when nine States acceded to and ratified it. In that convention some delegates from the (now) free States, and some from Virginia, felt and talked about slavery just as Mr. Lincoln feels and talks, just as Wendell Phillips feels and talks, just as [Horace] Greeley feels and writes. Some others felt and talked just as we feel and write, that slavery is an injury to the interests of both slave and master. Georgia and South Carolina said in substance, "We do not think as you think; we do not seek to convert you, nor can you convert us. Count us out." Thereupon it was clear that Maryland, Delaware, the two Carolinas, Georgia and Virginia would form a separate confederacy, and the rest of the States possibly another, if slavery was insisted upon as one of the subjects of Federal cognizance.

The other States had the option either to ally themselves with slavery or to cut loose from it. They chose the former, and cannot now, with the slightest fairness, hold to the benefits and reject the burdens of their bargain.

—Reprinted as "President Lincoln's Last Speech," *Detroit Free Press*, November 29, 1863, p. 2.

e. Steve Forbes, *Forbes* magazine publisher and Republican presidential candidate, calling for a new birth of privatized Social Security and school vouchers (1999): The purpose of my campaign is to give new meaning to Lincoln's words at Gettysburg where he talked about a new birth of freedom, that this nation, under God, shall have a new birth of freedom. . . . We need a new birth of freedom for the freedom to be born. Freedom from fear of the IRS. Freedom for parents to choose schools that work for their children. Freedom for young people to choose where their Social Security taxes are invested. Freedom for parents to choose schools that work best not only for their children, but their grandchildren as well. —Quoted in "Republican Presidential Candidates Debate in Phoenix, Arizona," December 6, 1999, www.presidency.ucsb.edu/ws/index.php?pid=75089.

William Lloyd Garrison Jr., author and activist, opposing U.S. imperialism in Hawaii (1898)

With the acceptance of Hawaii from the hands of the conspirators who captured it by the naval connivance and aid of the United States, a new creed must be evolved to perpetuate the unjust conditions there existing. A justification has to be found for the diminutive oligarchy which controls, without the consent of the governed, a people as much entitled to self-government as President Dole. The denial of suffrage rights to the Hawaiians, treating truth as geographical, is a betrayal of democracy at home. What shall it profit a nation to conquer all the islands of the sea if thereby the surrender of its own vital principle is the price?

The advocates of the [Spanish-American] war truly say that we have come out of the conflict a different nation. Not, however, in the nobler sense which they would imply, but with that dangerous consciousness of brute strength, destructive to the spirit and tempting to emulation in paths leading to the abyss in which so many promising democracies have perished. To gain the Hawaiian islands by the loss of our belief in "a government of the people, for the people, and by the people" is a costly exchange. To obtain Cuba and Porto Rico at the expense of an increased standing army and navy is to pay a deadly price. To surrender the Monroe doctrine for the Philippines is to demonstrate that something more than the Spanish squadron went down under Dewey's guns at Manila. The old chart and compass which have served so well to keep the country clear of the rocks and shoals of international greed will be of little use on this new voyage of imperialism.

Lincoln's Gettysburg address . . . must be suppressed at Honolulu because [its sentiments are] dangerous utterances under a despotic oligarchy. Every politician henceforth must keep two sets of principles, one for home, the other for colonial consumption, and speak with double tongue.

—William Lloyd Garrison, "War and Imperialism Fatal to Self-Government," *Advocate of Peace* 60.9 (October 1898): 210–11.

Helen Gardener, women's rights advocate, applying the Declaration's "all men" to "all women" (1913)

The arguments against woman suffrage are, in point of fact, always in the ultimate analysis simply arguments against self-government. They are in the ultimate analysis based on opposition to our form of government. They are the arguments which have been used by king to serf in all the ages past, with woman now the disqualified unit instead of labor or poverty or any other "lower class."

If government is to rest upon suffrage at all—that is, upon the expressed will of anybody not a "king by divine right"—who is to decide that you are born with that divine right to vote, to express yourself in civic affairs, and that I am not? When and how did you get the right and where and how did I lose it?

That always puzzles me. I cannot remember when I lost it. How did one type of human units get the right to decide that another type of human units shall not have liberty of conscience and expression? I never could understand that. If it is a divine right, what particular streak of divinity has been discovered in man that women lack?

If it is not a natural, inherent, human right, then they say it is a "conferred privilege." Now, who conferred it? On what basis did they confer it, and where did they get it to confer?

Has the supply run out? Is not special privilege in government, in the final analysis, simply a wrong and an outrage against which people have been fighting since history began? Kings claim to be born with this divine right. The founders of our government scouted the idea—for kings, but not for men. They announced to the world that we are born "free and equal," and that all just government is based upon the consent of the governed. They said—and both our President and Secretary of State said to us the other day in this patriotic organization of women—that this is a government of the people, by the people, and for the people. I hope that they realized, even when they were saying it, that it was only a glittering form of speech. I hope that they realized that it is in fact a government of all of the people by a half of the people for a few of the people.

—"Remarks of Helen B. Gardener," in *Hearings Before the Committee on Woman Suffrage* (Washington, DC: U.S. Government Printing Office, 1913), pp. 83–84.

Afro-American, *a Baltimore newspaper, lamenting, on the fiftieth anniversary of Lincoln's address, a government of, by, and for* white *people (1913)*

We are wondering whether Mr. Lincoln had the slightest idea in his mind that the time would ever come when the people of this country would come to the conclusion that by the "People" he meant only white people. No one can look over the conditions in the Southland as they prevail today and come to any other conclusions than that "government of the people, by the people, for the people," means anything else but government for all the people by the WHITE people. In not one southern state, whether formerly in rebellion or otherwise, but that the government is in the hands of the white people, and is administered solely for the benefit of the white people. The teeming millions of Negroes in the South are not considered when it comes to a question of government, only so far as the white people of that section may feel inclined.

Today the South is in the saddle, and with the single exception of slavery, everything it fought for during the days of the Civil War, it has gained by repression of the Negro within its borders. And the North has quietly allowed it to have its own way. . . .

The Negro has been loyal all the way through, even under the most adverse circumstances. And when Mr. Lincoln called for Negro volunteers, the call came back to him with the answer: "We are coming Father Abraham, one hundred thousand strong." And they came and fought and died, and their blood consecrated almost every battlefield from the Potomac to the Gulf. Today that blood is crying from the ground in every Southern State. Will the voice be heard? If it is not heard, little will the great reunion of the "Blue and Gray" on the battlefield of Gettysburg, or elsewhere, do towards carrying this great country on and on to the highest pinnacle of civilization. . . .

It would be wise, just at this juncture, to study well the words of the immortal Lincoln, and in order that the government of the people, by the people and for the people shall not perish from the earth, to recall the fact that at least part of the people of this country are Negroes and at the same time human beings, and civilized human beings at that; struggling towards the light, as God has given them to see the light.

—"A Government of the People," *Afro-American,* July 5, 1913, p. 4.

Wayne MacVeagh, former Union soldier and U.S. attorney general, defining for German immigrants the meaning of America (1915)

The simple truth, which [President Wilson] has been so unwilling to recognize, is that there exists an impassable chasm between a citizen of the United States and a subject of the German Emperor, and there is no possible political alchemy whereby the political standards of the one can be transmuted into the political standards of the other. No matter where a man is born or how he is reared, when he comes to manhood he instinctively prefers to be a citizen or a subject. . . .

We only ask [German Americans] . . . to make their choice—to be loyal either to the fundamental principles of our Government or those of the government of the Kaiser, and to believe that they cannot be half loyal to the one and half loyal to the other. They must be wholly American, or wholly German, and if they really prefer the German system of government, they should return thither and enjoy it; but if they propose to continue to live here, then they must be loyal to the American system, and there is no possibility for them of mistaking what that system is.

Thomas Jefferson declared it to the whole world when he said the just rights of all governments depend upon the consent of the governed, and Abraham Lincoln at Gettysburg, in a few simple words, stamped it forever upon the history of mankind, in his immortal aspiration, that government of the people, by the people and for the people should never perish from the earth. Whoever accepts without reservation those two principles of government is a loyal American. Whoever pretends to accept them and is at heart disloyal to them is unworthy of American citizenship and ought to be deprived of it, for it is an impassable chasm which those honestly on one side can never pass over to the other.

—Wayne MacVeagh, "The Impassable Chasm," *North American Review* 202.716 (July 1915): 34.

H. L. Mencken, journalist and satirist, on Lincoln's words as beautiful nonsense (1922)

The Gettysburg speech is at once the shortest and the most famous oration in American history. Put beside it, all the whoopings of the Websters, Sumners and Everetts seem gaudy and silly. It is eloquence brought to a pellucid and almost child-like perfection—the highest emotion reduced to one graceful and irresistible gesture. Nothing else precisely like it is to be found in the whole range of oratory. Lincoln himself never even remotely approached it. It is genuinely stupendous.

But let us not forget that it is oratory, not logic; beauty, not sense. Think of the argument in it! Put it into the cold words of everyday! The doctrine is simply this: that the Union soldiers who died at Gettysburg sacrificed their lives to the cause of self-determination—"that government of the people, by the people, for the people," should not perish from the earth. It is difficult to imagine anything more untrue. The Union soldiers in that battle actually fought against self-determination; it was the Confederates who fought for the right of their people to govern themselves. What was the practical effect of the battle of Gettysburg? What else than the destruction of the old sovereignty of the States, i.e., of the people of the States? The Confederates went into battle an absolutely free people; they came out with their freedom subject to the supervision and vote of the rest of the country—and for nearly twenty years that vote was so effective that they enjoyed scarcely any freedom at all. Am I the first American to note the fundamental nonsensicality of the Gettysburg address? If so, I plead my aesthetic joy in it in amelioration of the sacrilege.

—H. L. Mencken, *Prejudices: Third Series* (New York: Knopf, 1922), pp. 174–75.

Carl Sandburg, poet and author, reading the Gettysburg Address as part Lincoln, part Jefferson (1954)

[Lincoln] had stood that day, the world's foremost spokesman of popular government, saying that democracy was yet worth fighting for. What he meant by "a new birth of freedom" for the nation could have a thousand interpretations. The taller riddles of democracy stood up out of the address. It had the dream touch of vast and furious events epitomized for any foreteller to read what was to come. His cadences sang the ancient song that where there is freedom men have fought and sacrificed for it, and that freedom is worth men's dying for. For the first time since he became President he had on a dramatic occasion declaimed, howsoever it might be read, Jefferson's proposition which had been a slogan of the Revolutionary War—"All men are created equal"—leaving no other inference than that he regarded the Negro slave as a man. His outwardly smooth sentences were inside of them gnarled and tough with the enigmas of the American experiment.

—Carl Sandburg, *Abraham Lincoln: The Prairie Years and the War Years* (New York: Harcourt, Brace & World, 1954), p. 447.

Walter Judd, U.S. Representative (R-MN) and outspoken anti-Communist, enlisting Lincoln and God into the Cold War (1960)

Lincoln and the Republican Party led our country through the crisis of 100 years ago. Now we are engaged in a greater conflict—the whole planet is in the throes of the mightiest conflict in all history. It is a world civil war. What is it about? It is about exactly the same thing as then: Is Government of the people, by the people, and therefore for the people to perish, literally, from the earth? . . . If we in America, of whatever political opinion at the moment, are to prove worthy of this most terrible testing in our Nation's life, we too must resolve with Lincoln, "that under God, this Nation shall have a new birth of freedom." It was under God that our freedom was born. Only under God can there be a rebirth. . . .

—Walter H. Judd, "Keynote Speech at the Republican National Convention, July 25, 1960," *Washington Post*, July 26, 1960, p. A8.

Willmoore Kendall, political scientist, leading a conservative assault on Lincoln's "heretical" reading of the Declaration and the Constitution (1967)

After Gettysburg, the idea ["that all men are created equal"] rapidly acquired *sensu stricto,* biblical status, which is to say: Like many perplexing sentences in Holy Scripture, it now comes readily to the lips—all too readily, one is tempted to say—as a statement that (a) must be correct, somehow, or one wouldn't hear it so often from such highly authoritative quarters, and (b) need not, cannot, be acted upon, because we are so far from clear as to what they mean. . . .

Lincoln's statement, we notice at once, breaks down into four distinct—to use his own words—"propositions." First, the United States, as a nation, was born in 1776. Second, the United States was conceived in liberty. Third, the United States, in the very act of being born, was "dedicated" to an overriding purpose—that is, began its life with an understanding of its own meaning that is best expressed in a single supreme symbol. Fourth, the proposition to which we are dedicated is "all men are created equal," and the supreme symbol that expresses our meaning as a nation is "equality." . . .

With two of the four explicit propositions set forth in the first sentence of the Gettysburg Address—the United States was conceived in liberty, the United States, in the fact of being born, was dedicated to an overriding purpose—I am in fullest agreement. . . . The remaining two of our four propositions are, from the standpoint of the American political tradition, *heretical*. . . .

Let us look first at Heresy Number One: "Fourscore and seven years ago our forefathers brought forth on this continent a new nation . . ." What Lincoln did in that opening phrase at Gettysburg . . . was to falsify the facts of history, and to do so in a way that precisely *confuses* our self-understanding as a people. The facts, as it happens, are extremely simple and, moreover, well-known to all of us save as we fall under the spell of Lincoln's rhetoric: The Declaration of Independence, as signed at Philadelphia, declared the independence of "the thirteen United States of America"—the independence not of a nation but of a baker's dozen of new sovereignties. . . . The Declaration was, in short, just what its plain language shows it to be, namely a notice served on the government of Great Britain that thirteen of the English colonies were dissolving the political bonds that had hitherto connected them with Great Britain, that, as I put it a moment ago, they—not *it,* but *they*—were henceforth going to govern *themselves,* and not be governed, or rather misgoverned, from faraway London. . . .

So much for the first of the two Lincoln propositions with which I am taking issue; and, happily (since my time grows short) we have, in disposing of it, largely disposed of the second one: "[The] new nation . . . [was] dedicated to the proposition that all men are created equal." Here we can rely not primarily on a simple appeal to history but a simple appeal to logic. If the Declaration of Independence did not bring forth a new nation, as it certainly did not, if it was *not* a solemn act by which a single people constituted itself an agent for action in *history,* then we cannot tear *from* the Declaration—that is, tear from its proper context—a single proposition, and do with it what Lincoln tries to do with the words "all men are created equal"; and if we cannot, then the whole case for our commitment to equality as a national goal crashes to the ground. We have *no* such commitment (unless—I do not exclude the possibility—we have acquired it at some later date); we have, collectively and individually, *no* obligation to promote the overriding purpose; the whole business is a further Lincolnian heresy. . . .

The proposition "all men are created equal" is so ambiguous as to merit classification as, for all practical purposes, meaningless and therefore useless— especially if, in reading it, we take into account the time at which it was written. . . . [But] even if we withdraw the objection that the proposition to which we are allegedly "dedicated" is meaningless . . . there remains *this* point that we have heard curiously little about from our egalitarian political scientists and historians.

The founding fathers at Philadelphia, who *did* deliberate, and *did* produce a document in which we the American people *do* constitute ourselves a nation, and *did* dedicate us to an overriding purpose, and *did* submit their handiwork for ratification by Us the American people, certainly had in front of them the Declaration of Independence . . . and seem to have decided . . . either first to ignore it (they *do* make no reference to it or repeat any of its language) or, second, to, if I dare say it, *repudiate* it—by forestalling any appeal back to it, and to its credo, of the kind that Lincoln is to make in the mid-nineteenth century. . . . In short: I find myself unable to read the Preamble of the Constitution (which we have never repudiated, never revised) as other than an express repudiation of the tenet of the Declaration's creed that might seem to commit us somehow to equality.

And I conclude: The Declaration of Independence does not commit us to equality as a national goal—for more reasons than you can shake a stick at.

—Willmoore Kendall, "Equality: Commitment or Ideal?" *Phalanx* 1 (Fall 1967), reprinted in *Intercollegiate Review* 24.2 (Spring 1989): 25–33.

Garry Wills, historian, on the magic trick Lincoln pulled out of his hat at Gettysburg (1992)

He would cleanse the Constitution—not, as William Lloyd Garrison had, by burning an instrument that countenanced slavery. He altered the document from within, by appeal from its letter to the spirit, subtly changing the recalcitrant stuff of that legal compromise, bringing it to its own indictment. By implicitly doing this, he performed one of the most daring acts of open-air sleight-of-hand ever witnessed by the unsuspecting. Everyone in that vast throng of thousands was having his or her intellectual pocket picked. The crowd departed with a new thing in its ideological luggage, that new constitution Lincoln had substituted for the one they brought there with them. They walked off, from those curving graves on the hillside, under a changed sky, into a different America. Lincoln had revolutionized the Revolution, giving people a new past to live with that would change their future indefinitely.

—Garry Wills, *Lincoln at Gettysburg: The Words That Remade America* (New York: Simon & Schuster, 1992), p. 38.

Eliot Spitzer, lawyer and former Democratic governor of New York, on Americans as sacrifice avoiders (2010)

How quickly we forget. Just days ago, on Memorial Day—a day of gratitude, respect, and celebration—the words of President Lincoln's Gettysburg Address were read at ceremonies across the nation. The phrase from that speech that always sticks with me is the challenge President Lincoln set forth for us: "Resolve that these dead shall not have died in vain." He implored us not to shy away from the sacrifices we too have an obligation to shoulder in order to advance the "unfinished work" that remained—not merely winning the Civil War and ending slavery, but the continued creation of a nation with opportunity for all.

The question confronting the United States today is whether the notion of sacrifice—personal and collective—still has enough traction in our society to enable us to overcome the range of problems we face. For as much as we might honor the men and women in our armed forces for whom sacrifice is all too real, we know that in almost every matter of importance, Americans have become masters of "sacrifice avoidance." Every problem is turned into a positive-sum game—spending more, rather than making hard choices; shifting burdens to future generations whose voices can't be heard; pushing the obligations off to another day or on to another group. . . .

Just think about it. After reading the Gettysburg Address, does it seem onerous to ask for slightly higher marginal tax rates for the top 5 percent, those who benefited so remarkably from the excesses of the boom years, in order to fund the necessary investment in social infrastructure?

After reading the Gettysburg Address, does the idea of a carbon tax to finally move us away from an oil and old-energy dependence that is fouling not only the Gulf of Mexico but our entire climate, foreign policy, and economy seem so outrageous? Given the accomplishments of our global competitors, surely it makes sense to consider longer school days and school years. Don't the concerns voiced by those who would have to sacrifice somewhat—whether teachers, parents, or students—to accommodate this national imperative seem somewhat less compelling after reading the Gettysburg Address?

After reading the Gettysburg Address, don't the bleating self-important concerns of investment bankers whose multimillion-dollar bonuses might be jeopardized by a somewhat more rigorous regulatory structure seem downright offensive?

Yet our dedication to the sacrifices needed to complete the unfinished business that President Lincoln referred to is absent. The voice we need to hear right now is President Obama's—evoking the language of his great predecessors, from Lincoln to Franklin Roosevelt—inspiring in all of us a greater sense of national purpose.

—Eliot Spitzer, "Read the Gettysburg Address," *Slate*, June 4, 2010, www.slate.com/id/2256012/.

Vietnam Veterans Memorial

❧ MAYA LIN, 1982 ❧

THE Vietnam Veterans Memorial is a text of sorts. Its reflective black granite face is covered with words: names of over fifty-eight thousand American soldiers who died or went missing in the Vietnam War. "The memorial is analogous to a book in many ways," writes Maya Lin (b. 1959), a Chinese-American architect who designed it in 1981 as a twenty-one-year-old Yale undergraduate. "Note that on the right-hand panels the pages are set ragged right and on the left they are set ragged left, creating a spine at the apex as in a book."[1] Norman Hannah, who served in the foreign service in Southeast Asia, refers to this memorial as an "open book" that "makes our honored dead people of that book."[2]

The decision to include these names harks back to earlier war memorials that inventoried the dead, including one at Yale in the Woolsey Hall Rotunda past which Lin walked nearly every day as a college student. It also looks forward to what has become a tradition in American memorialization. The Oklahoma City National Memorial includes 168 empty chairs, each bearing the name of a person killed in the terrorist attack on the Murrah Building in that city on April 19, 1995. The 9/11 memorial at Ground Zero in Lower Manhattan remembers each victim by name.

The Vietnam Veterans Memorial was the brainchild of Jan Scruggs, an infantry corporal who served in Vietnam. In 1979 he founded the Vietnam Veterans Memorial Fund (VVMF), which raised the necessary money, secured a site in Constitutional Gardens on the Mall in Washington, D.C., and sponsored a design competition that drew 1,421 submissions. In May 1981, a jury of eight architects and sculptors named Lin the winner.

Lin's design called for two polished black granite walls, meeting in a *V* at a 125-degree angle, with one wall pointing to the east at the Roman obelisk that is the Washington Monument and the other to the west at the Greek temple that is the Lincoln Memorial. These triangular walls were to taper over a distance of 200 feet each from 10 feet high at the apex down to a point entering the earth at the edge. The names would be etched into the granite chronologically, beginning in the center with the beginning of the war, moving to the right edge, starting up again on the left edge, and concluding with the end of the war in the center. In this way, the Vietnam War would become as much a part of the American conversation as Washington's Revolution and Lincoln's Civil War.

Lin saw her creation less as a sculpture than as a place—a place where Americans could go to think about the war without being told what to think and to speak with the dead without being told what to say. Her design, by refusing to offer an official statement about the war—initially it did not even include the word "Vietnam"—left it up to individual visitors to bring to the site their own understandings of the war.

Just as *Adventures of Huckleberry Finn* has stimulated debates about individual freedom versus community responsibility and about America's original sin of slavery, the Vietnam Veterans Memorial has sparked conversation about the propriety of the Vietnam War, and about war and peace more broadly. Initial responses to the design were quite positive, including among veterans groups. Conservative columnist James Kilpatrick, for example, predicted that "this will be the most moving war memorial ever erected; . . . each of us may remember what he wishes to remember—the cause, the heroism, the blunders, or the waste."[3] But all this was happening in the Reagan years, when U.S. politics was taking a sharp turn to the right and U.S. foreign policy was assuming a more aggressive posture. Angry over decades of liberal leadership in Washington, conservatives had launched a bitter culture war over, among other things, the legacy of the 1960s. Lin's design was caught in the crossfire, attacked by vocal Vietnam veterans, conservative columnists, Reagan administration officials, and Republican legislators.

Critics denounced the proposed memorial as a "black gash of shame and sorrow."[4] They read the *V*-shape as a peace sign—a thumbs-up in minimalist code to the antiwar movement, and a middle finger to Reagan's notion of the Vietnam War as a "noble cause." Journalist Tom Wolfe denounced the wall as "a tribute to Jane Fonda."[5] The *National Review* labeled it an "Orwellian glop."[6] Congressman

Henry Hyde (R-IL) called it a "Black Hole of Calcutta."[7] James Webb, a Vietnam veteran who would later serve as a U.S. Senator from Virginia, foresaw "a wailing wall for future anti-draft and anti-nuclear demonstrators."[8] Columnist Patrick Buchanan spread rumors about a Communist sympathizer on the jury.[9] And a letter to the editor of the *Washington Post* compared the winning design to "an outside urinal of German beer garden design."[10] Other critics called Lin's project inane, meaningless, elitist, depressing, perverse, and insulting.

Opponents advanced five main objections to the design. First, it was black rather than white, the color of most other monuments and memorials on the Mall. Tom Carhart, a West Point graduate, Vietnam veteran, and unsuccessful entrant in the design competition, was particularly fixated on the color, referring to the proposed memorial as a "black trench" and a "black pit" while insisting that black is "the universal color of shame and sorrow and degradation."[11] Second, it was below ground level, which signified to opponents something shameful, hidden, and buried away. Third, it was abstract. What was needed was a realistic and heroic design—something more like the Iwo Jima Memorial, depicting soldiers triumphantly raising the American flag. Fourth, it was for elites rather than ordinary soldiers—"something for New York intellectuals," in the words of businessman Ross Perot, who put up $160,000 for the design competition but later withdrew his support.[12] Finally, and most important, opponents argued that the design was antiwar. According to the competition's rules, the memorial was supposed to be apolitical, and Lin consistently maintained that her memorial said nothing about the propriety of the Vietnam War. Nonetheless, opponents believed that her refusal to sanctify the war as noble was tantamount to labeling it ignoble.

Supporters responded by referring to the proposed memorial as pure, beautiful, and eloquent in its simplicity. But the objections gathered force. In January 1982, Interior Secretary James Watt informed the VVMF that he would not approve permits for the memorial until some modifications had been made. Changing the color of the wall was off the table after George Price, a retired African-American general, testified at a January 1982 meeting about the meaning of black. "Black is not a color of shame," he insisted. "Color meant nothing on the battlefields of Korea and Vietnam. . . . Color should mean nothing now."[13] Opponents continued to press for other changes, however, and they got what they wanted when the powers that be in Congress, the VVMF, the Reagan administration, and the Commission of Fine Arts (the federal agency overseeing the project) agreed to add to the design an American flag and a realistic statue of soldiers by the sculptor Frederick Hart.

By early 1982, Scruggs was referring to the memorial as a "political football."[14] Others gravitated toward a more martial metaphor, observing that this contest over the shape of the memorial, the legacy of the Vietnam War, and the meaning of America itself now amounted to an "art war." Architect Harry Weese, who had served on the jury that chose Lin's design, blasted the Reagan administration for making art by subcommittee. "It's as if Michelangelo had the Secretary of the Interior climb onto the scaffold and muck around with his work," he said.[15] Others charged that opponents were motivated less by artistic or even political calculations than by sexism, racism, and anti-intellectualism. (Lin, after all, was a woman, an Asian American, and a Yalie.)

Breaking a long silence, Lin told the *Washington Post* in July 1982 that the controversy was a "farce," but she saved her harshest words for Hart, whom she accused of "drawing mustaches on other people's portraits." The memorial, she argued, should be built as designed: "Past a certain point . . . it's not worth compromising. It becomes nothing."[16] Hart responded in kind. "It doesn't relate to ordinary people and I don't like art that is contemptuous of life," he said of Lin's project. "Lin's piece is a serene exercise in contemporary art done in a vacuum with no knowledge of the subject. It's nihilistic—that's its appeal."[17] Later that year, at an October meeting on the compromise, Lin again dug in:

> *What is realistic? Is any one man's interpretation better able to convey an idea than any other's? Should it not be left to the observer? The original design gives each individual the freedom to reflect upon the heroism and sacrifice of those who served. It is symbolic of individual freedom, which this country stands for.*

Lin then insisted that the visitor's experience of the memorial "should not be interrupted visually by the abrupt verticality of a flag pole, or conceptually by a sculpture that forces a specific interpretation."[18]

In the end, political rather than artistic calculations carried the day. The powers that be agreed to add a statue and a flag, so a statue and a flag it would be. The question was where these additions would be placed. Conservative critics wanted them atop and at the center of the original design, which Lin said would turn her piece into a mere "retaining wall."[19] Ultimately, the Commission of Fine

Arts decided to place both elements at some distance from "The Wall," as Lin's design was coming to be called.

This outcome—"a political pastiche of heroism and loss," wrote columnist Ellen Goodman—frustrated almost everyone. But Goodman thought this frustration was appropriate for a conflict that had divided the nation like no other since the Civil War. "Instead of a resolution, we have an artistic collision of ideas, an uncomfortable collage of our Vietnam legacy," she wrote. "Maybe, just maybe, that's fitting."[20]

One hundred and fifty thousand people attended the dedication of the Vietnam Veterans Memorial on November 13, 1982. Almost immediately, the controversy dissipated. Kilpatrick, one of Lin's most stalwart supporters, had predicted that the memorial would "pack an unforgettable wallop."[21] It did. Veterans and their loved ones came by the thousands, and by the thousands they wept. Long before Hart's statue, *The Three Soldiers,* was dedicated on November 11, 1984, the Vietnam Veterans Memorial had become the most emotionally charged site in the nation's capital and one of the most frequently visited. It was featured on the covers of *Newsweek* and *Time* and soon was drawing over 3 million visitors annually.

But the controversy was not over. On November 11, 1993, the Vietnam Women's Memorial, depicting three uniformed women attending to a wounded male soldier, was dedicated on the site over Lin's strenuous objections. But The Wall remains the beating heart of the memorial, drawing visitors away from the proliferating statuary to an emotional encounter with the names.

Today this memorial is an American Lourdes—a pilgrimage site where the living come to commune with the dead and to reckon with their own mortality in the medium of the mirror that is The Wall. When visitors approach, they do so slowly, as if entering into the aura of St. Peter's Cathedral. When they break the reverential silence that amplifies the site, they speak in hushed tones. If The Wall is simple, it is deceptively so, since it invites all sorts of complex and contradictory interpretations.

According to architect William Hubbard, "The Vietnam monument does not speak."[22] But it does. Most plainly, it speaks its names. But it has more to say than that. Lin was influenced, as were many baby boomers, by the view that Americans are death deniers, turning a blind eye to the undeniable fact of mortality. More than any other voice in America today, Lin's memorial shouts down that denial. It does not say, with General Sherman, that "war is hell." It does insist, however, that war has a cost. Whether war is worth that cost neither Lin nor her memorial will say. But the site—"the saddest place in America"—insists that the costs of war must be counted, at a minimum, in the lives of the individual soldiers it claims as its own.[23] "The most successful memorials of modern times have . . . not been about victory as such but about the single, incontrovertible truth of war: that it kills a lot of people," writes architecture historian Vincent Scully. That is why this memorial is in his estimation "America's greatest such monument—if we except the battlefields themselves."[24]

The Vietnam Veterans Memorial may not have healed the nation, as Scruggs had hoped, but it is therapy in stone to those who come to find a name, to touch and kiss it, to pray or throw back a beer, and perhaps to leave behind letters, photographs, dog tags, or combat boots—objects initially classified as "lost and found," but now saved each day by National Park Service rangers. Early critics described the wall as an open wound, and Lin had conceived of it from the start as a cut into the earth, with the black granite side stanching the wound. The wound inflicted on America's body politic by the Vietnam conflict remains. But there is healing of a sort in airing the antagonisms that this war engendered. Was it a noble cause or an unjust war of imperial aggression? Are the soldiers who died in it heroes or victims or both? Is the United States a land of the free, or has its commitment to freedom given way to commitments to lesser things?

Like other books in *The American Bible*, the Vietnam Veterans Memorial speaks with many voices. James Webb called it "a Rorschach for what you think about Vietnam."[25] As Lin intended, you can read into it what you will. Part of what makes a book a classic is its ability to be interpreted in different ways—a desideratum for any text that wants to be heard across time and space. The Vietnam Veterans Memorial does just that. Critics call it ambiguity. Defenders call it art. But it is also the way of the American Bible.

Vietnam Veterans Memorial ❧

DALE R BUIS * CHESTER M OVNARD * MAURICE W FLOURNOY * ALFONS A BANKOWSKI * FREDERICK T GARSIDE * RALPH W MAGEE * GLENN MATTESON * LESLIE V SAMPSON * EDGAR W WEITKAMP Jr * OSCAR B WESTON Jr * THEODORE G FELAND * GERALD M BIBER * JOHN M BISCHOFF * ODIS D ARNOLD * WALTER H MOON * BRUCE R JONES * FLOYD STUDER * JAMES T DAVIS * HERMAN K DURRWACHTER Jr *FRED M STEUER * TOM J CRESS * THEODORE J BERLETT * MILO B COGHILL * FERGUS C GROVES II * ROBERT D LARSON * JOSEPH M FAHEY Jr * FLOYD M FRAZIER * STANLEY G HARTSON * EDWARD K KISSAM Jr * JACK D LETOURNEAU * GLEN F MERRIHEW * LEWIS M WALLING Jr * ROBERT L WESTFALL   CHARLES A PULLIAM * AL SUMINGGUIT PADAYHAG * IVAN P WHITLOCK * MILTON D BRITTON * BARNEY KAATZ * JAMES GABRIEL Jr * WAYNE E MARCHAND * BILLIE L BEARD * RONALD E LEWIS * HEWETT F COE * GEORGE E COLLIER * ROBERT L GARDNER * WALTER R McCARTHY Jr * WILLIAM F TRAIN III * ROBERT L SIMPSON * DON J YORK * JOSEPH A GOLDBERG * HAROLD L GUTHRIE * JAMES E LANE[26]

COMMENTARY

Maya Lin, architect, describing the memorial in her winning application (1981)

Walking through this park-like area, the memorial appears as a rift in the earth—a long, polished, black stone wall, emerging from and receding into the earth. Approaching the memorial, the ground slopes gently downward, and the low walls emerging on either side, growing out of the earth, extend and converge at a point below and ahead. Walking into the grassy site contained by the walls of this memorial we can barely make out the carved names upon the memorial's walls. These names, seemingly infinite in number, convey the sense of overwhelming numbers, while unifying those individuals into a whole. For this memorial is meant not as a monument to the individual, but rather as a memorial to the men and women who died during this war, as a whole.

The memorial is composed not as an unchanging monument, but as a moving composition, to be understood as we move into and out of it; the passage itself is gradual, the descent to the origin slow, but it is at the origin that the meaning of this memorial is to [be] fully understood. At the intersection of these walls, on the right side, at this wall's top is carved the date of the first death. It is followed by the names of those who have died in the war, in chronological order. These names continue on this wall, appearing to recede into the earth at the wall's end. The names resume on the left wall, as the wall emerges from the earth, continuing back to the origin, where the date of the last death is carved, at the bottom of this wall. Thus the war's beginning and end meet; the war is "complete," coming full-circle, yet broken by the earth that bounds the angle's open side, and contained within the earth itself. As we turn to leave, we see these walls stretching into the distance, directing us to the Washington Monument to the left and the Lincoln Memorial to the right, thus bringing the Vietnam Memorial into historical context. We, the living, are brought to a concrete realization of these deaths.

Brought to a sharp awareness of such a loss, it is up to each individual to resolve or come to terms with this loss. For death is in the end a personal and private matter, and the area contained with this memorial is a quiet place meant for personal reflection and private reckoning. The black granite walls, each 200 feet long and 10 feet below ground at their lowest point (gradually ascending toward ground level) effectively act as a sound barrier, yet are of such a height and length so as not to appear threatening or enclosing. The actual area is wide and shallow; allowing for a sense of privacy and the sunlight from the memorial's southern exposure along with the grassy park surrounding and within its wall contribute to the serenity of the area. Thus this memorial is for those who have died, and for us to remember them.

—Maya Lin, *Boundaries* (New York: Simon & Schuster, 2000), p. 4:05.

Wolf Von Eckardt, art critic, refusing to label Lin's design abstract (1981)

It seemed too much to expect that a worthy memorial design could emerge from the mess that was Vietnam. But it did. . . . Lin's design has been called "minimal art," whatever that means. There is nothing minimal about this concept. Nor is it abstract, in the sense of being apart from human experience. It is, rather, a direct evocation of an emotional experience, which, one way or another, is what art is all about. Being unconventional—as unconventional as Stonehenge or the Eiffel Tower—the design may not instantly be grasped. . . . But once Lin's concept is experienced, it is hard to imagine any better solution to the problems a Vietnam Veterans Memorial poses.

—Wolf Von Eckardt, "Of Heart and Mind: Vietnam War Memorial; The Serene Grace of the Vietnam Memorial," *Washington Post,* May 16, 1981, p. B1.

Charles Krauthammer, columnist, calling the design "meaningless" (1981)

This memorial says one thing: only the dead, nothing besides, remain. Its purpose is to impress upon the visitor the sheer human waste, the utter meaningless of it all. It is an unfortunate choice of memorial. Memorials are built to give context and, possibly, meaning to suffering that is otherwise incomprehensible. We do not memorialize bus accidents, which by nature are contextless, meaningless. To treat the Vietnam dead like the victims of some monstrous traffic accident is more than a disservice to history.

—Charles Krauthammer, "Washington Diarist: Memorials," *New Republic,* May 23, 1981, p. 43.

James Kilpatrick, columnist, on the emotional impact of the memorial (1982)

Nothing I had heard or written had prepared me for the moment. I could not speak. I wept. . . . This memorial has a pile driver's impact. No politics. No recriminations. Nothing of vainglory or of glory either. . . . The memorial carries a message for all ages: this is what war is all about.

—James J. Kilpatrick, "The Names," *Washington Post,* September 21, 1982, p. A19.

Michael Scrogin, Baptist minister, praising the memorial as both "wailing wall" and "altar" (1983)

The memorial is a work of art, even great art. It evokes so much. It is a wailing wall. It is a mirror; in fact, one sees oneself reflected in its polished surface. It is an altar littered with the evidence of burdens laid down. . . . It is a symbol of the valley of the shadow of death. It is a last, enduring body count. It is a book of the generations—even as the Bible lists generations: "And this is the book of the generations of the sons of Noah: Ham, Shem, Japheth." And this is the book of the generations of Vietnam: Andrew, Robert, William. It is a Sphinx that will endlessly pose its riddle to those who seek power and will, let us pray, devour those who cannot answer or who answer poorly. It is a scar upon the monumental landscape of our capital; like all scars, it is at once evidence of a wound's healing and a reminder of its hurt.

—Michael Scrogin, "Symbol of the Valley of the Shadow," *Christian Century,* January 5–12, 1983, p. 8.

Ronald Reagan, fortieth U.S. president, urging forgiveness at the dedication of The Three Soldiers statue (1984)

It's been said that these memorials reflect a hunger for healing. Well, I do not know if perfect healing ever occurs, but I know that sometimes when a bone is broken, if it's knit together well, it will in the end be stronger than if it had not been broken. I believe that in the decade since Vietnam the healing has begun, and I hope that before my days as Commander in Chief are over the process will be completed.

There were great moral and philosophical disagreements about the rightness of the war, and we cannot forget them because there is no wisdom to be gained in forgetting. But we can forgive each other and ourselves for those things that we now recognize may have been wrong, and I think it's time we did.

—Ronald Reagan, "Remarks at the Dedication of *The Three Soldiers* Statue at the Vietnam Veterans Memorial," November 11, 1984, www.reagan.utexas.edu/archives/speeches/1984/111184a.htm.

Gloria Emerson, war correspondent, fantasizing about confronting the architects of war with the names of the dead (1985)

Do you know what I'd do? I'd chain all of [the politicians] to that haunting Vietnam memorial and have them read—slowly—every name aloud. Then the war would end for me. Take all of them, all of them who gave us the war—all of them who, like McNamara, began to doubt that the war could be won and still kept it going. Chain them to the memorial for several days, if need be, and have them read each name aloud. Wouldn't that be something? Justice at last.

—Quoted in "Hearts and Minds," *Newsweek,* April 15, 1985, p. 67.

Charles Griswold, philosopher, on the questions the memorial asks (1986)

The VVM is, in my opinion, fundamentally interrogative; it does *not* take a position as to the answers. It implies some terrible questions: Did these individuals die in vain? Was their death in keeping with our nation's best traditions as symbolized by the nearby monuments? For what and when should Americans die in war? That the person contemplating the monument is implicated in these questions is also emphasized by another crucial aspect of this memorial, namely that the polished black granite functions as a mirror. This fact gives added depth to the monument and mitigates any sense of its being a tomb. In looking at the names one cannot help seeing oneself looking at them. On a bright day one also sees the reflections of the Washington or Lincoln memorials along with one's own reflection. The dead and living thus meet, and the living are forced to ask whether those names should be on that wall, and whether others should die in similar causes. You are forced to wonder where you were then and what role you played in the war.

—Charles L. Griswold, "The Vietnam Veterans Memorial and the Washington Mall: Philosophical Thoughts on Political Iconography," *Critical Inquiry* 12.4 (Summer 1986): 711.

Bill Clinton, forty-second U.S. president, invoking Lincoln's Second Inaugural in an effort to bind up the wounds caused by the Vietnam War (1993)

Some have suggested that it is wrong for me to be here with you today because I did not agree a quarter of a century ago with the decision made to send the young men and women to battle in Vietnam. Well, so much the better. Here we are celebrating America today. Just as war is freedom's cost, disagreement is freedom's privilege, and we honor it here today. But I ask all of you to remember the words that have been said here today. And I ask you at this monument: . . . can any Commander in Chief be in any other place but here on this day? I think not.

Many volumes have been written about this war and those complicated times. But the message of this memorial is quite simple: These men and women fought for freedom, brought honor to their communities, loved their country, and died for it. They were known to all of us. There's not a person in this crowd today who did not know someone on this wall. Four of my high school classmates are there. Four who shared with me the joys and trials of childhood and did not live to see the three score and ten years the Scripture says we are entitled to.

Let us continue to disagree, if we must, about the war. But let us not let it divide us as a people any longer.

You heard General Powell quoting President Lincoln: "With malice toward none and charity for all let us bind up the nation's wounds." Lincoln speaks to us today across the years. Let us resolve to take from this haunting and beautiful memorial a renewed sense of our national unity and purpose, a deepened gratitude for the sacrifice of those whose names we touched and whose memories we revere, and a finer dedication to making America a better place for their children and for our children, too.

—William J. Clinton, "Remarks at a Memorial Day Ceremony at the Vietnam Veterans Memorial," May 31, 1993, www.presidency.ucsb.edu/ws/index.php?pid=46641.

GOSPELS

First Inaugural Address

❧ THOMAS JEFFERSON, 1801 ❧

U.S. POLITICAL LIFE is pockmarked by culture wars—passionate and often bitter contests over what America means and who are its rightful heirs. It is also marked by repeated efforts to defuse these partisan passions. Patrick Henry, in an era when factionalism was based on region rather than party, told his fellow delegates at the First Continental Congress in 1774: "The distinctions between Virginians, Pennsylvanians, New Yorkers, and New Englanders, are no more. I am not a Virginian, but an American."[1] In 1861, Lincoln concluded his First Inaugural Address with: "We are not enemies, but friends. We must not be enemies."[2] Closer to our own time, Illinois Senator Barack Obama said at the 2004 Democratic National Convention: "There's not a liberal America and a conservative America—there's the United States of America. There's not a black America and white America and Latino America and Asian America—there's the United States of America."[3] However, the most remarkable of these efforts at bipartisanship, and the one they all recall, is the First Inaugural Address of Thomas Jefferson (1743–1826).

In seventeenth-century England, writes historian Richard Hofstadter, "Party was associated with painfully deep and unbridgeable differences in national politics, with religious bigotry and clerical animus, with treason and the threat of foreign invasion, with instability and dangers to liberty." America's founders too "looked upon parties as sores on the body politic."[4] George Washington, in his 1796 Farewell Address of September, had delivered a stern warning "against the baneful effects of the spirit of party." The emergent party system, which pitted his Federalists against Jefferson's Republicans (also known as the Democratic-Republicans), was in his view the "worst enemy" of good government—a "fire not to be quenched."[5] But Washington's warning did not put out this unquenchable fire, which scorched the political landscape in the angriest presidential campaign in American history.

In the election of 1800, which makes early twenty-first century Republican-Democratic acrimony look like country club bridge, character assassination was the order of the day. Federalists accused Jefferson of all sorts of infidelities to God and country. Massachusetts Federalist Theophilus Parsons called him the "great arch priest of Jacobinism and infidelity."[6] The *Connecticut Courant* intimated that he might be a secret Jew or Muslim.[7] Another Federalist stalwart, Alexander Hamilton (whose advocacy of a national bank would eventually land him on the ten-dollar bill), spoke of saving America from the "fangs of Jefferson" even as Republicans spoke of saving the nation from the "talons of Monarchists."[8] Soon each side was openly questioning whether America could survive rule by the opposing party. "The country is so divided and agitated, as to be in some danger of civil commotions," Secretary of the Treasury Oliver Wolcott told Hamilton.[9] According to the *Connecticut Courant,* there was "scarcely a possibility that we shall escape a civil war."[10]

Jefferson and his running mate, Aaron Burr, defeated John Adams and his running mate, Charles Pinckney, but in this era where the electoral college did not distinguish between presidential and vice-presidential votes (a mess later cleaned up by the Twelfth Amendment), Jefferson and Burr tied, so the election was thrown into the Federalist-heavy House. As House members burned through ballot after ballot without a winner, many feared that America's first culture war would devolve into an actual war. After thirty-six ballots, however, the House awarded the presidency to Jefferson.

Adams left town in a huff on the morning of Jefferson's inauguration, a pomp-free affair that saw America's third president walking from his boardinghouse to the Capitol building, dressed as "a plain citizen, without any distinctive badge of office."[11] Would Jefferson meet pique with pique?

Jefferson was the "American Sphinx"; though he wrote "all men are created equal," he owned slaves, and he likely fathered children with Sally Hemings, a slave at Monticello.[12] But there is no mystery about Jefferson's intellect. A renowned polymath, Jefferson was one of America's great writers and thinkers. So much so that President Kennedy famously quipped, at a White House dinner for Nobel Prize winners, that he was grateful to find himself among "the most extraordinary collection of talent, of human knowledge, that has ever been gathered together at the White House, with the possible exception of when Thomas Jefferson dined alone." According to Kennedy, the Man from Monticello "could calculate an eclipse, survey an estate, tie an artery, plan an edifice, try a cause, break a horse, and dance the minuet."[13] What he could not do was speak in public. In fact, his inaugural address, the first in the new capital city of Washington, D.C., was barely audible. But he gave the Washington *National Intelligencer* a copy of the speech, which was published the same day and widely reprinted. A Philadelphia broadside used capital letters to call attention to what everyone immediately recognized as the heart of the address: "WE ARE ALL REPUBLICANS; WE ARE ALL FEDERALISTS."[14]

Was this speech as conciliatory as this sentence sounds—"a lofty appeal for the restoration of harmony and affection"?[15] Or was it "a partisan act of the most ingenious kind"—a cynical effort to co-opt his opponents?[16] Or were Jefferson's words, as Noah Webster—ever the agitated Federalist—argued, "susceptible . . . of a double construction"?[17]

In his address, Jefferson outlines his domestic and foreign policies, including: "Peace, commerce, and honest friendship with all nations, entangling alliances with none" and "the support of the state governments in all their rights, as the most competent administrations for our domestic concerns, and the surest bulwarks against anti-republican tendencies." He let it be known that he was going to kill the Alien and Sedition Acts, which had been used to stifle Jeffersonian newspapers. And he spoke plainly of the power of reason to combat error under circumstances of free speech and toleration. But he also took pains to reconcile himself to his political enemies. Or, as Chief Justice John Marshall, who administered the presidential oath at the inauguration, wrote of the speech: "It is in general well judged and conciliatory. It is in direct terms giving the lie to the violent party declamation which has elected him."[18]

In fact, under the circumstances, it was a remarkably conciliatory speech— "better liked by our party than his own," in the words of Massachusetts Federalist George Cabot.[19] Jefferson included in his outline of the "creed of our political faith" some of the core concerns of his Federalist opponents, including "the honest payment of our debts and sacred preservation of the public faith." Addressing (albeit indirectly) fears of many New England clergy that God would withdraw His blessing from America if an infidel were elected president, he referred to the United States as "a chosen country" and concluded his address with a prayer. Most important, Jefferson urged his fellow Americans to "unite in common efforts for the common good." In first-person-plural rhetoric, which Lincoln would later employ in his Gettysburg Address, Jefferson said, "Let us then, fellow citizens, unite with one heart and one mind, let us restore to social intercourse that harmony and affection without which liberty, and even life itself, are but dreary things. . . . Every difference of opinion is not a difference of principle. We have called by different names brethren of the same principle. We are all republicans: we are all federalists."

Over the course of U.S. history, Jefferson's First Inaugural has been widely praised. Biographer Fawn Brodie called the speech "one of the great seminal papers in American political history" and assessed its impact as "almost Biblical."[20] Nonetheless, the "revolution of 1800," as Jefferson called it, was not so revolutionary as he claimed.[21]

Jefferson's message of unity did not turn the apocalypse of the election into a peaceful millennium in which the demon of political discord was bound and gagged for a thousand years (or even one). Newspapers did not repent of their partisanship. Politicians still preached hatred and revenge. And each party continued to accuse the other of betraying the Constitution. Some in his own party accused Jefferson of selling out. Some in the opposition accused him of hypocrisy, since the road Jefferson charted here was by no means a middle path. Like Washington before him, he saw factionalism ending not because the two parties would learn to get along but because one of them would go away. In fact, in an 1802 letter Jefferson spoke of his desire to "sink federalism into an abyss from which there shall be no resurrection."[22] Which is precisely what happened. Though Federalists controlled national politics from the founding to the election of 1800, they never again controlled the White House, House, or Senate.

The election of 1800 bequeathed to the country a two-party system that would continue to produce culture wars for centuries to come. But Jefferson's First Inaugural is rightly remembered for its call for national reconciliation. It may not be, as one Jefferson biographer has claimed, that this address "will always be to good government what the Sermon on the Mount is to religion."[23] But it is scripture of a sort. It remains the gold standard for Americans seeking to knit the nation together across party lines.

First Inaugural Address 🦅

Friends and Fellow Citizens,

Called upon to undertake the duties of the first Executive office of our country, I avail myself of the presence of that portion of my fellow citizens which is here assembled to express my grateful thanks for the favor with which they have been pleased to look towards me, to declare a sincere consciousness that the task is above my talents, and that I approach it with those anxious and awful presentiments which the greatness of the charge, and the weakness of my powers so justly inspire. A rising nation, spread over a wide and fruitful land, traversing all the seas with the rich productions of their industry, engaged in commerce with nations who feel power and forget right, advancing rapidly to destinies beyond the reach of mortal eye; when I contemplate these transcendent objects, and see the honour, the happiness, and the hopes of this beloved country committed to the issue and the auspices of this day, I shrink from the contemplation and humble myself before the magnitude of the undertaking. Utterly indeed should I despair, did not the presence of many, whom I here see, remind me, that, in the other high authorities provided by our Constitution, I shall find resources of wisdom, of virtue, and of zeal, on which to rely under all difficulties. To you, then, gentlemen, who are charged with the sovereign functions of legislation, and to those associated with you, I look with encouragement for that guidance and support which may enable us to steer with safety the vessel in which we are all embarked, amidst the conflicting elements of a troubled world.

During the contest of opinion through which we have past, the animation of discussions and of exertions has sometimes worn an aspect which might impose on strangers unused to think freely, and to speak and to write what they think; but this being now decided by the voice of the nation, announced according to the rules of the Constitution all will of course arrange themselves under the will of the law, and unite in common efforts for the common good.

All too will bear in mind this sacred principle, that though the will of the majority is in all cases to prevail, that will, to be rightful, must be reasonable; that the minority possess their equal rights, which equal laws must protect, and to violate would be oppression. Let us then, fellow citizens, unite with one heart and one mind, let us restore to social intercourse that harmony and affection without which liberty, and even life itself, are but dreary things.

And let us reflect that having banished from our land that religious intolerance under which mankind so long bled and suffered, we have yet gained little if we countenance a political intolerance as despotic, as wicked, and capable of as bitter and bloody persecutions. During the throes and convulsions of the ancient world, during the agonising spasms of infuriated man, seeking through blood and slaughter his long lost liberty, it was not wonderful that the agitation of the billows should reach even this distant and peaceful shore; that this should be more felt and feared by some and less by others; and should divide opinions as to measures of safety; but every difference of opinion is not a difference of principle. We have called by different names brethren of the same principle. We are all republicans: we are all federalists.

If there be any among us who would wish to dissolve this Union, or to change its republican form, let them stand undisturbed as monuments of the safety with which error of opinion may be tolerated, where reason is left free to combat it. I know indeed that some honest men fear that a republican government cannot be strong; that this government is not strong enough. But would the honest patriot, in the full tide of successful experiment, abandon a government which has so far kept us free and firm, on the theoretic and visionary fear, that this government, the world's best hope,[a,b] may, by possibility, want energy to preserve itself? I trust not.

I believe this, on the contrary, the strongest government on earth. I believe it the only one, where every man, at the call of the law, would fly to the standard of the law, and would meet invasions of the public order as his own personal concern.—Sometimes it is said that man cannot be trusted

a. Abraham Lincoln, sixteenth U.S. president, conjuring Jefferson's phrase in an appeal for perseverance during the Civil War (1862): The fiery trial through which we pass will light us down, in honor or dishonor, to the latest generation. We say that we are for the Union. The world will not forget that we say this. We know how to save the Union. The world knows we do know how to save it. We—even we here—hold the power and bear the responsibility. In giving freedom to the slave, we assure freedom to the free—honorable alike in what we give and what we preserve. We shall nobly save or meanly lose the last, best hope of earth. —Abraham Lincoln, "Annual Message to Congress," December 1, 1862, in John G. Nicolay and John Hay, eds., *Abraham Lincoln: Complete Works* (New York: Century, 1894), 2:276–77.

b. Bill Clinton, forty-second U.S. president, defining the hope of America during the two-hundredth birthday celebration of the Capitol (1993): This is a moment of unity in this great city of ours so often known for its conflicts. In this moment, we all agree, we know in our minds and feel in our hearts the words that Thomas Jefferson spoke in the first Inaugural Address ever given on these grounds. He said that people of little faith were doubtful about America's future, but he believed our Government was the world's best hope. What was that hope? The hope that still endures that in this country every man and woman without regard to race or region or station in life would have the freedom to live up to the fullest of his or her God-given potential; the hope that every citizen would get from Government not a guarantee but the promise of an opportunity to do one's best, to have an equal chance, for the most humble and the most well born, to do what God meant for them to be able to do. —William J. Clinton, "Remarks on the 200th Anniversary of the Capitol and the Reinstallation of the Statue of Freedom," October 23, 1993, www.presidency.ucsb.edu/ws/index.php?pid=46006.

with the government of himself. Can he then be trusted with the government of others? Or have we found angels, in the form of kings, to govern him? Let history answer this question.

Let us then, with courage and confidence, pursue our own federal and republican principles; our attachment to union and representative government. Kindly separated by nature and a wide ocean from the exterminating havoc of one quarter of the globe; too high minded to endure the degradations of the others, possessing a chosen country, with room enough for our descendants to the thousandth and thousandth generation, entertaining a due sense of our equal right to the use of our own faculties, to the acquisitions of our own industry, to honor and confidence from our fellow citizens, resulting not from birth, but from our actions and their sense of them, enlightened by a benign religion, professed indeed and practised in various forms, yet all of them inculcating honesty, truth, temperance, gratitude and the love of man, acknowledging and adoring an overruling providence, which by all its dispensations proves that it delights in the happiness of man here, and his greater happiness hereafter; with all these blessings, what more is necessary to make us a happy and a prosperous people?

Still one thing more, fellow citizens, a wise and frugal government, which shall restrain men from injuring one another, shall leave them otherwise free to regulate their own pursuits of industry and improvement, and shall not take from the mouth of labor the bread it has earned. This is the sum of good government; and this is necessary to close the circle of our felicities.

About to enter, fellow citizens, on the exercise of duties which comprehend every thing dear and valuable to you, it is proper you should understand what I deem the essential principles of our government, and consequently those which ought to shape its administration. I will compress them within the narrowest compass they will bear, stating the general principle, but not all its limitations.

Equal and exact justice to all men, of whatever state or persuasion, religious or political:—peace, commerce, and honest friendship with all nations, entangling alliances with none:[c]—the support

---

c. James Monroe, fifth U.S. president, articulating the Monroe Doctrine (1823): In the wars of the European powers in matters relating to themselves we have never taken any part, nor does it comport with our policy so to do. It is only when our rights are invaded or seriously menaced that we resent injuries or make preparation for our defense. With the movements in this hemisphere we are of necessity more immediately connected, and by causes which must be obvious to all enlightened and impartial observers. The political system of the allied powers is essentially different in this respect from that of America. This difference proceeds from that which exists in their respective Governments; and to the defence of our own, which has been achieved by the loss of so much blood and treasure, and matured by the wisdom of their most enlightened citizens, and under which we have enjoyed unexampled felicity, this whole nation is devoted. We owe it, therefore, to

of the state governments in all their rights, as the most competent administrations for our domestic concerns, and the surest bulwarks against anti-republican tendencies:—the preservation of the General government in its whole constitutional vigor, as the sheet anchor of our peace at home, and safety abroad: a jealous care of the right of election by the people, a mild and safe corrective of abuses which are lopped by the sword of revolution where peaceable remedies are unprovided:—absolute acquiescence in the decisions of the majority, the vital principle of republics, from which is no appeal but to force, the vital principle and immediate parent of the despotism:—a well disciplined militia, our best reliance in peace, and for the first moments of war, till regulars may relieve them:—the supremacy of the civil over the military authority:—economy in the public expence, that labor may be lightly burthened:—the honest payment of our debts and sacred preservation of the public faith:—encouragement of agriculture, and of commerce as its handmaid:—the diffusion of information, and arraignment of all abuses at the bar of the public reason:—freedom of religion; freedom of the press; and freedom of person, under the protection of the Habeas Corpus:—and trial by juries impartially selected.

These principles form the bright constellation, which has gone before us and guided our steps through an age of revolution and reformation. The wisdom of our sages, and blood of our heroes have been devoted to their attainment:—they should be the creed of our political faith; the text of civic instruction, the touchstone by which to try the services of those we trust; and should we wander from them in moments of error or of alarm, let us hasten to retrace our steps, and to regain the road which alone leads to peace, liberty and safety.

I repair then, fellow citizens, to the post you have assigned me. With experience enough in subordinate offices to have seen the difficulties of this the greatest of all, I have learnt to expect that it will rarely fall to the lot of imperfect man to retire from this station with the reputation, and the favor, which bring him into it. Without pretensions to that high confidence you reposed in our first and greatest revolutionary character, whose pre-eminent services had entitled him to the first place in his country's love, and destined for him the fairest page in the volume of faithful history, I ask so much confidence only as may give firmness and effect to the legal administration of your affairs. I shall often go wrong through defect of judgment. When right, I shall often be thought wrong by those whose positions will not command a view of the whole ground. I ask your indulgence for my own errors, which will never be intentional; and your support against

candour and to the amicable relations existing between the United States and those powers to declare that we should consider any attempt on their part to extend their system to any portion of this hemisphere as dangerous to our peace and safety. With the existing colonies or dependencies of any European power we have not interfered and shall not interfere. —James Monroe, "State of the Union," December 2, 1823, http://teaching americanhistory.org/library/index.asp?document=1225.

the errors of others, who may condemn what they would not if seen in all its parts. The approbation implied by your suffrage, is a great consolation to me for the past; and my future solicitude will be, to retain the good opinion of those who have bestowed it in advance, to conciliate that of others by doing them all the good in my power, and to be instrumental to the happiness and freedom of all.

Relying then on the patronage of your good will, I advance with obedience to the work, ready to retire from it whenever you become sensible how much better choices it is in your power to make. And may that infinite power, which rules the destinies of the universe, lead our councils to what is best, and give them a favorable issue for your peace and prosperity.[24]

COMMENTARY

Alexander Hamilton, founding father and leading Federalist, approving Jefferson's address (1801)

In referring to this speech, we think it proper to make a public declaration of our approbation of its contents. We view it as virtually a candid retraction of past misapprehensions, and a pledge to the community, that the new President will not lend himself to dangerous innovations, but in essential points will tread in the steps of his predecessors. . . .

—Alexander Hamilton, "Address, to the Electors of the State of New-York," March 21, 1801, in John C. Hamilton, ed., *The Works of Alexander Hamilton* (New York: Trow, 1851), 7:740.

Noah Webster, lexicographer and ardent Federalist, criticizing Jefferson's speech (1801)

You tell us that "every difference of opinion is not a difference of principle; that we are all Republicans—all Federalists." It follows from these declarations, that, in your opinion, the parties have contended not for *principles,* but for *unimportant opinions.* . . . But this concession criminates you and your friends; for unimportant concerns can never justify men in violent and animated exertions to change an administration.

—Noah Webster Jr., "A Letter to the President of the United States," in *Miscellaneous Papers, on Political and Commercial Subjects* (New York: Beldon, 1802), p. 4.

Benjamin Rush, physician and founding father,
lauding Jefferson's magnanimity (1801)

You have opened a new era by your speech on the 4th of March in the history of the United States. Never have I seen the public mind more generally or more agreeably affected by any publication. Old friends who had been separated by party names and a *supposed* difference of *principle* in politics for many years shook hands with each other immediately after reading it, and discovered, for the first time, that they had differed in *opinion* only, about the best means of promoting the interests of their common country. It would require a page to contain the names of all the citizens (formerly called Federalists) who have spoken in the highest terms of your speech. . . . I need hardly tell you how much every sentiment and even word in it accord with my feelings and principles.

—Benjamin Rush to Thomas Jefferson, March 12, 1801, in L. H. Butterfield, ed., *Letters of Benjamin Rush* (Princeton, NJ: Princeton Univ. Press, 1951), 2:831.

Port Folio, *Federalist magazine, refusing the olive branch (1801)*

The federalist and the democrat are in a state of eternal hostility toward each other, as much as the dog and the cat, and it is to be hoped they never will be more congenial.

—"Domestic Occurrences," *Port Folio*, August 22, 1801, p. 270, quoted in Catherine O'Donnell Kaplan, *Men of Letters in the Early Republic* (Chapel Hill: Univ. of North Carolina Press, 2008), p. 164.

Quarterly Christian Spectator, *precursor to the* Yale Review *literary magazine, calling in Christ's name for an end to political partisanship (1835)*

A variety of causes have contributed to divide our citizens into hostile political parties. It is not our purpose to investigate the origin, the principles, or the comparative merits of these parties. We pronounce their very existence in a republic to be wrong, essentially wrong. They are injurious to religion, and dangerous to free governments. . . . If the citizens were under the influence of the gospel, mere difference of opinion on political subjects would not array them against each other in hostile bands. Instead of having the spirit of combatants, they would feel "like brethren of the same principle," and would say, in the language of a distinguished statesman, "We are all federalists, we are all republicans." . . .

Religion and civil policy, duty and interest, require that the spirit of party should be extinguished, and that the minds of the people should be brought under the influence of the spirit of the gospel; that all political combinations which retard the progress of moral reform should be done away, and that the energies of all men should be employed in promoting the kingdom of the Redeemer.

—"Christian Politics," *Quarterly Christian Spectator*, December 1, 1835, p. 540.

William Seward, incoming secretary of state, advising Abraham
Lincoln on a draft of his First Inaugural Address (1861)

Your case is quite like that of *Jefferson*. He brought the first Republican party into power against and over a party ready to resist and dismember the Government. Partisan as he was, he sank the partisan in the patriot, in his inaugural address; and propitiated his adversaries by declaring, "We are all Federalists; all Republicans." I could wish that you would think it wise to follow this example, in this crisis. Be sure that while all your administrative conduct will be in harmony with Republican principles and policy, you cannot lose the Republican party by practicing, in your advent to office, the magnanimity of a victor.

—William H. Seward to Abraham Lincoln, February 24, 1861, in Frederick W. Seward, *Seward at Washington* (New York: Derby and Miller, 1891), p. 512.

Henry Commager, historian, invoking Jefferson to
restore "liberalism's good name" (1979)

It is astonishing that the term liberal is now a dirty word. What are the distinguishing features of that liberalism that has now become so fashionable to regard with suspicion?

First, a passion for what Thomas Jefferson called "the illimitable freedom of the human mind" and an "uncompromising hostility of every form of tyranny over the minds of men," whether that be political, religious or military.

Second, a repudiation of the tyranny of ignorance, of poverty and of vice, because these deny or inhibit the exercise of true freedom.

Third, a faith in reason and in the ability of men to govern themselves when their minds are liberated by education and their judgments protected by the orderly processes of the law.

Fourth, respect for the dignity of every individual—a respect that requires equal rights and equal justice in law and society.

Fifth, an acceptance of the will of the majority as long as that will operates under the law, with respect for the rights and interests of minorities.

Sixth, a commitment to the principle that the earth belongs to the living, not the dead, and that while we have an obligation to preserve what is best in the past, our primary fiduciary obligation is to posterity.

It will not escape those familiar with American history that much of this agenda is also the agenda of conservatism. In the United States, liberalism and conservatism have been, from the beginning, two sides of the same coin, and our greatest liberals—Thomas Jefferson, Abraham Lincoln, and Franklin D. Roosevelt—also have been our greatest conservatives. . . .

By insisting on a hard and fast division between conservatives and liberals, between Republicans and Democrats, many of today's conservatives ignore the fact that since President Woodrow Wilson's Administration the two parties have wrestled themselves into each other's clothes.

It was Wilson who sponsored government intervention into the economy and who launched the nation on the road to world power; it was the Republican Party under Presidents Harding, Coolidge and Hoover that, by a kind of knee-jerk reaction, took refuge in "liberal" opposition to Big Government, a liberalism so extreme that it rejected government intervention even in the face of the greatest depression in our history.

In his first inaugural address, given in 1801, Thomas Jefferson said, "We are all republicans." We should heed his words. It is time to end the futile quarrel between "liberals" (who often demonstrate as little awareness of their own history as "conservatives") and conservatives. If our society is to recover the unity that it must have to survive, it must recognize that we are all Democrats, we are all Republicans, we are all federalists, we are all nationalists, we are all liberals, we are all conservatives.

—Henry Commager, "Restoring Liberalism's Good Name," *Boston Globe,* December 13, 1979, p. 21.

John Anderson, independent candidate for president, pressing beyond traditional political labels (1980)

The outdated quarrel between liberalism and conservatism, which the two major parties seem about to resume, has ceased to illuminate our most pressing public problems. . . . We are all liberals, we are all conservatives, we all believe that prosperity without justice is unacceptable, and that justice without prosperity is unattainable.

—"Remarks by Congressman John Anderson," *Proceedings of the National Governors' Association Annual Meeting 1980* (Washington, DC: National Governors' Association, 1981), p. 62.

Joseph Ellis, historian, reading Jefferson's speech (and Jefferson himself) as Manichaean to the core (1997)

But Jefferson did not really mean what Hamilton and all the other commentators thought they heard him say. Part of the problem was actually a matter of translation. In the version of his address printed in the *National Intelligencer* and then released to the newspapers throughout the country, the key passage read: "We are all Republicans—we are all Federalists." By capitalizing the operative terms, the printed version had Jefferson making a gracious statement about the overlapping goals of the two political parties. But in the handwritten version of the speech that Jefferson delivered, the key words were not capitalized. Jefferson was therefore referring not to the common ground shared by the two parties but to the common belief, shared by all American citizens, that a republican form of government and a federal bond among the states were most preferable. Since one would have been hard pressed to discover a handful of American citizens who disagreed with this observation, his statement was more a political platitude than an ideological concession. The impression that Jefferson had publicly retracted his previous statements about the party conflict as a moral struggle between the forces of light and the forces of darkness was, as it turned out, badly mistaken.

—Joseph J. Ellis, *American Sphinx: The Character of Thomas Jefferson* (New York: Knopf, 1997), p. 182.

Bill Clinton, forty-second U.S. president, invoking Jefferson after being asked whether the Supreme Court was stealing the 2000 election from Al Gore (2000)

We've had this happen before. In 1800 Thomas Jefferson was elected in a very divisive, highly partisan election. . . . He gave a very conciliatory Inaugural Address, saying, "We are all Federalists; we're all Republicans," and led to a whole new era in American politics, out of what was an exceedingly divisive election. . . .

So I think it depends upon whether the people believe that this whole thing plays out in a fair way. So that's why I've encouraged the American people to just relax, take a deep breath, recognize that a result of this kind is always possible in a democratic election that's hard-fought, and that the most important thing is that, when it's all said and done, that people believe that all the issues were resolved in a fair way.

—William J. Clinton, "Interview with Terence Hunt and Walter M. Mears of the Associated Press," November 14, 2000, www.presidency.ucsb.edu/ws/index.php?pid=1040.

Jeff Jacoby, conservative columnist, calling for unity after the Bush/Kerry election (2004)

For four years, Americans watched and listened as President Bush was demonized with a savagery unprecedented in modern American politics. For four years they saw him likened to Hitler and Goebbels, heard his supporters called brownshirts and racists, his administration dubbed "the 43rd Reich." For four years they took it all in: "Bush" spelled with a swastika instead of an "s," the depictions of the president as a drooling moron or a homicidal liar, the poisonous insults aimed at anyone who might consider voting for him. And then on Tuesday they turned out to vote and handed the haters a crushing repudiation.

Bush was reelected with the highest vote total in American history. He is the first president since 1988 to win a majority of the popular vote. He increased his 2000 tally by 8 million votes and saw his party not only keep its majorities in the House and Senate, but enlarge them. And he did it all in the face of an orgy of hatred. . . .

I told several colleagues on Tuesday that I knew what I was going to write if Kerry won the election. I would have said that the refusal of so many liberals and Democrats to accept Bush as a legitimate president had badly infected American politics since 2000, and that it would be disastrous if conservatives and Republicans allowed themselves to become equally envenomed. I planned to write that while I'd had many tough things to say about Kerry over the course of this campaign—and while I wasn't backing away from any of them—the voters had now spoken and their judgment had to be respected. When he took the oath of office, Kerry would become my president, too.

Well, Kerry didn't win, so this is a different column. But 55 million people voted for him, and that is no small thing. However much I may disagree with the choice they made, I don't regard those voters as fools or knaves or idiots. I regard them as fellow Americans. That is how we should all regard each other when an election season comes to a close.

In his concession speech yesterday, Kerry said that when he telephoned Bush to congratulate him, they spoke of "the desperate need for unity, for finding the common ground, coming together. Today I hope that we can begin the healing."

It was a furious contest for power, but the election is over, and the fury should end. We are all Republicans, we are all Democrats. And none of us should be seduced by the haters.

—Jeff Jacoby, "Big Loss for the Bush Haters," *Boston Globe,* November 4, 2004, p. 15.

First Inaugural Address

❧ FRANKLIN DELANO ROOSEVELT, 1933 ❧

*P*OLITICS IS ONLY intermittently a rational enterprise driven by policies and their efficient execution. Emotions drive its logic more often than data. Political masters such as Franklin Delano Roosevelt (1882–1945) and Ronald Reagan appeal to our hearts. Our feelings crown them the winners of debates and elections. As much as we like to believe that we vote based on our favorite candidates' plans or legislative accomplishments, we are far more likely to go with our gut, which itself is attuned to such intangibles as a smile or a laugh. The question, in other words, is not just whether we like their policies. It is whether we like (or loathe) them.

Over the course of U.S. history, many a candidate has gone far on fearmongering. Generations of politicians have wielded power based on anxieties about immigrants, Communists, terrorists, gays. Fear of African Americans was a staple of Democratic politics in the early twentieth century; fear of Islam is a staple of Republican politics today. But fear will take you only so far. All of the nation's most revered political figures have exuded optimism. Barack Obama rode to the White House on the back of a can-do mantra: "Yes We Can." This same spirit animated the presidential campaigns of the "Man from Hope" Bill Clinton. But both Obama and Clinton drew in turn on the modern-day master of hope, Ronald Reagan, while Reagan learned at the feet of Franklin Delano Roosevelt.[1]

In terms of policy, Roosevelt and Reagan were obviously miles apart. For Roosevelt, an unprecedented expansion of the federal government was the solution to the problem of the Great Depression. And that problem was brought on by fat-cat financiers. For Reagan, big government was the problem, and entrepreneurs the solution.

But why sweat the small stuff? Both Roosevelt and Reagan understood that politics really isn't about arguments. Both knew that success in their profession turned on the blink rather than the long view. Each had a sense of humor, moral clarity, personal charm, an awareness of his own intellectual limits, and firm faith in the goodwill of the American people. Each was a powerful public speaker (Roosevelt on the radio, Reagan on television). Perhaps most important, each knew how to lead, and when he did the American people followed. Churchill famously said that meeting Roosevelt was "like opening your first bottle of champagne."[2] Even his political opponents said similar things about Reagan's effervescent personality, which bubbled over with hope, optimism, purpose, and pride. In other words, if FDR gave the conservative revolution of the Reagan years the demons against which it would define itself—liberalism and the New Deal— he also gave Reagan the style and spirit that each "next Ronald Reagan" would find so difficult to reproduce. And nowhere is that style, and that spirit, more evident than in Roosevelt's First Inaugural Address of March 4, 1933.

The election of 1932 had been fought to a great extent over the role the federal government should play in the U.S. economy. Very little, said Hoover. Lots, said Roosevelt, who in his acceptance speech at the Democratic National Convention had pledged "a new deal for the American people." American voters opted overwhelmingly for Roosevelt, who captured 472 electoral votes to Hoover's 59. So FDR had every reason to be proud as he stood to deliver his inauguration day speech.

The American people, by contrast, had every reason to be fearful. In an era before food stamps and Social Security, two out of every five Americans were out of work. Farm prices were collapsing. Factories were closing. The banking system was convulsing. The stock market, which had put an end to the Roaring Twenties by diving on "Black Thursday," October 24, 1929, was still searching for a bottom. Meanwhile, Fascism, Communism, and Nazism loomed overseas.

Into this grim situation rode the Ronald Reagan of the 1930s, and what he brought was optimism. In a speech that inaugurated the longest presidency in American history, Roosevelt mentioned policies and made proposals. But what he really did was provide hope. In the eighteenth century, political theorist Edmund Burke had written, "No passion so effectually robs the mind of all its powers of acting and reasoning as *fear*."[3] FDR was determined to rob fear of these powers. "This is a national consecration," Roosevelt began, in homiletic language, and then got right to the point: "So, first of all, let me assert my belief that the only thing we have to fear is fear itself—nameless, unreasoning, unjustified terror which paralyzes needed efforts to convert retreat into advance."

This line, one of the most often quoted in the annals of American politics, would come to symbolize FDR's presidency, so it should not be surprising that there are disagreements over how Roosevelt came to utter it. The speech was drafted by Raymond Moley, a Columbia University law professor and part of Roosevelt's "brain trust." But according to Moley this line originated with Louis Howe, FDR's closest adviser and "the President's Other I."[4] It is not clear where Howe got these lines. Henry David Thoreau, in his journal for September 7, 1851, had written, "Nothing is so much to be feared as fear," and similar views had been expressed earlier by Montaigne ("The thing I fear most is fear") and Francis Bacon ("Nothing is terrible except fear itself").[5] Closer to Roosevelt's time, Julius Barnes, chairman of the board of the National Chamber of Commerce had said in a 1931 news conference, "In a condition of this kind, the thing to be feared most is fear itself."[6]

Who gets credit for this line matters less, however, than the effect it had on the American people. Although Roosevelt was not the father of his country, he told his fellow citizens the sort of thing parents are always telling their children: everything is going to be okay. Then, standing tall with neither top hat nor overcoat to protect him from the chill wind, he delivered the bad news in a long and sorry litany: moribund industry, frozen farm markets, lost savings, rising taxes, skyrocketing unemployment. "Only a foolish optimist can deny the dark realities of the moment," he said grimly.

Roosevelt quoted from the Bible—in times like these, how could he not?— but he refused to launch into a typical jeremiad. He would not follow the example of Woodrow Wilson, who shook his finger at the American people in his moralistic inaugural address. Neither would he attribute their troubles to God. "We are stricken by no plague of locusts," he said, and "the American people have not failed." Whatever plagues had stricken the nation had come at the hands of the "money changers"—a reference to Mark 11:15, where an enraged Jesus runs the "money changers" out of the Jerusalem temple.

Today Roosevelt's First Inaugural is remembered for "we have nothing to fear but fear itself," perhaps because these words came to be applied to the president's personal battle with polio, which eventually restricted him to a wheelchair. But in the spring of 1933 it was Roosevelt's preaching against the "rulers of the exchange" and the "evils of the old order" that got the presses rolling. Significantly, Roosevelt included no broadside here against capitalism. He did insist that "happiness lies not in the mere possession of money," and he sneered at "the mad chase of evanescent profits." But he did not indict bankers for being bankers or businessmen for being businessmen. He indicted them, instead, for their moral failures. Paraphrasing Proverbs 29:18, he said, "They have no vision, and when there is no vision the people perish." He called these "unscrupulous" financiers false leaders, and he urged the American people to follow a true leader instead.

But this "verbal scourging," as the *Nation* called it, did not instill confidence.[7] What accomplished that was Roosevelt's promise to act, or more precisely the reassurance that even in these dire straits acting would not come to naught. In what the *New York Times* described as "a Jacksonian speech, a fighting speech," Roosevelt declared "war against the emergency."[8] Drawing repeatedly on martial metaphors, he spoke of retreats and advances and "lines of attack." He spoke of U.S. citizens as "a trained and loyal army, willing to sacrifice for the good of a common discipline." In the sort of alchemy that a great speech can perform, he transformed personal hardships into sacrifice for the common good.

But Roosevelt did more than declare war and recruit an army. He made himself this army's leader—the commander in chief of the assault on the Great Depression that would come to be known as the New Deal. In the spirit of laissez-faire, Hoover had kept his hands off the machinery of capitalism, trusting that the economy would somehow right itself. FDR was hands-on. "With this pledge taken," he said in a speech that used the word "leadership" no fewer than seven times, "I assume unhesitatingly the leadership of this great army of our people dedicated to a disciplined attack upon our common problems."

All this was "feasible" under the prevailing constitutional system of checks and balances and the separation of powers, Roosevelt said, adding almost as an aside that "it is to be hoped" that the Constitution would be "wholly adequate" to the task. But this was no aside. What if Congress or the courts refused to fall in line? Roosevelt did not say. Instead, he professed his faith that Congress would anoint his crusade, by granting him, if necessary, "broad executive power"—"as great as the power that would be given to me if we were in fact invaded by a foreign foe."

Influential journalist Walter Lippmann had earlier urged FDR to serve for a time as a benevolent dictator unrestrained by Congress or the courts. "The situation is critical, Franklin," Lippmann told FDR. "You may have no alternative but to assume dictatorial powers."[9] But such talk caused much consternation, particularly as the bills started to pour out of Congress, radically centralizing American economic and political power and concentrating that power in the Oval Office. In an article headlined "Roosevelt Gets Power of Dictator," journalist Arthur Krock observed less than a week after the inauguration that Congress had already surrendered its constitutional prerogatives by vesting in Roosevelt "more arbitrary authority than any American statesman has had since the Constitution was framed."[10] Years later, the Beat writer William Burroughs, in a piece of dystopian science fiction called *Roosevelt After Inauguration,* would depict FDR, "dressed in the purple robes of a Roman emperor," beating Congress and the Supreme Court into submission via an army of "purple-assed baboons."[11]

Franklin Roosevelt is now such a saint in the American imagination that it is hard to remember how polarizing he was during his lifetime. Today most rankings of the greatest American presidents include FDR in the top three, typically after Lincoln and Washington.[12] But during his presidency, Roosevelt was seen as either a demon or a redeemer—a class warrior or a tireless champion of the poor and the downtrodden. Almost none of this friction was apparent in the days surrounding his inauguration, however. On the strength of his "New Deal" promise, he had won the 1932 election in a landslide that had also put both houses of Congress firmly in the hands of the Democrats. So Democrats and Republicans alike hailed his words as the cure for what ailed us. United States Steel chairman Myron Taylor spoke for many when he said, "I hasten to re-enlist to fight the depression to its end."[13] Thousands more expressed their approval through personal letters to the White House, typically remarking not so much on what their president *said,* but how it made them *feel.* "Never, since the news of the Armistice reached this country, have I had such a vibrant and electric feeling come over me, as when you made your inaugural address," wrote Albert Davies of Rutherford, New Jersey, while Morris Sterns of Columbus, Georgia, wrote, "This noon your inaugural address electrified us! Its clarity, logic and sincerity struck us with the force and simplicity of Lincoln's Speech at Gettysburg." The Reverend Dr. Edmund Trotman of St. Augustine's Protestant Episcopal Negro Church in Asbury Park, New Jersey, saw America's new president as "a modern Joshua" selected "to lead his people in the great crisis."[14]

But critics will be critics, and they did what they do. Edmund Wilson, who would go on to describe Tolkien's *The Lord of the Rings* as "juvenile trash," heard too many echoes of President Wilson in President Roosevelt's words, and an oversupply of theology—"the old unctuousness, the old pulpit vagueness."[15] Wilson also worried about an impending dictatorship, an anxiety more widely shared than articulated in March 1933. But as Roosevelt remade America in the image of his First Inaugural, the complaints started to roll in from both liberals and conservatives. On the left, some complained that Roosevelt was not going far enough to bring the American dream to African Americans and the poor. Socialist leader Norman Thomas joked that Roosevelt was carrying out much of his economic program—"in a coffin."[16] Meanwhile, the American Liberty League, formed in 1934 by conservative businessmen (the Du Ponts) and disaffected Democrats (Al Smith) to oppose Roosevelt from the right, denounced New Deal initiatives such as the Tennessee Valley Authority as huge steps in the direction of a "socialist State" and likened Roosevelt's centralization of economic planning to Communism and Fascism:

> *King George III was the symbol of autocratic power against which the Colonies revolted. The twenty-seven grievances enumerated in the Declaration of Independence were directed specifically against him. Under New Deal laws and usurpations of authority, autocratic power to plan the course of economic affairs has become centered in the President of the United States. In Italy Mussolini and in Germany Hitler typify autocracy and a planned economic order.[17]*

Closer to home, FDR was also challenged by the Supreme Court, which cut down a series of his legislative darlings, prompting Roosevelt to respond with a notorious (and ultimately unsuccessful) effort to pack the Court with his hand-picked appointees.

Historical writing on Roosevelt follows many of these same interpretive lines. Liberals praise Roosevelt as a bold reformer and champion of the poor, characterizing his New Deal as the "Third American Revolution" (after the Revolutionary War and the Civil War).[18] Radicals and some conservatives see Roosevelt as a stealth conservative who prevented a real revolution by shoring up the capitalist system with cosmetic reforms at a moment when it might plausibly have been overthrown. The New Deal, in short, was "corporate liberalism"—a good deal for corporations and a raw deal for the rest of us.[19] A growing number of conservatives and libertarians attack Roosevelt for selling American values down the river and particularly for declaring war on liberty by increasing the size and expanding the scope of the federal government. Some historians split the difference, interpreting the New Deal as a "halfway revolution."[20]

FDR's career after his first inauguration would include three more presidential election victories—an unprecedented twelve-year run in the White House that would not end until his death on April 12, 1945—and the successful prosecution of World War II. It would also include many influential speeches, including his popular "fireside chats," which, like his First Inaugural, added much to America's conversation about itself. Building on the key theme in his First Inaugural, his January 6, 1941, State of the Union speech delineated "four freedoms" that all people everywhere had every right to enjoy: freedom of speech and expression; freedom of worship; freedom from want; and freedom from fear. Later that year, in a speech calling on Congress to declare war on Japan, Roosevelt would describe December 7, 1941, when the Japanese attacked Pearl Harbor, as "a date which will live in infamy."[21] But the First Inaugural was his best and most important speech. Roosevelt's reassuring words *did* lift the American mood and in so doing began to heal the economy. They also set the course for the most transformative presidency of the twentieth century.

Although this speech is remembered for the "fear itself" line, what really matters are the ends to which FDR's fearlessness was put. A gateway drug into the New Deal, this speech gave the American people an inkling of the sort of society FDR wanted to create, and as they swooned he made it happen. The result was both the modern presidency—a form of executive leadership to which the Reagan Revolution of the 1980s was somehow more coda than corrective—and modern America. Liberals and conservatives disagree about whether the New Deal ended the Great Depression. And there is no end to disputes about Roosevelt's virtues and vices. But there is no doubting that Roosevelt's four terms in office redefined liberalism and remade America in its image.

On the eve of his inaugural address, the most intimate encounters most Americans had with the federal government came when they were picking up their mail at the local post office. There was no safety net for the elderly or the unemployed. There were no federal guarantees for bank deposits. And there was almost no regulation of business or the financial markets. After his inaugural address we got the minimum wage, unemployment compensation, and an alphabet soup of federal agencies, not least the Social Security Administration and the Federal Deposit Insurance Corporation. For better or for worse, Thoreau's vision of a minimalist government—"That government is best which governs least"[22]— had given way to "action, and action now."

First Inaugural Address ❧

This is a day of national consecration, and I am certain that on this day my fellow Americans expect that on my induction into the Presidency I will address them with a candor and a decision which the present situation of our people impels. This is preeminently the time to speak the truth, the whole truth, frankly and boldly. Nor need we shrink from honestly facing conditions in our country today. This great Nation will endure as it has endured, will revive, and will prosper. So, first of all, let me assert my firm belief that the only thing we have to fear is fear itself [a,b,c]—nameless, unreasoning, unjustified terror which paralyzes needed efforts to convert retreat into advance.

a. Lyndon B. Johnson, thirty-sixth U.S. president, on how FDR energized him as a boy (1964): I remember the first President I ever saw, and the greatest President I ever knew. I saw him stand up one day in his braces, with pain in his legs, and anguish in his face, but vision in his head and hope in his eyes. . . . It was a rainy, cold day in March 1933. The banks were popping in the country just like popcorn, just like firecrackers going off at Christmastime. . . . People were burning their corn. Cotton was selling for 5 cents. You couldn't find a job and relief lines were longer than from here to that airport I landed at, and that is 15 miles away. But this man stood up in that time when things weren't near as good as they are today, with the braces on his legs, out of his wheelchair, and he grabbed that microphone, and he stuck his chin up, and his jaw out, and he said, "The only thing we have to fear is fear itself," and he electrified a nation, and he saved a republic. —Lyndon B. Johnson, "Remarks at the Municipal Park, South Gate, California," October 11, 1964, www.presidency.ucsb.edu/ws/index.php?pid=26588.

b. Bill Clinton, forty-second U.S. president, praising FDR as a model for overcoming personal adversity (1997): [FDR] said over and over again in different ways that we had only to fear fear itself. We did not have to be afraid of pain or adversity or failure, for all those could be overcome. He knew that, of course, because that is exactly what he did. And with his faith and the power of this example, we did conquer them all, depression, war, and doubt. Now we see that faith again alive in America. We are grateful beyond measure for our own unprecedented prosperity. But we must remember the source of that

In every dark hour of our national life a leadership of frankness and vigor has met with that understanding and support of the people themselves which is essential to victory. I am convinced that you will again give that support to leadership in these critical days.

In such a spirit on my part and on yours we face our common difficulties. They concern, thank God, only material things. Values have shrunken to fantastic levels, taxes have risen, our ability to pay has fallen, government of all kinds is faced by serious curtailment of income, the means of exchange are frozen in the currents of trade, the withered leaves of industrial enterprise lie on every side, farmers find no markets for their produce, and the savings of many years in thousands of families are gone. More important, a host of unemployed citizens face the grim problem of existence, and an equally great number toil with little return. Only a foolish optimist can deny the dark realities of the moment.

And yet our distress comes from no failure of substance. We are stricken by no plague of locusts. Compared with the perils which our forefathers conquered, because they believed and were not afraid, we have still much to be thankful for. Nature still offers her bounty, and human efforts have multiplied it. Plenty is at our doorstep, but a generous use of it languishes in the very sight

---

faith. . . . By showing President Roosevelt as he was, we show the world that we have faith that in America you are measured for what you are and what you have achieved, not for what you have lost. And we encourage all who face their difficulties and overcome them not to give in to fear but to believe in their possibilities. —William J. Clinton, "Remarks at the Dedication of the Franklin Delano Roosevelt Memorial," May 2, 1997, in *Public Papers of the Presidents of the United States, William J. Clinton, 1997* (Washington, DC: U.S. Government Printing Office, 1999), 1:532.

c. Jonathan Alter, journalist, commenting on the senselessness of the notion that only fear is fearsome (2006): [This] line was a specimen of inspired nonsense, no different in substance than Hoover's jawboning, except for the fact that it came from a different jaw, one jutting confidently. If FDR were truly showing "candor" and speaking "the whole truth, frankly and boldly," why would he pretend that the only thing the United States had to fear was fear itself? Some of the terror was irrational, but there were plenty of other real things to fear: the loss of one's fortune or job or dignity, not to mention the consequences to family and health. Some fears—like the panic of the wealthy over what Roosevelt would do with their gold—were misplaced; others—worry over putting food on the table—were immediate. The widespread fear of a collapse of the banking system was neither "nameless," "unreasoning," nor "unjustified." All of this is true and irrelevant. Great leadership—like great theater—is often about the suspension of disbelief, the audience's surrender of questions, an embrace of hope and redemption. —Jonathan Alter, *The Defining Moment: FDR's Hundred Days and the Triumph of Hope* (New York: Simon & Schuster, 2006), p. 217.

of the supply. Primarily, this is because the rulers of the exchange of mankind's goods have failed through their own stubbornness and their own incompetence, have admitted their failure, and have abdicated. Practices of the unscrupulous money-changers stand indicted in the court of public opinion, rejected by the hearts and minds of men.

True, they have tried, but their efforts have been cast in the pattern of an outworn tradition. Faced by failure of credit, they have proposed only the lending of more money. Stripped of the lure of profit by which to induce our people to follow their false leadership, they have resorted to exhortations, pleading tearfully for restored confidence. They know only the rules of a generation of self-seekers. They have no vision, and when there is no vision the people perish.

Yes, the money changers have fled from their high seats in the temple of our civilization. We may now restore that temple to the ancient truths. The measure of the restoration lies in the extent to which we apply social values more noble than mere monetary profit. Happiness lies not in the mere possession of money; it lies in the joy of achievement, in the thrill of creative effort. The joy, the moral stimulation, of work no longer must be forgotten in the mad chase of evanescent profits. These dark days, my friends, will be worth all they cost us if they teach us that our true destiny is not to be ministered unto but to minister to ourselves, and to our fellow men.

Recognition of that falsity of material wealth as the standard of success goes hand in hand with the abandonment of the false belief that public office and high political position are to be valued only by the standards of pride of place and personal profit. And there must be an end to a conduct in banking and in business which too often has given to a sacred trust the likeness of callous and selfish wrongdoing. Small wonder that confidence languishes, for it thrives only on honesty, on honor, on the sacredness of obligations, on faithful protection, and on unselfish performance. Without them, it cannot live.

Restoration calls, however, not for changes in ethics alone. This Nation asks for action, and action now.[d]

---

d. Barack Obama, president-elect, applying the lessons of the Great Depression to the Great Recession (2008): Yesterday, we received another painful reminder of the serious economic challenge our country is facing when we learned that 533,000 jobs were lost in November alone, the single worst month of job loss in over three decades. That puts the total number of jobs lost in this recession at nearly 2 million. . . . We need action—and action now. That is why I have asked my economic team to develop an economic recovery plan for both Wall Street and Main Street that will help save or create at least two and a half million jobs, while rebuilding our infrastructure, improving our schools, reducing our dependence on oil, and saving billions of dollars. We won't do it the old Washington

Our greatest primary task is to put people to work. This is no unsolvable problem if we face it wisely and courageously. It can be accomplished in part by direct recruiting by the government itself, treating the task as we would treat the emergency of a war but at the same time, through this employment, accomplishing great—greatly needed projects to stimulate and reorganize the use of our natural resources.

Hand in hand with this we must frankly recognize the overbalance of population in our industrial centers and by engaging on a national scale in a redistribution endeavor to provide a better use of the land for those best fitted for the land. Yes, the task can be helped by definite efforts to raise the values of agricultural products and with this the power to purchase the output of our cities. It can be helped by preventing realistically the tragedy of the growing loss through foreclosure of our small homes and our farms. It can be helped by insistence that the Federal, the State, and the local governments act forthwith on the demand that their cost be drastically reduced. It can be helped by the unifying of relief activities which today are often scattered, uneconomical, and unequal. It can be helped by national planning for and supervision of all forms of transportation and of communications and other utilities that have a definitely public character. There are many ways in which it can be helped, but it can never be helped merely by talking about it.

We must act and act quickly.

And finally, in our progress towards a resumption of work we require two safeguards against a return of the evils of the old order. There must be a strict supervision of all banking and credits and investments. There must be an end to speculation with other people's money. And there must be provision for an adequate but sound currency.

These, my friends, are the lines of attack. I shall presently urge upon a new Congress, in special session, detailed measures for their fulfillment, and I shall seek the immediate assistance of the forty-eight states.

Through this program of action we address ourselves to putting our own national house in order and making income balance outgo. Our international trade relations, though vastly important, are in point of time and necessity secondary to the establishment of a sound national economy. I favor as a practical policy the putting of first things first. I shall spare no effort to restore world trade by international economic readjustment, but the emergency at home cannot wait on that accomplishment. The basic thought that guides these specific means of national

---

way. We won't just throw money at the problem. We'll measure progress by the reforms we make and the results we achieve—by the jobs we create, by the energy we save, by whether America is more competitive in the world. —Barack Obama, "The President-Elect's Radio Address," December 6, 2008, www.presidency.ucsb.edu/ws/index.php?pid=85034.

recovery is not narrowly nationalistic. It is the insistence, as a first consideration, upon the interdependence of the various elements in all parts of the United States of America, a recognition of the old and permanently important manifestation of the American spirit of the pioneer. It is the way to recovery. It is the immediate way. It is the strongest assurance that the recovery will endure.

In the field of world policy I would dedicate this nation to the policy of the good neighbor—the neighbor who resolutely respects himself and, because he does so, respects the rights of others— the neighbor who respects his obligations and respects the sanctity of his agreements in and with a world of neighbors.

If I read the temper of our people correctly, we now realize as we have never realized before our interdependence on each other, that we cannot merely take but we must give as well, that if we are to go forward, we must move as a trained and loyal army, willing to sacrifice for the good of a common discipline, because without such discipline no progress can be made, no leadership becomes effective. We are, I know, ready and willing to submit our lives and property to such discipline because it makes possible a leadership which aims at the larger good. This I propose to offer, pledging that the larger purposes will bind upon us, bind upon us all as a sacred obligation, with a unity of duty hitherto evoked only in times of armed strife.

With this pledge taken, I assume unhesitatingly the leadership of this great army of our people dedicated to a disciplined attack upon our common problems.

Action in this image, action to this end, is feasible under the form of government which we have inherited from our ancestors. Our Constitution is so simple, so practical, that it is possible always to meet extraordinary needs by changes in emphasis and arrangement without loss of essential form. That is why our constitutional system has proved itself the most superbly enduring political mechanism the modern world has ever seen. It has met every stress of vast expansion of territory, of foreign wars, of bitter internal strife, of world relations. And it is to be hoped that the normal balance of executive and legislative authority may be wholly equal, wholly adequate, to meet the unprecedented task before us. But it may be that an unprecedented demand and need for undelayed action may call for temporary departure from that normal balance of public procedure. I am prepared under my constitutional duty to recommend the measures that a stricken nation in the midst of a stricken world may require. These measures, or such other measures as the Congress may build out of its experience and wisdom, I shall seek within my constitutional authority to bring to speedy adoption. But in the event that the Congress shall fail to take one of these two courses, in the event that the national emergency is still critical, I shall not evade the clear course of duty that will then confront me. I shall ask the Congress for the one remaining instrument to meet the crisis: broad executive power to wage a war against the emergency, as great as the power that would be given to me if we were in fact invaded by a foreign foe.[e]

For the trust reposed in me I will return the courage and the devotion that befit the time. I can do no less.

We face the arduous days that lie before us in the warm courage of the national unity,[f] with the clear consciousness of seeking old and precious moral values, with the clean satisfaction that comes from the stern performance of duty by old and young alike. We aim at the assurance of a rounded, a permanent national life. We do not distrust the future of essential democracy. The people of the United States have not failed. In their need they have registered a mandate that they want direct, vigorous action. They have asked for discipline and direction under leadership. They have made me the present instrument of their wishes. In the spirit of the gift, I take it.

In this dedication of a nation we humbly ask the blessing of God. May he protect each and every one of us. May he guide me in the days to come.[23]

---

e. Eleanor Roosevelt, First Lady, expressing misgivings about the powers being invested in her husband (1933): [The applause that followed this line was] a little terrifying. You felt that they would do *anything*—if only someone would tell them *what* to do. —Quoted in Joseph P. Lash, *Eleanor and Franklin* (New York: Signet, 1973), p. 478.

f. George W. Bush, forty-third U.S. president (2001): Today [three days after 9/11] we feel what Franklin Roosevelt called the warm courage of national unity. This is a unity of every faith and every background. It has joined together political parties in both houses of Congress. It is evident in services of prayer and candlelight vigils and American flags, which are displayed in pride and wave in defiance. Our unity is a kinship of grief and a steadfast resolve to prevail against our enemies. And this unity against terror is now extending across the world. —George W. Bush, "Remarks at the National Day of Prayer and Remembrance Service," September 14, 2001, Washington, DC, www.presidency.ucsb .edu/ws/index.php?pid=63645.

COMMENTARY

*George Throop, Washington University chancellor, lauding FDR's
address for its middle-of-the-road moderation (1933)*

It is at once sane without conservatism and progressive without radicalism and
points toward that liberal path believed in and desired by a great majority of our
people.

—Quoted in "Nation's Leaders Pleased with Inaugural Address," *Boston Globe,* March 6, 1933, p. 5.

*H. L. Mencken, journalist and satirist, fretting about
putting his life in a dictator's hands (1933)*

Mr. Roosevelt's appeal to the American people, in his inaugural address, to
convert themselves into "a trained and loyal army willing to sacrifice for the good
of a common discipline," and his somewhat mysterious demand, immediately
following, that they "submit" their *lives* as well as their property to "such
discipline"—this appeal and demand, as everyone knows, have met with a hearty
response, and almost all of us are now looking forward confidently to that "larger
good" which he promised in the same breath.

We have had two dictatorships in the past, one operated by Abraham Lincoln
and the other by Woodrow Wilson. Both were marked by gross blunders and
injustices. At the end of each the courts were intimidated and palsied, the books
bristled with oppressive and idiotic laws, thousands of men were in jail for their
opinions, and great hordes of impudent scoundrels were rolling in money. . . .
Thus I hesitate to go with Dr. Roosevelt all the way. My property, it appears, is
already in his hands, but for the present, at least, I prefer not to hand over my
life.

This, of course, is not because I have any doubt about the right hon. gentleman's *bona fides.* On the contrary, I have the utmost confidence in his good
intentions, and I believe further that he has carried on his dictatorship so far
with courage, sense and due restraint. But it is always well, when anything of
the sort is set up in a presumably free country, to scrutinize it very carefully and
even biliously, lest it get out of hand.

—H. L. Mencken, "A Time to Be Wary," *Evening Sun* (Baltimore), March 13, 1933, in *On Politics: A Carnival
of Buncombe,* ed. Malcolm Moos (Baltimore: Johns Hopkins Univ. Press, 1996), pp. 276–78.

William Lemke, U.S. Representative (R-ND), on FDR's "about-face" between his inauguration and the passage of the Emergency Banking Act days later (1933)

The President drove the money changers out of the Capitol on March 4th and they were all back on the 9th.

—Quoted in Robert S. McElvaine, *The Great Depression: America, 1929–1941* (New York: Three Rivers, 1993), p. 140.

Charles Coughlin, populist Catholic priest who had earlier lauded the New Deal as "Christ's Deal," now denouncing FDR as a "Judas" (1936)

As far as the National Union [for Social Justice] is concerned, no candidate for Congress can campaign, go electioneering for, or support the great betrayer and liar, Franklin D. Roosevelt, he who promised to drive the money changers from the temple and succeeded in driving the farmers from their homesteads and the citizens from their homes in the cities. . . . Is it democracy for the President of this nation to assume power over Congress, to browbeat the Congress and to insist that his "must" legislation be passed? . . . Is it democracy, I ask those who cling to the party of Andrew Jackson, to have our country filled with plutocrats or bureaucrats and their banks filled with unpayable debts, all to save the bankers? . . . I ask you to purge the man who claims to be a Democrat from the Democratic Party, and mean Franklin Double-Crossing Roosevelt.

—Charles Coughlin, "Text of Father Coughlin's Address to Townsendites," *New York Times*, July 17, 1936, p. 6.

Richard Hofstadter, historian, finding continuities between FDR and Hoover in ideas but a huge gap in temperament (1948)

At the heart of the New Deal there was not a philosophy but a temperament. The essence of this temperament was Roosevelt's confidence that even when he was operating in unfamiliar territory he could do no wrong, commit no serious mistakes. From the standpoint of an economic technician this assurance seemed almost mad at times. . . . And yet there was a kind of intuitive wisdom under the harum-scarum surface of his methods. When he came to power, the people had seen stagnation go dangerously far. They wanted experiment, activity, trial and error, anything that would convey a sense of movement and novelty. . . . [Though] Roosevelt had been reared on a social and economic philosophy rather similar to Hoover's, he succeeded at once in communicating the fact that his temperament was antithetical. When Hoover bumbled that it was necessary only to restore confidence, the nation laughed bitterly. When Roosevelt said, "The only thing we have to fear is fear itself," essentially the same threadbare half-true idea, the nation was thrilled.

—Richard Hofstadter, *The American Political Tradition: And the Men Who Made It* (1948; New York: Vintage, 1989), pp. 411–12.

Ronald Reagan, fortieth U.S. president, praising his Democratic hero at the centennial of his birth (1982)

Franklin Roosevelt was the first President I ever saw. I remember the moment vividly. It was in 1936, a campaign parade in Des Moines, Iowa. What a wave of affection and pride swept through that crowd as he passed by in an open car—which we haven't seen a President able to do for a long time—a familiar smile on his lips, jaunty and confident, drawing from us reservoirs of confidence and enthusiasm some of us had forgotten we had during those hard years. Maybe that was FDR's greatest gift to us. He really did convince us that the only thing we had to fear was fear itself.

—Ronald Reagan, "Remarks at a White House Luncheon Celebrating the Centennial of the Birth of Franklin Delano Roosevelt," January 28, 1982, www.presidency.ucsb.edu/ws/index.php?pid=42798.

James Ostrowski, attorney and libertarian, ripping FDR's "embarrassingly Bolshevik philosophy" (2001)

This is everybody's favorite President? I haven't heard such overblown, overstuffed, cliched, incoherent, floatingly abstract socialist nonsense since Bill Clinton's first inaugural. . . . [Consider] the big line, endlessly quoted, rarely analyzed, never criticized: "So first of all let me assert my firm belief that the only thing we have to fear . . . is fear itself." . . . It's best not to think too much about this passage because you will get a headache. It's gibberish. Try this on: the only thing we have to fear is people who say we should fear people who say that fear is our only fear. . . . On March 4, 1933, the only thing we had to fear was—FDR himself.

—James Ostrowski, "Fear Itself: FDR's Inaugural Address," January 18, 2001, http://alpha.mises.org/daily/591/Fear-Itself-FDRs-Inaugural-Address.

Bob Bussel, historian, examining the Occupy Wall Street movement through the lens of FDR's First Inaugural (2011)

As President Obama contemplates how he should react to the frustration and outrage being expressed by the Occupy Wall Street movement, he might consider how a predecessor, Franklin Roosevelt, responded to similar circumstances eight decades ago.

Amid the hardship of the Great Depression, social movements sprang up to protest Wall Street's irresponsibility that had plunged the nation into economic crisis. . . . In response to this pressure from below, President Roosevelt established protections for workers, curbed corporate and banking misconduct, and created a social welfare system to protect Americans in times of need.

Just as importantly (and here is where President Obama should be taking notes, given the implacable congressional opposition he faces), Roosevelt reassured troubled Americans by conveying his empathy for their plight. From the outset he validated popular anger toward Wall Street by identifying those responsible for the nation's economic collapse.

At his first inauguration, he announced that "the money changers have fled their high seats in the temple of our civilization." During his re-election campaign in 1936, he condemned "economic royalists who . . . sought to regiment the people, their labor and their property." Before signing legislation mandating a federal minimum wage, FDR proclaimed: "Do not let any calamity-howling executive with an income of $1,000 a day . . . tell you . . . that a wage of $11 a week is going to have a disastrous effect on all American industry." . . .

Just before he became president, Barack Obama sent similar signals when he declared his support for workers in Chicago whose employer had refused to grant their final paychecks and benefits after announcing a plant closure. . . . Since then, Obama has appeared reluctant to declare his full solidarity with the other 99 percent. . . .

However, as a candidate who raised social expectations when he spoke of "the fierce urgency of now," President Obama's political future hinges on his ability to reawaken the spirit of hope and change that animated his election. . . . By "going toward people's centers" and focusing on "the stuff that makes them tick," Obama could perhaps have his own "Roosevelt moment." The Occupy Wall Street movement provides him the opportunity to redeem the promise of his presidency. The other 99 percent are waiting to see if he will seize it.

—Bob Bussel, "Protests Give Obama a Chance for a 'Roosevelt Moment,'" *Register-Guard* (Eugene, OR), November 2, 2011, www.registerguard.com/web/opinion/27106301–47/roosevelt-obama-president-nation-workers.html.csp.

"The Speech"

❧ RONALD REAGAN, 1964 ❧

RONALD REAGAN (1911–2004) had some memorable turns of phrase during his acting career and as governor of California and president of the United States. As a bedridden George Gipp in *Knute Rockne, All American* (1940), he said, "Win just one for the Gipper!" As president, he labeled the Soviet Union the "evil empire" in remarks to the National Association of Evangelicals in 1983; four years later in a speech at the Brandenburg Gate in Berlin he challenged Soviet leader Mikhail Gorbachev: "Tear down this wall!" But Reagan's most influential speech came two decades earlier, on October 27, 1964, just a week before a presidential election pitting the Republican Senator from Arizona, Barry Goldwater, against the incumbent Democrat, Lyndon Baines Johnson. Officially entitled "A Time for Choosing," it is widely referred to as "The Speech."

Reagan had delivered this message many times before on behalf of General Electric, which employed him from 1954 to 1962 to host its weekly television show, *General Electric Theater,* and to preach its "free market, anti-union, anti-Communist, anti-welfare creed" in motivational meetings at GE facilities nation-wide.[1] But he adapted this stock speech to the exigencies of the Goldwater campaign and delivered it from a Hollywood studio to television viewers nationwide.

Before this address, which columnist David Broder has characterized as "the most successful political debut since William Jennings Bryan electrified the 1896 Democratic Convention with the 'Cross of Gold' speech," Reagan was known as a fifty-something B-movie actor on the cusp of retirement.[2] In his political life, he had been a Democrat—a backer of FDR and the New Deal, and a union president for the Screen Actors Guild. But he testified against Communist influence in Hollywood before the House Committee on Un-American Activities in 1947, and he campaigned for both Dwight Eisenhower and Richard Nixon. In 1962, he registered as a Republican, and in 1964 he endorsed Goldwater.

Paid for by California businessmen, this thirty-minute speech was taped in front of a live audience and broadcast in black and white. It was later rebroadcast twice nationally and over a hundred times in local markets. Like any good conversion story, it begins with a confession: Reagan fessing up to his former life as a Democrat. But Reagan then charts a course for the Republican Party that he would follow to the White House, and Republicans would follow until his death in 2004, and beyond.

Although there are glimpses here of the "Great Communicator" to come, Reagan's demeanor is surprisingly serious. He includes a few of the folksy anecdotes that will come to characterize his State of the Union speeches, including a tale of a woman who filed for divorce so she could get more welfare money. He also tells some jokes and offers some statistics. As is fitting for the man who turned "God Bless America" into a presidential mantra, he praises not only "the patriots at Concord bridge" but also Moses, Jesus, and the Christian martyrs. And he calls for a politics that attends to what is "morally right." But the themes of the speech are martial—fighting Communism abroad and big government at home.

Strikingly absent from "The Speech" is the cosmic optimism that allowed Americans to meet this bellicosity with a smile. Reagan is preaching fear, not hope. There are notes of American exceptionalism, including an oft quoted reference to the United States as "the last stand on Earth." But there is no mention of a "shining city on the hill." The dominant theme is that the country is fading fast. What we get here is the Reagan mystique without his trademark ebullience.

Reagan's main argument on the domestic side is that Johnson's Great Society was not so great. Gazing across America, Reagan sees an "assault on freedom" in farms and cities alike—a fat federal government getting fatter each day and striding in the process away from the libertarianism of the founding fathers and toward the totalitarianism of "Marx, Lenin, and Stalin." Regarding foreign policy, Reagan argues, America is "at war with the most dangerous enemy that has ever faced mankind." And the worst possible strategy in conducting this war is appeasement. Unfortunately, appeasing the Soviet Union is precisely what

Democrats like Johnson were doing, Reagan says. So surrender is what they will be doing next.

Uniting the domestic and foreign policy portions of "The Speech" is the specter of Communism abroad and creeping socialism at home. The choice facing American citizens is not between two men, Reagan argues. It is between two philosophies: free enterprise and big government, individual liberty and totalitarian collectivism, the freedom of capitalism and the slavery of the welfare state, the founding ideals of the United States and the founding ideals of the Soviet Union.

Reagan concludes with a mashup of Lincoln and FDR that again presents American voters with a stark choice. "You and I have a rendezvous with destiny," he says. "We will preserve for our children this, the last best hope of man on Earth, or we will sentence them to take the last step into a thousand years of darkness."

"The Speech," which according to *Time* magazine "provided just about the only dramatic moments in the whole, dreary Goldwater campaign," did little for Goldwater, but it remade Reagan.[3] Johnson won the presidency with 61 percent of the popular vote, while Goldwater took only his native Arizona and five southern states. This rout led many to conclude that the future of the Republican Party lay with Eisenhower-style moderates. Instead of burying conservative Republicans, however, the 1964 election paved the way for their resurrection and for the rebirth of Reagan as a political star.

Almost immediately after this speech aired, Republican leaders were anointing Reagan as their party's next great hope. The California businessmen who paid for the broadcast were urging him to compete for the governor's mansion in California *and* to set his sights on the White House. Reagan was elected governor of California in 1966 and 1970. Beginning in the late 1970s, he skillfully cultivated the support of the Moral Majority and other organizations on the Christian Right, which supported him enthusiastically as a man of God and an opponent of abortion. In the 1980 presidential election, Reagan defeated the incumbent Jimmy Carter in a landslide, and in 1984 against Walter Mondale he carried every state except for Mondale's home state of Minnesota.

Reagan's presidency started swimmingly, with the release on inauguration day, January 20, 1981, of the fifty-two American hostages who had been held captive for over a year in Iran. In March, Reagan was shot in an assassination attempt, but he recovered quickly and graciously—"Honey, I forgot to duck," he told his wife,

Nancy—and cashed in on the popularity earned by his grace under fire. He took a hard line against the Professional Air Traffic Controllers Organization and against Communists in the Soviet Union and Central America. But his administration was best known for "Reaganomics"—its policy of stimulating the economy by cutting taxes. When accompanied by sharp increases in the military budget, this policy—"voodoo economics" according to critics—led to record deficits and ballooning debt. But a recovering economy and a seemingly inexhaustible wellspring of charisma turned Reagan into one of the most beloved figures in modern American politics.

Today Reagan is widely revered as the George Washington of the Reagan Revolution and the founding father of contemporary conservatism. But Reagan was more a pragmatist than a revolutionary, and the Republican Party today now stands far to the right of its standard bearer. Though he confronted the Soviet Union with a policy of "peace through strength," Reagan also sat down with the Soviet leader Mikhail Gorbachev to reduce nuclear weapons. His three appointees to the Supreme Court included one right-winger (Scalia) and two moderates (Kennedy and O'Connor). He did little to cut back on entitlement programs such as Social Security and Medicare. And he worked closely with Democrats throughout his presidency, raising taxes in 1982 and 1984 and passing a bipartisan overhaul of the tax code in 1986 that lowered individual and corporate tax rates even as it closed loopholes for corporations and tax shelters for the wealthy.

Today many Republican politicians aspire to be the next Ronald Reagan, and many more refer to "The Speech" as a watershed in their own lives. But there is a dissenting voice among deficit hawks, who refuse to divinize a man who oversaw a tripling of the debt ceiling from $985 billion in 1981 to $2.8 trillion in 1987. David Frum has also criticized Reagan for cajoling his fellow Republicans into something bordering on hatred of government. "There are things only government can do," he wrote in 2008, "and if we conservatives wish to be entrusted with the management of the government, we must prove that we care enough about government to manage it well."[4]

But Reagan gave contemporary conservatism more than a demigod. He also gave it a political philosophy (or perhaps a political theology), which he articulated first and most fully in "The Speech." Whenever Republicans today blast Democrats as socialists, whenever they say that government is the problem rather than the solution, they are tipping their hat to the Great Communicator.

"The Speech" 🌿

I have spent most of my life as a Democrat. I recently have seen fit to follow another course. I believe that the issues confronting us cross party lines. Now, one side in this campaign has been telling us that the issues of this election are the maintenance of peace and prosperity. The line has been used, "We've never had it so good."

But I have an uncomfortable feeling that this prosperity isn't something on which we can base our hopes for the future. No nation in history has ever survived a tax burden that reached a third of its national income. Today, 37 cents of every dollar earned in this country is the tax collector's share, and yet our government continues to spend $17 million a day more than the government takes in. We haven't balanced our budget 28 out of the last 34 years. We have raised our debt limit three times in the last twelve months, and now our national debt is one and a half times bigger than all the combined debts of all the nations in the world. We have $15 billion in gold in our treasury—we don't own an ounce. Foreign dollar claims are $27.3 billion, and we have just had announced that the dollar of 1939 will now purchase 45 cents in its total value.

As for the peace that we would preserve, I wonder who among us would like to approach the wife or mother whose husband or son has died in South Vietnam and ask them if they think this is a peace that should be maintained indefinitely. Do they mean peace, or do they mean we just want to be left in peace? There can be no real peace while one American is dying someplace in the world for the rest of us. We are at war with the most dangerous enemy that has ever faced mankind in his long climb from the swamp to the stars, and it has been said if we lose that war, and in doing so lose this way of freedom of ours, history will record with the greatest astonishment that those who had the most to lose did the least to prevent its happening. Well, I think it's time we ask ourselves if we still know the freedoms that were intended for us by the Founding Fathers.

Not too long ago two friends of mine were talking to a Cuban refugee, a businessman who had escaped from Castro, and in the midst of his story one of my friends turned to the other and said, "We don't know how lucky we are." And the Cuban stopped and said, "How lucky you are! I had someplace to escape to." In that sentence he told us the entire story. If we lose freedom here, there is no place to escape to. This is the last stand on Earth. And this idea that government is beholden to the people, that it has no other source of power except to sovereign people, is still the newest and most unique idea in all the long history of man's relation to man. This is the issue of this election. Whether we believe in our capacity for self-government or whether we abandon the American revolution and confess that a little intellectual elite in a far-distant capital can plan our lives for us better than we can plan them ourselves.

You and I are told increasingly that we have to choose between a left or right, but I would like to suggest that there is no such thing as a left or right. There is only an up or down—up to a man's age-old dream, the ultimate in individual freedom consistent with law and order—or down to the ant heap of totalitarianism. And regardless of their sincerity, their humanitarian motives, those who would trade our freedom for security have embarked on this downward course.

In this vote-harvesting time, they use terms like the "Great Society," or as we were told a few days ago by the President, we must accept a "greater government activity in the affairs of the people." But they have been a little more explicit in the past and among themselves—and all of the things that I now will quote have appeared in print. These are not Republican accusations. For example, they have voices that say, "The cold war will end through acceptance of a not undemocratic socialism." Another voice says that the profit motive has become outmoded, it must be replaced by the incentives of the welfare state; or our traditional system of individual freedom is incapable of solving the complex problems of the 20th century.

Senator Fulbright has said at Stanford University that the Constitution is outmoded. He referred to the President as our moral teacher and our leader, and he said he is hobbled in his task by the restrictions in power imposed on him by this antiquated document. He must be freed so that he can do for us what he knows is best. And Senator Clark of Pennsylvania, another articulate spokesman, defines liberalism as "meeting the material needs of the masses through the full power of centralized government." Well, I for one resent it when a representative of the people refers to you and me—the free man and woman of this country—as "the masses." This is a term we haven't applied to ourselves in America. But beyond that, "the full power of centralized government"—this was the very thing the Founding Fathers sought to minimize. They knew that governments don't control things. A government can't control the economy without control-ling people. And they know when a government sets out to do that, it must use force and coercion to achieve its purpose. They also knew, those Founding Fathers, that outside of its legitimate functions, government does nothing as well or as economically as the private sector of the economy.

Now, we have no better example of this than the government's involvement in the farm economy over the last 30 years. Since 1955, the cost of this program has nearly doubled. One-fourth of farming in America is responsible for 85 percent of the farm surplus. Three-fourths of farming is out on the free market and has known a 21 percent increase in the per capita consumption of all its produce. You see, that one-fourth of farming is regulated and controlled by the federal government. In the last three years we have spent $43 in the feed grain program for every bushel of corn we don't grow.

Senator Humphrey last week charged that Barry Goldwater as President would seek to elimi-nate farmers. He should do his homework a little better, because he will find out that we have had a decline of 5 million in the farm population under these government programs. He will also find that the Democratic administration has sought to get from Congress an extension of the farm program to include that three-fourths that is now free. He will find that they have also asked for the right to imprison farmers who wouldn't keep books as prescribed by the federal government. The Secretary of Agriculture asked for the right to seize farms through condemnation and resell them to other individuals. And contained in that same program was a provision that would have allowed the federal government to remove 2 million farmers from the soil.

At the same time, there has been an increase in the Department of Agriculture employees. There is now one for every 30 farms in the United States, and still they can't tell us how 66 shiploads of grain headed for Austria disappeared without a trace and Billie Sol Estes never left shore.

Every responsible farmer and farm organization has repeatedly asked the government to free the farm economy, but who are farmers to know what is best for them? The wheat farmers voted against a wheat program. The government passed it anyway. Now the price of bread goes up; the price of wheat to the farmer goes down.

Meanwhile, back in the city, under urban renewal the assault on freedom carries on. Private property rights are so diluted that public interest is almost anything that a few government planners decide it should be. In a program that takes from the needy and gives to the greedy, we see such spectacles as in Cleveland, Ohio, a million-and-a-half-dollar building completed only three years ago must be destroyed to make way for what government officials call a "more compatible use of the land." The President tells us he is now going to start building public housing units in the thousands where heretofore we have only built them in the hundreds. But FHA and the Veterans Administration tell us that they have 120,000 housing units they've taken back through mortgage foreclosures. For three decades, we have sought to solve the problems of unemployment through government planning, and the more the plans fail, the more the planners plan. The latest is the Area Redevelopment Agency. They have just declared Rice County, Kansas, a depressed area. Rice County, Kansas, has two hundred oil wells, and the 14,000 people there have over $30 million on deposit in personal savings in their banks. When the government tells you you're depressed, lie down and be depressed.

We have so many people who can't see a fat man standing beside a thin one without coming to the conclusion that the fat man got that way by taking advantage of the thin one. So they are going to solve all the problems of human misery through government and government planning. Well, now, if government planning and welfare had the answer and they've had almost 30 years of it, shouldn't we expect government to almost read the score to us once in a while? Shouldn't they be telling us about the decline each year in the number of people needing help? The reduction in the need for public housing?

But the reverse is true. Each year the need grows greater, the program grows greater. We were told four years ago that 17 million people went to bed hungry each night. Well, that was probably true. They were all on a diet.[a] But now we are told that 9.3 million families in this country are poverty-stricken on the basis of earning less than $3,000 a year. Welfare spending is 10 times greater than in the dark depths of the Depression. We are spending $45 billion on welfare. Now do a little arithmetic, and you will find that if we divided the $45 billion up equally among those 9 million poor families, we would be able to give each family $4,600 a year, and this added to their present income should eliminate poverty! Direct aid to the poor, however, is running only about $600 per family. It would seem that someplace there must be some overhead.

So now we declare "war on poverty," or "You too can be a Bobby Baker!" Now, do they honestly expect us to believe that if we add $1 billion to the $45 million we are spending . . . one more program to the 30-odd we have—and remember, this new program doesn't replace any, it just duplicates existing programs—do they believe that poverty is suddenly going to disappear by magic? Well, in all fairness I should explain that there is one part of the new program that isn't duplicated. This is the youth feature. We are now going to solve the dropout problem, juvenile delinquency, by reinstituting something like the old CCC camps, and we are going to put our young people in camps, but again we do some arithmetic, and we find that we are going to spend each year just on room and board for each young person that we help $4,700 a year! We can send them to Harvard for $2,700! Don't get me wrong. I'm not suggesting that Harvard is the answer to juvenile delinquency.

But seriously, what are we doing to those we seek to help? Not too long ago, a judge called me here in Los Angeles. He told me of a young woman who had come before him for a divorce. She had six children, was pregnant with her seventh. Under his questioning, she revealed her husband was a laborer earning $250 a month. She wanted a divorce so that she could get an $80 raise. She is eligible for $330 a month in the Aid to Dependent Children Program. She got the idea from two women in her neighborhood who had already done that very thing.

Yet anytime you and I question the schemes of the do-gooders, we are denounced as being against their humanitarian goals. They say we are always "against" things, never "for" anything. Well,

a. Paul Krugman, columnist, blasting Reagan and his heirs for chuckling in the face of poverty (2007): In 1960, John F. Kennedy, who had been shocked by the hunger he saw in West Virginia, made the fight against hunger a theme of his presidential campaign. After his election he created the modern food stamp program, which today helps millions of Americans get enough to eat. But Ronald Reagan thought the issue of hunger in the world's richest nation was nothing but a big joke. . . . Today's leading conservatives are Reagan's heirs. If you're poor, if you don't have health insurance, if you're sick—well, they don't think it's a serious issue. In fact, they think it's funny. —Paul Krugman, "Conservatives Are Such Jokers," *New York Times*, October 5, 2007, p. A25.

the trouble with our liberal friends is not that they are ignorant, but that they know so much that isn't so. We are for a provision that destitution should not follow unemployment by reason of old age, and to that end we have accepted Social Security as a step toward meeting the problem.

But we are against those entrusted with this program when they practice deception regarding its fiscal shortcomings, when they charge that any criticism of the program means that we want to end payments to those who depend on them for a livelihood. They have called it insurance to us in a hundred million pieces of literature. But then they appeared before the Supreme Court and they testified that it was a welfare program. They only use the term "insurance" to sell it to the people. And they said Social Security dues are a tax for the general use of the government, and the government has used that tax. There is no fund, because Robert Byers, the actuarial head, appeared before a congressional committee and admitted that Social Security as of this moment is $298 billion in the hole. But he said there should be no cause for worry because as long as they have the power to tax, they could always take away from the people whatever they needed to bail them out of trouble! And they are doing just that.

A young man, 21 years of age, working at an average salary . . . his Social Security contribution would, in the open market, buy him an insurance policy that would guarantee $220 a month at age 65. The government promises $127. He could live it up until he is 31 and then take out a policy that would pay more than Social Security. Now, are we so lacking in business sense that we can't put this program on a sound basis so that people who do require those payments will find that they can get them when they are due . . . that the cupboard isn't bare? Barry Goldwater thinks we can.

At the same time, can't we introduce voluntary features that would permit a citizen who can do better on his own to be excused upon presentation of evidence that he had made provisions for the non-earning years? Should we allow a widow with children to work, and not lose the benefits supposedly paid for by her deceased husband? Shouldn't you and I be allowed to declare who our beneficiaries will be under these programs, which we cannot do? I think we are for telling our senior citizens that no one in this country should be denied medical care because of a lack of funds. But I think we are against forcing all citizens, regardless of need, into a compulsory government program, especially when we have such examples, as announced last week, when France admitted that their Medicare program was now bankrupt. They've come to the end of the road.

In addition, was Barry Goldwater so irresponsible when he suggested that our government give up its program of deliberate planned inflation so that when you do get your Social Security pension, a dollar will buy a dollar's worth, and not 45 cents' worth?

I think we are for an international organization where the nations of the world can seek peace. But I think we are against subordinating American interests to an organization that has become so structurally unsound that today you can muster a two-thirds vote on the floor of the General

Assembly among the nations that represent less than 10 percent of the world's population. I think we are against the hypocrisy of assailing our allies because here and there they cling to a colony, while we engage in a conspiracy of silence and never open our mouths about the millions of people enslaved in Soviet colonies in the satellite nation.

I think we are for aiding our allies by sharing of our material blessings with those nations which share in our fundamental beliefs, but we are against doling out money government to government, creating bureaucracy, if not socialism, all over the world. We set out to help 19 countries. We are helping 107. We spent $146 billion. With that money, we bought a $2 million yacht for Haile Selassie. We bought dress suits for Greek undertakers, extra wives for Kenyan government officials. We bought a thousand TV sets for a place where they have no electricity. In the last six years, 52 nations have bought $7 billion worth of our gold, and all 52 are receiving foreign aid from this country.

No government ever voluntarily reduces itself in size. Government programs, once launched, never disappear. Actually, a government bureau is the nearest thing to eternal life we'll ever see on this Earth. Federal employees number 2.5 million, and federal, state, and local, one out of six of the nation's workforce is employed by the government. These proliferating bureaus with their thousands of regulations have cost us many of our constitutional safeguards. How many of us realize that today federal agents can invade a man's property without a warrant? They can impose a fine without a formal hearing, let alone a trial by jury, and they can seize and sell his property in auction to enforce the payment of that fine. In Chico County, Arkansas, James Wier overplanted his rice allotment. The government obtained a $17,000 judgment, and a U.S. marshal sold his 950-acre farm at auction. The government said it was necessary as a warning to others to make the system work. Last February 19 at the University of Minnesota, Norman Thomas, six-time candidate for President on the Socialist Party ticket, said, "If Barry Goldwater became President, he would stop the advance of socialism in the United States." I think that's exactly what he will do.

As a former Democrat, I can tell you Norman Thomas isn't the only man who has drawn this parallel to socialism with the present administration. Back in 1936, Mr. Democrat himself, Al Smith, the great American, came before the American people and charged that the leadership of his party was taking the [party] of Jefferson, Jackson, and Cleveland down the road under the banners of Marx, Lenin, and Stalin. And he walked away from his party, and he never returned to the day he died, because to this day, the leadership of that party has been taking that party, that honorable party, down the road in the image of the labor socialist party of England. Now it doesn't require expropriation or confiscation of private property or business to impose socialism on a people. What does it mean whether you hold the deed or the title to your business or property if the government holds the power of life and death over that business or property? Such machinery already exists. The government can find some charge to bring against any concern it chooses to prosecute. Every businessman has his own tale of harassment. Somewhere a perversion has taken place. Our natural, inalienable rights are now considered to be a dispensation of government, and freedom has never been so fragile, so close to slipping from our grasp as it is at this moment. Our Democratic opponents seem unwilling to debate these issues. They want to make you and I believe that this is a contest between two men . . . that we are to choose just between two personalities.

Well, what of this man that they would destroy? And in destroying, they would destroy that which he represents, the ideas that you and I hold dear. Is he the brash and shallow and trigger-happy man they say he is? Well, I have been privileged to know him "when." I knew him long before he ever dreamed of trying for high office, and I can tell you personally I have never known a man in my life I believe so incapable of doing a dishonest or dishonorable thing.

This is a man who in his own business, before he entered politics, instituted a profit-sharing plan, before unions had ever thought of it. He put in health and medical insurance for all his employees. He took 50 percent of the profits before taxes and set up a retirement program, a pension plan for all his employees. He sent checks for life to an employee who was ill and couldn't work. He provided nursing care for the children of mothers who work in the stores. When Mexico was ravaged by floods from the Rio Grande, he climbed in his airplane and flew medicine and supplies down there.

An ex-GI told me how he met him. It was the week before Christmas during the Korean War, and he was at the Los Angeles airport trying to get a ride home to Arizona for Christmas, and he said that there were a lot of servicemen there and no seats available on the planes. Then a voice came over the loudspeaker and said, "Any men in uniform wanting a ride to Arizona, go to runway such-and-such," and they went down there, and there was this fellow named Barry Goldwater sitting in his plane. Every day in the weeks before Christmas, all day long, he would load up the plane, fly to Arizona, fly them to their homes, then fly back over to get another load.

During the hectic split-second timing of a campaign, this is a man who took time out to sit beside an old friend who was dying of cancer. His campaign managers were understandably impatient, but he said, "There aren't many left who care what happens to her. I'd like her to know I care." This is a man who said to his 19-year-old son, "There is no foundation like the rock of honesty and fairness, and when you begin to build your life upon that rock, with the cement of the faith in God that you have, then you have a real start." This is not a man who could carelessly send other people's sons to war. And that is the issue of this campaign that makes all of the other problems I have discussed academic, unless we realize that we are in a war that must be won.

Those who would trade our freedom for the soup kitchen of the welfare state have told us that they have a utopian solution of peace without victory. They call their policy "accommodation."

And they say if we only avoid any direct confrontation with the enemy, he will forget his evil ways and learn to love us. All who oppose them are indicted as warmongers. They say we offer simple answers to complex problems. Well, perhaps there is a simple answer—not an easy answer—but simple: If you and I have the courage to tell our elected officials that we want our national policy based upon what we know in our hearts is morally right.

We cannot buy our security, our freedom from the threat of the bomb by committing an immorality so great as saying to a billion now in slavery behind the Iron Curtain, "Give up your dreams of freedom because to save our own skin, we are willing to make a deal with your slave masters." Alexander Hamilton said, "A nation which can prefer disgrace to danger is prepared for a master, and deserves one." Let's set the record straight. There is no argument over the choice between peace and war, but there is only one guaranteed way you can have peace—and you can have it in the next second—surrender.

Admittedly there is a risk in any course we follow other than this, but every lesson in history tells us that the greater risk lies in appeasement, and this is the specter our well-meaning liberal friends refuse to face—that their policy of accommodation is appeasement, and it gives no choice between peace and war, only between fight and surrender. If we continue to accommodate, continue to back and retreat, eventually we have to face the final demand—the ultimatum. And what then? When Nikita Khrushchev has told his people he knows what our answer will be? He has told them that we are retreating under the pressure of the Cold War, and someday when the time comes to deliver the ultimatum, our surrender will be voluntary, because by that time we will have weakened from within spiritually, morally, and economically. He believes this because from our side he has heard voices pleading for "peace at any price" or "better Red than dead," or as one commentator put it, he would rather "live on his knees than die on his feet." And therein lies the road to war, because those voices don't speak for the rest of us.

You and I know and do not believe that life is so dear and peace so sweet as to be purchased at the price of chains and slavery. If nothing in life is worth dying for, when did this begin—just in the face of this enemy? Or should Moses have told the children of Israel to live in slavery under the pharaohs? Should Christ have refused the cross? Should the patriots at Concord Bridge have thrown down their guns and refused to fire the shot heard 'round the world? The martyrs of history were not fools, and our honored dead who gave their lives to stop the advance of the Nazis didn't die in vain. Where, then, is the road to peace? Well, it's a simple answer after all.

You and I have the courage to say to our enemies, "There is a price we will not pay." There is a point beyond which they must not advance. This is the meaning in the phrase of Barry Goldwater's "peace through strength." Winston Churchill said that "the destiny of man is not measured by material computation. When great forces are on the move in the world, we learn we are spirits—not animals." And he said, "There is something going on in time and space, and beyond time and space, which, whether we like it or not, spells duty."

You and I have a rendezvous with destiny. We will preserve for our children this, the last best hope of man on Earth, or we will sentence them to take the last step into a thousand years of darkness.

We will keep in mind and remember that Barry Goldwater has faith in us. He has faith that you and I have the ability and the dignity and the right to make our own decisions and determine our own destiny.

Thank you very much.[5]

COMMENTARY

Lou Cannon, biographer, demythologizing "The Speech" (1982)

Most of Reagan's address was *standard, antigovernment boilerplate* larded with emotional denunciations of Communism and a celebration of individual freedom. His statistics were sweeping and in some cases dubious. His best lines were cribbed from Franklin Roosevelt.

—Lou Cannon, *Reagan* (New York: Putnam, 1982), p. 13.

Howard Means, author, comparing Reagan to Darth Vader in the context of the debate over the Gramm-Rudman balanced budget bill (1986)

Think of the scene as George Lucas, the Star Wars mastermind, might have staged it. As the Death Star fires away, the camera drifts in on that fearsome mask Darth Vader wears and we begin to hear Reagan speaking—a pastiche of the stump speeches he built his reputation on two decades and more ago. . . .

"Because no government ever voluntarily reduces itself in size, government programs once launched never go out of existence. A government agency is the nearest thing to eternal life."

That's the voice of the true ideological purist—the shady emperor who lurks in the galactic mists beyond Darth Vader. And in the Death Star scenario, that voice drives Gramm-Rudman.

Private charity takes over government's welfare role. Other money-consuming federal functions—Amtrak, power administrations in the West and the like—are farmed out to private business to sink or swim on their merits. The whole concept of the eternality of government programs is turned on its ear, of economic necessity and by congressional fiat.

In fact, a kind of Judgment Day is loosed on the federal role in American life: Government is blown away, and Congress is powerless to stop it. Darth Vader's voice will not fade. The Reagan revolution is cemented in place.

—Howard Means, "Empire Strikes Back: 'Darth' Reagan's Death Star Fights Welfare State," *Orlando Sentinel,* March 30, 1986, p. H1.

Jeff Flake, U.S. Representative (R-AZ), proposing an alternative budget in Reagan's name (2001)

Mr. Chairman, about 35 years ago Ronald Reagan stood and said it was a time for choosing. I believe it was the greatest speech ever delivered. He said, now is the time we choose whether we believe in our own capacity for self-government, or whether we "confess that a little intellectual elite in a far-distant capital can plan our lives for us better than we can plan them ourselves." Mr. Chairman, I never thought I would be in that far-distant capital, but I am here; and I do not pretend that I have any great knowledge. I have only been here a few short months, and I have not had any epiphany about how to spend people's money better than they can spend it themselves. This budget, better than any budget being offered on the floor, honors those principles: limited government, economic freedom and individual responsibility.

—Jeff Flake, *Congressional Record,* March 28, 2001, p. 4812.

Lee Edwards, biographer, analyzing "The Speech" as a "masterpiece" (2004)

The speech resonated with conservatives because it was a masterpiece of political fusionism, articulating traditional conservative, libertarian, and anti-Communist positions. It provided a conservative answer to the two major problems of modern American history—Communism and collectivism—insisting that Communism had to be defeated, and that the federal government had become dangerously large and intrusive and had to be rolled back, not managed.

—Lee Edwards, *The Essential Ronald Reagan: A Profile in Courage, Justice, and Wisdom* (Lanham, MD: Rowman & Littlefield, 2004), p. 49.

Gary Kamiya, writer and Salon.com cofounder, on this speech as "one of those uncanny cultural artifacts that contains within it not just words, gestures, and ideas, but a future" (2009)

The Speech is disturbing because it shows the paranoid, millenarian side of American conservatism, unleavened by Reagan's Main Street sunniness. But it is also disturbing because it presents that right-wing vision in its pure form, unsullied by history. The Speech predates Reagan's entry into the world of politics, with its compromises and accommodations. As president, Reagan ended up backing away from some of his most cherished ideals. He raised taxes, reached agreement with the Communists, folded his cards in the face of terrorism, increased the federal deficit, and expanded the federal government. Reagan never abandoned his rhetoric of good versus evil, but it turned out not to apply to the real world. The Speech allows us to imagine an alternative Reaganist future, in which he lives up to his words—a world where he really does bomb the Soviet Union, get rid of Social Security, and end the progressive income tax. The Speech is a kind of distillation of Reagan's Platonic right-wing essence. Like Keats's "Grecian Urn," it freezes him, an immortal figure from a strange, lost part of the American id, eternally raging against Communism, big government, and liberal traitors. . . .

The Speech tapped into the primordial American myth: untrammeled individuality. There must be a territory for Huck Finn to light out to, a promised land where authority—or government—does not reach. In this always beckoning frontier, all the hindrances that drag Americans down are left behind. Businessmen can run their businesses as they like, free from the plague of do-gooder bureaucrats. White people need not carry the spurious cross of racial guilt. Unruly and ungrateful minorities—pinkos and softies and degenerates and pointy-heads and uppity women—are shown their place. Above all, the profoundly destabilizing specter of relativism, of compromise, of moral ambiguity, is banished. No longer need Americans accommodate themselves to evil. A divine certainty stretches from sea to shining sea.

This is as much a metaphysical wish as it is a political platform. It is a sermon as much as a speech. And it is in the gap between those two things—the space between the dream of absolute freedom and the reality of a fallen world—that America forever stumbles.

—Gary Kamiya, "Ronald Reagan," in Greil Marcus and Werner Sollors, eds., *A New Literary History of America*, www.newliteraryhistory.com/ronaldreagan.html.

Kevin Baker, blogger, tapping "The Speech" as the "most overrated political speech" ever (2010)

Conservatives often like to refer nostalgically to "The Speech." . . . They rarely quote it, though, and for good reason. [It] is a frequently hysterical, frequently hilarious rant. It's not just loaded with such Reagan trademarks as wildly exaggerated statistics on government spending and spurious anecdotes about government bureaucrats ("sixty-six shiploads of grain headed for Austria disappeared without a trace") and mothers having seven children and getting divorced so they can get a little more welfare. Nor is it just completely callous toward anyone below the poverty level ("We were told four years ago that seventeen million people went to bed hungry each night. Well, that was probably true. They were all on a diet!"). More important, The Speech revealed complete ignorance about the most fundamental ways in which American government and society worked. This included farm price supports (he claimed the Johnson administration "asked for the right to imprison farmers who wouldn't keep books as prescribed by the federal government"), youth programs ("we're going to put our young people in camps"), Medicare ("France admitted that their Medicare program is now bankrupt. They've come to the end of the road."), the Federal Reserve Board ("our government [must] give up its program of deliberate planned inflation"), and foreign aid ("we bought a two-million-dollar yacht for Haile Selassie. We bought dress suits for Greek undertakers, extra wives for Kenya government officials. We bought a thousand TV sets for a place where they have no electricity. In the last six years, fifty-two nations have bought seven billion dollars worth of our gold, and all fifty-two are receiving foreign aid from this country"). To top it all off, Reagan appropriated an FDR line, saying, "You and I have a rendezvous with destiny," and somehow failed to attribute it.

The popular wisdom is that The Speech was at least a seminal moment in the modern conservative movement, the archetype for what would become Reagan's standard stump speech and the star turn that first won him wide recognition. Reagan himself would write, with his usual exuberance: "The speech raised eight million dollars and soon changed my entire life." In fact, it drew little notice outside right-wing circles and would be entirely remodeled by the time its author was running for President. As Reagan thundered, out of the blue, near the crescendo of The Speech, "Somewhere a perversion has taken place." Uh-huh.

—Kevin Baker, "American Heritage: Overrated/Underrated Issue," July 23, 2010, http://kevinbaker.info/b/american-heritage-overratedunderrated-issue-mayjune–2000/.

Sarah Palin, Alaska governor, evoking Reagan as she urges Americans to "put their faith in God, not government" (2011)

["The Speech"] gave birth to the Reagan Revolution because it was more than just a campaign address. It was a call to action against a fundamental threat to freedom. It was given by a former Democrat who had been a union leader who had left his party because his party had left him. Reagan saw the dangers in LBJ's Great Society. He refused to sit down and be silent as our liberties were eroded by an out-of-control centralized government that overtaxed and overreached in utter disregard of Constitutional limits. He saw our nation at a critical turning point.

We could choose one direction or the other: socialism or freedom and free markets. Collectivism or individualism. In his words, we could choose "the swamp or the stars." . . .

But just days ago, in [President Obama's] State of the Union address . . . we were told, "No, the era of big government is here to stay, and you're going to pay for it whether you want to or not." . . . It's the same old tax and spend policies, or rather now it's borrow and spend, then tax the job creators. But we'll no longer call it government spending. For a while we called it "stimulus," but that didn't work because clearly it didn't stimulate anything but a Tea Party. So now, they'll call it "investing." . . .

So, yes, we are at a crossroads, and this is a time for choosing. And the choices before us are as clear now as they were in 1964. Do we still believe in the values that this country was founded on—God-given individual liberty, and limited government, and free-market capitalism? Or do we surrender to big government and a corporatist agenda? Do we believe we can compete and succeed by individual initiative? Or do we need government to take care of us and to plan for us?

—Sarah Palin, remarks at Young America's Foundation Reagan 100 Celebration, Santa Barbara, CA, February 4, 2011, www.sarahpac.com/posts/governor-palins-for-young-americas-foundations-reagan–100-celebration-at-the-reagan-ranch-center-speech.

ACTS

The Pledge of Allegiance

1892, 1954

EVERY FOURTH OF JULY, in the village of Barnstable, Massachusetts, after the parade is over and before the pie-eating contests and sack races to come, a child stands underneath an American flag and leads villagers of all ages in the Pledge of Allegiance. This scene is repeated across the nation and throughout the year at civic events, naturalization ceremonies, Boy and Girl Scout meetings, and Miss America pageants. Given how singers stumble over the lyrics of "The Star-Spangled Banner," there is probably no patriotic formula that is more widely known and recited by Americans today than the Pledge of Allegiance.

This patriotic creed first appeared in print on September 8, 1892, in the Boston-based *The Youth's Companion* magazine. Initially, it read, "I pledge allegiance to my Flag and the Republic for which it stands: one Nation indivisible, with Liberty and Justice for all."[1] President Benjamin Harrison urged America's schoolchildren to recite the Pledge, and over time it became a fixture, first, in public schools and, later, in parochial and private schools.

The original Pledge of Allegiance was written by Francis Bellamy (1855–1931), a former Baptist minister, as part of a nationwide effort to commemorate the four-hundredth anniversary of Christopher Columbus's arrival in the New World. Bellamy was a Christian socialist who saw the Pledge as a way to counteract the selfishness and materialism of Gilded Age capitalism. But he was also a "race-conscious nativist" who saw the Pledge as a way to assimilate even the "vilest elements" into a nation that "was built purely of Anglo-Saxon stuff."[2] In short, his pledge aimed to socialize the economy and "Americanize the alien."[3] It allayed two anxieties Bellamy shared with many white middle-class Americans at the end of the nineteenth century: first, that the greed of capitalism was overtaking civic piety; and, second, that rapid immigration was turning the United States into the "dumping ground of Europe."[4]

These anxieties changed over time, and the Pledge changed with them. During the 1920s—a decade that would see, thanks to the Johnson-Reed Act of 1924, severe restrictions on immigration—some patriots at the American Legion and the Daughters of the American Revolution worried that "my Flag" was unduly ambiguous. It could refer to the Irish or the German flag. To eliminate this ambiguity, the phrase "my Flag" gave way in the early 1920s to "the flag of the United States of America." Gridley Adams, the United States Flag Foundation director who fought (over Bellamy's objections) for this rewrite, explained: "I did not like those words 'my flag,' believing that any alien or Hottentot could, and with all sincerity, pledge allegiance to whatever National emblem he held in his mind's eye. I wanted the Pledge of Allegiance to be *specifically* American."[5]

Various salutes, including one that looked perilously like the Nazi salute, came and went, only to be replaced by today's practice of reciting the Pledge with the right hand over the heart. In 1942, the U.S. Congress adopted a Flag Code that officially made this pledge the nation's own. In 1954, President Eisenhower signed legislation inserting into the Pledge the words "under God."

State efforts to mandate Pledge recitation in public schools repeatedly met with resistance. In 1911 in Perth Amboy, New Jersey, a fourteen-year-old girl refused to recite the Pledge because she was a British citizen. In 1912 a ten-year-old boy in Camden, New Jersey, refused because his parents were socialists. In 1916, an eleven-year-old African-American boy refused on the grounds that the flag stood for racial oppression. In 1918 a nine-year-old Mennonite girl refused on pacifist grounds. Other religious protests followed—by Jehovites in Denver, Colorado; by members of the Elijiah Voice Society in Bellingham, Washington; and by Church of God members in Oklahoma City.

Legislation requiring Pledge recitation in public schools was initially upheld by the Supreme Court in *Minersville School District v. Gobitis* (1940), but after this decision, issued amid war hysteria, prompted over eight hundred cases of violence against Jehovah's Witnesses (the religious community that brought the suit), the nation's highest court abruptly reversed itself in *West Virginia State Board of Education v. Barnette* (1943). "If there is any fixed star in our constitutional constellation, it is that no official, high or petty, can prescribe what shall be orthodox in politics, nationalism, religion, or other matters of opinion, or force citizens to confess by word or act their faith therein," wrote Justice Robert Jackson for the court's 6–3 majority.[6]

All these legal challenges concerned the coercive character of a wholly secular pledge. The controversy intensified as various constituencies agitated for a place for God in the Pledge during the post–World War II religious revival. The key player here was America's largest Catholic fraternal organization, the Knights of Columbus, which led a grassroots campaign to underscore the differences between "Judeo-Christian" America and godless Communism by adding "under God" to the Pledge. Prodded by constituents who were themselves prodded by a series of Hearst newspaper editorials, members of Congress introduced legislation to sanctify the Pledge with God's presence. Their efforts went nowhere until President Eisenhower heard a sermon on February 7, 1954, at Washington's New York Avenue Presbyterian Church. In this sermon, delivered in the church attended by President Lincoln during his White House years, the Reverend George Docherty argued that Americans faced "a theological war" against "modern, secularized, godless humanity" and that adding "under God" to the Pledge was as good a way as any to wage it.[7]

One sponsor of the "under God" legislation, Louis Rabaut, a Democratic congressman from Michigan, argued that the revised Pledge would teach American schoolchildren "the real meaning of America." And for him too this meaning was theological. The "unbridgeable gap between America and Communist Russia is a belief in Almighty God," he said.[8] But what did it mean during the Cold War to affirm that the United States is "under God"? And what might it mean today?

The most obvious reading is theological: there is a God and the United States has some special relationship with Him. But this interpretation of Americans as God's chosen people can go two ways. America could be favored by God, under His protection, and the righteous recipient of His blessing. Or America could be the recipient of God's righteous wrath—under God's judgment. The problem with these theological readings is that neither is likely to withstand constitutional scrutiny, since both seem to violate the establishment clause of the First Amendment. An alternative reading, utilized by "under God" proponents, interprets this phrase historically. To say that the United States is "under God" means that Americans have historically understood their experiment to be guided by the Almighty. Whether God actually exists and whether this "God" really has any special relationship with Americans, there are references to God aplenty in sources such as the Declaration of Independence and Lincoln's Second Inaugural Address.

These and other questions concerning the Pledge would come to trouble future judges, but they did not trouble many in Eisenhower's America. On Flag Day, June 14, 1954, President Eisenhower signed into law a resolution adding "under God" to the Pledge. The next year Congress passed legislation requiring the printing of "In God We Trust" on all U.S. currency. In 1956, "In God We Trust" replaced *E Pluribus Unum* ("Out of many, one") as the country's official motto. "Without God," Eisenhower said, "there could be no American form of Government, nor an American way of life. Recognition of the Supreme Being is the first— the most basic—expression of Americanism."[9]

During the 1960s, controversy about the Pledge focused more on politics than religion. Some objected to the Pledge on the grounds that it trampled on First Amendment free speech protections. Many more objected because of their conviction that the United States was not, in fact, a nation with "liberty and justice for all." There might be liberty and justice for the rich and the straight, but not for the poor and homosexuals. Others said America was not really indivisible, because of the yawning gap between black and white society. So to recite its words or even to stand silently while others did so was to implicate yourself in a lie. Defenders of the Pledge responded by insisting that its words are not reportorial but aspirational; they describe not the nation we are but the nation we hope to become.

Beginning in the 1980s, the Pledge became a wedge issue in the culture wars. In the 1988 presidential election, Republican candidate George H. W. Bush attacked Democratic candidate Michael Dukakis for vetoing, during his stint as Massachusetts governor, a bill that would have mandated Pledge recitation in the commonwealth's public schools.[10] Campaigning for Bush, Reagan claimed the Pledge for the Republican Party, which he described as "the party of working people; the family; the neighborhood; the defense of freedom; and, yes, the American flag and the Pledge of Allegiance to 'one nation under God.'" The Democratic Party, by contrast, was "the party of 'no'—'no' to holding a line on taxes, 'no' to spending cuts, 'no' to the line-item veto, 'no' to the balanced budget amendment, 'no' to the Pledge of Allegiance."[11]

In this way, a practice originally created to foster national unity became a partisan political weapon, positioning Reagan, Bush, and other Republicans as the patriotic party. This move prompted some Democrats to liken the Pledge to loyalty oaths in totalitarian regimes. It also brought out libertarian critics. In 2002, Minnesota's governor Jesse Ventura vetoed a mandatory Pledge bill. The United States is a free country, he said, and here "patriotism is voluntary."[12] But the first serious legal challenge to "under God" came on June 26, 2002, when the Ninth Circuit U.S. Court of Appeals ruled that these words violated the First Amendment's establishment clause. By turning what had been a patriotic pledge into a "religious recitation," the Ninth Circuit reasoned, Congress had effectively established monotheism as the country's official religion.

Backlash against this decision was swift and strong. In an outpouring of patriotic sentiment that anticipated the impromptu singing of "God Bless America" on the Capitol steps after 9/11, members of Congress gathered on the day of this decision to recite the Pledge, with a clear emphasis on "under God." Senator Robert Byrd (D-WV), who had voted for the "under God" resolution as a House member in 1954, sharply denounced both the "stupid judge" who wrote the decision and the "atheist lawyer" who brought the suit. "I, for one, am not going to stand for this country's being ruled by a bunch of atheists," he said. "If they do not like it, let them leave."[13] On Flag Day, 2004, the Supreme Court overturned the lower court's ruling but side-stepped the First Amendment question by ruling that Michael Newdow, the atheist who had brought the suit on behalf of his daughter, lacked standing to sue.

Today questions about the Pledge linger. Is the patriotism this ritual fosters *true* patriotism? What does it mean to call the United States "one nation under God"? Is this "under God" clause prescriptive or descriptive? Does it turn the Pledge into a state-sponsored prayer? Or is the Pledge an empty rite of "ceremonial deism"?[14] Finally, where does this monotheistic language leave atheists, who affirm fewer than one god, and polytheists, who affirm more? Are such citizens somehow un-American?

The irony of the Pledge of Allegiance is that an act designed to foster unity seems to have done just the opposite. According to historian Richard Ellis, this somehow makes sense in a nation ever anxious about its identity. Here "proud assertion of liberal principles coexists side-by-side with racial and ethnic anxieties," he writes. "The nation's liberal dreams are not separable from its racial and ethnic nightmares. The liberal hope invites the illiberal fear, and the Pledge of Allegiance embodies both."[15]

The Pledge of Allegiance

> I pledge allegiance to the flag of the United States of America,
> and to the republic for which it stands, one nation under God,
> indivisible, with liberty and justice for all.

COMMENTARY

Robert Jackson, Supreme Court justice, overturning a law
requiring public school students to recite the Pledge (1943)

Struggles to coerce uniformity of sentiment in support of some end thought essential to their time and country have been waged by many good, as well as by evil, men. Nationalism is a relatively recent phenomenon, but, at other times and places, the ends have been racial or territorial security, support of a dynasty or regime, and particular plans for saving souls. As first and moderate methods to attain unity have failed, those bent on its accomplishment must resort to an ever-increasing severity. . . . Those who begin coercive elimination of dissent soon find themselves exterminating dissenters. Compulsory unification of opinion achieves only the unanimity of the graveyard.

It seems trite but necessary to say that the First Amendment to our Constitution was designed to avoid these ends by avoiding these beginnings. There is no mysticism in the American concept of the State or of the nature or origin of its authority. We set up government by consent of the governed, and the Bill of Rights denies those in power any legal opportunity to coerce that consent. . . .

The case is made difficult not because the principles of its decision are obscure, but because the flag involved is our own. Nevertheless, we apply the limitations of the Constitution with no fear that freedom to be intellectually and spiritually diverse or even contrary will disintegrate the social organization. To believe that patriotism will not flourish if patriotic ceremonies are voluntary and spontaneous, instead of a compulsory routine, is to make an unflattering estimate of the appeal of our institutions to free minds. We can have intellectual individualism and the rich cultural diversities that we owe to exceptional minds only at the price of occasional eccentricity and abnormal attitudes. When they are so harmless to others or to the State as those we deal with here, the price is not too great. But freedom to differ is not limited to things that do not matter much. That would be a mere shadow of freedom. The test of its substance is the right to differ as to things that touch the heart of the existing order.

—Justice Robert Jackson, majority opinion in *West Virginia State Board of Education v. Barnette*, 319 U.S. 624 (1943).

George Docherty, Presbyterian minister, arguing for the insertion of "under God" in the Pledge in a sermon that influenced President Eisenhower (1954)

Let me describe what the "American Way of Life" is. It is going to the ball game and eating pop-corn, and drinking Coca Cola, and rooting for the Senators. It is shopping in Sears & Roebuck. It is losing heart and hat on a roller coaster. It is driving on the right side of the road and putting up at motels on a long journey. It is being bored with television commercials. It is setting off firecrackers with your children on the Fourth of July. It is sitting for seven hours to see the pageantry of the Presidential Inauguration.

But it is deeper than that.

It is gardens with no fences to bar you from the neighborliness of your neighbor. It is the perfume of honeysuckle, and the sound of katydids in the warm night air of summer, when you go out into the garden, the children long ago asleep, and you feel the pulse and throb of nature around you. It is Negro spirituals and colonial architecture. It is Thanksgiving turkey and pumpkin pie. It is the sweep of broad rivers and the sea of wheat and grass. . . .

And where did all this come from?

It has been with us so long, we have to recall it was brought here by people who laid stress on fundamentals. They called themselves Puritans because they wished to live the pure and noble life purged of all idolatry and enslavement of the mind, even by the Church. They did not realize that in fleeing from tyranny and setting up a new life in a new world, they were to be the Fathers of a Mighty Nation.

These fundamental concepts of life had been given to the world from Mount Sinai, where the moral law was graven upon Tablets of Stone, symbolizing the universal application to all men. And they came from the New Testament, where they [were heard] in the words of Jesus of Nazareth, the Living Word of God for the world.

This is the "American Way of Life." Lincoln saw this clearly. History for him was the Divine Comedy, though he would not use that phrase. The providence of God was being fulfilled.

Wherefore, Lincoln claims that it is "UNDER GOD" that this nation shall know a new birth of freedom. And by implication, it is under God that "government of the people, by the people, and for the people shall not perish from the earth." . . .

Now, all this may seem obvious until one sits down and takes these implications of freedom really seriously. For me, it came in a flash one day sometime ago when our children came home from school. Almost casually, I asked what happened at school when they arrived there in the morning. They described to me, in great detail, and with strange solemnity, the ritual of the salute to the flag. . . .

And I came to a strange conclusion. There was something missing in this Pledge, and that which was missing was the characteristic and definitive factor in the "American Way of Life." Indeed, apart from the mention of the phrase "the United States of America," this could be the pledge of any republic. . . .

What, therefore, is missing in the Pledge of Allegiance that Americans have been saying on and off since 1892, and officially since 1942? It is the one fundamental concept that completely and ultimately separates Communist Russia from the democratic institutions of this country. This was seen clearly by Lincoln. "One nation UNDER GOD."

We face, today, a theological war. It is not basically a conflict between two political philosophies [or] between two economic systems. . . . It is Armageddon, a battle of the gods. It is the view of man as it comes down to us from the Judeo-Christian civilization in mortal combat against modern, secularized, godless humanity.

The only point I make in raising the issue of the Pledge of Allegiance is that it seems to me to omit this theological implication that is inherent within the "American Way of Life." It should be "one nation, indivisible, under God." . . .

Some might assert this to be a violation of the First Amendment to the Constitution. It is quite the opposite. . . . If we were to add the phrase, "under the Church," . . . it would be dangerous. . . . But one of the glories of this land is that it has opened its gates to all men of every religious faith. . . . So, it must be "UNDER GOD" to include the great Jewish community, and the people of the Moslem faith, and the myriad of denominations of Christians in the land.

What, then, of the honest atheist?

Philosophically speaking, an atheistic American is a contradiction in terms. Now don't misunderstand me. . . . These men, and many I have known, are fine in character, and in their obligations as citizens and good neighbors, quite excellent. But they really are "spiritual parasites." And I mean no term of abuse in this. I'm simply classifying them. A parasite is an organism that lives upon the life force of another organism without contributing to the life of the other. These excellent ethical seculars are living upon the accumulated spiritual capital of a Judeo-Christian civilization, and at the same time, deny the God who revealed the divine principles upon which the ethics of this country grow.

—"Sermon Preached by Dr. George M. Docherty, New York Avenue Presbyterian Church, on Sunday, February 7, 1954," www.post-gazette.com/nation/20020819pledge0819p1.asp.

Dwight Eisenhower, thirty-fourth U.S. president, on the new Pledge as a "spiritual weapon" (1954)

From this day forward, the millions of our school children will daily proclaim in every city and town, every village and rural school house, the dedication of our nation and our people to the Almighty. To anyone who truly loves America, nothing could be more inspiring than to contemplate this rededication of our youth, on each school morning, to our country's true meaning.

Especially is this meaningful as we regard today's world. Over the globe, mankind has been cruelly torn by violence and brutality and, by the millions, deadened in mind and soul by a materialistic philosophy of life. Man everywhere is appalled by the prospect of atomic war. In this somber setting, this law and its effects today have profound meaning. In this way we are reaffirming the transcendence of religious faith in America's heritage and future; in this way we shall constantly strengthen those spiritual weapons which forever will be our country's most powerful resource, in peace or in war.

—Dwight D. Eisenhower, "Statement by the President Upon Signing Bill to Include the Words 'Under God' in the Pledge to the Flag," June 14, 1954, www.presidency.ucsb.edu/ws/?pid=9920.

Ronald Reagan, fortieth U.S. president, arguing at a prayer breakfast that the 1960s took America out from under the protection of God (1984)

When John Kennedy was running for President in 1960, he said that his church would not dictate his Presidency any more than he would speak for his church. Just so, and proper. But John Kennedy was speaking in an America in which the role of religion—and by that I mean the role of all churches—was secure. Abortion was not a political issue. Prayer was not a political issue. The right of church schools to operate was not a political issue. And it was broadly acknowledged that religious leaders had a right and a duty to speak out on the issues of the day. . . . The climate has changed greatly since then. And since it has, it logically follows that religion needs defenders against those who care only for the interests of the state. . . .

We establish no religion in this country, nor will we ever. We command no worship. We mandate no belief. But we poison our society when we remove its theological underpinnings. We court corruption when we leave it bereft of belief. All are free to believe or not believe; all are free to practice a faith or not. But those who believe must be free to speak of and act on their belief, to apply moral teaching to public questions. . . .

Without God, there is no virtue, because there's no prompting of the conscience. Without God, we're mired in the material, that flat world that tells us only what the senses perceive. Without God, there is a coarsening of the society. And without God, democracy will not and cannot long endure. If we ever forget that we're one nation under God, then we will be a nation gone under.

—Ronald Reagan, "Remarks at an Ecumenical Prayer Breakfast in Dallas, Texas," August 23, 1984, www.presidency.ucsb.edu/ws/?pid=40282.

Alfred Goodwin, U.S. Court of Appeals judge, ruling the "under God" Pledge unconstitutional (2002)

In the context of the Pledge, the statement that the United States is a nation "under God" is a profession of a religious belief, namely, a belief in monotheism. The recitation that ours is a nation "under God" is not a mere acknowledgment that many Americans believe in a deity. Nor is it merely descriptive of the undeniable historical significance of religion in the founding of the Republic. Rather, the phrase "one nation under God" in the context of the Pledge is normative. To recite the Pledge is not to describe the United States; instead, it is to swear allegiance to the values for which the flag stands: unity, indivisibility, liberty, justice, and—since 1954—monotheism. A profession that we are a nation "under God" is identical, for Establishment Clause purposes, to a profession that we are a nation "under Jesus," a nation "under Vishnu," a nation "under Zeus," or a nation "under no god," because none of these professions can be neutral with respect to religion.

—Judge Alfred Goodwin, majority opinion, *Newdow v. U.S. Congress*, Ninth Circuit U.S. Court of Appeals, No. 00–16423 (2002).

Hillary Clinton, U.S. Senator (D-NY), joining hundreds of other members of Congress in opposing the Ninth Circuit's ruling (2002)

I am surprised and offended by the decision. . . . While our men and women in uniform are battling overseas to preserve the freedom that we all cherish, we should never forget the blessings of divine providence that undergird our nation. That includes the freedom to recite the Pledge of Allegiance in our nation's schools.

—Quoted in Helen Kennedy, "I Pledge . . . Er . . . Never Mind: Pledge of Allegiance Unconstitutional, Says Court," *New York Daily News*, June 27, 2002, p. 5.

Jay Lapidus, rabbi, arguing that generic references to God trivialize religion (2002)

In your criticism of the federal appeals court ruling that the words "under God" in the Pledge of Allegiance violate the First Amendment, you say, "A generic two-word reference to God tucked inside a rote civic exercise is not a prayer." . . . By your own words, you have demonstrated how God and religion have become trivialized in American society. Regular, sincere prayer at a house of worship or in private and the performance of God's commandments—not generic, rote civic exercises, slogans on money or imposing religion on atheists—are what truly serve God.

—Jay S. Lapidus, letter to the editor, *New York Times*, June 28, 2002, p. A26.

Anna Quindlen, columnist, denouncing the revised Pledge as jingoistic (2002)

[Eisenhower said the "under God" legislation] would help us to "remain humble." Humility had nothing to do with it. Americans are not a humble people. Instead, the pledge had become yet another cold-war litmus test. The words "under God" were a way to indicate that America was better than other nations . . . and adding them to the pledge was another way of excluding, of saying that believers were real Americans and skeptics were not.

—Anna Quindlen, "Indivisible? Wanna Bet?" *Newsweek*, July 15, 2002, p. 64.

William Safire, columnist, siding with Newdow (2004)

The only thing this time-wasting pest Newdow has going for him is that he's right. Those of us who believe in God don't need to inject our faith into a patriotic affirmation and coerce all schoolchildren into going along. The key word in the pledge is the last one.

—William Safire, "Of God and the Flag," *New York Times*, March 24, 2004, www.nytimes.com/2004/03/24/opinion/of-god-and-the-flag.html.

Emma Martens, Boulder, Colorado, high-school student, offering a secular alternative to the post-1954 Pledge (2007)

I pledge allegiance to the flag and my constitutional rights with which it comes. And to the diversity, in which our nation stands, one nation, part of one planet, with liberty, freedom, choice, and justice for all.

—Vanessa Miller, "Boulder High Students to Protest Pledge of Allegiance," *Daily Camera*, September 27, 2007, www.dailycamera.com/archivesearch/ci_13088217#axzz0fkCAtxxf.

EPISTLES

Farewell Address

GEORGE WASHINGTON, 1796

𝒰NDER THE leadership of George Washington (1732–1799) the United States was relatively united. In his First Inaugural Address, delivered on April 30, 1789, Washington allowed himself to hope that "no local prejudices or attachments, no separate views nor party animosities" would stand in the way of the common good.[1] Fisher Ames, who represented Massachusetts in the first U.S. Congress, offered that hope substance. Later in 1789, he observed "embryos of faction," which had spawned "two parties," one dominated by Northern Federalists like himself and the other by Southern opponents of Federalism.[2] Nonetheless, whatever "sparks of passion" had been lit during this First Congress "went out for want of tinder," Ames wrote. "There is less party spirit, less of the acrimony of pride when disappointed of success, less personality, less intrigue, cabal, management, or cunning than I ever saw in a public assembly."[3]

And so it went at the relatively placid origins of the American experiment. To be sure, there were political differences between the Federalist party, which favored authority and a strong central government, and the Republican party (also known as the Democratic-Republican party), which championed liberty and the rights of states. But as the editor of the pro-Jefferson *General Advertiser*, Benjamin Bache, observed in 1790, there were "no party disputes to raise the printer's drooping spirits."[4] For the most part, it was *e pluribus unum:* "out of many, one." And the magician behind that sleight-of-hand was George Washington.

America's patriarch did more than symbolize national unity, however. He worked hard to foster moderation and civility in his own Cabinet, and beyond.

Thomas Jefferson and Alexander Hamilton—the two great personalities serving under Washington—were according to Jefferson "daily pitted in the cabinet like two cocks."[5] They fought about a national bank and the French Revolution, and about the ideas that were coming to define America. In an August 23, 1792, letter to Jefferson, Washington begged for "charity for the opinions and acts of one another in governmental matters."[6] In a letter to Hamilton dated three days later, he pleaded for a "middle course"—for "mutual forbearances and temporising yieldings on all sides." "Without these," Washington continued, "I do not see how the Reins of Government are to be managed, or how the Union of the States can be much longer preserved."[7]

Washington preserved the union. He was "the linchpin that—to the extent one man could do so—held together a fragile Revolution and afterward a federal union torn by domestic and foreign controversies."[8] But his vision of a politics of civility and moderation proved to be quixotic. Historians disagree on the temperature of the partisanship that heated up during Washington's second term, but nearly all resort to metaphors of combustion to describe, as one historian put it, "the partisan fires that blazed like a raging inferno" through much of the 1790s.[9] The French Revolution, which saw the storming of the Bastille in 1789 and the guillotining of Louis XVI and Marie Antoinette in 1793, stoked that inferno, as partisans of pro-British Federalists, on the one hand, and pro-French Jeffersonians, on the other, worked the bellows from both sides.

Domestic crises also roiled the nation. Washington's decision to meet the antitax resistance movement known as the Whiskey Rebellion with force—he led a militia of nearly 13,000 men (larger than the army he commanded in the Revolution) into western Pennsylvania in 1794—and then to follow that action by denouncing the antitax societies that inspired it as "incendiaries of public peace and order" angered Republicans ever wary of the military might of the federal government.[10]

Washington tried to remain above the fray, but the fray soared up to meet him. As the 1790s wore on, opponents said he was taking on monarchical airs, that he was besotted by the British, and that he was betraying the principles of Revolution and Declaration alike. According to one historian, "In town and country some men now spat at the mention of his name, denounced him as a monocrat and an Anglomaniac, and prayed for his removal from office."[11] Deeply stung by these personal attacks, Washington decided to retire from public life.

In the long term, Washington's retirement to domestic tranquility at Mount Vernon established a two-term precedent that would be honored by all U.S. presidents until FDR's four-term run. In the short term, his retirement set off the starting gun for the first contested presidential run in U.S. history.

Instead of informing Congress or the Supreme Court of his retirement decision, Washington decided to inform the American people directly, and to use the occasion to offer some paternal advice. Washington had been America's preeminent symbol of national unity both as a general and as a president, and he wanted to leave behind a message of unity. Writing a century later, Woodrow Wilson ably summarized what would come to be known as Washington's Farewell Address. His "mature and last counsel to the little nation he loved," wrote Wilson, was "to preserve it intact, and not degrade it in the using; to put down party spirit, make religion, education, and good faith the guides and safeguards of their government, and keep it national and their own by excluding foreign influences and entanglements."[12]

To put this in more formulaic terms, Washington's Farewell Address made three main points: first, it warned against the "baneful effects of the spirit of party"; second, it warned against entangling alliances; third, it commended religion as a "pillar" of good government. All three of these elements have echoed through the American centuries and are fiercely debated today. Has political partisanship gone too far? Should the United States flex its muscles around the globe? How entangled should religion be in U.S. politics?

This "noble document," as Wilson described it, was not really an address, because it was never delivered orally.[13] It was first published on September 19, 1796, by *Claypoole's American Daily Advertiser* of Philadelphia, and appeared shortly thereafter in virtually every major American newspaper (and some in Europe). And like so many other books in the American Bible it was a "collaborative effort."[14] While considering retirement in 1792, Washington had asked James Madison to draft a valedictory. Now he turned to his former Treasury Secretary, Alexander Hamilton. Historians use different metaphors to describe this collaboration—Hamilton the draftsman and Washington the architect, for example—but there is widespread agreement that, whereas Hamilton was the stylist and ghostwriter who provided the words, Washington was the author of its ideas and the editor in chief of the final product.

George Washington led the colonists to victory in the Revolutionary War, oversaw the drafting of the Constitution, and served as the first U.S. president. So he has been rightly described as the "Foundingest Father."[15] Upon his death in 1799, Washington was the first person enshrined in the American pantheon, and he still lords over it. "If there was a Mount Olympus in the new American Republic," writes historian Joseph Ellis, "all the lesser gods were gathered farther down the slope."[16] His accomplishments, in war and in peace, are one reason he came to be seen not merely as America's Moses but also as "the Father and Saviour of his Country."[17] But Washington's words too were seen as sacred, chief among them his Farewell Address.

Washington begins this address by announcing his retirement. He then turns to his central theme: the preservation of the Union, which in his view was threatened by entangling alliances abroad and partisan politics at home. Many scholars have interpreted this farewell as a foreign policy brief for the sort of "neutrality" that now characterizes the Swiss. And much of this "foreign policy of independence" does focus on international matters.[18] Washington argues that "foreign influence is one of the most baneful foes of republican government." He warns of the "evils" produced by "inveterate antipathies against particular nations, and passionate attachments for others." In other words, he speaks of other nations as a mother speaks of her children, refusing to name a favorite. To love or hate another nation too deeply "is in some degree to become a slave . . . to its animosity or to its affection," he says. "The great rule" in U.S. foreign policy, Washington says in a series of passages that have made this address "the seminal statement of American isolationism," is "to steer clear of permanent Alliances with any portion of the foreign world."[19]

But Washington also had domestic reasons for being so wary of entanglements with foreign nations. He knew from experience how the 1794 Jay Treaty had agitated Americans, chiefly over their relative sympathies for Great Britain (whom the treaty favored) and France (whom it did not). He had also witnessed French officials trying to "tamper with domestic factions." And here we arrive at the heart of Washington's valedictory, for although this document is doubtless a declaration of independence from foreign intrigue, it is also and more centrally a declaration of war on any sort of identity politics that threatens the common good.

At a time when U.S. citizens were still coming to think of themselves as one people—Jefferson referred to Virginia as "my country" in the 1790s—Washington urges his fellow Americans to remember their revolutionary past, to revel in their common culture, and to respect the Constitution as "sacredly obligatory upon all." He warns them against two evil spirits threatening to divide the Union: the spirit of sectionalism and the "spirit of party." There are significant differences between Easterners and Westerners, Washington observes, and between the commercial North and the agricultural South. So it is tempting to succumb to the "jealousies and heartburnings" of "local interests and views." But he exhorts his fellow Americans to see themselves as *Americans* first—to revel in the "name of American" rather than local designations.

Washington speaks most passionately, however, about the "baneful effects of the spirit of party." He calls the emergent party system the "worst enemy" of government and, in a paraphrase of Mark 9:44, he describes factionalism as a sort of hell: a "fire not to be quenched." On the "mischief's of the spirit of party," he offers this litany of sins:

> *It serves always to distract the public councils and enfeeble the public administration. It agitates the community with ill-founded jealousies and false alarms, kindles the animosity of one part against another, foments occasionally riot and insurrection. It opens the door to foreign influence and corruption, which finds a facilitated access to the government itself through the channels of party passions.*

Finally, Washington addresses the church/state question in a coda barely discussed in his time, but now a matter of much controversy. Freethinkers today argue that morality need not rest on a religious foundation. *Good Without God* (2009) by Harvard's Humanist chaplain Greg Epstein makes this argument in its title.[20] But according to Washington there is no morality without religion, and no republic without morality. Drawing on architectural metaphors, Washington writes of "religion and morality" as the "indispensable supports," "great pillars," and "firmest props" of true government. But as this choice of metaphors implies, his concerns are practical rather than theological. What do religion and morality uphold? "Political prosperity" and "human happiness"—things of this world. In other words, religion is good because it is useful. Like education, virtue, and trade, it is needed for a strong and secure republic.

Shortly after the Farewell Address appeared, the "unquenchable fire" of partisan politics burst into flames. During the election of 1800, the political battle between Federalists and Republicans turned into a cosmic battle between God and the devil in which each side accused the other of treason and sedition. The Federalist *Gazette of the United States* called rank-and-file Republicans "the very *refuse* and *filth* of society,"[21] while the Republican *Aurora* judged John Adams "blind, bald, crippled, toothless."[22] All this invective spread via its own sort of web, which extended in this case to popular pamphlets and not so private letters (the blogs of the day).

In his last public speech, delivered in March 1799, Patrick Henry tried to cool this partisan fever. "United we stand, divided we fall," he said. "Let us not split into factions which must destroy that union upon which our existence hangs."[23] Jefferson did the same in his First Inaugural Address in 1801, calling on his fellow citizens to be "united with one heart and one mind."[24] But partisanship proceeded apace. Newspapers did not repent of their partisanship. Politicians did not repent of their hatred. Each party continued to accuse the other of betraying the Revolution and trampling on the Constitution. "We have no Americans in America," a bitter John Adams complained in 1801.[25]

One reason Washington's Farewell Address failed to becalm this roiling "spirit of party" is because it was "a piece of partisan politics" itself.[26] Among the powers of parties is their capacity to change the conversation, and one way they do that is by putting everyone involved in their partisan place. Both George W. Bush and Barack Obama promised during their presidential campaigns to bring a conciliatory spirit to a warring government, but each found it impossible to govern in that spirit. In his Farewell Address, Washington seems committed to channeling the antiparty spirit, but repeatedly succumbs to partisanship. As if by instinct, and against his better judgment, he finds it impossible not to stick his poison pen to his political enemies. When he speaks of "ambitious, corrupted, or deluded citizens (who devote themselves to the favorite nation)," he obviously means Jeffersonians. When he speaks of foreigners trying to manipulate public opinion through the "arts of seduction," who can doubt he is speaking of the French?

In the end, Washington's standpoint was closer to nonpartisanship than bipartisanship. His hope was not for cooperation across party lines. He hoped instead for something that was already hopelessly nostalgic: the abolition of party altogether. In practical terms, Washington was not asking for the Jeffersonians and the Federalists to become friends; he was asking the Jeffersonians to become Federalists.

Given the fighting spirit lurking inside this supposedly "neutral" document, it should not be surprising that it did not inspire Jefferson's foot soldiers to fall on their swords. William Duane, a Jeffersonian journalist who would later be arrested under the Alien and Sedition Acts, wrote shortly after the Farewell Address appeared that Washington's "advice for the future is but a defence for the past."[27] And some common folk without access to a printing press doubtless shouted for joy as word of Washington's retirement circulated. But most Americans seem to have treated the news as a sort of little death—a foreboding of another parting to come. Which is to say that Washington's apotheosis did not begin upon his death on December 14, 1799; it began three years earlier with the publication of his adieu to the American people.

Of all the books in the American Bible, Washington's Farewell Address was canonized the quickest. Almost immediately after it appeared, commentators were speaking of it as a sort of scripture. In language reminiscent of Deuteronomy 6:6–7—"And these words, which I command thee this day, shall be in thine heart: And thou shalt teach them diligently unto thy children"—true believers spoke of Washington's political creed being "engraven" or "written" on their hearts and vowed to hand it down to future generations. The *New Jersey Journal* called the address a "testimonial of affection from the BRIGHTEST MIRROR OF DEITY that ever existed."[28]

After he was laid to rest, Washington's valedictory was quoted in eulogies and reprinted as a last testament, almost like a hero's dying words. Americans now spoke of it in one breath with the Constitution and the Declaration of Independence. Even as Jeffersonians were consolidating control over the federal government, Washington's Farewell Address was becoming "the supreme expression of the American political community."[29]

Like any classic, Washington's testament means different things to different people. It has been described as a defense of Washington's administration, a campaign tract, a sermon on behalf of the public display of religion, a political manifesto for the Federalists, a rebuke of the Jeffersonians, a mercantilist tract for commercial expansionism, a retirement notice, a warning against the French meddling in American affairs, a brief on behalf of the Constitution, a warning against interventionism, a warning against isolationism, and a plea for nonpartisan unity. It was (and is) all of these things.

Washington's words were widely evoked when President James Monroe promulgated the Monroe Doctrine (1823), which pledged that America would not interfere in Europe while demanding that European nations leave Central and South America alone. During the sectional crisis of the mid-nineteenth century, Daniel Webster used them to praise the sacredness of the union, while John Calhoun used them to justify secession. In the midst of the Civil War, President Lincoln issued a proclamation on February 19, 1862, recommending that Americans assemble to "celebrate the anniversary of the birth of the Father of his Country" and to read aloud "his immortal Farewell Address."[30] Three days later, a joint session of Congress did just that.

References to the speech slackened in the early twentieth century, only to be revived with the rise of the Religious Right, which emphasized neither Washington's antiparty message nor his isolationism but his commendation of religion as a bulwark of the republic. Since the 1980s, groups such as the Moral Majority have demanded "equal billing" for Washington's views alongside Thomas Jefferson's famous metaphor of a "wall" strictly separating church and state.[31] In recent years, as party politics paralyzed Congress's ability to respond to the Great Recession of 2008, ordinary citizens and pundits alike quoted Washington's words in letters to the editor, urging their elected representatives to put patriotism over party.

In some respects, Washington's Farewell Address must be judged a failure. On each of his three main themes—partisanship, entangling alliances, and religion— he said little that was new.[32] And his main goal—to quell party passions—failed miserably. So why has this speech been treated so kindly by posterity?

There are two reasons. First, because Washington gives voice here to our own disquiet about partisanship. No matter how devoted we may be to the Democrats or the Republicans, almost all of us know, to borrow from another American Savior, that the "better angels of our nature" are forever calling us to put the common good first. In other words, the failure here is not Washington's, but our own. We return to his address because, like any good sermon, it calls out our sins and inspires us to repent. The second reason for this document's enduring popularity is straightforward: we want some words to remember him by, and these are the words he gave us.

Farewell Address

Friends and Citizens:

The period for a new election of a citizen to administer the executive government of the United States being not far distant, and the time actually arrived when your thoughts must be employed in designating the person who is to be clothed with that important trust, it appears to me proper, especially as it may conduce to a more distinct expression of the public voice, that I should now apprise you of the resolution I have formed, to decline being considered among the number of those out of whom a choice is to be made. . . .

I shall carry it with me to my grave, as a strong incitement to unceasing vows that heaven may continue to you the choicest tokens of its beneficence; that your union and brotherly affection may be perpetual; that the free Constitution, which is the work of your hands, may be sacredly maintained; that its administration in every department may be stamped with wisdom and virtue; that, in fine, the happiness of the people of these States, under the auspices of liberty, may be made complete by so careful a preservation and so prudent a use of this blessing as will acquire to them the glory of recommending it to the applause, the affection, and adoption of every nation which is yet a stranger to it.

Here, perhaps, I ought to stop. But a solicitude for your welfare, which cannot end but with my life, and the apprehension of danger, natural to that solicitude, urge me, on an occasion like the present, to offer to your solemn contemplation, and to recommend to your frequent review, some sentiments which are the result of much reflection, of no inconsiderable observation, and which appear to me all-important to the permanency of your felicity as a people. These will be offered to you with the more freedom, as you can only see in them the disinterested warnings of a parting friend, who can possibly have no personal motive to bias his counsel. Nor can I forget, as an encouragement to it, your indulgent reception of my sentiments on a former and not dissimilar occasion.

Interwoven as is the love of liberty with every ligament of your hearts, no recommendation of mine is necessary to fortify or confirm the attachment.

The unity of government which constitutes you one people is also now dear to you. It is justly so, for it is a main pillar in the edifice of your real independence, the support of your tranquility at home, your peace abroad; of your safety; of your prosperity; of that very liberty which you so highly prize. But as it is easy to foresee that, from different causes and from different quarters, much pains will be taken, many artifices employed to weaken in your minds the conviction of this truth; as this is the point in your political fortress against which the batteries of internal and external enemies will be most constantly and actively (though often covertly and insidiously) directed, it is of infinite moment that you should properly estimate the immense value of your national union to your collective and individual happiness; that you should cherish a cordial, habitual, and immovable attachment to it; accustoming yourselves to think and speak of it as of the palladium of your political safety and prosperity; watching for its preservation with jealous anxiety; discountenancing whatever may suggest even a suspicion that it can in any event be abandoned; and indignantly frowning upon the first dawning of every attempt to alienate any portion of our country from the rest, or to enfeeble the sacred ties which now link together the various parts.

For this you have every inducement of sympathy and interest. Citizens, by birth or choice, of a common country, that country has a right to concentrate your affections. The name of American, which belongs to you in your national capacity, must always exalt the just pride of patriotism more than any appellation derived from local discriminations. With slight shades of difference, you have the same religion, manners, habits, and political principles. You have in a common cause fought and triumphed together; the independence and liberty you possess are the work of joint counsels, and joint efforts of common dangers, sufferings, and successes.

But these considerations, however powerfully they address themselves to your sensibility, are greatly outweighed by those which apply more immediately to your interest. Here every portion of our country finds the most commanding motives for carefully guarding and preserving the union of the whole.

The North, in an unrestrained intercourse with the South, protected by the equal laws of a common government, finds in the productions of the latter great additional resources of maritime and commercial enterprise and precious materials of manufacturing industry. The South, in the same intercourse, benefiting by the agency of the North, sees its agriculture grow and its commerce expand. Turning partly into its own channels the seamen of the North, it finds its particular navigation invigorated; and, while it contributes, in different ways, to nourish and increase the general mass of the national navigation, it looks forward to the protection of a maritime strength, to which itself is unequally adapted. The East, in a like intercourse with the West, already finds, and in the progressive improvement of interior communications by land and water, will more and more find a valuable vent for the commodities which it brings from abroad, or manufactures at home. The West derives from the East supplies requisite to its growth and comfort, and, what is perhaps of still greater consequence, it must of necessity owe the secure enjoyment of indispensable outlets for its own productions to the weight, influence, and the future maritime strength of the Atlantic side of the Union, directed by an indissoluble community of interest as one nation. Any other tenure by which the West can hold this essential advantage, whether derived from its own separate strength, or from an apostate and unnatural connection with any foreign power, must be intrinsically precarious.

While, then, every part of our country thus feels an immediate and particular interest in union, all the parts combined cannot fail to find in the united mass of means and efforts greater strength, greater resource, proportionably greater security from external danger, a less frequent interruption of their peace by foreign nations; and, what is of inestimable value, they must derive from union an exemption from those broils and wars between themselves, which so frequently afflict neighboring countries not tied together by the same governments, which their own rival ships alone would be sufficient to produce, but which opposite foreign alliances, attachments, and intrigues would stimulate and embitter. Hence, likewise, they will avoid the necessity of those overgrown military establishments which, under any form of government, are inauspicious to liberty, and which are to be regarded as particularly hostile to republican liberty. In this sense it is that your union ought to be considered as a main prop of your liberty, and that the love of the one ought to endear to you the preservation of the other.

These considerations speak a persuasive language to every reflecting and virtuous mind, and exhibit the continuance of the Union as a primary object of patriotic desire. Is there a doubt whether a common government can embrace so large a sphere? Let experience solve it. To listen to mere speculation in such a case were criminal. We are authorized to hope that a proper organization of the whole with the auxiliary agency of governments for the respective subdivisions, will afford a happy issue to the experiment. It is well worth a fair and full experiment. With such powerful and obvious motives to union, affecting all parts of our country, while experience shall not have demonstrated its impracticability, there will always be reason to distrust the patriotism of those who in any quarter may endeavor to weaken its bands.

In contemplating the causes which may disturb our Union, it occurs as matter of serious concern that any ground should have been furnished for characterizing parties by geographical discriminations, Northern and Southern, Atlantic and Western; whence designing men may endeavor to excite a belief that there is a real difference of local interests and views. One of the expedients of party to acquire influence within particular districts is to misrepresent the opinions and aims of other districts. You cannot shield yourselves too much against the jealousies and heartburnings which spring from these misrepresentations; they tend to render alien to each other those who ought to be bound together by fraternal affection. . . .

To the efficacy and permanency of your Union, a government for the whole is indispensable. No alliance, however strict, between the parts can be an adequate substitute; they must inevitably experience the infractions and interruptions which all alliances in all times have experienced. Sensible of this momentous truth, you have improved upon your first essay, by the adoption of a constitution of government better calculated than your former for an intimate union, and for the efficacious management of your common concerns. This government, the offspring of our own choice, uninfluenced and unawed, adopted upon full investigation and mature deliberation, completely free in its principles, in the distribution of its powers, uniting security with energy, and containing within itself a provision for its own amendment, has a just claim to your confidence and your support. Respect for its authority, compliance with its laws, acquiescence in its measures, are duties enjoined by the fundamental maxims of true liberty. The basis of our political systems is the right of the people to make and to alter their constitutions of government. But the Constitution which at any time exists, till changed by an explicit and authentic act of the whole people, is sacredly obligatory upon all. The very idea of the power and the right of the people to establish government presupposes the duty of every individual to obey the established government.

All obstructions to the execution of the laws, all combinations and associations, under whatever plausible character, with the real design to direct, control, counteract, or awe the regular deliberation and action of the constituted authorities, are destructive of this fundamental principle, and of fatal tendency. They serve to organize faction, to give it an artificial and extraordinary force; to put, in the place of the delegated will of the nation the will of a party, often a small but artful and enterprising minority of the community; and, according to the alternate triumphs of different parties, to make the public administration the mirror of the ill-concerted and incongruous projects of faction, rather than the organ of consistent and wholesome plans digested by common counsels and modified by mutual interests.

However combinations or associations of the above description may now and then answer popular ends, they are likely, in the course of time and things, to become potent engines, by which cunning, ambitious, and unprincipled men will be enabled to subvert the power of the people and to usurp for themselves the reins of government, destroying afterwards the very engines which have lifted them to unjust dominion.

Towards the preservation of your government, and the permanency of your present happy state, it is requisite, not only that you steadily discountenance irregular oppositions to its acknowledged authority, but also that you resist with care the spirit of innovation upon its principles, however specious the pretexts. One method of assault may be to effect, in the forms of the Constitution, alterations which will impair the energy of the system, and thus to undermine what cannot be directly overthrown. In all the changes to which you may be invited, remember that time and habit are at least as necessary to fix the true character of governments as of other human institutions; that experience is the surest standard by which to test the real tendency of the existing constitution of a country; that facility in changes, upon the credit of mere hypothesis and opinion, exposes to perpetual change, from the endless variety of hypothesis and opinion; and remember, especially, that for the efficient management of your common interests, in a country so extensive as ours, a government of as much vigor as is consistent with the perfect security of liberty is indispensable. Liberty itself will find in such a government, with powers properly distributed and adjusted, its surest guardian. It is, indeed, little else than a name, where the government is too feeble to withstand the enterprises of faction, to confine each member of the society within the limits prescribed by the laws, and to maintain all in the secure and tranquil enjoyment of the rights of person and property.

I have already intimated to you the danger of parties in the State, with particular reference to the founding of them on geographical discriminations. Let me now take a more comprehensive view, and warn you in the most solemn manner against the baneful effects of the spirit of party generally.[a]

This spirit, unfortunately, is inseparable from our nature, having its root in the strongest passions of the human mind. It exists under different shapes in all governments, more or less stifled, controlled, or repressed; but, in those of the popular form, it is seen in its greatest rankness, and is truly their worst enemy.

The alternate domination of one faction over another, sharpened by the spirit of revenge, natural to party dissension, which in different ages and countries has perpetrated the most horrid enormities, is itself a frightful despotism. But this leads at length to a more formal and permanent despotism. The disorders and miseries which result gradually incline the minds of men to seek security and repose in the absolute power of an individual; and sooner or later the chief of some prevailing faction, more able or more fortunate than his competitors, turns this disposition to the purposes of his own elevation, on the ruins of public liberty.

Without looking forward to an extremity of this kind (which nevertheless ought not to be entirely out of sight), the common and continual mischiefs of the spirit of party are sufficient to make it the interest and duty of a wise people to discourage and restrain it.

It serves always to distract the public councils and enfeeble the public administration. It agitates the community with ill-founded jealousies and false alarms, kindles the animosity of one part

---

a. E. Burritt Smith, judge, condemning the captivity of political parties to corporate interests (1898): Not even Washington foresaw that in our time a superstitious regard for party names would place our local governments under the control of private interests. . . . The motive power behind party organizations was changed from principles to money. The rapid extension and consolidation of railroads and other enterprises of great public moment by private corporations furnished to their officials the motive for securing control of our municipal and certain of our State governments. Political parties become less and less the organs of public opinion, and more and more instruments for despoiling the public. —Quoted in "E. Burritt Smith on Politics: Breaking Away from the Party Lines and Return to Self-Government Is Advocated," *Chicago Daily Tribune*, March 14, 1898, p. 10.

against another, foments occasionally riot and insurrection.[b] It opens the door to foreign influence and corruption, which finds a facilitated access to the government itself through the channels of party passions. Thus the policy and the will of one country are subjected to the policy and will of another.

There is an opinion that parties in free countries are useful checks upon the administration of the government and serve to keep alive the spirit of liberty. This within certain limits is probably

---

b. Lyndon Johnson, thirty-sixth U.S. president, warning against "reckless factions" in 1960s America (1964): So long as there has been an America, there have always been white and black, red and brown, Protestant and Catholic, Quaker and Jew, German and Dutch, Italian and Swede, rich and poor, capital and labor. And I would remind you good people tonight that these distinctions have never stood in our way, and they do not stand in our way tonight.

The one division that our forefathers most feared, the division that they warned us against, was the division of extreme factionalism. Jefferson warned against it, Hamilton and Madison warned against it. In his Farewell Address, the first President, George Washington, warned against it. . . .

Well, my fellow countrymen, in this year of 1964, those are words and those are warnings that all responsible Americans must remember. From the election of 1789 to the election of 1960, the choices for the American Presidency have never meant changes in the broad purposes of the American people. But that is not the choice this year. There are abroad in this responsible land reckless factions, contemptuous toward the will of majorities; callous toward the plight of minorities; arrogant toward allies; belligerent toward adversaries; careless toward peace. These factions wear many names. They espouse many causes. Standing together they confront the American people and they demand that you make a choice. They demand that you choose a doctrine that is alien to America—that would lead to a tragic convulsion in our foreign relations; a doctrine that flaunts the unity of our society and searches for scapegoats among our people. It is a doctrine that invites extremism to take over our land. It is a doctrine that plays loosely with human destiny, and this generation of Americans will have no part of it.

I have great faith in the American people. They are neither sick in spirit nor faint in moral courage. They have never been more capable of choosing for themselves what they think is right or wrong. They will reject a spirit of party which Washington once said "agitates the community with ill-founded jealousies and false alarms, or kindles the animosity of one party against another." Those are the words of the first President. But I believe that spirit must be the spirit of the next President, and every President who follows him. —Lyndon B. Johnson, "Remarks in Harrisburg at a Dinner Sponsored by the Pennsylvania State Democratic Committee," September 10, 1964, www.presidency.ucsb.edu/ws/index.php?pid=26494.

true; and in governments of a monarchical cast, patriotism may look with indulgence, if not with favor, upon the spirit of party. But in those of the popular character, in governments purely elective, it is a spirit not to be encouraged. From their natural tendency, it is certain there will always be enough of that spirit for every salutary purpose. And there being constant danger of excess, the effort ought to be by force of public opinion, to mitigate and assuage it. A fire not to be quenched, it demands a uniform vigilance to prevent its bursting into a flame, lest, instead of warming, it should consume.[c]

It is important, likewise, that the habits of thinking in a free country should inspire caution in those entrusted with its administration, to confine themselves within their respective constitutional spheres, avoiding in the exercise of the powers of one department to encroach upon another. The spirit of encroachment tends to consolidate the powers of all the departments in one, and thus to create, whatever the form of government, a real despotism. A just estimate of that love of power, and proneness to abuse it, which predominates in the human heart, is sufficient to satisfy us of the truth of this position. The necessity of reciprocal checks in the exercise of political power, by dividing and distributing it into different depositaries, and constituting each the guardian of the public weal against invasions by the others, has been evinced by experiments ancient and modern; some of them in our country and under our own eyes. To preserve them must be as necessary as to institute them. If, in the opinion of the people, the distribution or modification of the constitutional powers be in any particular wrong, let it be corrected by an amendment in the way which the Constitution designates. But let there be no change by usurpation; for though this, in one instance, may be the instrument of good, it is the customary weapon by which free governments are destroyed. The precedent must always greatly overbalance in permanent evil any partial or transient benefit, which the use can at any time yield.

---

c. Walter Lippmann, writer and critic, denouncing the bitter partisanship at the end of the 1940 presidential election campaign (1940): The time to remember the wisdom of Washington [on "the baneful effects of the spirit of party"] is now when it is hard to follow it, now when the spirit he warned us against is rampant, now when the foul blows are being struck. For let us have no illusions about it. These are foul blows. To say that [the Republican candidate] Mr. Willkie is preferred by Hitler is to strike a foul blow. . . . The partisans of Mr. Willkie, who will agree that this Democratic charge of "appeasement" is a foul blow, will—one might hope—also agree that the charge of "warmongering" [made against the Democratic president FDR] is a no less foul and a no less dangerous blow. . . . These two calumnies have no place in this campaign. If unhappily, the spirit of partisanship is too fierce to let men repudiate them both this week, then next week they must both be repudiated as a patriotic duty. —Walter Lippmann, "Two Super-Smears," *Daily Boston Globe*, October 29, 1940, p. 14.

Of all the dispositions and habits which lead to political prosperity, religion and morality are indispensable supports. In vain would that man claim the tribute of patriotism, who should labor to subvert these great pillars of human happiness, these firmest props of the duties of men and citizens.[d,e] The mere politician, equally with the pious man, ought to respect and to cherish them. A volume could not trace all their connections with private and public felicity. Let it simply be asked: Where is the security for property, for reputation, for life, if the sense of religious obligation desert the oaths which are the instruments of investigation in courts of justice? And let us with caution indulge the supposition that morality can be maintained without religion.[f,g] Whatever may be conceded to the influence of refined education on minds of peculiar structure, reason and experience both forbid us to expect that national morality can prevail in exclusion of religious principle.[h,i]

---

d. W. T. Willey, lawyer, Methodist layman, and future U.S. Senator from West Virginia, enlisting George Washington in the nineteenth-century missionary effort to Christianize the West (1854): "Of all the dispositions and habits which lead to political prosperity," said President Washington in his farewell address, "religion and morality are indispensable supports." . . . It is not, therefore, as Christians only, but as patriots also, that the various Churches should exert themselves to meet the early settlers in our territories with the Bible, and indoctrinate the public mind there, from the very beginning, with the principles of our holy Christianity. —W. T. Willey, "The Spirit and Mission of Methodism," *Methodist Quarterly Review* (January 1854): 73.

e. Ignatius Smith, Dominican priest, challenging Americans to revive the spirit of Washington in the midst of the Great Depression (1933): The Father of the Nation . . . linked the happiness of our people and the success of our Nation with the profession of religious belief, the worship of God and the practice of impeccable morality. For this he lived, for this he spoke to Congress and the people, for this he prayed to his God and ours. On this Washington's birthday we are not a happy people, we cannot be counted successful in the solution of the basic problems of our Government. Neither can we be called a nation of believers, with so many indifferent to the claims of the Almighty; nor a nation of worshippers, with so many of our churches depopulated; nor a nation of morally correct men and women, with the penal institutions of the land overcrowded, the moral fiber of the people collapsing. There is hope, not so much in new legislation, new leaders or new ideals as on the return to the old state on which Washington based the happiness of the people and found success for the Nation—a return to religion, worship and decent moral life. —Quoted in "Legion Men Told Religion Is Vital," *Washington Post*, February 23, 1933, p. 7.

f. Ronald Reagan, fortieth U.S. president, arguing at a prayer breakfast for the importance of religion in American life (1984): Those who created our country—the Founding Fathers and Mothers—understood that there is a divine order which transcends the human order.

They saw the state, in fact, as a form of moral order and felt that the bedrock of moral order is religion. The Mayflower Compact began with the words, "In the name of God, amen." The Declaration of Independence appeals to "Nature's God" and the "Creator" and "the Supreme Judge of the world." Congress was given a chaplain, and the oaths of office are oaths before God. . . . George Washington referred to religion's profound and unsurpassed place in the heart of our nation quite directly in his Farewell Address in 1796. . . . Washington voiced reservations about the idea that there could be a wise policy without a firm moral and religious foundation. . . . I believe that George Washington knew the City of Man cannot survive without the City of God, that the Visible City will perish without the Invisible City. —Ronald Reagan, "Remarks at an Ecumenical Prayer Breakfast in Dallas, Texas," August 23, 1984, www.reagan.utexas.edu/archives/speeches/1984/82384a.htm.

g. J. Matt Barber, attorney, enlisting Washington's views of religion and morality in his war on the "high priest of secular-socialism," President Obama (2010): I'll say it: I agree with George Washington. Those godless, postmodern secular-socialists, who, today, hold the reins of government, are unpatriotic. Fringe leftists like Barack Obama, Nancy Pelosi and Harry Reid seek to "subvert" Washington's "great pillars" of "religion and morality" and are distinctly un-American for it. Part and parcel of Obama's agenda has been to push, at a fever pitch, the most extremist pro-abortion, pro-homosexual, anti-Christian agenda in American history. Indeed, in contrast with the deeply held religious and moral values embraced by our Founding Fathers, today's America is governed by an "immoral" and "irreligious" chief executive. Barack Obama is the high priest of secular-socialism. He seeks to undermine—if not altogether dismantle—the American exceptionalism that, hitherto, has been fundamentally woven throughout our national fabric. He aspires to the lowest common denominator. He seeks to uproot Ronald Reagan's "shining city on a hill" and relocate the "land of the free and the home of the brave" to a much lower altitude, alongside those Euro-Marxist nations he so admires and wistfully desires to emulate. —J. Matt Barber, "Time to Reunite Church and State," *Oregon Magazine*, 2010, http://oregonmag.com/Barber1210.html.

h. R. F. Bishop, Methodist minister, condemning the publication of newspapers on the Sabbath (1889): With the spirit embodied in these words the Sunday newspaper most certainly clashes. . . . The attempts now making to secularize the Sabbath are really attempts to destroy it. A secular Sabbath was dreamed of by the insanity that inaugurated the French Revolution. It is talked of nowadays by the thoughtless, the avaricious, and the ignorant—and by them alone. It is much to be regretted that good newspapers should seem to lend themselves to the work of destroying the holiest things of our civilization—a work which commands the loud applause of anarchists and saloonists, while it brings grief to thousands of Christian patriots. —R. F. Bishop, "The Sunday Newspaper: Rev. Dr. Bishop of Alexandria Submits a Dissenting View," *Washington Post*, June 2, 1889, p. 4.

It is substantially true that virtue or morality is a necessary spring of popular government.[j] The rule, indeed, extends with more or less force to every species of free government. Who that is a sincere friend to it can look with indifference upon attempts to shake the foundation of the fabric?[k]

Promote then, as an object of primary importance, institutions for the general diffusion of knowledge. In proportion as the structure of a government gives force to public opinion, it is essential that public opinion should be enlightened.

---

i. Alan Wolfe, political scientist, taking Washington to task for insisting that freedom must rest on a shared religion (2000): Ever since Washington's time, the nation has tried to untangle the riddle of just which religion should provide this guidance. A religion broad enough to include diverse believers would lack the content to inspire devotion. A religion specific enough to speak compellingly would necessarily exclude minorities. . . . Today we face the same problem described by George Washington, but without any obvious solution. For Washington, political freedom required a common morality, undergirded by a common religion. If he was right, then America cannot have political freedom. And there are some voices in America certain that Washington was right. Look around, they say, and see at once what happens when the bonds of morality are loosened: Divorce, abortion and crime rates shoot up; young people lack guidance; secular humanists dominate the schools and media. A president engages in improper sex, lies about it and is barely punished. Early Christians worried that Americans, unless they believed in God, would go to hell. Some contemporary Christians believe America already has. . . .

But there is another way to approach the issue. We could begin by acknowledging that George Washington was wrong. Freedom does not require common religious values. We are a far freer society now than we were in 1800. Just ask the descendants of former slaves, or women, recent immigrants or non-believers. And we have become freer in the absence of either a Protestant establishment or a pervading myth of a Judeo-Christian tradition. . . . We have become so religiously diverse a society, and our religious practices so accepting of choice, that we no longer need fear a takeover of our public institutions by any single religious tradition. . . .

It is already clear that efforts by conservative Christians to impose their view of faith on the country have failed. America will easily survive any attempts in the present political campaign to invoke God for one side or the other. Creationism has not defeated evolution in any part of the United States, even in the South. We find ourselves in a novel situation. Instead of wondering how we can retain our freedom amid religious diversity, we can instead marvel at the fact that our diversity has strengthened our freedom. —Alan Wolfe, "Religious Diversity as a Key to Religious Freedom," Forward, November 10, 2000, p. 9.

j. William Jennings Bryan, Democratic leader and anti-imperialist, asserting that Americans have turned their back on morality, thanks to robber barons at home and war abroad (1902): What has become of this "necessary spring" when ship-subsidy grabbers, trust magnates,

As a very important source of strength and security, cherish public credit. One method of preserving it is to use it as sparingly as possible, avoiding occasions of expense by cultivating peace, but remembering also that timely disbursements to prepare for danger frequently prevent much greater disbursements to repel it, avoiding likewise the accumulation of debt, not only by shunning occasions of expense, but by vigorous exertion in time of peace to discharge the debts which unavoidable wars may have occasioned, not ungenerously throwing upon posterity the burden which we ourselves ought to bear. The execution of these maxims belongs to your representatives, but it is necessary

---

and other representatives of a privileged class are accorded high seats in the national councils, and make and unmake laws according to their own whims and to the advantage of their own interests? What has become of the "necessary spring" when we are appropriating millions of dollars in order to carry on a war of conquest, in order to subjugate a people who are fighting for principles declared by Washington and the men of his time to be true principles, and in their truth eternal as the stars? —William Jennings Bryan, "Warnings of a Parting Friend," in *The Commoner Condensed* (New York: Abbey Press, 1902), p. 42.

k. *Afro-American* (Baltimore), calling for religious instruction in public schools during World War I (1914): These are noble and prophetic words well worthy of serious consideration while the Devil is holding high carnival in Europe. This is a Christian government. And this law is written, not in the Constitution of the United States, but upon the tablets of the hearts of the people who make up this republic. In all the great moral triumphs of this country this religious principle is the means of victory. As great and incomparable as is our public school system, its one great and dangerous weakness is its lack in cultivating that kind of morality which is the outcome of a sincere conviction and belief in God. It is said we must not teach "religion" in the public schools. We must keep out religion. And, if it be meant by such a declaration that people must be selected to teach our children, who do not sincerely, in their hearts, believe in God,—then, we would readily answer, "we ought to obey God, rather than man." . . . The banishment of "God's Most Holy Word" from the schools of our country beyond all doubt "attempts to shake the foundations of the fabric" of our national government. . . . If the people of this country really believe in God, one of the best ways to set forth that belief is in informing the young in our schools of the sovereignty, power, and qualities of the Supreme Being. Without this, we cannot rest secure in the conviction that our resources are sufficient to protect us from the devil and hell now being realized in other parts of the world. From the primary school until one leaves college, offers a magnificent opportunity for teachers who are as godly as they are intellectual, to deepen and impress the sense of God's rightful sovereignty, which will inure to the stability and perpetuity of the republic. On the other hand, the nation or people who refuse to acknowledge the Almighty as the very center of their life, will, sooner or later, be brought to dust and ashes. —"Religion and the State," *Afro-American* (Baltimore), August 15, 1914, p. 3.

that public opinion should co-operate. To facilitate to them the performance of their duty, it is essential that you should practically bear in mind that towards the payment of debts there must be revenue; that to have revenue there must be taxes; that no taxes can be devised which are not more or less inconvenient and unpleasant; that the intrinsic embarrassment, inseparable from the selection of the proper objects (which is always a choice of difficulties), ought to be a decisive motive for a candid construction of the conduct of the government in making it, and for a spirit of acquiescence in the measures for obtaining revenue, which the public exigencies may at any time dictate.

Observe good faith and justice towards all nations; cultivate peace and harmony with all. Religion and morality enjoin this conduct; and can it be, that good policy does not equally enjoin it—It will be worthy of a free, enlightened, and at no distant period, a great nation, to give to mankind the magnanimous and too novel example of a people always guided by an exalted justice and benevolence. Who can doubt that, in the course of time and things, the fruits of such a plan would richly repay any temporary advantages which might be lost by a steady adherence to it? Can it be that Providence has not connected the permanent felicity of a nation with its virtue? The experiment, at least, is recommended by every sentiment which ennobles human nature. Alas! is it rendered impossible by its vices?

In the execution of such a plan, nothing is more essential than that permanent, inveterate antipathies against particular nations, and passionate attachments for others,[1] should be excluded; and that, in place of them, just and amicable feelings towards all should be cultivated. The nation which indulges towards another a habitual hatred or a habitual fondness is in some degree a slave. It is a slave to its animosity or to its affection, either of which is sufficient to lead it astray from its duty and its interest. Antipathy in one nation against another disposes each more readily to

---

1. Garry Wills, historian, lamenting the failure of American leaders to heed Washington's warning during the Cold War (1984): We have experienced the baleful effects arising from the "permanent, inveterate antipathies against particular Nations and passionate attachments for others." We have seen the world in terms of permanent blocs, where what is done by one part is taken as done by that whole. We entered Korea and Vietnam under the assumption that those countries were the instruments of China, and China of Russia. We delayed the split between Russia and China by denying that such a thing could occur. We welcomed the support of any nation so long as it was anti-Soviet, to the damage of our influence in the third world. We supported colonial powers if they were nonsocialist and opposed anti-colonial ones if they were socialist. We froze our responses by making them dependent on a single ideological test. What Russia was for we had to be against, and vice versa. Could there be a more complete fulfillment of the Farewell Address's warning? —Garry Wills, *Cincinnatus: George Washington and the Enlightenment* (Garden City, NY: Doubleday, 1984), p. 95.

offer insult and injury, to lay hold of slight causes of umbrage, and to be haughty and intractable, when accidental or trifling occasions of dispute occur. Hence, frequent collisions, obstinate, envenomed, and bloody contests. The nation, prompted by ill-will and resentment, sometimes impels to war the government, contrary to the best calculations of policy. The government sometimes participates in the national propensity, and adopts through passion what reason would reject; at other times it makes the animosity of the nation subservient to projects of hostility instigated by pride, ambition, and other sinister and pernicious motives. The peace often, some-times perhaps the liberty, of nations, has been the victim.

So likewise, a passionate attachment of one nation for another produces a variety of evils. Sympa-thy for the favorite nation, facilitating the illusion of an imaginary common interest in cases where no real common interest exists, and infusing into one the enmities of the other, betrays the former into a participation in the quarrels and wars of the latter without adequate inducement or justification.^m It leads also to concessions to the favorite nation of privileges denied to others which

---

m. George Ball, diplomat, detailing the disastrous consequences of America's "passionate attachment" to Israel (1985): The wisdom of Washington's advice has recently been dra-matically validated by an incident that has confused and angered American citizens—the sky-jacking of TWA Flight 847 during which a group of Lebanese Shias killed one Amer-ican Marine and held hostage the remaining 152 American passengers. As we all know, the affair quickly became a television obsession that absorbed the rapt attention of mil-lions of people all over the world. In America, at least, it was watched with anxiety and bitterness—and almost complete incomprehension. Why, troubled Americans asked, were the Shias doing this dreadful thing to our countrymen when, so far as they knew, our country had never done anything to harm them? . . . Although few realized it at the time, what the exhausting television ordeal revealed to all the world was the latest chapter in a particularly ill-conceived and unedifying episode—Israel's invasion of Lebanon and America's role in that misguided enterprise. . . . [B]efore we close the book on the agoniz-ing hostage crisis, we should rethink the whole episode. This time we should not focus obsessively on what alternative steps might have been taken after the hostages had been seized; instead we should scrutinize the incident in the larger context of our Middle East policy and the dangers inherent in the conditioned reflex that characterizes our relations with Israel and that impels us to give uncritical support to almost every initiative any Israeli government may launch. For let us not overlook the fact that repeated experience is more and more validating George Washington's admonition that a passionate attachment to another country ". . . by infusing into one the enmities of the other, betrays the former into a participation in the quarrels and wars of the latter, without adequate inducement or justification." I can think of no better demonstration of that thesis than the searing melodrama of Flight 847. —George W. Ball, "The Passionate Attachment," *The Washing-ton Report on Middle East Affairs* 8 (November 4, 1985), p. 9.

is apt doubly to injure the nation making the concessions; by unnecessarily parting with what ought to have been retained, and by exciting jealousy, ill-will, and a disposition to retaliate, in the parties from whom equal privileges are withheld. And it gives to ambitious, corrupted, or deluded citizens (who devote themselves to the favorite nation), facility to betray or sacrifice the interests of their own country, without odium, sometimes even with popularity; gilding, with the appearances of a virtuous sense of obligation, a commendable deference for public opinion, or a laudable zeal for public good, the base or foolish compliances of ambition, corruption, or infatuation.

As avenues to foreign influence in innumerable ways, such attachments are particularly alarming to the truly enlightened and independent patriot. How many opportunities do they afford to tamper with domestic factions, to practice the arts of seduction, to mislead public opinion, to influence or awe the public councils. Such an attachment of a small or weak towards a great and powerful nation dooms the former to be the satellite of the latter.

Against the insidious wiles of foreign influence (I conjure you to believe me, fellow-citizens) the jealousy of a free people ought to be constantly awake, since history and experience prove that foreign influence is one of the most baneful foes of republican government. But that jealousy to be useful must be impartial; else it becomes the instrument of the very influence to be avoided, instead of a defense against it. Excessive partiality for one foreign nation and excessive dislike of another cause those whom they actuate to see danger only on one side, and serve to veil and even second the arts of influence on the other. Real patriots who may resist the intrigues of the favorite are liable to become suspected and odious, while its tools and dupes usurp the applause and confidence of the people, to surrender their interests.

The great rule of conduct for us in regard to foreign nations is in extending our commercial relations, to have with them as little political connection as possible. So far as we have already formed engagements, let them be fulfilled with perfect good faith. Here let us stop. Europe has a set of primary interests which to us have none; or a very remote relation. Hence she must be engaged in frequent controversies, the causes of which are essentially foreign to our concerns. Hence, therefore, it must be unwise in us to implicate ourselves by artificial ties in the ordinary vicissitudes of her politics, or the ordinary combinations and collisions of her friendships or enmities.

Our detached and distant situation invites and enables us to pursue a different course. If we remain one people under an efficient government, the period is not far off when we may defy material injury from external annoyance; when we may take such an attitude as will cause the neutrality we may at any time resolve upon to be scrupulously respected; when belligerent nations, under the impossibility of making acquisitions upon us, will not lightly hazard the giving us provocation; when we may choose peace or war, as our interest, guided by justice, shall counsel.

Why forego the advantages of so peculiar a situation? Why quit our own to stand upon foreign ground? Why, by interweaving our destiny with that of any part of Europe, entangle our peace and prosperity in the toils of European ambition, rivalship, interest, humor or caprice?

It is our true policy to steer clear of permanent alliances with any portion of the foreign world; so far, I mean, as we are now at liberty to do it; for let me not be understood as capable of patronizing infidelity to existing engagements. I hold the maxim no less applicable to public than to private affairs, that honesty is always the best policy. I repeat it, therefore, let those engagements be observed in their genuine sense. But, in my opinion, it is unnecessary and would be unwise to extend them.

Taking care always to keep ourselves by suitable establishments on a respectable defensive posture, we may safely trust to temporary alliances for extraordinary emergencies.

Harmony, liberal intercourse with all nations, are recommended by policy, humanity, and interest. But even our commercial policy should hold an equal and impartial hand; neither seeking nor granting exclusive favors or preferences; consulting the natural course of things; diffusing and diversifying by gentle means the streams of commerce, but forcing nothing; establishing (with powers so disposed, in order to give trade a stable course, to define the rights of our merchants, and to enable the government to support them) conventional rules of intercourse, the best that present circumstances and mutual opinion will permit, but temporary, and liable to be from time to time abandoned or varied, as experience and circumstances shall dictate; constantly keeping in view that it is folly in one nation to look for disinterested favors from another; that it must pay with a portion of its independence for whatever it may accept under that character; that, by such acceptance, it may place itself in the condition of having given equivalents for nominal favors, and yet of being reproached with ingratitude for not giving more. There can be no greater error than to expect or calculate upon real favors from nation to nation. It is an illusion, which experience must cure, which a just pride ought to discard. . . .

In relation to the still subsisting war in Europe, my proclamation of the twenty-second of April, 1793, is the index of my plan. Sanctioned by your approving voice, and by that of your representatives in both houses of Congress, the spirit of that measure has continually governed me, uninfluenced by any attempts to deter or divert me from it.

After deliberate examination, with the aid of the best lights I could obtain, I was well satisfied that our country, under all the circumstances of the case, had a right to take, and was bound in duty and interest to take, a neutral position. Having taken it, I determined, as far as should depend upon me, to maintain it, with moderation, perseverance, and firmness. . . .

The inducements of interest for observing that conduct will best be referred to your own reflections and experience. With me a predominant motive has been to endeavor to gain time to our country to settle and mature its yet recent institutions, and to progress without interruption to that degree of strength and consistency which is necessary to give it, humanly speaking, the command of its own fortunes.

Though, in reviewing the incidents of my administration, I am unconscious of intentional error, I am nevertheless too sensible of my defects not to think it probable that I may have committed many errors. Whatever they may be, I fervently beseech the Almighty to avert or mitigate the evils to which they may tend. I shall also carry with me the hope that my country will never cease to view them with indulgence; and that, after forty-five years of my life dedicated to its service with an upright zeal, the faults of incompetent abilities will be consigned to oblivion, as myself must soon be to the mansions of rest.

Relying on its kindness in this as in other things, and actuated by that fervent love towards it, which is so natural to a man who views in it the native soil of himself and his progenitors for several generations, I anticipate with pleasing expectation that retreat in which I promise myself to realize, without alloy, the sweet enjoyment of partaking, in the midst of my fellow-citizens, the benign influence of good laws under a free government, the ever-favorite object of my heart, and the happy reward, as I trust, of our mutual cares, labors, and dangers.

Geo. Washington[33]

COMMENTARY

John Quincy Adams, sixth U.S. president, asking what Washington would do about "entangling alliances" with Latin America (1826)

Among the inquiries which were thought entitled to consideration before the determination was taken to accept the invitation [to a diplomatic congress in Latin America] was that whether the measure might not have a tendency to change the policy, hitherto invariably pursued by the United States, of avoiding all entangling alliances and all unnecessary foreign connections.

Mindful of the advice given by the father of our country in his Farewell Address, that the great rule of conduct for us in regard to foreign nations is, in extending our commercial relations, to have with them as little political connection as possible, and faithfully adhering to the spirit of that admonition, I cannot overlook the reflection that the counsel of Washington in that instance, like all the counsels of wisdom, was founded upon the circumstances in which our country and the world around us were situated at the time when it was given; that the reasons assigned by him for his advice were that Europe had a set of primary interests which to us had none or a very remote relation; that hence she must be engaged in frequent controversies, the causes of which were essentially foreign to our concerns; that our *detached* and *distant* situation invited and enabled us to pursue a different course. . . .

Compare our situation and the circumstances of that time with those of the present day, and what, from the very words of Washington then, would be his counsels to his countrymen now? Europe has still her set of primary interests, with which we have little or remote relation. Our distant and detached situation with reference to Europe remains the same. But we were then the only independent nation of this hemisphere, and we were surrounded by European colonies, with the greater part of which we had no more intercourse than with the inhabitants of another planet. These colonies have now been transformed into eight independent nations, extending to our very borders, seven of them Republics like ourselves, with whom we have an immensely growing commercial, and *must* have and have already important political, connections; with reference to whom our situation is neither distant nor detached; whose political principles and systems of government, congenial with our own, must and will have an action and counter action upon us and ours to which we cannot be indifferent. . . .

The acceptance of this invitation, therefore, far from conflicting with the counsel or the policy of Washington, is directly deducible from and conformable to it.

—John Quincy Adams to the House of Representatives of the United States, March 15, 1826, in James Richardson, ed., *A Compilation of the Messages and Papers of the Presidents* (Washington, DC: U.S. Government Printing Office, 1896), 2:337–38.

Daniel Webster, U.S. Senator from Massachusetts, urging the importance of union in a speech on the centennial of Washington's birth (1832)

Among other admonitions, Washington has left us, in his last communication to his country, an exhortation against the excesses of party spirit. A fire not to be quenched, he yet conjures us not to fan and feed the flame. Undoubtedly, Gentlemen, it is the greatest danger of our system and of our time. Undoubtedly, if that system should be overthrown, it will be the work of excessive party spirit, acting on the government, which is dangerous enough, or acting in the government, which is a thousand times more dangerous. . . .

In that last paper he conjures [Americans] to regard that unity of government which constitutes them one people as the very palladium of their prosperity and safety, and the security of liberty itself. He regarded the union of these States less as one of our blessings, than as the great treasure-house which contained them all. Here, in his judgment, was the great magazine of all our means of prosperity; here, as he thought, and as every true American still thinks, are deposited all our animating prospects, all our solid hopes for future greatness. . . . If we might regard our country as personated in the spirit of Washington . . . how should he answer him who has ventured to talk of disunion and dismemberment? Or how should he answer him who dwells perpetually on local interests, and fans every kindling flame of local prejudice? How should he answer him who would array State against State, interest against interest, and party against party, careless of the continuance of that unity of government which constitutes us one people?

—Daniel Webster, *The Character of Washington: A Speech by Daniel Webster at a Public Dinner on the 22nd of February, 1832, in Honor of the One Hundredth Birthday of George Washington* (Washington, DC: United States George Washington Bicentennial Celebration, 1932), pp. 9–12.

Robert Walker, U.S. Senator from Mississippi, calling on the United States to aid the Hungarian revolution (1851)

I contend, Mr. President, that what was our policy in our infancy and weakness, has ceased to be our *true* policy now that we have reached to manhood and strength. And I deny, what is so often asserted, that either Washington or any of the founders of the Republic, ever recommended that the neutral *policy* of our early days should become an established *principle,* to govern the conduct of the country in the days of its maturity and power. . . . Now, when mature and strong, shall we supinely and timidly look on, and see all the morals, justice, and principles of international law violated, without interposing? . . .

And what principle or rule of that law should be more dear to America, than that which secures the right of the masses to rise and throw off the yoke of oppression through the medium of revolution, and this too in a fair and single-handed contest with the oppressor? But, while this principle is thus dear and important to our country and the cause of liberty, shall we never raise our voice or hand to defend or sustain it, but erase and expunge it, by conceding the right of despots to perpetually violate it? . . . Or shall Hungary, struggling alone and friendless against the tyranny of Austria, with victory and triumph already perching upon her republican standard, be again trampled to the dust—enslaved and chained by intermeddling Russia? And all this without a murmur or a blow from the land of Washington and Franklin? God forbid! . . .

No one can believe that, with the present and growing intelligence of the world, despotisms and republics can much longer occupy the earth together. The flame of conflict is already kindled; the blood of one or the other must quench it. Between the spirits of the two political existences, there can be no compromise; one or the other must quit the world. In the struggle we cannot remain neutral if we would—and it is useless longer to disguise the fact. For one, I throw off all disguise. I am for the cause of liberty and free Government, against slavery and despotism, throughout the globe. . . .

When the people of [Russia or Austria] rise up and seek to throw off the yoke, or break the chain that galls them, and the other would interfere to prevent them, this becomes an *international concern*. . . . I would recommend *war* in such an extremity, when merely moral means had proved unavailing. Nor would I delay or wait for the cooperation of England—though I am not one of those who would decline it. An alliance for such an occasion would not conflict with the policy or advice of Washington. He never condemned alliances temporary and for the occasion. He only declared that "it is your policy to steer clear of *permanent* alliances." He did not ever recommend that this "policy" should be permanent and perpetual; but for such time only as would enable you "to gain time to your country to settle and mature its institutions, and to progress without interruption to that degree of strength and consistency which is necessary to give it the command of its own fortunes." I believe that such time has been gained, and that our country has reached the required condition; and so far from condemning and declining the occasional cooperation of other countries in such a cause, I would approve and accept it, as I would, indeed, invite it.

—Robert J. Walker, *Congressional Globe*, December 16, 1851, pp. 105–6.

Woodrow Wilson, twenty-eighth U.S. president, arguing during World War I that Washington's words demand overseas enforcement of "the rights of mankind" (1916)

You know that we have always remembered and revered the advice of the great Washington, who advised us to avoid foreign entanglements. By that I understand him to mean avoid being entangled in the ambitions and the national purposes of other nations. . . . It does not mean that we are to avoid the entanglements of the world, for we are part of the world, and nothing that concerns the whole world can be indifferent to us. We always want to hold the force of America to fight—for what? Not merely for the rights of property, or of national ambition, but for the rights of mankind. Nothing that concerns humanity, nothing that concerns the essential rights of mankind, can be foreign or indifferent to us. But in fighting for these things, my fellow citizens, we ought to have a touchstone. . . .

Now the touchstone is this: On our own part, absolute singleness of heart and purpose in our allegiance to America, and then a justification of that allegiance to America by holding the doctrine that is truly American—that the states of

America were set up to vindicate the rights of man and not the rights of property or the rights of self-aggrandizement and aggression. . . .

So that when we look forward to the years to come—I wish could say the months to come—and to the end of this war, we want all the world to know that we are ready to lend our force without stint or limit to the preservation of peace in the interest of mankind. The world is no longer divided into little circles of interest. The world no longer consists of neighborhoods. The world is linked together in a common life and interest such as humanity never saw before, and the starting of wars can never again be a private and individual matter for the nations. What disturbs the life of the whole world is the concern of the whole world.

And it is our duty to lend the full force of this nation—moral and physical—to a league of nations which shall see to it that nobody disturbs the peace of the world without submitting his case first to the opinion of mankind. When you are asked, "Aren't you willing to fight?" reply, yes, you are waiting for something worth fighting for; that you are not looking about for petty quarrels, but that you are looking about for that sort of quarrel within whose intricacies are written all the texts of the rights of man. You are looking for some cause which will elevate your spirit, not depress it, some cause in which it seems a glory to shed human blood if it be necessary, so that all the common compacts of liberty may be sealed with the blood of free men.

—Woodrow Wilson, "An Address in Omaha," October 5, 1916, in Arthur S. Link, ed. *The Papers of Woodrow Wilson* (Princeton, NJ: Princeton Univ. Press, 1982), 38.347–48.

Henry Cabot Lodge, U.S. Senator (R-MA), opposing America's entry into the League of Nations (1919)

We abandon entirely by the proposed [League of Nations] constitution the policy laid down by Washington in his Farewell Address and the Monroe Doctrine. It is worse than idle, it is not honest, to evade or deny this fact, and every fair-minded supporter of this draft plan for a league admits it. I know that some of the ardent advocates of the plan submitted to us regard any suggestion of the importance of the Washington policy as foolish and irrelevant. Perhaps it is. Perhaps the time has come when the policies of Washington should be abandoned; but if we are to cast them aside I think that at least it should be done respectfully and with a sense of gratitude to the great man who formulated them. . . .

Washington declared against permanent alliances. He did not close the door on temporary alliances for particular purposes. Our entry into the war just closed was entirely in accord with and violated in no respect the policy laid down by Washington. When we went to war with Germany we made no treaties with the nations engaged in the war against the German Government. The President was so careful in this direction that he did not permit himself ever to refer to the nations by whose side we fought as "allies," but always as "nations associated with us in the war." . . . Now, in the twinkling of an eye, while passion and emotion reign, the Washington policy is to be entirely laid aside and we are to enter upon a permanent and indissoluble alliance. That which we refuse to do in war we are to do in peace deliberately, coolly, and with no war exigency. Let us not overlook the profound gravity of this step.

—Henry Cabot Lodge, "Constitution of the League of Nations," *Congressional Record,* February 28, 1919, pp. 4521–28.

Harold Preece, writer, relegating Washington's isolationism to an early historical epoch in an article in an NAACP publication (1938)

Our friends who advocate isolation are honest even when they are deceiving themselves. Their political economy is derived, however, from a period when America was thirteen struggling provinces isolated in time and space from the rest of the universe. When Washington delivered his memorable farewell address, he was speaking to a nation still semi-feudal, a country with a working-class composed of chattel-slaves in the South and independent artisans in the North. The gigantic monopolies were yet unborn, and the American flag had not yet begun to follow the American dollar around the world. . . .

At this present stage of history, with America a leading power, it is suicidal for us to imagine that we can build a wall between ourselves and the rest of the world. Is it not clear from the successive examples of Ethiopia, Spain, and now China, that peace is as much of an international problem as war? We vainly imagine that we can sit contentedly by our own firesides until the storm is finished. Every factory of the Fascist nations simply increases our own danger, and at the same time checks the forces of peace over the entire world.

—Harold Preece, "A Labor Boycott for Peace," *The Crisis,* February 1938, p. 42.

Harry Truman, thirty-third U.S. president, recalling opposition from isolationists as he implemented his Cold War policy of containment (1956)

I could never quite forget the strong hold which isolationism had gained over our country after World War I. Throughout my years in the Senate I listened each year as one of the Senators would read Washington's Farewell Address. . . . For the isolationists this address was like a biblical text. . . . They all quoted the first President in support of their assorted aims. . . .

After World War II it was clear that without American participation there was no power capable of meeting Russia as an equal. . . . Inaction, withdrawal,

"Fortress America" notions could only result in handing to the Russians vast areas of the globe now denied to them. . . .

I knew that George Washington's spirit would be invoked against me. . . . But I was convinced that the policy I was about to proclaim was indeed as much required by the conditions of my day as was Washington's by the situation in his era and Monroe's doctrine by the circumstances which he then faced. . . .

This declaration of policy soon began to be referred to as the "Truman Doctrine." This was, I believe, the turning point in America's foreign policy, which now declared that wherever aggression, direct or indirect, threatened the peace, the security of the United States was involved.

—Harry S. Truman, *Memoirs: Volume Two, Years of Trial and Hope* (Garden City, NY: Doubleday, 1956), pp. 101–6.

Michael Hirsh, journalist, contending that Americans must confront the new global order with "a more inclusive exceptionalism" (2002)

Even now, the idea that borders do not mean much anymore is not an easy one for Americans to stomach. Clinton, the "globalization" president, was constantly harping on this theme, but it never really resonated. One of the nation's founding myths, after all, is that of exceptionalism: America is a place apart, protected by its oceans. Such hopes as George Washington's farewell plea for insularity in 1796 or Thomas Jefferson's warning against entangling alliances sprang from the fact that Americans had a national life of their own, gloriously isolated from Europe and Asia, lording over the western hemisphere. . . .

Americans must now embrace what might seem a contradiction in terms: a more inclusive exceptionalism, which recognizes that what separates the United States from the world is no longer nearly as significant as what binds it to the world. Especially in today's world, where both opportunities and threats have become globalized, the task of securing freedom means securing the international system. The United States faces a tradeoff of time-honored American ideals: to preserve the most central of its founding principles, freedom, it must give up one of its founding myths, that of a people apart.

—Michael Hirsh, "Bush and the World," *Foreign Affairs* 81.5 (September/October 2002): 24.

Antonin Scalia, Supreme Court justice, arguing that Ten Commandments displays in Kentucky courthouses are constitutional (2005)

Those who wrote the Constitution believed that morality was essential to the well-being of society and that encouragement of religion was the best way to foster morality. . . . President Washington opened his Presidency with a prayer . . . and reminded his fellow citizens at the conclusion of it that "reason and experience both forbid us to expect that National morality can prevail in exclusion of religious principle." . . .

Nor have the views of our people on this matter significantly changed. Presidents continue to conclude the Presidential oath with the words "so help me God." Our legislatures, state and national, continue to open their sessions with prayer led by official chaplains. The sessions of this Court continue to open with the prayer, "God save the United States and this Honorable Court." Invocation of the Almighty by our public figures, at all levels of government, remains commonplace. Our coinage bears the motto "IN GOD WE TRUST." And our Pledge of Allegiance contains the acknowledgment that we are a Nation "under God." As one of our Supreme Court opinions rightly observed, "We are a religious people whose institutions presuppose a Supreme Being." . . .

With all of this reality (and much more) staring it in the face, how can the Court *possibly* assert that "the First Amendment mandates governmental neutrality between . . . religion and nonreligion," . . . and that "[m]anifesting a purpose to favor . . . adherence to religion generally" . . . is unconstitutional? Who says so? Surely not the words of the Constitution. Surely not the history and traditions that reflect our society's constant understanding of those words. Surely not even the current sense of our society.

—Justice Antonin Scalia, dissenting opinion, *McCreary County v. American Civil Liberties Union,* 545 U.S. 844 (2005).

Joseph Lieberman, U.S. Senator (D-CT), explaining why he is crossing the aisle to endorse Republican John McCain for president (2008)

Every day across our country, millions of our fellow citizens are facing very big and real problems. . . . But when they look to Washington, all too often they don't see their leaders coming together to tackle these problems. Instead, they see Democrats and Republicans fighting each other, rather than fighting for the American people.

I don't have to tell you that we were blessed in this country to have a great generation of founders. And they foresaw the danger of this kind of senseless partisanship. In fact, our first president, George Washington, in his farewell address, warned that the spirit of party could be the worst enemy of our democracy and enfeeble our government's ability to do its job. . . .

And that brings me directly to why I am here tonight. What, after all, is a Democrat like me doing at a Republican convention like this? Well, I'll tell you what: I'm here to support John McCain because country matters more than party. . . .

I think you know that both of the presidential candidates this year have talked about changing the culture of Washington, about breaking through the partisan gridlock and the special interests that are poisoning our politics, but, my friends, only one of them has actually done it. . . . In the Senate, during the three-and-a-half years that Senator Obama has been a member, he has not reached across party lines to accomplish anything significant, nor has he been willing to take on powerful interest groups in the Democratic Party to get something done. And I'd just ask you to contrast that with John McCain's record of independence and bipartisanship. . . .

So, tonight, I want to ask you, whether you are an independent, a Reagan Democrat, a Clinton Democrat, or just a plain-old Democrat, this year, when you vote for president, vote for the person you believe is best for our country, not for the party you happen to belong to.

—Joseph Lieberman, "Address at the Republican National Convention in St. Paul," September 2, 2008, www.presidency.ucsb.edu/ws/?pid=78572.

Conservapedia, a conservative alternative to Wikipedia, quoting from Washington's address in the opening line of its entry on "conservative" (2012)

A conservative is someone who adheres to the principles of personal responsibility, moral values, and limited government, agreeing with George Washington's Farewell Address that "religion and morality are indispensable supports" to political prosperity.

—Conservapedia, "Conservative," www.conservapedia.com/Conservative.

*T*HE UNITED STATES is founded on laws, but it also stands on metaphors, and in American life there is no more controversial metaphor than Thomas Jefferson's "wall of separation between church and state." Although this image has achieved canonical status, it does not appear in the First Amendment, which begins, "Congress shall make no law respecting an establishment of religion, or prohibiting the free exercise thereof." This portion of the First Amendment is typically divided into two religious clauses: the establishment clause (concerning "an establishment of religion") and the free-exercise clause (concerning religious liberty). Jefferson's metaphor is an attempt to say what the establishment clause means. And what it means to Jefferson is that church and state should be strictly separated.

Jefferson's architectural metaphor first appears in a January 1, 1802, letter to Baptists from Danbury, Connecticut. On October 7, 1801, the Danbury Baptist Association wrote to congratulate Jefferson on his recent "appointment to the chief Magistracy in the United States" and to express its hope that God would strengthen him "for the arduous task which providence and the voice of the people have called [him]."[1] But they also presented to their new president their tradition's teachings on the proper relationship between church and state. And they called on Jefferson to support their cause.

The Danbury Baptists lived in a state in which Congregationalism was the established church. Although the First Amendment prohibited the federal government from establishing a national church or preferring one denomination over another, no such prohibition applied to the states (at least not yet). Connecticut's taxpayer-funded Congregational establishment lived on until 1818, and Baptists saw this arrangement as unfair and un-American.

Although Baptists are often associated today with the Religious Right and the commingling of religion and politics, Baptists in the early republic were strict separationists. As a religious minority, they did not want their religious liberty trampled upon by Congregationalists or Episcopalians. But they also had a more principled objection to the marriage of church and state. They believed that governmental support for any particular religious denomination violated the religious freedom and liberty of conscience of members of other denominations. "Religion is at all times and places a matter between God and individuals," Danbury's Baptists wrote, yet "what religious privileges we enjoy (as a minor part of the state) we enjoy as favors granted, and not as inalienable rights."

When Jefferson received this letter, he was still reeling from the venomous election of 1800. Federalists had attacked Jefferson as a libertine, a coward, and a Jacobin intent on remaking America in the image of France. But the most serious charge was that Jefferson was an atheist whose ascent to the presidency would set Americans against one another and turn God against His chosen people. New England divines led the charge, branding Jefferson "a confirmed infidel" notorious for "vilifying the divine word, and preaching insurrection against God."[2] Timothy Dwight, the president of Yale, a Congregationalist minister, and a spitfire Federalist, warned that Jefferson's election would result in Bibles being "cast into a bonfire." So the faithful across New England took to safeguarding their scriptures by burying them in their backyards or hanging them down wells.[3]

Jefferson's friends responded to these charges by promising Catholics, Jews, Baptists, and other religious minorities that a vote for their candidate was a vote for religious liberty. They also criticized Federalists for trying to turn the Almighty into a party hack. Jefferson didn't oppose true religion, the Connecticut Republican Abraham Bishop argued, but he stood steadfast against "that kind of religion, which is made a foot-ball or stalking horse, and which operates only to dishonour God and ruin man."[4] Meanwhile, Jefferson fulminated in private against this *"genus irritable vatum"* ("irritable tribe of priests") who, he was convinced, harbored a secret agenda: to establish a national church and turn America into a Christian nation. Jefferson even went so far as to compare his persecution at the hands of New England clerics to the crucifixion of Jesus: "From the clergy I expect no mercy. They crucified their Saviour, who preached that their kingdom was not of this world."[5]

Jefferson won the election, and in his First Inaugural Address, delivered on March 4, 1801, he tried to demonstrate that he was a friend of true religion. He spoke of "acknowledging and adoring an overriding Providence" and asked for the blessings of "that Infinite Power which rules the destinies of the universe."[6] The Danbury Baptists' letter presented another opportunity to speak to the question of the role of religion in the new republic, and Jefferson seized upon it.

Well aware that his response would be widely read, he took care in crafting it, circulating a draft to two New England politicians in his Cabinet, Postmaster General Gideon Granger and Attorney General Levi Lincoln. In a note to Lincoln, Jefferson confided that he intended to use the letter as a way of "sowing useful truths and principles among the people, which might germinate and become rooted among their political tenets."[7] In the final version of his letter, Jefferson deleted at Lincoln's suggestion sections that might have offended the religious sensibilities of pious New Englanders, including an extended justification of his refusal to declare national days of fasting and thanksgiving. Jefferson affirmed his long-standing belief that religion was a private matter. He then stated that the First Amendment did more than prohibit a national religion. It also built "a wall of separation between church and state."

When Jefferson sent this letter there was no consensus concerning how far or how freely religion should range into political affairs. And there was certainly no consensus that the public square was supposed to be naked of religious influences. As a result, no wall of separation between church and state was erected. There were chaplains in the U.S. military services and prayers to start sessions of Congress. When presidents raised their right hand to swear their allegiance to a godless Constitution they did so with their other hand upon a Bible. In their inaugural addresses, they invoked God.

In *Reynolds v. United States,* a controversial 1878 case involving a Mormon bigamist, the Supreme Court declared that Jefferson's language "may be accepted almost as an authoritative declaration of the scope and effect of the [First] amendment."[8] But Jefferson's metaphor was otherwise forgotten until the 1940s, when the Supreme Court revisited it in a series of controversial decisions that, among other things, prohibited the preaching of religion in the public schools.

Since that time, Jefferson's metaphor has dominated debates inside and outside the courtroom about the right relationship between church and state and the proper role of religion in public life. Is the United States a secular state or a Christian nation? What did the founders intend by the First Amendment? Strict separationists argue that they did not want religion to have any role in the federal government, so they view with alarm any intrusion of religious reasons into public debates. "The United States wasn't founded as a Christian country," argues historian Jon Butler. "Religion played very little role in the American Revolution and it played very little role in the making of the Constitution."[9]

Opponents of strict separationism argue that, in the founders' minds, social order depended on virtue, and virtue depended on religion. Or, as the Northwest Ordinance of 1787 put it, "Religion, morality, and knowledge [are] . . . necessary to good government and the happiness of mankind."[10] Therefore, the founders could not have intended to turn American public life into a religion-free zone. According to this camp, Jefferson's metaphor badly distorted the meaning of the establishment clause. And the Supreme Court's unwarranted use of this metaphor transformed "secular humanism" into the de facto national religion of the United States. Jefferson's phrase "is a metaphor based on bad history, a metaphor which has proved useless as a guide to judging," wrote Supreme Court justice William Rehnquist. "It should be frankly and explicitly abandoned."[11]

Often drowned out on this constitutional battlefield are the voices of people of faith who believe that church and state must remain separate not for secular reasons but for religious ones—to safeguard the integrity of the church. "For most members of the Founding Generation," writes Yale law professor Stephen Carter, "the idea of separating church and state meant protecting the church from the state—not the state from the church."[12] Danbury's Baptists stood in solidarity with this "Founding Generation." So did Rhode Island's founder Roger Williams, who wrote in 1644 of a "hedge or wall of separation between the garden of the church and the wilderness of the world."[13]

Democrats used to stand with Williams, Jefferson, and the Danbury Baptists. Since the defeat of John Kerry by George W. Bush in the presidential contest of 2004, however, the Democratic Party has gotten religion. In a country in which nearly everyone believes in God, it just doesn't make sense anymore to be the party that is trying to banish God from public life. During the 2008 election season, Democratic presidential candidates gathered for debates on questions of faith and morals, and Barack Obama routinely referred to himself as a "committed Christian." On February 3, 2011, at the National Prayer Breakfast in Washington, D.C., he spoke of how he "came to know Jesus Christ for myself and embrace Him as my lord and savior." That used to be the language of the Religious Right, but at least for now it is Democratic rhetoric too.

"Letter to the Danbury Baptists"

To messers. *Nehemiah Dodge, Ephraim Robbins, and Stephen S. Nelson, a committee of the Danbury Baptist Association in the state of Connecticut.*

Gentlemen ~

The affectionate sentiments of esteem and approbation which you are so good as to express towards me, on behalf of the Danbury Baptist Association, give me the highest satisfaction. My duties dictate a faithful and zealous pursuit of the interests of my constituents, and in proportion as they are persuaded of my fidelity to those duties, the discharge of them becomes more and more pleasing.

Believing with you that religion is a matter which lies solely between Man and his God, that he owes account to none other for his faith or his worship, that the legitimate powers of government reach actions only, and not opinions, I contemplate with sovereign reverence that act of the whole American people which declared that their legislature should "make no law respecting an establishment of religion, or prohibiting the free exercise thereof," thus building a wall of separation between Church and State. Adhering to this expression of the supreme will of the nation in behalf of the rights of conscience, I shall see with sincere satisfaction the progress of those sentiments which tend to restore to man all his natural rights, convinced he has no natural right in opposition to his social duties.

I reciprocate your kind prayers for the protection and blessing of the common father and creator of man, and tender you for yourselves and your religious association, assurances of my high respect and esteem.

Th. Jefferson[14]

COMMENTARY

Hugo Black, Supreme Court justice, evoking Jefferson in applying the First Amendment to state laws (1947)

The "establishment of religion" clause of the First Amendment means at least this: neither a state nor the Federal Government can set up a church. Neither can pass laws which aid one religion, aid all religions, or prefer one religion over another. Neither can force nor influence a person to go to or to remain away from church against his will or force him to profess a belief or disbelief in any religion. No person can be punished for entertaining or professing religious beliefs or disbeliefs, for church attendance or non-attendance. No tax in any amount, large or small, can be levied to support any religious activities or institutions, whatever they may be called, or whatever form they may adopt to teach or practice religion. Neither a state nor the Federal Government can, openly or secretly, participate in the affairs of any religious organizations or groups, and vice versa. In the words of Jefferson, the clause against establishment of religion by law was intended to erect "a wall of separation between church and State." . . . That wall must be kept high and impregnable. We could not approve the slightest breach.

—Justice Hugo Black, majority decision, *Everson v. Board of Education*, 330 U.S. 1 (1947).

Felix Frankfurter, Supreme Court justice, ruling against efforts to commingle secular and religious instruction in public schools (1948)

We find that the basic Constitutional principle of absolute Separation was violated when the State of Illinois, speaking through its Supreme Court, sustained the school authorities of Champaign in sponsoring and effectively furthering religious beliefs by its educational arrangement.

Separation means separation, not something less. Jefferson's metaphor in describing the relation between Church and State speaks of a "wall of separation," not of a fine line easily overstepped. The public school is at once the symbol of our democracy and the most pervasive means for promoting our common destiny. In no activity of the State is it more vital to keep out divisive forces than in its schools, to avoid confusing, not to say fusing, what the Constitution sought to keep strictly apart. "The great American principle of eternal separation"—Elihu Root's phrase bears repetition—is one of the vital reliances of our Constitutional system for assuring unities among our people stronger than our diversities. It is the Court's duty to enforce this principle in its full integrity.

We renew our conviction that: "We have staked the very existence of our country on the faith that complete separation between the state and religion is best for the state and best for religion." If nowhere else, in the relation between Church and State, "good fences make good neighbors."

—Justice Felix Frankfurter, majority decision, *McCollum v. Board of Education*, 133 U.S. 203 (1948).

John F. Kennedy, U.S. Senator (D-MA), promising during his presidential run to keep his Catholicism out of his politics (1960)

I believe in an America where the separation of church and state is absolute, where no Catholic prelate would tell the president, should he be Catholic, how to act, and no Protestant minister would tell his parishioners for whom to vote; where no church or church school is granted any public funds or political preference; and where no man is denied public office merely because his religion differs from the president who might appoint him or the people who might elect him. I believe in an America that is officially neither Catholic, Protestant nor Jewish; where no public official either requests or accepts instructions on public policy from the Pope, the National Council of Churches or any other ecclesiastical source; where no religious body seeks to impose its will directly or indirectly upon the general populace or the public acts of its officials; and where religious liberty is so indivisible that an act against one church is treated as an act against all.

—John F. Kennedy, "Speech to the Greater Houston Ministerial Association, Houston, Texas," September 12, 1960, www.presidency.ucsb.edu/ws/index.php?pid=25773#axzz1ZYhIu6am.

Potter Stewart, Supreme Court justice, dissenting in a case outlawing official prayer in public schools (1962)

The Court's task, in this as in all areas of constitutional adjudication, is not responsibly aided by the uncritical invocation of metaphors like the "wall of separation," a phrase nowhere to be found in the Constitution. What is relevant to the issue here is not the history of an established church in sixteenth-century England or in eighteenth-century America, but the history of the religious traditions of our people, reflected in countless practices of the institutions and officials of our government.

At the opening of each day's Session of this Court we stand, while one of our officials invokes the protection of God. Since the days of John Marshall, our Crier has said, "God save the United States and this Honorable Court." Both the Senate and the House of Representatives open their daily Sessions with prayer. Each of our Presidents, from George Washington to John F. Kennedy, has, upon assuming his Office, asked the protection and help of God.

The Court today says that the state and federal governments are without constitutional power to prescribe any particular form of words to be recited by any group of the American people on any subject touching religion. One of the stanzas of "The Star-Spangled Banner," made our National Anthem by Act of Congress in 1931, contains these verses:

> Blest with victory and peace, may the heav'n rescued land
> Praise the Pow'r that hath made and preserved us a nation.
> Then conquer we must, when our cause it is just.
> And this be our motto, "In God is our trust."

In 1954, Congress added a phrase to the Pledge of Allegiance to the Flag so that it now contains the words "one Nation *under God,* indivisible, with liberty and justice for all." In 1952, Congress enacted legislation calling upon the President each year to proclaim a National Day of Prayer. Since 1865, the words "IN GOD WE TRUST" have been impressed on our coins.

Countless similar examples could be listed, but there is no need to belabor the obvious. It was all summed up by this Court just ten years ago in a single sentence [in *Zorach v. Clauson*]: "We are a religious people whose institutions presuppose a Supreme Being."

—Justice Potter Stewart, dissenting opinion, *Engel v. Vitale,* 370 U.S. 421 (1962).

Stephen Carter, law professor, defending the use of religious reasons in the public square (1993)

We are trying, here in America, to strike an awkward but necessary balance, one that seems more and more difficult with each passing year. On the one hand, a magnificent respect for freedom of conscience, including the freedom of religious belief, runs deep in our political ideology. On the other hand, our understandable fear of religious domination of politics presses us, in our public personas, to be wary of those who take their religion too seriously. The public balance reflects our private selves. We are one of the most religious nations on earth, in the sense that we have a deeply religious citizenry; but we are also perhaps the most zealous in guarding our public institutions against explicit influences. One result is that we often ask our citizens to split their public and private selves, telling them in effect that it is fine to be religious in private, but there is something askew when those private beliefs become the basis for public action.

—Stephen L. Carter, *The Culture of Disbelief: How American Law and Politics Trivialize Religious Devotion* (New York: Basic Books, 1993), p. 8.

David Barton, evangelical minister and conservative activist, objecting to making Jefferson's private words public policy (2001)

Earlier Courts had always viewed Jefferson's Danbury letter for just what it was: a *personal, private* letter to a specific group. There is probably no other instance in

America's history where words spoken by a single individual in a private letter—words clearly divorced from their context—have become the sole authorization for a national policy.

—David Barton, "The Separation of Church and State," January 2001, www.wallbuilders.com/LIBissues
Articles.asp?id=123.

Philip Hamburger, law professor, describing Jefferson's metaphor as "dogma" and "sacrosanct" (2002)

By the middle of the twentieth century, the idea of separation between church and state had become an almost irresistible American dogma. In the decades that followed, the justices of the U.S. Supreme Court and myriad other Americans would continue to develop this American freedom. They would explore its application to school prayer, to religious displays on public land, and to government subsidies for private schools and charities. Some Americans would recognize that they could not take separation literally and would question the breadth of its application, but they would rarely reject or altogether abandon the metaphor. Even as Americans wondered about separation's meaning, they treated its constitutional legitimacy as sacrosanct. Having enshrined the doctrine of separation in their Constitution, they deferred to it with reverence and viewed any dissent from it as profoundly un-American.

—Philip Hamburger, *Separation of Church and State* (Cambridge, MA: Harvard Univ. Press, 2002), p. 478.

Jeffrey Stout, philosopher, justifying religious appeals in public life (2004)

For most religious people, integrity requires that they refuse to "separate their lives into a private sphere and a public sphere." The "wall of separation" between church and state does not run through the heart of believers. So unless these people stop being religious, as seems unlikely, the pundits and philosophers who want political deliberation to be conducted in a completely secularized way are fighting a losing battle. But if that is true, and a large segment of the citizenry is in fact relying on religious premises when making political decisions, it behooves all of us to know what those premises are. Premises left unexpressed are often premises left unchallenged.

—Jeffrey Stout, "Thoughts on Religion and Politics," in E. J. Dionne Jr. et al., *One Electorate Under God?* (Washington, DC: Brookings Institution, 2004), p. 194.

Jimmy Carter, thirty-ninth U.S. president, decrying "radical changes" in the relationship between religion and politics (2005)

I happen to be a Christian, and I think my religion teaches me that you should render unto Caesar the things that are Caesar's and unto God the things that are

God's. And Thomas Jefferson, one of our Founding Fathers, said that we should build a wall between the church and state. That wall is being deliberately and ostentatiously, not secretly, broken down. So, there has been an increasing merger in this country of fundamentalism on the religious side, fundamentalism on the political side, and the two have come together.

—Jimmy Carter, interview with Jon Stewart, *The Daily Show,* December 5, 2005, www.thedailyshow.com/watch/mon-december–5–2005/jimmy-carter-pt--1.

Focus on the Family, an evangelical organization devoted to defending "family values," championing a revolution in jurisprudence (2008)

The so-called "wall of separation between church and state" has done more damage to America's religious and moral tradition than any other utterance of the Supreme Court. While the First Amendment was originally intended to prevent the establishment of a national religion and thus ensure religious liberty, the Supreme Court's misuse of the "separation of church and state" phrase has fostered hostility toward, rather than protection of, religious freedom.

This phrase has been used by the Court to outlaw Ten Commandments displays in public buildings, prayer and Bible reading in schools, clergy and even student invocations at school events, and other public acknowledgements of God. Such decisions clearly negate the Founding Father's presupposition of America's Christian identity. It is time to return the First Amendment back to its original meaning and revive the rich faith-filled heritage of America's public life. . . .

The First Amendment's guarantees were intended as a check on the power of government. They were never intended as a check on religion's influence on the government. One of the strengths of our Constitution and the success that we have enjoyed as a country derives from our "unalienable rights" endowed by our Creator. The whole purpose of government is, according to the Declaration of Independence, "to secure these rights." . . .

Ironically, the more that courts cleanse the public square of all vestiges of religion and morality, the further we travel from the hope of Jefferson's best work, the Declaration of Independence, and toward his warning that "whenever any form of government becomes destructive of these ends . . ." change is necessary. We're not advocating a revolution of arms, but of jurisprudence.

—Focus on the Family, "Cause for Concern (Church/State)," 2008, www.focusonthefamily.com/socialissues/law-and-the-courts/separation-of-church-and-state/cause-for-concern.aspx.

On April 12, 1963, a group of eight Protestant, Catholic, and Jewish clergy from Alabama issued a public statement meant to stake out a middle ground between segregationists and civil rights protesters in Birmingham, Alabama. They admitted there were "racial problems" in their state, but they called demonstrations "unwise and untimely." Protesters should pursue their goals "in the courts and in negotiations among local leaders, and not in the streets," they wrote. Repeatedly referring to Birmingham's problems as "local," these clergy praised city police for their "calm" and cast a wary eye on "outsiders" stirring up trouble through "extreme" actions. Among these alleged outsiders was the Reverend Martin Luther King Jr., who read the clergy's statement, published in the *Birmingham News,* from a jail cell in Birmingham.[1]

King, a Baptist minister from Atlanta who in the mid-fifties had led the Montgomery bus boycott that would turn Rosa Parks into an American icon, was now serving as president of the Southern Christian Leadership Conference (SCLC). The Reverend Fred Shuttlesworth had invited King, as SCLC president, to Birmingham to lead "Project C" (for "confrontation"): a campaign of boycotts and demonstrations against segregation.

King was looking for a way to jump-start a stalled civil rights movement, and in Birmingham's notoriously racist Commissioner of Public Safety Eugene "Bull" Connor he got what he was looking for. Shuttlesworth sent a representative to city hall to request a parade permit, which was required by a city ordinance. "Arch-segregationist" Connor said no.[2] Connor also filed for and received a court order against parading without a permit. Defiantly, King and Shuttlesworth decided to act nonetheless. On Good Friday, April 12, 1963, they led a march of fifty-two protesters carefully confined to city sidewalks. They were arrested and jailed. In order to draw attention to the cause, King refused to post bail and remained in jail until April 20.

While in solitary confinement, he read the public statement of the eight Alabama clergy. His response, "Letter from Birmingham Jail," is now a classic in American civil religion, "compelling in its logic, passionate in its embrace of freedom, elegant in its language and unassailable in its appeal for equality and justice."[3] Drafted in the margins of a newspaper and polished after King got out of jail, it first appeared in an abbreviated form in the *New York Post Sunday Magazine* on May 19 and in *Christianity and Crisis* on May 27. It was published in full, also in May, as an American Friends Service Committee pamphlet, and in the June 12 issue of *Christian Century*. In July, the first half was read into the *Congressional Record*. King's friend and colleague, the Reverend Wyatt Walker, called "Letter from Birmingham Jail" a "twentieth-century Magna Carta for human rights."[4] A letter to the editor of *Ebony* magazine read, "It should have the impact of Paul's letter to the Corinthians or John Milton's *Paradise Lost*."[5]

Meanwhile, the Birmingham campaign continued to move forward. On May 2, in what would come to be called the "Children's Crusade," more than a thousand high-school and college students marched to the front lines—a strategy sharply criticized by Attorney General Robert Kennedy and black nationalist Malcolm X. The police carried hundreds off to jail. When hundreds more turned up the next day, Connor responded with force. Soon photos of black teenagers being blasted by high-pressure fire hoses and attacked by ferocious police dogs were running in the *New York Times* and *Life* magazine. President Kennedy said the photos made him "sick."[6] They also made King an international hero. "The civil rights movement should thank God for Bull Connor," the president would later remark. "He's helped it as much as Abraham Lincoln."[7]

The Birmingham campaign concluded on May 10 when SCLC leaders agreed to end the demonstrations and local leaders agreed to release the protesters and desegregate downtown stores. Ten days later the U.S. Supreme Court ruled that Birmingham city ordinances mandating segregation were unconstitutional.[8] In June, President Kennedy, announcing in a televised address that "the time has come for this nation to fulfill its promise," called on Congress to pass a civil rights bill.[9] In August, six leading civil rights groups organized the March on Washington, where King gave his famous "I Have a Dream" speech. King was named *Time* Person of the Year in 1963, and one year later became the youngest person to receive the Nobel Peace Prize. Meanwhile, the U.S. Congress passed the Civil Rights Act in 1964 and the Voting Rights Act in 1965.

After King's assassination on April 4, 1968, in Memphis, Tennessee, his letter "made the final transformation from an eloquent and inspiring example of protest literature into an apparent God-breathed epistle."[10] Today there is a federal holiday in King's honor, and a Martin Luther King Jr. National Memorial on the Mall in Washington, D.C. King's "Letter from Birmingham Jail" is widely regarded as *the* manifesto of the civil rights movement and a classic in international protest literature. Widely anthologized, it is read across the United States by high-school and college students, and across the world—from Beijing's Tiananmen Square to the Arab Spring uprisings in Cairo—by protesters agitating for freedom and democracy.

But this letter is also a *summa theologica* of King's thought, drawing on virtually all of the intellectual resources he gathered in the black church, as an undergraduate in sociology at Morehouse, in his Ph.D. program in systematic theology at Boston University, and in close to a decade in the civil rights movement. It ranges widely across a remarkable array of sources both ancient and modern, secular and religious, enlisting in his sacred cause Paul and Socrates, Augustine and Aquinas, T. S. Eliot and Martin Luther. (Oddly, King does not refer either to Thoreau or Gandhi, both major inspirations in the theory and practice of civil disobedience.)

Considering the charge that he is an "outside agitator," King has two replies. The first is that it is not true. He serves as the president of the SCLC, which operates in every Southern state, including Alabama. Moreover, he was invited to Birmingham by a local affiliate. King's second response to this label is that the distinction between insider and outsider is moot. Did the Old Testament prophets confine their jeremiads to their hometowns? Did the apostle Paul preach the gospel only in Tarsus? Besides, who said that Birmingham is separate from Atlanta or Boston? "Injustice anywhere is a threat to justice everywhere," King writes. "We are caught in an inescapable network of mutuality, tied in a single garment of destiny. Whatever affects one directly, affects all indirectly."

King's response to charges of extremism also moves from local situations to universal principles. First, he denies that he is an extremist. "I stand in the middle of two opposing forces in the Negro community," he says, with complacent African Americans on his right and Black Muslims on his left. But then he proudly takes up the "extremist" mantle, standing alongside Jesus ("an extremist for love") and Amos ("an extremist for justice").

"Letter from Birmingham Jail" also offers a concise primer on the strategy of "nonviolent direct action." King explains each of its four steps—"collection of the facts to determine whether injustices exist; negotiation; self-purification; and direct actions"—and demonstrates how each has been employed in Birmingham. Like Thoreau before him, he advances an argument for the moral and legal "responsibility to disobey unjust laws."

At the heart of the letter, however, is King's rejection of the Alabama clergy's call for patience. Since the Renaissance, two hallmarks of the liberal tradition have been its belief in the goodness of human nature and its belief in the inevitability of human progress. The clergy who criticized the Birmingham protests were convinced that desegregation would eventually come to Alabama, because the good people of Alabama would eventually come to see the errors of their ways. Influenced by his intellectual hero the Protestant theologian Reinhold Niebuhr and more broadly by the Christian doctrine of sin, King does not believe that humans are naturally good, so he does not believe that progress is inevitable. "This 'Wait,'" he writes, "has almost always meant 'Never.'" So he rejects calls for patience. "We know through painful experience that freedom is never voluntarily given by the oppressor; it must be demanded by the oppressed," he writes.

King then turns to children in America. In an emotional appeal tucked inside what is otherwise a carefully reasoned argument, King writes of children who "have seen vicious mobs lynch [their] mothers and fathers" and "hate filled policemen curse, kick and even kill [their] black brothers and sisters." He speaks of black parents having to tell their daughter that "Funtown is closed to colored children" and then watching "ominous clouds of inferiority beginning to form in her little mental sky."

Like the civil rights movement itself, this letter is both political and religious. King writes as both a Christian minister and an American citizen. He addresses not only eight white clergymen in Alabama but also the president and white and black "moderates" throughout the United States. He refers to the Jewish thinker Martin Buber, the Declaration of Independence, and the Constitution. Rooted firmly in the prophetic tradition, which runs from Old Testament firebrands to Puritan divines to Lincoln to Niebuhr, he calls the church to task, for concerning itself more with heavenly salvation than with justice here and now. He calls America to task too for failing to live up to its commitment to freedom. Nonetheless, he remains hopeful. Like the Israelites on their Exodus march, Americans will reach their goal "because the goal of America is freedom."

Not everyone agreed with this letter or with the confrontational strategy King and his collaborators pursued in Birmingham. Moderates such as the Reverend Joseph Jackson, the African-American president of the National Baptist Convention, opposed King's civil disobedience in the name of "law and order."[11] Radicals such as Eldridge Cleaver referred to King's nonviolence policy as "self-flagellating."[12] None of the eight clergy to whom King addressed his letter has ever responded in kind, but Rabbi Milton Grafman, the only Jew to sign the statement, complained at a 1978 conference, "Now this letter is studied in English courses and sociology courses, and I get at least one letter a semester asking me if I'm still a bigot."[13]

In the 1970s, a group of black theologians proposed adding King's letter to the Bible.[14] That is unlikely. But the effort speaks to the scriptural status it enjoys in contemporary American life.

"Letter from Birmingham Jail" ❧

16 April 1963

My Dear Fellow Clergymen:

While confined here in the Birmingham city jail, I came across your recent statement calling my present activities "unwise and untimely." Seldom do I pause to answer criticism of my work and ideas. If I sought to answer all the criticisms that cross my desk, my secretaries would have little time for anything other than such correspondence in the course of the day, and I would have no time for constructive work. But since I feel that you are men of genuine good will and that your criticisms are sincerely set forth, I want to try to answer your statement in what I hope will be patient and reasonable terms.

I think I should indicate why I am here in Birmingham, since you have been influenced by the view which argues against "outsiders coming in." I have the honor of serving as president of the

Southern Christian Leadership Conference, an organization operating in every southern state, with headquarters in Atlanta, Georgia. We have some eighty-five affiliated organizations across the South, and one of them is the Alabama Christian Movement for Human Rights. Frequently we share staff, educational and financial resources with our affiliates. Several months ago the affiliate here in Birmingham asked us to be on call to engage in a nonviolent direct action program if such were deemed necessary. We readily consented, and when the hour came we lived up to our promise. So I, along with several members of my staff, am here because I was invited here. I am here because I have organizational ties here.

But more basically, I am in Birmingham because injustice is here. Just as the prophets of the eighth century B.C. left their villages and carried their "thus saith the Lord" far beyond the boundaries of their hometowns, and just as the Apostle Paul left his village of Tarsus and carried the gospel of Jesus Christ to the far corners of the Greco-Roman world, so am I compelled to carry the gospel of freedom beyond my own hometown. Like Paul, I must constantly respond to the Macedonian call for aid.

Moreover, I am cognizant of the interrelatedness of all communities and states. I cannot sit idly by in Atlanta and not be concerned about what happens in Birmingham. Injustice anywhere is a threat to justice everywhere. We are caught in an inescapable network of mutuality, tied in a single garment of destiny. Whatever affects one directly, affects all indirectly. Never again can we afford to live with the narrow, provincial "outside agitator" idea. Anyone who lives inside the United States can never be considered an outsider anywhere within its bounds.

You deplore the demonstrations taking place in Birmingham. But your statement, I am sorry to say, fails to express a similar concern for the conditions that brought about the demonstrations. I am sure that none of you would want to rest content with the superficial kind of social analysis that deals merely with effects and does not grapple with underlying causes. It is unfortunate that demonstrations are taking place in Birmingham, but it is even more unfortunate that the city's white power structure left the Negro community with no alternative.

In any nonviolent campaign there are four basic steps: collection of the facts to determine whether injustices exist; negotiation; self-purification; and direct action. We have gone through all these steps in Birmingham. There can be no gainsaying the fact that racial injustice engulfs this community. Birmingham is probably the most thoroughly segregated city in the United States. Its ugly record of brutality is widely known. Negroes have experienced grossly unjust treatment in the courts. There have been more unsolved bombings of Negro homes and churches in Birmingham than in any other city in the nation. These are the hard, brutal facts of the case. On the basis of these conditions, Negro leaders sought to negotiate with the city fathers. But the latter consistently refused to engage in good faith negotiation.

Then, last September, came the opportunity to talk with leaders of Birmingham's economic community. In the course of the negotiations, certain promises were made by the merchants— for example, to remove the stores' humiliating racial signs. On the basis of these promises, the Reverend Fred Shuttlesworth and the leaders of the Alabama Christian Movement for Human Rights agreed to a moratorium on all demonstrations. As the weeks and months went by, we realized that we were the victims of a broken promise. A few signs, briefly removed, returned; the others remained. As in so many past experiences, our hopes had been blasted, and the shadow of deep disappointment settled upon us.

We had no alternative except to prepare for direct action, whereby we would present our very bodies as a means of laying our case before the conscience of the local and the national community. Mindful of the difficulties involved, we decided to undertake a process of self-purification. We began a series of workshops on nonviolence, and we repeatedly asked ourselves: "Are you able to accept blows without retaliating?" "Are you able to endure the ordeal of jail?" We decided to schedule our direct action program for the Easter season, realizing that except for Christmas, this is the main shopping period of the year. Knowing that a strong economic-withdrawal program would be the by-product of direct action, we felt that this would be the best time to bring pressure to bear on the merchants for the needed change.

Then it occurred to us that Birmingham's mayoral election was coming up in March, and we speedily decided to postpone action until after election day. When we discovered that the Commissioner of Public Safety, Eugene "Bull" Connor, had piled up enough votes to be in the runoff, we decided again to postpone action until the day after the runoff so that the demonstrations could not be used to cloud the issues. Like many others, we waited to see Mr. Connor defeated, and to this end we endured postponement after postponement. Having aided in this community need, we felt that our direct action program could be delayed no longer.

You may well ask: "Why direct action? Why sit-ins, marches and so forth? Isn't negotiation a better path?" You are quite right in calling for negotiation. Indeed, this is the very purpose of direct action. Nonviolent direct action seeks to create such a crisis and foster such a tension that a community which has constantly refused to negotiate is forced to confront the issue. It seeks so to dramatize the issue that it can no longer be ignored. My citing the creation of tension as part of the work of the nonviolent resister may sound rather shocking. But I must confess that I am not afraid of the word "tension." I have earnestly opposed violent tension, but there is a type of constructive, nonviolent tension which is necessary for growth. Just as Socrates felt that it was necessary to create a tension in the mind so that individuals could rise from the bondage of myths and half-truths to the unfettered realm of creative analysis and objective appraisal, so must we see the need for nonviolent gadflies to create the kind of tension in society that will help men rise from the dark depths of prejudice and racism to the majestic heights of understanding and brotherhood.

The purpose of our direct action program is to create a situation so crisis-packed that it will inevitably open the door to negotiation. I therefore concur with you in your call for negotiation. Too long has our beloved Southland been bogged down in a tragic effort to live in monologue rather than dialogue.

One of the basic points in your statement is that the action that I and my associates have taken in Birmingham is untimely. Some have asked: "Why didn't you give the new city administration time to act?" The only answer that I can give to this query is that the new Birmingham administration must be prodded about as much as the outgoing one, before it will act. We are sadly mistaken if we feel that the election of Albert Boutwell as mayor will bring the millennium to Birmingham. While Mr. Boutwell is a much more gentle person than Mr. Connor, they are both segregationists, dedicated to maintenance of the status quo. I have hope that Mr. Boutwell will be reasonable enough to see the futility of massive resistance to desegregation. But he will not see this without pressure from devotees of civil rights. My friends, I must say to you that we have not made a single gain in civil rights without determined legal and nonviolent pressure. Lamentably, it is an historical fact that privileged groups seldom give up their privileges voluntarily. Individuals may see the moral light and voluntarily give up their unjust posture; but, as Reinhold Niebuhr has reminded us, groups tend to be more immoral than individuals.

We know through painful experience that freedom is never voluntarily given by the oppressor; it must be demanded by the oppressed. Frankly, I have yet to engage in a direct action campaign that was "well timed" in the view of those who have not suffered unduly from the disease of segregation. For years now I have heard the word "Wait!" It rings in the ear of every Negro with piercing familiarity. This "Wait" has almost always meant "Never." We must come to see, with one of our distinguished jurists, that "justice too long delayed is justice denied."

We have waited for more than 340 years for our constitutional and God-given rights. The nations of Asia and Africa are moving with jetlike speed toward gaining political independence, but we still creep at horse-and-buggy pace toward gaining a cup of coffee at a lunch counter. Perhaps it is easy for those who have never felt the stinging darts of segregation to say, "Wait." But when you have seen vicious mobs lynch your mothers and fathers at will and drown your sisters and brothers at whim; when you have seen hate filled policemen curse, kick and even kill your black brothers and sisters; when you see the vast majority of your twenty million Negro brothers smothering in an airtight cage of poverty in the midst of an affluent society; when you suddenly find your tongue twisted and your speech stammering as you seek to explain to your six-year-old daughter why she can't go to the public amusement park that has just been advertised on television, and see tears welling up in her eyes when she is told that Funtown is closed to colored children, and see ominous clouds of inferiority beginning to form in her little mental sky, and see her beginning to distort her personality by developing an unconscious bitterness toward white people; when you have to concoct an answer for a five-year-old son who is asking: "Daddy, why do white people treat colored people so mean?"; when you take a cross-county drive and find it necessary to sleep night after night in the uncomfortable corners of your automobile because no motel will accept you; when you are humiliated day in and day out by nagging signs reading "white" and "colored"; when your first name becomes "nigger," your middle name becomes "boy" (however old you are) and your last name becomes "John," and your wife and mother are never given the respected title "Mrs."; when you are harried by day and haunted by night by the fact that you are a Negro, living constantly at tiptoe stance, never quite knowing what to expect next, and are plagued with inner fears and outer resentments; when you are forever fighting a degenerating sense of "nobodiness"—then you will understand why we find it difficult to wait. There comes a time when the cup of endurance runs over, and men are no longer willing to be plunged into the abyss of despair. I hope, sirs, you can understand our legitimate and unavoidable impatience.

You express a great deal of anxiety over our willingness to break laws. This is certainly a legitimate concern. Since we so diligently urge people to obey the Supreme Court's decision of 1954 outlawing segregation in the public schools, at first glance it may seem rather paradoxical for us consciously to break laws. One may well ask: "How can you advocate breaking some laws and obeying others?" The answer lies in the fact that there are two types of laws: just and unjust. I would be the first to advocate obeying just laws. One has not only a legal but a moral responsibility to obey just laws. Conversely, one has a moral responsibility to disobey unjust laws. I would agree with St. Augustine that "an unjust law is no law at all."

Now, what is the difference between the two? How does one determine whether a law is just or unjust? A just law is a man-made code that squares with the moral law or the law of God. An unjust law is a code that is out of harmony with the moral law. To put it in the terms of St. Thomas Aquinas: An unjust law is a human law that is not rooted in eternal law and natural law. Any law that uplifts human personality is just. Any law that degrades human personality is unjust. All segregation statutes are unjust because segregation distorts the soul and damages the personality. It gives the segregator a false sense of superiority and the segregated a false sense of inferiority. Segregation, to use the terminology of the Jewish philosopher Martin Buber, substitutes an "I-it" relationship for an "I-thou" relationship and ends up relegating persons to the status of things. Hence segregation is not only politically, economically and sociologically unsound, it is morally wrong and sinful. Paul Tillich has said that sin is separation. Is not segregation an existential expression of man's tragic separation, his awful estrangement, his terrible sinfulness? Thus it is that I can urge men to obey the 1954 decision of the Supreme Court, for it is morally right; and I can urge them to disobey segregation ordinances, for they are morally wrong.

Let us consider a more concrete example of just and unjust laws. An unjust law is a code that a numerical or power majority group compels a minority group to obey but does not make binding on itself. This is *difference* made legal. By the same token, a just law is a code that a majority compels a minority to follow and that it is willing to follow itself. This is *sameness* made legal.

Let me give another explanation. A law is unjust if it is inflicted on a minority that, as a result of being denied the right to vote, had no part in enacting or devising the law. Who can say that the legislature of Alabama which set up that state's segregation laws was democratically elected? Throughout Alabama all sorts of devious methods are used to prevent Negroes from becoming registered voters, and there are some counties in which, even though Negroes constitute a majority of the population, not a single Negro is registered. Can any law enacted under such circumstances be considered democratically structured?

Sometimes a law is just on its face and unjust in its application. For instance, I have been arrested on a charge of parading without a permit. Now, there is nothing wrong in having an ordinance which requires a permit for a parade. But such an ordinance becomes unjust when it is used to maintain segregation and to deny citizens the First-Amendment privilege of peaceful assembly and protest.

I hope you are able to see the distinction I am trying to point out. In no sense do I advocate evading or defying the law, as would the rabid segregationist. That would lead to anarchy. One who breaks an unjust law must do so openly, lovingly, and with a willingness to accept the penalty. I submit that an individual who breaks a law that conscience tells him is unjust, and who willingly accepts the penalty of imprisonment in order to arouse the conscience of the community over its injustice, is in reality expressing the highest respect for law.

Of course, there is nothing new about this kind of civil disobedience. It was evidenced sublimely in the refusal of Shadrach, Meshach and Abednego to obey the laws of Nebuchadnezzar, on the ground that a higher moral law was at stake. It was practiced superbly by the early Christians, who were willing to face hungry lions and the excruciating pain of chopping blocks rather than submit to certain unjust laws of the Roman Empire. To a degree, academic freedom is a reality today because Socrates practiced civil disobedience. In our own nation, the Boston Tea Party represented a massive act of civil disobedience.

We should never forget that everything Adolf Hitler did in Germany was "legal" and everything the Hungarian freedom fighters did in Hungary was "illegal." It was "illegal" to aid and comfort a Jew in Hitler's Germany. Even so, I am sure that, had I lived in Germany at the time, I would have aided and comforted my Jewish brothers. If today I lived in a Communist country where certain principles dear to the Christian faith are suppressed, I would openly advocate disobeying that country's antireligious laws.

I must make two honest confessions to you, my Christian and Jewish brothers. First, I must confess that over the past few years I have been gravely disappointed with the white moderate. I have almost reached the regrettable conclusion that the Negro's great stumbling block in his stride toward freedom is not the White Citizen's Counciler or the Ku Klux Klanner, but the white moderate, who is more devoted to "order" than to justice; who prefers a negative peace which is the absence of tension to a positive peace which is the presence of justice; who constantly says: "I agree with you in the goal you seek, but I cannot agree with your methods of direct action"; who paternalistically believes he can set the timetable for another man's freedom; who lives by a mythical concept of time and who constantly advises the Negro to wait for a "more convenient season." Shallow understanding from people of good will is more frustrating than absolute misunderstanding from people of ill will. Lukewarm acceptance is much more bewildering than outright rejection.

I had hoped that the white moderate would understand that law and order exist for the purpose of establishing justice and that when they fail in this purpose they become the dangerously structured dams that block the flow of social progress. I had hoped that the white moderate would understand that the present tension in the South is a necessary phase of the transition from an obnoxious negative peace, in which the Negro passively accepted his unjust plight, to a substantive and positive peace, in which all men will respect the dignity and worth of human personality. Actually, we who engage in nonviolent direct action are not the creators of tension. We merely bring to the surface the hidden tension that is already alive. We bring it out in the open, where it can be seen and dealt with. Like a boil that can never be cured so long as it is covered up but must be opened with all its ugliness to the natural medicines of air and light, injustice must be exposed, with all the tension its exposure creates, to the light of human conscience and the air of national opinion before it can be cured.

In your statement you assert that our actions, even though peaceful, must be condemned because they precipitate violence. But is this a logical assertion? Isn't this like condemning a robbed man because his possession of money precipitated the evil act of robbery? Isn't this like condemning Socrates because his unswerving commitment to truth and his philosophical inquiries precipitated the act by the misguided populace in which they made him drink hemlock? Isn't this like condemning Jesus because his unique God-consciousness and never-ceasing devotion to God's will precipitated the evil act of crucifixion? We must come to see that, as the federal courts have consistently affirmed, it is wrong to urge an individual to cease his efforts to gain his basic constitutional rights because the quest may precipitate violence. Society must protect the robbed and punish the robber.

I had also hoped that the white moderate would reject the myth concerning time in relation to the struggle for freedom. I have just received a letter from a white brother in Texas. He writes: "All Christians know that the colored people will receive equal rights eventually, but it is possible that you are in too great a religious hurry. It has taken Christianity almost two thousand years to accomplish what it has. The teachings of Christ take time to come to earth." Such an attitude stems from a tragic misconception of time, from the strangely irrational notion that there is something in the very flow of time that will inevitably cure all ills. Actually, time itself is neutral; it can be used either destructively or constructively. More and more I feel that the people of ill will have used time much more effectively than have the people of good will. We will have to repent in this generation not merely for the hateful words and actions of the bad people but for the appalling silence of the good people. Human progress never rolls in on wheels of inevitability; it comes through the tireless efforts of men willing to be co-workers with God, and without this hard work, time itself becomes an ally of the forces of social stagnation. We must use time creatively, in the knowledge that the time is always ripe to do right. Now is the time to make real the promise of democracy and transform our pending national elegy into a creative psalm of brotherhood. Now is the time to lift our national policy from the quicksand of racial injustice to the solid rock of human dignity.

You speak of our activity in Birmingham as extreme. At first I was rather disappointed that fellow clergymen would see my nonviolent efforts as those of an extremist. I began thinking about the fact that I stand in the middle of two opposing forces in the Negro community. One is a force of complacency, made up in part of Negroes who, as a result of long years of oppression, are so drained of self-respect and a sense of "somebodiness" that they have adjusted to segregation; and in part of a few middle-class Negroes who, because of a degree of academic and economic security and because in some ways they profit by segregation, have become insensitive to the problems of the masses. The other force is one of bitterness and hatred, and it comes perilously close to advocating violence. It is expressed in the various black nationalist groups that are springing up across the nation, the largest and best known being Elijah Muhammad's Muslim movement. Nourished by the Negro's frustration over the continued existence of racial discrimination, this movement is made up of people who have lost faith in America, who have absolutely repudiated Christianity, and who have concluded that the white man is an incorrigible "devil."

I have tried to stand between these two forces, saying that we need emulate neither the "do nothingism" of the complacent nor the hatred and despair of the black nationalist. For there is the more excellent way of love and nonviolent protest. I am grateful to God that, through the influence of the Negro church, the way of nonviolence became an integral part of our struggle.

If this philosophy had not emerged, by now many streets of the South would, I am convinced, be flowing with blood. And I am further convinced that if our white brothers dismiss as "rabble-rousers" and "outside agitators" those of us who employ nonviolent direct action, and if they refuse to support our nonviolent efforts, millions of Negroes will, out of frustration and despair, seek solace and security in black-nationalist ideologies—a development that would inevitably lead to a frightening racial nightmare.

Oppressed people cannot remain oppressed forever. The yearning for freedom eventually manifests itself, and that is what has happened to the American Negro. Something within has reminded him of his birthright of freedom, and something without has reminded him that it can be gained. Consciously or unconsciously, he has been caught up by the *Zeitgeist*, and with his black brothers of Africa and his brown and yellow brothers of Asia, South America and the Caribbean, the United States Negro is moving with a sense of great urgency toward the promised land of racial justice. If one recognizes this vital urge that has engulfed the Negro community, one should readily understand why public demonstrations are taking place. The Negro has many pent-up resentments and latent frustrations, and he must release them. So let him march; let him make prayer pilgrimages to the city hall; let him go on freedom rides—and try to understand why he must do so. If his repressed emotions are not released in nonviolent ways, they will seek expression through violence; this is not a threat but a fact of history. So I have not said to my people: "Get rid of your discontent." Rather, I have tried to say that this normal and healthy discontent can be channeled into the creative outlet of nonviolent direct action. And now this approach is being termed extremist.

But though I was initially disappointed at being categorized as an extremist, as I continued to think about the matter I gradually gained a measure of satisfaction from the label. Was not Jesus an extremist for love: "Love your enemies, bless them that curse you, do good to them that hate you, and pray for them which despitefully use you, and persecute you." Was not Amos an extremist for justice: "Let justice roll down like waters and righteousness like an ever flowing stream." Was not Paul an extremist for the Christian gospel: "I bear in my body the marks of the Lord Jesus." Was not Martin Luther an extremist: "Here I stand; I cannot do otherwise, so help me God." And John Bunyan: "I will stay in jail to the end of my days before I make a butchery of my conscience." And Abraham Lincoln: "This nation cannot survive half slave and half free." And Thomas Jefferson: "We hold these truths to be self-evident, that all men are created equal." So the question is not whether we will be extremists, but what kind of extremists we will be. Will we be extremists for hate or for love? Will we be extremists for the preservation of injustice or for the extension of justice? In that dramatic scene on Calvary's hill three men were crucified. We must never forget that all three were crucified for the same crime—the crime of extremism. Two were extremists for immorality, and thus fell below their environment. The other, Jesus Christ, was an extremist for love, truth and goodness, and thereby rose above his environment. Perhaps the South, the nation and the world are in dire need of creative extremists.

I had hoped that the white moderate would see this need. Perhaps I was too optimistic; perhaps I expected too much. I suppose I should have realized that few members of the oppressor race can understand the deep groans and passionate yearnings of the oppressed race, and still fewer have the vision to see that injustice must be rooted out by strong, persistent and determined action. I am thankful, however, that some of our white brothers in the South have grasped the meaning of this social revolution and committed themselves to it. They are still all too few in quantity, but they are big in quality. Some—such as Ralph McGill, Lillian Smith, Harry Golden, James McBride Dabbs, Ann Braden and Sarah Patton Boyle—have written about our struggle in eloquent and prophetic terms. Others have marched with us down nameless streets of the South. They have languished in filthy, roach-infested jails, suffering the abuse and brutality of policemen who view them as "dirty nigger-lovers." Unlike so many of their moderate brothers and sisters, they have recognized the urgency of the moment and sensed the need for powerful "action" antidotes to combat the disease of segregation.

Let me take note of my other major disappointment. I have been so greatly disappointed with the white church and its leadership. Of course, there are some notable exceptions. I am not unmindful of the fact that each of you has taken some significant stands on this issue. I commend you, Reverend Stallings, for your Christian stand on this past Sunday, in welcoming Negroes to your worship service on a nonsegregated basis. I commend the Catholic leaders of this state for integrating Spring Hill College several years ago.

But despite these notable exceptions, I must honestly reiterate that I have been disappointed with the church. I do not say this as one of those negative critics who can always find something wrong with the church. I say this as a minister of the gospel, who loves the church; who was nurtured in its bosom; who has been sustained by its spiritual blessings and who will remain true to it as long as the cord of life shall lengthen.

When I was suddenly catapulted into the leadership of the bus protest in Montgomery, Alabama, a few years ago, I felt we would be supported by the white church. I felt that the white ministers, priests and rabbis of the South would be among our strongest allies. Instead, some have been outright opponents, refusing to understand the freedom movement and misrepresenting its leaders; all too many others have been more cautious than courageous and have remained silent behind the anesthetizing security of stained-glass windows.

In spite of my shattered dreams, I came to Birmingham with the hope that the white religious leadership of this community would see the justice of our cause and, with deep moral concern, would serve as the channel through which our just grievances could reach the power structure. I had hoped that each of you would understand. But again I have been disappointed.

I have heard numerous southern religious leaders admonish their worshipers to comply with a desegregation decision because it is the law, but I have longed to hear white ministers declare: "Follow this decree because integration is morally right and because the Negro is your brother." In the midst of blatant injustices inflicted upon the Negro, I have watched white churchmen stand on the sideline and mouth pious irrelevancies and sanctimonious trivialities. In the midst of a mighty struggle to rid our nation of racial and economic injustice, I have heard many ministers say: "Those are social issues, with which the gospel has no real concern." And I have watched many churches commit themselves to a completely otherworldly religion which makes a strange, un-Biblical distinction between body and soul, between the sacred and the secular.

I have traveled the length and breadth of Alabama, Mississippi and all the other southern states. On sweltering summer days and crisp autumn mornings I have looked at the South's beautiful churches with their lofty spires pointing heavenward. I have beheld the impressive outlines of her massive religious education buildings. Over and over I have found myself asking: "What kind of people worship here? Who is their God? Where were their voices when the lips of Governor Barnett dripped with words of interposition and nullification? Where were they when Governor Wallace gave a clarion call for defiance and hatred? Where were their voices of support when bruised and weary Negro men and women decided to rise from the dark dungeons of complacency to the bright hills of creative protest?"

Yes, these questions are still in my mind. In deep disappointment I have wept over the laxity of the church. But be assured that my tears have been tears of love. There can be no deep disappointment where there is not deep love. Yes, I love the church. How could I do otherwise? I am in the rather unique position of being the son, the grandson and the great-grandson of preachers. Yes, I see the church as the body of Christ. But, oh! How we have blemished and scarred that body through social neglect and through fear of being nonconformists.

There was a time when the church was very powerful—in the time when the early Christians rejoiced at being deemed worthy to suffer for what they believed. In those days the church was not merely a thermometer that recorded the ideas and principles of popular opinion; it was a thermostat that transformed the mores of society. Whenever the early Christians entered a town, the people in power became disturbed and immediately sought to convict the Christians for being "disturbers of the peace" and "outside agitators." But the Christians pressed on, in the conviction that they were "a colony of heaven," called to obey God rather than man. Small in number, they were big in commitment. They were too God-intoxicated to be "astronomically intimidated." By their effort and example they brought an end to such ancient evils as infanticide and gladiatorial contests.

Things are different now. So often the contemporary church is a weak, ineffectual voice with an uncertain sound. So often it is an archdefender of the status quo. Far from being disturbed by the presence of the church, the power structure of the average community is consoled by the church's silent—and often even vocal—sanction of things as they are.

But the judgment of God is upon the church as never before. If today's church does not recapture the sacrificial spirit of the early church, it will lose its authenticity, forfeit the loyalty of millions, and be dismissed as an irrelevant social club with no meaning for the twentieth century. Every day I meet young people whose disappointment with the church has turned into outright disgust.

Perhaps I have once again been too optimistic. Is organized religion too inextricably bound to the status quo to save our nation and the world? Perhaps I must turn my faith to the inner spiritual church, the church within the church, as the true *ekklesia* and the hope of the world. But again I am thankful to God that some noble souls from the ranks of organized religion have broken loose from the paralyzing chains of conformity and joined us as active partners in the struggle for freedom. They have left their secure congregations and walked the streets of Albany, Georgia, with us. They have gone down the highways of the South on tortuous rides for freedom. Yes, they have gone to jail with us. Some have been dismissed from their churches, have lost the support of their bishops and fellow ministers. But they have acted in the faith that right defeated is stronger than evil triumphant. Their witness has been the spiritual salt that has preserved the true meaning of the gospel in these troubled times. They have carved a tunnel of hope through the dark mountain of disappointment.

I hope the church as a whole will meet the challenge of this decisive hour. But even if the church does not come to the aid of justice, I have no despair about the future. I have no fear about the outcome of our struggle in Birmingham, even if our motives are at present misunderstood. We will reach the goal of freedom in Birmingham and all over the nation, because the goal of America is freedom. Abused and scorned though we may be, our destiny is tied up with America's destiny. Before the pilgrims landed at Plymouth, we were here. Before the pen of Jefferson etched the majestic words of the Declaration of Independence across the pages of history, we were here. For more than two centuries our forebears labored in this country without wages; they made cotton king; they built the homes of their masters while suffering gross injustice and shameful humiliation—and yet out of a bottomless vitality they continued to thrive and develop. If the inexpressible cruelties of slavery could not stop us, the opposition we now face will surely fail. We will win our freedom because the sacred heritage of our nation and the eternal will of God are embodied in our echoing demands.

Before closing I feel impelled to mention one other point in your statement that has troubled me profoundly. You warmly commended the Birmingham police force for keeping "order" and "preventing violence." I doubt that you would have so warmly commended the police force if you had seen its dogs sinking their teeth into unarmed, nonviolent Negroes. I doubt that you would so quickly commend the policemen if you were to observe their ugly and inhumane treatment of Negroes here in the city jail; if you were to watch them push and curse old Negro women and young Negro girls; if you were to see them slap and kick old Negro men and young boys; if you were to observe them, as they did on two occasions, refuse to give us food because we wanted to sing our grace together. I cannot join you in your praise of the Birmingham police department.

It is true that the police have exercised a degree of discipline in handling the demonstrators. In this sense they have conducted themselves rather "nonviolently" in public. But for what purpose? To preserve the evil system of segregation. Over the past few years I have consistently preached that nonviolence demands that the means we use must be as pure as the ends we seek. I have tried to make clear that it is wrong to use immoral means to attain moral ends. But now I must affirm that it is just as wrong, or perhaps even more so, to use moral means to preserve immoral ends. Perhaps Mr. Connor and his policemen have been rather nonviolent in public, as was Chief Pritchett in Albany, Georgia, but they have used the moral means of nonviolence to maintain the immoral end of racial injustice. As T. S. Eliot has said: "The last temptation is the greatest treason: To do the right deed for the wrong reason."

I wish you had commended the Negro sit-inners and demonstrators of Birmingham for their sublime courage, their willingness to suffer and their amazing discipline in the midst of great provocation. One day the South will recognize its real heroes. They will be the James Merediths, with the noble sense of purpose that enables them to face jeering and hostile mobs, and with the agonizing loneliness that characterizes the life of the pioneer. They will be old, oppressed, battered Negro women, symbolized in a seventy-two-year-old woman in Montgomery, Alabama, who rose up with a sense of dignity and with her people decided not to ride segregated buses, and who responded with ungrammatical profundity to one who inquired about her weariness: "My feets is tired, but my soul is at rest." They will be the young high-school and college students, the young ministers of the gospel and a host of their elders, courageously and nonviolently sitting in at lunch counters and willingly going to jail for conscience' sake. One day the South will know that when these disinherited children of God sat down at lunch counters, they were in reality standing up for what is best in the American dream and for the most sacred values in our Judaeo-Christian heritage, thereby bringing our nation back to those great wells of democracy which were dug deep by the founding fathers in their formulation of the Constitution and the Declaration of Independence.

Never before have I written so long a letter. I'm afraid it is much too long to take your precious time. I can assure you that it would have been much shorter if I had been writing from a comfortable desk, but what else can one do when he is alone in a narrow jail cell, other than write long letters, think long thoughts and pray long prayers?

If I have said anything in this letter that overstates the truth and indicates an unreasonable impatience, I beg you to forgive me. If I have said anything that understates the truth and indicates my having a patience that allows me to settle for anything less than brotherhood, I beg God to forgive me.

I hope this letter finds you strong in the faith. I also hope that circumstances will soon make it possible for me to meet each of you, not as an integrationist or a civil rights leader but as a fellow clergyman and a Christian brother. Let us all hope that the dark clouds of racial prejudice will soon pass away and the deep fog of misunderstanding will be lifted from our fear-drenched communities, and in some not too distant tomorrow the radiant stars of love and brotherhood will shine over our great nation with all their scintillating beauty.

Yours for the cause of Peace and Brotherhood,

Martin Luther King, Jr.[15]

COMMENTARY

Martin Luther King Jr., reflecting on his famous letter in a Playboy interview with Alex Haley (1965)

PLAYBOY: One of the highlights of [the Birmingham] campaign was your celebrated "Letter from a Birmingham Jail." . . . Do you feel that subsequent events have justified the sentiments expressed in your letter?

MARTIN LUTHER KING: I would say yes. . . . By now, nearly a million copies of the letter have been widely circulated in churches of most of the major denominations. It helped to focus greater international attention upon what was happening in Birmingham. And I am sure that without Birmingham, the march on Washington wouldn't have been called—which in my mind was one of the most creative steps the Negro struggle has taken. . . . It was also the image of Birmingham which, to a great extent, helped to bring the Civil Rights Bill into being in 1963. Previously, President Kennedy had decided not to propose it that year, feeling that it would so arouse the South that it would meet a bottleneck. But Birmingham, and subsequent developments, caused him to reorder his legislative priorities.

—*Playboy,* January 1965, www.alex-haley.com/alex_haley_martin_luther_king_interview.htm.

Bayard Rustin, civil rights and gay rights pioneer, criticizing the Palestine Liberation Organization (1979)

Looking back on the history of the P.L.O., one thing has become abundantly clear: The P.L.O. from the day of its creation in 1964 has never once uttered a word in support of any form of nonviolent resistance, peaceful relations between Israelis and Palestinians, or a political solution to the complex problems in the Middle East. By contrast, black leaders in America . . . never once in the long history of the civil rights struggle countenanced violence or terrorism.

Dr. King, in his letter from the Birmingham jail, included a story to illustrate the rewards of perseverance in the nonviolent tradition. He wrote about a 72-year-old black woman who walked a long distance every day during [a] bus boycott. Frequently she was jeered by hostile whites; she was tired and physically weak, but she refused to use the buses. Someone asked her why she continued to support the nonviolent protest. Her response, I believe, will always be precious: "My feets is tired," she said, "but my soul is at rest." By shunning and condemning the terrorism of the P.L.O. we too can be assured that our souls will be at rest, as we preserve our tradition of nonviolence.

—Bayard Rustin, "To Blacks: Condemn P.L.O. Terrorism," *New York Times,* August 30, 1979, p. A21.

James Cone, theologian, on segregation as a "double contradiction" of American values (1991)

King's "Letter" was an eloquent and now classic statement of his theological and political views. It contained nothing new, nothing that he had not said in other sermons, addresses, and essays to white America, but when he restated what he had been saying for nearly eight years, it acquired a moral power that shook the conscience of the members of the white churches in America, especially northern liberals. King stated that nothing was more tragic for the church and the American dream than the continued existence of segregation. He saw segregation as a double contradiction: of America's democratic faith and of its religious heritage. Of the two contradictions, according to King, the religious one was the worst.

—James H. Cone, *Martin and Malcolm and America: A Dream or a Nightmare* (Maryknoll, NY: Orbis, 1991), p. 140.

Jesse Jackson, civil rights activist and Democratic politician, likening the Christian Coalition to the white clergy who prompted King's letter (1995)

Dr. King's "Letter from Birmingham Jail" was written to the Christian coalition. The white ministers in Birmingham—who had never raised their voices for racial justice or general equality or the rights of workers to organize—publicly challenged him for coming to Birmingham and demanded to know what his motives were. So the "Letter from Birmingham Jail" was to the Christian coalition, and yet here they are now—still having never raised their voices for racial justice or for general equality or for the rights of workers, or for the poor and the disenfranchised and the dispossessed. By definition, there are no Jewish members of the Christian Coalition. There are just a smattering of blacks—just enough for the Coalition to cover itself. Fundamentally, if you look at their positions—whether it's on South Africa or Haiti or civil rights or racial justice—there is a spirit there that does not reflect the compassion or the character of the faith. They've franchised the name, but their positions do not reflect the character of the faith.

—Quoted in John Nichols, "Jesse Jackson," *Progressive* 59.1 (January 1995): 31.

Nanette Lee Reynolds and Eleanor Josaitis, civil rights activists, applying King's letter to post-9/11 racial profiling (2002)

In many parts of the country bigots have used the tragedy [of 9/11] as an opportunity to physically assault and verbally harass people who "look Middle Eastern" or happened to have Muslim names. At least one man, a Sikh from India, was killed. . . .

Fortunately, tragedy also has a way of inspiring good deeds. In many communities around the country, non-Muslim women sought out their Muslim sisters and volunteered to escort them on outings. On some university campuses, women wore head coverings in an attempt to show solidarity with their female Muslim schoolmates. . . .

On this 73rd birthday of Dr. Martin Luther King Jr., there is something ironic about these developments: it's taken the worst domestic terrorist act in American history to help bring us a few more baby steps closer to the realization of the vision of brotherhood and community nursed by this apostle of love and nonviolence. This kind of coming together is, we think, another chapter in Dr. King's enduring legacy. . . .

"Injustice anywhere is a threat to injustice everywhere," Dr. King wrote in his "Letter from Birmingham Jail." "We are caught in an inescapable network of mutuality, tied up in a single garment of destiny. What affects one directly, affects all indirectly."

There is something prescient about that comment, given the perceived attacks on civil liberties in recent months. No segment of this population exists in isolation. And, as Dr. King would have seen it, nor could any group afford to. Therefore, the problem of the central city is not just the problem of the people who live there; it is our problem. The arbitrary profiling at airports and borders of people of young men of Middle Eastern ancestry is not just the problem of the two million-plus Americans of Middle Eastern descent; it is our problem.

—Nanette Lee Reynolds and Eleanor Josaitis, "Sept. 11 Puts Unique Twist on the Legacy of Dr. Martin Luther King Jr.," *Michigan Chronicle*, January 23, 2002, p. 7.

Sarah Palin, former Alaska governor, using King's "eloquent letter" to argue for a greater role for conservative Christianity in the public square (2010)

[King's] famous "Letter from Birmingham Jail" was both a refutation of racial segregation and a repudiation of those who opposed civil disobedience in pursuit of civil rights—a *refudiation,* if you will—cast in explicitly religious terms. . . . Martin Luther King, Jr.'s, appeal to our religious faith and the morality that it informs eventually succeeded, and thank God for that. Just as our Founders couldn't foresee America surviving in liberty without religion, it's hard to see how slavery could have been abolished and civil rights achieved in an America without religious faith and values. No one objected to the civil rights movement's grounding in Christianity, seeing it as somehow offensive to Americans of other faiths, let alone harmful to atheists. . . . And yet this selective evocation of religious tolerance continues today when Americans are lectured about who can exercise their freedom of religion, and under what circumstances.

—Sarah Palin, *America by Heart: Reflections on Family, Faith, and Flag* (New York: HarperCollins, 2010), pp. 241–44.

EPILOGUE

CRIPTURES do a lot of heavy lifting in the world's religions—so much so that many observers confuse what the Bible and the Qur'an *say* with what Christianity and Islam *are*. Faith says that scriptural authority comes from God. Historically speaking, this authority comes from the ancients—people in first-century Palestine or the seventh-century Arabian Peninsula who recorded the truth as they saw it. But if scriptures are going to speak to living people, they need to adapt to contemporary circumstances, and such work cannot be done by the dead.

Many religions have "open canons," which adapt through ongoing revelation. This is the strategy of the Church of Jesus Christ of Latter-day Saints, popularly known as the Mormons. In the 1970s, Donny Osmond tried to explain on national television why the LDS Church would not permit men of African ancestry to become priests. In June 1978, LDS president Spencer Kimball announced a new revelation from God allowing ordination to the priesthood "without regard for race or color." This development can be seen as hypocrisy or delusion. For 148 years God banned men of African descent from the priesthood, but in the summer of 1978 He changed His mind? However, this openness to new revelation can also be seen as a laudable effort to adapt to changing circumstances.

Other religions have "closed canons." The list of books in the Catholic Bible was debated at a series of early church councils and fixed by the fourth century. During the sixteenth-century Reformation, Protestants distanced themselves from Catholics in part by adopting a different Bible, which exiled some books of the Catholic Bible to the Apocrypha. Religions with closed canons change with the times not by adding new revelations but by creatively reinterpreting old ones. In fact, all long-standing religions have vibrant traditions of commentary that allow their scriptures to live and breathe—to speak in new languages and new technologies to new political and economic realities.

The American Bible is amorphous. No convention met to decide, once and for all, which books are "in" and which are "out." But its canon is clearly open, with books coming and going with shifts in the political and cultural winds. The Constitution allows for new amendments. If a new speech is given that resonates like Sojourner Truth's "Ain't I a Woman?" it can become American scripture. So can a new novel or a new song. But the American Bible adapts first and foremost by reinterpretation. In fact, many of our past additions are themselves reinterpretations. The Gettysburg Address amends the Declaration of Independence, and "I Have a Dream" amends the Gettysburg Address.

All this is to say that America's conversation about itself is, in a sense, "rabbinic," with its own "House of Hillel" and "House of Shammai" offering competing interpretations. Here Federalists and Anti-Federalists square off over the Constitution. So do Abraham Lincoln and Stephen Douglas in their famous Lincoln-Douglas debates and, closer to our own time, "loose" and "strict" constructionists. Americans today disagree fiercely about the Supreme Court's decision on abortion in *Roe v. Wade* and Thomas Jefferson's metaphor of a "wall of separation between church and state." If Ronald Reagan rose from the grave today to deliver "The Speech," many Americans would give him a standing ovation, but others would sit and boo. Consensus eludes us; conflict is endemic to American public life.

Nowhere is this conflict more plain, or more painful, than on *the* question in the American Bible: the question of race. How to make sense of a "land of liberty" in which twelve of the first eighteen presidents were slaveholders? When George Washington died, the "Father of our Country" was lording over 316 slaves at Mount Vernon. During his life, the "Apostle of Liberty" Thomas Jefferson owned some 600 human beings. This paradox at the heart of the American experiment— "the world's fairest hope linked with man's foulest crime," according to Herman Melville[1]—was written into the Constitution, which protected both slavery and the slave trade. It was not resolved until the Civil War. But the Civil War did not put an end to racism. Neither did the civil rights movement. Over the course of U.S. history, Americans have struggled to make sense of their legacies of slavery and segregation by wrestling with books such as *Adventures of Huckleberry Finn* and *The Autobiography of Malcolm X*. And racism has never been confined here to what Booker T. Washington called "The Negro Problem."[2] The treatment of Indians by Americans was in some ways more brutal. And roughly 120,000 Japanese Americans were incarcerated in internment camps during World War II.

Of course, Americans have found other things to argue about, including whether the United States is a Christian nation or a secular one, whether the Declaration of Independence or the Constitution is preeminent, and whether liberty depends on states' rights or a strong central government. Paradoxically, however, all this conflict seems to have brought us closer.

This book shows why this is the case, and how it happened. The United States is not held together by one common creed. Americans have not fused into a "melting pot." The country continues to be multiethnic and multireligious, with fierce partisanship on both ends of the political spectrum. What holds the nation together is a sentiment that John Stuart Mill called "fellow-feeling." And from where does this sentiment come? In theory, it could come, as Mill proposed, from "united public opinion."[3] But such unity has been elusive here. What brings us together is practice—the practice of listening to and arguing about voices from our shared past.

Emile Durkheim started a revolution in sociology when he observed that when societies say "God" they really mean "us." Revelation was in his view an expression not of the mind of the Almighty but of the needs of society. The power we feel in the midst of a ritual is "collective effervescence."[4] Whether this is true of baptism or the Bible, it is clearly the case for the Pledge of Allegiance and other books in *The American Bible*. When we say that the Declaration is "sacred" or the Gettysburg Address is "immortal," what are we saying? We are doubtless asserting something about the power of these words, but more fundamentally we are asserting something about ourselves—these texts are our texts; in the past, they may have divided or united us (or both), but in either case they tell us who we are and who we hope to be.

To be an American is to engage in this common conversation. It is to ask, "What would Jefferson do?" about the budget deficit or the role of religion on Capitol Hill, and "What would Lincoln do?" about affirmative action or gay marriage. The core texts in *The American Bible* speak in their own voices, to be sure. FDR has his say, as does JFK. And when they speak, we listen. But these voices conflict with one another, and sometimes they contradict themselves. So "we the people" need to decide what each voice means and how to choose among their incompatible ideals.

In recent years, historians have demonstrated that classic utterances long thought to be the products of individual genius were actually collaborative works. In *American Scripture*, Pauline Maier proves that the Declaration of Independence was by no means the work of Jefferson alone. She also demonstrates how, over time, the Declaration came to mean "what the American people chose to make of it."[5] Similarly, the Vietnam Veterans Memorial was art by committee—a work of our own hands—and since its construction it has been reinterpreted by millions of Americans, who have seen not only themselves and the Vietnam War but also their country in the mirror that is The Wall. King's "I Have a Dream" speech was also produced by a cast of thousands. Without the civil rights movement and the March on Washington (both collective acts), this sermon never would have been delivered. And without the millions of Americans who responded to King's words with a collective "Amen," it would not have been remembered. The French sociologist Danièle Hervieu-Léger speaks of religion as a "chain of memory" that binds us to each other by binding us to the past.[6] The same is true of the American Bible.

The United States is a "nation of competing readers and competing readings," but this competition debate is something "we the people" do together.[7] Consider any given book in *The American Bible*. The core text appeals in some way to American values. It tells us who we are and the ends toward which we are straining. Maybe it tells us we are God's New Israel. Maybe it tells us capitalism is king. Either way, what makes its voice vital is controversy—the arguments and counterarguments, interpretations and reinterpretations it generates. None of these books is killed by criticism. In fact, criticism makes each stronger. Like the Constitution, which lives through the interpretations of Supreme Court justices, legal scholars, and ordinary Americans, the American Bible lives through commentaries, which are as much a part of American scripture as the primary texts themselves. These commentaries drive our politics, inspire social action, and animate debates about who is—and who is not—a true American. To read them is to see how American public life works—how it allows for dissent even as it channels it, how it anoints heroes and then cuts them down to size. The conversation these commentaries inspire defines us, telling us, in our own words, what we have been and what we will become.

This conversation is the rite of the republic, but it is not lorded over by any high priest. To be sure, Franklin and King and Reagan all have pride of place here. But the sacred syllables of this rite can be uttered by any of us. When the American Bible speaks, "we the people" listen, but only because we have written it ourselves.

Sometimes this speaking and listening settles things. Slavery is now illegal, and women have the right to vote. But the broader questions are never settled. In 1782, the French sojourner to the New World J. Hector St. John de Crèvecoeur asked, "What then is the American, this new man?"[8] Americans decided in 1790 that only "free white persons" can be naturalized U.S. citizens. They extended citizenship to blacks born in the United States in 1870, to Native Americans in 1924, and to Asian immigrants in 1952. Through the efforts of suffragists, they decided that "this new man" can also be a woman. But Crèvecoeur's question lives on. And the conversation it spurs is our collective practice.

There are, to be sure, moments in American history when debate divides us, and divides us dangerously. These moments occur when one side anathematizes the other as "un-American," accusing it of consorting with the enemy or dancing with the devil—sedition, treason, heresy. In these moments, compromise may become impossible. What self-respecting citizen will split the difference with evil incarnate? The Civil War, which claimed six hundred thousand lives, or 2 percent of the U.S. population, was one of these moments. And the human toll it took is another reminder that words matter. But such bloodshed is by no means the norm. Neither is the epidemic of incivility of recent years. Debate exposes tensions by giving the dissenter a voice, but in so doing it tends to defuse them. In this way, debate functions alongside voting as a core ritual in American public life. Neither of these practices puts an end to our disagreements. Elections recur. Debates are revisited. But each offers the assurance that *your* voice will be heard by *us*.

Of course, this only works if a wide variety of voices *are* heard and if the conversation manages to be both informed and civil. Unfortunately, these desiderata are in short supply nowadays. The deep-throated voiceovers in negative campaign ads are rarely informed or civil. And the millionaires and billionaires behind them speak on behalf of the special interests the founders unanimously decried as "factions."

We hear a lot today from political activists about the Constitution and the founders. We hardly ever hear about Washington's warnings against the "mischiefs of the spirit of party" or about Lincoln's "We are not enemies, but friends. We must not be enemies."[9] Sometimes these voices are not as consistent as we might like. Jefferson didn't just remind us that "we are all Federalists, we are all Republicans."[10] He also denounced the Federalists as "enemies of our Constitution" and described their time in power as a "reign of witches."[11] And even Washington's Farewell Address had some partisanship in it. So there is no golden age to revisit.

There are voices that call us up and out of the muck in which we are mired, however. In fact, there is a long tradition of a "vital center" in American politics, forever redirecting us away from partisan politicking and toward the common good.[12] There is Thomas Paine insisting that we are all the better for a diversity of opinion among us. There is Patrick Henry affirming, "I am not a Virginian, but an American."[13] Closer to our own time, there is Barack Obama pledging his allegiance not to blue states or red states but to the United States. And there is George W. Bush, after the closest presidential election since 1800, saying, "Our nation must rise above a house divided. . . . Republicans want the best for our nation. And so do Democrats."[14] None of these men were saints. But at least on these occasions, each was possessed by something other than the spirit of party.

Like the Constitution itself, the American Bible is a living document possessed by a spirit of adaptation. In each new generation, we the living converse with each other and with the dead—with journalist H. L. Mencken and Chief Joseph and abolitionist Frederick Douglass and less famous writers of letters to the editor—about how to make the United States more free, more equal, more democratic, more just. In the process, we reassess how we are living up to our ideals and take practical steps to create a union a little better than the one we have today.

Part of what makes this conversation dynamic is its mix of patriotic and prophetic voices. Much of our talk about our nation is celebratory. We anoint our patriots as saints. We assert that the business of America is God's business. We damn our enemies as evildoers. We boast of America as a "shining city on a hill." But the American Bible also speaks in a different voice. Harking back to the Exodus story and the biblical books of Jeremiah and Amos, this prophetic voice says that America has lost its way and challenges it to repent of its wrongdoing. Thoreau refuses to pay his taxes. Eisenhower warns of the military-industrial complex. Malcolm X says that the American dream has become a nightmare.

This prophetic voice has been muted in recent years. Those who celebrate the virtues of the "greatest nation on earth" are a dime a dozen.[15] Those who chastise us for our vices are in short supply. Increasingly, both political parties tell us what we want to hear, and almost no one dares to call for genuine sacrifice. Democrats push for more government services and higher taxes; Republicans push for fewer government services and lower taxes. What we get is the easy stuff: more services and lower taxes. The hard choices are put off to the next election, the next generation.

We Americans are at our best when we face hard facts and make tough choices—when we see ourselves not as chosen but as "almost chosen," poised between the real and the ideal, struggling to bend the arc of American history toward purposes worthy of the effort. This unsettled yet creative state of "in between" can only be maintained, however, if we keep in mind both our lofty ideals and how far we continue to fall short of them. The American Bible does this work. It admits that "unjust laws exist" and that racism is still with us.[16] It calls the United States the "world's best hope" even as it laments the fact that this hope has been squandered.[17] It says, "We have it in our power to begin the world over again," yet criticizes what we have done with our military might.[18] It asks hard questions: "Will we be extremists for hate or for love?"; "Can there not be a government in which majorities do not virtually decide right and wrong, but conscience?"[19]

To wrestle with these difficult questions does not make everything okay. It does not magically redirect the energies of Democrats and Republicans from petty partisanship toward the common good. It does not make our many gods one. It does not resolve the unresolvable tensions in our founding documents. But it does do something. What it does is bring us together into something like a middle path, where we can engage in a civil and informed conversation about our common life. This conversation reacquaints us with ancestors who wrote and responded to the letters and lamentations, psalms and proverbs that make up the American Bible. Equally important, it puts us in touch with one another—male and female, Democrat and Republican, white and black, the living and the dead.

It is not un-American to criticize any book in the American Bible. Look Lincoln in the eye and tell him you don't give a hoot about equality. Tell King you have a different dream. More power to you. No one here is divine. No idea is dogma. But as you criticize Lincoln or King or Bush or Obama, know what you are doing. You are not opting out of America; you are opting in. Americans speak different languages and worship different gods. They join competing political parties. But they come together to argue. This is our shared practice, and it makes us a community as surely as the Mass brings together Catholics or the sermon brings together Protestants. Agreement cannot hold us together, because we do not agree. Not even the Constitution itself can constitute America. What constitutes us is this ongoing conversation about our law and our prophets and the many questions they left unresolved.

ACKNOWLEDGMENTS

$\mathcal{T}$HIS BOOK obviously depends on prior generations who wrote the classics of American public life, and on the many commentators who kept these texts alive by debating them. Closer to home, it depends on family members, friends, and colleagues who contributed to this book. Eric Baldwin was my chief research assistant and main sounding board from start to finish. I also received expert research help from Marthe Hesselmans, Marilyn Mellowes, Laura Montorio, Cristine Hutchison-Jones, and Chris Leveroni. Colleagues in American history who read and commented on various books in this "Bible" include Julie Byrne, Kirsten Fischer, Lauren Winner, and Edward Blum. I also benefited from discussions of the project with my colleagues in the Department of Religion at Boston University, and with David Chappell, Thomas Tweed, and many other scholars elsewhere.

I continue to benefit from a wonderfully supportive team at HarperOne, including publisher Mark Tauber, associate publisher Claudia Boutote, and my crack publicist, Julie Burton. My editor, Roger Freet, responded to this project with his usual combination of hard work and good cheer, and somehow struck just the right balance of "get it done" and "get it right." I am also grateful for the work of his assistants Christina Bailly and Babette Dunkelgrun. This book presented some unusual challenges in the design department. Here I have to thank HarperOne's Michele Wetherbee, Suzanne Quist, and Terri Leonard. The permissions were close to unmanageable, but Kris Ashley at Belvedere Editorial and Research managed them well.

My agent, Sandra Dijkstra, continues to be a terrific advocate, as are Elise Capron and other members of her West Coast team. Finally, I want to thank my partner, Meera Subramanian, for dealing with the crazy schedule this book presented with more cheer and support than any writer could expect, and my daughters, Molly and Lucy, for reminding me every day why I started this project in the first place.

NOTES

Introduction

1. Abraham Lincoln, "Gettysburg Address," http://avalon.law.yale.edu/19th_century/gettyb.asp.

2. Thomas Paine, *The Rights of Man* (1791–92), chap. 4, www.constitution.org/tp/rightsman2.htm. See, however, John Jay, "Federalist No. 2," www.constitution.org/fed/federa02.htm: "Providence has been pleased to give this one connected country to one united people—a people descended from the same ancestors, speaking the same language, professing the same religion, attached to the same principles of government, very similar in their manners and customs, and who, by their joint counsels, arms, and efforts, fighting side by side throughout a long and bloody war, have nobly established general liberty and independence."

3. Gordon Wood, *The Idea of America: Reflections on the Birth of the United States* (New York: Penguin, 2011), p. 322.

4. Noah Webster Jr., *An American Selection of Lessons in Reading and Speaking* (Hartford, CT: Hudson & Goodwin, 1789), p. 2.

5. "Thomas Jefferson: A Film by Ken Burns," interview transcripts, Gore Vidal, www.pbs.org/jefferson/archives/interviews/Vidal.htm.

6. George Chambers, quoted in *Proceedings and Debates of the Convention of the Commonwealth of Pennsylvania to Propose Amendments to the Constitution* (Harrisburg, PA: Packer, Barrett, and Parke, 1838), 4.483.

7. Merrill D. Peterson, *The Jefferson Image in the American Mind* (New York: Oxford Univ. Press, 1960), p. 9.

8. Garry Wills, *Lincoln at Gettysburg: The Words That Remade America* (New York: Simon & Schuster, 1992), p. 172.

9. Quoted in Linda Holmes, "Why Read Moby-Dick?': A Passionate Defense of the 'American Bible,'" www.npr.org/blogs/monkeysee/2011/10/18/141429619/why-read-moby-dick-a-passionate-defense-of-the-american-bible.

10. John Updike, "A Sage for All Seasons," *Guardian*, June 25, 2004, www.guardian.co.uk/books/2004/jun/26/classics.

11. Jeffrey M. Jones, "Democratic Party ID Drops in 2010, Tying 22-Year Low," January 5, 2011, www.gallup.com/poll/145463/democratic-party-drops-2010-tying-year-low.aspx.

12. "Congress: Republicans," www.pollingreport.com/cong_rep.htm; "Congress: Democrats," www.pollingreport.com/cong_dem.htm.

13. Jeff Zeleny and Megan Thee-Brenan, "New Poll Finds a Deep Distrust of Government," *New York Times*, October 25, 2011, p. 1.

14. "Video and Transcript of Jon Stewart's Closing Speech at Rally to Restore Sanity," www.examiner.com/political-buzz-in-national/video-and-transcript-of-jon-stewart-s-closing-speech-at-rally-to-restore-sanity.

15. Henry Commager, "Restoring Liberalism's Good Name," *Boston Globe*, December 13, 1979, p. 21. Commager is borrowing from an Abraham Lincoln story about two men fighting their way into each other's coats—a story Lincoln applied to the Federalists and the Jeffersonians (Lincoln to H. L. Pierce and others, April 6, 1859, in Andrew A. Lipscomb and Albert E. Bergh, eds., *The Writings of Thomas Jefferson* [Washington, DC: Thomas Jefferson Memorial Association, 1903], 1:xvi).

16. See Stuart Butler and Edmund Haislmaier, *A National Health System for America* (Washington, DC: Heritage Foundation, 1989), p. 1.

17. Abraham Lincoln, "First Inaugural Address," March 4, 1861, http://avalon.law.yale.edu/19th_century/lincoln1.asp.

18. Horace M. Kallen, "Democracy Versus the Melting-Pot: A Study of American Nationality," *Nation*, February 25, 1915, www.expo98.msu.edu/people/Kallen.htm.

The Exodus Story

1. Bruce Feiler, *America's Prophet: Moses and the American Story* (New York: William Morrow, 2009), p. 4.

2. Sarah H. Bradford, *Harriet Tubman: The Moses of Her People* (New York: Lockwood, 1886); Martin Luther King Jr., "I've Been to the Mountaintop," Memphis, Tennessee, April 3, 1968, www.americanrhetoric.com/speeches/mlkivebeentothemountaintop.htm.

3. Abraham Lincoln, "Address to the Senate of New Jersey," Trenton, New Jersey, February 21, 1861, reprinted in John G. Nicolay and John Hay, eds., *Abraham Lincoln: Complete Works* (New York: Century, 1894), 1:688.

4. Martin Luther King Jr., Nobel Prize acceptance speech, December 11, 1964, www.nobelprize.org/nobel_prizes/peace/laureates/1964/king-lecture.html.

5. Albert J. Raboteau, "American Salvation: The Place of Christianity in Public Life," *Boston Review*, April/May 2005, http://bostonreview.net/BR30.2/raboteau.php.

6. Nehemiah 9:7–25, KJV.

John Winthrop, "A Model of Christian Charity" (1630)

1. Perry Miller, *Errand into the Wilderness* (Cambridge, MA: Harvard Univ. Press, 1956).

2. For an excellent discussion of the sermon, including its composition and delivery, see Francis J. Bremer, *John Winthrop: America's Forgotten Founding Father* (New York: Oxford Univ. Press, 2003), pp. 174–84.

3. Quoted in Eve LaPlante, *American Jezebel: The Uncommon Life of Anne Hutchinson, the Woman Who Defied the Puritans* (New York: HarperSanFrancisco, 2004), p. 130.

4. Peter J. Gomes, "Best Sermon: A Pilgrim's Progress," *New York Times*, April 18, 1999, p. 101, http://theater.nytimes.com/library/magazine/millennium/m1/gomes.html; Andrew Delbanco, *The Puritan Ordeal* (Cambridge, MA: Harvard Univ. Press, 1989), p. 72.

5. Thomas Jefferson, "First Inaugural Address," March 4, 1801, www.princeton.edu/~tjpapers/inaugural/infinal.html; Abraham Lincoln, "First Inaugural Address," March 4, 1861, www.vlib.us/amdocs/texts/19linc1.htm.

6. Edmund S. Morgan, "John Winthrop's 'Model of Christian Charity' in a Wider Context," *Huntington Library Quarterly* 50.2 (Spring 1987): 145–46.

7. Peter J. Gomes, *The Good Book: Reading the Bible with Mind and Heart* (New York: HarperSanFrancisco, 2002), pp. 62–63.

8. Gordon S. Wood, *Empire of Liberty: A History of the Early Republic, 1789–1815* (New York: Oxford Univ. Press, 2009).

9. John Winthrop, "A Model of Christian Charity" (1630), http://religiousfreedom.lib.virginia.edu/sacred/charity.html.

Thomas Paine, *Common Sense* (1776)

1. Benjamin Franklin to Richard Bache, September 30, 1774, in Jared Sparks, ed., *The Works of Benjamin Franklin* (Boston: Hilliard, Gray, 1839), 8:137.

2. Scott Liell, *46 Pages: Thomas Paine, Common Sense, and the Turning Point to American Independence* (Philadelphia: Running Press, 2003), p. 51.

3. John Adams, *Autobiography*, in Charles Francis Adams, ed., *The Works of John Adams* (Boston: Little and Brown, 1850), 2:509. In a June 22, 1819, letter to Thomas Jefferson, Adams described *Common Sense* as a "poor, ignorant, malicious, short-sighted, crapulous mass" (Charles Francis Adams, ed., *The Works of John Adams* [Boston: Little, Brown, 1856], 10:380).

4. John Adams to Abigail Adams, March 19, 1776, in Charles Francis Adams, ed., *Familiar Letters of John Adams and His Wife Abigail Adams During the Revolution* (New York: Hurd and Houghton, 1876), p. 146.

5. Pauline Maier, *American Scripture: Making the Declaration of Independence* (New York: Vintage, 1998), p. 31.

6. Craig Nelson, "Thomas Paine and the Making of 'Common Sense,'" *New England Review* 27.3 (2006): 237.

7. Martin Luther King Jr., "I Have a Dream," Washington, D.C., August 28, 1963, http://avalon.law.yale.edu/20th_century/mlk01.asp.

8. Bernard Bailyn, "Thomas Paine: A Reappraisal of 'Common Sense,' the Most Extraordinary Pamphlet of the American Revolution," *Unesco Courier*, July 1976, p. 28.

9. Theodore Roosevelt, *Gouverneur Morris* (Boston: Houghton, Mifflin, 1888), p. 289.

10. Thomas Paine to Henry Laurens, January 14, 1779, in Philip S. Foner, ed., *The Complete Writings of Thomas Paine* (New York: Citadel, 1945), 2:1163.

11. Josiah Bartlett to John Langdon, January 13, 1776, quoted in John Sanderson, ed., *Biography of the Signers to the Declaration of Independence,* 2nd ed. (Philadelphia: Brown and Peters, 1828), 1:268.

12. Nelson, "Thomas Paine and the Making of 'Common Sense,'" 245. There are no complete sales data for *Common Sense,* so estimates vary widely. Many scholars converge on 150,000, perhaps in an effort to arrive in the neighborhood of Paine's own estimate of 120,000 (Thomas Paine to Henry Laurens, January 14, 1799, in Foner, ed., *Complete Writings of Thomas Paine,* 2:1162–63). Some go as high as half a million. Here I follow the more conservative estimate of 75,000 presented in Trish Loughran, "Disseminating *Common Sense:* Thomas Paine and the Problem of the Early National Bestseller," *American Literature* 78.1 (March 2006): 17.

13. George Washington to Joseph Reed, January 31, 1776, quoted in Joseph N. Moreau, ed., *Testimonials to the Merits of Thomas Paine* (Burlington, NJ: Taylor, 1861), p. 8.

14. J. Adams, *Autobiography,* in C. F. Adams, ed., *Works of John Adams,* 2:507; John Adams to James Warren, May 12, 1776, www.masshist.org/publications/apde/portia.php?id=PJA04d092. In a less restrained moment, Adams referred to Paine as "a mongrel between pigg and puppy, begotten by a wild boar on a bitch wolf" (John Adams to Benjamin Waterhouse, October 29, 1805, in Worthington Chauncey Ford, ed., *Statesman and Friend: Correspondence of John Adams with Benjamin Waterhouse, 1784–1822* [Boston: Little, Brown, 1927], p. 31).

15. Adams to Waterhouse, October 29, 1805, in Ford, ed., *Statesman and Friend,* p. 31.

16. Edmund Randolph, *History of Virginia,* ed. Arthur H. Shaffer (Charlottesville: Univ. Press of Virginia, 1970), p. 234; George Washington to Joseph Reed, April 1, 1776, in Jared Sparks, ed., *The Writings of George Washington* (Boston: Russell, Odiorne, and Metcalf, 1834), p. 347; Benjamin Franklin to M. le Veillard, April 15, 1787, in Benjamin Franklin, *Autobiography of Benjamin Franklin,* ed. John Bigelow (Philadelphia: Lippincott, 1869), p. 370.

17. Sean Wilentz, "The Air Around Tom Paine," *New Republic,* April 24, 1995, p. 36.

18. Quoted in Foner, ed., *Complete Writings of Thomas Paine,* 1:xlii.

19. J. Adams, *Autobiography,* in C. F. Adams, ed., *Works of John Adams,* 3:93.

20. Thomas Paine to George Washington, July 30, 1796, quoted in James Cheetham, *The Life of Thomas Paine* (New York: Southwick and Pelsue, 1809), p. 208.

21. Dixon Wecter, "Hero in Reverse," *Virginia Quarterly Review* (Spring 1942): 251, www.vqronline.org/articles/1942/spring/wecter-hero-reverse/.

22. Wecter, "Hero in Reverse," p. 243. Wecter's essay begins with this ditty:

Poor Tom Paine! There he lies:
Nobody laughs and nobody cries.
Where he has gone or how he fares
Nobody knows and nobody cares.

23. Moncure Conway, *The Life of Thomas Paine,* 2 vols. (New York: Putnam, 1892); James C. Young, "Edison Speaks for Tom Paine," *New York Times,* June 7, 1915, p. 1. According to Conway, the effect of *Common Sense* "has never been paralleled in literary history" (1:187). Edison admitted, however, that, among the founding fathers, Paine was "the most misunderstood and the object of greatest calumny."

24. Jill Lepore, "A World of Paine," in Alfred F. Young, Gary B. Nash, and Ray Raphael, eds., *Revolutionary Founders: Rebels, Radicals, and Reformers in the Making of the Nation* (New York: Knopf, 2011), p. 89. "In the comic-book version of history that serves as our national heritage, where the founding Fathers are like the Hanna-Barbera SuperFriends," Lepore writes, "Paine is Aquaman to Washington's Superman and Jefferson's Batman" (p. 89).

25. Irving Kristol, "The American Revolution as a Successful Revolution," in *Neo-Conservatism: Selected Essays, 1949–1995* (New York: Free Press, 1995), pp. 235–52.

26. George H. W. Bush, "Address to the Nation Announcing Allied Military Action in the Persian Gulf," January 16, 1991, www.presidency.ucsb.edu/ws/index.php?pid=19222.

27. Christopher Hitchens, "The Actuarial Radical: Common Sense About Thomas Paine," *Grand Street* 7.1 (Autumn 1987): 67–77. The Anglo-American Hitchens calls Paine "the greatest Englishman and the finest American" (p. 67).

28. Arthur Herman, "The First Neoconservative," *Wall Street Journal,* September 22, 2006, p. 4, http://online.wsj.com/article/SB115888035208870663.html.

29. The quote was from Paine's "these are the times that try men's souls" essay from *The Crisis* and reads: "Let it be told to the future world . . . that in the depth of winter, when nothing but hope and virtue could survive, . . . that the city and the country, alarmed at one common danger, came forth to meet [it]." See Barack Obama, "Inaugural Address," January 20, 2009, www.presidency.ucsb.edu/ws/index.php?pid=44.

30. Thomas Paine, *Common Sense* (1776), www.gutenberg.org/files/147/147-h/147-h.htm.

The Declaration of Independence (1776)

1. Pauline Maier, *American Scripture: Making the Declaration of Independence* (New York: Knopf, 1997), p. 47.

2. Garry Wills, *Inventing America: Jefferson's Declaration of Independence* (Garden City, NY: Doubleday, 1978), p. xxv.

3. Rufus Choate to the Maine Whig State Central Committee, August 9, 1856, in Samuel Gilman Brown, *The Works of Rufus Choate* (Boston: Little, Brown, 1862), 1:215.

4. Abraham Lincoln, "Address in Independence Hall, Philadelphia, February 22, 1861," in John G. Nicolay, ed., *The Complete Works of Abraham Lincoln* (New York: Tandy, 1894), 6:157, http://lincoln.lib.niu.edu/cgi-bin/philologic/getobject.pl?c.2923:1.lincoln. When he praised Jefferson, Lincoln did so largely on the basis of his contributions to the Declaration. "All honor to Jefferson," he wrote in 1858, "to the man who, in the concrete pressure of a struggle for national independence by a single people, had the coolness, forecast, and capacity, to introduce [into a] merely revolutionary document an abstract truth, applicable to all men and all times, and so to embalm it there, that to-day, and in all coming days, it shall be a rebuke and a stumbling block to the harbingers of reappearing tyranny [and] oppression" (Abraham Lincoln to H. L. Pierce et al., April 6, 1858, http://lincoln.lib.niu.edu/cgi-bin/philologic/getobject.pl?c.2453:6:1.lincoln).

5. "Lincoln's Reply to Douglas," Galesburg, Illinois, October 7, 1858, in John G. Nicolay and John Jay, eds., *Abraham Lincoln: Complete Works* (New York: Century, 1894), 1:437.

6. Joseph J. Ellis, "Jefferson's View: Three American Memorials Trace the Nation's Racial Progress," *Los Angeles Times,* October 19, 2011, p. A15.

7. "Declaration of Sentiments," in Elizabeth Cady Stanton, *A History of Woman Suffrage* (Rochester, NY: Fowler and Wells, 1881), p. 70, www.fordham.edu/halsall/mod/senecafalls.asp.

8. Frederick Douglass, "What to the Slave Is the Fourth of July?," July 5, 1852, Rochester, New York, http://teaching americanhistory.org/library/index.asp?document=162.

9. According to Maier, "The remaking of the Declaration of Independence no less than its original creation was not an individual but a collective act that drew on the words and thoughts of many people, dead and alive, who struggled with the same or closely related problems" (*American Scripture,* p. xx).

10. Charles Sumner, Senate speech, February 4, 1872, in *Charles Sumner: His Complete Works* (Boston: Lee and Shepard, 1900), 19:308. "Sir, it precedes the Constitution in time, as it is more elevated in character," Sumner adds in a debate with Wisconsin Senator Matthew Hale. "The Constitution is a machine, great, mighty, beneficent. The Declaration supplies the principles giving character and object to the machine. The Constitution is an earthly body, if you please; the Declaration is the soul" (p. 305).

11. Vernon Louis Parrington, *Main Currents in American Thought: An Interpretation of American Literature from the Beginnings to 1920,* vol. 1 (New York: Harcourt, Brace, 1930), p. 285.

12. Robert F. Gibbs, "The Spirit of '89: Conservatism and Bicentenary," *University Bookman* 14 (Spring 1974): 54.

13. Willmoore Kendall and George W. Carey, "Preface to This Edition," in their *The Basic Symbols of the American Political Tradition* (Washington, DC: Catholic Univ. of America Press, 1995), p. xv. Kendall and Carey make an additional argument with important implications for interpreting not only this document, but every other book in the American Bible. Assume that the Declaration *does* have the sort of binding status that Charles Sumner claimed it has. Assume as well that the heart and soul of this document can be found in its listing of self-evident truths. Even then, who says the equality clause is preeminent among the five listed? And who is to decide whether equality or liberty, for example, gets the upper hand when the document itself provides no means for selecting among these competing goods?

14. Declaration of Independence (1776), www.archives.gov/exhibits/charters/declaration_transcript.html.

Noah Webster, The Blue-Back Speller (1783–)

1. Samuel Campbell, quoted in Harry R. Warfel, *Noah Webster: Schoolmaster to America* (New York: Macmillan, 1936), p. 73; William Cobbett, *Porcupine's Works* (London: Cobbett and Morgan, 1801), 9:29, 200, 45–46.

2. Thomas Jefferson, *The Writings of Thomas Jefferson,* ed. Paul Leicester Ford (New York: Putnam, 1897), 8:80.

3. Jill Lepore, *A Is for American: Letters and Other Characters in the Newly United States* (New York: Knopf, 2002), p. 39.

4. Lepore, *A Is for American,* p. 5.

5. Noah Webster Jr., *Dissertations on the English Language* (Boston: Isaiah Thomas, 1789), p. 179.

6. Noah Webster to Joseph Priestley, January 20, 1800, in Harry R. Warfel, ed., *Letters of Noah Webster* (New York: Library Publishers, 1953), p. 215.

7. Noah Webster Jr., *Sketches of American Policy* (Hartford, CT: Hudson and Goodwin, 1785), p. 48.

8. Webster, *Dissertations on the English Language,* p. 22.

9. Noah Webster to John Canfield, January 7, 1783, in Noah Webster Papers, New York Public Library, quoted in Lawrence J. Friedman, *Inventors of the Promised Land* (New York: Knopf, 1975), p. 30.

10. Henry Steele Commager, "Schoolmaster to America," in *Noah Webster's American Spelling Book* (New York: Bureau of Publications, Teacher's College, Columbia Univ., 1962), p. 1.

11. Howard Lamar, quoted in Joshua Kendall, *The Forgotten Founding Father: Noah Webster's Obsession and the Creation of an American Culture* (New York: Putnam, 2010), p. 6.

12. Noah Webster Jr., *The American Spelling Book* (Wilmington, DE: Bonsal & Niles, 1800?), p. 149, www.merrycoz .org/books/spelling/SPELLER.HTM.

13. Noah Webster Jr., *A Grammatical Institute of the English Language in Three Parts: Part III* (1785), quoted in Warfel, *Noah Webster,* p. 86.

14. Quoted in E. Jennifer Monaghan, *A Common Heritage: Noah Webster's Blue-Back Speller* (Hamden, CT: Archon, 1983), p. 37.

15. Joseph J. Ellis, *After the Revolution: Profiles of Early American Culture* (New York: Norton, 2002), p. 175.

16. Webster, *American Spelling Book*, pp. 60, 52, 77.

17. This is a fairly typical estimate for an era lacking precise data on bestsellers. In *Golden Multitudes: The Story of Best Sellers in the United States* (New York: Macmillan, 1947), Frank Luther Mott estimates sales of 60 to 65 million through 1890 (p. 299). An advertisement published in 1872 put sales for the prior year at just under 1 million copies. See *Legal Opinion* 4.5 (November 30, 1872): 460.

18. Quoted in Warfel, *Noah Webster,* p. 74.

19. "Highways and Byways," *Chautauquan* 30.5 (February 1900): 452.

20. Commager, "Schoolmaster to America," p. 1.

21. Commager, "Schoolmaster to America," p. 12.

22. Webster, *American Spelling Book*, pp. 52, 54.

The Constitution (1787)

1. Mortimer J. Adler and William Gorman, *The American Testament* (New York: Praeger, 1975).

2. Akhil Reed Amar, *America's Constitution: A Biography* (New York: Random House, 2006), p. 467. On "popular constitutionalism," see also Larry D. Kramer, *The People Themselves: Popular Constitutionalism and Judicial Review* (New York: Oxford Univ. Press, 2004); and Bruce Ackerman, "The Living Constitution," *Harvard Law Review* 120.7 (May 2007): 1737–1812. "[My proposal] puts the People, not the Court, at the center of constitutional development," writes Ackerman. "It insists that ordinary Americans, led by such figures as Franklin Roosevelt and Martin Luther King, Jr., have made as large a constitutional contribution as the generations led by George Washington and Abraham Lincoln—and that the job of the Supreme Court is to recognize this point when making sense of the living Constitution" (1804–5). Michael Kammen's exhaustive *A Machine That Would Go of Itself: The Constitution in American Culture* (New York: Knopf, 1986) also stresses popular constitutionalism.

3. George Washington to Benjamin Harrison, January 18, 1784, http://gwpapers.virginia.edu/documents/constitution/ 1784/harrison.html.

4. George Washington to James Madison, November 5, 1786, http://gwpapers.virginia.edu/documents/constitution/ 1784/madison2.html.

5. Hugh Blair Grigsby, *The History of the Virginia Federal Convention of 1788* (Richmond: Virginia Historical Society, 1890), 1:32, n. 36.

6. Centinel (a.k.a. Samuel Bryan), "Number 1," *Independent Gazeteer* (Philadelphia), October 5, 1787, www .constitution.org/afp/centin01.htm.

7. Amos Singletary speech at the Massachusetts Constitutional Convention, January 25, 1788, quoted in Jonathan Eliot, ed., *The Debates in the Several State Conventions* (Philadelphia: Lippincott, 1836), 2:102, http://teaching americanhistory.org/ratification/elliot/vol2/massachusetts0125.html.

8. James Madison, "Federalist No. 10," *Daily Advertiser,* November 22, 1787, www.constitution.org/fed/federa10 .htm. Madison writes: "The smaller the society, the fewer probably will be the distinct parties and interests composing it; the fewer the distinct parties and interests, the more frequently will a majority be found of the same party; and the smaller the number of individuals composing a majority, and the smaller the compass within which they are placed, the more easily will they concert and execute their plans of oppression. Extend

the sphere, and you take in a greater variety of parties and interests; you make it less probable that a majority of the whole will have a common motive to invade the rights of other citizens; or if such a common motive exists, it will be more difficult for all who feel it to discover their own strength, and to act in unison with each other. . . . Hence, it clearly appears, that the same advantage which a republic has over a democracy, in controlling the effects of faction, is enjoyed by a large over a small republic."

9. *New York Independent,* September 26, 1861, and National Reform Association, "Memorial to Congress" (1864), both quoted in *Proceedings of the National Convention to Secure the Religious Amendment of the Constitution of the United States, Held in Pittsburg, February 4, 5, 1874* (Philadelphia: Christian Statesman Association, 1874), pp. 54, 7.

10. George Washington, Farewell Address, 1796, http://avalon.law.yale.edu/18th_century/washing.asp.

11. Caleb Cushing, *A Reply to the Letter of J. Fenimore Cooper* (Boston: Buckingham, 1834), p. 76.

12. Amar, *America's Constitution,* p. xi.

13. *Gompers v. United States,* 233 U.S. 604 (1914). Holmes writes, "But the provisions of the Constitution are not mathematical formulas having their essence in their form; they are organic, living institutions transplanted from English soil." Justice Charles Evans Hughes took this position to its perhaps illogical extreme when he said, in a speech before the Elmira Chamber of Commerce on May 3, 1907, "We are under a Constitution, but the Constitution is what the judges say it is" (*Addresses and Papers of Charles Evans Hughes* [New York: Putnam, 1908], p. 139).

14. Robert Bork, *The Tempting of America: The Political Seduction of the Law* (New York: Simon & Schuster, 1990), p. 218.

15. Jack N. Rakove, *Original Meanings: Politics and Ideas in the Making of the Constitution* (New York: Knopf, 1996), p. 6. Rakove also argues that the notion of "original intent" is self-contradictory, since it was not the intent of the framers to have their intentions set in stone.

16. An Ngram Viewer search for the first ten amendments shows mentions of "First Amendment" in books written in American English moving up sharply around 1940 and "Fourth Amendment" mentions moving up sharply around 1960. The next most discussed amendment in the Bill of Rights in the twentieth century is the Fifth.

17. William Lloyd Garrison, quoted in Wendell Phillips Garrison and Francis Jackson Garrison, *William Lloyd Garrison* (New York: Century, 1889), 3:412.

18. Charles Beard, editorial, quoted in Ellen Nore, *Charles A. Beard: An Intellectual Biography* (Carbondale: Southern Illinois Univ. Press, 1983), p. 9.

19. Amar, *America's Constitution,* p. 472.

20. See Terry Bouton, *Taming Democracy: "The People," the Founders, and the Troubled Ending of the American Revolution* (Oxford: Oxford Univ. Press), 2007.

21. "The Constitution," 1787, www.archives.gov/exhibits/charters/constitution_transcript.html.

Brown v. Board of Education (1954)

1. Claude Sitton, "Two White Schools in New Orleans Are Integrated," *New York Times,* November 15, 1960, p. 1.

2. John Steinbeck, *Travels with Charley: In Search of America* (New York: Bantam, 1962), p. 255.

3. Although the Supreme Court heard the cases from these five locations together, it issued a separate opinion in the Washington, D.C., case—*Bolling v. Sharpe,* 347 U.S. 497 (1954)—because the Fourteenth Amendment guarantee of equal protection applies only to states, and therefore not to the District of Columbia. The *Bolling* case turned instead on the due process clause of the Fifth Amendment.

4. *New York Amsterdam News,* quoted in "Editorial Excerpts from the Nation's Press on Segregation Ruling," *New York Times,* May 18, 1954, p. 19.

5. *Plessy v. Ferguson,* 163 U.S. 537 (1896).

6. James Reston, "A Sociological Decision; Court Founded Its Segregation Ruling on Hearts and Minds Rather Than Laws," *New York Times,* May 18, 1954, p. 14.

7. Gwen Bergner, "Black Children, White Preference: *Brown v. Board,* the Doll Tests, and the Politics of Self-Esteem," *American Quarterly* 61.2 (June 2009): 299–332.

8. C. Vann Woodward, "Look Away, Look Away," *Journal of Southern History* 59.3 (August 1993): 490.

9. James Jackson Kilpatrick, *The Sovereign States: Notes of a Citizen of Virginia* (Chicago: Henry Regnery, 1957), p. 256.

10. See "Editorial Excerpts from the Nation's Press on Segregation Ruling," p. 19.

11. *Annual of the Southern Baptist Convention,* 1954, p. 407, quoted in Andrew M. Manis, *Southern Civil Religions in Conflict: Civil Rights and the Culture Wars* (Macon, GA: Mercer Univ. Press, 2002), p. 96.

12. "Bloodstains on White Marble Steps," *Daily News,* May 18, 1954, quoted in Waldo E. Martin Jr., ed., *Brown v. Board*

of Education: A Brief History with Documents (Boston: Bedford/St. Martin's, 1998), p. 204. Brown, the Daily News added, was "the first step, or an opening wedge, toward mixed marriages, miscegenation, and the mongrelization of the human race."

13. David L. Chappell, A Stone of Hope: Prophetic Religion and the Death of Jim Crow (Chapel Hill: Univ. of North Carolina Press, 2004), p. 160.

14. Richmond News Leader, editorial, June 1, 1955, quoted in Benjamin Muse, Ten Years of Prelude: The Story of Integration Since the Supreme Court's 1954 Decision (New York: Viking, 1964), p. 29.

15. "Southern Manifesto," Congressional Record, March 12, 1956, pp. 4459–60, www.pbs.org/wnet/supremecourt/rights/sources_document2.html.

16. Michael J. Klarman, "The Puzzling Resistance to Political Process Theory," Virginia Law Review 77.4 (May 1991): 807.

17. "Table 1," Harrell R. Rodgers Jr. and Charles S. Bullock, "School Desegregation: A Policy Analysis," Journal of Black Studies 2.4 (June 1972): 412.

18. "Segregation and Democracy," National Review, January 25, 1956, p. 5; Cincinnati Enquirer, quoted in "Editorial Excerpts from the Nation's Press on Segregation Ruling," p. 19.

19. J. Harvie Wilkinson III, From Brown to Bakke: The Supreme Court and School Integration, 1954–1978 (New York: Oxford Univ. Press, 1979), p. 6; Alonzo N. Smith, "Separate Is Not Equal: Brown v. the Board of Education of Topeka, Kansas," project essay for "Separate Is Not Equal: Brown v. Board of Education" exhibition, Smithsonian National Museum of American History (2004), http://americanhistory.si.edu/brown/resources/index.html, p. 25.

20. For "ambiguous," see, e.g., Lani Guinier, "From Racial Liberalism to Racial Literacy: Brown v. Board of Education and the Interest-Divergence Dilemma," Journal of American History 91.1 (June 2004): 92. For "hollow": Gerald Rosenberg, The Hollow Hope: Can Courts Bring About Social Change? (Chicago: Univ. of Chicago Press, 1991). See also James T. Patterson, Brown v. Board of Education: A Civil Rights Milestone and Its Troubled Legacy (New York: Oxford Univ. Press, 2001).

21. Gerald N. Rosenberg, "Brown Is Dead! Long Live Brown!: The Endless Attempt to Canonize a Case," Virginia Law Review 80.1 (February 1994): 165.

22. Guinier, "From Racial Liberalism to Racial Literacy," p. 93.

23. Kenneth L. Karst, Belonging to America: Equal Citizenship and the Constitution (New Haven, CT: Yale Univ. Press, 1989), p. 74.

24. J. M. Balkin and Bruce A. Ackerman, What Brown v. Board of Education Should Have Said: The Nation's Top Legal Experts Rewrite America's Landmark Civil Rights Decision (New York: New York Univ. Press, 2001), p. 5.

25. Cheryl Brown Henderson, "Dedication Ceremony—Henderson Remarks," Topeka, Kansas, May 17, 2004, http://brownvboard.org/content/dedication-ceremony-henderson-remarks.

26. Brown v. Board of Education, 347 U.S. 483, www.law.cornell.edu/supct/html/historics/USSC_CR_0347_0483_ZO.html.

Roe v. Wade (1973)

1. Lee Gidding quoted in Michael T. Malloy, "Despite Court's Ruling Abortion Fight Goes On," National Observer, February 3, 1973, quoted in Eva R. Rubin, ed., The Abortion Controversy: A Documentary History (Westwood, CT: Greenwood, 1994), p. 144.

2. United States Catholic Conference, "Documentation on the Right to Life and Abortion," Washington, DC, 1974, pp. 59–60, quoted in Rubin, ed., The Abortion Controversy, p. 141.

3. Patrick T. Conley and Robert J. McKenna, "The Supreme Court on Abortion—Dissenting Opinion," Catholic Lawyer #19 (Winter 1973): 25.

4. Michael E. Kinsley, Curse of the Giant Muffins and Other Washington Maladies (New York: Summit, 1987), p. 28.

5. Guttmacher Institute, "States Enact Record Number of Abortion Restrictions in First Half of 2011," July 13, 2011, www.guttmacher.org/media/inthenews/2011/07/13/index.html. For a spoof of these measures, see "New Law Requires Women to Name Baby, Paint Nursery Before Getting Abortion," www.theonion.com/video/new-law-requires-women-to-name-baby-paint-nursery,14393/.

6. Justice Sandra O'Connor, dissenting opinion (with Justices White and Rehnquist), Akron v. Akron Center for Reproductive Health, 462 U.S. 416 (1983), www.law.cornell.edu/supct/html/historics/USSC_CR_0462_0416_ZD.html.

7. Lydia Saad, "Americans Still Split Along 'Pro-Choice,' 'Pro-Life' Lines," www.gallup.com/poll/147734/americans-split-along-pro-choice-pro-life-lines.aspx; Harris Poll, "Attitudes to Abortion and Roe vs. Wade Are Now Almost

Identical to Attitudes in 2005 and 2006," August 11, 2009, www.reuters.com/article/2009/08/11/idUS107894+11-Aug-2009+BW20090811.

8. *Roe v. Wade,* 410 U.S. 113 (1973), www.law.cornell.edu/supct/html/historics/USSC_CR_0410_0113_ZO.html.

Harriet Beecher Stowe, *Uncle Tom's Cabin* (1852)

1. Annie Fields, ed., *Life and Letters of Harriet Beecher Stowe* (Boston: Houghton, Mifflin, 1897), p. 377. This quote also appears years earlier in various advertisements for the book.

2. "From the *Morning Post,* Boston," *The Living Age,* July 10, 1852, p. 61.

3. This legend first appears in print in 1897. See Fields, ed., *Life and Letters of Harriet Beecher Stowe,* p. 269.

4. *New York Herald,* paraphrased in "Mrs. Stowe and Her Assailants," *National Era,* May 12, 1853, http://utc.iath.virginia.edu/notices/noar01jt.html.

5. "Uncle Tom's Cabin," *Daily Picayune* (New Orleans), February 11, 1853, http://utc.iath.virginia.edu/proslav/prar97gt.html.

6. "Speech of Theodore Parker," *The Liberator,* February 25, 1853, http://utc.iath.virginia.edu/notices/noar02agt.html.

7. David S. Reynolds, *Mightier Than the Sword:* Uncle Tom's Cabin *and the Battle for America* (New York: Norton, 2011), p. 145.

8. Reynolds, *Mightier Than the Sword,* pp. xii, 175.

9. Harriet Beecher Stowe, "Introduction," in *Uncle Tom's Cabin; Or, Life Among the Lowly* (Boston: Houghton, Mifflin, 1887), p. x.

10. Harriet Beecher Stowe, *Uncle Tom's Cabin; or, Life Among the Lowly* (Boston: Jewett, 1852), p. 322.

11. William G. Allen, letter to the editor, *Frederick Douglass' Paper,* May 20, 1852, http://utc.iath.virginia.edu/reviews/rere03at.html. "I have one regret, with regard to the book," Allen added, "and that is that the chapter favoring colonization was ever written." See also William Lloyd Garrison, writing in *The Liberator* (March 26, 1852): "The work, towards its conclusion, contains some objectionable sentiments respecting African colonization, which we regret to see" (http://utc.iath.virginia.edu/reviews/rere02at.html).

12. George Frederick Holmes, "Uncle Tom's Cabin," *Southern Literary Messenger,* December 1852, p. 371, http://utc.iath.virginia.edu/reviews/rere24bt.html.

13. *Courier and Enquirer* (New York), October 8, 1852, quoted in "Uncle Tom's Cabin," *New York Observer,* October 21, 1852, http://utc.iath.virginia.edu/proslav/prar11at.html.

14. George Graham, "Black Letters; or Uncle Tom-Foolery in Literature," *Graham's Magazine,* February 1853, pp. 209–15, http://utc.iath.virginia.edu/reviews/rere25at.html.

15. George Fitzhugh, *Cannibals All! Or, Slaves Without Masters* (Richmond, VA: A. Morris, 1857).

16. George M. Frederickson, *The Black Image in the White Mind: The Debate on Afro-American Character and Destiny, 1817–1914* (New York: Harper, 1971), pp. 97–129.

17. James Baldwin, "Everybody's Protest Novel," in *Notes of a Native Son* (Boston: Beacon, 1955), p. 14.

18. Reynolds, *Mightier Than the Sword,* p. 256; "Malcolm X: Dr. King Is an Uncle Tom," www.youtube.com/watch?v=-Rr-aRxItpw.

19. Alfred Kazin, "Introduction," in Harriet Beecher Stowe, *Uncle Tom's Cabin* (New York: Bantam Classics, 2003), p. ix.

20. John W. De Forest, "The Great American Novel," *Nation,* January 8, 1868, pp. 27–29.

21. Jane P. Tompkins, *Sentimental Designs: The Cultural Work of American Fiction, 1790–1860* (New York: Oxford Univ. Press, 1985), p. 134.

22. Stowe, *Uncle Tom's Cabin* (1852).

Mark Twain, *Adventures of Huckleberry Finn* (1884)

1. H. L. Mencken, "The Burden of Humor," *Smart Set* 39:6 (February 1913): 152; "H. L. Mencken on Mark Twain," *Chicago Daily Tribune,* February 8, 1925, p. E3.

2. Andrew Lang, "The Art of Mark Twain," *Illustrated London News,* February 14, 1891, p. 222.

3. Jonathan Arac, *Huckleberry Finn as Idol and Target: The Functions of Criticism in Our Time* (Madison: Univ. of Wisconsin Press, 1997), p. 18.

4. Justin Kaplan, "Born to Trouble: One Hundred Years of *Huckleberry Finn,*" in Gerald Graff and James Phelan, eds., *Adventures of Huckleberry Finn: A Case Study in Critical Controversy,* 2nd ed. (Boston: Bedford/St. Martin's, 2004), p. 375; Lionel Trilling, "Introduction," in Mark Twain, *The Adventures of Huckleberry Finn* (New York: Rinehart, 1948), p. ix.

5. Sacvan Bercovitch, "Deadpan Huck: Or, What's Funny About Interpretation," *The Kenyon Review* 24.3/4 (Summer/Autumn 2002): 132.

6. *San Francisco Chronicle,* March 15, 1885, p. 6, quoted in Victor Fischer, "Huck Finn Reviewed: The Reception of 'Huckleberry Finn' in the United States, 1885–1897," *American Literary Realism, 1870–1910* 16.1 (Spring 1983): 14.

7. Joel Chandler Harris to Samuel Clemens, June 1, 1885, Mark Twain Project Online, quoted in Fischer, "Huck Finn Reviewed," p. 16.

8. *New York World,* March 2, 1885, quoted in Fischer, "Huck Finn Reviewed," p. 8.

9. *Boston Evening Traveler,* March 5, 1885, p. 1, quoted in Fischer, "Huck Finn Reviewed," p. 10.

10. *New York World,* March 2, 1885, quoted in Fischer, "Huck Finn Reviewed," p. 7.

11. *Boston Transcript,* March 17, 1885, quoted in James S. Leonard et al., *Satire or Evasion? Black Perspectives on Huckleberry Finn* (Durham, NC: Duke Univ. Press, 1992), p. 2.

12. *San Francisco Chronicle,* March 29, 1885, p. 4, quoted in Fischer, "Huck Finn Reviewed," p. 24.

13. *Boston Daily Globe,* March 17, 1885, p. 2, quoted in Shelley Fisher Fishkin, *Was Huck Black? Mark Twain and African-American Voices* (New York: Oxford Univ. Press, 1993), p. 115.

14. S. L. Clemens, letter to the editor, *Boston Daily Advertiser,* April 2, 1885, p. 2, quoted in Fischer, "Huck Finn Reviewed," p. 26.

15. Ernest Hemingway, *Green Hills of Africa* (New York: Scribner, 1935), p. 22. Like many readers, Hemingway was unimpressed by the book's conclusion. "If you read it you must stop where the Nigger Jim is stolen from the boys. That is the real end. The rest is just cheating," he wrote.

16. Arac, *Huckleberry Finn as Idol and Target,* p. 21.

17. Trilling, "Introduction," pp. xv, vi.

18. Arac, *Huckleberry Finn as Idol and Target,* p. vii; T. S. Eliot, introduction to *Adventures of Huckleberry Finn* (New York: Chanticleer, 1950), quoted in M. Thomas Inge, *Huck Finn Among the Critics: A Centennial Selection* (Frederick, MD: Univ. Publications of America, 1985), pp. 103, 111.

19. T. S. Eliot, "American Literature and the American Language," *Sewanee Review* 74.1 (Winter 1966): 13.

20. Neil Schmitz, "On American Humor," *Partisan Review* 47.4 (1980): 562.

21. Quoted in Mike Sager and Molly Moore, "Huck Is Given a Reprieve in Fairfax Schools," *Washington Post,* April 13, 1982, p. A1.

22. Quoted in Mike Sager, "Mark Twain School Trying to Censor Huck," *Washington Post,* April 8, 1982, p. A1.

23. Kaplan, "Born to Trouble," p. 378.

24. George F. Will, "Huck at a Hundred," *Newsweek,* February 18, 1985, p. 92.

25. Ralph Ellison, "Twentieth-Century Fiction and the Black Mask of Humanity," *Confluence* (December 1953): 3–21.

26. Toni Morrison, *Playing in the Dark: Whiteness and the Literary Imagination* (Cambridge, MA: Harvard Univ. Press, 1992), p. 57.

27. W. D. Howells, *My Mark Twain: Reminiscences and Criticisms* (New York: Harper, 1910), p. 101.

28. William Styron, "Huck, Continued," *New Yorker,* June 26, 1995, p. 132.

29. Mark Twain, *Adventures of Huckleberry Finn* (New York: Harper & Brothers, 1912), http://etext.virginia.edu/toc/modeng/public/Twa2Huc.html.

Ayn Rand, *Atlas Shrugged* (1957)

1. Christopher Hitchens, "The Moral Necessity of Atheism," Sewanee University, Sewanee, Tennessee, February 23, 2004, www.youtube.com/watch?v=4wYR6e9Z6es; William F. Buckley, "A Conversation with William F. Buckley, Jr.," June 17, 2003, www.charlierose.com/view/interview/1922. Hitchens continues, "So to have a book strenuously recommending that people be more self-centered seems to be, as the Anglican Church used to say in its critique of Catholicism, a work of supererogation."

2. John Blades, "1000 Years of Progress: Books," *Chicago Tribune,* December 20, 1990, p. 11.

3. Esther B. Fein, "Book Notes," *New York Times,* November 20, 1991, p. C26.

4. "100 Best Novels," www.modernlibrary.com/top-100/100-best-novels/.

5. Whittaker Chambers, "Big Sister Is Watching You," *National Review,* December 28, 1957, pp. 594–96; Nick Gillespie, "Ready for Her Close-up," *Wilson Quarterly* 33.4 (Autumn 2009): 97. Of the Chambers review, Gillespie added, "It makes Mark Twain's legendary 'Fenimore Cooper's Literary Offenses' read like a love letter" (p. 97).

6. Quoted in Jonathan Chait, "Paul Ryan and Ayn Rand," *New Republic,* December 28, 2010, www.tnr.com/blog/jonathan-chait/80552/paul-ryan-and-ayn-rand.

7. Quoted in "Hearing of the Senate Judiciary Committee," Federal News Service, September 13, 1991.

8. Susan Brownmiller, "Ayn Rand: A Traitor to Her Own Sex," in Mimi Reisel Gladstein and Chris Matthew Sciabarra, eds., *Feminist Interpretations of Ayn Rand* (University Park: Pennsylvania State Univ. Press, 1999), pp. 63–65; "Question Period: Noam Chomsky on Being Censored, CHRC Censorship, Ayn Rand, Robert Nozick and Libertarianism," *Western Standard,* December 8, 2008, http://westernstandard.blogs.com/shotgun/2008/12/question-period.html; Onkar Ghate, "*Atlas Shrugged:* America's Second Declaration of Independence," www.aynrand.org/site/.../atlas_shrugged_2nd_dec_tea_party.pdf.

9. Gerald Clarke, "Publishing Was His Line," *Time,* August 22, 1977, p. 76.

10. Ayn Rand, *Letters of Ayn Rand,* ed. Michael S. Berliner (New York: Plume, 1997), p. 157.

11. Claudia Roth Pierpont, "Twilight of the Goddess," *New Yorker*, July 24, 1995, p. 79.

12. Ayn Rand, "The Sanction of the Victims" (1981), www.aynrand.org/site/PageServer?pagename=reg_ar_sanction.

13. Charles Colson, "Two-Minute Warning: Atlas Shrugged and So Should You," May 10, 2011, www.youtube.com/watch?v=ZhbE8NDTY0c.

Francis Scott Key, "The Star-Spangled Banner" (1814)

1. Francis Scott Key to John Randolph, quoted in F. S. Key-Smith, *Francis Scott Key: Author of the Star-Spangled Banner* (Washington, DC: Key-Smith, 1911), pp. 78, 76.

2. Key to Randolph, p. 78.

3. John S. Skinner, "Attack of the British on Baltimore—Mr. Ingersoll's History," *Baltimore Patriot and Commercial Gazette,* May 29, 1849, p. 2, quoted in George J. Svejda, *History of the Star-Spangled Banner from 1814 to the Present* (Washington, DC: Division of History, Office of Archeology and Historic Preservation, 1969), p. 72.

4. Quoted in "Not One National Song: A Chance for Patriotic American Composers," *New York Times,* August 25, 1889, p. 5. See also John Philip Sousa, "What Our National Anthem Should Be," *New York Times,* August 26, 1928, p. 69.

5. Quoted in Svejda, *History of the Star-Spangled Banner,* pp. 361, 365.

6. Baltimore *Sun,* August 25, 1923, p. 6, quoted in Svejda, *History of the Star-Spangled Banner,* p. 363.

7. Quoted in Georgia Dullea, "'O Say, Can . . .' How Does It Go Again?," *New York Times,* July 6, 1976, p. 1.

8. "Union musician," letter to the editor, *Evening Star,* September 2, 1968, p. A14, quoted in Svejda, *History of the Star-Spangled Banner,* p. 446.

9. Cynthia Janovy, "Roseanne Barr's High Art," *New York Times,* August 1, 1990, p. A21.

10. John Gettings, "Star-Mangled Banner," www.infoplease.com/spot/starmangledbanner.html.

11. Quoted in David Montgomery, "An Anthem's Discordant Notes: Spanish Version of 'Star-Spangled Banner' Draws Strong Reactions," *Washington Post,* April 28, 2006, p. A1.

12. Quoted in David R. Sands, "National Anthems a Cultural Feat," *Washington Times,* August 20, 2007, p. A12.

Irving Berlin, "God Bless America" (1938)

1. Quoted in Robert Kimball and Linda Emmet, eds., *The Complete Lyrics of Irving Berlin* (New York: Knopf, 2001), p. 321.

2. "What Makes a Song: A Talk with Irving Berlin," *New York Times,* July 28, 1940, p. 80.

3. Sheryl Renee Kaskowitz, "As We Raise Our Voices: A Social History and Ethnography of 'God Bless America,' 1918–2010," Ph.D. dissertation, Harvard University, 2010, p. 201.

4. Kaskowitz, "As We Raise Our Voices," pp. 222, 275.

5. Kaskowitz, "As We Raise Our Voices," pp. 260, 263.

6. William Safire, "God Bless Us," *New York Times,* August 27, 1992, p. A23.

7. Michael Kinsley, "God Bless You and . . . You Know the Rest," *Slate,* January 26, 2001.

Woody Guthrie, "This Land Is Your Land" (1940)

1. Colman McCarthy, "We Need a People's Anthem," *Washington Post,* December 16, 1989, p. A34.
2. Bruce Springsteen and Pete Seeger, " 'This Land Is Your Land' Live," www.youtube.com/watch?v=Hkc2LcimvoA.
3. Studs Terkel, "Foreword," in Ed Cray, *Ramblin' Man: The Life and Times of Woody Guthrie* (New York: Norton, 2004).
4. Woody Guthrie to Alan Lomax, September 19, 1940, quoted in Richard A. Reuss, "Woody Guthrie and His Folk Tradition," *Journal of American Folklore* 83.329 (July–September 1970): 291.
5. Olin Downes and Elie Siegmeister, *A Treasury of American Song* (New York: Howell, Soskin, 1940), p. 338.
6. John Steinbeck, quoted in Reuss, "Woody Guthrie and His Folk Tradition," p. 280.
7. Bob Dylan, *Chronicles: Volume One* (New York: Simon & Schuster, 2004), p. 344.
8. "Woody Guthrie Home Town Ends Ban on Claiming Him," *New York Times,* November 25, 1972, p. 37.
9. Quoted in Joe Klein, *Woody Guthrie: A Life* (New York: Knopf, 1980), p. 126.
10. "This Land!," www.youtube.com/watch?v=z8Q-sRdV7SY.

Benjamin Franklin, "Remember that time is money" (1748)

1. Benjamin Franklin, "Advice to a Young Tradesman," in *The Works of Benjamin Franklin,* ed. Jared Sparks (Boston: Hilliard, Gray, 1836), 2:87.
2. Rev. M. N. Olmsted, "Shout for Freedom," *Ladies' Repository,* June 1858, p. 338.
3. Max Weber, *The Protestant Ethic and the Spirit of Capitalism,* trans. Talcott Parsons (Mineola, NY: Dover, 2003), p. 48.
4. Commentary: A Farmer, letter to the editor, *American Farmer,* May 20, 1825, p. 67; Louis Agassiz, quoted in Henry Greenough, *Ernest Carroll, or Artist-life in Italy: A Novel* (Boston: Ticknor and Fields, 1858), p. 52; "Mark Twain in New York," *Stars and Stripes,* June 23, 1870, in Paul Fatout, ed., *Mark Twain Speaks for Himself* (West Lafayette, IN: Purdue Univ. Press, 1997), p. 62; Austin Phelps, quoted in "Young People's Christian Endeavor," *Assembly Herald,* April 1899, p. 241; Abraham Joshua Heschel, *The Sabbath: Its Meaning for Modern Man* (New York: Farrar, Straus & Giroux, 1951), p. 76; Peter F. Drucker, *The Effective Executive* (New York: Harper & Row, 1966), pp. 25–26; Richard J. Callahan Jr., "Sacred Time," in Gary Laderman and Luis Leon, eds., *Religion and American Cultures: An Encyclopedia of Traditions, Diversity, and Popular Expressions* (Santa Barbara, CA: ABC-CLIO, 2003), 1:598; David Marcus, "Time in the Age of Immediacy," *Dissent,* April 28, 2010, www.dissentmagazine.org/atw.php?id=10.

Benjamin Franklin, "God helps those who help themselves" (1758)

1. John Heywood, *The Proverbs, Epigrams, and Miscellanies of John Heywood,* ed. John S. Farmer (London: Early English Drama Society, 1906), p. 366; Algernon Sidney, *Discourses Concerning Government* (Edinburgh: Hamilton and Balfour, 1750), 1:298; Benjamin Franklin, "The Way to Wealth," in *Poor Richard's Almanac* (Philadelphia: Franklin and Hall, 1758), quoted in Jared Sparks, ed., *The Works of Benjamin Franklin* (Boston: Hilliard, Gray, 1836), 2:95.
2. Commentary: Orson Hyde, "Gathering the Saints—Perpetual Emigrating Fund," Salt Lake City, October 8, 1854, in Brigham Young et al., *Journal of Discourses* (London: Richards, 1855), 2:65; Malcolm X with Alex Haley, *The Autobiography of Malcolm X* (New York: Grove, 1965), p. 195; Bill McKibben, "The Christian Paradox: How a Faithful Nation Gets Jesus Wrong," *Harper's,* August 2005, http://harpers.org/archive/2005/08/0080695; Bill O'Reilly, "Keep Christ in Unemployment," December 9, 2010, www.billoreilly.com/column?pid=30748; Barack Obama, "Remarks by the President on the American Jobs Act," Eastfield College, Mesquite, Texas, October 4, 2011, www.whitehouse.gov/the-press-office/2011/10/04/remarks-president-american-jobs-act.

Patrick Henry, "Give me liberty or give me death" (1775)

1. Patrick Henry, quoted in William Wirt, *Sketches of the Life and Character of Patrick Henry* (Philadelphia: James Webster, 1817), p. 123.
2. Lyndon B. Johnson, "We Shall Overcome," Washington, DC, March 15, 1965, http://voicesofdemocracy.umd.edu/johnson-we-shall-overcome-speech-text/.
3. Commentary: Henry Highland Garnet, "An Address to the Slaves of the United States of America," National Negro Convention, Buffalo, New York, August 16, 1843, reprinted in his *A Memorial Discourse* (Philadelphia: Wilson, 1865), p. 50; William Jennings Bryan, "Imperialism," Indianapolis, August 8, 1900, www.greatamericandocuments

.com/speeches/bryan-imperialism.html; Harry S. Truman, "Remarks to Delegates to the Fifth Annual Conference on Citizenship," Washington, D.C., May 23, 1950, www.presidency.ucsb.edu/ws/index.php?pid=13506&st=patrick +henry&st1=#axzz1aVSue9pL; "Notes of the Changing Times," *Kiplinger's Personal Finance,* April 1950, p. 45; John F. Kennedy, "Excerpts of Remarks of Senator John F. Kennedy, Public Rally, Hotel Theresa, New York, New York," October 12, 1960, www.presidency.ucsb.edu/ws/index.php?pid=25785#axzz1aVSue9pL.

Abigail Adams, "Remember the ladies" (1776)

1. Abigail Adams to John Adams, March 31, 1776, in Charles Francis Adams, ed., *Familiar Letters of John Adams and His Wife Abigail Adams During the Revolution* (New York: Hurd and Houghton, 1876), pp. 149–50. See also images of these letters in the Adams Family Papers collection of the Massachusetts Historical Society: www.masshist.org/digitaladams/aea/letter/.

2. John Adams to Abigail Adams, April 14, 1776, in C. F. Adams, ed., *Familiar Letters of John Adams and His Wife,* p. 155.

3. Abigail Adams to John Adams, May 7, 1776, in C. F. Adams, ed., *Familiar Letters of John Adams and His Wife,* p. 169.

4. Edith B. Gelles, *Abigail and John: Portrait of a Marriage* (New York: Morrow, 2009), p. 77.

5. John Adams to James Sullivan, May 26, 1776, http://press-pubs.uchicago.edu/founders/documents/v1ch13s10.html.

6. Commentary: John Adams to Abigail Adams, April 14, 1776, in C. F. Adams, ed., *Familiar Letters of John Adams and His Wife,* p. 155; Elizabeth Cady Stanton, Susan B. Anthony, and Matilda Joslyn Gage, *History of Woman Suffrage* (New York: Fowler & Wells, 1881), 1:32–34; Emily Taft Douglas, *Remember the Ladies: The Story of Great Women Who Helped Shape America* (New York: Putnam, 1966), pp. 7–8, 49, 51; Letty Cottin Pogrebin, "Sexism Rampant," *New York Times,* March 19, 1976, p. 32; Carl N. Degler, *At Odds: Women and the Family in America from the Revolution to the Present* (New York: Oxford Univ. Press, 1980), p. 190; Abigail Adams Tea Party Patriots, "A Letter to John Adams," http://abigailadamsteapartypatriots.com/?page_id=10.

Sojourner Truth, "Ain't I a woman?" (1851)

1. Sojourner Truth, *Narrative of Sojourner Truth* (Battle Creek, MI: Review and Herald Office, 1884), p. 24.

2. Sojourner Truth, "Ain't I a Woman?," Women's Rights Convention, Akron, Ohio, December 1851, www.fordham.edu/halsall/mod/sojtruth-woman.asp.

3. There are many versions of Truth's speech. Shortly after the convention, one appeared in the New York *Tribune* on June 6, 1851, and another in the *Anti-Slavery Bugle* on June 21, 1851. A third was reported twelve years later, on May 2, 1863, in the *National Anti-Slavery Standard* by Frances Gage, the well-known advocate for women's rights who organized the convention. Gage was responding, in part, to a major article about Truth written by Harriet Beecher Stowe ("Sojourner Truth, the Libyan Sibyl," *Atlantic Monthly,* April 1863, pp. 473–81). Gage's version contains the classic refrain (though here it appears as "Ar'n't I a woman?"). The other two versions do not, though the *Tribune* reads, "She said she was a woman." The earlier accounts present Truth's words in standard English, while Gage attributes to her a heavy Southern accent. Scholars have pored over these competing texts like scriptures from the Dead Sea Scrolls, reading differences in rhetoric and dialect against the historical contexts in which each was produced. Some have concluded that Gage inserted the refrain to strengthen the impact of Truth's speech, making her, in effect, the "author" of this classic line. Others argue that, even if the refrain was added later, it accurately reflects what Truth said. These arguments aside, the speech is widely celebrated today as "Ain't I a Woman?" and it has taken its place as such in the American canon. For a reading of the three versions discussed here, see, e.g., Erlene Stetson and Linda David, *Glorying in Tribulation: The Lifework of Sojourner Truth* (East Lansing: Michigan State Univ. Press, 1994), pp. 114–18.

4. Stetson and David, *Glorying in Tribulation,* p. 112.

5. Nell Irvin Painter, *Sojourner Truth: A Life, a Symbol* (New York: Norton, 1997), pp. 160–61.

6. Hillary Rodham Clinton, "Tribute to Sojourner Truth," Washington, D.C., April 28, 2009, www.state.gov/secretary/rm/2009a/04/122342.htm.

7. Michelle Obama, "Remarks by the First Lady at the Sojourner Truth Bust Unveiling," Washington, D.C., April 28, 2009, www.whitehouse.gov/the-press-office/remarks-first-lady-sojourner-truth-bust-unveiling.

8. Commentary: Gloria Steinem, "Women and Power," *New York,* December 23, 1968, http://nymag.com/news/features/50175/; Donna Haraway, "Ecce Homo, Ain't (Ar'n't) I a Woman, and Inappropriate/d Others: The Human in a Post-Humanist Landscape," in Judith Butler and Joan Scott, eds., *Feminists Theorize the Political* (New York: Routledge, 1992), p. 92; Nell Irvin Painter, "Representing Truth: Sojourner Truth's Knowing and Becoming Known," *Journal of American History* 81.2 (September 1994): 480–81; Gwen Moore, *Congressional Record,* March 18, 2010, pp. H1637–38.

Abraham Lincoln, "With malice toward none, with charity for all" (1865)

1. Abraham Lincoln, "Second Inaugural Address," March 4, 1865, www.ourdocuments.gov/doc.php?flash=true&doc=38&page=transcript.

2. Theodore Roosevelt, speech, Republican Club, New York, February 13, 1905, in Alfred Henry Lewis, ed., *A Compilation of the Messages and Speeches of Theodore Roosevelt, 1901–1905* (New York: Bureau of National Literature and Art, 1906), p. 560. On this as Lincoln's best speech, see Ronald C. White Jr., *Lincoln's Greatest Speech: The Second Inaugural* (New York: Simon & Schuster, 2002); and James Tackach, *Lincoln's Moral Vision: The Second Inaugural Address* (Jackson: Univ. Press of Mississippi, 2002). According to Garry Wills, the Second Inaugural "complements and completes the Gettysburg Address. It is the only speech worth to stand with it" (*Lincoln at Gettysburg: The Speech That Remade America* [New York: Simon & Schuster, 1992], p. 189).

3. Frederick Douglass, *Life and Times of Frederick Douglass* (Hartford, CT: Park, 1882), p. 441. The *Richmond Examiner* complained on March 8, 1865, that the address "reads like the tail of some old sermon" (quoted in "Very Late from Richmond: The Rebel Papers," *New York Times,* March 12, 1865, p. 1).

4. William Lee Miller, "Lincoln's Second Inaugural: The Zenith of Statecraft," in Kenneth L. Deutsch and Joseph R. Fornieri, eds., *Lincoln's American Dream: Clashing Political Perspectives* (Washington, DC: Potomac, 2005), p. 343.

5. John McClintock, *Discourse Delivered on the Day of the Funeral of President Lincoln* (New York: Bradstreet, 1865), p. 17.

6. Herman Melville, "The Martyr," in M. A. De Wolfe Howe, ed., *The Memory of Lincoln* (Boston: Small, Maynard, 1899), p. 35.

7. Commentary: *Chicago Times,* March 6, 1865, quoted in Herbert Mitgang, *Abraham Lincoln: A Press Portrait* (New York: Fordham Univ. Press, 2000), p. 440; Abraham Lincoln to Thurlow Weed, March 15, 1865, in Charles W. Moores, ed., *Lincoln Addresses and Letters* (New York: American Book, 1914), p. 217; quoted in "Leader with Malice Toward None Needed, Willkie Says," *St. Petersburg Times,* February 12, 1944, pp. 1–2; Jonathan Alter, "Trickle-Down Hate," October 26, 1998, *Newsweek,* p. 44; White, *Lincoln's Greatest Speech,* pp. 164–65; Jonathan Zimmerman, "Celebrating Osama bin Laden's Death Is Anti-American . . . and Not Very Biblical," *Christian Science Monitor,* May 2, 2011, www.csmonitor.com/Commentary/Opinion/2011/0502/Celebrating-Osama-bin-Laden-s-death-is-anti-American-and-not-very-biblical.

Chief Joseph, "I will fight no more forever" (1877)

1. "Surrender Speech of Chief Joseph," www2.gsu.edu/~eslmlm/chiefjoseph.html.

2. Two main versions of Chief Joseph's oration circulated in the press not long after the war's end. A "short version," typically of one sentence, first appeared on October 26, 1877, in the *Chicago Times,* where Chief Joseph reportedly said, "From where the sun stands, forever and ever, I will never fight again." A longer version, in excess of one hundred words, first appeared in the *Bismarck Tri-Weekly Tribune* on that same day, but gained national attention a few weeks later in *Harper's Weekly* (November 17, 1877). In both of these sources, the long version reads: "Tell General Howard I know his heart. What he told me before, I have it in my heart. I am tired of fighting. Our chiefs are killed; LOOKING GLASS is dead, TA-HOOL-HOOL-SHUTE is dead. The old men are all dead. It is the young men who say 'Yes' or 'No.' He who led on the young men is dead. It is cold, and we have no blankets; the little children are freezing to death. My people, some of them, have run away to the hills, and have no blankets, no food. No one knows where they are—perhaps freezing to death. I want to have time to look for my children, and see how many of them I can find. Maybe I shall find them among the dead. Hear me my chiefs! I am tired; my heart is sick and sad. From where the sun now stands I will fight no more forever." For a careful examination of these and other sources, see Haruo Aoki, "Chief Joseph's Words," *Idaho Yesterdays* 33.3 (1989): 16–21. In a review of the Ken Burns documentary "The West," one critic referred to this "fictional speech" as "some of the most memorable words that a white man has ever created for a native orator" (Clyde A. Milner II, "Sometimes the Magic Works," *Montana: The Magazine of Western History* 47.1 [Spring 1997]: 70).

3. George Venn, "Soldier to Advocate: C. E. S. Wood's 1877 Diary of Alaska and the Nez Perce Conflict," *Oregon Historical Quarterly* 106.1 (Spring 2005): 65.

4. Commentary: George Truman Kercheval, "Joseph the Second," in *Lend a Hand,* April 1890, p. 250; J. W. Powell, *Fourteenth Annual Report of the Bureau of Ethnology to the Secretary of the Smithsonian Institution, 1892–93* (Washington, DC: U.S. Government Printing Office, 1896), 2:715; Helen Addison Howard, *War Chief Joseph* (Caldwell, ID: Caxton, 1941), p. 282; Mark H. Brown, "The Joseph Myth," *Montana: The Magazine of Western History* 22.2 (Winter 1972): 14; Marlon Brando with Robert Lindsey, *Brando: Songs My Mother Taught Me* (New York: Random

House, 1994), pp. 382–83; Bill Clinton, "Remarks to the People of the Navajo Nation," Shiprock, New Mexico, April 17, 2000, www.presidency.ucsb.edu/ws/?pid=58134; Gerald Vizenor, "Native American Narratives: Resistance and Survivance," in Robert Paul Lamb and G. R. Thompson, eds., *A Companion to American Fiction: 1865–1914* (Malden, MA: Blackwell, 2005), pp. 225, 227.

Calvin Coolidge, "The business of America is business" (1925)

1. Calvin Coolidge, "Address to the American Society of Newspaper Editors," Washington, D.C., January 17, 1925, www.presidency.ucsb.edu/ws/index.php?pid=24180.

2. Commentary: William Allen White, *Calvin Coolidge, The Man Who Is President* (New York: Macmillan, 1925), p. 218; Stephen Wise, Madison Square Garden speech, November 3, 1928, quoted in Melvin I. Urofsky, *A Voice That Spoke for Justice: The Life and Times of Stephen S. Wise* (Albany: State Univ. of New York Press, 1982), p. 181; Shirley Chisholm, "The Business of America Is War, and It Is Time for a Change," in Warren J. Halliburton, *Historic Speeches of African Americans* (New York: Watts, 1993), pp. 140–43; Russell Baker, "American Knighthood," *New York Times,* April 4, 1972, p. 43; Arthur Ochs Sulzberger, "Business and the Press: Is the Press Anti-Business?," March 14, 1977, Detroit, in *Vital Speeches of the Day* 43.14 (May 1, 1977):426; Tom Shales, "Super Football, Super Television," *Washington Post,* February 1, 1988, p. B1; George Will, "A Land Fit for Heroes," *Newsweek,* March 11, 1991, p. 78; Wendell Berry, *Sex, Economy, Freedom and Community* (New York: Pantheon, 1993), p. 10; Ralph Nader, *In Pursuit of Justice: Selected Writings 2000–2003* (New York: Seven Stories, 2004), p. 69.

Franklin Delano Roosevelt, "I pledge you, I pledge myself, to a new deal for the American people" (1932)

1. Franklin D. Roosevelt, "Address Accepting the Presidential Nomination at the Democratic National Convention," Chicago, July 2, 1932, www.presidency.ucsb.edu/ws/index.php?pid=75174.

2. Ronald Reagan, *An American Life: The Autobiography* (New York: Simon & Schuster, 1990), p. 66; Will Rogers, quoted in Robert A. Caro, *Master of the Senate: The Years of Lyndon Johnson* (New York: Knopf, 2002), p. 355.

3. Paul Krugman, "Franklin Delano Obama?," *New York Times,* November 10, 2008, www.nytimes.com/2008/11/10/opinion/10krugman.html. See also the *Time* magazine cover, "The New New Deal" (November 24, 2008), which depicts Obama as a latter-day FDR.

4. Commentary: Quoted in Ray Tucker, "Ickes—and No Fooling," *Collier's,* September 30, 1933; Herbert Hoover, "The Challenge to Liberty," *Saturday Evening Post,* September 8, 1934, p. 69, www.restoreliberty.com/CTL9-8-1934.htm; quoted in Robert S. McElvaine, *The Great Depression: America, 1929–1941* (New York: Times Books, 1993), p. 240; Carl N. Degler, "The Third American Revolution," in *Out of Our Past: The Forces That Shaped Modern America* (New York: Harper, 1959), p. 416; William E. Leuchtenburg, *Franklin D. Roosevelt and the New Deal: 1932–1940* (New York: Harper & Row, 1963), p. 347; Barton J. Bernstein, "The New Deal: The Conservative Achievements of Liberal Reform," in Barton J. Bernstein, ed., *Towards a New Past: Dissenting Essays in American History* (New York: Pantheon, 1968), pp. 264–65; Samuel Eliot Morison, *The Oxford History of the American People* (New York: New American Library, 1972), 3:302; Ronald Reagan, "Remarks at the Franklin D. Roosevelt Library 50th Anniversary Luncheon," January 10, 1989, www.presidency.ucsb.edu/ws/?pid=35350; Amity Shlaes, *The Forgotten Man: A New History of the Great Depression* (New York: HarperCollins, 2007), pp. 12–13; Jim Powell, "FDR's New Deal, Obama's New New Deal and High Unemployment," August 18, 2011, http://townhall.com/columnists/jimpowell/2011/08/18/fdrs_new_deal,_obamas_new_new_deal__and_high_unemployment.

John F. Kennedy, "Ask not what your country can do for you—ask what you can do for your country" (1961)

1. Quoted in Mark Harris, "Two Poets," *Life,* December 1, 1961, p. 110.

2. For similar lines by Oliver Wendell Holmes Jr. and Warren Harding, see Thurston Clarke, *Ask Not: The Inauguration of John F. Kennedy and the Speech That Changed America* (New York: Henry Holt, 2004), p. 78. See, too, Peter Marshall, "Why Should God Bless America?," September 15, 1940, in Peter J. Marshall, ed., *The Wartime Sermons of Dr. Peter Marshall* (Dallas, TX: Clarion Call Marketing, 2005), p. 9. "When are we going to say to [our legislators] that we don't want to hear any longer about what we can *get* from our country, but we do want to hear what we can *give* to our country?" Marshall asks.

3. James Reston, "Washington: President Kennedy's Inaugural—Speech or Policy?," *New York Times,* January 22, 1961, p. E10.

4. John D. Morris, "Inaugural Widely Praised by Both Sides of Congress," *New York Times,* January 21, 1961, p. 1; "Presidential Approval Ratings—Gallup Historical Statistics and Trends," www.gallup.com/poll/116677/presidential-approval-ratings-gallup-historical-statistics-trends.aspx.

5. According to the Pew Research Center, admonitions to sacrifice are rapidly disappearing from political life. See Jodie T. Allen. "Ask Not . . . ," http://pewresearch.org/pubs/1078/ask-not-kennedy-inaugural-sacrifice.

6. Commentary: Milton Friedman, *Capitalism and Freedom* (Chicago: Univ. of Chicago Press, 1962), pp. 1–2; Robert N. Bellah, "Civil Religion in America," *Daedalus* 96.1 (Winter 1967): 5. Richard Nixon, "Second Inaugural Address," January 20, 1973, www.presidency.ucsb.edu/ws/index.php?pid=4141; "1985 Tribute by President Reagan," McLean, Virginia, June 24, 1985, www.jfklibrary.org/About-Us/About-the-JFK-Library/History/1985-Tribute-by-President-Reagan.aspx; quoted in " 'Ask Not': 50 Years Since JFK Inaugural Address," January 20, 2011, www.cbsnews.com/stories/2011/01/20/politics/main7264846.shtml; Barack Obama, "Remarks Honoring the 50th Anniversary of President John F. Kennedy's Inauguration," Washington, DC, January 20, 2011, www.presidency.ucsb.edu/ws/index.php?pid=88921&st=&st1=#axzz1Zdn5ZHN7.

Ronald Reagan, "evil empire" (1983)

1. Ronald Reagan, *An American Life: The Autobiography* (New York: Simon & Schuster, 1990), p. 569.

2. Ronald Reagan, "Remarks at the Annual Convention of the National Association of Evangelicals," Orlando, Florida, March 8, 1983, www.presidency.ucsb.edu/ws/?pid=41023.

3. Henry Steele Commager, quoted in Bill Peterson, "Reagan's Use of Moral Language to Explain Politics Draws Fire," *Washington Post,* March 23, 1983, p. A15; Nancy Reagan, quoted in Rev. Michael H. Wenning, "Benediction," Ronald Reagan Interment Services, June 11, 2004, in Robert W. Ney, ed., *Ronald Reagan, Late a President of the United States: Memorial Tributes Delivered in Congress* (Washington, DC: U.S. Government Printing Office, 2005), 11:lvii.

4. "Reverend Reagan," *New Republic,* April 4, 1983, pp. 7–9.

5. Hugh Sidey, "The Right Rev. Ronald Reagan," *Time,* March 21, 1983, p. 24.

6. Ronald Reagan, "The President's News Conference," January 29, 1981, www.presidency.ucsb.edu/ws/index.php?pid=44101.

7. "World News Tonight," ABC News Transcripts, May 31, 1988.

8. Ronald Reagan, "Remarks on East-West Relations at the Brandenburg Gate," West Berlin, June 12, 1987, www.presidency.ucsb.edu/ws/index.php?pid=34390.

9. George W. Bush, "State of the Union Address," January 29, 2002, www.presidency.ucsb.edu/ws/index.php?pid=29644.

10. Commentary: Anthony Lewis, "Onward, Christian Soldiers," *New York Times,* March 10, 1983, p. A27; Tom Wicker, "Two Dangerous Doctrines," *New York Times,* March 15, 1983, p. A25; His Holiness Pimen, "An Open Letter to: His Excellency, Mr. Ronald Wilson Reagan," *New York Times,* April 3, 1983, p. E16; quoted in Don Phillips, "O'Neill: Mondale Must Attack 'Cold, Mean' Reagan," United Press International, July 19, 1984; "Reagan's Soviet Speech," *National Review,* February 10, 1984, p. 17; Strobe Talbott, *The Russians and Reagan* (New York: Vintage, 1984), p. 33; William F. Buckley Jr., "So Long, Evil Empire?" (June 2, 1988), in *Happy Days Were Here Again: Reflections of a Libertarian Journalist,* ed. Patricia Bozell (New York: Basic Books, 2008), p. 77; quoted in Louis Errol, "Islam, the New Evil Empire," *New York Daily News,* September 9, 2010, p. 28.

Henry David Thoreau, "Civil Disobedience" (1849)

1. Stanley Cavell, *The Senses of Walden* (New York: Viking, 1972), p. 33; Vernon Louis Parrington, *The Romantic Revolution in America, 1800–1860* (New York: Harcourt, Brace, 1927), p. 400.

2. Originally delivered as two lectures in Concord in January and February 1848, this essay was first published as "Resistance to Civil Government" in *Aesthetic Papers* (1849), an obscure journal that folded after one issue. It later appeared as "Civil Disobedience" in Henry D. Thoreau, *A Yankee in Canada, with Anti-Slavery and Reform Papers* (Boston: Ticknor and Fields, 1866).

3. Randall Stewart, "The Growth of Thoreau's Reputation," *College English* 7.4 (January 1946): 213; Linck Johnson, "The Life and Legacy of 'Civil Disobedience,' " in Joel Myerson et al., eds., *The Oxford Handbook of Transcendentalism* (New York: Oxford Univ. Press, 2010), p. 629.

4. Robert Louis Stevenson, "Henry David Thoreau: His Character and Opinions," *Cornhill Magazine,* June 1800, http://thoreau.eserver.org/stevens1.html.

5. Henry James, *Hawthorne* (New York: Harper, 1880), p. 94. Concerning Thoreau's parochialism, William Sloane Kennedy replied: "It is not absolutely necessary that the thinker should travel much, and especially not the mystic. All we require of such is catholicity and breadth in their reading and thinking. Thoreau, as is well known, was thoroughly read in the Ethnic Scriptures, in Greek literature, and in old English poetry. But he was pre-eminently antiquarian, autochthonous, patriotic—loving his country with manly devotion and enthusiasm. Mr. James aspires, I believe, to be cosmopolitan. But it is surely better to be patriotic first, and cosmopolitan second, than to be cosmopolitan first, and patriotic last, or not at all" ("A New Estimate of Thoreau," *Penn Monthly* 11 [October 1880]: 795).

6. Ralph Waldo Emerson, "Thoreau," *Atlantic Monthly,* August 1862, p. 241, www.theatlantic.com/magazine/archive/1862/08/thoreau/6418/; Harold Bloom, *Henry David Thoreau,* Bloom's Classic Critical Views (New York: Infobase, 2008), p. ix.

7. "Thoreau's Works in New Edition," *New York Times,* July 6, 1907, p. BR427; "Thoreau Comes into His Own," November 20, 1927, p. BR1. See also Gilbert P. Coleman, "Thoreau and His Critics": "Probably no writer in America can lay claim to a sounder foundation for fame than Thoreau" (*Dial,* June 1, 1906, p. 352).

8. "Americanizing the Titmen," *Freeman* 6 (December 1922): 343.

9. Stanley Edgar Hyman, *The Promised End: Essays and Reviews, 1942–1962* (Cleveland: World, 1963), p. 24. "At his best," Hyman continues, "Thoreau wrote the only really first-rate prose ever written by an American, with the possible exception of Abraham Lincoln" (p. 27).

10. John F. Kennedy telegram, quoted in Walter Harding, "The Centennial of Thoreau's Death," *Thoreau Society Bulletin* 79 (Spring 1962): 1.

11. "Civil Disobedience," www.youtube.com/watch?v=4TK7g89AnnI. This oft-cited quote has been attributed to Thomas Paine, Thomas Jefferson, and others. Thoreau was likely borrowing here from the motto of *The United States Magazine and Democratic Review,* a New York–based magazine to which he contributed two articles in 1843: "The best government is that which governs least." He may also have been drawing on Emerson, who wrote in his essay "Politics" (1844), "Hence the less government we have the better,—the fewer laws, and the less confided power."

12. Henry David Thoreau, "Resistance to Civil Government," in Elizabeth P. Peabody, ed., *Aesthetic Papers* (Boston: The Editor, 1849), pp. 189–211, http://thoreau.eserver.org/civil.html.

Dwight Eisenhower, Farewell Address (1961)

1. George Washington, Farewell Address, 1796, http://avalon.law.yale.edu/18th_century/washing.asp.

2. Dwight D. Eisenhower, "Farewell Address," January 17, 1961, www.presidency.ucsb.edu/ws/index.php?pid=12086&st=&st1=#axzz1YzNDMpZX.

3. "Foreign Relations: For a True and Total Peace," *Time,* April 27, 1953, www.time.com/time/magazine/article/0,9171,818270,00.html.

4. Dwight D. Eisenhower, "The Chance for Peace," April 16, 1953, www.presidency.ucsb.edu/ws/index.php?pid=9819.

5. Andrew J. Bacevich, "The Tyranny of Defense Inc.," *Atlantic,* January/February 2011, www.theatlantic.com/magazine/archive/2011/01/the-tyranny-of-defense-inc/8342/. The data in this paragraph comes from this same source.

6. Bryce Harlow memo to Eisenhower and Nixon, DDE's Post-Presidential Papers, Special Names Series, Box 6, Harlow Bryce 1961 (3), www.eisenhower.archives.gov/research/online_documents/farewell_address/1961_03_17_Memo_for_DDE_and_RN.pdf.

7. Blanche Wiesen Cook, *Dwight David Eisenhower: Antimilitarist in the White House* (St. Charles, MO: Forum, 1974).

8. George McGovern, "The Military-Industrial Complex Eight Years Later," Yeshiva University speech, quoted in "McGovern Decries Military Influence," *New York Times,* December 9, 1968, p. 41. "We will lose the American dream," McGovern added, "if we continue to pursue the illusion of security through arms."

9. Richard J. Barnet, *The Economy of Death* (New York: Atheneum, 1969), quoted in Christopher Lehmann-Haupt, "On Slaying the Military-Industrial Hydra," *New York Times,* October 13, 1969, p. 43.

10. Richard Nixon, "Air Force Academy Commencement Address," June 4, 1969, www.presidency.ucsb.edu/ws/index.php?pid=2081.

11. Michael Weisskopf, "The Military-Industrial Complex: 25 Years Later," *Washington Post,* January 17, 1986, p. A8.

12. Cyrus Sanati, "Harsh New Realities for the Military Industrial Complex," *Fortune,* September 12, 2011, http://features.blogs.fortune.cnn.com/2011/09/12/harsh-new-realities-for-the-military-industrial-complex/.

13. Bacevich, "The Tyranny of Defense Inc."

14. Eisenhower, "Farewell Address."

Martin Luther King Jr., "I Have a Dream" (1963)

1. Quoted in David J. Garrow, "Betraying the March," *Christian Science Monitor,* August 28, 2003, www.csmonitor.com/2003/0828/p09s02-coop.html.

2. *Washington Daily News,* August 26, 1963, quoted in Richard Reeves, *President Kennedy: Profile of Power* (New York: Simon & Schuster, 1994), p. 564.

3. John Lewis, *Walking with the Wind: A Memoir of the Movement* (New York: Simon & Schuster, 1998), pp. 222, 226.

4. Lewis, *Walking with the Wind,* p. 221.

5. Michael Eric Dyson, *I May Not Get There with You: The True Martin Luther King, Jr.* (New York: Free Press, 2000), p. 16.

6. "America's Gandhi: Rev. Martin Luther King Jr.," *Time,* January 3, 1964, www.time.com/time/magazine/article/0,9171,940759,00.html.

7. Malcolm X with Alex Haley, *The Autobiography of Malcolm X* (New York: Ballantine, 1965), p. 303.

8. Drew D. Hansen, *The Dream: Martin Luther King and the Speech That Inspired a Nation* (New York: HarperCollins, 2003), pp. 221–22.

9. Andrew Young, quoted in "God in America: The Soul of a Nation," www.pbs.org/godinamerica/transcripts/hour-five.html; Pearl Diver, "I Have a Dream, 2009 Edition," http://pearl-diving.blogspot.com/2009/01/martin-luther-king-has-dream-gay.html.

10. Martin Luther King, Jr., *Why We Can't Wait* (New York: New American Library, 1963), p. 137. In the 1990s, state referenda, led by California's Proposition 209, sought to outlaw affirmative action in the name of a "color-blind" society. The California Republican Party ran a television advertisement featuring a clip of King delivering his "content of their character" line, followed by a voice-over saying, "Martin Luther King was right . . . let's get rid of all discrimination." John Lewis called the ad "almost obscene." Coretta Scott King said that her husband supported affirmative action and that "those who suggest he did not . . . are misrepresenting his beliefs and, indeed, his life's work." See Derrick Z. Jackson, "Twisting King's Dream," *Boston Globe,* October 25, 1996, p. A19.

11. "King's 'I Have a Dream' Is Greatest Political Speech of the Century," *Jet,* January 17, 2000, pp. 4–6.

12. Amaad Rivera, Jeannette Huezo, Christina Kasica, and Dedrick Muhammad, *State of the Dream 2009: The Silent Depression* (Boston: United for a Fair Economy, 2009), pp. 39, iii.

13. Langston Hughes, "Harlem," in *Selected Poems of Langston Hughes* (New York: Vintage, 1990), p. 268.

14. Martin Luther King Jr., "I Have a Dream," August 28, 1963, http://avalon.law.yale.edu/20th_century/mlk01.asp.

Malcolm X, *The Autobiography of Malcolm X* (1965)

1. See http://entertainment.time.com/2011/08/30/all-time-100-best-nonfiction-books; www.modernlibrary.com/top-100/100-best-nonfiction; and http://legacy.www.nypl.org/research/chss/events/booklist.html.

2. Ossie Davis, "Eulogy at the Funeral of Malcolm X," Faith Temple Church of God, New York, February 27, 1965, www.africawithin.com/malcolmx/eulogy.htm.

3. "Malcolm X Scores U.S. and Kennedy," *New York Times,* December 2, 1963, p. 21.

4. "Death and Transfiguration," *Time,* March 5, 1965, p. 23; "Malcolm X," *New York Times,* February 22, 1965, p. 20. See also the New York *Herald Tribune:* "The slaying of Malcolm X has shown again that hatred, whatever its apparent justification, however it may be rationalized, turns on itself in the end. . . . Now the hatred and violence he preached has overwhelmed him and he has fallen at the hands of Negroes" (quoted in Charles E. Wilson, "Leadership: Triumph in Leadership Tragedy," in John Henrik Clarke, ed., *Malcolm X: The Man and His Times* [New York: Macmillan, 1969], p. 28); and Eliot Fremont-Smith, "An Eloquent Testimony": "It is probably fair to say that the majority of the public regards Malcolm X . . . as a violence-preaching 'Black Muslim' racial agitator who reaped his own bloody death" (*New York Times,* November 5, 1965, p. 35).

5. Manning Marable, *Living Black History: How Reimagining the African-American Past Can Remake America's Racial Future* (New York: Basic, 2006), p. 136.

6. Richard Brent Turner, *Islam in the African-American Experience,* 2nd ed. (Bloomington: Indiana Univ. Press, 2003), p. 185.

7. Martin Luther King Jr., "Letter from Birmingham Jail," April 16, 1963, www.thekingcenter.org/archive/document/letter-birmingham-city-jail-0.

8. Michael Eric Dyson, "Who Speaks for Malcolm X? The Writings of Just About Everybody," *New York Times,* November 29, 1992, p. BR29.

9. Martin Luther King Jr., "I've Been to the Mountaintop," Memphis, Tennessee, April 3, 1968, www.americanrhetoric

.com/speeches/mlkivebeentothemountaintop.htm. King also presents a litany of recollections of America's founding documents that begins with "But somewhere I read of the freedom of assembly. Somewhere I read of the freedom of speech . . ."

10. Malcolm X with Alex Haley, *The Autobiography of Malcolm X* (New York: Ballantine, 1992): "When whites had rifles in their homes, the Constitution gave them the right to protect their home and themselves. But when black people even spoke of having rifles in their homes, that was 'ominous'" (p. 394).

11. Malcolm X, *The Autobiography,* p. 422.

12. Eliot Fremont-Smith, "An Eloquent Testament," *New York Times,* November 5, 1965, p. 35.

13. Warner Berthoff, "Witness and Testament: Two Contemporary Classics," *New Literary History* 2.2 (Winter 1971): 321.

14. I take it as axiomatic that every autobiographical work is a work of the imagination; important facts are left out, while others are embellished or invented. So I do not object to Manning Marable's depiction of portions of the autobiography as "fictive" (*Malcolm X: A Life of Reinvention* [New York: Viking, 2011], p. 481). Malcolm's book opens with a dramatic scene he could not have witnessed, because he was still in his mother's womb. Members of the Ku Klux Klan, hooded and armed, surround his home in Omaha, Nebraska. They shout for his father to come out, but he is away. So they tell his mother to pack up and leave because "good Christian white people" are not going to stand idly by while his father, a Baptist preacher, spreads the "back to Africa" teachings of black nationalist Marcus Garvey. Later we learn that Malcolm's father was killed by white racists. According to Bruce Perry, who tracked down Malcolm's mother for an interview, nothing of the sort ever happened with the Klan and, according to a newspaper article, Little died not in a dramatic racist attack, but in a banal accident: he was run over by a streetcar (*State Journal* [Lansing, Michigan], September 28, 1931, www.brothermalcolm.net/family/eldeath.html).

15. Marable, *Living Black History,* p. 148. "Talk about a full-circle book. This will be it!" Haley wrote to his Doubleday editors after Malcolm announced his break from the Nation of Islam in March 1964. "From the toughest anti-white demagogue the land has ever produced to, now, 'All are brothers!'" (p. 159). It should be noted, however, that the metamorphosis of Malcolm X into El-Hajj Malik El-Shabazz is attested to not only in the autobiography, but also in various speeches and interviews Malcolm gave on his own. "I no longer subscribe to sweeping indictments of any one race," he told the *Egyptian Gazette* on August 25, 1964. "I can state in all sincerity that I wish nothing but freedom, justice, and equality, life, liberty, and the pursuit of happiness for all people" (quoted in Clarke, ed., *Malcolm X,* p. 302).

16. Albert E. Stone, "Modern American Autobiography: Texts and Transactions," in John Paul Eaken, ed., *American Autobiography: Retrospect and Prospect* (Madison: Univ. of Wisconsin Press, 1991), p. 101.

17. James Cone, *Malcolm and Martin and America: A Dream or a Nightmare* (Maryknoll, NY: Orbis, 1992), pp. 246, 270–71.

18. Quoted in Coretta Scott King, *My Life with Martin Luther King, Jr.* (New York: Holt, Rinehart and Winston, 1969), p. 256.

19. James Baldwin, "Malcolm and Martin," *Esquire,* April 1972, pp. 94, 201.

20. Marable, *Malcolm X,* p. 482.

21. George Breitman, ed., *Malcolm X Speaks* (New York: Grove, 1990), p. 26. See also his May 13, 1964, speech at the University of Ghana: "I'm from America but I'm not an American. I didn't go there of my own free choice" (in Steve Clark, ed., *Malcolm X Talks to Young People: Speeches in the U.S., Britain, and Africa* [New York: Pathfinder, 1991], p. 11).

22. Walt Whitman, *Leaves of Grass* (Philadelphia: Rees Welsh, 1882), p. 78.

23. Cornel West, *Race Matters* (Boston: Beacon Press, 2001), p. 103.

24. bell hooks, "Malcolm X: The Longed-For Feminist Manhood," in *Outlaw Culture: Resisting Representations* (New York: Routledge, 1994).

25. Marshall Frady, "The Children of Malcolm," *New Yorker,* October 12, 1992, p. 79. The irony, of course, is that this "authentic" voice speaks to us first and foremost through the *Autobiography of Malcolm X,* where it is mixed throughout with the far more moderate voice of Alex Haley.

26. Cone, *Martin and Malcolm and America,* p. 39.

27. Touré, "We Need a Malcolm X Day," *Time,* January 20, 2012, http://ideas.time.com/2012/01/20/we-need-a-malcolm-x-day/.

28. Rasheed Ziyad, quoted in Isabel Wilkerson, "Young Believe Malcolm X Is Still Speaking to Them," *New York Times,* November 18, 1992, p. B7.

29. George Santayana, *The Character and Opinion of the United States* (New York: Scribner, 1920), quoted in John Bartlett, ed., *Familiar Quotations,* 14th ed. (Boston: Little, Brown, 1968), p. 867.

30. Malcolm X with Alex Haley, *The Autobiography of Malcolm X* (New York: Ballantine, 1965), pp. 217–20, 369–73, 400–405, 412–13, 415, 417–18.

Abraham Lincoln, Gettysburg Address (1863)

1. Horace Greeley, *Greeley on Lincoln* (New York: Baker & Taylor, 1893), p. 66.
2. Garry Wills: *Lincoln at Gettysburg: The Words That Remade America* (New York: Simon & Schuster, 1992), p. 101.
3. Wills, *Lincoln at Gettysburg,* p. 145.
4. Wills, *Lincoln at Gettysburg,* p. 147.
5. See Gabor Boritt, *The Gettysburg Gospel: The Lincoln Speech That Nobody Knows* (New York: Simon & Schuster, 2006).
6. "From Gettysburg, Pa.: The Consecration of the Battle Cemetery," *Chicago Tribune,* November 21, 1863, p. 1. See also "The Heroes of July," *New York Times,* November 20, 1863, which reported "long continued applause" (p. 1).
7. *Chicago Times,* November 20, 1863; *Harrisburg Patriot and Union,* November 20, 1863; *Springfield Republican,* November 20, 1863, http://rmc.library.cornell.edu/gettysburg/ideas_more/reactions_p1.htm.
8. "The President at Gettysburg," *Chicago Times,* November 23, 1863, http://teachingamericanhistory.org/library/index.asp?document=1721.
9. "A Mistake in Bronze," *Art World* 2.3 (June 1917): 213.
10. Joseph E. Stiglitz, "Of the 1%, by the 1%, for the 1%," *Vanity Fair,* May 2011, www.vanityfair.com/society/features/2011/05/top-one-percent-201105.
11. Desmond Tutu, quoted in Robert D. McFadden, "Tutu Assails U.S. on Pretoria Ties," *New York Times,* October 28, 1984, p. 19.
12. "Pravda Says Inauguration Reflects 'Government of, for, by Millionaires,'" *Los Angeles Times,* January 21, 1985, http://articles.latimes.com/1985-01-21/news/mn-14215_1_millionaires.
13. Lincoln speech in debate with Stephen Douglas, Charlestown, Illinois, September 18, 1858, in John G. Nicolay and John Hay, eds., *Abraham Lincoln: Complete Works* (New York: Century, 1894), 1:369.
14. This version is based on the so-called Bliss copy, made for Colonel Alexander Bliss, and now located in the Lincoln Room of the White House. This copy is the only version Lincoln signed. See http://americanhistory.si.edu/documentsgallery/exhibitions/gettysburg_address_2.html.

Maya Lin, Vietnam Veterans Memorial (1982)

1. Maya Lin, "Making the Memorial," *New York Review of Books,* November 2, 2000, www.nybooks.com/articles/archives/2000/nov/02/making-the-memorial/?page=1. See also Robert Campbell, "An Emotive Place Apart," *American Institute of Architects Journal* 72 (May 1983): 150–51. Campbell sees Lin's wall as "a huge book, open at a place where it both begins and ends, and its text, its long march of names, has made it, you realize, a memorial to individual human beings rather than to any larger but vaguer concept of country or sacrifice or victory or heroism" (p. 151).
2. Norman B. Hannah, "Open Book Memorial," *National Review,* December 11, 1981, p. 1476.
3. James J. Kilpatrick, "Finally, We Honor the Vietnam Dead," *Washington Post,* November 11, 1981, p. A27.
4. Tom Carhart, "Insulting Vietnam Vets," *New York Times,* October 24, 1981, p. A23.
5. Tom Wolfe, "Art Disputes War: The Battle of the Vietnam Memorial," *Washington Post,* October 13, 1982, p. B4.
6. "Stop That Monument," *National Review,* September 18, 1981, p. 1064.
7. Henry J. Hyde to Republican colleagues, December 30, 1981, http://digital.lib.lehigh.edu/trial/vietnam/r3/october/.
8. James H. Webb Jr., "Reassessing the Vietnam Veterans Memorial," *Wall Street Journal,* December 18, 1981, p. 22.
9. Patrick Buchanan, "An Insulting Memorial," *Chicago Tribune,* December 26, 1981, p. 11.
10. David De Vault, letter to the editor, *Washington Post,* July 17, 1982, p. A22.
11. Tom Carhart, Commission of Fine Arts meeting transcript, October 13, 1981, http://digital.lib.lehigh.edu/trial/vietnam/r3/october/; and Carhart, "Insulting Vietnam Vets," p. A23. Carhart was wrong about black being a universal color of sorrow. In Vietnam that color is white.
12. H. Ross Perot telephone call to Scruggs, quoted in Jan C. Scruggs and Joel L. Swerdlow, *To Heal a Nation: The Vietnam Veterans Memorial* (New York: Harper & Row, 1985), p. 68.
13. Quoted in Scruggs and Swerdlow, *To Heal a Nation,* p. 100.
14. Quoted in Michael J. Weiss, "Vietnam War Memorial Flap: Is It a 'Black Wall of Shame'?," *Washingtonian,* March 1982, http://digital.lib.lehigh.edu/trial/vietnam/r3/february/.
15. Quoted in Isabel Wilkerson, "'Art War' Erupts Over Vietnam Veterans Memorial," *Washington Post,* July 8, 1982, p. D3.
16. Rick Horowitz, "Maya Lin's Angry Objections," *Washington Post,* July 7, 1982, p. B1.

17. Frederick Hart, quoted in Phil McCombs, "Let Me Count the Ways," *Washington Post,* May 11, 1983, p. B7.

18. Maya Lin, testimony at the Commission of Fine Arts meeting, October 13, 1982, unpublished transcript, pp. 153–54, http://digital.lib.lehigh.edu/trial/vietnam/r4/1982/.

19. Lin, testimony at the Commission of Fine Arts meeting, pp. 153–54.

20. Ellen Goodman, "A Monument to Our Discomfort," *Washington Post,* September 25, 1982, p. A25.

21. James J. Kilpatrick, "Vietnam War Memorial," letter to the *National Review,* October 16, 1981, p. 1170.

22. William Hubbard, "A Meaning for Monuments," *Public Interest* 74 (Winter 1984): 27.

23. Thurston Clarke, *Ask Not: The Inauguration of John F. Kennedy and the Speech That Changed America* (New York: Henry Holt, 2004), p. 5.

24. Vincent Scully, "The Terrible Art of Designing a War Memorial," *New York Times,* July 14, 1991, p. 28.

25. James Webb, quoted in Elinda Beck with Mary Lord, "Refighting the Vietnam War," *Newsweek,* October 25, 1982, p. 30.

26. "Panel 01E of the Vietnam Veterans Memorial," www.virtualwall.org/ipanels/ipan01e.htm. This list was modified at the site via personal observations.

Thomas Jefferson, First Inaugural Address (1801)

1. The only record of Henry's speech survives in the notes of John Adams. See Charles Francis Adams, ed., *The Works of John Adams* (Boston: Little and Brown, 1850), 2:367.

2. Abraham Lincoln, "First Inaugural Address," March 4, 1861, http://avalon.law.yale.edu/19th_century/lincoln1.asp.

3. Barack Obama, "Keynote Address at the 2004 Democratic National Convention," July 27, 2004, www.presidency.ucsb.edu/ws/index.php?pid=76988.

4. Richard Hofstadter, *The Idea of a Party System: The Rise of Legitimate Opposition in the United States, 1780–1840* (Berkeley: Univ. of California Press, 1969), pp. 12, 2.

5. George Washington, Farewell Address, 1796, http://avalon.law.yale.edu/18th_century/washing.asp. "A fire not to be quenched" alludes to two parallel passages in the Gospel of Mark (9:44, 48), each of which refers to hell as a place where "the fire is not quenched."

6. Theophilus Parsons to John Jay, May 5, 1800, in John Jay, *The Correspondence and Public Papers of John Jay,* ed. Henry P. Johnson (New York: Putnam, 1893), 4:270.

7. "No one seems to know," the *Connecticut Courant* complained on August 18, 1800, "whether Mr. Jefferson believes in the heathen mythology or, in the alcoran [Qur'an]; whether he is a Jew or a Christian; whether he believes in one God, or in many; or in none at all" (quoted in Susan Dunn, *Jefferson's Second Revolution* [Boston: Houghton Mifflin, 2004], p. 148).

8. Alexander Hamilton to Theodore Sedgwick, May 4, 1800, www.myloc.gov/Exhibitions/creatingtheus/BillofRights/Electionof1800/ExhibitObjects/FederalistsFearFangsofJefferson.aspx; *Aurora* (Philadelphia), December 16, 1800, quoted in Richard N. Rosenfeld, *American Aurora* (New York: St. Martin's, 1997), p. 890.

9. Oliver Wolcott to Alexander Hamilton, October 2, 1800, in George Gibbs, ed., *Memoirs of the Administrations of Washington and John Adams, Edited from the Papers of Oliver Wolcott, Secretary of the Treasury* (New York: n.p., 1846), 2:431.

10. *Connecticut Courant,* September 20, 1800, quoted in Charles O. Lerche Jr., "Jefferson and the Election of 1800: A Case Study in the Political Smear," *William & Mary Quarterly* 5:467 (October 1948): 480.

11. *National Intelligencer,* March 6, 1801, quoted in Samuel Clagett Busey, "The Centennial of the First Inauguration of a President at the Permanent Seat of the Government," *Records of the Columbia Historical Society, Washington, D.C.* 5 (1902): 98.

12. Joseph J. Ellis, *American Sphinx: The Character of Thomas Jefferson* (New York: Knopf, 1997). On the vast literature on Jefferson and Hemings, see "Thomas Jefferson and Sally Hemings: A Brief Account," www.monticello.org/site/plantation-and-slavery/thomas-jefferson-and-sally-hemings-brief-account.

13. John F. Kennedy, "Remarks at a Dinner Honoring Nobel Prize Winners of the Western Hemisphere," April 29, 1962, www.presidency.ucsb.edu/ws/index.php?pid=8623.

14. *Speech of Thomas Jefferson, President of the United States, Delivered at His Installment, March 4, 1801, at the City of Washington* (Philadelphia: Matthew Carey, 1801), reprinted in Noble E. Cunningham Jr., *The Inaugural Addresses of President Thomas Jefferson, 1801 and 1805* (Columbia: Univ. of Missouri Press, 2001), p. 27.

15. Merrill D. Peterson, *Thomas Jefferson and the New Nation: A Biography* (New York: Oxford Univ. Press, 1970), p. 656.

16. Stephen Howard Browne, *Jefferson's Call for Nationhood* (College Station: Texas A&M Press, 2002), p. 23.

17. Noah Webster Jr., "A Letter to the President of the United States," in *Miscellaneous Papers, on Political and Commercial Subjects* (New York: Beldon, 1802), p. 2.

18. John Marshall to Charles Pinckney, March 4, 1801, in Herbert A. Johnson, Charles T. Cullen, and Charles F. Hobson, eds., *The Papers of John Marshall* (Chapel Hill: Univ. of North Carolina Press, 1990), 6:89–90.

19. George Cabot to Rufus King, March 20, 1801, in *The Life and Correspondence of Rufus King* (New York: Putnam, 1896), 3:408.

20. Fawn M. Brodie, *Thomas Jefferson: An Intimate History* (New York: Norton, 1974), p. 336. According to historian Barbara Oberg, "It would be hard to find words that have rung more loudly through American political history" ("Decoding an American Icon: The Textuality of Thomas Jefferson," *Text* 15 [2003]: 10).

21. Thomas Jefferson to Judge Spencer Roane, September 6, 1819, in Paul Leicester Ford, ed., *The Works of Thomas Jefferson* (New York: Putnam, 1905), 12:136.

22. Thomas Jefferson to Levi Lincoln, October 25, 1802, in Paul Leicester Ford, ed., *The Writings of Thomas Jefferson* (New York: Putnam, 1897), 8:176.

23. Thomas E. Watson, *The Life and Times of Thomas Jefferson* (New York: Appleton, 1903), p. 398.

24. Thomas Jefferson, "Inaugural Address," *National Intelligencer,* March 4, 1801, in Thomas Jefferson, *The Papers of Thomas Jefferson,* ed. Barbara B. Oberg (Princeton, NJ: Princeton Univ. Press, 2006), pp. 148–52, www.princeton.edu/~tjpapers/inaugural/infinal.html.

Franklin Delano Roosevelt, First Inaugural Address (1933)

1. During his early life as a radio broadcaster and film and television actor, Reagan was a staunch New Deal Democrat. "I cast my first vote for Roosevelt and the full Democratic ticket," he writes in his autobiography, and "I soon idolized FDR" (Ronald Reagan, *An American Life: The Autobiography* [New York: Simon & Schuster, 1990], p. 66). Reagan ended his acceptance speech at the 1980 Republican National Convention with words from Roosevelt's acceptance speech at the 1932 Democratic National Convention. In 1982, Reagan signed legislation authorizing the building of the FDR memorial that now stands on the National Mall in Washington, D.C. And his 1984 campaign theme—"morning in America"—was pure FDR. Reagan eventually voted for Roosevelt four times, and even after he left the Democratic Party in 1962—or, as he put it, the Democratic Party left him—he continued to revere Roosevelt, whom he praised as "an American giant" (Ronald Reagan, "Remarks at a White House Luncheon Celebrating the Centennial of the Birth of Franklin Delano Roosevelt," January 28, 1982, www.presidency.ucsb.edu/ws/index.php?pid=42798). No wonder the *New York Times* referred to him as "Franklin Delano Reagan" ("Franklin Delano Reagan," *New York Times,* July 20, 1980, p. E20; "The New Old Deal," *New York Times,* January 28, 1982).

2. Quoted in Richard Langworth, ed., *Churchill by Himself: The Definitive Collection of Quotations* (New York: PublicAffairs, 2011), p. 371.

3. Edmund Burke, *The Works of the Right Honourable Edmund Burke* (London: George Bell, 1889), p. 88.

4. "A Birthday Posie," *New York Times,* January 15, 1935, p. 18.

5. Henry David Thoreau, *The Writings of Henry David Thoreau* (Boston: Houghton Mifflin, 1906), 8:468. For Montaigne, Francis Bacon, and others, see John Hollander, "Fear Itself," *Social Research* 71.4 (Winter 2004): 865–86.

6. Quoted in "Business to Make Stabilization Study," *New York Times,* February 9, 1931, p. 3.

7. "The Faith of Roosevelt," *Nation,* March 15, 1933, 278.

8. Arthur Krock, "100,000 at Inauguration," *New York Times,* March 4, 1933, p. 1.

9. Quoted in Ronald Steel, *Walter Lippmann and the American Century* (Boston: Little, Brown, 1980), p. 300.

10. Arthur Krock, "Roosevelt Gets Power of Dictator," *New York Times,* March 11, 1933, p. 7.

11. William S. Burroughs, "Roosevelt After Inauguration," in James Grauerholz and Ira Silverberg, eds., *Word Virus: The William S. Burroughs Reader* (New York: Grove, 1998), pp. 109–12.

12. The Siena Research Institute's polls of scholars conducted in 1982, 1990, 1994, 2002, and 2010 all placed Franklin Roosevelt first ("America's Presidents: Greatest and Worst," www.siena.edu/...research/Presidents%20Release_2010_final.pdf). A 1996 poll by historian Arthur Schlesinger Jr. saw FDR tied with George Washington for second, behind Abraham Lincoln ("Rating the Presidents: Washington to Clinton," *Political Science Quarterly* 11.2 [Summer 1997]: 179–90).

13. Myron Taylor, quoted in "Leaders Here Praise Address as 'Strong,'" *New York Times,* March 5, 1933, p. F6.

14. Letters quoted in Davis W. Houck, *FDR and Fear Itself: The First Inaugural Address* (College Station: Texas A&M Univ. Press, 2002), pp. 10–11. Significantly, Houck describes the address as "a speech first and foremost to be experienced, felt" (p. 10).

15. Edmund Wilson, "Washington: Inaugural Parade," 1933, in *American Earthquake* (New York: Farrar, Straus & Giroux, 1958), pp. 478–79.

16. Quoted in Tom Hayden, *Reunion: A Memoir* (New York: Collier, 1989), p. 472.

17. "TVA 'Socialism' Hit by Liberty League," *New York Times*, May 27, 1935, p. 9; "Warns of New George III," *New York Times*, November 11, 1935, p. 4.

18. Carl N. Degler, "The Third American Revolution," in *Out of Our Past: The Forces That Shaped Modern America* (New York: Harper & Row, 1970), pp. 379–413.

19. Ronald Radosh, "The Myth of the New Deal," in Ronald Radosh and Murray N. Rothbard, eds., *A New History of Leviathan: Essays on the Rise of the American Corporate State* (New York: Dutton, 1972), pp. 146–87. On this argument's libertarian side, see John Thomas Flynn, *The Roosevelt Myth* (New York: Devin-Adair, 1948): "The figure of Roosevelt exhibited before the eyes of our people is a fiction. There was no such being as that noble, selfless, hard-headed, wise and farseeing combination of philosopher, philanthropist and warrior which has been fabricated out of pure propaganda and which a small collection of dangerous cliques in this country are using to advance their own evil ends" (p. 419). Conrad Black, a businessman and author of a massive Roosevelt biography that describes his subject as "the most important person of the twentieth century," is far kinder. "He was a reformer," Black writes, "and also one of the very greatest conservatives in American history." See Conrad Black, *Franklin Delano Roosevelt: Champion of Freedom* (New York: PublicAffairs, 2003), p. 1122; and Conrad Black, "Roosevelt and the Revisionists," *National Review*, March 5, 2009, www.nationalreview.com/articles/227009/roosevelt-revisionists/conrad-black.

20. William E. Leuchtenburg, *Franklin D. Roosevelt and the New Deal* (New York: Harper Torchbooks, 1963), p. 347.

21. Franklin D. Roosevelt, "Address to Congress Requesting a Declaration of War with Japan," December 8, 1941, www.presidency.ucsb.edu/ws/index.php?pid=16053.

22. Henry David Thoreau, "Resistance to Civil Government," in Elizabeth P. Peabody, ed., *Aesthetic Papers* (Boston: The Editor, 1849), pp. 189–211, http://thoreau.eserver.org/civil.html.

23. There are considerable differences between the prepared text of this speech and the speech Roosevelt delivered. Most notably, Roosevelt added an opening line—"This is a day of national consecration"—which was not in his working draft. He also added various oral flourishes, including "yes" and "my friends." Typically, printed versions of the speech followed the prepared text. This version follows the spoken word. See Houck, *FDR and Fear Itself*, pp. 3–8.

Ronald Reagan, "The Speech" (1964)

1. Gary Kamiya, "Ronald Reagan," in Greil Marcus and Werner Sollors, eds., *A New Literary History of America* (Cambridge, MA: Harvard Univ. Press, 2009), www.newliteraryhistory.com/ronaldreagan.html.

2. David Broder and Stephen Hess, *The Republican Establishment: The Present and Future of the G.O.P.* (New York: Harper & Row, 1967), pp. 253–54.

3. "Republicans: Stage to Sacramento?," *Time*, July 30, 1965, p. 23.

4. David Frum, *Comeback: Conservatism That Can Win* (New York: Broadway, 2008), p. 19. "The most dangerous legacy Reagan bequeathed his party was his legacy of cheerful indifference to detail. . . . The next Republican president needs to master details, understand his options, and make decisions with care" (p. 19).

5. Ronald Reagan, "A Time for Choosing," October 27, 1964, www.reagan.utexas.edu/archives/reference/timechoosing .html.

The Pledge of Allegiance (1892, 1954)

1. "National School Celebration of Columbus Day," *The Youth's Companion*, September 8, 1892, p. 446. This original formulation did *not* include the word "to" before "the Republic," as many sources wrongly claim.

2. Francis Bellamy, quoted in Richard J. Ellis, *To the Flag: The Unlikely History of the Pledge of Allegiance* (Lawrence: Univ. Press of Kansas, 2005), pp. 32, 22.

3. Ellis, *To the Flag*, p. 42.

4. Ellis, *To the Flag*, p. 32. In an unpublished document dating to 1923, Bellamy drafted a list of anti-American foes the Pledge could be used to repel, namely: "red radicals . . . academic radicals . . . radical newspapers . . . large radical sections of Russian and Polish Jews . . . 'pink' radicals of older American stock among whom are many clergymen . . . pacifists." See his "A New Plan for Counter-Attack on the Nation's Internal Foes: How to Mobilize the Masses to Support Primary American Doctrines," May 1, 1923, 1, Francis Bellamy Papers, Rare Books and Special Collections, Rush Rhees Library, Univ. of Rochester, Rochester, NY, quoted in Ellis, *To the Flag*, p. 68.

5. Ellis, *To the Flag,* p. 66.

6. *West Virginia State Board of Education v. Barnette,* 319 U.S. 624 (1943).

7. "Sermon preached by Dr. George M. Docherty, New York Avenue Presbyterian Church, on Sunday, February 7, 1954," www.post-gazette.com/nation/20020819pledge0819p1.asp.

8. Louis Rabaut, *Congressional Record,* February 12, 1954, p. 1700.

9. Dwight D. Eisenhower, "Remarks Recorded for the 'Back-to-God' Program of the American Legion," February 20, 1955, www.presidency.ucsb.edu/ws/index.php?pid=10414#axzz1Zw1STdnk.

10. Ellis, *To the Flag,* p. 173.

11. Ronald Reagan, "Remarks at a Republican Campaign Rally in Mesquite, Texas," November 5, 1988, www.reagan .utexas.edu/archives/speeches/1988/110588c.htm; Ronald Reagan, "Remarks at a Republican Party Rally in Cape Girardeau, Missouri," September 14, 1988, www.reagan.utexas.edu/archives/speeches/1988/091488e.htm.

12. Jesse Ventura, quoted in Ellis, *To the Flag,* p. 194.

13. Robert Byrd, *Congressional Record,* June 26, 2002, p. S6103.

14. Justice William J. Brennan Jr. in *Lynch v. Donnelly,* 465 U.S. 668 (1984).

15. Ellis, *To the Flag,* p. 216.

George Washington, Farewell Address (1796)

1. George Washington, "First Inaugural Address," April 30, 1789, http://avalon.law.yale.edu/18th_century/wash1.asp.

2. Fisher Ames to George Richards Minot, November 30, 1791, in Seth Ames, ed., *Works of Fisher Ames with a Selection from His Speeches* (Boston: Little, Brown, 1854), 1:104.

3. Fisher Ames to George Richards Minot, July 8, 1789, in Ames, ed., *Works of Fisher Ames,* 1:61.

4. *General Advertiser* (Philadelphia), October 3, 1790, later reprinted in *Aurora,* October 23, 1790, quoted in Donald H. Stewart, *The Opposition Press of the Federalist Period* (Albany: State Univ. of New York Press, 1969), p. 32.

5. Thomas Jefferson to Dr. Jones, March 5, 1810, in H. A. Washington, ed., *The Writings of Thomas Jefferson* (New York: Derby & Jackson, 1859), 5:510.

6. George Washington to Thomas Jefferson, August 23, 1792, in Worthington Chauncey Ford, ed., *The Writings of George Washington, 1790–1794* (New York: Putnam, 1891), 12:174.

7. George Washington to Alexander Hamilton, August 26, 1792, in *The Papers of Alexander Hamilton,* ed. Harold Coffin Syrett (New York: Columbia Univ. Press, 1967), 11:276–77.

8. Don Higginbotham, ed., *George Washington Reconsidered* (Charlottesville: Univ. Press of Virginia, 2001), "Introduction," p. 6.

9. John Ferling, *Adams vs. Jefferson: The Tumultuous Election of 1800* (New York: Oxford Univ. Press, 2004), p. 57.

10. George Washington to Burgess Ball, September 25, 1794, http://oll.libertyfund.org/?option=com_staticxt &staticfile=show.php%3Ftitle=848&chapter=102147&layout=html&Itemid=27.

11. Alexander DeConde, "Washington's Farewell, the French Alliance, and the Election of 1796," *Mississippi Valley Historical Review* 43.4 (March 1957): 645.

12. Woodrow Wilson, *George Washington* (New York: Harper, 1897), p. 308.

13. Wilson, *George Washington,* p. 308.

14. Joseph J. Ellis, *His Excellency: George Washington* (New York: Vintage, 2005), p. 234.

15. Ellis, *His Excellency,* p. xiv.

16. Joseph J. Ellis, "The Farewell: Washington's Wisdom at the End," in Higginbotham, ed., *George Washington Reconsidered,* p. 213.

17. *Maryland Journal & Baltimore Daily Advertiser,* September 17, 1896, quoted in Victor Hugo Paltsits, ed., *Washington's Farewell Address* (New York: New York Public Library, 1935), p. 64.

18. Samuel Flagg Bemis, "Washington's Farewell Address: A Foreign Policy of Independence," *American Historical Review* 39.2 (January 1934): 250–68.

19. Ellis, *His Excellency,* p. 235.

20. Greg Epstein, *Good Without God: What a Billion Nonreligious People Do Believe* (New York: Morrow, 2009).

21. "An Observer," writing in the *Gazette of the United States,* August 5, 1800, reprinted in Charles Brockden Brown, *Arthur Mervyn or, Memoirs of the Year 1793, with Related Texts,* ed. Philip Barnard and Stephen Shapiro (Indianapolis, IN: Hackett, 2008), p. 415.

22. *Aurora*, April 27, 1798, in Richard N. Rosenfeld, *American Aurora* (New York: St. Martin's, 1997), p. 94.

23. William Wirt Henry, *Patrick Henry: Life, Correspondence and Speeches* (New York: Scribner, 1891), 2:610.

24. Thomas Jefferson, "First Inaugural Address," March 4, 1801, http://avalon.law.yale.edu/19th_century/jefinau1.asp.

25. John Adams to Benjamin Stoddert, March 31, 1801, in Charles Francis Adams, ed., *The Works of John Adams* (Boston: Little, Brown, 1854), 9:582.

26. Alexander DeConde, "Washington's Farewell, the French Alliance, and the Election of 1796," *Mississippi Valley Historical Review* 43.4 (March 1957): 648.

27. Jasper Dwight (a.k.a. William Duane), *A Letter to George Washington, President of the United States: Containing Strictures on His Address of the Seventeenth of September, 1796* (Philadelphia: The Author, 1796), p. 42.

28. Quoted in Paltsits, ed., *Washington's Farewell Address*, p. 69.

29. Stephen E. Lucas, "Review of *A Sacred Union of Citizens: George Washington's Farewell Address and the American Character*," *Journal of American History* 84.4 (March 1998): 1493.

30. "By the President of the United States of America: A Proclamation," February 19, 1862, http://memory.loc.gov/cgi-bin/ampage?collId=llsl&fileName=012/llsl012.db&recNum=1316.

31. Nathan A. Forrester Jr., "Equal Billing: On Religion, Washington's Views Should Be Considered, Too," *Texas Review of Law & Politics* 12.1 (Fall 2007): 207–221.

32. The view that America had interests distinct from those of Europe and should avoid getting involved in European conflicts was commonplace—over a decade earlier Jefferson was already calling it "a maxim with us, and . . . a wise one"—and had been expressed earlier by many leading Americans, including Thomas Paine, John Adams, James Madison, and Alexander Hamilton (Bemis, "Washington's Farewell Address," pp. 260–61). In fact, the iconic expression of this view comes not from Washington, but from Jefferson, who in his First Inaugural Address in 1801 famously said (in words often wrongly attributed to Washington), "Peace, commerce, and honest friendship with all nations, entangling alliances with none." American political thinking was also full of Washington's antiparty spirit. Edmund Burke, the eighteenth-century Irish political philosopher and darling of modern American conservatism, famously saw something good about parties, an idiosyncratic view that inspired this postmortem doggerel by one William Goldsmith: "Here lies our good Edmund. / Who, born for the universe, / narrowed his mind. / And to party gave up / what was meant for mankind" (quoted in Nancy L. Rosenblum, "A Political Theory of Partisanship and Independence," in John C. Green and Daniel J. Coffey, eds., *The State of the Parties: The Changing Role of Contemporary American Parties*, 6th ed. [Lanham, MD: Rowman & Littlefield, 2011], p. 289). But early American political thought was almost unanimously antiparty. In the *Federalist Papers*, Madison and Hamilton deplored parties. John Adams called them "the greatest political evil under our Constitution." And Ben Franklin wrote of "the infinite mutual abuse of parties, tearing to pieces the best of characters." "If there was one point of political philosophy upon which these men, who differed on so many things, agreed quite readily," historian Richard Hofstadter writes of the founders, "it was their common conviction about the baneful effects of the spirit of party" (*The Idea of the Party System* [Berkeley: Univ. of California Press, 1969], pp. 2–3). On religion too Washington was no innovator. About his now famous statement that religion and morality are "indispensable supports," historian Mark A. Noll writes, "With one exception, the other founders believed much the same thing" (*America's God: From Jonathan Edwards to Abraham Lincoln* [New York: Oxford Univ. Press, 2002], p. 204). That exception, of course, was Thomas Jefferson.

33. Washington, Farewell Address.

Thomas Jefferson, "Letter to the Danbury Baptists" (1802)

1. Danbury Baptist Association to Thomas Jefferson, October 7, 1801, Thomas Jefferson Papers, Manuscript Division, Library of Congress, Washington, D.C., in Daniel L. Dreisbach and Mark David Hall, eds., *The Sacred Rights of Conscience* (Indianapolis, IN: Liberty Fund, 2009), p. 526.

2. John Mason, quoted in Robert M. S. McDonald, "Was There a Religious Revolution of 1800?," in James Horn, Jan Ellen Lewis, and Peter S. Onuf, eds., *The Revolution of 1800: Democracy, Race, and the New Republic* (Charlottesville: Univ. of Virginia Press, 2002), p. 182.

3. Quoted in McDonald, "Was There a Religious Revolution of 1800?," p. 173.

4. Abraham Bishop, *Connecticut Republicanism: An Oration on the Extent and Power of Political Delusion* (Albany, NY: Barber, 1801), pp. 49–50.

5. Thomas Jefferson to Benjamin Rush, September 23, 1800, in Andrew A. Lipscomb and Albert E. Bergh, eds., *The Writings of Thomas Jefferson* (Washington, DC: Thomas Jefferson Memorial Association, 1903), 10:174; Thomas Jefferson to Levi Lincoln, August 26, 1801, in Paul Leicester Ford, ed., *The Works of Thomas Jefferson* (New York: Putnam, 1905), 9:290.

6. Thomas Jefferson, "First Inaugural Address," March 4, 1801, http://avalon.law.yale.edu/19th_century/jefinau1.asp.

7. Thomas Jefferson to Levi Lincoln, January 1, 1802, in Lipscomb and Bergh, eds., *The Writings of Thomas Jefferson,* 10:305.

8. *Reynolds v. United States,* 98 U.S. 145 (1878).

9. Quoted in Rick Shenkman, "An Interview with Jon Butler . . . Was America Founded as a Christian Nation?," History News Network, December 19, 2004, http://hnn.us/articles/9144.html.

10. Northwest Ordinance, 1787, www.ourdocuments.gov/doc.php?flash=true&doc=8&page=transcript.

11. *Wallace v. Jaffree,* 472 U.S. 38.

12. Stephen L. Carter, *The Culture of Disbelief: How American Law and Politics Trivialize Religious Devotion* (New York: Basic Books, 1993), p. 115.

13. Roger Williams, "Mr. Cotton's Letter Lately Printed, Examined and Answered," in *The Complete Writings of Roger Williams* (Providence, RI: Providence, 1866), 1:392, quoted in Perry Miller, *Roger Williams: His Contribution to the American Tradition* (Indianapolis, IN: Bobbs-Merrill, 1953), p. 98.

14. Thomas Jefferson, "Letter to the Danbury Baptists," January 1, 1802, www.loc.gov/loc/lcib/9806/danpre.html.

Martin Luther King Jr., "Letter from Birmingham Jail" (1963)

1. "Public Statement by Eight Alabama Clergymen," *Birmingham News,* April 13, 1963, p. 2, www.thekingcenter.org/archive/document/letter-birmingham-city-jail-0.

2. "Dogs, Kids and Clubs," *Time,* May 10, 1963, www.time.com/time/magazine/article/0,9171,830260,00.html.

3. Hillary Kaell and Marilyn Mellowes, "American Scripture," www.pbs.org/godinamerica/american-scripture/.

4. Wyatt Walker, quoted in S. Jonathan Bass, *Blessed Are the Peacemakers: Martin Luther King, Jr., Eight White Religious Leaders, and the "Letter from Birmingham Jail"* (Baton Rouge: Louisiana State Univ. Press, 2001), p. 145.

5. Herwald M. Price, letter to the editor, *Ebony,* August 1963, pp. 16–17.

6. Robert Dallek, *An Unfinished Life: John F. Kennedy, 1917–1963* (Boston: Little, Brown, 2003), p. 594.

7. John F. Kennedy, quoted in William A. Nunnelly, *Bull Connor* (Tuscaloosa: Univ. of Alabama Press, 1991), p. 164.

8. See *Shuttlesworth v. Birmingham,* 373 U.S. 262 (1963). In 1967 the U.S. Supreme Court ruled against the Reverend Shuttlesworth in a case that upheld the court order restricting him from marching. In 1969, however, the Supreme Court ruled for Shuttlesworth in a separate but related case he brought against the city of Birmingham, finding that the city's ordinance against parading without a permit amounted to an unconstitutional restriction on free speech. See *Walker v. Birmingham,* 388 U.S. 307 (1967), and *Shuttlesworth v. Birmingham,* 394 U.S. 147 (1969).

9. John F. Kennedy, "Radio and Television Report to the American People on Civil Rights," June 11, 1963, www.presidency.ucsb.edu/ws/index.php?pid=9271.

10. Bass, *Blessed Are the Peacemakers,* p. 148.

11. Joseph Jackson, "Annual Address," National Baptist Convention, Detroit, Michigan, September 10, 1964, http://teachingamericanhistory.org/library/index.asp?document=642.

12. Eldridge Cleaver, *Soul on Ice* (New York: McGraw-Hill, 1968), p. 108.

13. Milton Grafman, quoted in Howell Raines, "Parley Focuses on Social Changes in Birmingham," *New York Times,* November 16, 1978, p. A20.

14. Kenneth A. Briggs, "Black Theologians Want to Add a Letter by Dr. King to the Bible," *New York Times,* August 5, 1989, p. 42.

15. Martin Luther King Jr., "Letter from Birmingham Jail," April 16, 1963, in *Why We Can't Wait* (New York: Harper & Row, 1964), pp. 77–100. See also www.thekingcenter.org/archive/document/letter-birmingham-city-jail-0.

Epilogue

1. Herman Melville, "Misgivings" (1861), www.poetryfoundation.org/poem/182550.

2. Booker T. Washington, *The Negro Problem: A Series of Articles by Representative American Negroes* (New York: Pott, 1903).

3. John Stuart Mill, *Considerations on Representative Government* (New York: Harper, 1862), p. 310.

4. Emile Durkheim, *The Elementary Forms of the Religious Life,* trans. Joseph Ward Swain (London: Allen & Unwin, 1915), p. 226.

5. Pauline Maier, *American Scripture* (New York: Knopf, 1997), p. 208.

6. Danièle Hervieu-Léger, *Religion as a Chain of Memory* (New Brunswick, NJ: Rutgers Univ. Press, 2000).

7. Frank Kelleter, "A Dialectics of Radical Enlightenment," in Greil Marcus and Werner Sollors, eds., *A New Literary History of America* (Cambridge, MA: Harvard Univ. Press, 2009), p. 101.

8. J. Hector St. John de Crèvecoeur, *Letters from an American Farmer* (1782; New York: Fox, Duffield, 1904), p. 54.

9. George Washington, Farewell Address, 1796, http://avalon.law.yale.edu/18th_century/washing.asp; Abraham Lincoln, "First Inaugural Address," March 4, 1861, www.presidency.ucsb.edu/ws/index.php?pid=25818.

10. Thomas Jefferson, "First Inaugural Address," March 4, 1801, www.princeton.edu/~tjpapers/inaugural/infinal.html.

11. Thomas Jefferson to T. M. Randolph, February 2, 1800, and Thomas Jefferson to John Taylor, June 1, 1798, in Andrew A. Lipscomb, ed., *The Writings of Thomas Jefferson* (Washington, DC: Thomas Jefferson Memorial Association, 1903), 10.150, 10.44.

12. For one expression of this idea, see Arthur M. Schlesinger Jr., *The Vital Center: The Politics of Freedom* (Boston: Houghton Mifflin, 1949).

13. Quoted in Charles Francis Adams, ed., *The Works of John Adams* (Boston: Little and Brown, 1850), 2:367.

14. George W. Bush, "Address in Austin Accepting Election as the 43rd President of the United States," December 13, 2000, www.presidency.ucsb.edu/ws/index.php?pid=84900.

15. "Governor George Pataki Announces Formation of Revere America," April 15, 2010, www.revereamerica.org/News/Governor-George-Pataki-Announces-Formation-of-Revere-America.aspx.

16. H. D. Thoreau, "Resistance to Civil Government," in Elizabeth P. Peabody, *Aesthetic Papers* (Boston: The Editor, 1849), p. 197.

17. Jefferson, "First Inaugural Address."

18. Thomas Paine, *Common Sense* (1776), in Moncure Daniel Conway, ed., *The Writings of Thomas Paine* (New York: Putnam, 1894), 1:118.

19. Martin Luther King Jr., "Letter from Birmingham Jail" (1963), http://abacus.bates.edu/admin/offices/dos/mlk/letter.html; Thoreau, "Resistance to Civil Government," p. 180.

CREDITS

Chief Joseph, "I will fight no more forever"

Helen Howard: Used by permission of Caxton Press.

Mark Brown: Used by permission of *Montana, the Magazine of Western History*.

Ronald Reagan, "evil empire"

National Review editorial: Used by permission of *National Review*.

Henry David Thoreau, "Civil Disobedience"

Edwin Griswold: Originally published in 42 Tul. L Rev. 726 (1968). Reprinted with the permission of the Tulane Law Review Association, which holds the copyright.

Dwight Eisenhower, Farewell Address

Jack Shor: Used by permission of the author.

Martin Luther King Jr., "I Have a Dream"

Martin Luther King Jr., "I Have a Dream" speech: Reprinted by arrangement with the Heirs to the Estate of Martin Luther King Jr., c/o Writers House as agent for the proprietor New York, NY. Copyright 1963 Dr. Martin Luther King Jr; copyright renewed 1991 Coretta Scott King.

Malcolm X, *The Autobiography of Malcolm X*

Excerpts from the *Autobiography*: Excerpts used with permission from the family of Malcolm X.

Saturday Evening Post: "The Lesson of Malcolm X" article © 1964 SEPS licensed by Curtis Licensing, Indianapolis, IN. All rights reserved.

Abraham Lincoln, Gettysburg Address

Wilmoore Kendall: From Willmoore Kendall, "Equality: Commitment or Ideal?" Phalanx 1 (Fall 1967), reprinted in the *Intercollegiate Review* 24, no. 2 (Spring 1989). Reprinted here with permission of the Intercollegiate Studies Institute.

Eliot Spitzer: From *Slate,* © June 4, 2010 The Slate Group. All rights reserved. Used by permission and protected by the Copyright Laws of the United States. The printing, copying, redistribution, or retransmission of the Material without express written permission is prohibited.

Maya Lin, Vietnam Veterans Memorial

Maya Lin: Reprinted with the permission of Simon & Schuster, Inc., from BOUNDARIES by Maya Lin. Copyright © 2000 by Maya Lin Studio, Inc. All rights reserved. Audio rights by permission of International Creative Management, Inc. Copyright © 2000 by Maya Lin.

Michael Scrogin: Copyright © 1983 by the *Christian Century*. An excerpt of "Symbol of the valley of the shadow" by Michael Scrogin is reprinted with permission from the January 5–12, 1983, issue of the *Christian Century*.

Charles Griswold: Used by permission of the author.

Thomas Jefferson, First Inaugural Address

Henry Commager: From the *Boston Globe,* December 13, 1979. © 1979 *Boston Globe*. All rights reserved. Used by permission and protected by the Copyright Laws of the United States. The printing, copying, redistribution, or retransmission of this Content without express written permission is prohibited.

Jeff Jacoby: From the *Boston Globe,* November 4, 2004. © 2004 *Boston Globe*. All rights reserved. Used by permission and protected by the Copyright Laws of the United States. The printing, copying, redistribution, or retransmission of this Content without express written permission is prohibited.

Franklin Delano Roosevelt, First Inaugural Address

H. L. Mencken: Copyright 1933 by BALTIMORE SUN COMPANY. Reproduced with permission of BALTIMORE SUN COMPANY via Copyright Clearance Center.

James Ostrowski: Used by permission of www.mises.org.

Bob Bussel: Used by permission of the author.

Ronald Reagan, "The Speech"

Ronald Reagan: Used courtesy of the Ronald Reagan Presidential Foundation.

Paul Krugman: From *The New York Times*, October 5, 2007. © 2007 *The New York Times*. All rights reserved. Used by permission and protected by the Copyright Laws of the United States. The printing, copying, redistribution, or retransmission of this Content without express written permission is prohibited.

Howard Means: Used with permission of the *Orlando Sentinel* (1986).

Gary Kamiya: Reprinted by permission of the publisher from *1964, October 27 "The Last Stand on Earth," by Gary Kamiya* in A NEW LITERARY HISTORY OF AMERICA, edited by Greil Marcus and Werner Sollors, pp. 927–928, Cambridge, Mass.: The Belknap Press of Harvard University Press. Copyright © 2009 by the President and Fellows of Harvard College.

Kevin Baker: Used by permission of the author.

The Pledge of Allegiance

George Docherty: Used with permission of the New York Avenue Presbyterian Church.

Jay Lapidus: Used by permission of the author.

Emma Martens: Used by permission of the author.

George Washington, Farewell Address

J. Matt Barber: Used by permission of the author.

Alan Wolfe: Used by permission of the author.

Thomas Jefferson, "Letter to the Danbury Baptists"

Focus on the Family: Excerpted from the Focus on the Family website. Copyright © 2008 Focus on the Family. All rights reserved. International copyright secured. Used by permission.

Martin Luther King Jr., "Letter from Birmingham Jail"

Martin Luther King Jr., "Letter from Birmingham Jail": Reprinted by arrangement with the Heirs to the Estate of Martin Luther King Jr., c/o Writers House as agent for the proprietor New York, NY. *Copyright 1963 Dr. Martin Luther King Jr; copyright renewed 1991 Coretta Scott King.*

Bayard Rustin: From *The New York Times*, August 30, 1979. © 1979 *The New York Times*. All rights reserved. Used by permission and protected by the Copyright Laws of the United States. The printing, copying, redistribution, or retransmission of this Content without express written permission is prohibited.

INDEX

Entries for core texts appear in bold typeface.

Burke, J. W., 101

Burr, Aaron, 359

Burroughs, William, 376

Bush, George H. W., 48, 56, 65n, 148, 229, 411

Bush, George W., 134, 148, 181, 210, 216, 217, 226, 229, 264, 370–71, 425, 449, 455, 488; "Remarks at the National Day of Prayer and Remembrance Service" (Bush), 384n; "State of the Union Message to Congress 2002," 293

"Bush and the World" (Hirsh), 449

"business of America is business, The" (Coolidge), 8, 258–59, **259**

Bussel, Bob, 387–88

Butler, Frederick, 25–26

Butler, Jon, 455

Byrd, Robert, 412

Cabot, George, 360

Calhoun, John, 427

Callahan, Richard, Jr., 245

Camus, Albert, 11

"Canaanites, Cowboys, and Indians" (Warrior), 31–32

"Candidates at Bay, The" (Will), 69n

Cannon, Lou, 401

Carhart, Tom, 348, 509n 11

Carroll, James, 233

Carter, Jimmy, 12, 231, 391, 460–61

Carter, Stephen, 455, 459

"Case Against Thoreau, The" (Buranelli), 274

Cavell, Stanley, 268

Chambers, Whittaker, 200, 205–6, 500n 5

Character of Washington, The (Webster), 444–45

Chavez, Leo, 217

Cheatham, Kitty, 223–24

Chicago Daily Tribune, 219n, 432n

Chicago Times, 255, 332, 333, 503n 2; "The President at Gettysburg," 334–35n

Chief Joseph, 256–57, 488, 503n 2

Chisholm, Shirley, 259

Chomsky, Noam, 200

Christianity, 21; America as Christian nation, 2, 49–50, 78, 79n, 111, 113, 126–27, 200, 234–35, 435n, 436n, 437n, 452–61, 482; American Legion's Back to God program, 336n; *Atlas Shrugged,* Ayn Rand, and, 203, 211; Blue-Back Speller and, 100–101; "family values"

and, 203; "under God" added to Pledge of Allegiance, 332, 409, 410–11, 412, 459

"Christian Politics" (*Quarterly Christian Spectator*), 367

"Christmas Sermon on Peace, A" (King), 302

Churchill, Winston, 373, 400–401

Cincinnatus: George Washington and the Enlightenment (Wills), 439n

"Civil Disobedience" (Thoreau), 164, 185, 268–83, **272–78**, 505–6n 2, 506n 11

civil rights movement, 30, 32–33, 112, 220n, 270, 314, 333, 484; affirmative action, 134, 144, 297, 303, 507n 10; Bradley arguing for Martin Luther King Jr. holiday, 302–3; busing, 134; Civil Rights Act of 1964, 134, 297, 302, 303, 463; gradualism, 131; "I Have a Dream" (King), 294–307, **298–301**, 334, 463, 484, 486; Kennedy and, 295, 335–36n; "Letter from Birmingham Jail" (King), 10, 462–82, **466–79**; Lincoln's views and, 333; 1968 Olympics and, 217; school desegregation, 129–45 (*see also Brown v. Board of Education*); Voting Rights Act of 1965, 248, 297, 302, 464. *See also* King, Martin Luther Jr.; Malcolm X

Civil War, 1, 22, 27–28, 38, 66–67n, 77, 111, 112, 114, 122, 177, 254, 341, 427, 484, 487; Gettysburg Address and, 332. *See also* Confederate States of America; Lincoln, Abraham

Cizik, Richard, 265

Cleage, Albert, 30–31, 324–25

Cleaver, Eldridge, 466

Clinton, Hillary, 252, 417

Clinton, William J. "Bill," 149, 229, 231, 257, 314, 372, 387, 449; interview with Terence Hunt and Walter M. Mears of AP, 370; on Jefferson, 363n, 370; "Remarks at a Memorial Day Ceremony at the Vietnam Veterans Memorial," 355–56; "Remarks at the Dedication of the FDR Memorial," 379–80n; "Remarks on the 200th Anniversary of the Capitol . . . ," 363n; State of the Union address 1996, 260, 272

Cobbett, William, 55

Coffin, William Sloan, 232

Colbert, Stephen, 12, 181

Cold War, 133, 140, 264, 284, 342, 394, 400, 410, 418, 439n, 448–49

Colson, Chuck, 203, 211

Commager, Henry Steele, 13, 65n, 100, 102, 105, 264, 368–69, 491n 15

Common Sense (Paine), 52–72, **57–69**, 74, 167, 492n 3, 493n 12, 493n 23

Complete History of the United States of America, A (Butler), 25–26

"How the Great Men of Other Nations Regard Our National Character" (*Oberlin Evangelist*), 44–45

Hubbard, William, 350

Hubler, Richard G., 58n

Huckleberry Finn as Idol and Target (Arac), 188

Hughes, Charles Evans, 496n 13

Hughes, Langston, 298

Hume, David, 2

Humphrey, Hubert, 303, 394

Hungarian Revolution, 445–46

Hurston, Zora Neale, 20

Hutchinson, Anne, 35

Hyde, Henry, 156, 348

Hyde, Orson, 247

Hyman, Stanley Edgar, 269

I May Not Get There with You (Dyson), 304

Ickes, Harold, 261

Idea of America, The (Wood), 96–97

"I Have a Dream" (Jackson), 305–6

"I Have a Dream" (King), 2, 3, 10, 35, 294–307, **298–301**, 334, 463, 484, 486

"Image and Superscription of Caesar, The" (Ingalls), 219–20n

immigration, 57n, 67n, 219n

"Impassable Chasm, The" (MacVeagh), 340–41

Incidents in the Life of a Slave Girl (Jacobs), 310

"In Depth" (Nader), 209

"Indivisible? Wanna Bet?" (Quindlen), 418

Ingalls, John James, 219–20n

Ingersoll, Robert, 71

Inglis, Charles, 70

"In God We Trust," 411, 450, 459

"I pledge you, I pledge myself, to a new deal for the American people" (Roosevelt), 260–61, **261**

"I've Been to the Mountaintop" (King), 20, 30

"I will fight no more forever" (Chief Joseph), 256–57, **257**, 503n 2

Jackson, Jesse, 240, 480–81

Jackson, Jesse, Jr., 305–6

Jackson, Joseph, 466

Jackson, Justice Robert, 410, 413–14

Jacobs, Harriet, 310

Jacoby, Jeff, 370–71

James, Henry, 269

James, William, 310

Jay, John, 110, 491n 2

Jefferson, Mildred, 155

Jefferson, Nationalism, and the Enlightenment (Commager), 65n

Jefferson, Thomas, 4, 8, 11, 12, 13, 15, 36, 44, 248, 272, 421, 427, 433n, 449, 484, 510n 7, 514n 32; Declaration of Independence and, 5, 74, 75, 76, 77, 79n, 82n, 93, 96–97, 340, 461, 485–86, 494n 4; First Inaugural Address, 5, 358–71, **362–66**, 425, 454, 487, 510n 1, 511n 20, 514n 32; Gore Vidal on, 4; great seal of the United States and, 19; "Letter to the Danbury Baptists," 452–61, **456**; on Noah Webster, 98; Paine and, 55, 57; Rush's letter to (1801), 367; "wall of separation between church and state," 13, 452, 454, 455, 456, 457, 458, 460, 461, 484

Jeffersonians, 421, 425–26, 491n 15

Johnson, James Weldon, 20, 177, 179

Johnson, Lyndon B., 13, 202, 248, 389, 391, 394, 395; "Remarks at the Municipal Park, South Gate, CA," 379n; "Remarks in Harrisburg at a Dinner," 433n

Josaitis, Eleanor, 481

Joyce, James, 199

Judd, Walter H., 342

"Judging in a Government by Consent" (Thomas), 127

Kallen, Horace, 15

Kamiya, Gary, 402–3

Kaplan, Justin, 195–96

Kaskowitz, Sheryl, 228, 229

Kaye, Harvey, 72

Kazin, Alfred, 167, 282–83

Kelly, Michael, 241

Kemp, Jack, 334

Kendall, Willmoore, 342–44

Kennedy, John F., 6, 10, 12, 13, 249, 270, 308, 359–60, 396n, 416; address as President-Elect to Massachusetts legislators, 45–46; address to Massachusetts legislators, 45–46; "Ask not what your country can do for you . . . ," 262–63, **263**, 504–5n 2; civil rights and, 294–95, 335–36n, 463–64; missile gap and, 286; "Speech to the Greater Houston Ministerial Association," 458

Kennedy, Robert F., 295, 297, 463

Kennedy, Robert F., Jr., 50

Kennedy, William Sloane, 506n 5